palgrave macmillan law masters

constitutional and administrative law

Series editor: Marise Cremona

Business Law   Stephen Judge
Company Law   Janet Dine and Marios Koutsias
Constitutional and Administrative Law   John Alder
Contract Law   Ewan McKendrick
Criminal Law   Jonathan Herring
Employment Law   Deborah J. Lockton
Evidence   Raymond Emson
Family Law   Kate Standley and Paula Davies
Intellectual Property Law   Tina Hart, Simon Clark and Linda Fazzani
Land Law   Mark Davys
Landlord and Tenant Law   Margaret Wilkie, Peter Luxton and Desmond Kilcoyne
Legal Method   Ian McLeod
Legal Theory   Ian McLeod
Medical Law   Jo Samanta and Ash Samanta
Sports Law   Mark James
Torts   Alastair Mullis and Ken Oliphant
Trusts Law   Charlie Webb and Tim Akkouh

If you would like to comment on this book, or on the series generally, please write to lawfeedback@palgrave.com.

palgrave macmillan law masters

constitutional and administrative law

john alder

Emeritus Professor of Law, Newcastle University

Visiting Professor of Law, Bangor University

ninth edition

palgrave
macmillan

This edition first published 2013 by PALGRAVE MACMILLAN

Palgrave Macmillan in the UK is an imprint of Macmillan Publishers Limited, registered in England, company number 785998, of Houndmills, Basingstoke, Hampshire RG21 6XS.

Palgrave Macmillan in the US is a division of St Martin's Press LLC, 175 Fifth Avenue, New York, NY 10010.

Palgrave Macmillan is the global academic imprint of the above companies and has companies and representatives throughout the world.

Palgrave® and Macmillan® are registered trademarks in the United States, the United Kingdom, Europe and other countries.

ISBN: 978–1–137–28144–9   paperback

This book is printed on paper suitable for recycling and made from fully managed and sustained forest sources. Logging, pulping and manufacturing processes are expected to conform to the environmental regulations of the country of origin.

A catalogue record for this book is available from the British Library.

Contents

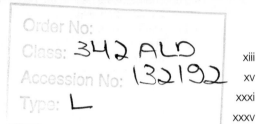

Preface

As in previous editions my aims are firstly to explain the main principles of United Kingdom constitutional law in the context of the political and legal values that influence their development and secondly to draw attention to the main controversies. I hope that the book will provide a self-contained text for those new to the subject and a starting point for more advanced students.

In this edition there is a new Chapter 20, on administrative justice, which brings together the treatment of tribunals, inquiries and ombudsmen and adds a section on 'regulation', an area of government which is increasingly raising constitutional problems about accountability and independence. The chapter on constitutional reform has been removed in favour of dealing with reforms (and the absence of any coherent method of reform) in particular contexts.

I have updated the book and provided further discussion of key cases to keep abreast of the shifts in the importance of different aspects of the constitution. Issues concerning security, respect for family life, freedom of the press, devolution, and the right to a fair trial have particularly engaged the courts. Other issues have arisen central to the study of constitutional law. These include parliamentary supremacy, parliamentary privilege and the relationship between statute and the royal prerogative. These show that longstanding academic controversies have practical contemporary implications. The reforms proposed by the present government in respect of the House of Lords and the electoral system have come to nothing. However the little publicised Fixed Term Parliaments Act 2011 has come into force making an important change to the separation of powers, the powers of the Prime Minister and the political cycle. As usual constitutional change has been driven by short-term political expediency.

Part I concerns general principles. These include basic constitutional concepts and issues (Chapter 1), a broad account of the moral and political ideals that have influenced the constitution (Chapter 2) and the sources of the constitution (Chapter 3). Chapters 4 offers a brief overview of the history of the constitution, emphasising significant events in relation to the contemporary law but without trying to suggest that there is some inevitable historical progression. Chapter 5 provides an overview of the main institutions of government, the most important aspects of which are expanded in later chapters. Pervasive legal values and doctrines are considered in Chapters 6, 7 and 8.

Part II concerns international relationships. Chapter 9 explains the various ways in which international requirements are filtered into our domestic constitution, the ambivalent position of dependent territories and the responses of the courts to international issues. Chapter 10 discusses the most important international influence, namely the EU, which is firmly anchored into domestic law.

Part III is concerned with the powers of the central government institutions and the relationship between them. Parts IV and V deal with the rights of the individual against government. Part IV concerns judicial review of government action, the core of administrative law and with administrative justice which comprises methods of challenging government action within the government structure (although what were once called administrative tribunals should now be considered primarily as part of the judicial system). Part V deals with the fundamental rights of the individual primarily in relation to topics that relate to the political freedoms that underpin democracy and the rule of law. These include freedom of expression and assembly, secrecy and national security.

I am grateful particularly to Rob Gibson at Palgrave Macmillan for his excellent advice and support. I am also grateful for the comments of anonymous reviewers of the previous editions. I have updated this edition on the basis of material available to me on 31 March 2013. Further updates can be found on the companion website: www. palgrave.com/law/alder9e

John Alder
April 2013

Table of cases

Table of legislation

Author note

Specific references to books and articles in the text are to writings that expand on the point in question. The Further Reading at the end of each chapter discusses fundamental and controversial general issues for those who require greater depth or more ideas and points of view. Short references in the text are to the Further reading. Unless otherwise stated, the main classical works cited throughout are as follows:

Bagehot, *The English Constitution,* ed Crossman (8th edn, Fontana/Collins 1963)

Dicey, *An Introduction to the Study of the Law of the Constitution* (8th edn, Macmillan 1915, referenced as last edition for which Dicey was himself responsible); (10th edn, Macmillan 1958, ed. ECS Wade)

Hobbes, *Leviathan*, ed Minogue (Dent 1973)

Locke, *Two Treatises of Government*, ed Laslett (Cambridge University Press 1960)

Mill, *Utilitarianism, On Liberty and Considerations of Representative Government*, ed Acton (Dent 1972)

Montesquieu 'L'Esprit des Lois', extracted in Stirk and Weigall (eds), *An Introduction to Political Ideas* (Pinter 1995)

Paine, *The Thomas Paine Reader*, eds Foot and Kramnick (Penguin 1987)

Part I

The framework of the constitution

Chapter 1

Introduction: constitutional themes and structures

1.1 The nature of a constitution: general issues

A constitution provides the fundamental principles that form the governing framework of an organisation. Any organisation might have a constitution; for example. most golf clubs do so. In our case the organisation is the state. A state is recognised throughout the world as an independent geographical territory.

A constitution has two worthy purposes: firstly to enable the organisation to run effectively in the light of its goals; secondly to prevent those in charge of the organisation from abusing their powers. Thus the late Lord Bingham, a leading judge, suggested that 'any constitution, whether of a state, a trade union, a college, a club or other institution seeks to lay down and define...the main offices in which authority is vested and the powers which may be exercised (or not exercised) by the holders of those offices' (*R v Secretary of State for Foreign and Commonwealth Affairs, ex p Quark Fishing Ltd* [2006] [12]).

Friedrich (*Limited Government: A Comparison* (Prentice Hall 1974) 21) displays a romantic approach to the idea of a constitution that stresses the (assumed) consent of the community: 'a constitution is the ordering and dividing of the exercise of political power by that group in an existent community who are able to secure the consent of the community and who thereby make manifest the power of the community itself'.

Perhaps it is fanciful to assume a necessary connection between the securing of power and community consent unless by consent is meant only acquiescence in the sense of the absence of resistance to whoever is in power.

Constitutional law deals with the following matters:

- the choosing and removing of rulers;
- the relationship between the different branches of the government;
- the accountability of the government;
- the dividing up of powers geographically, for example, the relationship between the central government and the devolved governments of Scotland, Wales and Northern Ireland; by those with a taste for jargon this is sometimes called 'multi-layered' constitutionalism;
- the relationship between the state and overseas bodies;
- the rights of the citizen in relation to government.

There is no hard and fast difference between constitutional law and administrative law. Administrative law deals with particular government functions such as immigration or taxation or the work of the numerous regulators, special tribunals and inquiries that decide disputes involving government action. This book does not attempt to cover administrative law comprehensively since the subject has its own separate texts. Chapters 17, 18 and 19 on judicial review of administrative action deal with the core of administrative law which is the legal accountability of the government. Other matters such as 'regulation,' tribunals, public inquiries and ombudsmen are discussed in Chapter 20.

In almost all countries the constitution comprises a special document or set of documents set above the ordinary law. This is known as a written constitution or a Basic Law. In addition to setting out the main principles of the government structure and sometimes a list of individual rights, a written constitution may proclaim, usually in a preamble, some grand vision or moral message about the nature and purposes of the society (eg the US Constitution, the German, Basic Law). Importantly, a written constitution usually has a status superior to the rest of the law, in the sense that it can be altered only by a special procedure such as a public referendum or a special vote in the legislature. The constitution is therefore protected against manipulation by the government of the day.

The UK has no written constitution of this kind and no grand vision about the nature of our society. Our constitution such as it is composed of numerous ordinary laws and other rules and practices which have emerged from time to time to deal with particular issues. Its legal principles and rules, if written down at all, are to be found in the same documents as the sources of any law, namely:

▶ Acts of Parliament (statutes) made by the regime in power at the time dealing with particular issues; thus constitutional statutes are scattered throughout the centuries each dealing with a particular matter.
▶ Cases decided by the courts dealing with matters of constitutional importance. Again these are scattered and can arise in many and various contexts.

Rules from these two sources can be changed in the same way as any other law. In other words they are constitutional only because of the matters they deal with. New Zealand has an unwritten constitution similar to our own. Israel is also sometimes said to lack a written constitution but unlike the UK has an organised collection of legislation recognised as constitutional by the Supreme Court. The constitution of Saudi Arabia is the Koran.

There are also many rules, practices and customs which are not law in that they cannot be directly enforced by the courts. They get their force only because they are consistently obeyed. The most important of these are known as 'constitutional conventions' (Section 3.4). Many basic constitutional arrangements rely on conventions; for example, the existence of and most of the powers of the Prime Minister. Unlike laws, conventions are not set out in any authoritative written texts but exist only in the collective imagination of the officials who run the government. The citizen therefore has no independent way of ensuring that conventions are not abused.

Some writers describe our constitution as 'part written' meaning that some but not all of its rules are written down but only in the same ways as any other law. This seems unhelpful in as-much as it does not capture the notion of a special constitutional document.

Our constitution is often described as 'organic' meaning that it develops naturally in the light of changing circumstances. We should not therefore expect the constitution to be straightforward and logical. It is a product of historical development and practical compromises generated by rival groups of power hungry persons. In another metaphor the UK constitution is sometimes compared to a ramshackle old house under constant repair and renovation and made of numerous bits and pieces. It has also been compared with the implication that it is 'sound and lasting' to the work of bees making a honeycomb (see *R (Jackson) v Attorney General* [2005] 4 All ER 1253 [125] Lord Hope).

It has often been suggested that we do not have a constitution in any meaningful sense. The democratic activist Thomas Paine (1737–1809), labelled the British government as 'power without right'. In *The Rights of Man*, Paine asserted that without a written constitution authorised directly by the people there was no valid constitution (1987, 220–21, 285–96). Similarly, Ridley (1988) claims that the UK has no constitution since he believes that constitutions must be superior to the government of the day and not changeable by it. Without a written constitution the UK seems to fail this test. Insofar as the constitution has a special status, this is based on no more than self-restraint due to respect for principles that are regarded by those in power as fundamental or 'constitutional'.

However, whether or not we have a constitution in a strict sense, the term 'constitutionalism' applies to the UK as a widely shared political belief. Constitutionalism is the belief that a state should have arrangements that limit the powers of the rulers. It includes both legal and political limits on government. It requires government officials to be accountable for their actions to an independent body, although not necessarily a court. It requires a separation of powers between different governmental organs and proper controls within each governmental organ. In a democracy it requires frequent elections open to all and subject to rules which prevent any candidate from having an unfair advantage.

1.2 The foundations of a constitution

A constitution can of course adopt any form of government. The most widely accepted explanation of the foundations of a constitution is a 'positivist' one. According to this theory a constitution is valid or 'legitimate' if enough of the people whom it concerns, both officials and the public, accept it so as to make it broadly effective. Thus the foundations of the law depend on a political state of affairs. UK law takes this pragmatic view in the context, for example, of recognising the legality of a rebellion (see *Madzimbamuto v Lardner-Burke* [1969] 1 AC 645: takeover of a British colony by a group of white settlers held not valid because they were not yet fully in control).

Possible reasons for the 'legitimacy' (acceptance) of a constitution such as love of power, fear, sycophancy, apathy, self-interest, ideological belief, herd instinct and so on are irrelevant to its legal validity. On the other hand a general belief among the people that the constitution is morally good, or at least that it is in their interests, might help the rulers stay in power.

'Legitimacy' might also refer to an external standard that can be used to assess the constitution. The problem here of course is to identify what this is. Lawyers, for example, might refer to 'the rule of law', meaning widely accepted vague values such as justice as identified by themselves. Related to this are 'natural law' theories in which a constitution is valid only if it conforms to a set of objective moral principles. Apart from the question of who decides what these principles are it may be preferable to treat moral principles as a standpoint for criticising a constitution rather than confusing this with questions of legal validity.

Building on a famous essay by Isaiah Berlin (Section 2.4) Daintith and Page (*The Executive in the Constitution* (Oxford University Press 1999) ch 1) classify those who attempt to understand our unwritten constitution as 'foxes', 'hedgehogs', 'rude little boys' and 'Humpty Dumpties'. A fox regards the constitution as no more than a collection of working practices developed by the government enterprise. A hedgehog looks for a single grand overarching principle such as 'the rule of law'. It is unlikely that in a matter as complex as government any single principle is credible. A rude little boy therefore asserts that the emperor has no clothes, the constitution being a fiction disguising a power struggle between control freaks. Humpty Dumpties, who probably include most academic commentators, seek to explain the constitution on the basis of theories of their own such as liberalism, fairness, social welfare and so on, sometimes claiming that these ideals are inherent in the rules. We shall meet examples of each approach throughout this book.

1.3 Basic constitutional concepts

Three related ideas have influenced many modern constitutions including our own. These are 'sovereignty', the rule of law and the separation of powers. Sovereignty means ultimate power without limit. In any constitution it might be difficult to locate sovereignty. Some such as Hobbes (Section 2.3) and Carl Schmidt argue that there must always be a sovereign in this sense. Someone must be capable of having the last word in any conceivable dispute particularly in an emergency where the ordinary law runs out. The sovereign need not be a single person. In the UK the conventional view is that the sovereign is Parliament as a combination of the monarch, the House of Lords and the House of Commons. Moreover the legal sovereign is not necessary the political sovereign. For example, although Parliament has legal power to make any law, politically it is unlikely to be able to make a law that the international money markets would seriously object to.

The primary meaning of the rule of law is relatively uncontroversial, namely, that it is desirable to have rules known in advance which are binding on government and governed alike. This helps the organisation to run effectively by keeping order and producing certainty. However this ignores the content of the rules, whether they are morally good or bad, and the question of who makes them. For example, a concentration camp might be subject to the rule of law in this sense. A wider version of the rule of law invokes certain moral and political ideas which are claimed to be especially associated with law in the sense of government by rules. These include openness, equality and freedom policed by independent courts. Thus the rule of law places judges rather than elected politicians in the driving seat. Whether this is desirable is a political issue that pervades the subject of constitutional law.

The separation of powers requires that government be divided up into different branches of equal status and importance. From both a political and a legal perspective this is to prevent any one branch of government having dominant power. Each branch can restrain the others since any major decision would require the cooperation of all branches. Governments usually comprise three primary branches. The legislature is the primary lawmaker, the judiciary settles disputes about the meaning and application of the law and the executive carries out all the other government functions, implementing and enforcing the law. Crucially in contemporary society the executive proposes most new laws to the legislature.

Different countries have reached different conclusions as to the extent of the separation of powers since there is a trade-off between the interests of government efficiency which points away from a separation and the desire to prevent abuse of power. For example, the USA has a strict separation but in the UK separation is more limited. In the USA, a member of the executive headed by the President cannot be a member of the legislature but in the UK ministers who head the executive must (by convention) be members of Parliament. We seem to prefer strong government to limited government.

Some constitutions make grandiose claims to shared ideals and purposes. For example, the Constitution of Ireland refers to 'seeking to promote the common good with due observance of Prudence, Justice and Charity so that the dignity and freedom of the individual may be assured, true social order attained, the unity of our country restored and concord established with other nations'. The French Constitution famously refers to 'the Rights of Man' and the 'equality and solidity of the peoples who compose [the Republic]' (Art 1). The UK constitution makes no such claims, at least explicitly.

Many constitutions contain a list of basic rights of the citizen. These rights vary reflecting the political culture of the ruling group in question. Constitutions also vary in the extent to which the courts may police these rights. In the family of liberal democratic states to which the UK belongs these rights are primarily 'negative' rights in the sense of rights not to be interfered with by the state. They include the right to life, the right to personal freedom, the right to a fair trial, the right to privacy and family life, the right to freedom of expression, the right to assembly and association, the right to freedom of religion and the right to protection for property. 'Positive rights', such as the right to a decent standard of living, the right to a good environment and the right to medical care, might be regarded as equally important, but because these require hard political choices between priorities and large-scale public expenditure they are regarded as a matter for the ordinary political process rather than as firm legal rights. Enforcement by a court would be practically impossible. Nevertheless some positive rights appear in many constitutions, for example, those of Poland and Portugal. Some constitutions, for example, that of Switzerland, also impose duties on citizens such as military service and voting.

1.4 Written and unwritten constitutions: advantages and disadvantages

As we have seen, most constitutions are set out in a single document or related group of documents. These are sometimes superior to all other kinds of law in that laws which conflict with the constitution can be struck down by the courts. They also often contain 'entrenched' provisions which protect the constitution from being changed by the government of the day, for example, a referendum of the people or a two-thirds majority of the lawmaking assembly.

Even a written constitution will not include all the rules needed for governing the country but will include the most basic rules. This varies considerably between different states. For example, the methods of voting are important by any standards but do not feature in many constitutions other than general requirement of fairness and equality. Some constitutions, such as that of the US, are relatively short and expressed in general terms. Others, like that of Portugal, run to hundreds of detailed pages.

1.4.1 The merits of a written constitution

There is no agreement as to whether it is preferable to have a written constitution although proposals for one are regularly made. The content of a written constitution and an unwritten one can be the same. The main advantages of a written constitution seem to be its relative certainty and ease of public access and the political advantage of providing a focus for the consent and loyalty of the community that is independent of the personalities of the day. In the USA, for example, there is considerable reverence for the written constitution. In the UK the Queen provides such a focus which many would regard as degrading. The political journalist Walter Bagehot (1826–77) thought that mystical reverence for royalty was essential to the authority of the 'English' constitution.

If it can be changed only by a special procedure (entrenchment) and permits the courts to override unconstitutional acts of government a written constitution provides some assurance that important rules are outside the control of temporary ruling elites. However a written constitution does not necessarily include these features. Indeed one reason why almost every other country has a written constitution is that the constitution was created following a revolution or major political disturbance in that country resulting in a new regime producing a written constitution to suit itself.

Moreover a written constitution may be far from certain. It is likely to be drafted in vague general language interpreted in the light of the politics of the day and so changing its meaning from time to time. For example in *Plessey v Ferguson* 163 US 537 (1896) the US Supreme Court held that racial segregation was constitutional under the 14th amendment of the Constitution ('equal protection of the law') and in *Brown v Board of Education* 347 US 483 (1954) that it was not. Similarly in *Lochner v New York* 198 US 45 (1905) the Supreme Court held that it was unconstitutional under the same provision for the law to regulate the relations between employer and employee but in *West Coast Hotels v Parish* 300 US 379 (1937), a 'new deal', case the court upheld a law protecting women's wages UK (contrast *Roberts v Hopwood* [1925] AC 578 in the UK: local authority could not protect women's wages).

Even in the absence of a written constitution there are devices within UK law capable of limiting the ability of governments to make constitutional changes.

▶ It is arguable that an ordinary law could 'entrench' a special rule by providing that the rule could be changed only by a special process such as a referendum (Section 8.4.3).
▶ The courts may give special weight to matters that they consider to be constitutional. Thus it has been suggested that certain statutes are 'constitutional statutes' and certain rights, such as freedom of speech, constitutional rights which require the lawmaker to use very clear language to repeal or override (*Thorburn v Sunderland City Council* [2002] 4 All ER 156: European Communities Act 1972, *R(Brynmawr Foundation School Governors v Welsh Ministers* [2011] EWHC (admin) 519: Government of Wales Act 2006; *R (Bancoult) v Secretary of State for Foreign and Commonwealth Affairs* [2008] 4 All ER 1055 [151]: right to reside in the UK (Section 9.5) but see Lord Hoffmann [45]). However what counts as a constitutional statute or right is unclear and it is doubtful whether the term means more than 'important' (Sections 6.6, 8.4.5, 21.2).
▶ The House of Lords Constitutional Committee examines the constitutional aspects of bills and reviews constitutional developments (see Caird [2012] PL 4). There is also a House of Commons Political and Constitutional Reform Committee which considers general questions of constitutional reform.
▶ Proposed legislation that Parliament regards as 'of first-class constitutional importance' is examined by a committee of the whole House rather than by the normal 'standing committee' (Section 13.3.1).

▶ There is authority that compensation can be awarded against a public official who violates a 'constitutional right' even where no loss or damage has occurred (*Ashby v White* (1703) 2 Lord Raym. 938: right to vote).

A written constitution may strengthen the political legitimacy of the courts. Thus in *Cullen v Chief Constable of the RUC* [2004] 2 All ER 237, 46, Lord Hutton said that a written constitution has a special significance. He referred to a right which a democratic assembly representing the people has enshrined in a written constitution. In the latter case a person who has suffered harm can recover damages, the written constitution being 'clear testimony that an added value is attached to the protection of that right'. Similarly in *Ghaidan v Mendosa* [2004] 3 All ER 411 at 178, Lord Millet said that a written constitution would give the court greater legitimacy in reviewing legislation under the Human Rights Act 1998.

A possible advantage of a written constitution is that it encourages a rationalistic process of constitutional design which ideally creates a constitution as a logical scheme which is relatively stable. On the other hand it can be argued that in a matter as large and open to disagreement as a constitution, human beings are not capable of sensible grand designs and that the flexible trial and error approach favoured in the UK is preferable. Edmund Burke (1729–97), a prominent parliamentarian and conservative thinker, claimed that the constitution has special status by virtue of its being rooted in long-standing custom and tradition. Burke regarded attempts to engineer constitutions on the basis of abstract reason as ultimately leading to tyranny. This is because he believed that humans, with their limited understanding and knowledge, are inevitably at the mercy of unforeseen events and that reasoning based on abstract general principles, by trying to squeeze us into rigid templates, is a potential instrument of oppression:

> the age of chivalry is gone…That of sophisters, economists and calculators has succeeded; and the glory of Europe is extinguished for ever. (Burke, Reflections on the Revolution in France (1790))

Along the same lines as Burke, it is sometimes said that a written constitution encourages the use of abstract, linguistic, legalistic techniques at the expense of the underlying political realities and human interests. However courts have often emphasised the need for a broad and flexible approach to constitutional interpretation that stresses the underlying moral and political context (eg *Robinson v Secretary of State for Northern Ireland* [2002] UKHL 32). Indeed the language of a written constitution may be very vague, leaving plenty of room for disagreement. This gives the courts, undemocratic though they are, considerable power.

1.4.2   The merits of the unwritten constitution

Our pragmatic mixture of ordinary laws and political conventions is said to have the advantage of practicality in that it responds to particular issues that arise from time to time and can easily adapt to changing circumstances. Dicey considered that our constitution is strengthened by the fact that much of it is embedded in the fabric of the common law which gets its strength from practical issues generated from below and is and not imposed from above in a constitution that can be torn up (Section 6.4.2).

It has been suggested that (along with a temperate climate) the organic, slow and evolutionary development of 'the mess that is Britain's constitution' encourages values such as freedom and democracy to develop and mature with less upheaval and bloodshed than radical reform might entail (see Kellner, *Democracy: 1000 Years in Pursuit of British Liberty* (Mainstream 2009) 28–29). Superficially at least our unwritten constitution does have a coherent structure as a parliamentary or representative democracy which has evolved gradually out of struggles between monarchs and other interests and indeed has been copied in many written constitutions.

It is argued that a written constitution is likely to be in the hands of the courts who would inevitably be drawn into political controversy and their independence questioned as is the case with the US Supreme Court the decisions of which often reflect the balance between left and right members of the panel. However, whether the courts should have a larger political role does not depend on a written constitution but primarily on whether the courts can overturn legislation passed by Parliament (Section 8.4).

There is disagreement as to whether in an unwritten constitution it is worth labelling some rights as 'constitutional rights' in order to stress their importance. On the one hand Lord Steyn has remarked that to classify a right as constitutional strengthens its value in that the court is virtually always required to protect it (quoted by Cooke, in Andenas and Fairgrieve (2009, 691)). In *R v Secretary of State for the Home Dept, ex p Simms* [1999] 2 AC 115 at 412: right of a prisoner of access to the press, Lord Hoffmann stated that we apply 'principles of constitutionality little different from those which exist in countries where the power of the legislature is expressly limited by a constitutional document'. On the other hand in *Watkins v Secretary of State for the Home Dept* (2006): prisoner's access to a lawyer, the House of Lords rejected this argument on the ground that without a written constitution the notion of a constitutional right is too vague.

Claims to flexibility carry the price that our system is vulnerable to manipulation by those in power for self-serving reasons. It is widely acknowledged that people with power can easily abuse their power, albeit sometimes accidentally or for good motives. Those who seek power are sometimes over-endowed with self-confidence and prone to identify the public interest with their own interests.

Political thinkers over the centuries have worried about the corruptibility of those in power:

now it is a universally observed fact, that the two evil dispositions in question, the disposition to prefer a man's selfish interests to those he shares with other people, and his immediate and direct interests to those which are indirect and remote, are characterised most especially called forth and fostered by the possession of power... this is the meaning of the universal tradition, grounded on universal experience, of men's being corrupted by power. (Mill, 1972, 242)

John Adams, one of the founders of the US Constitution, asserted that:

despotism, or unlimited sovereignty or absolute power, is the same in a majority of a popular assembly, an aristocratic council, an oligarchical junta, and a single emperor. (Letter to Thomas Jefferson, 13 November 1815)

It is doubtful whether any constitution written or otherwise can entirely prevent powers being concentrated in the hands of a network of personal, family and professional associates. 'Oligarchy', government by the few, is arguably the natural state of politics. Powerful interest groups such as the media and financial interests can influence the conduct of government through privileged access by providing money in return for favours, by publicity against unhelpful politicians or by offering jobs to former politicians and officials. Indeed, according to the *Democratic Audit* 2012 (Joseph Rowntree Trust) the proportion of major UK companies with direct connections to members of the UK Parliament is many times greater than that found in other established democracies. This might be related to the fact that so much of our constitution depends on conventions and understandings among the network of politicians and officials.

It has been suggested that the complexity and subtlety of the UK's arrangements make it impractical and divisive to reduce the constitution to writing, an argument convenient to those enjoying power. In particular there may be disagreement as to what rules or principles are truly 'constitutional'. There is no doubt that rules concerning the circumstances in which a government should lose office are constitutional, but what of local government which exists to provide relatively limited services for local communities? The debate would turn on the political issue of whether Britain should be a highly centralised or a dispersed democracy.

In the end it is arguable that whether or not the constitution is written is relatively unimportant other than a matter of convenience in identifying particular rules or principles. Underlying political factors are far more important. We shall now consider some of these.

1.5 The legal and the political constitution

Constitutional law depends heavily on its political context. Although our primary concern is law it is necessary to relate this to the political environment. For the purposes of studying constitutional law, it is useful to distinguish as a working matter between law and politics.

Unfortunately there is no agreed meaning of 'politics' nor of 'law'. For now it is enough to say that 'law' means rules, principles and standards that are enforced ultimately by the physical force of the state. Laws are recognised solely because they are made by designated procedures (in the UK by the courts and Parliament, the lawmaking assembly). In our system of constitutionalism because they ultimately involve force against individuals, laws should ideally be interpreted by independent courts. In a broad sense 'politics' means the struggle for power between different interest groups and in this sense law is a distinctive aspect of politics in that it depends on and is influenced by political forces.

Law can be distinguished from other aspects of politics in at least the following respects:

- It relies on impersonal and usually written sources of authority in the form of binding general rules.
- It emphasises the desirability of certainty, coherence and impartial and independent public procedures such as courts for settling disputes.
- Politics is concerned primarily with outcomes, for which law is only one among several instruments, and is more willing than law to use emotions, personal relationships, rewards and compromises in order to achieve those outcomes.

A way of framing the political context of especial importance to lawyers is the metaphor derived from Harlow and Rawlings (2009), of 'red light' and 'green light' theories of Public Law (a term that we can treat as meaning the same as Constitutional and

Administrative Law). Red lighters emphasise the protection of individual rights. They would cut back government to a minimum in order to protect individual freedom. 'Green lighters' favour the collective goals of society which they believe are best carried out by the government through democratic mechanisms. They therefore see the role of law as being primarily to enable government to achieve important public goals such as education, health and social welfare. Green light theory does not of course deny the importance of the individual but emphasises collective and community values such as democratic participation. These metaphors therefore seem essentially to represent the familiar left and right wing division of politics. In a democracy such as the UK constitution claims to be, it is important to keep both these views open since permanent agreement is likely to be impossible. Thus we must expect the law to be a messy compromise: 'in Harlow and Rawlings terms', yellow light.

Griffith famously distinguished between the 'legal' constitution and the 'political constitution'. He remarked that 'the constitution of the United Kingdom lives on, changing from day to day for the constitution is no more and no less than what happens. Everything that happens is constitutional. And if nothing happened that would be constitutional also' (1979, 19). On one reading this suggests that there is nothing at all behind the idea of a constitution. However Griffith may merely be pointing out that the constitution is a mixture of competing forces, of which law in the shape of courts is only one and not the most important. The relationship between them is determined by political events and is constantly changing (see Gee, 2008; Loughlin, 'John Griffith: An Appreciation' [2010] PL 643, 649).

The term 'political constitution' is confusing and has different meanings, sometimes conflicting and sometimes overlapping. These different meanings may influence how one might resolve basic constitutional problems, most notably whether the courts or the elected lawmaker should have the last word.

1. A fundamental political belief as a result of which the legal constitution is created. In the UK this might be the revolution of 1688 in which James II was deposed in favour of arrangements controlled by supporters of Parliament (Section 4.5). Some argue that the creation of what is now the European Union (EU) is such a principle but a more widely held view is that the EU is the creation of established principles of international treaty law and part of UK law by virtue of statute (Section 10.1).
2. The belief that all constitutional actors, including of course judges, are influenced by political bias favouring certain interests (usually in favour of the status quo (see Griffith, 1979)). Given that no human being is likely to be entirely without personal views, complete impartiality is impossible although judges are trained to be open-minded and self-critical. The law provides safeguards for judicial impartiality which broadly speaking distinguishes between general political views which must be accepted and specific connections with the parties or issues, i these not being acceptable (Section 18.4). However the judiciary is predominantly recruited from a limited social and economic group, this being prosperous, white, privately educated, middle-aged males, a group which is also strongly represented in the executive branch of government. Unlike other European countries there is no separate judicial profession. Senior judges are mainly recruited from successful practitioners in the courts with existing judges playing a prominent part in the recruitment process (Section 7.8.2).

3. Much of the UK constitution comprises rules and principles that are not law in the sense that they are not enforceable in the courts but rely on political pressures and voluntary consent (Chapter 3).

4. Political activity and institutions operate within a framework designated by law (Hickman, 2005). This suggests that law rather than politics is the basis of the constitution but does not explain where law gets its authority. It gives the courts a starring role.

5. By contrast, fundamental *political* principles such as democracy underpin all aspects of the constitution, give law its authority and pervade the law (Gee and Webber, 2010). These provide the framework within which law operates.

6. The fact that the courts are often required to settle disputes concerning the other branches of government and so enter politically controversial territory. This arises especially in relation to membership of the EU, the Human Rights Act 1998, devolution of limited powers to Scotland Wales and Northern Ireland and the courts' general powers of judicial review.

7. A preference for political solutions reached by democratic methods rather than solutions imposed by unelected judges. Griffith (1979, 335–36) (2001) thought that constitutional decisions should be made by political bodies rather than by courts because he thought that judges are likely to be biased in favour of established authority and because Parliament is likely to be better informed.

The legal and the political constitution are interrelated in various ways. For example:

▶ Politics provides the purposes and values that underpin the constitution and give the law its content.

▶ Law operates as a delivery mechanism for particular political policies written into legislation.

▶ The accountability of government: constitutionalism, is both legal and political. There is legal accountability to the courts through the courts' powers of judicial review of government decisions to ensure that they comply with the law. There is political accountability to Parliament in the form of the concept of 'responsible government' which requires the government to justify its actions to Parliament. However, for several reasons including the domination of Parliament by the executive and limited resources political accountability is weak. Other than the right to vote periodically for individual MPs there is no direct accountability to the people.

▶ Conversely, values especially concerned with the legal process in the courts, which can be summarised as fairness and justice, feed into the political process. For example, how far should anti-terrorist policies be subject to the right to a fair trial (Section 23.7.2)?

▶ Within the law itself there is disagreement between different judges and groups of lawyers about political values. Because the limits of language mean that rules can never be entirely clear or complete, judges may be influenced by their political beliefs in deciding between competing arguments. The best we can expect is an open and self-aware mind. Endless disagreement underlies both law and politics and dissents are commonplace in judicial decisions. See Dickson in Lee (ed), From *House of Lords to Supreme Court: Judges and the Process of Judging* (Oxford Hart Publishing 2011). This is one reason why a diverse judiciary may be desirable (Section 5.4).

- ▶ Politics determines the actual power relationship between the different branches of government: lawmaker, executive, judges, military and so on. For example, even if in law the Parliament as the lawmaker is supreme; if members of Parliament are weak, self-seeking and subservient the executive is likely to be dominant.
- ▶ In many countries with written constitutions the courts have the power to overturn laws that they deem to be unconstitutional. The conventional view is that the UK courts have no such power (but see Section 8.5). This power is not dependent on a written constitution except in the sense that a written constitution may make the matter clear. It would therefore be possible for the UK courts to have such a power Whether the courts should have such a power depends on the underlying political values of society, namely, whether appointed judges or elected politicians should have the last word. Thus in the USA the Constitution did not specifically deal with the matter but the Supreme Court regarded it as implicit in the Constitution as a fundamental law that the courts should have such a power (*Marbury v Madison* (1803) 1 Cranch 6). This became the political consensus.

1.6   The dignified and efficient constitution: deceiving the people?

It is often said that the glue which holds the unwritten UK constitution together is the propensity of the British to subservience and deference to officialdom. Writing in the mid-nineteenth century, Walter Bagehot (1902) regarded social class deference and superstition as the 'magic' ingredients that animated the constitution. Bagehot took a jaundiced view of the political sophistication of ordinary people and thought that government could only work effectively if its authority is buttressed by traditional institutions which command people's imagination and make them deferential to the rulers.

Bagehot distinguished between what he called the 'dignified' and the 'efficient' parts of the constitution. The dignified parts give the constitution its authority and encourage people to obey it. They involve the trappings of power, notably the monarchy that underpins the central government (Section 14.6), and the mystique of ceremony and ritual. Bagehot thought that it would be dangerous to shed the light of reality upon the monarchy since doing so would expose it as a sham. The efficient part of the constitution, which Bagehot located primarily in the Cabinet carries out the working exercise of power behind the scenes. From this perspective all government boils down to an oligarchy of like-minded people in the form of a 'king' and his courtiers.

The distinction between the dignified and the efficient performs a useful function in a democracy by preventing working politicians from claiming to embody the state, a technique adopted by tyrants throughout history. For example, the monarch and Parliament have authority, the latter because it is elected, while the government has power without authority in its own right. It gets its authority only from Parliament.

On the other hand the dignified element can reinforce tyranny by hiding reality. The 'noble lie' postulated by Plato in his *Republic* is designed to keep people happy with their designated roles: when humans were formed in the earth the rulers had gold mixed with them, the military silver and the workers lead. Even Plato's pupils found this hard to swallow but they thought that it is sometimes right to lie in the interests of the state. There is similar thinking today. In *McIlkenny v Chief Constable of the West Midlands Police* [1980] at 239–40, Lord Denning MR took the view that it was better for the 'Birmingham Six' to remain wrongly convicted than to face the 'appalling vista' of the police being found to be guilty of perjury, violence and threats. The Scott Report into the sale of arms to Iraq (*Report of the Inquiry into the Export of Defence Equipment and Dual Use Goods to Iraq and Related Prosecution* (HC 1995–96, 115)) revealed that ministers and civil servants regarded it as being in the public interest to mislead Parliament, if not actually to lie, over government involvement in arms sales to overseas regimes. The Constitutional Reform Act 2010 prevents disclosure under the Freedom of Information Act 2000 of all correspondence between the Prince of Wales and ministers on the ground that it would weaken public confidence in the monarchy if people knew that the heir to the throne attempted to influence government (Section 23.2.1; see also *Guardian* 16 September 2010).

1.7 Types of constitution

There are several traditional ways of classifying constitutions. It must be emphasised that these are ideals or models and there is no reason to assume that any particular constitutions completely fits into any single category. The types are:

> *Federal and unitary. I*n a federal state (such as the USA and Germany) the various powers of government are divided between different geographical units and a central government. Each level has its own constitution and courts and is protected against intervention by the others. The UK is a unitary state. In a unitary state there may be subordinate units such as the devolved governments of Scotland, Northern Ireland and Wales but ultimate power is held by the centre.
>
> How powers are allocated varies according to the history and political concerns of the state in question. There may be demarcation problems to be resolved by the courts, so federal constitutions have a strong legalistic element. There is usually a single citizenship of the central state, the federal government being responsible for foreign affairs, defence and major economic matters, while private law issues are the responsibility of the states. Criminal offences, social regulation and public services may be allocated to either level.
>
> Usually particular matters are given to the federal level, with the residue left with the states, but the converse sometimes applies (eg in Canada). Switzerland provides an extreme example of a constitution where both the powers of the federal government and its personnel are severely limited in favour of the autonomy of the cantons. The relative political power of each level depends on the circumstances of each country and cannot necessarily be discovered from the law itself.
>
> Federalism is practicable where the component units have sufficient in common economically and culturally to enable them to cooperate, while at the same time each unit is sufficiently distinctive to constitute a community in its own right but not sufficiently powerful to aspire to a role on the international stage. Thus a delicate balance must be struck. The US and Australia are relatively successful federations, whereas Canada with its split between English-speaking and French-speaking regions is less stable. Yugoslavia with its many ethnic tensions was tragically unsuccessful once Soviet control was removed.
>
> During the late nineteenth century there were some advocates of a federal UK as a way of avoiding home rule for Ireland. Dicey (1915, 171), the influential Victorian constitutional lawyer, strongly opposed federalism, claiming that it tends towards

conservatism, creates divided loyalties and elevates legalism to a primary value, making the courts the pivot on which the constitution turns and perhaps threatening their independence. Devolved government is therefore a pragmatic compromise (cf Olowofoyeku, 'Decentralising the United Kingdom: The Federal Argument' (1999) 3 Edinburgh LR 57).

The Royal Commission on the Constitution (Cmnd 5460, 1973) argued against a federal constitution for the UK on the following grounds:

▶ There would be a lack of balance since the units are widely different in economic terms, with England being dominant.
▶ A federal regime would be contrary to our constitutional traditions in that it would elevate the courts over political machinery.
▶ The UK was thought to require central and flexible economic management since its resources are unevenly distributed geographically, much of it comprising thinly populated hills.
▶ Apart from Northern Ireland, regional issues were not high on the agenda of the main parties, which suggested that there was little public desire for federalism. However more recent claims that EU law is superior to Parliament (Section 8.4.4) and the political strength of devolution, particularly in Scotland, mean that at a political level there may be a tendency towards federalism.

Rigid and flexible. This concerns whether it is easy for those in power to change the constitution. In legal terms some constitutions are rigid in that a special process such as a referendum of the people may be required to change them. This is known as 'entrenchment'. In the UK no special process is required. However the courts may resist interpreting laws so as to undermine what they regard as constitutionally important matters. Whether a constitution is easy to change depends more on politics than on law. Any constitution can be ignored or overthrown.

Parliamentary and presidential. The UK has an extreme parliamentary system. In a parliamentary system such as that of many western European countries the people choose representatives who form the legislature, Parliament. The head of government is the Prime Minister (the Chancellor in Austria and Germany), chosen by the Parliament. The Prime Minister chooses and removes ministers, who are the leaders of the executive government. Sometimes, as in the UK, these must also be members of the legislature. Parliament scrutinises government activities, consents to laws and provides the government with finance. It can ultimately dismiss the executive by withdrawing its support. Parliamentary government therefore looks strong and accountable. However in practice the executive is likely to be dominant, if only because of the human tendency to defer to leaders.

In a parliamentary system there is usually a separate head of state who formally represents the state and is the source of its authority but has little political power, except perhaps as a safety mechanism in the event of a serious political breakdown. In some states, including the UK, the head of state is a hereditary monarch and thus relatively independent of political pressures. In republican states the head of state is elected either by Parliament or by the people.

The device of a separate head of state in the parliamentary system has the advantages of separating the authority of the state from its political powers. In a parliamentary system the Prime Minister and other members of the executive are merely government employees who cannot identify themselves with the state as such and so claim reflected glory and immunity from criticism. The head of state has a symbolic role and also ensures continuity in the constitution. For example, if the government were to collapse, it would be the responsibility of the head of state to ensure that government continued. Apart from this exceptional situation the Queen has little personal political power (Section 14.4), so that any respect due to her as representing the state does not carry the risk of tyranny.

In a presidential system such as that of the US, the leader of the executive, the President, is elected directly by the people independently of the legislature and holds office for a fixed period, subject in some countries such as France (which has a complex mixture of the two systems) to dismissal by the legislature. The President is usually also the head of state. Presidential government therefore gives the voter a greater choice. On the other hand without a strong input from the legislature accountability might be weak and when the legislature and President represent different political parties it might be difficult for the government to work effectively since its proposed laws might be blocked by the legislature.

Unicameral or bicameral. A unicameral constitution has a single lawmaking assembly. A bicameral constitution has two assemblies, each of which operates as a check on the other, the balance between them depending on the circumstances of the particular country. In the US, for example, the Senate, the upper house, represents the states which comprise the federal system, with the legislature of each state, irrespective of its size, choosing two members, whereas Congress, the lower and larger house, is elected by the people generally, each state being represented according to the size of its population. Some European constitutions, such as those of Denmark, Sweden and Greece, are unicameral, and in most European constitutions the upper house cannot override the lower house. It is questionable whether an upper house serves a useful purpose other than in a federal system on the US model, where each house can check the other from importantly different perspectives.

The UK constitution is bicameral. The lower house, the House of Commons, with about 646 members, is elected from the UK as a whole. The upper house, the House of Lords, with about 740 members, is mainly appointed by the Prime Minister, in contrast to other European countries, where the upper houses are mainly elected. The House of Lords cannot normally override the Commons but serves as a revising chamber to scrutinise and amend legislation proposed by the lower house, thus providing an opportunity for second thoughts.

Monarchy, aristocracy and democracy. In a tradition dating back at least to Aristotle, there are three fundamental types of government: monarchy, or rule by one person; aristocracy, literally rule by a group of the 'best' people; and democracy, rule by the many or the people as a whole. According to Aristotle, each form of constitution has its virtues but also corresponding vices or deviations. The virtues exist when the ruler rules for the benefit of others; the vices when the ruler rules for the benefit of him or herself. Monarchy is usually inherited within a family, so that the holder's power is not dependent on temporary political forces. According to Aristotle, the main merit of monarchy is its authority and independence since monarchs have a quasi-godlike status. The corresponding defect is despotism. The merit of aristocracy is wisdom; its defect is oligarchy (rule by a selfish group). The merit of democracy is consent of the community; its defect is instability leading to mob tyranny. Aristotle postulated a vicious cycle in which a monarch becomes a despot, is deposed by an aristocracy, which turns into an oligarchy and is overthrown by a popular rebellion. The ensuing democracy degenerates into chaos, resolved by the emergence of a dictator, who takes on the characteristics of a monarch, and so on. Aristotle therefore favoured what he called 'polity', a 'mixed government' combining all three (but loaded in favour of the middle classes) and with checks and balances between different branches of government.

Modern constitutions draw on all three elements. In those European countries where monarchy remains, the powers of the monarch are invariably limited, in some cases being purely ceremonial. The UK constitution is sometimes called a 'constitutional monarchy', meaning that the powers of the monarch are limited by law and in our case by convention. The UK retains an aristocratic element in the form of the House of Lords, one of the two parts of Parliament. However the House of Commons, the members of which are elected as representatives of the people, is the more powerful part of Parliament.

However a cynical view, 'the iron law of oligarchy', claims that whatever form the constitution takes power will inevitably accumulate in the hands of a group of selfish cronies – a king by whatever name and his courtiers. In contemporary conditions this might well be a political party: 'who says organisation says oligarchy...the oligarchical structure of the building suffocates the basic democratic principle' (Michels, quoted in Lipset, *Political Parties* (Free Press 1966)).

Monist and Dualist. This concerns how far the constitution is receptive to international law in the form, for example, of treaties between nations or resolutions of the United Nations (UN). In a monist state a treaty once ratified (confirmed) by the state is automatically part of that state's domestic law. For example the Basic Law of the German Federal Republic Art. 25 states that the general principles of international law take precedence over domestic law and directly create rights and duties. The UK is a dualist state, more inward looking in which international law is not binding in domestic law unless it has been adopted as part of our law in the ordinary way usually by an Act of Parliament.

The UK constitution could be summarised as:

- unwritten;
- *with an incomplete separation of powers*: the judiciary being independent but the executive and legislature partly combined;
- based on the rule of law and accountable government;
- unitary;
- flexible;
- a constitutional monarchy;
- parliamentary;
- a representative democracy with an aristocratic element;
- bicameral;
- dualist.

1.8　Public and private law

Constitutional law is the most basic aspect of 'public law'. It is controversial as to whether there is a useful distinction between public law and 'private law'. Broadly, public law governs the relationship between the government and individuals and that between different governmental agencies. Private law concerns the relationship between individuals and also deals with private organisations such as companies. For reasons connected with a peculiarly English notion of the rule of law (Section 6.4.1) the distinction between public law and private law is less firmly embedded here than in the continental legal systems that inherited the distinction from Roman law. It was believed by the likes of Dicey that the liberties of the individual are best secured if the same law, broadly private law, governs officials and individuals alike so that officials have no special powers or status.

Attractive though this may be, it is arguably unrealistic given the huge powers that must be vested in the state to meet public demand for large-scale public services and government controls over daily life and the movement of the population.

Some writers have rejected the distinction between public and private law, at least on the level of fundamental principle, arguing that the same basic values and concepts pervade all law and that any given function could be carried out by the state or a private body (Section 19.5). This is particularly important today, when it is politically fashionable to entrust public services to profit-making private bodies. Moreover there are numerous bodies not directly connected with the government which exercise vast powers over individuals, such as sporting and professional disciplinary bodies, trade unions and financial bodies. Outside the core functions of keeping order and defence, there is no agreement in the UK as to what the proper sphere of the state is and which bodies are subject to public law.

Conversely the Crown has the same legal powers as a private person, so government makes extensive use of private law in the contexts, for example, of contracts for the procurement of goods and equipment, employment and property. In this context the government's economic power is so great and its activities so wide-ranging that it might be argued that these powers should be treated as having a distinctive public law character. At a very general level the rejection of the distinction between public and private law may be defensible. It is difficult to deny that values such as fairness and openness are common to the private and public sectors, and organisations such as charities that carry out functions for the benefit of the public on a non-profit basis have elements both of the public and of the private. A typical example is social housing, which is currently provided by numerous charitable and other housing associations, but with powerful government agencies behind the scenes setting standards, dictating objectives and punishing defaulters.

There are however important distinctions between public law and private law. These include the following:

▶ The government represents the whole community and its officials have no self-interest of their own. By contrast a private company and an individual both have a legitimate self-interest, including the profit motive. It follows that government should be accountable to the community as a whole for its actions. In the case of a private body by contrast accountability might be regarded as an unacceptable intrusion on its freedom.

▶ Arguably private law is fundamentally different from public law in that it concerns the voluntary interaction of individuals, calling for compromises, recognition of agreed solutions and concessions to vulnerability, whereas public law calls predominantly for general principles designed to structure and contain power. For example, in private law a promise made is normally binding, whereas this is not so in public law (Section 19.5).

▶ The government has the ultimate responsibility to protect the community against disruption and external threats. For this purpose it must be entrusted with special powers to use force. As we shall see in Chapter 23, concerning emergencies, it may be difficult or impossible to reconcile this with our belief that all power should be curbed by law.

▶ The distinction between public and private law has particular implications in two main contexts. Firstly there is the question of the scope of judicial review of decisions made by powerful bodies. This is limited to 'functions of a public nature' (Section 19.5). Secondly the protection of the Human Rights Act 1998 applies mainly against public bodies and against bodies certain of whose functions are public functions (Section 22.4.1). A similar approach is taken in both contexts, the matter depending upon the extent to which the body in question is linked to the central government, for example, whether the body in question has special powers, whether it is controlled or financed by the government and the public importance of its functions.

1.9   The direction of the constitution: reform

There is widely shared belief that the constitution should not be subject to radical reforms but should evolve naturally, particular problems being dealt with as they arise. Hence there is strong resistance to altering the House of Lords on the basis that 'it works' (Section 12.3). This places constitutional reform at the mercy of the party politics of the day rather than subject to a special process designed to consider the long term public interest (eg current attempts at press reform, Section 23.3). Some commentators assert that there are general forces guiding the direction of the constitution. The 'Whig' view of history optimistically claims to find a progression from tyranny to democracy (Section 4.1). In this vein Oliver (2009) suggests that four tendencies underlie constitutional reform. The first is towards 'principles'. These have been developed by the courts, for example, the 'legitimate expectation' (Section 18.3) and 'proportionality' (Section 18.2), and also from within government, for example, the 'Seven Principles of Public Life' (Section 5.11). The second tendency is towards 'governance', meaning reforming governmental processes. This would include, for example, the modernisation of parliamentary procedures. The third tendency albeit perhaps hesitant and sporadic, is that of strengthening 'citizenship' in the sense of equality, for example the Human Rights Act 1998. Oliver's fourth tendency is 'separation'. This would include devolution and the reforms to the court system made by the Constitutional Reform Act 2005 which enhance the separation of powers (Sections 7.5.3, 7.6.2). Bogdanor (*The New British Constitution* Oxford Hart Publishing (2009)), finds a tendency albeit imperfect, towards dispersing power away from the centre and towards 'juridification' in the sense of using law rather than politics.

Contemporary issues have placed the traditional model of the constitution under strain. In particular, the authority of state constitutions are challenged by globalisation, which in this context includes the following:

▶ the commitment to free markets by the powerful countries who control the main international organisations (the UN, the International Monetary Fund and the World Bank);

▶ a commitment albeit less concrete to international human rights and environmental standards and the bringing to justice of political leaders who engage in international crimes such as genocide and torture;

- the ease with which money can be moved around the world;
- the international nature of problems such as terrorism, environmental protection and financial failure. State laws are sometimes ineffective, for example, in dealing with terrorism, human trafficking and financial corruption;
- the fact that individual countries are increasingly dependent on others for resources and security.

The constitution provides filter mechanisms which to a certain extent recognise and control the influences of international actions and relationships on our own law and vice versa (Section 9.7) but otherwise the law has not adapted to globalisation. International affairs are still based on seventeenth-century ideas of self-contained sovereign states.

A constitution might be regarded as managing perpetual disagreement while scholars and politicians continue an apparently fruitless search for objectivity. A constitution will always contain gaps and uncertainties and produce unstable compromises. Moreover there may be values in the constitution – personal privacy is an example – which cannot easily be embodied in clear rules so that they are best undefined as providing only a general sense of direction or an attitude (see Lord Hoffmann in *Wainwright v Home Office* [2003] 4 All ER 969 at 979).

Indeed it might sometimes be better to avoid trying to resolve fundamental disagreement and to let sleeping dogs lie. The blurring or absence of a rule may indicate a deliberate choice to leave a controversial question unanswered: a constitutional abeyance. Thus in *R (Chaytor) v A-G* [2010] EWCA crim. 1910 at [46] the Court of Appeal said that 'it would be to the public disadvantage for the constitutional relationship between the courts and Parliament to be tested to destruction'. Silence might also contribute to stability by confining decisions to matters essential to the issue in hand.

Constitutional silences therefore might discourage us from looking too closely into controversial areas into which it might be wiser not to venture. It invites disputing factions to take comfort in the belief that the constitution does not rule out their concerns. Examples include the question of whether European law prevails over parliamentary sovereignty (Section 8.4), whether Parliament can override certain basic principles of Scottish law (Section 9.4.2) and the relationship between Parliament and the courts.

Summary

- Having read this chapter, you should have a general idea of some basic constitutional concepts and how they relate to the UK. Constitutions deal with the fundamental framework of government and its powers, reflecting the political interests of those who design and operate them and providing mechanisms for the control of government. The constitution does not adequately address the international dimension of modern government.

- The UK constitution is unwritten in the sense that there is no special constitutional document giving the constitution a status superior to the ordinary law. The constitution is made up of many ordinary laws and political conventions. Any special status depends on courts and officials giving it special weight when making decisions.

- The ultimate aim of a constitution is to manage disagreement in circumstances where collective action on behalf of the whole community is required.

- There is an underlying dispute as to how far constitutional disputes should be settled by courts or by elected bodies.

Summary cont'd

▶ There is a tendency in any form of government for powers to gravitate towards a single group so that a primary concern of constitutional law is to provide checks and balances between different branches of government. We introduced the basic concepts of sovereignty, the rule of law, separation of powers and fundamental rights. These are discussed in detail in later chapters.

▶ Political and legal aspects of a constitution should be distinguished, although the boundary between them is leaky and they have different perspectives. The legal aspects of the constitution are a distinctive part of the wider political context, each influencing the other. There are also important constitutional principles in the form of conventions and practices operating without a formal legal basis.

▶ The distinction between written and unwritten constitutions is of some but not fundamental importance. We compared the main advantages and disadvantages of written and unwritten constitutions without committing ourselves to one or the other since the matter is one for political choice. The UK constitution is an untidy mixture of different kinds of law practices and customs and has a substantial informal element, lending itself to domination by personal networks.

▶ We introduced various formal definitions of a constitution without suggesting they were helpful. Different definitions tend to emphasise particular political or legal biases.

▶ We outlined the main classifications of constitutions, emphasising that these are models and that actual constitutions need not closely correspond to any pure model. The UK constitution is strongly parliamentary but weakly monarchical, with perhaps a tendency towards federalism.

▶ The distinction between public law and private law is important, particularly in the context of the Human Rights Act 1998 and of judicial review of powerful bodies. The courts have adopted a pragmatic approach.

▶ Disagreement is inherent in political disputes and may not be resolvable by rational means. In this context we discussed the concept of incommensurability. Constitutional silences or 'abeyances' play a useful role mainly by avoiding confrontation in respect of issues that are inherently controversial.

Exercises

1.1 You are discussing constitutional law with an American who claims that the UK has no constitution. What does she mean and how would you respond?

1.2 Sir John Laws ('The Constitution, Morals and Rights' [1996] PL 622 described a constitution as: 'that set of legal rules which govern the relationship in a state between the ruler and the ruled'. To what extent is this an adequate description of the UK constitution?

1.3 In what sense does the UK have a 'political constitution'?

1.4 How well does the UK constitution fit the various methods of classifying constitutions mentioned in this chapter?

1.5 'It is both a strength and a potential weakness of the British constitution, that almost uniquely for an advanced democracy it is not all set down in writing' (Royal Commission on the Reform of the House of Lords, *Wakeham Report* (Cm 4534, 2000)). Discuss.

1.6 Should the courts have the power to overturn legislation?

1.7 Compare the merits of the parliamentary and presidential systems of government.

1.8 What arrangements are there in the UK for constitutional reform?

Further reading

Note: The Further Reading marked * might usefully be tackled towards the end of the student's course, when fuller knowledge of the subject will have been gained.

*Bamforth and Leyland (eds), *Public Law in a Multi-Layered Constitution* (Hart 2003) ch 1

*Barber, *The Constitutional State* (Oxford University Press 2010)

Barker, 'Against a Written Constitution' [2008] PL 11

Bellamy, *Political Constitutionalism* (Cambridge University Press 2007) ch 1

Bogdanor and Vogenauer, 'Enacting a British Constitution: Some Problems' [2008] PL 38

*Ewing, 'The Politics of the British Constitution' [2000] PL 405

Feldman, 'None, One or Several? Perspectives on the UK's Constitution' (2005) 64 CLJ 329

Feldman, ' "Which in Your Case You Have Not Got": Constitutionalism at Home and Abroad' (2011) 62 CLP 117

Finer, Bogdanor and Rudden, *Comparing Constitutions* (Oxford University Press 1995) ch 1

*Gee, 'The Political Constitutionalism of JAG Griffith' (2008) 28 LS 20

*Gee and Webber, 'What Is a Political Constitution?' (2010) 30 OJLS 273

Griffith, 'The Common Law and the Political Constitution' (2001) 117 LQR 42.

Griffith, 'The Political Constitution' (1979) 42 MLR 1

Harlow and Rawlings, *Law and Administration* (3rd edn, Cambridge University Press 2009) ch 1

Hennessy, *The Hidden Wiring: Unearthing the British Constitution* (Gollancz 1995) Prologue, ch. 1

*Hickman, 'In Defence of the Legal Constitution' (2005) 55 U Toronto LJ 981

House of Lords Select Committee on the Constitution, *The Process of Constitutional Change* (HL 2010–12, 117) and Government Response Cm 8181

*Loughlin, *Foundations of Public Law* (Oxford University Press 2010) ch 10

Loughlin, *Sword and Scales* (Hart 2005)

Loveland, 'A Critique of the Political Constitution' (2006) 122 LQR 340

Marshall, 'The Constitution: Its Theory and Interpretation' in Bogdanor (ed), *The British Constitution in the Twentieth Century* (Oxford University Press 2003) 29–35

Mc Cormick, *Institutions of Law* (Oxford University Press 2007) chs 1–4, 10

McIlwain, *Constitutionalism Ancient and Modern* (Cornell University Press 1947) ch. 1

Munro, *Studies in Constitutional Law* (2nd edn, Butterworths 1999) ch 1

Oliver, *Constitutional Reform in the United Kingdom* (Oxford University Press 2003)

Oliver, 'The United Kingdom Constitution in Transition: From Where to Where?' in Adenas and Fairgrieve (eds), *Tom Bingham and the Transformation of the Law* (Oxford University Press 2009)

Poole, 'Tilting at Windmills? Truth and Illusion in the Political Constitution' (2007) 70 MLR 250

Ridley, 'There Is No British Constitution: A Dangerous Case of the Emperor's Clothes' (1988) 41 Parliamentary Aff 340

Ward, *The English Constitution: Myths and Realities* (Hart 2004)

Chapter 2
Underlying political traditions

2.1 Introduction

Western European constitutions have been influenced by three broad and overlapping political traditions. They are loosely termed 'liberalism', 'republicanism' and 'communitarianism'. Each emphasises a different aspect of human nature and privileges different values. Liberalism is a relatively modern notion. It is based on the notions of individual self-determination and limited government focusing on rights and freedom. It assumes that the individual is the best judge of how he or she should live and that the state should not prefer one way of life over another. It therefore concentrates on limiting the power of the state. Republicanism is an ancient notion inherited from classical Greece. It favours the concept of the 'virtuous citizen'. Drawing upon our social and cooperative nature as what Aristotle called 'political animals'. Republicanism concentrates on political involvement as equal citizens in governing ourselves and preventing any elite becoming dominant. Communitarianism goes further in a collective direction. It emphasises our nature as herd animals that live by copying each other. It emphasises the virtues of sympathy and mutual support within the customs and traditions in which different communities are embedded. It is particularly concerned to protect the interests of groups such as ethnic minorities.

We would not expect a particular constitution to fit into any single set of values but would expect to find values associated with all three traditions scattered throughout the constitution, with some more prominent than others depending on the circumstances at any given time. Moreover, each tradition has varying shades, so that in many contexts their practical conclusions overlap.

The three traditions might differ especially as to the extent to which they would protect fundamental rights such as freedom of expression. Liberalism would place an especially high value on individual freedom of expression, for example in the US Constitution. Republicanism would regard freedom of expression primarily as an instrument to ensure citizen participation in government and not as an end in itself. Republicanism and liberalism would concur in placing an especially high value on political freedom. To a communitarian, freedom of expression may be regarded as divisive, selfish and frustrating community values.

Liberalism is the dominant tradition behind the UK constitution. Liberalism developed gradually from the seventeenth century originating most prominently with the first Lord Shaftsbury (1621–83) and John Locke (1632–1704) in defence of the English revolution. Liberalism is sometimes invoked by the courts. For example according to Lord Steyn in *Roberts v Parole Board* [2006]: 'in our system the working assumption is that Parliament legislates for a European liberal democracy which respects fundamental rights'. Unfortunately liberalism has several meanings (below) so that such a generalisation is not particularly useful.

The communitarian tradition is less prominent in the UK than in other European countries. For example the French Constitution places' liberty, equality and fraternity together. Elsewhere the Canadian Constitution is widely regarded as emphasising the communitarian tradition. See Cram, *Contested Words: Legal Restrictions on Freedom of*

Speech in Liberal Democracies (Ashgate, 2006). Within the UK, the provisions for devolved governments in Scotland, Wales and Northern Ireland embody communitarian elements especially in the case of Northern Ireland concerning the interests of the different communities in the Province (Section 16.3).

2.2 Liberalism

It is difficult to identify concrete principles on which all liberals agree. However, the following might be the main principles of liberalism:

▶ Liberalism emphasises the interests of the individual rather than the collective interests of the community. The state exists only to protect the interests of the individual.

▶ The interests of all individuals except those who harm others are worthy of equal concern and respect. This of course begs the question as to what counts as 'harm'. It might for example merely mean interference which the rulers themselves find unpleasant.

▶ Individuals should be free to follow their own chosen way of life ('autonomy'). Liberalism attempts to place constraints on government in the interests of individual freedom and to give the individual an area of private life that is out of bounds for the state. Liberal laws are therefore tolerant of minorities and dissenters. A problem here is how far to tolerate a dissenter who threatens the security of the liberal state itself. The state should not favour one way of life over another. This is particularly problematic and embodies what is claimed to be a fatal contradiction within liberalism. Liberalism obviously favours its own, liberal way of life, but the state might have to choose between conflicting interests some being non-liberal, for example an authoritarian religion. Similarly given that the state has to fund itself from taxation, unless it were to tax everyone equally, it has to make choices as to whom to tax, thus sometimes encouraging or discouraging particular ways of life

▶ Liberalism claims to be rational. It seeks a constitution that free and equal people would rationally support. It recognises that there is likely to be irreducible disagreement even among people of good will and so favours caution about state intervention.

▶ Liberalism is international and favours cooperation between nations. Thus liberals broadly support organisations, such as the EU, that attempt to override national interests. An extreme version of liberalism, neo-liberalism, would use force to impose 'freedom' on other nations, thus exemplifying the paradox that, according to opponents of liberalism, undermines liberalism. Neo-liberalism lay behind the invasion of Iraq carried out by the UK in 2002.

Liberalism is not universally admired, sometimes being condemned as selfish and uncaring and favouring the individual over the group. A modest defence of liberalism is that at least it tries to make room for other beliefs, recognising the 'lurking doubt' in all human affairs and the desire to avoid conflicts. Liberal societies have been relatively stable and peaceful. Even if there is some objective truth as to how to live, it has so far eluded the human race. Indeed the desire for peace was the historical origin of liberalism as a response to the religious conflicts that disrupted Europe during the sixteenth and seventeenth centuries. Once the bond supplied by a dominant religion had been dissolved, it became impossible to govern people of widely different beliefs without either conferring a large amount of individual freedom or resorting to oppression, which would ultimately destroy the community.

Liberalism is not wedded to any particular form of government. Liberals usually support democracy as the form of government most likely to secure individual freedom but unlike republicanism do not value democracy as an end in itself, having no objection in principle to securing individual rights through the undemocratic means of a court. Moreover, in contrast to republicanism, liberalism is not especially interested in whether citizens directly participate in governmental decision making but accepts government by an elite accountable to citizens.

Liberalism would emphasise in particular the following:

1. Decision makers must be open and accountable. It must be borne in mind that mechanisms for making a decision maker accountable are not the same for each kind of decision maker. For example it is arguably wrong to elect judges, since election risks compromising the independence of a court. Conversely the arguments for elected lawmakers are strong since they can be removed if they make laws to which the people object. In both cases it is normally important that the decision-making process be open and public, but sometimes confidentiality may be a competing concern, for example in cases involving the methods of the secret security services (see Section 23.3) and in order to protect vulnerable people such as children.
2. Government power must be limited and no single institution should have the last word so as irrevocably to close off debate. For example the lawmaker must not be able to bind future lawmakers (Chapter 9), and court decisions should allow dissenting judgements. The courts have an important role in protecting individuals against abuse of power and safeguarding fundamental rights but there must be checks and balances between the courts and the lawmaker.
3. Individual rights are respected but are not necessarily absolute. There is considerable disagreement within liberalism as to when individual rights can be overridden.
4. Departures from treating everyone equally must be justified. There must, in particular, be equal access to courts of law, and public office must be open to anyone with suitable qualifications.

2.3 Varieties of liberalism in constitutional thought

There are many varieties of liberalism, each applying the basic ingredients of freedom and equality in different ways. The following classical writers have influenced the development of constitutional thought in the UK and exemplify particular points on the map.

2.3.1 Thomas Hobbes (1588–1679): the impersonal state and individualism

A fundamental change in political thinking emerged in the sixteenth century when the church and the state became separated. The idea of the state as an impersonal organisation intended to serve everyone was revived from classical antiquity by republican thinkers such as Machiavelli. Hobbes was one of the earliest English exponents of this approach and, although not a liberal, generated ideas that are basic to liberalism.

Hobbes published his most influential work, *Leviathan*, in 1651 (1973) following a time of widespread political unrest when England was in the grip of religious turmoil and civil war between an authoritarian king and an equally authoritarian Parliament dominated by religious interests. (Of his other works, *The Elements of Law* is of particular interest.) He tried to explain the rationale of legal authority without drawing upon religion. Hobbes doubted whether it was possible to discover objective truth about anything. He had a strongly individualistic approach based on the equality of all citizens. He believed that human affairs involve endless disagreement and therefore that a constitution has solid foundations only in the minimum on which it is possible rationally to agree.

As with many liberal thinkers, Hobbes' idea of government was based on an imaginary 'social contract' according to which free and equal people would choose to give up their natural freedom in exchange for the benefits of government. This symbolises that government depends on the consent of the governed, hence Hobbes' relevance to contemporary democratic ideas. The controversial question is what form of government free and equal people would agree to, and to this question there is no generally accepted answer. According to Hobbes, the need for someone to settle disputes and keep order is the basic purpose of government. There must therefore be a single ultimate ruler, a sovereign, 'Leviathan', who has unlimited power and ultimately rules by force, to whom the people consent to surrender their natural freedom. Under that ultimate sovereign there can be many different detailed government arrangements.

Hobbes did not believe that humans are inherently wicked but thought that we are self-seeking and that our different ideas of good inevitably set us in conflict with each other – a war of 'all against all' – so that without government we would destroy each other. According to Hobbes, outside the private sphere of family and personal relationships we are motivated by three impulses: competition, fear and the desire for power over others. We constantly strive to fulfil new desires in a never-ending and ultimately doomed search for what he called 'felicity'. Hobbes therefore argued that any government is better than none and that 'the concord of many cannot be maintained without power to keep them all in awe' (*Elements of Law* XIX, 4).

Hobbes' most famous passage encapsulates both his basic principle and the beauty of his language:

> Hereby it is manifest that during the time men live without a common Power to keep them all in awe, they are in that condition which is called Warre; and such a warre, as is of every man against every man ... In such condition, there is no place for Industry: because the fruit thereof is uncertain; and consequently no Culture of the Earth, no Navigation, nor use of the commodities that may be imported by Sea; no commodious Building; no Instruments of moving and removing such things as require much force; no knowledge of the face of the Earth; no account of Time; no Arts; no Letters; no Society; and which is worst of all, continuall feare, and danger of violent death; And the life of man, solitary, poore, nasty, brutish and short. (1973, 65)

Hobbes' hypothetical contract is made between the people, who agree with each other to surrender their natural freedom to the sovereign. The sovereign is not itself a party to the social contract. This produces a 'covenant', a one-sided promise, to obey Leviathan. In order to minimise disagreement the sovereign must be a single unitary body, an 'artificial man'. This could be either a monarch or an assembly. Hobbes' sovereign has no special qualifications for ruling but is merely the representative of the community. The obligation of the sovereign derives from its gratitude to the people for the free gift of power.

Hobbes believed that humans have certain 'natural' rights based on keeping promises, respect for individual freedom and equality: 'Do not that to another, which thou wouldest not have done to thyself' (1973, 14, 15). He also believed, anticipating modern liberalism that the ruler has a duty to leave the people as much liberty as possible without hurt to the public (*Elements of Law* XXVIII). However according to Hobbes, natural rights are no more than rational hopes or expectations and have no binding force unless the lawmaker chooses to protect them.

Hobbes believed that because the sovereign itself needs security the interests of the sovereign and the people naturally coincide. The sovereign therefore needs to keep the people happy. It may be that the money provided by business interests coupled with modern technology, with its surveillance devices and weapons, makes a lawmaker less dependent on the happiness of the people than was the case in Hobbes' time.

Hobbes' government has two crucial features. Firstly, because of the uncertainty of human affairs, Leviathan must have unlimited power since otherwise there would be the very disagreement that the sovereign exists to resolve. Hobbes thought that, although some forms of government may be better than others, by definition the sovereign can never act unjustly to a subject because the subject has agreed to accept every decision of the sovereign. Secondly the sovereign exists for a single purpose, the welfare of his subjects, and has no authority to act for any other purpose. Thus the sovereign should act 'so that the giver shall have no just occasion to repent him of his gift' and 'all the duties of the rulers are contained in this one sentence, the safety of the people is the supreme law'. (By 'safety' Hobbes meant not just the preservation of life but general justice and well-being; see *Elements of Law* XXVIII, 1.) However Hobbes was clear that it is for the ruler alone to decide whether it needs to exercise its powers, and he provided no legal remedy against a ruler that exceeded its power, regarding the matter as one for divine retribution.

Hobbes' ideas although perhaps representing a one-sided view of human nature are relevant to the modern constitution in that they identify recurring themes and claims. They include the following:

▶ Government depends on the consent of the people and is the representative of the people.
▶ The minimum to be expected from government and the constitution is the keeping of order and the protection of the people.
▶ A single sovereign source of absolute power to resolve disagreement. In our case the doctrine of parliamentary supremacy reflects Hobbes' idea, as does the belief that in an emergency the executive should be entrusted with very wide powers (see Section 23.1). Indeed the German political theorist Carl Schmidt (a Nazi supporter) argued that, in view of the possibility of 'the exception' (ie an emergency), a sovereign must have absolute power always available. The contemporary question, contrary to Hobbes, is whether there should be any individual rights that are sacrosanct.
▶ All citizens are equal. No one should have powers or rights or be subject to special obligations based on factors such as birth, custom, social status or religion.
▶ Freedom is the natural state of affairs as opposed to a gift bestowed by authority. According to Hobbes, 'right is that liberty which the law leaves us' (*Elements of Law* XXIX, 5). It is true that the sovereign can make any law but unless it positively does

so the individual is free to do what he or she likes: 'freedom lies in the silence of the laws'. Conversely however there cannot be any guaranteed rights without law.
- ▶ The separation of politics from religion, church from state.
- ▶ The distinction between the public and the private spheres. In relation to areas of life not controlled by the state, namely those where public order and safety are not at risk, what I do is not the state's business.
- ▶ Laws concern external behaviour not matters of personal belief or conscience. For example under Article 9 of the European Convention on Human Rights (ECHR), freedom of religious belief is absolute but the 'manifestation of religion' can be restricted on certain public interest grounds (see Section 21.4.3).

Hobbes was not concerned with republican issues of participation in government. Nor did he tackle the problem of how to make government accountable. He believed that by a 'natural law' the sovereign must respect the trust placed in him by the people. He did not deal with the problem that in all but the simplest societies, power must in practice be divided up and rulers must rely on advisers, thereby creating potential disagreements. Hobbes however recognised that some methods of government might be better than others and in the later part of his work *The Dialogues (ed Copsey (University of Chicago Press 1971))* made many suggestions, such as that the sovereign should consult the Parliament.

Hobbes disliked the common law because it is made by courts. In a long-running dispute with Coke, the Lord Chief Justice, Hobbes attacked the view of the judges that law is 'artificial reason' that resides in the learning of an elite group (themselves) as a childish fiction. He recognised a place for rules derived from natural reason which must be applied where there are gaps in the written law but thought that these depend on the tacit consent of the sovereign (*Elements of Law* XXIX, 10). This dispute is echoed today in several contexts where one school of thought claims that the courts are the guardians of the values of the community (see Sections 8.4, 8.5, 17.1, 20.1).

2.3.2   John Locke (1632–1704): individual rights and majority government

Locke is widely regarded as a founder of modern liberalism and constitutionalism. Locke's writings (*Second Treatise of Government*, 1690) supported the 1688 revolution, which founded our present constitution against the claims of absolute monarchy. They also influenced the US Constitution. His approach was grounded in the Protestant religion, which stressed individual conscience and self-improvement by hard work. Locke believed that individuals had certain natural rights identified by reasoning about human nature and existing, as he saw it, to serve God. These are life, health, freedom and property. For him, the purpose of government is to protect these rights, particularly property, in the exceptional cases where conflicts arise. To this extent Locke's government serves the same function as that of Hobbes. However unlike Hobbes, Locke's government has limited powers. Hobbes' and Locke's contrasting views still underlie the debate about the nature of the constitution.

According to Locke, the people first hypothetically contract with each other unanimously to establish a government and then choose an actual government by majority vote. The government as such does not enter into a contract but takes on a trust or 'covenant', a one-sided promise, whereby it undertakes to perform its functions of protecting natural rights and advancing well-being. Thus, unlike Hobbes' Leviathan,

Lockes' government is limited by the covenant it makes. Locke's basic principles can be found in modern liberal constitutions. Firstly, there is the idea that government depends on the consent of the people. According to Locke, government should be appointed and dismissed periodically by a majority vote representing those with a stake in the community. Locke justified majority voting on the basis that the majority commands most force but recognised that there is no logical reason why a majority should be 'right' in relation to any particular issue. Secondly, Locke was concerned to limit the power of government in order to protect the rights and freedoms of the individual. This is perhaps the most distinctive feature of liberalism, although liberals do not agree how this should be done, for example whether by courts or democratic mechanisms. Locke himself did not favour detailed legal constraints on government, regarding the contribution of lawyers as 'the Phansies and intricate contrivances of men, following contrary and hidden interests put into words' (1960, para 12). He relied on dividing up government power so that no one branch can be dominant: the separation of powers (Chapter 7). He also insisted that governments should periodically be held to account by means of elections and upheld as a last resort the right to rebel against a government that broke its trust.

Thirdly, Locke promoted 'toleration' of different ways of life provided they did not upset the basic political framework. For example he did not favour toleration of Catholics, whom he regarded as subversive. Moreover, he drafted the Constitution of Carolina to accommodate slaves as property since this advanced the economic system of the day. This apparent double standard is one of the alleged contradictions of liberalism. Thus liberalism downgrades some interests in order to protect itself, this being a justification often used today to defend illiberal laws aimed at terrorism but in their language of wider scope (Chapter 22).

2.3.3   David Hume (1711–76), Jeremy Bentham (1748–1832), John Stuart Mill (1806–73): utilitarianism

Welfare liberalism. The most influential version of welfare liberalism is utilitarianism. Utilitarians believe that what is the right thing to do depends solely on its consequences This of course begs the question of what counts as a good consequence. In the context of a constitution, this might be anything designated by the lawmaker. In the case of utilitarianism, it is the satisfaction of the wishes of as many people as possible an approach which is attractive to the mindset of officials but not necessarily to the lawyer since it sidesteps questions of fairness and justice. The case of *Copsey* (Section 2.4) is an example.

David Hume whose ideas influence the common law was a founder of utilitarianism. He thought that government is a matter of practical compromise. He rejected the social contract as a fiction and regarded ideals of abstract justice as myths useful for persuading people to conform. Hume advocated a pragmatic society based on coordinating individual interests. He believed that our limited knowledge, strength and altruism provided the moral basis for a legal system. Contrasting with Hobbes, Hume thought that self-interest and our natural sympathy for others would generate basic principles of cooperation, including respect for private property, voluntary dealings and keeping promises. Hume favoured the common law as a vehicle for this, which he described as a happy combination of circumstances, according to which the law is developed pragmatically in the light of changing social practices and values.

Jeremy Bentham is the most celebrated utilitarian. He gave intellectual respectability to the idea of an all-powerful central government making general laws and accountable to a majority of the people. Using the slogan 'the greatest happiness of the greatest number', Bentham measured utility by counting people's actual demands, giving each equal weight ('each counts for one and none for more than one') and refusing to treat any preference as better than any other: ('pushpin is as good as poetry'). Bentham's version of utilitarianism involves strong democratic controls to ensure that the law represents public opinion (see generally Craig, 'Bentham, Public Law and Democracy' [1989] PL 407). Bentham regarded law and courts as subordinate to utilitarian considerations. In particular he regarded legal certainty and judicial independence, what we call the 'rule of law', as a sham. He thought that the idea of natural rights promoted by Locke was 'nonsense on stilts', claiming that rights were simply legal mechanisms, that law is merely a tool of government and public opinion is the ultimate authority.

Utilitarianism is replete with problems, particularly in relation to justice and fairness. For example, utilitarianism is consistent with slavery in that the standard of living of a majority might be held to outweigh the loss of freedom of a minority. A utilitarian could reasonably think that innocent people could be shot in order to disperse a public meeting or kept in jail even if wrongly convicted in order to preserve public confidence in the police (see Lord Denning in *McIlkenny v Chief Constable of the West Midlands Police* [1980] at 239–40). Utilitarianism also finds difficulty with the notion of rights and obligations. Why should I pay you what I have promised if I now discover a better use for the money? Can utilitarianism really give equal weight to all preferences without some non-utilitarian filter to exclude 'irrational' or 'immoral' preferences such as those of paedophiles? These and other problems have been widely discussed without a conclusion.

John Stuart Mill tried to reconcile utilitarianism with liberal individualism by claiming that maximising individual freedom is the best way to advance general welfare since it encourages the virtues of creativity. He believed that happiness could best be achieved by experimenting with different ways of life. This led to Mill's emphasis on freedom of expression and his influential 'harm' principle, namely that the only ground on which the state should interfere with freedom is to prevent harm to others. The state should not normally interfere paternalistically to protect a person for his or her own good. However this begs the question of what counts as 'harm' since harm can be defined as anything we dislike. For example does harm include 'offence' if someone makes fun of my religious beliefs (Chapter 20)?

Mill did not apply his harm principle to those who were unable fully to make rational judgements, such as children, a principle that, uncomfortably, Mill seemed to extend to colonised peoples. Moreover distortions creep in. For example Mill was less egalitarian than Bentham, since for Mill preferences were not equal. Mill favoured the 'higher' and more intellectual and artistic capacities of the human mind. He was also a romantic, reminding us that ideas such as justice may not be purely rational, in the sense of being possible to pin down as legal rules, but have an emotional and spiritual dimension (see Ward, 'The Echo of a Sentimental Jurisprudence' (2002) 15 L & Critique 107).

However Mill departed from strict utilitarianism in two ways. Firstly, he believed that a person who makes independent choices does not unthinkingly follow the majority is to be especially valued as having a better 'character'. Secondly, in contrast with Bentham's insistence that all pleasures are of equal value he thought that the higher and more intellectual pleasures enjoyed by a well-educated minority were better than the lower pleasures enjoyed by the mob Thus although Mill emphasised that the individual is the best judge of how he or she should live, some ways of life, notably those of the creative artist or intellectual are objectively better than others and can be favoured by the state. On the other hand Mill would not have welcomed the contemporary practice of giving privileged access to government to business and financial interests.

The conflict between the different recipes of Mill and Bentham are reflected in contemporary legal and political issues, especially in relation to the question of the compromise between individual rights (Mill) and the wishes of the majority (Bentham). Not surprisingly there is no overarching general principle. Outcomes depend largely on the mix of individuals and circumstances prevailing at the time. Sometimes, most notably in the increased respect given to minorities since the 1960s, Mill's values triumph. In other areas most obviously that of state surveillance a version of the general welfare has prevailed over individual freedom (Section 23.5).

A general issue is influenced by the different versions of liberalism presented by Bentham and Mill. There is an influential school of thought most prominently promoted by the American theorist Ronald Dworkin that the courts should be the pre-eminent guardians of the (liberal) moral values of the community. The courts are depicted in a manner long claimed by common lawyers as wise and objective moral philosophers with special access to the values of the community (Section 4.5). According to Dworkin the courts should focus on the protection of rights which should prevail over utilitarian principles which are the special concern of the other branches of government. However it is not obvious that the courts are any better at deciding moral issues than Parliament. Both Bentham and Mill preferred political to legal mechanisms, including a strong system of checks and balances between different branches of government and a belief in democracy. However Mill was not a wholehearted democrat. His elitist strain led him to favour decision making by experts and he favoured slewing voting rights in favour of the wealthy and educated.

2.3.4   Market liberalism (neo-liberalism): Friedrich Hayek (1899–1992)

Market liberalism claims to provide an objective method of resolving disputes. It is a form of utilitarianism. Market liberalism is concerned with harnessing what it regards as the primary human impulse of self-interest, in pursuit of the common good. It does so by encouraging competition between free individuals relying on the allegedly objective measure of money. It gives the state a limited but strong role as an allegedly neutral umpire to ensure that free competition takes place. Its latest incarnation, neo-liberalism, has no compunction in using force to ensure conformity to its idea of freedom thereby illustrating what opponent of liberalism regard as liberalism's inbuilt contradiction.

Market liberalism is currently fashionable in the UK government circles. A market liberal constitution requires a strong highly centralised government as envisaged by Hobbes (Section 2.3.1). The UK constitution is therefore well suited to market liberalism as it is to any single minded ideology since the sovereign Parliament can easily be controlled by a cohesive group. For example there are no restrictions preventing the state from transferring any of its functions to the private market (Contrast the German Basic Law: education).

Hayek was the outstanding champion of the relationship between market liberalism and the law. According to Hayek, the state has neither the knowledge nor the competence to plan people's lives, and efficient solutions are best found through free interchange in the market, the price mechanism acting as a store of knowledge of supply and demand. The market encourages people to produce goods that others want. It also respects individual freedom since people can decide for themselves what they want to buy or sell.

There is no necessary connection between market liberalism and a liberal belief in individual freedom in moral and social matters. A market liberal such as the former British Prime Minister Margaret Thatcher might claim to harness valuable human impulses in the economic sphere while suppressing what he or she regards as harmful human impulses elsewhere. As a form of utilitarianism market liberalism does not value freedom for its own sake but only as a means to an end, this end being wealth maximisation. Moreover the poor may be excluded from the market and many 'goods' for example the environment are not easily reduced to a market.

Hayek seems to assume, contrary to Hobbes, that within a society which maximises individual freedom, shared understandings will emerge on which enough people agree for life to be harmonious, what he called the 'spontaneous order'. Hayek relied on the notion of the rule of law as a framework of certain general rules within which we can be 'free' to plan our lives (Chapter 6). Following Hume (above), in this respect favoured the common law since it produces rules generated from below by individual cases.

Liberals do not usually regard particular economic policies or public service provisions as constitutional matters to be treated as part of the overriding framework of government but treat them as subjects of democratic choice. However, according to 'public choice' theory (an application of market liberalism to the government itself), politicians and officials are driven by self-interest. Thus, if left alone, they will try to maximise their incomes, expand their territories and minimise their workloads. Since the 1980s this view of official behaviour has strongly influenced Parliament and the executive while the courts have perhaps displayed the older liberalisms of Locke and Mill. Market liberalism may be attractive to politicians and officials partly because it provides an allegedly objective means of making policy since, according to market liberalism, the market can never be wrong. Thus the role of the law is only to ensure that the market operates as freely as possible.

Examples are the contemporary practices of privatisation, and outsourcing such as that of the railways, the utility companies, some health services, schools and prisons, and the splitting up of many civil service operations into semi-autonomous 'executive agencies' run on the model of private business (Section 15.8). Where goods and services cannot actually be competed for, regulatory mechanisms are created to simulate competitive price mechanisms, for example by setting targets and standards with accompanying rewards and penalties (Section 20.4).

2.3.5   Welfare liberalism: John Rawls (1921–2000): liberal justice and equality

Welfare liberalism recognises that individual freedom and market freedom may be of little value unless we have the basic resources public and private to live fulfilled and comfortable lives as social beings. Welfare liberalism therefore overlaps with communitarianism. (In the USA the term 'liberal' is commonly used to mean this form of liberalism). Welfare liberalism if it is to operate at a constitutional level therefore requires positive protections for human goods such as health, security, education, dignity, friendship and leisure. Parliamentary supremacy means that UK law is capable of participating in these protections but there is little specific protection for welfare goals. The Human Rights Act 1998 concentrates on individual freedoms (but see Art 8 ECHR: respect for family life, Section 20.4). However, European Union law which has priority over domestic law has a strong welfare element.

An influential version of welfare liberalism based on the social contract device is that of John Rawls:

> Our exercise of political power is proper and hence justifiable only when it is exercised in accordance with a constitution the essentials of which all citizens may be reasonably expected to endorse in the light of principles and ideas acceptable to them as reasonable and rational. This is the liberal principle of legitimacy. (*Political Liberalism* (Columbia University Press 1993) 217)

One problem with this is its reliance on the word 'reasonably', since we may disagree as to what is reasonable. Who decides what is 'reasonably expected' in a society made up of people with many different beliefs? To answer this question Rawls constructed an imaginary 'original position' in which a representative group of people ignorant of their own circumstances, including sex, race or wealth, decide what would be a just constitution (*A Theory of Justice* (Oxford University Press 1972)). The purpose of this 'veil of ignorance' is to ensure equality and the removal of self-interested influences. However it also reduces the parties to clones, thinking as one and therefore not making an agreement at all in any real sense. Rawls was of course aware of this and later introduced the watered-down notion of an 'overlapping consensus'. This is a settlement that people from a wide variety of backgrounds might be prepared to acknowledge as reasonable. However underlying all this is the liberal assumption that people want to agree and might be willing to compromise. It is by no means obvious that this is the case. Rawls acknowledges this, claiming that his arguments are political rather than philosophical and apply only in a community that is broadly sympathetic to liberal values ('Justice as Fairness: Political Not Metaphysical' in Freeman (ed), *Collected Papers* (Harvard University Press 1999); but see Skidelsky and Skidelsky, *How Much is Enough? The Love of Money and the Case for the Good Life* (Allen Lane 2012), objecting to Rawls's idea of a neutral state as a misreading of liberalism).

Rawls identifies two fundamental 'principles of justice'. The first is that 'each person is to have an equal right to the most extensive basic liberty compatible with a similar liberty for others'. These liberties operate in the constitutional sphere. They include political freedoms, freedom of speech, personal liberty and the right to hold private property. This has priority over the second principle, the 'difference principle', which is concerned with allocating the resources of society: 'Social and economic inequalities are to be arranged so that they are both (a) reasonably expected to be to everyone's advantage, and (b) attached to positions and offices open to all.' Rawls is prepared to redistribute resources from rich to poor on the ground that much wealth is accumulated by chance, either through inheritance or through abilities that we happen to be born with. We therefore owe a duty to help the less fortunate. However fundamental freedoms cannot be overridden in the interests of some other social goal. This distinguishes a liberal for a communitarian perspective.

2.3.6 Liberal pluralism: group liberalism

Liberal pluralism, sometimes called 'identity politics' or 'the politics of recognition', is similar to communitarianism and not always regarded as a kind of liberalism (see

Anderson, *Constitutional Rights after Globalism* (Hart 2005); Cover, 1983; Galston, 2005). It requires the state to respect the identities and way of life of different groups such as national, religious, ethnic or sexual minorities, as well as political associations, trade unions, vocational groups and the like. It may therefore conflict with other liberal ideas of equality. The groups protected by pluralism might be disadvantaged because of the stereotype of the 'normal' person represented by the ruling group, in our case the white, able-bodied, heterosexual, culturally Christian male.

As Baroness Hale pointed out in *In re G (Adoption) (Unmarried Couple)* [2009] 1 AC 173 [122] the protection of unpopular minorities is a particular duty of the courts. Liberal pluralism requires active steps to ensure that all such groups have the leverage to participate fully in the life of the community and to express their own identity against that of the dominant group, for example by being represented in public institutions, using their own language and giving effect to their own law and courts, as in the case of Islamic and Jewish laws. It is not enough merely to tolerate or attempt to integrate such groups into the mainstream, as is the dominant approach of UK law, since this implies only limited acceptance. The danger of identity politics is that it might encourage hostility between different groups, since its extreme 'identity' implies rejecting outsiders.

Liberal pluralism might therefore conflict with other kinds of liberalism, particularly where the values of the group conflict with more individualistic values; for example a religious sect might claim that corporal punishment is part of its religion (*R (Williamson) v Secretary of State for Education and Employment* [2005] 2 All ER 1: religious claim overridden by interests of child). A group might also claim that its way of life should be supported by the state, for example religious schools, or should have special treatment to compensate for past injustices.

Liberal pluralism would put less stress on equality and rationality than would other forms of liberalism. Thus there is the problem of a group whose values are authoritarian: the famous liberal dilemma of 'tolerating intolerance'. According to Lord Walker in *Williamson* [60], 'in matters of human rights the courts should not show liberal tolerance only to tolerant liberals.' For example a common liberal claim is that liberalism contains universal truths derived from reason, and a liberal law should not permit a religious group to prevent its members leaving it. However such freedom might be unacceptable to a religion which teaches, along the lines of positive freedom (Section 2.4), that compulsion is in a person's best interests. Some liberals suggest the proper approach is that the members of any group must accept that the state, in order to protect itself, can override their interests provided the decision process used is fair to all interests. However there may not be agreement as to what a fair process means (see Raz, 'Multiculturalism' (1998) 11 *Ratio Juris* 193).

In terms of constitutional arrangements, we would expect liberal pluralists to emphasise open and dispersed government and the equal representation of minority groups in public institutions such as the judiciary. The different devolved arrangements in Scotland, Northern Ireland and Wales (Chapter 16) could be presented as embodying this. It is often suggested that one part of the legislature, the House of Lords, might comprise representatives of important interest groups. At present the only such groups represented in Parliament are the aristocracy and Church of England bishops (Section 12.2). Liberal pluralism would also favour voluntary mechanisms to enable individuals to participate in society, for example tax breaks for charities and other voluntary bodies ('civil society').

Liberal pluralism might not be sympathetic to the idea of an overarching state law and might be required to respect different interpretations of the law according to the culture and traditions of different religious or ethnic groups and to allow particular groups to use their own form of dispute resolution machinery, including courts. In the UK voluntary methods of arbitration are permitted in respect of commercial disputes, and a variety of forms of marriage are recognised. However these are subject to overriding requirements of the general law.

2.4   Freedom

The idea of freedom is central to liberalism. Some regard freedom as an end in itself: 'he who desires in liberty anything other than itself is born to be a servant' (De Tocqueville, *L'Ancien Regime*, 1856). However it is difficult to regard freedom as an end in itself, let alone the highest end. Do we, for example, regard Hitler's freedom to pursue his interests as something good in itself, although offset by the harm he did? Moreover freedom may conflict with 'equality' since the strong are free to exploit the weak.

Freedom has different, vague and sometimes conflicting meanings. At the most basic level liberalism contains a conflict between two ideas of freedom. This affects the extent to which different political groups regard state intervention as a good or bad thing.

1. *Traditional or negative freedom* meaning the absence of interference is what most of us understand by freedom. For example, negative social freedom as presented by Mill (Section 2.3) concentrates on the individual as 'author of his own life', that is freeing the individual from interference by the state. Economic liberalism relies on the idea of the free market and the belief that competing individuals pursuing their own self-interests are more likely to produce generally good outcomes than the state. The role of the state is a limited one of ensuring that the free market operates smoothly: a government with as few powers as possible beyond the basic functions of defence and keeping order.

   Social and economic freedom do not necessarily go together politically and do not lead to any particular conclusion as to how freedom should be protected, whether by a court or by democratic means. Arguably economic liberalism depends on a certain degree of social conformity in order to ensure that enough people buy the goods on offer and to control those who lose out from the adverse consequences of competition.

   A fundamental problem with negative freedom is that some freedoms are more important than others. Thus the relative importance of competing freedoms, such as freedom of the press against privacy (eg *Campbell v MGN Ltd* [2004]), may be controversial and courts must sometimes choose between them an exercise in which the idea of negative freedom is unhelpful. There seems to be no common measure or litmus test to enable us to rank or compare different freedoms (eg *Copsey* below). Thus when the law restricts freedom in order to protect the freedom of others as liberalism recommends, for example by restricting demonstrators in order to protect those going to work, it is not maximising freedom but only redistributing freedom among different people according to the lawmakers' preference as to which freedom is more attractive. This leads to the second kind of freedom.

2. *Positive freedom*, an older idea, is freedom not to do what we want as such, but to control our lives by doing what is good for us. Freedom in this sense means

exercising the power of reason to make choices that enhance the possibilities of our lives, thus 'liberating' our higher nature from our animal instincts and allowing us to control our own destinies (autonomy). For example a drunk may have negative freedom but, having lost self-control, has no positive freedom. Plato (*c*428–*c*348BC), who recommended authoritarian rule, insisted: you are not free when you are slave to your desires. Freedom is mastery by the rational self, mastery by knowledge of what is really good. (Gorman, *Rights and Reason* (Acumen 2003) 33). Locke (Section 2.3) puts forward a version of positive freedom when he asserts that freedom means the exercise of specific rights protected by the law whereas Hobbes treats freedom as the absence of law: 'by Liberty, is understood ... the absence of external impediments' (Hobbes, 1973, ch 14, para 1).

The two kinds of freedom sometimes support each other since negative freedom enables us to exercise choices. However positive freedom is in one sense wider since it includes restrictions on our power to choose good things caused not just by interference by the state but also by social and economic conditions such as poverty or a bad environment. It requires government action to limit negative freedom, such as distributing resources such as education, wealth and health care to enable people to make genuine choices and so take control of their lives.

In another sense positive freedom is narrower in that it concentrates only on freedom to do good things. Positive freedom also allows us to claim paradoxically that obeying the law is 'freedom', in that law gives us a degree of rational choice by providing stability, which enables us to plan our lives. But the worm within positive freedom is the issue of who decides what is good (below).

Attitudes of negative and positive freedom towards law therefore differ. Negative freedom regards law as a restriction and concentrates on limiting state power, thus reflecting the red light perspective (Section 1.6). Positive freedom (green light) is open to greater government control since it is consistent with the state designating what are valuable choices. The distinction between positive and negative freedom sometimes underlies disagreements in the courts. For example in *Tomlinson v Congleton DC* [2003], the claimant had, despite warning notices, jumped into a pool owned by a local authority and broken his neck. The question was whether a local authority was obliged to do more to protect against this risk. Lord Hoffmann remarked from the negative freedom perspective that our liberal individualistic system meant that the nanny state should not be encouraged and that, given there was a clear warning notice, the claimant should be responsible for his own safety. By contrast Sedley LJ in the Court of Appeal had taken the view, characteristic of positive freedom, that the local authority should have taken precautions to guard people against their own irrationality.

According to Isaiah Berlin (2002), positive freedom has a sinister aspect. Who decides what is good and rational? As we saw in Chapter 1 human affairs are prone to disagreement. How does one compare and choose between different freedoms which are 'incommensurable', meaning that there is no objective way of measuring their importance? For example should one condone torture in the interests of good international relations (see *Jones v Ministry of Interior of Saudi Arabia* [2006] (Section 9.6.2)) or torture one person in order to save the lives, possibly, of many? Positive freedom might justify the state claiming that a particular way of life, for example one based on a religious cult, an economic theory or belonging to the European Union, is 'rationally' better than others and is therefore what the people would 'really' want if they could think properly, just as we say that someone who is drunk is not 'himself'. This justifies coercion in a person's 'own interests':

> Once I take this view I am in a position to ignore the actual wishes of men or societies, to bully, oppress, torture them in the name, and on behalf, of their real selves, in the secure knowledge that whatever is the true goal of man (happiness, performance of duty, wisdom, a just society, self-fulfillment) must be identical with his freedom – the free choice of his 'true', albeit often submerged and inarticulate self. (Berlin, 2002, 180)

For example a person detained in a hospital for 'his own good' could be claimed to be not 'detained' at all but freely submitting. Thus in *HM v Switzerland* [2002] the European Court of Human Rights held that placing a child in a foster home was not a 'deprivation of liberty' since it was a responsible measure in the child's own interests.

Berlin of course recognises that the state might sometimes have good reason for interfering with freedom. For example in *HM v Switzerland* Berlin's analysis would probably be that there was a deprivation of liberty, but one outweighed by a greater good. His point is that by lumping together freedom and other goods we are disguising hard choices between incommensurables. Thus Berlin is concerned that decision makers openly confront difficult choices. The best we can expect is a compromise that is widely acceptable.

Copsey v WBB Devon Clays Ltd [2005] illustrates the kind of compromise that has to be made. Neuberger LJ referred to 'enlightened capitalism and liberal democracy' in deciding that an employer could require a Christian employee to work on a Sunday. It was held that Article 9 of the ECHR, freedom to manifest religion, requires a balance to be struck between the reasonable needs of the employer and those of the employee, since Article 9 rights can be overridden on several grounds, including the 'rights and freedoms of others'. Perhaps a widely acceptable compromise was reached. The employer had seriously tried to accommodate the employee's Christian beliefs about Sunday working but in the circumstances this proved impossible and would cause unfairness to other workers. Thus the decision was based upon a subjective evaluation of the relative importance of the interests concerned. There is some indication in the case, although the judges were not fully agreed on this point, that freedom of contract is to be ranked especially highly, so that an employee is free to get another job. Mummery LJ went further in a liberal direction, holding that an employer was entitled to adopt a secular regime. The secular approach means that religious interests must not be given special weight or perhaps even feature in public life at all so as to ensure equality, but this conflicts with another cherished liberal belief, that of respecting an individual's choice of lifestyle.

2.5 Republicanism

There has been a recent revival of interest in republican ideas, stimulated by evidence of widespread apathy among voters and disenchantment with the integrity and competence of the political leadership (see eg Bellamy, 2007; Tomkins, 2005). Republicanism means far more than its popular sense of the absence of a monarchy. Republicanism and liberalism overlap, but republicanism stresses equal citizenship and citizen participation in the processes of government. Originating in ancient Greece, revived in the Renaissance and developed in the seventeenth and eighteenth centuries (Machiavelli, 1469–1527; Harrington, 1611–77; Montesquieu, 1689–1755), Rousseau (1712–88), republicanism builds on the idea of positive freedom (above). It stresses that the state exists for the benefit of all members of the community as free and equal citizens. Thus rulers have no rights of their own (other than as citizens) but only duties to the community.

Republicanism has two main aspects which stress different meanings of the idea of 'freedom' (above). Firstly, it embraces the notion of virtuous citizenship and political self-determination by citizens collectively as equal participants in a democratic process. Republicanism stresses the right and the duty of citizens to participate in government. Positive freedom (above) links with this republican idea of democracy since we can rationally control our own lives if we participate in collective decision making, what Constant (1767–1830) called 'the liberty of the ancients'. Thus positive freedom might favour compulsory voting. Rousseau (1712–78) for example famously wrote that we should be 'forced' to be free, meaning that true freedom lies in collective participation by voting in public affairs. He assumed that each person would vote rationally in accordance with the public interest (the 'general will' rather than his or her selfish interests, the will of all) and that the minority who disagree with the outcome must therefore be 'wrong' (see Rousseau, *The Social Contract*, trans Cole (The Constitution Society 1762) Book 2).

Republicanism ideally favours direct democracy by means of an assembly of all qualifying citizens (qualification to be determined by those currently in power). Ignoring possible technological solutions, this is of course difficult to achieve except in relation to small local areas. Therefore contemporary republicans such as Bellamy (2007) emphasise *representative* democracy by means of elected legislatures and also favour citizen participation through consultative mechanisms and the devolution of power to small units.

The principles of parliamentary supremacy, the devolution of powers to Scotland Wales and Northern Ireland and executive government responsible primarily to the elected House of Commons are broadly republican in character. Bellamy and Waldron (2001), drawing on the collectivist strain, suggest that improved democratic mechanisms are the appropriate republican safeguards rather than the courts' powers of judicial review.

The second form of republicanism invokes another meaning of freedom what Pettit (*Republicanism: A Theory of Freedom and Government* (Oxford University Press 1997)) calls 'freedom as non-domination' as opposed to liberalism's 'freedom as non interference.' The republicanism concern to ensure that no single person or group within the community can dominate others. This applies to private vested interests and democratic majorities as much as to government bodies. Apart from concern with a separation of powers between different branches of government and with protecting political freedoms, republicanism involves such questions as whether individuals should be able to buy access to political influence.

According to Pettit this strain of republicanism influenced the American Founding Fathers. Freedom as non-domination recognises that even if our rulers do not interfere with us and leave us to our own devices we are nevertheless not truly free since our liberty depends entirely on the goodwill of the rulers. We are slaves who are at the mercy of maybe a kind slave master but are in the demeaning position of depending on the arbitrary whim of another.

Freedom from domination therefore requires that the ruler be restricted by law from arbitrarily interfering with us whether for good or ill. It assumes that those in power cannot be trusted even if their motives are good and should therefore not have large discretionary powers. Thus this version of republicanism puts more faith in the courts than the democratic version. It is consistent with Dicey's version of the rule of law (Section 6.5). It can also be illustrated by the Constitutional Reform Act 2005 which places the independence of the judiciary, albeit imperfectly on a legal footing. Previously judicial independence was safeguarded largely by the self-restraint of the political and official community. It was widely accepted that the judges were in fact independent but public confidence was thought to require full legal protection (Section 7.7).

Republicanism does not regard state interference as intrinsically bad, but rejects only *arbitrary* interference. Interference is not arbitrary where it is carried for the benefit of those who are subject to the interference, in other words for the public good. By public good is meant benefit which is common to all as members of the community as opposed to the benefit of the rulers themselves or of sectional interests. Republican ideas therefore concentrate on constitutional mechanisms to ensure that government decisions are made for the public benefit.

These mechanisms include the following:

▶ the 'empire of law' (Harrington), or what we now refer to as the rule of law meaning that all government power is limited by and must exercised through legal rules announced in advance and binding both ruler and ruled;
▶ separation of powers in order to ensure that no person or group is dominant not only between executive, legislature and judiciary but in several other respects such as geographical jurisdictions;
▶ accountability mechanism such as fair elections, independent scrutiny of public appointments and other oversight bodies and openness in government decision making. According to Pettit a key principle is that of *contestability* by those who are subject to government, ie all citizens. It must be borne in mind that mechanisms for making a decision contestable are not the same for each kind of decision maker. For example from a republican perspective it is arguably wrong to elect judges however democratic this seems since election risks compromising the independence of a court. Conversely the arguments for elected lawmakers are strong since they can be removed if they make laws to which the people object. In both cases it is normally important that the decision-making process be open and public and that there are mechanisms for individual complaints and grievances.

Particular constitutions may reflect these requirements in different ways and in all likelihood imperfectly. The UK constitution with its commitment to representative and accountable government embodies general republican ideas but in some respects falls short of republican standards. For example democratic government is imperfectly realised since we have an unelected head of state in the shape of the Queen and one part of the legislature the House of Lords is also unelected. There is no attempt to insure that government gives access on an impartial basis to those who wish to influence it. Public offices are theoretically open to all but appointments often depend on the personal patronage of ministers.

Perhaps most importantly, large parts of the UK constitution are outside the law based only on informal practices or conventions or non-binding codes of conduct which rely heavily on trusting the rulers and their hand picked networks of associates from business, the professions and the media to act without self-interest (Section 3.4). Parliament sometimes enacts laws of draconian severity with little discussion, relying on assurances from the government that in practice the laws will be applied only in special and limited circumstances (such as anti-terrorism legislation. Republicanism stresses that it is not enough that rulers in fact rule wisely and benevolently. In the interests of dignity, equality and freedom, all limits on the rulers must be secured by law so that the ruler cannot abuse his or her power. Anything less relies only on hoping that the slavemaster will be kind. Occasionally the law will intervene as a panic response following a conspicuous abuse of power such as the recent scandal concerning MPs' expense claims (Section 11.7).

Nor do we have a full separation of powers since the executive forms part of Parliament the lawmaker. According to the orthodox view Parliament has unlimited law making power so that whichever group controls Parliament can exercise domination without legal constraint. The internal workings of Parliament are such that the will of the political party controlling the executive can be overcome only in exceptional circumstances (Section 13.1). On the other hand it could be argued that Parliament has imposed these fetters on itself and that MPs who represent the people could, if they so wished, free themselves from executive control (the price being less efficient government).

Republicans differ as to the best form of constitution. Drawing on classical virtues combined with modern communications technology, some republicans favour the notion of deliberative democracy, where disputes are settled by ensuring that citizens have the opportunity to participate directly in decision making. This seems to paint an idealised picture of groups of leisured and well-informed people with enough in common and sufficient good will to reach agreement.

Others regard this as unrealistic in a complex many sided society that depends on specialists and prefer a version of the representative system where ultimate power is vested in an assembly chosen by the people in free and fair elections to which the executive government is accountable (see Bellamy, 2007). Overlapping with communitarianism and group liberalism the emphasis might be on elections based on the various trades, professions, regions, ethnic and other groups in the community. Proposals to reform the House of Lords included these ideas (Section 11.2). The UK has provision for direct participation only exceptionally (see Section 2.8.2).

Those who support republicanism usually reject the notion that the courts should have the last word and regard the constitution as being safer in political hands. For example Tomkins (2005) places stress on the political doctrine that ministers are responsible to Parliament, regarding this as the golden principle of the constitution, while Bellamy (2007) stresses the importance of equal voting rights. Allan (2001) by contrast regards the courts as guardians of republican ideals and would permit them to disapply legislation that violated fundamental democratic values. This runs counter to the view that it is offensive to submit to unelected authority on fundamental matters and that participation is 'the right of rights' (see Waldron, 2001, 11, 12, 13).

Republicans are ambivalent about human rights. They recognise human rights, but in a more grudging way than liberals. A moderate republican would accept the idea of human rights, but as part of the general interest, and would therefore recognise more easily than a liberal that a right should give way to a social goal. It is sometimes suggested that the Human Rights Act 1998 embodies a moderate republican approach. Not only does it recognise that a social goal often overrides a right but it also leaves the final choice to Parliament rather than the court. However republicanism and liberalism would both give special importance but for different reasons to freedom of political expression (Section 22.1) An extreme version of republicanism would regard possession of a right as conditional upon being a good citizen.

Republican and liberal approaches are illustrated by the reasoning of the majority and minority in *R (Begum) v Head Teacher and Governors of Denbigh High School* [2007] AC 100. The House of Lords held that a ban on the wearing of a strict form of Muslim dress at a school was not an unlawful interference with the right of freedom of religion. Two lines of reasoning were used. The majority held that the right to religious freedom was not infringed at all. The child concerned could have attended other, more flexible schools, and the style of dress chosen was not required by mainstream Islamic doctrine. This is consistent with a republicanism that imposes a standard model of the good citizen. Lord Nicholls and Baroness Hale held that a right had been infringed but was overridden by the important social purpose of fostering a sense of community by means of a dress code. This is a nearer to the liberal approach because it recognises both the importance of the individual claim and that there is a dilemma. To the majority the right disappeared within the wider public good, so that the problem of balancing the two competing claims was avoided.

2.6 Equality

Liberalism and republicanism presuppose that all people are equal. However 'equality' has no clear meaning. Equality is merely a measure, the real question being 'equality of what?' For example liberalism emphasises equality between individual freedoms, whereas republicanism is concerned with equality in the political process. We can distinguish broadly between 'formal' equality and 'substantive' equality. This is reflected in different versions of the 'rule of law' (Section 6.3). Formal equality is about procedures and appearances. It requires that everyone's rights be treated the same in terms of the application of the law, for example the right to a fair trial. It does not mean that the contents of the rights are the same. That is a matter of substantive equality. For example a landlord has greater rights over a house than a tenant and can often afford to go to court and get legal advice more easily than a tenant, but the two sets of rights will be given equal consideration by a court. Unless we adopt the difficult position that everyone should be treated identically (which conflicts with freedom), substantive equality means only that we should not treat people differently without a good reason. Thus John Stuart Mill, widely regarded as a founder of British liberalism, said that 'all persons are deemed to have a right to equality of treatment except when some recognised social expediency requires otherwise' (1972, ch 5).

We may disagree about what counts as a good reason. This creates further conflicting concepts of equality. For example, while there is widespread consensus that we should not discriminate on grounds of personal characteristics such as race or gender, it is controversial whether there should be equality in respect of the distribution of wealth or public services (equality of outcome). Should resource allocation be based on need (equality of opportunity) or on merit (equality of desert)? Why should people who happen to be born with talents that suit the interests of the community be better off for that reason than those less fortunate? This raises political questions largely outside the scope of the law. Nevertheless equality is of primary importance in combating action that arbitrarily targets certain groups: even though, as with other grand sounding rights, the law sometimes permits other interests to override equality.

For example, the Equality Act 2010 imposes a duty on public bodies when making 'strategic' decisions to have regard to the desirability of reducing 'the inequalities of outcome which result from socio-economic disadvantage'. The Act also prohibits discrimination, meaning less favourable treatment, by private persons and public authorities on the ground of certain 'protected characteristics'. These are age; disability; gender reassignment; marriage and civil partnership; pregnancy and maternity; race (including colour, nationality, ethnic or national origins); religion or belief; sex; sexual orientation. However less favourable treatment can be justified if is a 'proportionate means of achieving a legitimate aim' (Section 18.1.1).

2.7 Communitarianism

A thread of communitarianism linked to traditional conservatism is represented by the eighteenth-century political thinker and MP Edmund Burke and more recently by the writings of Michael Oakshott (1901–90). Burke believed that the constitution should be supported by custom and tradition generated within the community and that rational attempts at constitution building are dangerous (Section 4.6). Burke believed in representative government but supported an inherited aristocratic element arguing that society was held together by respect for established rank and status. Burkian thinking finds modern expression in resistance to reform of the House of Lords (Section 12.3) and more generally in the heavy reliance on conventions, unwritten practices and understandings that characterises the UK constitution (Section 3.4).

In similar vein Oakshott distinguishes between civil association 'in which individuals and groups can pursue their freely chosen goals' by means of shared customs and understandings ('intimations') that cannot necessarily be formulated as rules (Burke's 'little platoons') and 'enterprise associations' where the rulers impose their own goals on society through prescriptive laws.

Mullender ((2012) 128 LQR 190), suggests that the decision of the Upper Tribunal in *Independent Schools Council v Charity Commission for England and Wales* [2012] 1 All ER 127 exemplifies the conflict between the two kinds of association. The Charities Act 2006 requires that all charities must show that their activities carry public benefit. Charitable status has large tax benefits. This is particularly problematic in the case of private schools. The Charity Commission which regulates charities and which consists of government appointees has been said to attempt to impose its own ideas of what a charity should be like (enterprise society). Accordingly it issued guidance 'Guidance' that there must be 'sufficient opportunity for people who cannot afford ... fees to benefit in a material way that is related to the charity's aim' (*Public Benefit and Fee Charging* (2008), 9). The Tribunal held that the Guidance was too interventionist and that beyond the minimum threshold that its purposes did not exclude the poor it was a matter for the trustees of each charity to decide how to run the school and that it is not for the Charity Commissioners or the Tribunal or the Court to impose their own ideas of what is or is not reasonable [229].

2.8 Democracy

Liberalism and republicanism share ideals of democracy, but there are different versions of democracy. Fear of democracy remains a significant theme of the constitutional debate in the UK. Democracy in the limited sense of a periodic right to vote in specified elections was introduced slowly and reluctantly between the mid-nineteenth and mid-twentieth centuries. Proposals to reform the House of Lords, which is currently wholly appointed, have foundered largely because of resistance to the idea of a wholly elected legislature (Section 12.3).

The courts recognise the importance of democracy by refraining for interfering with laws made by elected bodies with wide powers such as the Scottish Parliament other than in exceptional circumstances (see *AXA General Insurance Ltd v HM Advocate* [2012] 1 AC 868, Section 8.5.2). This restraint does not normally apply to decisions taken by officials on behalf of government (see *R (Bancoult) v Secretary of State for the Foreign and Commonwealth Office (No 2)* [2008] 4 All ER 1055). Indeed judicial review is intended to ensure that officials keep within the powers given to them by the democratic government.

Karl Marx famously said that democracy is the 'solved riddle of all constitutions. Here ... the constitution is brought back to its actual basis ... and established as the people's own work' (see Marks, *The Riddle of All Constitutions* (Oxford University Press 2000) 149). Similarly (perhaps) democracy has been defined as 'the people of a country deciding for themselves the contents of the laws that organise and regulate their political association' (Michaelman, 'Brennan and Democracy' (1998) 86 California LR 399–400).

According to this definition there is unlikely to be much democracy in the world and yet most states label themselves democracies. Michaelman's aspiration is the republican one of direct citizen self-government by active participation, sometimes called 'deliberative democracy'. This might be practicable in a village where everyone knows everyone else, but it is unrealistic in contemporary nation states comprising millions of strangers with conflicting goals and interests and where the complexity of society requires decisions to be made by specialists. Democracy also means government with the 'consent' of the people, a more slippery notion. The people cannot consent to anything until there are rules determining who counts as 'the people' and how they express their wishes. For example different voting formulae fixed by those currently in power produce very different outcomes (see Section 12.7). From the earliest times democracy has meant decisions made by a majority. The proposed European Constitution, quoting Thucydides (*c*460–400 BC), claims that: 'our constitution is called a democracy because power is in the hands not of a minority but of the greatest number'.

The justification for majoritarianism is not that a majority is likely to be 'right', since this is clearly untrue, but that majority voting is fair since it treats everyone equally. However majoritarianism has well-known problems. Firstly, unless there is a simple choice between only two options, the mathematics of majority voting will not necessarily produce a majority preference. Secondly, objections democracy dating back to the time of Plato (424–348 approx BC) include lack of expertise and susceptibility to persuasion by panic mongers or plausible villains or ideologues. Thus John Adams, one of the founders of the US Constitution, feared 'elective despotism', and De Tocqueville (1805–59), commenting on the newly formed US Constitution, referring to the 'tyranny of the majority', said:

> I am trying to imagine under what novel features despotism may appear in the world. In the first place, I see an innumerable multitude of men, alike and equal, constantly circling around in pursuit of the petty and banal pleasures with which they glut their souls ... Over this kind of men stands an immense, protective power which is alone responsible for

securing their enjoyment and watching over their fate. (*Democracy in America*, trans Lawrence (Fontana 1968) vol 2, 898)

There is therefore a tension between individual freedom on the one hand, and democracy on the other. This underlies important issues in constitutional law, in particular whether the courts should be empowered to overturn Acts of Parliament on constitutional grounds. Liberals are ambivalent about this. On the one hand judges could be regarded as undemocratic. On the other hand liberalism is not tied to democracy. A standard argument in this context is that there are certain fundamental requirements of democracy, such as freedom of expression, that should be protected by independent courts in case a democratic majority is seduced or panicked into overriding them. A republican answer is that it is those who are affected by the laws in question who should have an equal say in deciding what those laws should be, it being offensive to human dignity not to trust a democratic body (see Waldron, 2001; Bellamy, 2007).

2.8.1 Representative democracy

The characteristic form of modern democracy is 'representative democracy'. This applies in the UK. The ideal is that of government which the people can choose, call to account and remove. The people choose representatives directly, who appoint others to assist them subject to a clear chain of responsibility thus combining the advantages of specialist decision makers with control by the people. The representatives must explain their actions and must regularly submit themselves for re-election. A famous early statement is that of Fortescue (*On the Governance of the Kingdom of England*, 1537), who distinguished between *dominium regale*, the rule of the king alone, necessary in certain cases, for example to deal with an emergency, and *dominium politicum et regale*, the rule of the king with the assent of representatives of the community after discussion collectively in Parliament. More recently, in *R (Alconbury Developments) v Secretary of State for the Environment, Transport and the Regions* [2001], Lord Hoffmann informed us that in the UK: 'decisions as to what the general interest requires are made by democratically elected bodies or by persons accountable to them' (at 980).

Representative democracy favours the more individualistic versions of liberalism, since the citizen's only power is to vote as a private solitary act without any requirement for discussion. Representative democracy relies upon a passive population, provided that enough people vote to give those chosen some legitimacy. Republicans and communitarians who favour the active participation of citizens are less comfortable with representative democracy. Typically the people choose a lawmaking assembly as the highest branch of government. In a presidential system the people also vote for the head of state. Bentham and his utilitarian followers recommended that even judges be removable by the people since the people are the final court, but this is not the case in the UK.

Mill especially favoured representative democracy since it combines popular consent with a utilitarian reliance on experts. However, like many contemporary public officials, Mill distrusted 'the people'. He recommended slewing the voting system so that the highly educated had greater voting power. He also suggested that Parliament should include a quota of people with a 'national reputation' and that people on welfare benefits should be disqualified from voting on the ground they might be biased. He favoured a greater level of democracy at local level, not because it produced efficient government but in order to develop the abilities of local people to develop themselves by participating in public life. This does not apply to the contemporary UK constitution, where local government is substantially constrained by central government, so that local elected politicians have little significant power.

The term 'representative' is ambiguous. A representative assembly could be a 'portrait' or microcosm of those it represents, for example being representative in terms of the political balance of opinion or ethnic and racial groupings. Alternatively it could be an agent of the people, not having any specified composition but made up of people chosen for their personal qualities or party membership. The practical significance of this concerns different types of voting system designed to produce different outcomes (Section 12.5). The UK Parliament operates the agency model but the devolved regimes in Scotland, Wales and Northern Ireland combine both models.

Another basic issue is whether representatives are bound by the views of those who voted for them or should vote according to their own consciences. The UK constitution has traditionally taken the attitude that representatives must not be bound by any outside commitments. For example elected local authorities must not bind themselves in law to carry out any political mandate on which they are elected (eg *Bromley LBC v GLC* [1983]). However within Parliament the Whip system encourages MPs to vote blindly for their party. Proceedings in Parliament cannot be challenged in the courts.

Representative democracy provides mechanisms for ensuring that the government is accountable to the electorate. Accountability is an ambiguous idea but basically means that decisions must be explained and justified. The main accountability devices required by representative democracies are as follows:

▶ right to question the executive (Chapters 13, 15);
▶ policing financial limits on government spending (Chapter 13);
▶ internal control mechanisms within government (Chapter 15);
▶ judicial review (Chapters 17, 18, 19);
▶ public consultation and access to information (Chapters 22, 23).

Each of these depends on a separation of powers between different functions of government (Chapter 7) and on safeguarding basic freedoms, including the freedom to form political parties and the freedom of the press to criticise government. The European Court and the UK courts have stressed the special importance of political freedom of speech in connection with the democratic process (eg *Culnane v Morris* [2006]; *Bowman v UK* [1998]; *State of Mauritius v Khoyratty* [2006]).

2.8.2 Participatory democracy

Sometimes called 'deliberative' or 'direct democracy' participatory democracy promotes direct participation by individuals and groups in decisions which affect them. The UK constitution makes little provision for participation. Supporters of participation that it can harness 'reason' from a wide range of perspectives and enhances dignity and public education. However participants are voiceless without rules and leaders who stage-manage their involvement.

It is not clear how deliberative democracy can be organised. Notions such as town meetings have been proposed, although it is unclear what matters might be appropriate to their remit. Recognising that in a complex society full participation might be impracticable, many have argued (such as Hannah Ahrendt, 1906–75) that participation should apply to smaller units such as local government, charities and the workplace (civil society). Habermas suggests a form of deliberative democracy that he regards as appropriate to contemporary circumstances in which the state is merely one among numerous community organisations, each comprising activists 'deliberating' on equal terms. The role of the law is to coordinate these units and to ensure that the discussions are open, fair and equal ('Three Normative Models of Democracy' in *The Inclusion of the Other* (MIT Press 1996)).

Liberals, notably Mill, have objected that deliberative democracy is likely to attract busybodies, the self-promoting, the corrupt, the ignorant and cranks. It also favours the wealthy and leisured. However representative democracy is not immune from these distortions.

UK law provides for deliberative democracy only in a limited and piecemeal way:

- The jury system for serious criminal trials and in certain civil cases is the only example regarded as important enough to have constitutional status (Juries Act 1974). It has been suggested that citizens juries should be enlisted to make decisions in constitutional cases as a response to the problem that many see in fundamental rights being determined by unelected judges (see Ghosh, 2010).
- The devolved regimes of Wales and Northern Ireland contain some provision for public involvement.
- Statute provides for referendums (Political Parties, Elections and Referendums Act 2000, European Union Act 2011). However these are rarely held and are triggered by the government. Referendums were held in 1976 concerning continued membership of what is now the European Union, in 1979 and 1997 concerning devolution in Scotland, Wales and Northern Ireland, in 2004 concerning a proposal for a regional assembly in northeast England and in 2011 concerning proposed changes to the voting system (Section 2.5). There are also referendum provisions applying in Northern Ireland and Wales (Sections 16.3, 16.4). It is proposed at an unspecified time to hold a referendum in Scotland concerning possible Scottish independence from the UK. It is often argued that the use of referendums would threaten the equality protected by representative democracy since a referendum is liable to be manipulated by vested interests.
- The government usually consults interested parties and sometimes the public when important policies are proposed although there is no general legal requirement to do so. In some cases statute requires consultation and the courts can ensure that the process is fair and is not merely window dressing (Section 18.2). However, vested interests with informal links with government officials or who finances political parties may have an advantage in the consultation process.
- There are formal statutory public inquiries into many decisions relating to land development where those who can afford good lawyers have an advantage. The outcome is not normally binding on the government.
- There is also some participation in the provision for 'parish meetings' at local government level in small rural villages. However these have little power other than in relation to local amenities such as playgrounds. The Localism Act 2012 introduces direct public involvement in certain land use planning decisions

In recent years the courts seem to have adopted a more sympathetic approach to direct participation, at least in cases where machinery has been provided by statute. (Compare *Berkeley v Secretary of State for the Environment* [2000]: participation a right for its own sake, with *Bushell v Secretary of State for the Environment* [1981]: participation does not entitle full information.) Participatory democracy shares with representative democracy a concern with freedom of expression, particularly freedom of the press and with public access to information. Thus Lord Bingham pointed out in *McCartan Turkington-Breen v Times Newspapers* [2000] at 922 that a 'free, active, professional and enquiring press' was all the more important to support a participatory democracy since the majority of people can participate only indirectly.

2.8.3 Political parties: market democracy

Political parties are essential in a democracy. They publicise and coordinate different opinions and, as Edmund Burke somewhat idealistically asserted, make it possible to achieve by discussion a notion of the common good (*On the Present Discontents* (1770) vol II). Without them an elected assembly would be a rabble and democratic governments would be unable to coordinate their policies. In Burke's time MPs were usually of independent means as opposed to the paid functionaries of the present day, and party structures were relatively loose. A modern political party can usually exclude independently minded people as candidates for election and ensure that MPs vote in accordance with the party line.

Liberalism regards political parties as self-governing voluntary bodies even though they are central to government. In the interests of freedom there is resistance to legal controls over political parties, for example in respect of how they raise funds. On the other hand fair elections require certain controls – a tension characteristic of liberal democracy. For example in the US case of *Buckley v Valeo* [1976], restrictions on expenses for election advertising designed to ensure equal competition were held to violate the right to freedom of expression. A different view has been taken in the UK (Section 12.6.1).

'Market democracy', recognises the role of parties and argues that in contemporary circumstances elections provide only a limited choice. According to Weber (1864–1920) and Schumpeter (1883–1950), the voter's only power is to choose between products offered by competing party leaders who present themselves for election every few years. The vote provides the price mechanism.

Market democracy has significant implications for the constitution. No longer is the state the neutral umpire of Hobbes and Locke; it is a player in the game offering inducements for votes. In particular there is the danger that government will be captured by the vested interests of those who fund the parties. However supporters of market democracy argue that competition will ensure that one party is unlikely to stay in control permanently, provided that the electoral system properly reflects the range of opinion – a matter which is questionable in the UK. Society may have become too fragmented and diverse to fit into large-scale parties and may be represented more accurately by single issue or special interest pressure groups. Modern governments may therefore be chosen not on the basis of broad ideological or class differences but on the basis of the personalities of the individuals standing for election. Moreover market democracy encourages government policies to be expressed in terms of outcomes, targets and 'value for money' rather than in terms of fairness and justice. The emphasis on outputs also blurs the divide between the public and private sectors since the means by which outputs are delivered ceases to matter.

Summary

▶ Having read this chapter you should have some general perspectives which you can use to assess the UK constitution.

▶ Constitutions are underpinned by an assortment of sometimes conflicting political values. Of these liberalism has strong contemporary influence. Liberalism separates the individual from the state and emphasises limitations on state power in the interests of individual freedom. Liberalism overlaps with republicanism; however the latter stresses equal participation as citizens and emphasises duties rather than individual rights. Both favour limited government.

▶ Liberalism also treats individuals as equal, the two ideas being capable of conflicting. Formal equality relating to fair procedures is a prime concern of the law. Substantive equality relating to the distribution of resources is primarily a matter of pre-legal political choices.

▶ A review of significant writers who have influenced liberal ideas reveals different and sometimes conflicting forms of liberalism, depending on the importance and meaning given to individual freedom as opposed to the general public interest. These include liberal individualism, market liberalism, welfare liberalism and liberal pluralism.

▶ The distinction between positive and negative freedom illustrates the kinds of disagreements that arise within liberalism. Positive freedom emphasises our ability to choose reason to exercise choice and links with republican ideas of citizen participation in government. It may also lead to authoritarian attempts to impose rational solutions. Negative freedom is the freedom to be left alone. It may be seen as impractical and selfish.

▶ Republicanism can be contrasted with liberalism. Republicanism does not separate the individual from the state but favours the notion of the virtuous, politically active citizen. It is associated with positive freedom and treats freedom as the right to participate in government. It stresses limited government and (usually) democratic rather than judicial controls over government. There are limited republican elements in the UK constitution.

▶ A third tradition, communitarianism, is less influential in the UK. It is less sympathetic to human rights than liberalism and favours the interests of groups over those of individuals. The devolution provisions have communitarian elements. There are different kinds of democracy, including deliberative/participatory democracy, representative democracy and market democracy.

▶ There are differences between a parliamentary and a presidential democracy. The former concentrates legal power in the legislature and usually involves a separate head of state with limited power. However in practice the executive may come to dominate the legislature. The latter divides power between the executive and the legislature as equals but the President is both head of the executive and head of state.

▶ Democracy has several variations, the main ones being representative democracy, deliberative democracy and market democracy. Representative democracy is the basis of the UK constitution but market democracy is in practice pursued by the political parties. Democracy is underpinned by ideas of constitutionalism and the rule of law, and the courts give particular importance to freedom of speech and of the press in the context of democratic processes.

Exercises

2.1 How would (i) a liberal, (ii) a republican, (iii) a communitarian arrange for (a) the appointment of judges, (b) the method of lawmaking, (c) the settlement of a dispute as to whether a religious group should be permitted to have polygamous marriages?

2.2 What are the main principles of a republican form of constitution? Give examples of such principles in the UK constitution.

Exercises cont'd

2.3 Sedley (*London Review of Books*, 15 November 2001) describes a case where a French court upheld a ban on local funfairs where revellers had been permitted to shoot a dwarf from a cannon. The decision was made in the name of public morals and human dignity even though the dwarfs made their living from the spectacle and were among the chief opponents of the ban. Discuss in relation to the views of Locke, Mill and Bentham.

2.4 Discuss from the perspective of different forms of liberalism the following legislative proposals:
  (i) a ban on any religion that prevents its members from leaving it;
  (ii) provision for a free market in unwanted babies;
  (iii) a right for any person to have paid leave from work in order to practise his or her religion;
  (iv) a ban on any person convicted of a crime from voting;
  (v) a ban on 'faith schools'.

2.5 'A democratic constitution is in the end undemocratic if it gives all power to its elected government' (Sir John Laws, 'Law and Democracy' [1995] PL 73). Explain and discuss.

2.6 To what extent does the common law reflect liberal or republican ideals?

Further reading

Allan, *Constitutional Justice: A Liberal Theory of the Rule of Law* (Oxford University Press 2001)
Bellamy, *Political Constitutionalism* (Cambridge University Press 2007) chs 1, 3–6
Berlin, 'Two Concepts of Liberty' in Hardy (ed), *Liberty* (Oxford University Press 2002)
Crick, *Democracy: A Very Short Introduction* (Oxford University Press 2002)
Dworkin, *A Question of Principle (Oxford Clarendon Press 1986) Parts 1 and 3.*
Dyzenhaus, 'How Hobbes Met the Hobbes Challenge' (2009) 72 MLR 488
Etherton, 'Liberty, the Archetype, and Diversity' [2010] PL 727
Galston, *The Practice of Liberal Pluralism* (Cambridge University Press 2005)
Harden, *Liberalism, Constitutionalism and Democracy* (Oxford University Press 1999)
Hayek, 'Freedom and Coercion' in Miller (ed), *Liberty* (Oxford University Press 1991)
Kymlicka, 'Citizenship Theory' in *Contemporary Political Philosophy* (2nd edn, Oxford University Press 2002)
Laws, 'The Constitution: Morals and Right' [1996] PL 622
Leoni, *Freedom and the Law*, Princeton William Volker 1961.
Loughlin, *Foundations of Public Law* (Oxford University Press 2010) chs 3–6
Loughlin, 'Towards a Republican Revival' (2006) 26 OJLS 425
Morison, 'Models of Democracy: From Representation to Participation' in Jowell and Oliver (eds), *The Changing Constitution* (6th edn, Oxford University Press 2007)
Pettit, *Republicanism: A Theory of Freedom and Government* (Oxford University Press 1997) chs 1–3, 5, 6
Skinner, 'The Paradoxes of Political Liberty' in Miller (ed), *Liberty* (Oxford University Press 1991)
Tierney, 'Constitutional Referendums: A Theoretical Inquiry' (2009) 72 MLR 360
Tomkins, *Our Republican Constitution* (Hart 2005)
Tully, 'The Unfreedom of the Moderns' (2002) 65 MLR 204
Waldron, *Law and Disagreement* (Oxford University Press 2001)
Wolheim, 'A Paradox in the Theory of Democracy' in Laslett and Runciman (eds), *Philosophy, Politics and Society* (2nd ser, Blackwell 1969)

Chapter 3

The sources of the constitution

3.1 Introduction

As we saw in Chapter 1 the UK has no written constitution with a special legal status. The UK's unwritten constitution is constructed partly out of the general sources of law and relies partly on political 'conventions'. The legal sources include Acts of Parliament, the common law in the form of decisions of the higher courts, and the 'laws and customs of Parliament' made by each House in order to control its affairs. The conventional view is that statute law is the highest form of law in our constitution, although there is an argument that statute is subject to the 'rule of law', which is in the hands of the courts (see Section 8.5).

All constitutions rely to some extent on political understandings and practices even if they are not labelled as conventions but because our constitution is unwritten we rely more heavily on such rules than most countries. There is of course no intrinsic difference between the content of a convention and that of a law. Any convention can be enacted as a law (eg the 'Ponsonby' convention concerning the ratification of treaties (Section 9.5.1)).

There are also 'practices' which may be of fundamental constitutional significance even though they are not in any sense binding as rules. The most obvious of these is the existence of political parties through which contenders for power organise themselves. There is no legal or conventional requirement that there be political parties. Strictly speaking a political party is a private voluntary organisation, albeit regulated to prevent parties abusing the electoral process (Political Parties, Elections and Referendums Act 2000). Because the leader of the majority party in the House of Commons normally becomes the Prime Minister, the internal rules of each party for choosing its leader are of fundamental importance. Indeed it has been said that:

> parties have substituted for a constitution in Britain. They have filled all the vast empty spaces in the political system where a constitution should be and made the system in their own image. (Wright, quoted in Nolan and Sedley, 1997, 83)

3.2 Statute law

From the sixteenth century it became increasingly established that Parliament, in the sense of the monarch, the House of Lords and the House of Commons combining to enact statutes (Acts of Parliament), is the supreme lawmaker. The most radical constitutional changes have been made by statute. For example:

- Magna Carta 1215, of symbolic value rather than for its specific provisions, which recognised the principles that the monarch rules by consent (of the most powerful and wealthiest members of the community) and the right to a fair trial;
- Habeas Corpus Act 1640, which enacted the right to challenge arbitrary imprisonment (but as an ordinary statute was suspended several times to deal with government opponents);

- Bill of Rights 1688, which, following the 1688 revolution, subjected the Crown to Parliament;
- Act of Settlement 1700, which regulated succession to the Crown and gave the senior judges security of tenure;
- Act of Union with Scotland 1707;
- Parliament Acts 1911 and 1949, which made the House of Lords subordinate to the House of Commons; Life Peerages Act 1958 and House of Lords Act 1999, which reformed the composition of the House of Lords;
- European Communities Act 1972, which made European law part of UK law;
- Human Rights Act 1998, which incorporated provisions taken from the European Convention on Human Rights into UK law;
- Constitutional Reform Act 2005, which strengthened the independence of the judiciary;
- Constitutional Reform and Governance Act 2010, which despite its grand title makes relatively minor changes.

Many other statutes raise constitutional issues, such as those dealing with elections, complaints against government, controls over government finance, immigration, the media, police powers, the security services and freedom of information.

Two things might be noted about these statutes. Firstly they do not add up to a general constitutional code; they deal with specific issues and are usually responses to particular problems. Thus whether a statute is enacted depends mainly on the interests of the government of the day. For example, there are no statutes (other than some dealing with incidental matters such as pensions and salaries) limiting the powers of the Prime Minister or regulating the relationship between the executive and Parliament (contrast the devolved regimes in Scotland, Wales and Northern Ireland).

Secondly some statutes might have a special status and influence as symbolic of great events and important principles. This is true particularly of the Bill of Rights 1688 and also of Magna Carta 1215 (enacted 1297). Many of the general principles and sentiments behind Magna Carta are still invoked in constitutional debate. It established that in principle the King is subject to the law, in the sense of the customs of the realm that protected the rights of the landowners and local communities. It also foreshadowed the modern concept of proportionality in relation to penalties. Magna Carta remains of great symbolic value as capturing the essence of the rule of law and accountable government; for example 'to none will we sell: to no one will we delay or deny justice' (see *R v Secretary of State, ex p Phansopkar* [1976]: claim to right to reside in UK, right to a court hearing prior to deportation) and 'no freeman shall be taken or imprisoned or be outlawed or exiled or in otherwise destroyed ... but by ... the law of the land' (see *R (Bancoult) v Secretary of State* [2001], Section 9.4). Magna Carta also includes the principles of no taxation without representation and the right to a fair trial.

In *Thoburn v Sunderland City Council* [2002], Laws LJ, in the context of the European Communities Act 1972, spoke of a 'constitutional' statute, meaning a statute which the courts will not read as overridden by other statutes unless very clear language is used (Chapters 7, 9; see also *Robinson v Secretary of State for Northern Ireland* [2002]: devolution legislation). The problem here is that we may not agree as to what counts as a constitutional statute.

Statutory instruments might occasionally have constitutional importance. These are laws made by the executive under powers delegated by an Act of Parliament and are not subject to full democratic scrutiny. They usually concern very detailed and technical matters and are unlikely to raise general concerns. However ministers are sometimes given wide powers to alter Acts of Parliament themselves, for example in relation to the powers of regulators (see Section 5.9) Moreover, statutory instruments are used to create constitutions for some dependent territories (see Section 6.7).

3.3 The common law

The common law developed by judges on a case-by-case basis claims legitimacy as the embodiment of the values of the community given shape by precedent. Liberals and communitarians might both find the common law attractive, although republicans would have doubts about whether the common law meets the aspiration of citizen participation in government and might regret the emphasis of the law upon confrontation and rights rather than on compromise. However, from a republican angle it might be claimed that all citizens are on an equal footing in the courts (subject to the obvious objection that the wealthy are at a practical advantage in being able to afford high-level legal assistance).

Historically the common law predates Parliament as lawmaker since the common law emerged from customary laws that are sometimes claimed to go back to the ancient Britons. Indeed the idea of an ancient common law constitution, threatened by the pretensions of monarchs, is part of the rhetoric of English constitutional debate, designed to instil reverence for precedent. The common law was strengthened from the thirteenth century by the practice of the King's judges touring the country on his behalf as 'the fount of justice', with the main courts later gravitating to London. Although judges are in theory Crown servants, from the seventeenth century it was established that the King cannot act as a judge himself but is bound by the law as made by the judges (see *Prohibitions del Roy* [1607]). This is an important marker establishing a separation of powers of sorts.

There is a tension between the classical common law view of the constitution – advocated with varying degrees of emphasis by judges such as Coke (1552–1634), Hale (1609–76) and Mansfield (1709–93) and commentators such as Blackstone (1723–80) – and the modern political notion of the constitution as the application of unlimited democratic power vested in Parliament. Coke claimed that common law was the supreme arbiter of the constitution – an argument still pursued today (Chapter 8). According to Coke, the common law is a matter of reason, but:

> the artificial perfection of reason...gotten by long study and experience...No man (out of his private reason) ought to be wiser than the law, which is the perfection of reason. (Institutes, 1(21))

Artificial reason is apparently the collective wisdom of the judges. The classical view envisages the common law constitution as the product of the evolutionary development of community practices adapting the law in a practical way to meet changing circumstances Hale's famous metaphor of the Argonauts' ship has often been used, where the same ship in the sense of design and purpose that had set sail returns but has been so often mended that no piece of the original remains (Hale, *A History of the Common Law* (1713) 40).

Hobbes (Section 2.3) roundly condemned Coke's claims. He denied that there is anything special about lawyers' reasoning and refused to accept that custom and tradition in themselves carry any legal authority. According to Hobbes, the rule of law derives from authority, subject to 'natural reason' which is available to everyone. He objected to the common law on the ground that disagreement between judges picking over conflicting precedents creates the very uncertainty that the law exists to prevent. Jeremy Bentham (Chapter 2) also objected to the common law on the ground that relying on precedent was irrational. We might also be cynical about the notion that the common law represents community values and may regard it as the creation of professional lawyers, filtering experience through their own self-interest, even if unintentionally.

The distinctive characteristics of the common law have substantial influence on the constitution.

- ▶ The common law has largely developed through private law notions of personal liability and property rights, underlying Dicey's claim that the same rule of law applies to public bodies and private citizens alike (see Section 6.4). Arguably this has frustrated the development of public law principles designed to hold government to account.

- ▶ The common law can claim to be embedded in community values. Notions such as the reasonable person, 'reasonable expectations' and right-thinking members of society surface in common law argument.

- ▶ The common law can be a focus for open and public debate about competing versions of justice (see eg *White v South Yorkshire Police Authority* [1999]). The common law recognises disagreement about basic values appropriate to a democracy. Its driving force is dispute. Disagreement is kept open through the practices of separate opinions by individual judges and dissenting judgements. Judges can change their minds subject to the loose rules of binding precedent.

- ▶ Some liberals argue that the courts are the guardians of fundamental freedoms and in extreme cases should have the power to override an Act of Parliament (Sections 8.4, 8.5). The conventional approach, characteristic of the UK's reliance on voluntary practices, is that there is an 'understanding' among the personal networks that make up the institutions of government as to their respective roles and limits.

- ▶ It is difficult to reconcile the judges' common law power to make law with either the separation of powers (see Section 7.6.2) or democracy. Supporters of the common law usually argue that the common law supports democracy by protecting its basic values such as freedom of speech against the danger that an elected government might pervert democracy by becoming tyrannical. Against this it can be argued that there is nothing to prevent judges from supporting tyrannical governments and that it is offensive to entrust an unelected elite with the protection of fundamental values, the proper remedy against tyranny being to strengthen democratic mechanisms (see Waldron, *Law and Disagreement* (Oxford University Press 1999) 11, 12, 13).

- ▶ The courts are careful to respect the separation of powers to the extent that they are reluctant to develop common law principles in areas where Parliament has shown willingness to intervene (see *Re McKerr* [2004]: investigation of deaths; *Cambridge Water Co v English Counties Leather* [1994]: environmental protection).

3.4 Constitutional conventions

3.4.1 The nature of conventions

Conventions are rules and principles are not legally binding but are nevertheless important parts of the constitution. Conventions are binding primarily by virtue of their acceptance by those in power. (The term 'convention' literally means a 'coming together'). Conventions play a central part in the constitution. They deal with fundamental matters concerning the distribution of power and government accountability, for example the principle that the monarch must act on the advice of ministers is a convention. Thus conventions act to adjust the legal rules to the political reality. Dicey (1915) suggests that conventions reconcile legal sovereignty and political sovereignty. Allan (*Law, Liberty and Justice* (Oxford University Press 1993) 253) concludes that conventions 'give effect to the principle of governmental accountability that constitutes the structure of responsible government'.

Constitutional conventions deal mainly with the relationship between the different branches of government: the Crown, the executive and Parliament, ministers and the civil service, the Prime Minister and the Cabinet, the central government and the devolved governments. There are for example no legal rules requiring there to be either a Prime Minister or a Cabinet, and most of the powers of the Prime Minister are conventional. Many of the central principles of the political constitution are conventions namely that the monarch must assent to all bills presented to her by Parliament and the Crown must act through ministers who are collectively and individually accountable to Parliament. However the principle that the monarch cannot make law without the cooperation of Parliament is statutory (Bill of Rights 1688). Our mix of law and convention is therefore somewhat random and exemplifies how the UK constitution must be pieced together without a blueprint other than orthodox opinion. Conventions also show a reluctance to develop the constitution according to principles of abstract reason.

Unlike a law which gets its validity because it is made in public by a recognised process: a statute or a court judgement, a convention is valid only in as much as it are generally respected. Conventions are evidenced by the opinions of those in influential positions based usually on previous practice. This might be discovered in government records, in academic writing or even the biographies of past political grandees. There is no shortage of camp followers of the powerful willing to give a suitable opinion. However the views of the courts carry no weight in this matter.

Disputes as to the application of a convention must be settled by political means such as negotiation or parliamentary debate without the certainty of a conclusive outcome. For example no one is sure precisely what the 'Salisbury Convention' means. This requires the House of Lords to respect the 'mandate' which the electorate is assumed to have given to the government. However since the electorate votes only for individual local MPs the notion of the mandate is obscure assuming as it does that voters approved every aspect of the governing party's election manifesto. Moreover the Salisbury Convention was introduced at a time when the House of Lords had an inbuilt Conservative majority which, now that most of hereditary element has been ejected (Section 12.2), is no longer the case. (See HL Deb vol 672, col 275, 23 May 2005)

Another example comes from the General Election of 2010. When it appeared that a 'hung Parliament' without a clear majority to choose a Prime Minister was likely (as so it turned out), a self-selected group of civil servants, members of the Queen's entourage and invited academics drafted a set of principles to deal with the issue. (See Blackburn, 'The 2010 General Election and the Formation of the Conservative-Liberal Democrat Coalition Government' [2011] PL 30.) There was no publicly endorsed mechanism available.

In law if the monarch ignored the conventions and appointed a friend as Prime Minister nothing could directly be done. The appointment would be lawful and any. solution would be political. Probably Parliament would refuse to support the Prime Minister in a vote of confidence and refuse to raise taxes to support the executive, thereby making government impossible and forcing the Queen to respond to Parliament's wishes. However the Queen might be required to exercise her legal powers in a political crisis if for example no leader had the support of Parliament. (Chapter 14).

Conventions and law are sometimes intertwined in the sense that a law either assumes a convention or a convention has influenced the content of the law which cannot be understood without knowing the relevant convention. For example many royal prerogative powers, legally in the hands of the Queen, are lawfully exercised directly by ministers without reference to the Queen thus acknowledging the convention of ministerial responsibility (Section 15.7). Conventions can of course be turned into law by enacting them as statutes (eg the *Ponsonby Convention;* see Section 9.7.1 and the rules relating to dissolution of Parliament (Section 11.3)). Approval by a resolution of the House of Commons would give a convention greater authority but would not turn it into law unless it was enacted as a statute.

Many conventions are wholly unwritten, residing only in the opinions of those consulted about them. Some conventions and other practices and understandings are written down by officials in an uncoordinated profusion of 'protocols' 'concordats', 'memoranda', 'codes of practice' and the like. For example the *Ministerial Code* (2010) issued by the Cabinet Office comprises a mixture of conventions, advice about ethics, practice and administrative matters designed to guide ministers. The Cabinet Office is currently attempting to produce a comprehensive guide to constitutional practice. The mere fact that a principle has been put in writing does not in itself make it a convention but might be evidence of a convention.

The absence of an authoritative decision making process, or indeed any public and systematic discussion, reveals the absence of democratic legitimacy of conventions. Lord Simon of Glaisdale let the cat out of bag in evidence to the Joint Committee on Conventions (2005–06, HL 1212–1, HC 1212–1):

> the great thing about the Salisbury convention is that it works. Generally that is enough in this country...The last comment to make about it is that it is a constitutional convention and not constitutional law. In other words it is binding only politically and morally but not legally and only so long as it is convenient.

The obvious reaction to this is convenient to whom? There is also the republican argument (Chapter 2) that it is insulting to human dignity to rely on the goodwill of those in power to conform to proper standards of conduct. Respect for the equality of citizens requires that government be constrained by independent rules made democratically and known to all.

The UK constitution is not alone in generating conventions. Any constitution or set of formal rules is likely to be overlaid by unwritten customs and practices. This is partly because no set of written rules can deal with every possible situation but also because all written documents fall to be interpreted in the light of the assumptions and beliefs, moral and political, of the interpreter. In the case of a constitution there are numerous inputs of thousands of people over time so that the nuances of the constitution are in constant flux.

3.4.2 The main conventions

Conventions help to ensure that the constitution reflects contemporary political values and so as to manage evolutionary constitutional change without generating political controversy by attempting to reform legislation. Most conventions concern the relationship between different components of government.

▶ Conventions relating to the monarch (above) ensure that vestigial prerogative powers are normally exercised only by or in accordance with advice received from ministers, who are accountable to Parliament. However there are ill-defined circumstances in which ministerial advice need not be followed (Section 14.4).

▶ The chain of conventions embodied in the doctrine of ministerial responsibility to Parliament is of fundamental importance, being intended to ensure that the legal powers of the Crown are subject to democratic control. However the supposed chain of accountability is not complete. Dicey anticipated neither the dominance of the executive in Parliament, nor the dispersal of executive power to miscellaneous bodies, including private companies, outside the central government structure (Section 15.9). Moreover if ministerial accountability is to be effective it assumes that members of Parliament will act independently and not through party loyalty. Accountability to Parliament is often accountability to the minister's own party.

▶ Other conventions concern the relationship between the two Houses of Parliament. For example the 'Salisbury Convention' (Section 3.4.1) requires that the House of Lords should not oppose a measure sent to it by the Commons which was contained in the governing party's election manifesto except perhaps where the matter is the subject of deep public controversy (see Turpin and Tomkins, *British Government and the Constitution* (6th edn, Cambridge University Press 2007) 643–45, 652–53).

▶ New conventions have been introduced to meet new challenges, for example to deal with the relationship between the central government and the devolved governments of Scotland, Wales and Northern Ireland. The *Sewell Convention* requires that legislatures of the devolved territories should consent to any legislation made by Parliament that affects devolved matters (*Memorandum of Understanding* (Cm 5420, 1999)). There may also be a right of the Prince of Wales as heir to the Crown to meet with ministers, to obtain information from them, to comment on their policies and to argue for alternative policies, although this competes with the convention that the monarchy should not be involved with political controversy (see Brazier, 'The Constitutional Position of the Prince of Wales' [1995] PL 401).

A fashionable recent device is that of 'concordats' agreed between participants and intended to govern the relationship between different organs of government or to set out practices. These may have the status of convention, at least if they are generally acted upon. There are many of these between government departments, agencies and the devolved institutions of Scotland, Northern Ireland and Wales which clarify the relationship between these bodies. A Concordat made in 2004 between the government and the Lord Chief Justice concerning links between the judiciary and the executive underpins the reforms introduced by the Constitutional Reform Act 2005 (Section 11.2). These could be regarded as expressing conventions designed to secure the independence of the judiciary.

It is sometimes suggested that convention requires there to be a referendum before legislation is introduced making fundamental constitutional change. However this raises the problem of how we recognise a convention (Section 3.4.4). There have been few precedents for this and, subject to some statutory provision it is for the government to decide whether to hold a referendum (Section 2.7.2).

3.4.3 Identifying conventions

It is important to distinguish constitutional conventions from other forms of constitutional behaviour such as practices, traditions and legal principles. It is necessary in particular to distinguish between conventions and practices, because practices, however important, are not binding at all. The party system provides an example of a practice fundamental to the workings of the constitution which has no binding force. There is a logical gulf between practice (what is) and rule (what 'ought' to be), although it must be conceded that well-established practices carry at least a presumption that they ought to be continued. This seems to be a basic psychological fact about human motivation. Furthermore a practice ceases to exist if it is regularly broken. If a convention is broken, it ceases to exist only if no criticism follows. To this extent conventions are at the mercy of raw politics.

Sir Kenneth Wheare defined conventions as 'a rule of behaviour accepted as obligatory by those concerned in the working of the constitution' (*Modern Constitutions* (Oxford University Press 1966) 102). This emphasises that the crucial matter is the belief of the politicians to whom a convention applies that there is an obligation to act in a particular manner. A convention exists if, as a matter of fact, the belief is present (presumably held by most of those it affects?). But it is arguable that a convention ought to engage what politicians are actually bound to do and not merely what they consider their obligations to be. On the other hand who is to say what this should be?

Dicey famously defined conventions negatively as anything which is not law (1959, 24). He stated that apart from laws:

> The other set of rules consist of conventions, understandings, habits, or practices which, though they may regulate the conduct of several members of the sovereign power, of the Ministry, or of other officials, are not in reality laws at all since they are not enforced by the courts.

Since neither conventions nor non-binding practices are enforced by the courts, Dicey's test does not identify that which is a convention as opposed to non-binding practice. In this connection, Munro (1999, 81) argues that non-legal rules are best viewed as of one type provided we accept that conventions vary in stringency. Thus while conventions are obligatory, they do not all have the same degree of binding force. Some may have exceptions (such as the personal powers of the monarch; see Section 14.4); some may not be regarded as important. It may be difficult to decide whether a particular pattern of behaviour amounts to a convention or merely a working practice. For example doubt surrounds the role of the Cabinet the importance of which seems to depend on the whim of the prime minister at the time and the courage of the cabinet ministers (Section 15.4).

A consensus may be said to arise if there is substantial support for the proposed convention. Unanimity is not of course required although the notion of substantial is flimsy and open to abuse in favour of the views of friends of those in power. Evidence might be found through the political biographies or friendly persons regarded as constitutional experts. The impartial civil service is responsible for ensuring continuity in government (Section 15.8). The views of important non-elected officials may therefore be drawn upon such as Peter Hennessy's 'golden triangle' of Cabinet Secretary, the Queen's advisers and the Prime Minister's Principal Private Secretary (PPS) a was the case in 2010 (Section 3.4.1). Hennessy (1995, 45, 46) describes how officials monitor and record practice in a 'Precedent Book', which, characteristically of the UK constitution, is not open to public inspection. Officials and politicians refer to the records so contained and this may eventually lead to a consensus that the practice is obligatory. Moreover there is no shortage of academic and journalistic courtiers anxious to promote their opinions.

Hennessy (1995, 15–30) describes the UK constitution as generated by an inner circle of guardians mainly comprising senior officials and their friends. He recounts the Victorian conceit that conventions embody 'the general agreement of public men' about 'the rules of the game' (1995, 36, 37). Similarly Bogdanor described the UK constitution as 'a very peculiar constitution which no one intended whereby the government of the day decides what the constitution is' (ibid., 165). Horwitz has argued ('Why Is Anglo-American Jurisprudence Unhistorical?' [1997] OJLS 551) that conventions were developed as undemocratic devices to reassure the ruling class that constitutional fundamentals would continue to be developed within government largely beyond the influence of the rising middle classes following rapid extension of the franchise after the Reform Act 1867.

Jennings offered three tests to identify a convention (*The Law and the Constitution* (London University Press 1959) 136). First, are there any precedents? Second, do those operating the constitution believe that they are bound by a rule? Third, is there a constitutional reason for the convention? This has been accepted by the Canadian courts, although it is not clear why a court should have any say in the matter (*Reference re Amendment of the Constitution of Canada (Nos 1, 2 and 3)* (1982) 105 DLR (3d) 1).

In the absence of an authoritative decision maker such as a court there are plainly difficulties with precedents because there may be many occasions on which politicians disagree about the precedents they are supposed to follow. This uncertainty clouds even established conventional rules, such as the choice of a Prime Minister (Section 15.2). Sometimes precedent is unnecessary because a convention might be created by agreement, for example by the Cabinet, or even laid down unilaterally by the Prime Minister (for instance the *Sewell Convention*; see Section 16.1). It is arguable however that a rule which is laid down in this way is better described a 'soft law' to be put to the test and which becomes a convention only after it has gained general acceptance (see McHarg, 2008). A convention created by a formal agreement, such as a concordat (see Section 3.4.3), may perhaps be immediately binding.

Jennings' second test that those subject to it regard themselves as bound by the rule is subject to the difficulties discussed above in connection with Wheare and Dicey. Moreover the notion that conventions are essentially self-policing offends at least republican versions of constitutionalism since it denies the notion of limited government. Jenning's third requirement of a reason for the convention is also problematic. Who decides whether such a reason exists, and if the rule is in fact obeyed why should the reason matter? In the absence of an independent judge, the reason for a practice might depend upon contested political views as to what the constitution should be like.

3.4.4   The differences between law and convention

As we have seen, for Dicey the distinction between legal and political rules depended on the absence of direct power to enforce conventions through the courts. However many conventions function in a close relationship with laws since they direct how legal power will be exercised or prevent the exercise of anachronistic prerogative powers for example the convention that the Queen must assent to bills presented to her by Parliament. Conventions provide principles and values that form the context of the strict law; as Jennings famously said, 'flesh which clothes the dry bones of the law'.

Law and conventions have clear differences. Munro (1999) points out that a breach of the law does not call into question its existence or validity. He adds that individual laws do not rest upon consent – an unpopular law or a widely disregarded law is nevertheless a valid law. But a convention is valid only if it is accepted as binding. A law does not lapse if it becomes obsolete, yet a convention can disappear if it is not followed for a significant period, or if it is broken without objection.

Another difference which is of vital importance is that laws emanate from definite sources – the courts and Parliament – with an authoritative mechanism (the courts) for deciding what the rule means and how it applies. In the case of conventions there is no such authoritative source.

Nevertheless Dicey's distinction between law and convention has been criticised as too rigid. Some laws are less binding than others. For example procedural requirements stipulated by statute are sometimes 'directory only'. This means that such requirements need not always be obeyed (Section 18.2). Nor can importance be a distinguishing factor. Both laws and conventions deal with fundamental matters, and conventions can be as important as laws; indeed some conventions may be more important than some laws. On the other hand importance is irrelevant to the existence of a law but perhaps not to the existence of a convention. It is also said that conventions are different from laws because they lack certainty. Munro (1999) demonstrates that certainty is not the issue. He argues that some social rules, such as the rules of cricket, can be clearly stated but they are manifestly not laws. Moreover many laws are uncertain and while the courts certainly rely on precedent they are free to depart from precedents in many cases.

From a functionalist perspective (ie concerned with outcomes) Jennings, argued that law and convention are at root the same thing, each resting ultimately on public acquiescence and serving the same function, social control. Certainly the content of a convention is no different from that of a law, and a convention can be turned into law by enacting it as a statute. But this does not help on a detailed level for example to explain the different attitude of the courts to conventions and laws.

Perhaps the crucial distinction between convention and law concerns the attitude of the courts. The courts do not apply conventions directly. This means firstly that there is no remedy in the courts for breach of a convention as such, and secondly that the views of a court as to whether a particular convention exists and what it means are not binding. The existence and meaning of a convention are matters of fact that must be proved by evidence and not matters of law for the court.

On the other hand the courts do not ignore conventions. In particular a convention may form the political background against which the law has to be interpreted (see box). Furthermore statute may draw upon a particular convention, making it indirectly enforceable. For example section 36(2) of the Freedom of Information Act 2000 exempts government information from disclosure if it prejudices or is likely to prejudice the convention of the collective responsibility of ministers of the Crown.

The following cases illustrate the relationship between law and convention in the courts:

▶ In *Reference re Amendment of the Constitution of Canada* [1982], the Canadian Supreme Court, relying partly on British authority, recognised but refused to apply a convention. Under Canadian law any amendment to the Canadian Constitution required an Act of the UK Parliament following a request from the federal government of Canada. The Canadian government wished to amend the Constitution so as to free itself from this legal link with Britain. The UK Parliament would automatically pass any legislation requested by Canada.

▶ However there were important Canadian conventions on the matter. These required that the governments of the Canadian provinces be consulted about, and give their consent to, any proposed changes in the Constitution that affected federal–provincial relations. Some claimed that this had not been done. The Supreme Court was divided as to whether the convention in question existed. A majority held that it did, and went on to explain in some detail what the convention meant. Some of the judges doubted whether the court should have gone even this far, but as long as we remember that the court's view about the meaning of a convention is not in itself binding, it seems acceptable. In any event a larger majority held that, whatever the convention meant, it could not affect the legal rule that empowered the federal government to request an alteration to the Constitution. Thus the convention could not be enforced by legal remedies. The judges also denied that a convention can ever crystallise into law, for example by becoming established over a period of years. This seems to be equally true of English law (see Munro, 1999, 72ff).

▶ In *A-G v Jonathan Cape Ltd* [1975] the government sought to prevent publication of the diaries of Richard Crossman, a former Labour Cabinet minister. This involves balancing the confidential nature of any material against any public interest in favour of its disclosure. The government relied upon the convention of collective cabinet responsibility, arguing that this necessarily required that cabinet business remain confidential to cabinet ministers. The court refused to apply the convention as such. It held that the convention was relevant only to the problem of deciding where the public interest lay. His Lordship held that some of the diaries could be published because they dealt only with matters of historical interest and did not concern the activities of ministers still in office, which the convention was intended to protect. Thus the convention was a crucial strand in the argument but not the law itself (see further Jaconelli, 2005).

▶ In *Carltona Ltd v Comr for Works* [1943] the courts accepted the legitimacy of civil servants taking decisions that are in law the responsibility of the minister without reference to the minister personally. The reason for this was that, by convention, the minister is responsible to Parliament for the acts of civil servants in his department so that in law the civil servant can be deemed to be merely the instrument of the minister.

> ▶ In *R (Bancoult) v Secretary of State (No 2)* [2008] the government argued that an Order in Council made under the royal prerogative by the Crown was an exercise of sovereign power and could not be challenged in the courts. The House of Lords firmly rejected this argument as 'little more than a makeweight' (Lord Rodger at [106]) on the ground that in reality the order was made by a minister (see also *M v Home Office* [1993]).

3.4.5   Why conventions are obeyed

The main reason why conventions are obeyed is the adverse political consequences that might result from their breach. This is unsurprising since conventions are traditionally regarded as a matter of political ethics. It also produces the circularity that if a convention is not obeyed it may lose its binding force. For example the supposed convention that a minister should resign if there has been a serious wrongdoing in his or her department is usually ignored unless a minister loses political support (Section 15.7).

Dicey unsuccessfully tried to link breach of convention to breach of law. He stated (1959, 439ff) that conventions are not laws and so not enforced by the courts, but he argued that even the 'boldest political adventurer' would be restrained from breaching conventions because (at least in the case of some conventions) it would eventually lead to the offender coming into conflict with the courts and the law of the land (1959, 445–46). He gave as an example the consequences that might follow if Parliament did not meet at least once a year, or if a government did not resign after losing a vote of confidence. Dicey argued that the government would have the statutory authority neither for raising (some) taxes nor for spending money.

Not all conventions can be similarly treated. For example the appointment of a non-member of Parliament as a minister will not lead to a legal violation. The absence of adverse political repercussions may fortify ministers who give inaccurate parliamentary answers but this failure is unlikely to lead to a breach of the law (although such a statement might create a binding 'legitimate expectation'; see Section 17.9).

If some conventions were breached, Parliament might be compelled to intervene to prevent a recurrence. Most famously this occurred after the Lords refused to pass the Finance Bill 1909, thereby disregarding the conventional principle that the Lords should ultimately defer to the wishes of the elected Commons. The Parliament Act 1911 removed the veto power of the Lords in respect of most public bills. If the sovereign (without ministerial advice) were to refuse to grant royal assent to a bill passed by both Houses, the prerogative power to refuse would soon be removed by legislation.

It also seems that conventions are obeyed because they are part of a shared and respected system of values. This is evident in the commonly accepted definitions of conventions that emphasise the consent upon which they depend for their existence Jaconelli (2005) goes further and ventures the possibility that many conventions prescribe behaviour that is implicitly reciprocal. The party in power for the time being accepts the constraints that conventions impose upon its behaviour in the expectation that the opposition parties will do likewise when they attain office, However Jaconelli concedes that this would not apply to all conventions, such as those of an inter-institutional rather than inter-party kind, for instance the obligation of the monarch to assent to bills passed by both Houses. According to Jaconelli, prudence explains why such conventions are observed.

Conventions may apparently be breached or qualified (depending on one's viewpoint) as a safety valve where there is a conflict between what is normally constitutionally expected and current political consensus or expediency. In 1975 the Prime Minister 'suspended' the principle of collective Cabinet unanimity to allow ministers to express their views openly in a referendum campaign concerning membership of the European Economic Community (EEC). Any referendum on the future of sterling as the British currency might result in a similar temporary modification to collective ministerial responsibility.

3.4.6 Codification of conventions

Codification has different meanings and the fact that a set of rules is codified does not in itself determine the nature of the rules. Firstly it means an authoritative written version of the conventions in question. Strictly speaking this means turning the convention into law in the form of an Act of Parliament, although promulgation as a Standing Order or Resolution of Parliament would give it legal effect within Parliament itself. Conventions might also be codified in a less authoritative sense and not legally binding, for example in the form of a report of a parliamentary committee, a ministerial announcement, a concordat or a Memorandum of Understanding (see *Report of Joint Committee on Conventions* (2005–06, HL 1212–1, HC 1212–1).

The case for codification thus involves two distinct positions. The first asserts that conventions should be given legal force; the second that conventions might be codified within an authoritative text but remain as non-legal political practices, as at present. Even under the second version however, which has been adopted in Australia it is likely that the courts may rely on the codified conventions (see Sampford, '"Recognize and Declare": An Australian Experience in Codifying Constitutional Conventions' [1987] OJLS 369).

The second approach would to some extent address the lack of precision in some conventions and if it was intended to be a comprehensive code would enable us to say with certainty which usages are and which are not conventional. Establishing the certainty of conventions could also safeguard the neutrality of those who apply them. On the other hand this approach might create uncertainty, for example as to the status of any interpretation of a convention that a court might give if the matter arose in litigation.

The more adventurous position involving enactment as law has the important advantage that it is likely to generate public confidence in the integrity of government by reducing uncertainty and increasing openness and transparency. Authoritative versions of statutes must be widely published and the process of enactment is to some extent open and public. A recent example is the Constitutional Reform Act 2005. This reconfigured the relationship between the judges, Parliament and the executive in order to reinforce the principle of judicial independence (Sections 5.4, 7.7). This was so even though owing to various conventions and practices nobody seriously believed that the judiciary was not in fact independent. Another example is the Fixed Term Parliament Act 2011 which replaced conventions concerning the removal or resignation of a government (Section 11.3). (However these statutes made changes to the arrangements rather than merely enacting the conventions.)

On the other hand the enactment of conventions might damage the flexibility of the constitution and inhibit its evolutionary role in maintaining the relationship between the constitution and contemporary political values. It would be undesirable if conventions were to become fossilised and so impede further constitutional change. This might even prevent the development of qualifications limiting the scope of some conventions (as in the case of the 'suspension' of collective Cabinet unanimity in 1975).

The enactment of a convention would bring the matter within the scope of the courts. It is arguable that democratic issues for example whether a minister should resign ought to be a matter of collective political decision and fall outside the proper scope of the judicial function. But this depends on the particular convention. For example the *Sewell Convention* which restrains the UK Parliament from legislating in a matter within the powers of a devolved government does not seem to be inherently non justiciable. Moreover there is a concept of 'deference' whereby the court will refrain from looking closely into matters which it regards as inappropriate to the judicial function (Section 19.7.2)

There might be practical difficulties in systematic codification. It would be impossible to identify all usages that are currently conventional, and after a code was established further conventions might develop. A possible approach might be to enact only the most important and widely accepted conventions. This would place those selected outside the scope of the executive and locate more extensive power in Parliament. Constitutional development would then be a matter of statutory reform, which itself permit more open debate and discussion.

Summary

▶ The UK constitution is embodied in individual statutes and in the common law, which is claimed to derive from the values embedded in the community. Statutes and common law principles that are regarded as 'constitutional' are given special treatment but within a context of considerable uncertainty. The common law introduces an element of openness, independence and flexibility into the constitution, although it challenges the idea of democracy.

▶ The UK constitution is also embodied in customs and practices, the most important of which are conventions. Conventions are pragmatically intertwined with law but are not directly enforceable in the courts. There is therefore no authoritative mechanism for interpreting, identifying or enforcing conventions.

▶ Conventions are of fundamental importance in the UK constitution. In their best light they enable the constitution to evolve pragmatically in accordance with changing political values. In their worst light they allow the government of the day and its favourites to manipulate the constitution in their own interests, for example by recruiting sycophantic academics to endorse a particular interpretation of a convention.

▶ There is disagreement about the definition of a convention. Accordingly it is not always clear which forms of constitutional behaviour are conventions and which are mere practices. Conventions are binding rules of constitutional behaviour while mere practices are not.

▶ Conventions are distinct from law, firstly in that there are no authoritative formal tests for the validity of conventions and secondly because conventions are not directly enforced by the courts. However there is no inherent difference in the content of laws and conventions and the courts use conventions, as they do moral principles, to help interpret, develop and apply the law.

Summary cont'd

▶ Some commentators have argued that conventions could be incorporated into the law, but even if this is achieved how many such laws would be justiciable? Codification might offer certainty in respect of those conventions included in the code, but new conventions would be evolved after the code was introduced and some flexibility in adapting existing conventions might be lost. There may be scope for extending 'soft' forms of codification such as the Ministerial Code.

Exercises

3.1 'The British constitution presumes, more boldly than any other, the good faith of those who work it' (Gladstone). 'The constitution is "what happens"' (Griffith). Explain and compare these two statements.

3.2 To what extent does the common law influence the character of the UK constitution?

3.3 How are conventions recognised and enforced? Can they be distinguished from 'practices'?

3.4 '... the great thing about the Salisbury convention is that it works. Generally that is enough in this country...The last comment to make about it is that it is a constitutional convention and not constitutional law. In other words it is binding only politically and morally but not legally and only so long as it is convenient.' Lord Simon of Glaisdale Joint Committee on Conventions (2005–06, HL 1212–1, HC 1212–1). Discuss from the point of view of democracy.

3.5 Are conventions a desirable method of bringing about constitutional change?

3.6 What is the relationship between law and convention? Does it serve a useful purpose to distinguish between law and convention?

3.7 Should conventions be enacted into law or codified?

3.8 To what extent is silence a valuable constitutional device?

Further reading

Allott, 'The Theory of the British Constitution', in Gross and Harrison (eds) *Jurisprudence: Cambridge Essays* (Cambridge University Press 1992)

Bagehot, *The English Constitution* (2nd edn, Kegan Paul 1902) ch 1

Barber, 'Law and Constitutional Conventions' (2009) 125 LQR 294

Bogdanor and Vogenauer, 'Enacting a British Constitution: Some Problems' [2008] PL 38

Foley, *The Silence of Constitutions* (Routledge 1989)

Jaconelli, 'Do Constitutional Conventions Bind?' (2005) 64 CLJ 149

McHarg, 'Reforming the United Kingdom Constitution: Law, Convention, Soft Law' (2008) 71 MLR 853

Marshall, 'The Constitution: Its Theory and Interpretation' in Bogdanor (ed), *The British Constitution in the Twentieth Century* (Oxford University Press 2003) 36

Munro, *Studies in Constitutional Law* (2nd edn, Butterworths 1999) ch 3

Nolan and Sedley (eds) *The Making and Remaking of the British Constitution* (Blackstone 1997) ch 2

Postema, *Bentham and the Common Law Tradition* (Clarendon Press 1986) chs 1, 2

Sedley, 'The Sound of Silence: Constitutional Law without a Constitution' (1994) 110 LQR 270

Ward, *A State of Mind? The English Constitution and the Public Imagination* (Sutton 2000)

Wilson, 'The Robustness of Conventions in a Time of Modernisation' [2004] PL 407

Chapter 4

Historical outline

4.1 Introduction

This chapter highlights themes and events that have influenced the institutions of the UK constitution. (The devolved regions of Scotland Wales and Northern Ireland will be discussed in Chapter 16.) As we saw in Chapter 1, our unwritten constitution has evolved as the outcome of ever changing political pressures. This makes the historical context important as an aid to understanding. It is helpful to trace the gradual adjustment of institutions to different demands. History also helps to explain the survival of obsolete institutions which do not raise immediate problems and so have been left alone.

One view is that historical development is essentially random, driven by short term chances and personalities. Another view that there are large forces at work driving the constitution. Thus there may be a myth or story of how the constitution is justified. One such story, 'the Whig View of History', claims that the constitution is a happy unfolding progress from tyranny represented by the Norman kings towards democracy and responsible government. (The Whigs, part ancestors of the modern Liberal Democratic party, were the more progressive of the two parties that dominated politics between the end of the seventeenth century and the late nineteenth century, the other party being the Tories.)

The Whig story claims that our relatively peaceful constitutional development was achieved, through a happy mixture of strong central government in the form of Parliament and the Crown and dispersed local administration. There was popular consent through the substantial independence of towns and counties supervised benignly by royal officials (see eg Kellner, 2009). All government including the King was subject to the common law based on the customs of the realm. This ensured that absolutism never took root.

Another view is that the constitution is the outcome of an endless contest between rival factions competing for power against a background of a docile population. Political power is fragmented and elusive and there is no single source of ultimate power. The conflict between the Crown, and other claimants to power has always been dominated by money. Power lies with whichever group can provide money most effectively and changes hands in response to particular problems. The experience of the French revolution at the end of the eighteenth century reinforced a distrust for attempts at abstract constitution building.

In the following sections we shall outline some important stages in the development of the constitution.

4.2 The Saxon period: origins of the Crown

The monarchy is the oldest institution and in legal terms still the keystone of the constitution. In theory all legal power derives from the Crown. The withdrawal of the Romans in the fifth century put paid to a republican constitution. By the end of the tenth century 'England' as a loose unity comprising rival warlords headed by a King had emerged from rival kingdoms.

From pre-Norman times the hierarchical and centralised character of English society was apparent. According to the myth of the 'ancient constitution', the King ruled subject to the consent of a council, the Witan, representing the leading citizens. By the end of the tenth century a complex system of local government existed within the structure of counties that remains today. This was controlled by royal representatives in the shape of aldermen and sheriffs. (These offices survive today in characteristic English fashion as ceremonial and social.) There were local bodies within the counties organised into 'hundreds' and 'tithings' which acted as law enforcers, courts and tax collectors.

4.3 The medieval period: the beginning of parliamentary government and the common law

After the Norman Conquest (1066) the King claimed jurisdiction over the whole of England and by the sixteenth century over Wales. The power of the monarchy derived from the hierarchical feudal system of landowning, with the King at its apex. The chief landowners and church dignitaries (the two often overlapping) formed the King's council of advisors which he could summon at will and through which he issued laws. Some of the original powers of the monarch survive today in the form of the royal prerogative (Section 14.6.2). The army comprised private armies raised by the King and other landowners, each of which had a feudal obligation to provide the King with resources. Until the Wars of the Roses ushered in the Tudor regime (1487) the Crown was held by a succession of warlords supported by rival landowning families. There were many disputes as to the succession.

Henry II (1154-89) introduced a centralised but flexible legal regime in the shape of the common law. The *Assize of Clarendon* (1166) established the King's power to administer law through judges and juries throughout the land. Justice was carried out in the King's name by travelling judges and by local Justices of the Peace. By the reign of Edward 1 (1272–1307) the common law was established as a general system of law developed by the judges through decided cases. It was accepted that even the King was subject to the common law.

Magna Carta (1215) (named by virtue of its length not its content), was later promoted, notably in the seventeenth century by Chief Justice Coke, as a foundation of the rule of law and as representing an allegedly ancient common law. In *Magna Carta* (later annulled, revived and embellished), King John promised to rectify a list of grievances presented by leading landowners and clerics. The King was forced to commit what were previously unwritten customs to formal writings. Some of the rights listed in *Magna Carta* are fundamental today. These include the right to a fair trial by due process of law, the jury, no punishment except by law, and no taxation without consultation of those affected. The symbolic effect of *Magna Carta*, as later promoted, was immense as a foundation of the rule of law:

> no freeman shall be taken or imprisoned or be disseised of his freehold, or liberties or free customs or be outlawed or exiled or in any wise destroyed ... but by ... the law of the land

Although it is no longer directly in force, the underlying principles of *Magna Carta* have been invoked in modern cases and inspired other constitutions notably that of the USA (see Thompson, *Magna Carta: Its Role in the Making of the English Constitution* (Octagon 1972)).

The King originally made law and governed through a Council chosen by himself. The reign of Henry III (1216–72) saw constitutional conflict between the King who wished to rule through the royal household and the barons (the chief landowning families). Following the collapse of a period of baronial domination, Parliament, today the dominant institution of the constitution began to develop as a distinct institution.

Parliament originated early in the thirteenth century as a meeting of leading landowners and officials summoned personally by the King at irregular intervals to transact important governmental business often including hearing appeals from the courts. (The term means a 'parley or conference.') The House of Lords (which perhaps evolved from the Saxon Council of Elders, the *Witan*) was composed of the barons and church dignitaries. From time to time during the early thirteenth century representatives from other groups were summoned separately mainly to give information to the King.

Simon de Montfort Earl of Leicester (1208–65) is credited with founding the House of Commons as a counterforce to the Lords by insisting in 1265 that representatives of local dignitaries, authorised to speak for their communities be summoned together to Parliament, namely knights from country areas (the shires) and leading citizens from certain towns (burghers). This was the seed of the modern principle of representation. The first substantial representative Parliament was the 'Model Parliament' of 1295. Originally the Commons sent representatives to the House of Lords but from the middle of the fourteenth century met separately. The House of Lords was interested only in its own members and the two Houses made separate grants of money to the King. (In 1640 Charles 1 tried to summon the Lords alone but this was rejected as now constitutionally impossible.)

The King could decide when to summon Parliament and did so irregularly mainly when he needed to raise taxation. From the late thirteenth century the King in conjunction with Parliament began to make laws originally on the basis that Parliament was declaring the existing customs of the realm. A strong relationship developed between the House of Commons and the common lawyers which was important for the future. Parliament had the status of a high court, able to give final rulings on the law and to 'impeach' public officials for misconduct. Impeachment depends on a resolution of the House and is unlikely to be used today (although it was suggested that Tony Blair, the then Prime Minister, should be impeached over the decision to invade Iraq in 2002). The notion of the 'High Court of Parliament' is still used today (Sections 11.6, 13.5).

By the reign of Henry IV (1366–1413) the Commons claimed primacy over the House of Lords in respect of taxation matters an important precursor of contemporary principles. The Commons voted funds to the King in exchange for the redress of grievances a principle that echos in the modern Parliament. However, until the seventeenth century when royal pretensions became extravagant Parliament was largely deferential to the Crown.

During the fourteenth and fifteenth centuries which saw constant struggles between the King and the barons, representative parliaments gradually became an established feature of the constitution although law making was infrequent and demands for taxation irregular. The Speaker, a royal official was introduced as a link between the King and the Commons and the Commons claimed protection against outside interference (Section 11.4). There were claims in the reign of Richard 11 (1377–99) that, at least in judicial matters, Parliament was supreme.

The reasons for the rise of a representative parliament which was unique in Europe are obscure. It may be that Parliament which was usually deferential to the monarchy was a useful tool of the King against obstructive barons particularly when he needed to raise money.

The principle that the royal power required consent was recognised, by the end of the fifteenth century. Thus the leading common lawyer Sir John Fortesque (whose propaganda may have helped to bring about his claims) distinguished between *dominium regale*, as in France, where the King makes his own laws and *dominium politicum et regale*, where the people assent to laws made by the King (*The Difference between an Absolute and Limited Monarchy* (1471)). Fortequieu declared that 'nor does the King by himself or by his minister impose tall ages, subsidies, or any other burdens whatsoever on his subjects, nor change their laws nor make new ones, without the concession or assent of his whole realm expressed in Parliament' (*de Laudibus Leges Angliae*, 'In Praise of the Laws of England' (*c*1470)). Of course there is plenty of room for disagreement as to who count as 'the whole realm'. (See also *Duchy of Lancaster Case* [1567] 1 Plow 325.)

Thus by the beginning of the sixteenth century the structure of monarchy subject to Parliament and the common law was in place but with the monarch still the being dominant player.

4.4   The Tudor period: the creation of the state and the executive

This period introduced both new and revived political ideas (assisted by the introduction of the moveable type printing press into England in 1476). The Tudor period, spanning the sixteenth century, saw the emergence in Europe of the modern concept of the nation state as a self-contained impersonal structure served by a bureaucracy and with absolute authority within its territory (see Section 9.1). This replaced the more complex medieval regime in which Church, state and various interest groups such as landowners and trade groups coexisted uneasily.

The Reformation destroyed the dominance of the Catholic Church in England and was the context in which Henry VIII created the Church of England as a state religion. This led to a century of religious conflict which underlay the disputes between King and Parliament that culminated in the 1688 revolution. The Reformation had wider significance for the constitution by opening up a gulf which still exists, between pragmatic English constitutional ideas and the more rationalistic mainstream European tradition.

Medieval ideas of monarchy within common law clashed with newer ideas of absolute monarchy and the nation state. Throughout Europe the monarchy claimed to embody the new absolute notion of the state, although less so in England, where the common law and Parliament were established counterforces. Protestant notions of individualism and freedom of thought began to circulate widely as did classical republican ideas of equal citizenship (eg Sir John Harrington, 1561–1612) although the latter have not significantly influenced constitutional development in the UK.

The Reformation statutes showed that the monarch in conjunction with Parliament could make new laws of any kind as opposed merely to declaring the existing law. It was widely assumed but not settled that this involved unlimited legal power.

On the whole the Crown, Parliament and the common law courts worked harmoniously. Tudor monarchs had relatively little need to demand money from Parliament, since they had acquired considerable church property following the Reformation (1532–36) and had the proceeds of naval adventures and levies on the burgeoning overseas trade. However there was friction between Queen Elizabeth and Parliament concerning whether Parliament could discuss matters not raised before it by the Crown. This has echoes in the modern law of parliamentary privilege.

This period saw the emergence of the modern type of executive, comprising ministers, the most important of whom were styled secretaries of state; committees comprising the monarch's favourites and a bureaucratic structure of professional civil servants.

Parliament was still spoken of as a court reflecting the influence of lawyers in constitutional development and the fact that much government was carried out by court like procedures This has echos today (Section 18.3). However by the end of the sixteenth century it had become clear that Parliament was more than a court and was a proper law making assembly. Indeed an emerging doctrine of parliamentary supremacy was challenging the common law. Parliament was promoted as the personification of the important elements of the realm from the monarch downwards: 'The great corporation and body politic of the kingdom…with high, absolute and authentical powers' (Coke, 4th inst 2; see Holdworth, *History of English Law*, London Sweet and Maxwell 1945 IV, 181–187). The Crown was still the driving force in lawmaking although only in Parliament could the Crown exercise the fullest lawmaking power.

4.5   The seventeenth-century revolution: the supremacy of Parliament over the Crown

The seventeenth century saw harmony between the three branches of government disintegrating. The century was a crucible of ideas, including sovereignty, individual rights, representation and, to a limited extent, democracy. It was dominated by religious and financial conflicts between the Crown and Parliament. These led to the revolution of 1688, the foundation of the present constitution.

The Stuart monarchs ran out of money and were under military pressure from Scotland and Ireland. They claimed the right to exercise the royal prerogative to raise certain taxes without Parliament but respected the common law by subjecting their powers to scrutiny by the courts. The judges were servants of the Crown but asserted their independence from the Crown in deciding cases.

See e.g. *Bates Case*; (1606) 2 St Tr 371: King could tax import of currents since foreign affairs exclusively for King; *Darnall's Case: The Case of the Five Knights* (1627) 3 St Tr 1: the King could imprison without giving reasons; *R v Hampden* [1637] 3 ST Tr 825: King could tax for defence of the realm purposes: Seven Bishops Case (1688) 12 St. Tr. 133: King could not suspend the operation of statute (suspending power); but *Thomas v Sorrell* (1674) *Vaughan* 330, *Godden v Hales* [1686] 11 St Tr 1685: King could release from legal obligation (dispensing powers).

The position of the judges remained ambivalent since they could be dismissed by the King and the judgements of the day were full of disagreement. James 1 and Charles 1 both claimed that under the constitution the monarchy was the embodiment of the community and as the 'fount of justice' guardian of the people's rights, an interpretation contested by Parliament and somewhat more uneasily by the common lawyers.

In *Prohibitions del Roy* (1607) 12 Co Rep 64 a landmark decision of the Kings Bench, Coke CJ asserted that the King although nominally the head of the legal system could not personally adjudicate in the courts since the judges were the guardians of the 'artificial reason of the law' available only to a learned elite. As well promoting the self- serving notion that the law was a matter of professional expertise in the hands of a priesthood of lawyer this relates to modern ideas of the separation of powers and the rule of law Thus Coke's principle has been used to prevent ministers from hiding behind any special privileges of the Crown (see *M v Home Office* [1993] 3 All ER 537). Coke claimed that the law was 'the golden metwand' that if respected by the King would protect both citizens and himself. The seventeenth century philosopher Thomas Hobbes (see Section 2.3.1) strongly objected to what he regarded as Coke's inflated claims for the courts. Hobbes argued that the law should be based on ordinary reason accessible to all and not in the hands of an elite. See also *Case of Proclamations* [1611] 12 Co Rep 74: King could not make law by proclamation.

In 1621 Charles accepted the *Petition of Right* presented by Parliament which listed grievances about excess of royal power including taxation and, imprisonment without trial. However the King refused to regard this as binding and from 1629 attempted to rule without Parliament. However, when Charles attempted in 1639 to impose the Anglican prayer book on the Scots, the resulting uprising forced him to summon Parliament, the 'Long Parliament', which lasted from 1640 until 1660 albeit dormant or suspended for most of its life. The religious dimension was crucial. The Church of England, headed by the King, was confronted on the one hand by the Catholic Church and on the other by Protestant groups, who dominated Parliament.

A shortlived compromise was reached in 1641 when the Star Chamber and other special prerogative courts introduced by the Tudors to support an administrative state were abolished together with various other prerogative measures. These events left English legal culture with a suspicion of special jurisdictions over governmental matters and a preference for the ordinary courts, reflected in Dicey's idea of the rule of law (see Section 6.4).

In 1641 there was an uprising in Ireland which was widely blamed on the King. The King attempted to enter Parliament with soldiers and arrest a group of members for Treason. Civil war broke out in 1642, resulting in victory for Parliament in 1646.

There was a wide ranging constitutional debate at Putney between the ruling establishment of landowners and business interests led by Oliver Cromwell, and the more radical army rank and file, represented by the Levellers, who proposed a written constitution. This 'Agreement of the People' was based on religious freedom, equality before the law and universal male suffrage (later qualified by excluding servants and beggars). However Cromwell invoked custom and tradition in favour of more limited reforms. The Levellers, with their wider ideas of democracy, were defeated by force in 1649.

In 1649 Charles I was executed on the authority of Parliament, which was packed with army supporters. The House of Lords was abolished and a republic declared. In 1653 the remnants of Parliament were expelled and a military dictatorship, dominated by Protestants and with Cromwell as 'Lord Protector', was introduced. However after Cromwell's death in 1658 it seemed that chaos could best be avoided by restoring the traditional constitution. A self-appointed group of political leaders restored the Crown in 1660 in the form of Charles II, the heir of Charles I. The House of Lords was also restored.

Charles II (1660–85) and his brother, James II (1685–88), ruled on the basis that there had been no republic and the republican legislation was expunged from the statute book. Towards the end of Charles' reign, at a time when he was heavily subsidised by the French, anti-Catholic sentiment was revived. Catholicism was associated in the public mind with absolute monarchy, an association that still scars the constitution by preventing the monarch from being or marrying a Catholic (the present government proposes to abolish this restriction).

There was a substantial exodus abroad by Catholics and other religious minorities, thereby sowing the seeds of the American Revolution and adding to the problem of Ireland. The Exclusion Crisis (1679–81), in which Parliament attempted to bar Charles' Catholic brother, James, from the succession to the throne, reactivated the conflict between the monarchy and Parliament. Charles used his prerogative power to close Parliament and refused to summon Parliament again after 1681.

James II ruled with the support of Parliament from 1685. However James alienated both the main parties by favouring Catholics and attempting to override Parliament under the royal prerogative ('suspending and dispensing' powers). This had some success in the courts, at least to meet emergencies (*Thomas v Sorrell* (1674) *Vaughan* 330; *Godden v Hales* [1686] 11 St Tr 1165). James suspended the penal laws against Catholics in 1687 and 1688. He also displaced thousands of local parliamentary candidates who would not vote according to his wishes.

The foundations of the modern constitution were laid by the 1688 'Glorious' revolution when James dissolved Parliament and fled the country. A self-appointed 'Convention Parliament' combining landowning and commercial interests offered the Crown to the Protestant William of Orange and his wife, Mary (James's daughter), supported by the Dutch military. The common law courts sided with Parliament which may be one reason why the revolution was promoted as a revival of an established constitution rather than as a radical break with the past.

Indeed in political terms the 1688 revolution was relatively conservative, a compromise designed to satisfy the main financial and property interests. It was justified in two ways. On a Hobbesian premise, James II had abdicated, leaving a power vacuum which, according to the common law doctrine of necessity, must be filled in order to avoid chaos. On the other premise, based on Locke, James had broken his contract by violating property rights, so entitling the people to rebel. In Scotland and Ireland, continuing support for the Stuart monarchs was crushed by force.

The Convention promoted the Bill of Rights 1688 (still in force) dealing with the grievances against the Stuart Kings and based on the Petition of Rights of 1621 (above). It prohibited the Crown from exercising key powers without the consent of Parliament, including the powers to make laws, to tax, to keep a standing army in peacetime and to override legislation. It also protected freedom of speech and elections in Parliament, ensured that Parliaments were summoned regularly, protected jury trial and banned excessive bail. William and Mary then summoned a Parliament which ratified the Acts of the Convention (Crown and Parliament Recognition Act 1689). The Act of Settlement 1700 (still in force) provided for the succession to the Crown and gave superior court judges security of tenure and therefore independence from the Crown. Thus was founded the first 'constitutional monarchy' in western Europe. The Act of Settlement linked Church and state by requiring the monarch to be a member of the Church of England and not to marry a Catholic, contains safeguards to prevent a monarch born 'out of this Kingdom' embroiling the country in a foreign war and prohibits non-citizens from being members of Parliament or the Privy Council (see Sections 12.2, 12.4). The Meeting of Parliament Act 1694 (the Triennial Act) required Parliament to meet at least every three years (by convention it must meet annually) and limited the life of a Parliament to three years (now five years: Parliament Act 1911, Fixed Term Parliaments Act 2011).

Thus the 1688 settlement put in place the main legal structures we have today. It was based neither on democracy nor on the fundamental rights of the individual. The House of Lords was a powerful body and the House of Commons was largely made up of landowners and businessmen dependent on the patronage of the Lords. Thomas Paine, who fled the country in 1792 having been charged with sedition for denying that Britain had a constitution, said in *The Rights of Man* (1791–92):

> What is [the Bill of Rights 1688] but a bargain which the parts of the government made with each other to decide powers. You shall have so much and I will have the rest; and with respect to the nation, it said, for your share, you shall have the right of petitioning. This being the case the Bill of Rights is more properly a bill of wrongs and of insult. (Paine, 1987, 292)

The 1688 settlement also led to the creation of the Bank of England in 1694 as a semi-independent institution backed by Parliament which guaranteed the currency and through which the government could borrow money. This was an important reason for the successful expansion of the British government and the economy during the following century since it gave the Crown a secure source of funds.

4.6   The eighteenth and early nineteenth centuries: the parliamentary and party system

During this period the central structure of the UK constitution emerged, whereby power is concentrated in Parliament and the executive is chosen by Parliament and is responsible to it mainly through non-legally binding conventions. This places the third branch of government, the judiciary on the sidelines at the mercy of the other branches thereby raising questions about the separation of powers and judicial independence which remain unresolved. These concern the extent of parliamentary supremacy, interference with courts by parliament and the executive and judicial review of government decisions.

The monarch remained the head of the government, with power to assent to legislation, to appoint and dismiss l ministers and to summon and dissolve Parliament, but unable to raise taxes or make law without the cooperation of Parliament. The Crown retained certain other royal prerogative powers which still survive. For most of the eighteenth century the monarch claimed to run the executive personally although the Commons could dismiss a ministry of which it disapproved. The Crown ran what was in effect a political party known as the 'Court and Treasury Party', which it controlled by giving government jobs to its supporters and manipulating elections. The main parties, the Whigs and the Tories, alternated in forming governments, although coalition governments were common. The aristocracy were dominant and held most ministerial posts.

Politicians such as Edmund Burke, who entered Parliament in 1765, still influence contemporary debate. Burke favoured traditional ideas of monarchy, custom and the unwritten constitution as opposed to equality and abstract reason, which he feared would lead to chaos and tyranny. He grounded the constitution in the limited right to choose and remove a representative government (see Pocock (ed), *Reflections on the Revolution in France* (Hackett 1987)). Burke's rival Thomas Paine (see Section 4.5) favoured equality, broader ideas of democracy and the establishment of a code of fundamental rights.

A significant difference from the modern Parliament was that the party system was looser. Indeed the very existence of parties was controversial (eg lack of independence against rallying support for great causes). About half the MPs were independent of party allegiance and others frequently changed parties. One reason for the relative independence of MPs was that unlike today most MPs had private means and did not depend on their party for career advancement. Indeed an Act of 1710 (9 Anne c 5) imposed a property requirement on membership of the House of Commons (except for the eldest sons of peers and knights and the representatives of Oxford and Cambridge universities).

On the other hand the dominant political culture was adversarial and oligarchical, assuming a permanent contest between two elites led by aristocratic families. This adversarial culture has had important consequences for our contemporary constitution. In particular the 'first past the post' voting system, which gives the prize to the largest party with nothing for the runners-up, favours two dominant parties at the expense of other parties. However, the House of Lords could veto legislation although the Commons controlled the raising and spending of money by the Crown. At a time when most European states were absolute monarchies, the British constitution was widely admired from outside as a stable regime. The notion of the 'mixed constitution' was promoted, in which monarch, Lords and Commons acted as checks on each other in a balanced clockwork-like machine. The leading legal commentator Blackstone (1723–80) announced that the royal assent to legislation meant that the King could not propose evil but could prevent it. Blackstone also emphasised the importance of the rule of law and the independence of the judges.

From inside Britain the picture was more blurred. The electoral system was not democratic and bore little relationship to the distribution of the population. Only about 4 per cent of the population had the right to vote. Elections were largely controlled by aristocratic families by bribery or by selecting candidates. There was a property qualification to vote in the rural counties. In the boroughs (towns) the right to vote depended on local charters and customs. In many cases this was attached to particular property and could be bought. There were numerous 'rotten boroughs' that only had a handful of electors, sometimes in the gift of particular families. For example in 1830 Gatton (patron Sir John Wood) had two MPs and seven voters. At the other extreme the expanding cities had few, if any, representatives. The younger sons of members of the House of Lords were often guaranteed seats in the Commons.

Turning to the judicial branch, the British system of responsible government that concentrates power in the central executive and enables it to control the legislature makes the position of the third branch, the judiciary, vulnerable. Indeed Jefferson, a founder of the US constitution thought that the system of responsible government was inevitably corrupt (Stevens (2004) 2). Judges had obtained security against dismissal and loss of pay by the executive in the Act of Settlement 1701. The same Act excluded judges from membership of the House of Commons but not of the House of Lords of which many judges were members. Until the early twentieth century, judges were politically appointed and were often former ministers or military men. Until the reign of George III (1760–1820) judges had to be reappointed on the death of a monarch.

During the eighteenth and early nineteenth centuries the rhetoric of the rule of law was promoted. The constitution was portrayed as a delicately balanced machine held in place by law; as George III put it, 'the most beautiful balance ever framed' (Briggs, *The Age of Improvement* (Longman 1959) 88). The rule of law protected individual rights imagined as being grounded in ancient common law tradition:

> The poorest man may in his cottage bid defiance to all the forces of the Crown. It may be frail, its roof may shake, the wind may blow through it, the storm may enter, the rain may enter, but the king of England cannot enter. (Lord Brougham, *Historical Sketches of Statesmen in the Time of George III* (1845)

It was widely asserted that the relative stability and economic prosperity of that period was connected with a commitment to the rule of law. By contrast 'France with its demagoguery, revolt, beheadings and ... unruly mobs stood in English 'common sense' as a dreadful warning of all that can go wrong, a sort of conceptual opposite to England's altogether more sensible ways' (Pugh, 'Lawyers and Political Liberalism in Eighteenth and Nineteenth Century England' in Halliday and Karpick *Lawyers and the Rise of Western Political Liberalism: From the Eighteenth to the Twentieth Centuries* (Clarendon Press 1997) 168).

The record of the rule of law was mixed. It protected rights in the formal sense that everyone had access to the same courts and whatever rights a person had were usually adjudicated impartially. However Parliament passed harsh laws for the benefit of its supporters, which the courts were required to apply. These included the notorious anti-poaching 'Black Acts' (see Thompson, *Whigs and Hunters* (Allen Lane 1975)), periodic suspension *Habeas Corpus, blasphemy and sedition laws* and the Corresponding Societies Act 1799, which outlawed radical political and cultural organisations. The taxation system put the burden upon consumption as opposed to property, thus penalising the poor.

The courts protected property rights and personal security strongly (eg *Leach v Money* [1765]; *Entick v Carrington* (1765); *Wolfe Tone's Case* [1798]). The common law rejected slavery within England albeit reluctantly (*Somersett's Case* [1772]). Freedom of expression was less clearly protected, other than that of MPs (Section 11.6). Indeed, because laws are often vague, reformers such as Bentham, thought the law's claim to objectivity and balance were spurious and that the constitution was held together by aristocratic power and influence. 'Talk of balance, ne'er will it do: leave that to Mother Goose and Mother Blackstone' (Bentham, *Works*, quoted by Loughlin, 'John Griffith: An Appreciation', [2010] PL 649).

Some contemporary themes are emerging. The constitution relies heavily on personal relationships within the governing elite. Patronage is exercised by the Prime Minister and political parties, who nominate candidates for election and recommend peerages and public appointments. The common law and Parliament are in tension. Judicial independence while acknowledged has frail protection.

4.7 The nineteenth century: reforms and democracy

During the nineteenth century the political and economic circumstances of Britain changed. Rural communities dominated by aristocratic landowners were eclipsed by cities dependent upon industrial production and overseas trade. This led to a rapidly increasing urban population, and the enactment of statutes acquiring land on a large scale for public works such as railway building. By the middle of the nineteenth century the modern doctrine that Parliament has unlimited power become the orthodoxy as it is today but the position has never been fully resolved partly because the common law is an alternative (Section 8.5.6).

Successive governments were weak and corrupt dominated by networks of wealthy families and industrialists. There were, demands for democratic government by radical organisations notably the Chartists (1837–54). Uprisings took place throughout Europe notably in 1848 which was a year of revolution. However uprising in Britain was on a lesser scale and followed economic fluctuations rather than a strong public desire for democracy. Public unrest was sometimes put down brutally (eg the 'Peterloo' massacre of reform campaigners in Manchester (1819)). This led to the notorious 'Six Acts' which severely limited political freedoms and made criminal prosections easier.

Revolutionary pressures did however lead albeit gradually to a more democratic electoral system. During the nineteenth century the extension of voting rights to non-property owners was slowly and reluctantly conceded, resisted by liberal arguments that the freedom of talented people to develop themselves would be curtailed by the inflated demands of the masses. Democracy was also resisted on rule of law grounds by the likes of Dicey, who thought that it was unpredictable, and on communitarian grounds by Matthew Arnold (1822–88). Arnold (*Culture and Anarchy* (1869)) believed in a grand overarching concept of the public good and recommended an 'authority of culture', by which he seemed to mean a monarchy or the Platonic ideal of a wise ruling class. This approach is still canvassed in the context of reform of the House of Lords and pervades official culture.

Between the first Reform Act of 1832 and the Representation of the People Act 1948, which finally introduced equal voting rights for most adults, Parliament gradually and reluctantly extended the right to vote by reducing and eventually removing property qualifications. Many more electoral constituencies were created mainly in the urban areas corresponding to the distribution of the population. Secret ballots and a register of electors were introduced, reducing corruption and intimidation.

Utilitarianism and economics became the intellectual fashion. For much of the nineteenth century free market ideas were dominant but coupled with strong state activity to provide basic services and to remedy injustices. Local authorities were created to provide the roads, utilities and public health services necessary to support business interests but their powers were interpreted restrictively by the courts to prevent them providing more than basic welfare services (eg *A-G v Fulham Corp* [1921] 1 Ch 440).

During Queen Victoria's reign (1837–1901) the monarchy reshaped itself as a symbolic representative of the nation standing outside party politics. By the end of the nineteenth century it was becoming established that the Prime Minister and most senior ministers must be members of the House of Commons and, it was increasingly claimed, that the unelected House of Lords was subordinate to the House of Commons. Lord Salisbury was the last Prime Minister to sit in the House of Lords (1885–92) presiding over a regime notorious for nepotism.

The civil service which advises government and carries out its instructions was caught between two stools. On the one hand, efficiency required it to be distant from day-to-day politics. On the other hand, ministers required loyal servants. Civil service recruitment and training was improved during the nineteenth century competitive examinations replacing the previous method of personal patronage. Various 'Place Acts' barred many categories of public official from membership of Parliament.

The extension of democracy led to a debate about the place of common law. Traditionalists regarded the common law as a hedge against tyranny while reformers despised the common law as an enemy of progress, democracy and efficient management. During this period of developing democracy the courts endorsed the principle of parliamentary supremacy. In relation to the common law it is arguable that the broad justice-based system that predominated during the eighteenth century was challenged by more formalistic rule-based conceptions of law that suited the development of trade in the nineteenth century.

Utilitarian ideas produced radical reforms to the court system in the shape of the Judicature Acts 1873 and 1875 which introduced a unified court structure. However the anomaly of the House of Lords as part of Parliament being the final appeal body was restored by the Appellate Jurisdiction Act 1876. This was the result of a political deal concerning home rule in Ireland thus illustrating the way in which constitutional reform can be driven by short term party politics.

During the late nineteenth century the Lord Chancellor, who was a Cabinet minister and who also presided over the House of Lords became responsible for judicial appointments and the independence of the judiciary. This violation of the separation of powers was defended as a means of protecting the interests of the judges against the executive by giving them a voice in the Cabinet (Section 7.7). Thus judicial independence remained ambivalent. With the expansion of democracy that took place from the mid-nineteenth century, influential lawyers such as Dicey defended the idea of the rule of law against what they perceived as threats from both democratic ideas and the authoritarian influences of continental Europe. Dicey is often credited with coining the concept of the rule of law and his reformulation notable for emphasising the importance of the ordinary courts as opposed to specialist administrative powers remains influential today.

Until the early twentieth century many High Court judges were political appointments. Reflecting the nature of the constitution Lord Salisbury claimed that to have claimed that 'it is the unwritten law of our party system; that party claims should weigh very heavily in the disposal of the highest legal appointments. To ignore the party system would be a breach of the tacit convention in which politicians and lawyers have worked the constitution together'. (quoted by Stevens (2004) 11).

From the 1870s the question of Irish home rule dominated national politics. Indeed traditionalists such as Dicey feared that Parliamentary supremacy would be threatened.

4.8   The twentieth century: the rise of the executive

During the early years of the twentieth century there was persistent hostility between the House of Lords, which had an inbuilt Conservative majority, and the Liberal government. This concerned in particular the continuing issue of Irish home rule and also the reluctance of the Lords to approve high taxation for welfare purposes. Edward

VII attempted to intervene but died in the middle of the crisis in 1910. His successor George V reaffirmed the convention that the monarch must act on government advice. After a general election the Lords backed down. The Parliament Act 1911 endorsed the supremacy of the Commons by removing most of the powers of the House of Lords to veto legislation. (There is a good account of these events in Lady Hale's speech in *R (Jackson) v A-G* (2005).)

Various attempts at compromise over Irish home rule failed leading to violent rebellion. Most of Ireland left the UK in 1921 leaving the six counties of Northern Ireland as part of the UK but continuing to be bitterly divided (Section 16.3).

During the twentieth century the balance of power between Parliament and the executive moved strongly in favour of the executive. MPs were becoming professional politicians dependent for their livelihood on party support. Elections became the mass campaigns with which we are familiar today. After the First World War (1914–18) the moderately radical Liberal Party collapsed and the conservative Tories were confronted by the newly emergent Labour Party, then representing working-class interests and broadly in favour of a state with wide discretionary power.

Impelled by the demands of a larger electorate the executive began to increase in size and range of discretionary powers as successive governments provided a wider range of welfare services. These could be delivered only through large bureaucratic organisations making numerous detailed decisions, guided by a plethora of rules and technical specialists. During the twentieth century it became widely accepted that the state could regulate any aspect of our lives and that whether it should do so was a matter not for the constitution but for the everyday political contest.

The traditional sources of law, Acts of Parliament and the courts, were supplemented by an array of tools that enabled the executive to act relatively quickly and informally without detailed parliamentary scrutiny. These included delegated legislation made by government departments under powers given to them by statute and wide discretionary powers conferred on ministers and local authorities. Thousands of special tribunals staffed by government appointees were created to deal with the disputes generated by the expansion of state activity. These seemed to threaten the traditional idea of the rule of law according to which the same general law should apply to all administered in the ordinary courts.

Executive control over Parliament increased. Parliamentary processes were controlled by government supporters and were too amateurish and to enable executive action to be thoroughly scrutinised. Statutory provisions were introduced which attempted to exclude scrutiny of governmental decisions by the courts. It was therefore feared that the executive had outgrown the constraints both of the rule of law and political accountability to Parliament. The constitution made only limited responses to these developments. In the interwar period both ends of the political spectrum were worried. Some believed that the executive had taken over; others that an individualistically minded judiciary would frustrate social reforms. In 1928 Lord Chief Justice Lord Hewart a follower of Dicey published *The New Despotism*, in which he asserted that the rule of law was under threat from the executive. This led to the establishment of the Committee on Ministers' Powers, whose terms of reference were 'to report what safeguards were desirable or necessary to secure the constitutional principles of the sovereignty of Parliament and the supremacy of the law'. Described as having 'the dead hand of Dicey lying frozen on its neck', the Committee's report (Cmd 4060, 1932) gave the constitution a clean bill of health. It recommended some strengthening of the powers of Parliament in relation to delegated legislation (Statutory Instruments Act 1946) and asserted the importance of control by the ordinary courts over the executive. There was however a powerful dissent from the socialist Laski who argued that judges were frustrating legitimate democratic policies.

The *Report of the Committee on Administrative Tribunals and Inquiries* (Cmd 218, 1958, the Franks Committee) also recommended marginal reforms. These improved publicity, strengthened the powers of the courts, supplemented parliamentary scrutiny of the executive and introduced limited reform of the tribunal system (Tribunals and Inquiries Acts 1958 and 1992). More radical reforms of tribunals were made in 2006 (see Section 5.4). From the 1960s various 'ombudsmen' were set up to investigate complaints by citizens against government, but without enforceable powers (Section 5.5).

Later in the century there were wider concerns about democracy. In 1972 the UK became a member of what is now the European Union (European Communities Act 1972). Much European law has thereby become binding in UK law but is not made by an elected body and is subject only to limited democratic scrutiny. Concerns were also raised that the electoral system puts minorities into power and enables the large political parties to control both the executive and Parliament. These complaints amounted to fears that the constitution had degenerated into an oligarchy that did little more than allow the people to choose periodically between groups of cronies. Indeed in the eighteenth century the French philosopher Rousseau had asserted that the British were slaves except at election time.

During the middle years of the century reluctant to appear to be challenging democracy, the courts adopted a low profile. They deferred to government decisions and predominantly took a narrow technical approach to their work. This reinforced the notions that law was objective and that judges were independent and above politics. However from the 1960s for reasons which remain unexplained the courts woke up from what Sir Stephen Sedley has called their long sleep (in Andenas and Fairgrieve, 2009) and began to interfere more actively with government decisions. Landmark cases during the 1960s form the basis of contemporary administrative law. These include *Ridge v Baldwin* [1964] AC 40: the right to a fair hearing, *Anisminic v Foreign Compensation Commission* [1968] 2 AC 147: no exclusion of judicial review, *Conway v Rimmer* [1968] AC 910: disclosure of government information in evidence and *Padfield v Minister of Agriculture* [1968] AC 997: no unreviewable discretionary power.

Judicial independence depending as it does on executive self- restraint continued to be at risk. From the beginning of the century High Court and Court of Appeal judges began to be appointed from the ranks of practicing barristers. However until the 1960s about 25 per cent of High Court judges had been former MPs or parliamentary candidates and political appointments to the Appellate Committee of the House of Lords were common until the 1930s.

From the 1960s there was something of a sea change in Parliament as full time professional politicians replaced lawyers in the House of Commons (the workloads of the latter no longer facilitated part time work as MPs). Thus the longstanding collaboration of lawyers in running the constitution propounded by Lord Salisbury (above) had all but vanished.

However the Lord Chancellor, still combined membership of the executive with leadership of the judiciary and responsibility for appointing most judges. (The most senior judges were appointed by the Prime Minister.) Indeed in the 1980s an expanded Lord Chancellor's Department assumed control of the court and legal aid system.

This led to fears among the judiciary that their independence was at risk. Judicial independence was also compromised by the practice of appointing judges to hold special inquiries into politically controversial issues (Tribunals of Inquiry Act 1921 (Section 7.6.3)).

From the 1960s the courts were increasingly exposed to politics. Governments introduced partisan legislation such as promoting competition and restrictions upon trade unions. These sometimes involved specialist courts leading to pressure upon the notion of judicial impartiality. In the late 1980s the judicial review process was reformed and in some respects was made more widely accessible (Section 19.4). This raised the political profile of the judges. Moreover, well before the enactment of the Human Rights Act 1998 increasingly liberal judges were drawing upon human rights concepts. The obligation dating from 1972 to apply EU law sometimes against the interests of the government also put the judges under political scrutiny. There was sometimes vociferous criticism of the judges from government circles again leading to worries about judicial independence (see Stevens (2004), 16, 20, 26).

4.9   The present century: distrust and juridification

Despite the eulogies from the likes of Blackstone in the eighteenth century, the UK constitution is unbalanced. This is because it entrusts unlimited legal power to Parliament and enables Parliament to be politically dominated by the executive which in turn is subjected to pressure from business and financial interests. Thus the legal constitution depends on the political constitution. The notions of the separation of powers and in particular judicial independence are frail.

A series of scandals from 1980s onwards have exposed significant corruption, ambivalence and incompetence within central government and Parliament. They included the *Westland* affair, where ministers and civil servants appeared to conspire against each other (see Treasury and Civil Service Committee, 1985–6, HC 92), and the 'arms to Iraq' affair, which involved allegations that ministers had tried to cover up breaches of United Nations sanctions against Iraq (see Scott Report, 1996, HC 115 and 15.2). The exposure during 2009 of the extent to which MPs and Peers had been abusing their expense allowances has led to criminal convictions and the introduction of an independent statutory regulator for MPs (Section 11.7.2). There have been allegations that MPs, peers civil servants and ministers give privileges to and have received favours from business interests including 'cash for questions' to be raised by Members of Parliament in the House which resulted in criminal convictions. Allegations of the sale of peerages by the Prime Minister's office were investigated by the police in 2010 but without prosecutions. There have been concerns about wealthy business and media interests having privileged access to government, appointments to government agencies being influenced by personal networking and the 'revolving door' through which retired ministers and officials obtain jobs with private firms that they dealt with in government.

The ability of a powerful executive to invade Iraq in 2002 on the basis of false information given to Parliament and the restriction of traditional civil liberties under the umbrella of combating terrorism weakened faith in the democratic process. The courts responded by asserting their independence and to some extent resisting the erosion of rights most famously in *A v Secretary of State for the Home Department* (2005) where the House of Lords condemned the use of detention without trial against foreign terrorist suspects. However the government's response was to extend similar if lesser powers to UK citizens (Section 23.7). Iraq placed in question the extent of the Prime Minister's personal power under the royal prerogative (Section 14.6). However proposals to increase parliamentary control over the prerogative have come to nothing. The invasion of Iraq is currently the subject of an inquiry in 2011 led by Lord Chilcott. This has not yet reported apparently being hampered by a refusal of the government to disclose information.

Finally there have been concerns about police racism and corruption (see the *Stephen Lawrence Inquiry* (1999) London, Stationary Office), and doubts about the independence of the *Independent Police Complaints Authority*, for example the absence of successful prosecution against police officers for homicide since 1970 (Times, 20 July 2012). Of the three branches of government only the judiciary has so far been untainted.

Bogdanor (2009) claims that the UK constitution has recently been transformed. However the recent changes do not amount to systematic reform but have been responses to specific problems. They have dispersed some power away from the central executive and have strengthened the appearance of judicial independence. They have been described as 'juridification' meaning the introduction of a larger legal element and therefore a larger role for the courts into the constitution.

They include most importantly devolution of substantial law making and executive power to Scotland, Wales and Northern Ireland (1998) the arrangements being policed by the courts, and the Human Rights Act 1998 which makes many rights drawn from the European Convention on Human Rights enforceable in UK courts.

The separation of powers was strengthened by juridification in the shape of Constitutional Reform Act 2005 The Act replaced the House of Lords as the final appeal body with a separate Supreme Court. The new court has the same powers and composition as did its predecessor so that the reform may be cosmetic (Section 5.4). The primary reason for the reforms was to reinforce public confidence in the appearance of judicial independence. The Act also removed the Lord Chancellor, who is a member of the executive, from his traditional role as head of the judiciary and limited the Lord Chancellor's power over judicial appointments (Section 7.5.3). There was general agreement that the existing conventions and practices meant that the judges and less convincingly the Lord Chancellor were in fact independent. Indeed it has long been argued by those who favour the constitution as a network of personal relationships, that a close relationship between the branches of governments enables the interests of the judges to be represented more strongly in the other branches and vice versa.

The civil service (the appointed officials who serve ministers) which existed under a mixture of royal prerogative powers and conventions was placed on a statutory basis in 2010. This was largely cosmetic designed to reinforce civil service political impartiality (Section 15.7). There have been slightly more than cosmetic changes in parliamentary procedure which have made select committees of the House of Commons more independent of the executive (Section 13.5). More importantly the royal prerogative power exercised by the Prime Minister to dissolve Parliament and so trigger a general election was removed in 2011 in favour of a fixed term of five years which could be ended earlier by resolutions of the House of Commons. More ambitious proposals to place the remaining royal prerogative powers on a statutory basis so as to make them more easily accountable have come to nothing.

There was a large reduction in the number of hereditary peers eligible to sit in the House of Lords (1998) (this *increases* the power of the executive since it can now appoint more peers and further reform of the House of Lords has stalled). Following a referendum in 2011, proposals to reform the voting system for Parliament have failed and are unlikely to be renewed in the foreseeable future. However, the government proposes to reduce the membership of the House of Commons in 2015 to 600 from its present 650 a change that also increases the power of the executive.

A limited response to disquiet relating to the integrity of government has been 'semi juridification' a characteristically British retention of power within a closed circle. This involves government through 'codes of practice' created and policed by unelected bodies without a formal legal basis.

Summary

▶ The historical development of the constitution was driven by the gradual wresting of power from the monarch in favour of other interest groups focused mainly on Parliament.

▶ The 1688 revolution created a settlement that still forms the legal basis of the constitution. It made the Crown dependent on Parliament and attempted to combine respect for continuity and a balance of forces with the principle of parliamentary supremacy.

▶ During the eighteenth and nineteenth centuries the modern principles of responsible parliamentary government were developed mainly through conventions. This increased the power of the executive at the expense of Parliament and has left the judiciary in an ambivalent position which has yet to be fully resolved.

▶ Despite a tendency to corruption, democratic reforms were introduced during the nineteenth and early twentieth centuries but without being a complete democratic basis for the constitution. The House of Lords remains an unelected part of the legislature. The common law and independent courts are regarded as important checks on government but the independence of the judiciary has no special protection against infringement by the executive and Parliament. In the late nineteenth century the Lord Chancellor became responsible for the judiciary thereby blurring the separation of powers but possibly acting as a check on the executive. In recent years the courts have been more active than previously in challenging government action.

▶ Latterly there have been concerns about the increased power of the central executive and a growing public lack of confidence in the integrity of public officials. These factors have generated limited constitutional reforms. Concern for the independence of the judiciary has reduced the role of the Lord Chancellor produced a new Supreme Court and an independent judicial Appointments Commission. The relationship between the courts and Parliament remains unresolved with some judges claiming the power to override Parliament.

Exercises

4.1 To what extent was the 1688 settlement a constitutional revolution?

4.2 Does the history of the UK constitution reveal a march towards a greater democracy?

4.3 Do you agree with Jefferson that responsible government of the British type is inevitably corrupt?

4.4 'Herein consists the excellence of the English Government, that all parts of it form a mutual check on each other' (Blackstone, 1765). To what extent was this true in Blackstone's time and is it true today?

4.5 To what extent have the judges influenced the development of the constitution and to what extent are they protected against interference by the executive?

Further reading

Bogdanor, *The New British Constitution* (Hart 2009) ch 1
Chrimes, *English Constitutional History* (4th edn, Oxford University Press 1967)
Kellner, *Democracy: 1000 Years in Pursuit of British Liberty* (Mainstream 2009)
Loughlin, *Foundations of Public Law* (Oxford University Press 2010) chs 1, 2
Lyons, *Constitutional History of the United Kingdom* (Cavendish 2003)
McIlwain, *Constitutionalism Ancient and Modern* (Cornell University Press 1947) ch 4
Sedley, 'The Long Sleep' in Andenas and Fairgrieve (eds), *Tom Bingham and the Transformation of the Law* (Oxford University Press 2009)
Stevens, 'Reform in Haste and Repent at Leisure', (2004) 24 *Legal Studies* 1
Van Caenegem, *An Historical Introduction to Western Constitutional Law* (Cambridge University Press 1995). Wicks, *Evolution of a Constitution* (Hart 2006)

Chapter 5

An overview of the main institutions of the constitution

5.1 The basic structure of the constitution

The constitution has historically been dominated by the idea of monarchy. Unlike other European legal systems (see eg the Constitution of Ireland, Arts 4–6) the UK has no legal concept of the state. The nearest we have is the concept of the Crown (Section 14.1). Thus in *R v Preston* [1993] 4 All ER 638, Lord Mustill remarked: 'The Crown as the source of authority means that the UK has never found it necessary to create the notion of the "state" as a single legal entity' (at 663).

The UK constitution therefore regards government as a collection of separate institutions and persons. The various central government institutions have gained their separate identity over time by hiving off from original roles as servants or advisers to the monarch. Where legislation refers to the 'state' its meaning depends on the context, for example the community as a whole (*Chandler v DPP* [1964] AC 763), the 'sovereign power' (*General Medical Council v BBC* [1998] 1WLR 1573) or the executive branch of government (*D v NSPCC* [1978] AC 171). The civil service is unhelpfully defined as the 'civil service of the state' (Constitutional Reform and Governance Act 2010, s 3) (Section 15.8). Sometimes the 'state' refers to the whole system of government.

The non-statist nature of English law has at least the following important consequences:

▶ There is a distinction in statist constitutions between 'public law', which regulates the state itself and its relationship with citizens, and 'private law', which the state uses to regulate the relationship between its citizens. The UK constitution has not historically recognised such a distinction (see *Davy v Spelthorne BC* [1984] AC 262 (Section 19.6). The individualised nature of our public bodies means that officials are regarded as ordinary citizens embedded in the general private law. According to Dicey this is an important requirement of the rule of law (Section 6.5) in that unless a particular law provides otherwise, officials have no special powers or status and are individually responsible for any legal wrongs they commit. Thus the doctrine of *raison d'état* as a general justification for government power is not recognised (*Entick v Carrington* (1765) 19 St Tr 1029). There are some advantages in the UK approach. Particular decision-making bodies must be openly identified and cannot hide under the general state umbrella.

▶ However the contemporary fashion of farming out government functions to private bodies have led to attempts to distinguish between public and private law and between public and private bodies and functions, particularly in connection with judicial review of government action, European law, human rights and access to information. A successful definition of a public body or public function has yet to be produced and these terms are not defined in the same way in each context. Sometimes a statute provides for a list of bodies or functions regarded as public (eg Freedom of Information Act 2000 (Section 24.2)) but usually the notion of public function is left undefined. For example, the Civil Procedure Rules 2000 which deal with judicial review, refers to 'a feature or combination of features which impose a public character or stamp' (Section 19.5).

▶ In a statist system the state is both a creation of the law and the producer of law. Judges are the authoritative interpreters of the law but not its creators. Judicial opinions are regarded as making more concrete the laws emanating from the state but do not traditionally have an independent lawmaking role. By contrast the historical basis of the common law gives the courts an independent basis of legitimacy. The authority of the common law lies in community values. In the common law system judges are regarded as individuals charged with doing justice on behalf of the Crown. However in *R v Jones (Margaret)* [2006] 2 WLR 773, which concerned an attempt to accuse the government of a war crime in invading Iraq, Lord Hoffmann [65], expressed concern about the theoretical difficulty of the court taking action against the 'state' of which it is a part (but see *M v Home Office* [1993]: Crown, courts and ministers must be separated (Section 7.5.3)).

The constitution, labelled as a *Parliamentary democracy*, comprises the Queen as head of state and the three traditional branches of government: namely legislature, executive and judiciary. The legal part of the constitution is based on parliamentary supremacy. The political constitution is based on the parliamentary system of 'responsible government'.

The UK constitution has also been portrayed from three perspectives or 'models' (Le Seur in Feldman (ed) *English Public Law* (2nd edn Oxford University Press 2009), 1.86). These are not necessarily rivals but each provides a partial point of view. First there is the 'Crown' model which emphasises formal legal matters; second there is the 'Westminster model' which emphasises political matters and in particular the responsibility of ministers to Parliament. The third model is the 'multi-layered fragmented governance model'. This emphasises that government powers are increasingly split in uncoordinated ways between many different bodies both within the UK, for example, the devolved governments of Scotland, Wales and Northern Ireland and outside the UK (eg the EU). This is also primarily a political model but has implications for the central legal doctrine that Parliament is omnipotent.

The main structure of the constitution is as follows:

▶ According to the strict law the Queen heads all branches of government and is the source of all legal power. However the effect of an interlocking series of *conventions* is to ensure that the legal powers of the monarch are exercised in accordance with modern ideas of *responsible parliamentary government*. The office of Head of State is a *constitutional monarchy* with various formal functions in relation to the three branches of government but without significant political power except in extreme circumstances of constitutional breakdown (Section 14.4).

▶ Griffiths summarised the basic legal position as follows: 'Governments of the United Kingdom may take any action necessary for the proper government of the United

Kingdom as they see it, subject to two limitations. The first limitation is that they may not infringe the legal rights of others unless expressly authorised to do so under statute or the prerogative. The second limitation is that if they wish to change the law, whether by adding to their existing power or otherwise, they must obtain the consent of Parliament' ('The Political Constitution' (1979) 42 MLR 15).

5.2   The legislative branch

▶ The Queen in Parliament makes primary law in the form of Acts of Parliament (statutes). The Queen cannot make law without it being first proposed by Parliament (Bill of Rights 1688). By law the royal assent is needed for all Acts of Parliament so that in law the Queen could veto a bill. However by convention the Queen is obliged to give her assent to all bills submitted to her by Parliament.

▶ Parliament comprises the appointed (in law by the monarch by convention by the Prime Minister), House of Lords and the elected House of Commons. It has three main functions. Firstly, together formally with the Queen it is the primary legislature (lawmaker). Secondly, Parliament provides the government with money: taxes cannot be raised without the authority of Parliament (Bill of Rights 1688). Thirdly, as a matter of convention the executive is politically accountable to Parliament and ministers must appear before it to justify their actions.

▶ Parliament must meet at least every three years and so cannot be dispensed with (Meeting of Parliament Act 1694). By convention Parliament must meet annually.

▶ Parliament can dismiss the executive but the executive can no longer dismiss Parliament. The long standing prerogative power which enabled the Prime Minister to dissolve Parliament was abolished by the Fixed Term Parliaments Act 2011 which, despite its importance, was enacted with surprisingly little public debate (illustrating the casual nature of constitutional reform in the UK). Under the Act, Parliament is automatically dissolved at the end of five years and a general election held within a short time specified by statute. Within five years Parliament is dissolved following *either* a two-thirds vote of the whole of the House of Commons in favour of dissolution *or* failure to form a new government within 14 days of a majority vote in the Commons of no confidence in the government.

▶ Although Parliament is the lawmaker and any Member of Parliament can introduce a bill, in practice almost all laws are prepared by ministers who formally propose them to Parliament. Parliamentary procedure is to a large extent controlled by ministers. The main role of Parliament is therefore to scrutinise, amend and give consent to government legislation.

▶ The elected House of Commons is superior to the appointed House of Lords. Subject to an important exception The House of Lords cannot veto *public bills* introduced in the House of Commons but can delay a bill by no more about one year, in the case of a '*money bill*' by one month. The exception is a bill to prolong the life of a Parliament beyond five years. Thus the House of Lords provides a constitutional safeguard to prevent a government avoiding a general election.

▶ Parliamentary elections are conducted for members to represent local constituencies by the '*first past the post*' method. This gives victory to the candidate with the largest number of votes and ignores all other votes. FPP therefore makes it difficult for minority parties to gain seats. (Different voting systems apply in the devolved regimes of Scotland, Wales and Northern Ireland and for the London Assembly and Mayor (Section 12.5).)

5.3   The executive branch

▶ The core executive is the Crown. The term 'Crown' is used in this context rather than 'Queen' but it is unclear what the term means (Section 14.1). The Crown includes the Queen as its formal head, ministers (holders of specific Offices) and civil servants (other civilian crown employees). The armed forces are also servants of the Crown.

▶ Other public bodies of which there are many such as local authorities must be created by particular statutes. It depends on the particular statute whether they are part of the Crown or freestanding. The significance of this is that the Crown has certain special immunities and privileges (Section 14.5), There are no unifying constitutional principles and the UK lacks an umbrella legal concept of the 'state'.

▶ By convention the Queen must appoint as Prime Minister to lead the executive, the person who commands a majority of the House of Commons. This is normally the leader of the largest party. The Prime Minister could in law be dismissed by the Queen. However except in extreme circumstances (Section 14.4) the Prime Minister, along with all other ministers, is required to resign only following a vote of no confidence in the House of Commons. The Queen must appoint and dismiss other ministers on the advice of the Prime Minister.

▶ All ministers must be member of Parliament. Most must be members of the House of Commons including at least the Prime Minister and ministers directly concerned with government finance. Hence there is an incomplete separation of powers. The law prohibits many public officials from being members of the legislature (Section 12.4) but this does not apply to ministers.

▶ By convention the Cabinet, a committee of about 25 senior ministers chaired by the Prime Minister, is responsible for government policy, co-ordinating the work of government departments and major decisions. Latter the Cabinet may have declined in importance, thus illustrating the tenuous nature of conventions. Its role has arguably been usurped by strong overlord departments such as the Treasury and the Prime Minister's Office and by informal committees appointed by the Prime Minister (see Burch and Holiday, 'The Blair Government and the Core Executive' (2004) 39 Gov't & Oppos 1).

▶ Government powers are mainly conferred by statute on individual ministers but the Crown also has certain inherent common law powers under the *royal prerogative* which can be exercised independently of Parliament. These include important powers relating to foreign affairs such as making treaties and deploying the armed forces. The Crown also has the 'ordinary' powers in common with other persons such as owning property and making contracts but these cannot authorise violating the rights of anyone. These powers give the government considerable leverage, for example in property and business matters such as the sale and purchase of land, financial dealing, the arms, transport and medicines trades. Parliament can of course regulate or remove any Crown power. Other public bodies can be created only by statute and have no powers other than those specifically given to them by statute (see *R v Somerset CC, ex p Fewings* [1995] 1 All ER 513).

▶ By convention all powers of the Crown must be exercised either by the Queen on the advice of ministers or by ministers directly. A few largely ceremonial powers require the involvement of the Queen as head of state but otherwise any Crown power can be exercised by a minister. Thus convention and law have at this point merged.

▶ A minister can normally exercise any power through a civil servant (*Carltona Ltd v Comr for Works* (1943), Section 3.4.3). The civil service is a body of appointed Crown servants with the dual responsibility of providing impartial advice to the government and carrying out the day to day management and operations of the executive. The civil service is governed by a mixture of statute and royal prerogative. It is required to be loyal to the government of the day. Civil servants cannot be members of Parliament. In order to ensure impartiality ministers play no direct part in the appointment of civil servants other than being consulted in respect of the most senior appointments (Section 15.7).

▶ A special kind of civil servant, a 'special adviser' is not subject to the normal obligation of impartiality and is appointed directly by the minister as a political adviser. This has led to tensions with the regular civil service (Section 15.7). However special advisors cannot directly exercise any government powers.

▶ The principle of responsible or accountable government is fundamental to the constitution. Ministers are responsible to Parliament. This means firstly *collective responsibility* for government policy in the sense that a minister who disagrees must resign. There is also *individual responsibility* meaning that a minister must appear before Parliament and explain the conduct of his or her department.

▶ A civil service has no direct responsibility to Parliament but is responsible to the minister in charge of his or her department. The minister in turn is responsible to Parliament. Thus there is a chain of responsibility. However most government decisions are made by officials without the involvement of a minister and most departments sponsor semi independent 'agencies' to carry out routine functions. Ministerial responsibility has therefore been questioned where the minister is not personally involved (Sections 15.8.3, 15.8.4, 15.8, 15.10). Indeed senior civil servants are increasingly being directly questioned by parliamentary committees.

▶ There are no constitutional principles requiring any particular structure of government departments. In recent years the executive has become fragmented with about 650 separate bodies created for a variety of purposes including specialist expertise, independence from political pressure, and cost saving, for example the Environment Agency. Many of these bodies are concerned with regulating private activities and have enforcement powers (Section 20.4). They lack legal coherence. They are not normally part of the Crown. They are usually called 'non-departmental bodies' or more commonly 'quangos' (quasi autonomous non governmental organisations, a term which sums up their muddled character being neither part of the central executive nor private bodies. Loughlin (2010), has called them the 'Ephorate' (autocratic officials in ancient Greece) and effectively a new branch of government (Sections 15.8, 15.10).

▶ Quangos embody a fundamental constitutional dilemma in that the aspiration towards independence from political pressure conflicts with the need for accountability. Their accountability is uncertain since they are outside the direct chain of ministers and Parliament (Sections 15.8, 15.10, 20.4). In one sense these bodies could widen democracy by dispersing power. However their members are appointed by ministers typically from the familiar networks of personal associates who might be anxious to please their patron.

5.3.1   Political parties

There is no law or convention required for the existence of political parties and in law political parties are private associations. However because parliamentary elections are organised on the basis of political parties and the executive is formed from the dominant party in Parliament, parties are a central feature of constitutional practice. Indeed political parties are an inevitable feature of a democracy. The pressures of party conformity are both strengths and weaknesses of government accountability making independent scrutiny of legislation difficult but providing a clear focus of responsibility when things go wrong.

The Prime Minister is normally the leader of the largest party and chosen under internal party arrangements. Thus the party chooses the Prime Minister rather than the electorate. Among 25 Prime Ministers since 1900 only 10 have taken office following a general election. For example in 2007, Gordon Brown was chosen as leader by the Labour Party without opposition following the resignation of Tony Blair under pressure from his party. Brown was defeated in the General Election of 2010.

The regulation of political parties poses constitutional problems. These primarily concern the funding of the parties; whether this should be by private persons and organisations as it is the case at present. On the one hand to restrict private funding could be seen as an interference with a basic freedom of political expression (the line taken in the USA). On the other hand private funding could enable wealthy persons to buy influence both in Parliament and the executive.

5.4   The judicial branch

This section outlines the main constitutional features of the judiciary. Matters particularly affecting judicial independence and the separation of powers are discussed further in Chapter 7. The discussion is concerned primarily with England and Wales as Scotland and Northern Ireland have a separate court system, although all appeals from Northern Ireland and appeals in civil cases in Scotland are dealt with by the Supreme Court. (The internal structure of the court system will not be discussed here but can be studied in works on the English legal system.)

All courts must be created by statute and their powers are determined by statute. The courts act in the name of the Queen but an important aspect of the separation of powers is that, apart from certain powers relating to the Attorney General (Section 15.7.2), the executive cannot interfere in legal proceedings (*Prohibitions Del Roy* (1607) 12 Co Rep 64).

The right to a fair trial before an independent court is a fundamental feature of common law and also of the European Convention on Human Rights (ECHR). The concentration of power in the other two branches of government without any overriding safeguards for judicial independence makes the position of judges in the UK especially vulnerable. However it is sometimes suggested that in extreme cases the judges can override Parliament (Section 8.5.6).

The courts uphold the rule of law by means of judicial review of government action and by virtue of the fact that government officials are not generally protected against liability in the courts. Under the Human Rights Act 1998 the courts can scrutinise government decisions and Acts of Parliament for conformity with rights derived from the ECHR. However the 1998 Act does not empower the courts to overturn an Act of Parliament.

The highest appeal court, the Supreme Court, was created by the Constitutional Reform Act 2005. Previously for historical reasons the highest appellate body was part of Parliament, the Appellate Committee of the House of Lords, and its members sat in the House of Lords in its other roles. By making the highest appellate body a separate institution it was hoped to reinforce public confidence in the judges both internally and at international level.

The Supreme Court was introduced following a Cabinet reshuffle intended to remove the traditionally minded Lord Chancellor thus illustrating the pragmatic aspects of constitutional reform. However a principle was also involved, namely the independence of the judiciary which contemporary developments had put under pressure. The courts were becoming more 'political' in the sense that they are increasingly required to decide cases involving disputes between citizen and government under the Human Rights Act 1998. The courts are also required increasingly to adjudicate between governments by virtue of the devolution of powers to Scotland, Wales and Northern Ireland in 2000 and under EU law. Devolution appeals were heard by the Judicial Committee of the Privy Council which is technically part of the UK executive (Section 5.7). There were also worries that the previous arrangements violated Art 6 of the ECHR, the right to a fair trial before an independent court. Behind these particular concerns was a general agenda of 'modernising' the constitution in the sense of rationalising it rather than relying on tradition.

There was no serious doubt that at least since the 1930s the Law Lords were in fact independent of political pressures and many thought that the presence of the law lords in Parliament served the interests of constitutional balance well by providing a channel of mutual influence and understanding. Thus the characteristic English way of constitutionalism through personal relationships among the rulers clashed with republican ideas of government by law (Section 2.5).

The Supreme Court has the same jurisdiction as the former Appellate Committee of the House of Lords. It also took on the functions of the Judicial Committee of the Privy Council in relation to disputes about the powers of the devolved governments of Scotland, Wales and Northern Ireland.

However the Supreme Court is not the 'constitutional court' that some supporters of the reform would favour (see Hale, 'A Supreme Court for the United Kingdom?' (2002) 22 LS 36). The composition procedure and powers of the Supreme Court, have not changed significantly from the previous regime although eligibility for membership has been widened from exclusive reliance on senior judges (below). Unlike many overseas supreme courts it usually sits in panels of five rather then *en banc* (which would avoid any suspicion of packing the panel). However larger panels are used in important cases.

It hears appeals on all matters both public law and private law (although leave is required) from all the UK jurisdictions except Scottish criminal cases. Scotland has its own court system (Section 16.2.3). However under the Scotland Act 2012 ss 35–36 (not yet in force) issues of compatibility with Convention rights under the ECHR are decided by the Supreme Court even in Scottish criminal cases.

The Supreme Court judges between them must have knowledge or experience in the practice of the law of each part of the UK, thus acknowledging the differences between English law and that of the devolved regimes (s 27). However there are no quotas required and Wales which has the same legal system as England has no separate representation. Arguably the increasing powers of the Welsh Assembly should entail a separate jurisdiction (Section 16.4). As was its predecessor, the Supreme Court is unbalanced in relation with the devolved legal systems in that there are only two Scottish members and one from Northern Ireland (see Mc Clusky (2011) *The Supreme Court in Scotland: Final Report*, *Fraser v HM Advocate* [2011] UK SC 24).

It is premature to assess whether the introduction of the Supreme Court is more than cosmetic (see Kavanagh in Lee (ed) (2011)). In their previous incarnation as Law Lords the judges made decisions as independently as those so far made by the Supreme Court (eg *R v Secretary of State exparte Simms* [1999] 2 AC 115, *A v Secretary of State* (2005), *R (Jackson) v A-G* [2005] 4 All ER 1253). However as a separate institution the court has the potential, to evolve into a constitutional court which might eventually claim to override statutes (see Webber, 'Supreme Courts, independence and democratic agency', (2002) 24 *LS* 55, Steyn, 'Creating a Supreme court' *Counsel*, October 2003). The House of Lords as part of Parliament could not have done so. Thus the previous arrangements may have enjoyed stronger democratic checks.

The courts have traditionally been divided into *superior courts* and *inferior courts*. Superior courts include the High Court, which deals with major civil cases, the Court of Appeal and the Supreme Court. The High Court has power to decide its own jurisdiction and so can never act beyond its powers. High Court of Appeal and Supreme Court judges are 'Senior Judges'. They have strong protection against dismissal and reduction in salary (Section 7.7.3). Various specialised bodies are also designated as superior courts although the effect of this is unclear. A body designated as a superior court is not equivalent to the High Court (see *R (Cart) v Upper Tribunal* [2012] 1 AC 663), and the term 'superior court' has no clear legal consequences. Its main significance is probably in connection with the personal liability of the judge (Section 7.4). All other courts are *inferior courts*. Depending on the particular statute inferior court judges have a lesser degree of security of tenure and a lower level of protection against personal liability.

In addition to the courts system numerous special tribunals composed of both lawyers and lay persons decide matters allocated to them by particular statutes. They are essentially simplified versions of courts of law and provide simpler, cheaper and more expert ways of deciding relatively small or specialised disputes than the ordinary courts. These are most commonly disputes between individuals and government bodies. Tribunals were once called 'administrative tribunals' and were often regarded as closely bound up with the executive. Recent reforms have tied them more closely to the judicial system (Section 20.1).

Judges are formally appointed under particular statutes, in the case of senior judges by the Queen on the recommendation of the Lord Chancellor, who is a government minister, and in the case of junior judges and lay magistrates by the Lord Chancellor alone. There has been long concerns about the informal way in which judicial appointments have been made including private consultations within professional networks.

Under the Constitutional Reform Act 2005, except in the case of lay magistrates and some minor offices, a person recommended by an independent Judicial Appointments Commission must be appointed subject to the Lord Chancellor having a limited right of veto (Section 7.7.2). This reinforces the separation of powers while at the same time giving the democratic branch some input. However there is no direct input from elected bodies, for example along the lines of Senate hearings into the appointment of Supreme Court judges in the USA.

Other than lay magistrates and tribunal members, judges are normally appointed from senior practising barristers. Before the Tribunals, Courts and Enforcement Act 2007, judicial appointments were restricted to barristers and solicitors with rights of advocacy in the High Court for a prescribed period – usually ten or seven years. This contrasts with the position in other European countries where there is a separate judicial profession. The UK system has the advantage of drawing on talented people who are familiar with the workings of the court process. The disadvantage is that this might reinforce the perception of the legal system as a closed elite (the stereotype of white, elderly, privately educated males) which arguably hampers good judging and public confidence (see Etherton, 'Liberty, the archetype and diversity: a philosophy of judging', [2010] PL 727, Kirby in Lee (ed) (2011), Department of Constitutional Affairs, *Judicial Diversity Strategy* (2006)).

The 2007 Act was intended to increase judicial diversity. It introduces the general concept of the 'judicial appointments eligibility condition'. In addition to solicitors and barristers with rights of audience and experience (now of 5 or 10 years depending on the post and 15 years for the Supreme Court (Sched 10)), this allows persons with specified other qualifications and experience for the same period in 'law-related activities' to be considered for judicial appointments. Other law-related activates include teaching or research in addition to various forms of legal practice. The specified 'other qualifications' are however a limiting factor. They include only qualifications specified by the Lord Chancellor granted either by the Institute of Legal Executives (solicitors's assistants) or by other bodies authorised to confer rights of audience or conduct litigation (Courts and Legal Services Act 1990 ss 27, 28). The broader base of eligibility has not yet resulted in increased judicial diversity. (See Blackwell, 'Old Boys Networks, Family Connections and the English Legal Profession' (2012) PL 426.)

5.5 Local government

Local authorities exercise a range of functions within geographical areas based on urban conurbations (Unitary Authorities), traditional counties and areas within those counties namely Districts and Parishes (Communities in Wales). (Parishes have only limited functions relating primarily to local amenities their main role being consultative in relation to local land use planning matters.) There are special provisions for London (Greater London Authority Act 1999).

Local authorities take the form of an elected council which is a corporate body with both legislative and executive powers. They have tax-raising powers and might therefore be considered to have some constitutional significance. However local authorities have little financial independence, more than two-thirds of their resources being provided by central government in the form of grants or loans. Moreover their tax raising powers are regulated by central government. Local authorities are therefore accountable both to their electorate and the central executive thus distorting and confusing their accountability.

From both liberal and republican perspectives local government could be regarded as providing a check and balance on central government in the sense of an alternative source of democratic power. Thus Mill claimed that it is desirable in the interests of democracy and individual self-fulfilment for people to have closer contact with governmental bodies than is possible at central government level. In particular local democracy generates different political perspectives and healthy disagreement and debate. On the other hand, particularly where personal welfare services, health and education are concerned, it may be unfair for different levels of service to be provided in different, sometimes neighbouring, areas (see *R v Gloucestershire CC, ex p Barry* [1997] 2 All ER 1 for judicial disagreement).

Local authorities are entirely creatures of statute (a series of constantly changing local Government Acts based on the Local Government Act 1972) and as such are subject to comprehensive central government control. Local Authority geographical boundaries are decided by the Secretary of State on the advice of a Boundary Committee (Local Government and Public Involvement in Health Act 2007). Although changes to local authority areas are often matters of considerable public concern there is no provision for a public hearing although the representations by interested parties must be taken into account (s 9 (3)).

All local government powers derive from particular statutes sometimes requiring the consent of ministers for their exercise. Local authorities have executive powers in relation most importantly to land use planning, public health, education, housing, local amenities, waste collection, the environment and trade. They have limited lawmaking powers to make bylaws for prescribed purposes such as keeping order in public places and traffic control. Their main functions are to provide local political and strategic influence and deliver services designated by central government. This is usually subject to central government power to intervene by means of devices such as inspections, 'default powers' to take over a function and appeals. Central control is often exercised in characteristic British manner not by using formal legal powers, although these exist in abundance, but through advisory circulars and letters and personal contacts or for example through conferences and meetings. Thus there may be the appearance of local independence but without the substance. Some functions, such as housing and education, have been substantially removed from local control in favour of separate private and semi-public bodies regulated from the centre.

The Localism Act 2011 confers a general power on a local authority to do anything that an individual can do (of course without a specific statutory power this cannot involve violating legal rights of another). This power is subject to various limitations. Reflecting a constitutional fundamental it cannot be used to make a charge for performing any duty and without the agreement of the person concerned (see ss 2–4). Moreover this general power is subject to any specific statutory power that may exist and so is of limited significance.

Local government operates through a variety of structures. The council of an authority is a corporate body which exercises both law making and executive powers. Powers can be exercised flexibly (most powers can be delegated to committees, sub committees, officers, members of an executive (below) or other local authorities (Local Government Act 1972, s 101; Local Government Act 2000, s 13 (2)). Some authorities use a structure similar to that of central government based on a council leader and 'executive', (cabinet) responsible to the Council, others use an elected mayor and executive structure more akin to the presidential system (Local Government Act 2000). Under the Localism Act 2011 a referendum to introduce an elected mayor can be held in many cities. This has met with mixed approval.

From a liberal perspective, the weakness of local government threatens the checks and balances required to limit government. There is occasional provision for public consultation but such deliberative democracy (Chapter 2) is normally a matter for the discretion of the local authority (see eg Local Government Act 2000, ss 7, 27; Planning and Compulsory Purchase Act 2004, s 18).

The Localism Act 2011 introduces increased public involvement. There is a right to a referendum on any local issue triggered by a petition of at least 5 per cent of the local electorate. Proposals to increase council tax by at least 2% also require a referendum. The referendum is not binding. Subject to independent scrutiny a local authority is required to make an order giving planning permission to land use development proposed by a parish council or in certain cases a 'neighbourhood forum' comprising local residents and supported by a referendum of local electors. Land listed by the local authority as an 'asset of community value' nominated by a community organisation is protected against disposal. A local authority must also consider giving effect to a matter embodied in an 'expression of interest' put to it by a voluntary or community body or a charity or at least two local authority employees or other persons specified by the Secretary of State.

5.6   The police and the prosecution system

The police are connected with the judicial system so that in accordance with the separation of powers they should be independent of the executive. Moreover, from the origins of the police force (in London 1829), there has been a concern that policing should be on a local basis with democratic accountability in order to avoid the risk of a repressive police state under government control. An accommodation must be struck between these concerns. This issue underlies the constitutional position of the police.

Although they are officers of the Crown, in the sense that their common law powers derive from the Crown's duty to keep the peace, the police are not Crown servants. Control over the police has been split three ways, a complex and tension-ridden arrangement that can be justified as a liberal mechanism for controlling power.

Firstly there is the traditional status at common law of the 'constable' as an independent officer of the Crown with inherent powers of arrest, search and entry to premises, some common law and others statutory, and owing duties to the law itself to keep the peace (see Police Act 1996, s 10; *R v Metropolitan Police Comr, ex p Blackburn* [1968] 2 QB 118 at 136). All police officers and also prison officers are constables. Each police force is under the direction of its Chief Constable (in London the Metropolitan Police Commissioner) with regard to operational matters (Police Reform and Social Responsibility Act 2011, s 2, 4). Traditionally Chief Constables have been independent in relation to operational matters.

Secondly, there is a tradition that the organisation of the police should be locally based and subject to democratic control so as to avoid the concentration of power associated with a 'police state'. Under the Police Act 1996 local police forces are organised on the basis of counties and amalgamations of county units. There are special arrangements in London comprising the Metropolitan Police and the City of London Police Force (Greater London Authority Act 1999). Funding is provided by local authorities by means of a share of local taxation and central grants.

Local Police Forces were traditionally supervised by Local Police Authorities. These comprised a mixture of local councillors, magistrates and persons appointed by the Home Secretary, with elected members a bare majority. The presence of magistrates seems to violate the separation of powers reinforcing a common perception that magistrates have a privileged relationship with the police. Traditionally a local police authority must 'secure the maintenance of an effective and efficient police force'. This is normally taken to mean that the authority must provide resources but cannot decide operational priorities. Subject to the Secretary of State the police authority appointed and removed the Chief Constable and certain other senior officers.

The threefold division of responsibility means that accountability over the police is confused and weak. The Police Reform and Social Responsibility Act 2011 attempts to focus police accountability. The Act creates an elected Police and Crime Commissioner for each force to be elected every four years (s 50). The first elections were held on 15 November 2012 with little publicity. The Commissioner's functions include funding, an obligation to issue a 'Police and Crime Plan' and requirements of public consultation and publishing information about policies. In London the Mayor's Office for Policing and Crime has the equivalent functions.

The Commissioner must be a UK, Irish, or Commonwealth citizen with a right to live in the UK or an EU citizen. There are substantial disqualifications for standing for election (ss 65, 68). The Commissioner must be a registered voter for the area (Section 12.6), must not be a member of a police force or similar body nor the holder of certain posts that would disqualify from being an MP (full time judges, civil servants, armed forces, Section 12.4), nor member of an overseas legislature nor on the staff of a local authority. and must not be insolvent or convicted of an imprisonable offence. This has disqualified several candidates who were convicted of minor offences as children and not actually imprisoned (*Times* 11 August 2012). The same person cannot stand in more than one area. The Presiding Judge has issued Guidance that magistrates should resign if they are elected as Commissioners (*Times* 11 August 2012). This supports the separation of powers by removing the connection which applies to the existing local police authorities (above).

Regarding accountability there is a Police and Crime Panel the members of which are appointed by the relevant local authority or if it fails to do so by the Secretary of State (Sched 13). The panel scrutinises the work of the Commissioner including an annual report. However it has no power to examine documents. The panel can suspend a Commissioner who is charged with a serious offence (s 30). Otherwise the Commissioner appears to be accountable only at election time.

The Commissioner appoints the Chief Constable subject to a 'confirmation hearing' and report of the Police and Crime Panel (in London the Secretary of State). The Panel can veto an appointment by a two-thirds majority. The Secretary of State can make regulations as to the consequences of a veto which can enable him or herself to make the decision. The Commissioner can suspend or remove the Chief Constable. He or she must refer the decision to the panel but the panel cannot veto the Commissioner's decision (see s 38, s 48 Sched 8).

The relationship between the Commissioner and the traditionally independent Chief Constable is murky. The Commissioner is responsible for securing the maintenance of the police force in the area, thus setting its budget and securing that it is efficient and effective (s 1 (6)). It must 'hold the Chief Constable to account' (s 1 (8)) but has no direct powers to interfere with operational matters. However the Chief Constable must have regard to the Police and Crime Plan for the area (s 8(2)). This is subject to guidance by the Secretary of State (s 8(5)).

There is a debate as to whether this level of democracy is desirable since it might compromise the independence of the police. On the other hand an elected Commissioner is a democratic counterforce against political interference by central government, which might be a greater threat to police independence.

Thirdly, the central government has wide powers over police forces conferred by statute, usually upon the Home Secretary (Police Act 1996, Part II; Police Reform Act 2002). However except in London (s 82) the Home Secretary has no power to require the removal of a chief officer. The Home Secretary can provide funding, set objectives and make regulations concerning discipline and resources, including requiring the use of specified equipment. The Home Secretary can also require the merger of local forces and issue a national policing plan and 'policing protocol' concerning how police functions should be exercised (see Police Reform and Social Responsibility Act 2011, s 77, s 78). As usual the Home Office exercises informal influence through non-statutory 'advice', 'guidance' and personal networks.

Technical support for policing may be too expensive to provide locally and modern crime is no respecter of local boundaries. Therefore there are an increasing number of national bodies, including the National Police Data Bank, the Mutual Aid Coordinating Centre, the National Criminal Intelligence Service and the National Crime Squad (Police Act 1997) which carry out police operations, operating formally by agreement with local forces. They are regulated by central boards, the membership of which strikes a balance between a minority of independent persons appointed by the Secretary of State and nomination by chief officers and local police authorities from among their members. A Central Police Training and Development Authority has also been created (Criminal Justice and Police Act 2001), the objectives of which are decided by the Secretary of State, who can also give it detailed guidance and directions. There is therefore a considerable momentum towards a national police force.

Originally the police themselves conducted most prosecutions. However the Prosecution of Offences Act 1985 created a separate Crown Prosecution Service (CPS), which is under the control of the Director of Public Prosecutions (DPP). Crown prosecutors in local areas have powers to prosecute and conduct cases subject to discretion given by the DPP under the Act. The DPP is appointed by the Attorney General, who is answerable in Parliament for the CPS. In some cases the consent of the Attorney General is required for a prosecution, particularly where political or large commercial interests are involved. The Attorney General has conflicting roles. As well as being responsible for the prosecuting service, he is the government's chief legal adviser and a member of the government itself, appointed and dismissed by the Prime Minister. He also brings legal actions on behalf of the public interest against public bodies (Section 15.7). This blurring of roles is characteristic of the culture of UK government and attracts public suspicions of lack of independence. For example there has been unease in respect of particular decisions not to prosecute policemen alleged to have killed members of the public (see eg *New Statesman* 22 July 2010).

The CPS has power to take over most criminal prosecutions (s 3) or to order any proceedings to be discontinued (s 23). Except where an offence can only be prosecuted by a person named in the relevant statute (eg the Attorney General or a specified public authority), any individual may bring a private prosecution, but the CPS can take over such a prosecution (s 6(2)). The Police Complaints Authority has an independent role in investigating complaints against the police (Police Reform Act 2002; see *R (Green) v Police Complaints Authority* [2004] 2 All ER 209 for a useful general account of the process but a narrow approach to whether information should be disclosed).

5.7   The Privy Council

The Privy Council exercises both legislative and judicial powers. It is the descendant of the medieval 'inner council, *curia regis*' of trusted advisers to the King. Over the centuries most functions of the Privy Council were transferred either to Parliament or to ministers. Members are appointed by the Queen on the advice of the Prime Minister, and any British citizen is eligible. There are currently over 400 Privy Counsellors, including Cabinet ministers, senior judges and miscellaneous worthies who have gained the approval of the Prime Minister. The Cabinet is sometimes said to be a committee of the Privy Council, although there is no legal basis for this assumption. However Cabinet ministers and leading opposition politicians are invariably appointed Privy Counsellors. One reason for such appointments is that Privy Counsellors swear an oath of secrecy, thus assisting government business to be kept out of the public domain.

Apart from its judicial functions (discussed below), the role of the Privy Council is largely formal. Its approval is needed for certain important exercises of the royal prerogative, known as Prerogative Orders in Council, including for example laws for overseas territories, and also for Statutory Orders in Council, where Parliament gives power to the executive to make laws in this form. Approval is usually given by a small deputation of counsellors attending the Queen. The Privy Council also confers state recognition and legal personality by granting charters to bodies such as universities and professional, scientific and cultural organisations. It can exercise some degree of supervision over such bodies.

The Judicial Committee of the Privy Council is the final court of appeal for those few former British territories that choose to retain its services, in which capacity it is familiar with broad constitutional reasoning. It also has jurisdiction in respect of ecclesiastical courts, peerage claims, election petitions and appeals from the Channel Islands and the Isle of Man. Its former appeals jurisdiction in relation to the medical profession is now exercised by the Administrative Court and its powers in respect of devolution by the Supreme Court. The Judicial Committee comprises the Law Lords together with judges of the country under whose laws the appeal is heard. Not being strictly a court, the Judicial Committee can give advisory opinions to the government (Judicial Committee Act 1833, s 4), although this is rare.

5.8   The Church of England

The relationship between Church and state is ambivalent. On the one hand neither Christianity nor any other religion is part of the law as such (*Bowman v Secular Society* [1917] AC 406). On the other hand we do not have a formal separation between Church and state as existing in France or the US. The Church of England is the Established Church in England, and the Presbyterian Church of Scotland the Established Church in Scotland. The Church of England has certain links with the state, the result of the historical chance that Henry VIII was the founder of the Church of England. These links are sometimes justified even by supporters of other religions on the basis that the Church provides religious services open to all without discrimination and that it helps the state to curb the extremes of religious fanaticism.

There are several particular connections between the Church of England and the state:

▶ The monarch, as nominal head of the Church of England, must on succession be or become a member of the Church (Act of Settlement 1700, s 3) and must swear an oath to support the Established Churches of England and Scotland (Act of Union with Scotland 1706).

▶ Church laws (measures) are legally binding and must be approved by Parliament (Church of England Assembly (Powers) Act 1919).

▶ There are special ecclesiastical courts subject to control by the ordinary courts if they exceed their powers or act unfairly.

▶ The Queen, on the advice of the Prime Minister (which as usual is binding on her by convention), appoints bishops (see Ecclesiastical Jurisdiction Measure 1963).

▶ The 26 most senior bishops are members of the House of Lords until retirement.

▶ Finally everyone has certain rights in connection with baptisms, weddings and funerals.

A Church body is not a public body as such, at least for human rights purposes (see *Aston Cantlow and Wilmcote with Billesley PCC v Wallbank* [2003] 3 All ER 1213; Section 21.4.1). However particular functions available to the public, such as weddings and funerals, might be public functions and as such subject to control by the courts. The Anglican Church in Wales is not established (Welsh Churches Act 1914, a measure passed without the consent of the House of Lords).

5.9   Bodies monitoring government standards of behaviour

The informal nature of much of the UK constitution makes our arrangements heavily dependent on trusting those in power. A series of scandals from the 1980s onwards have exposed significant corruption, ambivalence and incompetence within central government and Parliament. They included the Westland affair, where ministers and civil servants appeared to conspire against each other (see Treasury and Civil Service Committee, 1985–6, HC 92), and the 'arms to Iraq' affair, which involved allegations that ministers had tried to cover up breaches of United Nations sanctions against Iraq (see Scott Report, 1996, HC 115 and Section 15.2).

There have also been continual allegations that MPs, peers civil servants and ministers give privileges to and have received favours from business interests. Legal controls over public standards are miscellaneous and fragmented. Conflicts of interest by Members of Parliament are regulated by internal parliamentary rules enforced by Parliament itself (Section 11.7). There are also certain controls, particularly during elections over donations to political parties (Section 12.6.2). There are statutory provisions aimed at preventing corruption by public officials. These include the Public Bodies (Corrupt Practices) Act 1889 and the Honours (Prevention of Corruption) Act 1925. The latter was enacted in response to the sale of peerages on behalf of the then Prime Minister, Lloyd George. It requires specific evidence of an offer or agreement to sell an honour. This is difficult to establish since such arrangements may be only implicit in informal conversations. For example after a long investigation during 2006/7 the CPS decided to bring no charges into allegations that peerages were being sold by the Blair government. There are provisions concerning misconduct in elections (Section 12.6) and common law offences of intentional abuse of public office and corruption which can be used at least in blatant cases. In 2008 there were convictions as a result of payments made to Members of Parliament for questions to be raised in the House (Section 5.9) and convictions in 2013 of police officers for receiving bribes from the press. Public officials are also subject to the ordinary criminal law but with some exemptions for MPs in relation to their core duties (see Section 11.6).

The *Committee on Standards in Public Life* covers the whole field of government. It was appointed in 1994 by the Prime Minister as a permanent advisory committee but has no statutory basis. Its terms of reference include the UK Parliament, UK members of the European Parliament, central and local government and other publicly funded bodies. The Committee reports to the Prime Minister so that there is no independent mechanism but its reports are published. The Committee does not investigate complaints against individuals. It has become highly influential. Its recommendations are widely followed and sometimes incorporated into law.

In its first report (1995, Cm 2850) under the chairmanship of Lord Nolan the Committee promulgated seven 'Principles of Public Life' representing the core values of public service. They are 'selflessness, integrity, objectivity, accountability, openness, honesty and leadership'. They are supported by what Nolan called 'common threads', these being mechanisms used to embed the principles into governmental institutions. These are codes of conduct, independent scrutiny and guidance and education.

The Nolan principles are enshrined in all governmental codes of conduct and in statutory provisions relating to government appointments. For example there is a Ministerial Code (2010), a Civil Service Code (2006), a Local Government Code and Codes of Conduct for MPs and the House of Lords. The codes are not usually enforceable by law and there is not always independent scrutiny. For example the Ministerial Code is enforced by the Prime Minister and the House of Lords Code by the House itself. The Code of Conduct for MPs is policed by the Parliamentary Standards Commissioner who reports to the Standards and Privileges Committee of the Commons (Section 11.7). The *Civil Service Code, Special Advisor's Code* and *Diplomatic Service Code* now have statutory backing but no specific enforcement mechanism (Constitutional Reform and Governance Act 2010).

The main scrutiny bodies will be discussed in their contexts. The Nolan principles regarding public appointments are particularly important. Against the background of a tradition that gives ministers large powers of discretion in appointments and a culture of personal networking, it is regarded as improper for politicians to interfere with senior public appointments. The formula of 'appointed on merit by fair and open competition' for public appointments has become standard usage. The Committee on Standards has promulgated general principles of appointment according to open and published criteria that public bodies should follow and with independent representation on appointment bodies. Some bodies but not those close to ministers are policed by a non-statutory Commissioner for Public Appointments (Section 15.9). The Nolan Committee also recommended that ministers should not be able to choose between shortlisted candidates (Tenth Report, 2004, Cm 6407). The government rejected this proposal.

There are both advantages and disadvantages of codes of conduct. Firstly those investigated may be more prepared to cooperate with a non-enforceable code. On the other hand unless there is independent enforcement such codes may not command public confidence. Moreover complaints may be made for party political reasons (see Tenth Report above). The formality of a legal code might discourage this. The vagueness of many of the codes is also a mixed blessing. On the one hand the codes are flexible and could produce negotiated outcomes which are practical and acceptable to the persons concerned. On the other hand the flexibility of the codes risks attempts to manipulate them. In a consultation paper the Committee on Standards warned that the codes might be undermined by appearing to be over-zealous or over-bureaucratic and attracting public cynicism (see *Getting the Balance Right: Implementing Standards of Conduct in Public Life*, 2003). The Committee particularly emphasised the principle of 'proportionality' which concerns adjusting processes to the particular context, taking account of the importance of the activity and the risks and costs involved. It also emphasised the importance of the culture of the particular organisation.

5.10 General weaknesses of the constitution

It is often asserted that democracy in the UK is seriously flawed (see eg Wilks-Heeg, Blick, Crose, *How Democratic is the UK? The 2012 Audit* (Rowntree Trust 2012)). Some manifestations of this are voter apathy, petty corruption and undue influence upon government by commercial and financial interests. Such problems go beyond the law and reside in our political culture. The heavy reliance of our constitution on unwritten convention and practices which are not legally binding encourages a culture among politicians and officials of taking decisions informally within networks of personal and professional associates outside mechanisms of public scrutiny or authority, what Lewis called 'networks of conviviality which obscure the workings of the British state' (Mc Auslen and McEldowney (eds), *Law, Legitimacy and the Constitution* (Sweet and Maxwell 1985), 125). Institutional structures and official culture have no firm concept of independence and objectivity and law is sometimes regarded as an external intrusion rather than the basis of government (see Stevens 'Reform in haste and repent at leisure' (2004) 24 LS, 16, 18, 20).

The following problems can be highlighted.

▶ *Domination of Parliament by the executive*. This is partly the result of our incomplete separation of powers where all ministers are Members of Parliament and in a position to dominate parliamentary business. MPs usually vote for their party automatically, even perhaps without reading the proposals in question. This is reinforced by the Whip system under which party Whips persuade individual MPs to vote appropriately. Apart from the tribalism which is inherent in political culture, MPs depend on the approval of the party leaders for advancement. Moreover under the convention of collective ministerial responsibility MPs who are government ministers must support the government or resign. About 100 MPs out of a total of about 650 are ministers. The abuse of executive domination was remarked on by Lord Bingham [41] and Lord Steyn [71] in *R (Jackson) v A-G* [2005] 2 All ER 1253. Lord Bingham thought that this was outside the concerns of the courts. Lord Steyn was more equivocal (Section 8.5.6). In the same case Lord Hope [125] relied on the characteristic British evasion that the constitution depends on 'mutual respect' between the institutions of government.

▶ *Wide discretionary powers* given by Parliament to public officials are defended on the basis that officials can be trusted not to misuse their powers. This may assist efficient government but it requires us to trust our rulers to an extent distasteful at least to republicans (Section 2.5, see eg RIPA 2000, Section 23.5, *Gwillan and Quinton v UK* [2010] ECHR App No 158/05).

▶ *Patronage*. Many public appointments and positions of privilege, most notably membership of the House of Lords and of Quangos but also positions as advisers or consultants are made by the Prime Minister or other senior ministers. There is no legal or parliamentary mechanism to prevent appointments being made from insider networks or to prevent the same persons being recycled through several positions. Through the 'revolving door' lucrative positions may be given to former ministers, military officers or senior officials on leaving the public service as 'consultants' or board members in private organisations related to their former areas of responsibility for example in the weapons industry. The press has exposed assiduous attempts by such persons to exploit their links with government (eg *Guardian* 16 October 2012). Safeguards comprise non-binding codes of practice policed by persons recruited from the same pool (Section 15.10). Some senior appointments involve the candidate appearing before a parliamentary committee but this has no binding force.

For example out of 775 sitting members of the House of Lords, 124 are connected with the financial services industry. The House of Lords Appointments Commission is dominated by existing members of the House of Lords (Section 12.2). Five out of eleven members of the House of Lords committee set up to review the 2011 Finance Bill held positions in banks (*Bureau of Investigative Journalism* (above)). MHRA the medicines regulatory body has members connected with commercial suppliers of medicines but no one from a patient group or representing the public. The Medical Research Council is chaired by a leader of a private weapons technology firm and the board includes commercial suppliers of drugs but no representatives from charities or public interest groups. The Rail Regulator's board includes members chosen from commercial interests but nobody from rail users or public interest groups. The Farming Regulation Task Force is similarly constituted with no one representing environmental interests. These arrangements have been described as a 'kind of shadow government drafting and enforcing polices, disbursing money, regulating businesses, quietly, unobtrusively without effective public scrutiny. When it is unbalanced, crawling with conflicts of interest it makes a nonsense of democracy'. (George Monbiot, *Guardian* 13 March 2012).

▶ *Influence of private wealth.* There are no provisions for preventing anyone having privileged access to the executive. There have been allegations that payments are being made for access to ministers. In 2008 there was a police investigation into allegations that the Prime Minister's Office was selling peerages. However this did not produce sufficient evidence for a prosecution (Section 12.2).

These matters are regulated by internal non-binding practices, such as recording official meetings with outside bodies, but not generally by law. Thus private business interests can exercise influence by lobbying either directly or by financing political parties or acting as government advisers.

For example in 2011 the financial services industry (mainly banks and insurance companies) successfully lobbied for tax reductions, lighter regulation and reductions in the pensions of the lower paid. Senior government advisors and MPs have active connections with lobbying groups and business interests. (See *Lobbying's Hidden Influence*, Bureau of Investigative Journalism, London, City University 2012, see also 13 September 2012; Peston, *Who Runs Britain?* London Hodder 2008.) The current inquiry under Lord Justice Leveson into the conduct of the press includes the relationship between the owners of media interests, police and government.

▶ *Secrecy.* Controlling the executive is difficult because of the strong culture of secrecy that pervades the operations of government. Supported by a deferential public culture there is a basic assumption that government documents are confidential and that to give public access to them would inhibit officials from being frank and would destroy public confidence in government by revealing inappropriate behaviour or incompetence. The contrary argument is that publicity increases trust and confidence.

For example the Justice and Security Bill which provides for some legal actions against the government to be tried in secret has been promoted as having the advantage that it spares the government from adverse publicity (see *Guardian* 25 September 2012). Members of the Privy Council which includes all senior ministers are required to swear an oath of secrecy.

Requirements to disclose government information are ambivalent. The Freedom of Information Act 2000 which allows anyone to request disclosure of most kinds of government information is subject to many restrictions and exemptions including a ministerial veto (Section 23.2.1). Moreover the private companies to which many government functions have been transferred are not subject to the Act and 'commercial confidentiality' is one of its exemptions. An independently minded parliamentary committee might press to see government documents, but MPs as such have no rights in the matter beyond those of the general public. Some official inquiries have a power to compel witnesses and documents (Section 20.3).

Secrecy is necessary for specific matters (eg national security (Section 23.1)), and to protect some business and private interests and dealings with foreign governments). Moreover the culture of informal networking might be reinforced by a wide requirement to disclose official information in that officials could resort to making decisions in private places without official records. The Butler Report (2004 HC 898) on the government's decision making process concerning the invasion of Iraq in 2002, referred critically to 'sofa government' which sidestepped formal cabinet discussions.

The courts are relatively open. They normally sit in public must give reasoned decisions and information must normally be disclosed in legal proceedings. Certain cases most controversially concerning national security (Sections 24.3.3, 24.3.4), and also to protect the independence of court proceedings and to protect vulnerable persons such as children (Section 23.2) require restrictions on publicity and disclosure.

▶ *Weak accountability*. The doctrine of ministerial responsibility means that civil servants who are responsible for detailed decision making, operate in secret and are shielded from public accountability for their actions. Moreover ministerial responsibility is haphazard, for example the responsible minister may have left office by the time a civil service blunder comes to light. There is no reliable mechanism for public scrutiny of civil service behaviour short of the drastic weapon of a legal action which requires full disclosure of information (eg the recent competition for rail franchises aborted due to civil service errors and with the ministers responsible moved elsewhere (see *Times* 4 October 2012).

Moreover, the absence of general principles regarding the structure of government has produced a profusion of different types of government agency including private bodies outside the core hierarchy of ministers and civil servants. This makes accountability vulnerable since responsibility may be shared between different bodies with nobody taking overall responsibility what Rhodes has called a 'hollowing out of the state (*Everyday Life in British Government* (Oxford University Press 2011, 2). There is accountability upwards to the ministers who appoint and influence these bodies but ministers may deny responsibility for the day to day activities of such bodies. Accountability 'downwards' to the public depends on the particular statute creating the body and is often discretionary or non existent (Section 15.10).

▶ *An unstable constitution*. This problem arises from the devolution of substantial law making powers to Scotland, Wales and Northern Ireland and the fact that it is only by virtue of convention that the UK government is restrained from overriding the devolved legislatures (Section 16.1). In Scotland at least there are political pressures for even larger powers including complete independence from the UK. Moreover England has no government of its own and relies on the UK Parliament. Thus Scottish MPs can vote in purely English matters an issue that has not been resolved (Section 16.5).

▶ *The foundation of the constitution*. This is another kind of instability. Although the orthodox view is that Parliament is supreme with unlimited power, the basis of this is controversial. It probably rests on no more than general acceptance among the ruling groups (Section 8.1). Parliamentary supremacy is increasingly regarded as politically unreal thus separating the legal from the political constitution. There have been several challenges to the principle of Parliamentary supremacy including a claim so far unfulfilled that the courts by virtue of the common law can override Parliament (Section 8.4).

▶ *Haphazard arrangements for constitutional reform*. There are no special provisions in UK law for constitutional reform such as special procedures in the legislature or referendums of the people. In *R (Southall) v Foreign Secretary* [2003] EWCA Civ 1002, it was said that there is no principle that fundamental constitutional change requires the approval of the electorate. This makes constitutional reform a matter of the politics of the government of the day and so vulnerable to party political bargaining (eg Sections 12.3, 12.5.8, 16.2.5). There is provision for a referendum on certain EU matters (Section 10.4) and referendums have been held spasmodically (concerning devolution (Section 16.1) and the voting system (Section 12.5.7)). Some constitutional changes have been brought about by political crises and have been preceded by a general election (eg the reduction of the powers of the House of Lords by the Parliament Act 1911).

Reforms may also be driven by the desire of a new government to appear radical (eg the package of reforms introduced by the 'New Labour' government in 1997 including devolution and the Human Rights Act 1998 (Section 22.1) and the limited reforms made when Gordon Brown became Prime Minister in 2007 (Section 15.7)). The reforms to the judiciary in the Constitutional Reform Act 2005 may have been precipitated by infighting within government (Section 5.4).

There is a school of thought that rejects radical constitutional reform in favour of letting the constitution evolve according to traditions and customs. From this perspective the constitution should be left to develop naturally tradition being a good in itself as evidence of the tried and trusted. This attitude has influenced in particular the many failed attempts to reform the House of Lords (Section 12.3) and the reforms to the Office of Lord Chancellor in 2005 (Section 7.5.3). However in *Hirst the UK (No 2)* (2006) 42 EHRR 41 the European Court of Human Rights rejected the UK's claim to deny the vote to prisoners partly on the ground that such decisions should be made by reasoned debate rather than unthinking tradition.

One result of this erratic approach to reform is that obsolete principles which do not raise short-term problems may remain unchanged. For example the connection between the Church of England, the monarchy and anti-Catholicism is still built into our constitution (Section 14.2) as is the hereditary aristocratic membership of the House of Lords and the survival of archaic institutions such as the Privy Council (Section 5.7) and archaic procedures in Parliament (eg Section 11.6.1).

Summary

▶ This chapter has identified the main features of the mix of law, conventions and political practice that forms the constitution and points out important sources of conflict which will be followed up in later chapters.

▶ The Crown, which in law is the executive branch of government, must be distinguished from the Queen personally as head of state.

▶ The Queen in Parliament is legally the supreme lawmaker but by convention the Queen must assent to all Bills presented by Parliament.

▶ Parliament comprises an unelected upper House with limited powers (House of Lords) and an elected lower House (House of Commons). The upper House is currently undergoing reform but there is disagreement as to what form this should take.

▶ By convention the executive is accountable to Parliament. In practice however the influence of political parties and the power of the Prime Minister mean that Parliament tends to be subservient to the executive.

▶ The Queen must appoint the leader of the majority party in the Commons as Prime Minister and must accept the Prime Minister's advice in appointing all other ministers and also senior judges and other public functionaries.

▶ There are conventions to safeguard democracy against both legislature and executive. The executive must have the support of Parliament. Parliament must meet annually. By law Parliament cannot last for more than five years, and before then by convention Parliament can remove the executive by a vote of confidence. The Prime Minister can also dissolve Parliament. The dissolution of Parliament triggers the summoning of a new Parliament, preceded by a general election. These mechanisms are weakened by the executive domination of Parliament. They are currently being reviewed.

▶ The executive formally comprises ministers of the Crown. Statutory powers are normally given to individual ministers and the central government is therefore fragmented.

▶ The Cabinet as the central policy-making body may be in decline with the rise of informal networks and powerful overlord departments.

▶ Permanent civil servants are of two kinds. The senior civil service is responsible for advising ministers, developing policy and making rules and decisions. Other civil servants usually organised as separately structured executive agencies are responsible for delivering policies at an operational level. Civil servants are shielded from public responsibility for their actions by the doctrine of ministerial responsibility.

▶ Special advisers are a distinct group of civil servants. They are political appointees of ministers and their jobs terminate when their minister leaves office. They are not subject to the duty of a civil servant to be impartial. There are tensions between special advisers and regular civil servants who may regard themselves as being sidelined. However special advisers cannot exercise any legal powers.

Summary cont'd

▶ According to the doctrine of ministerial responsibility, ministers are responsible to Parliament for the conduct of their departments and for agencies sponsored by their departments. The civil service is responsible to ministers but not directly to Parliament. Ministerial responsibility is becoming weaker and its scope and effect unclear.

▶ In recent years executive powers have been distributed across a wide variety of public and private bodies outside the central executive, known as 'quangos' again obscuring the convention of ministerial responsibility.

▶ The judiciary is usually regarded as subordinate to Parliament. There is a tension between the judiciary and the executive arising out of the courts' powers of judicial review. It has been suggested that the courts might override Parliament.

▶ The independence of the judiciary is vulnerable to the combined executive and legislature. Senior judges have strong security of tenure. The appointment of judges was previously made by the Lord Chancellor, and in the most senior cases the Prime Minister. Recent reforms have introduced the safeguard of an independent Judicial Appointments Commission. The creation of the Supreme Court even though it has no new powers has separated the judicial system formally from Parliament. It is debatable whether this is more than cosmetic. Further discussion of these matters is in Chapter 7.

▶ The police are regulated by an unstable combination of an elected Commissioner, local and central government.

▶ The Church of England has particular constitutional links with the state but is not a state religion.

▶ Weaknesses in the traditional methods of accountability have led to attempts to formulate standards of ethical conduct for persons holding public office. These do not generally have legal status and are enforced within government itself.

▶ The constitution's main weakness lies in the concentration of power at the centre exercised substantially outside legal controls coupled with the dispersal of low level government functions to a range of bodies both public and private leading to fragmented and uncertain accountability. However there has recently been increased 'juridification' of important aspects of the constitution and devolution of government to Scotland, Wales and Northern Ireland has introduced instability.

Exercises

5.1   Is it possible to identify the three most fundamental principles of the constitution? If so, what are they?

5.2   What mechanisms enable the executive to dominate Parliament? Are there any counter-mechanisms?

5.3   Is the Supreme Court a 'constitutional court'. If not should it be?

5.4   Jade the Chief Constable of Barsetshire instructs her force to give priority to protecting vulnerable persons against street crime and to ignore drug trafficking. Boris, the local Police and Crime Commissioner informs Jade that these policies are contrary both to the local Police and Crime Plan which gives priority to protecting 'persons of high net worth' and also to an objective set by the Home Secretary of combating drug trafficking. Jade continues the same policies. Advise her. Would your advice be affected if Jade was informed that, when he was 17 years old Boris had been fined for a driving offence?

5.4   Assess the arguments for and against the Church of England having special constitutional status.

5.5   To what extent is the UK constitution a republican constitution?

Further reading

Bogdanor, *The New British Constitution* (Hart Publishing 2009) chs 1, 2, 8, 10

Committee on Standards in Public Life, *Reports* <http://www.public-standards.gov.uk> (an excellent resource)

Cornes, 'Gains and Dangers of Losses' in Transition-the Leadership Functions in the United Kingdom's Supreme Court, Parameters and Prospects [2011] PL 509

Finer, Bogdanor and Rudden, *Comparing Constitutions* (Clarendon Press 1995) ch 2

House of Commons, *Government by Appointment: Opening up the Patronage State* (HC 2002–03, 165-I, Cm 6056)

Lee (ed) *From House of Lords to Supreme Court: Judges, Jurists and the Process of Judging* (Hart Publishing 2011)

Leigh, The Changing Nature of Local and Regional Democracy' in Jowell and Oliver (eds), *The Changing Constitution* (7th edn Oxford University Press 2011)

Leopold, 'Standards of Conduct in Public Life' in Jowell and Oliver (eds), *The Changing Constitution* (7th edn, Oxford University Press 2011)

Loughlin, *Foundations of Public Law* (Oxford University Press 2010) ch 15

Malleson, 'The Evolving Role of the UK Supreme Court' [2011] PL 754

Oliva, 'Church, State and Establishment in the UK in the 21st Century: Anachronism or Idiosyncrasy?' [2010] PL 482

Oliver, 'Standards of Conduct in Public Life: What Standards?' [1995] PL 497

Power Commission, *Power to the People: An Independent Inquiry into Britain's Democracy* (Rowntree Trust 2006)

Prosser, *The Regulatory Enterprise* (2010)

Sampson, *Who Runs This Place?* (John Murray 2004) chs 1–4, 7, 8

Steven, *The English Judges: Their Role in the Changing Constitution* (Hart Publishing 2002)

Van Gervan, 'Scandals, Political Accountability and the Rule of Law: Counting Heads?' in Andenas and Fairgrieve (eds), *Tom Bingham and the Transformation of the Law* (Oxford University Press 2009)

Wilks-Heeg, Blick and Crone, *How Democratic Is the UK? The 2012 Audit* (Rowntree Trust 2012)

Windlesham, 'The Constitutional Reform Act 2005: The Politics of Constitutional Change', [2006] PL 35

Woodhouse, 'Delivering Public Confidence: Codes of Conduct: A Step in the Right Direction' [2003] PL 511

Part II

Fundamental principles

Chapter 6
The rule of law

The nature of the rule of law

The concept of the rule of law has two strands of meaning. In its most basic sense the rule of laws means that it is desirable to be governed by rules. Rules helps us to plan our affairs with certainty free of the fear of arbitrary interference and to settle disputes peacefully. Rules restrain those in power from imposing their personal whims on us: 'a government of laws not men' in the much repeated phrase of Aristotle (third century bc). This is an aspect of the idea of 'constitutionalism' which means that the powers of government should be limited. Thus Aristotle encapsulated the idea of the rule of law: 'it is better for the law to rule than one of the citizens so even the guardians of the law are obeying the law'.

However, since the government makes the law, this tells us nothing about the content of the law. It is consistent with an authoritarian government making laws exclusively in the interests of its own supporters or one in which the law consists of the application of a sacred text. The second strand of meaning of the rule of law therefore includes moral and political values that underlie the law, of which the keystone is equality in the sense of universal access to independent courts. In *R (Corner House Research) v Director of the Serious Fraud Office* [2008] 4 All ER 927 [65], Moses said that the rule of law is nothing if it fails to constrain overweening power. In an even wider sense the rule of law is sometimes used as rhetorical shorthand for liberal values tending to the right wing of the political spectrum; for example 'the sanctity of individual freedom and the security of private property rights, ensured by representative constitutional government' (Ferguson, *Civilisation*, London Penguin Books 2012, 96).

The rule of law is widely recognised internationally albeit its meaning is rarely specified. For example, the preamble to the UN Universal Declaration of Human Rights refers to the rule of law as 'essential'. The principle is embodied in the European Convention on Human Rights (ECHR) in that where a state is permitted to interfere with a human right, its intervention must be 'prescribed by law' as well as being 'necessary' in a democratic society. The European Union claims to be based on the rule of law (Treaty of the European Union, Preamble). Article 28 of the German Basic Law refers to 'the principles of republican, democratic and social government based on the rule of law'.

Thus Republican thought especially cherishes the rule of law since it regards relying on the discretion of a ruler however benevolent as a form of slavery (Section 2.5).

The rule of law at least in its basic sense has less welcome aspects. Firstly it shields government officials from accountability in that they can shelter behind laws made by others when making controversial or unpleasant decisions. Secondly it enables lawyers, unelected by the people to exercise power. Thirdly the wealthy can take advantage of the law more effectively than the poor since they can afford better lawyers. Thus the rule of law is said to encourage the rich and powerful to harass people who cannot fight back (see Horowitz 1977). Indeed the law may become too burdensome. The UK produces about three times as much laws as other democratic states. This results in complexity and cost adding to our dependency upon lawyers.

In England the rule of law is claimed to go back to the Anglo-Saxon notion of a compact between ruler and ruled under which obedience to the King was conditional upon the King respecting customary law. It was famously invoked by the thirteenth century jurist Bracton as 'a bridle on power':

> the King should be under no man but under God and the Law because the Law makes him King. (quoted in *Burmah Oil Co Ltd v Lord Advocate* [1965] AC 75, 147)

The English version stresses the common law as law made by independent courts. This was a conscious break from the Roman law tradition, which regarded law as the will of the ruler. In the seventeenth century disputes between King and Parliament, emphasis was placed on the common law and on the independence of the judges from the King (see eg Crook J., dissenting in *R v Hampden* 3 St Trials 825, 1130 (1637) quoted in *Burmah Oil* above, 148). According to Coke cj (1552–1634), the rule of law protected both ruler and subject, the ruler against criticism, the subject against tyranny: 'The golden and straight metwand of the law and not the uncertain and eroded cord of discretion' (*Institutes* (c1647) published posthumously Part 4, 37, 41; see also *Prohibitions del Roy* [1607] 12 Co Rep. 64). The rule of law as proposed by Coke could of course also be regarded as a bid for power by lawyers.

John Locke, an ally of Parliament equated law with reason and freedom, which as we saw (Section 2.4) has its dangers:

> Law in its true notion is not so much the limitation as the direction of a free and intelligent agent to his proper interest and prescribes no further than is for the general good of those under that law ... for all the power the Government hath being only for the good of the Society, as it ought not to be Arbitrary and at Pleasure, so it ought to be exercised by established and promulgated Laws: that both the People may know their duty, and be safe and secure within the limits of the law, and the Rulers too kept within their due bounds not to be tempted by the Power they have in their hands, to imploy it to such purposes, and by such measures, as they would not have known and own not willingly. (Second Treatise on Government (1690) VI, 57; IX, 137)

During the mid-twentieth century, however, the rule of law became associated with a belief that conservative judges tended to defend the status quo against the policies of progressive governments (see Griffith, *The Politics of the Judiciary* (Fontana 1997)). More recently governments both right and left have resorted to authoritarian measures and there has been a revival of interest in wider versions of the rule of law as a means of protecting fundamental rights and liberal beliefs.

The Constitutional Reform Act 2005 assumes that the rule of law applies in the UK, asserting that:

> This Act does not adversely affect:
> (a) the existing constitutional principle of the rule of law, or
> (b) the Lord Chancellor's existing constitutional role in relation to that principle. As we shall see the rule of law is frequently invoked by UK judges.

The UK constitution is not wholly derived from the rule of law. The rule of law as understood in the UK is not the same as the German concept of *Rechstaat*, which means that the state and the constitution as a whole should be embodied in legal rights, a republican idea (see Section 2.5). The rule of law is far from this. As we have seen, in relation to much of the UK constitution there are no laws in place but only political understandings, or conventions, between members of the ruling elite. These are at best morally binding and are administered and policed by the same people that are subject to them. Thus our unwritten constitution is sometimes called a political constitution. Nominally independent bodies are sometimes appointed by the same ruling groups to police standards of official behaviour, for example the Commissioner for Public Appointments (see Section 5.3), but these typically have no legally enforceable powers. Parliamentary committees scrutinise government conduct but again these have no enforcement powers and Parliament itself is substantially controlled by the executive.

The meaning and importance of the rule of law are much contested. This is evidenced by the varying amount of space devoted to the topic in textbooks. There is a huge literature on the subject. The main areas of debate are as follows:

▶ Is the idea of the rule of law any more than empty rhetoric? There are many different views as to what the rule of law means so that it is sometimes regarded as signifying only that a law is good (see Box).
▶ Could an Act of Parliament be overridden on the ground that it conflicts with the rule of law, for example an Act that restricts access to the courts?
▶ Should the rule of law sometimes be overridden in favour of more important values? For example in an emergency should the government be free to act without constraint? Should rules sometimes give way to compassion or mercy or even to good relationships with dubious overseas governments?

Does the rule of law necessarily include questions as to whether a law is good or bad? At one extreme the rule of law merely claims that rules are a good thing in themselves. It tells us nothing about the content of those laws. From this perspective rules made by an evil tyrant, for example to kill all dissenters, comply with the rule of law. Is the regime of a tyrant who rules according to law however repressive, in some sense a better regime than one ruled by a dictator who governs by personal whims?

The following are examples of claims made for the rule of law:

▶ Good government, wealth and individual happiness depend on the rule of law. However, this may be perhaps more important to a successful community is that its political institutions are open and inclusive, dispersing power rather than concentrating it in a central authority. The UK constitution has managed over the years to disperse power significantly albeit without relinquishing ultimate central control, for example to dependent territories and to Scotland, Wales and Northern Ireland. However unlike the case in many countries local government remains firmly under central control.
▶ Bentham (see Section 2.3.3) was unhappy with what he called 'Judge and Co'. He thought it strange that courts should be bound by precedent since to him this merely reproduces errors. He also thought the common law, which he called 'dog law', was unjust in that we may be ignorant of the wrong until the case is decided (*Truth versus Ashhurst* (1823); see *R v Rimmington* [2005] UKHL 63 at [33]). He thought that laws should be no more than guidelines and in the end should give way to his master principle of the greatest happiness of the greatest number.

▶ The rule of law is also invoked as meaning that there is a duty to obey the lawful government. In *Brown v Stott* [2001] 2 All ER 97 Lord Hope said:

> The rule of law requires that every person be protected from invasion by the authorities of his rights and liberties. But the preservation of law and order on which the rule of law also depends, requires that those protections should not be framed in such a way as to make it impracticable to bring those who are accused of crime to justice. The benefits of the rule of law must be extended to the public at large and to the victims of crime also (at 128).

▶ In *Brown* the House of Lords held that the normal right to remain silent was overridden by a requirement to disclose the name of the driver of a car in connection with a drink-driving charge. This was because of the social importance of road safety. However it was also emphasised that any specific unfairness should be compensated for by ensuring that the proceedings were fair overall.

▶ The rule of law has been invoked as requiring an independent judiciary and that special jurisdictions such as tribunals to be subject to supervision by the ordinary courts to ensure fairness and consistency (see *R (Cart) v Upper Tribunal* (2012), Section 20.1 and as requiring exemptions from legal liability for example Article 9 of the Bill of Rights 1688 which protects parliamentary proceedings to be given a limited scope (see *R (Chaytor v AG* (2010) UKSC 52), Section 11.6.3.

▶ There are grandiose claims associating the rule of law with liberal beliefs such as dignity and freedom – for example in relation to the ECHR (see *Klass v Federal Republic of Germany* (1979–80) 2 EHRR 214; *Young, James and Webster v UK* [1982] 4 EHRR 38) and by the International Commission of Jurists, which equates the rule of law with 'the conditions which will uphold the dignity of man as an individual' (see Raz, *The Authority of Law* (Clarendon Press 1979) 210–11). For example in *Taylor v Chief Constable of the Thames Valley Police* [2004] 3 All ER 503 the Court of Appeal stressed the fundamental principle that a policeman must give clear reasons for arresting someone, Sedley LJ (at [58]) basing this on the value of human dignity.

▶ The rule of law is often claimed to be a necessary foundation of democracy. For example by ensuring that officials keep within the powers given to them by the people and treat people equally, the rule of law is said to be both the servant and policeman of democracy (see Lady Hale in *Ghaidan v Mendoza* [2004] 3 All ER 411 at [132]). However the idea of the rule of law long predates democracy. For example a constitution based on a sacred text is as much under the rule of law as a democratic constitution. It is arguable therefore that the rule of law as such is neutral between different law based systems of government. Its function is to promote and protect the particular regime.

▶ In one sense the rule of law seems to be at odds with democracy in that it depends on decisions being made by an elite of unelected judges. Thus Bellamy (2007) claims that the rule of law points in opposite directions. He is referring however to different understandings of what the rule of law means. On the one hand lawyers have used wider versions of the rule of law to assert the importance of the courts, meaning that access to the courts should not be impeded, that the courts should be able to control those in power and that fundamental rights should be respected (eg *M v Home Office* [1993] 3 All ER 537; *R v Secretary of State for the Home Dept, ex p Simms* [1999]; *R (Anderson) v Secretary of State* [2002] 4 All ER 1089 at [27], [39]). On the other hand those favouring political solutions use the narrower 'core' version, which they associate with the importance of the democratic process as producing valid laws that should be obeyed precisely because they have been through that process. From this perspective the judges have the more limited role of interpreting and applying laws validly made by Parliament but not pronouncing on their wisdom or their conformity to a higher law.

▶ The standard compromise is to say that the courts act as a safety valve defending the fundamental values of our democratic system against the possibility that elected politicians are panicked or deluded into harming it (Section 21.1).

6.2 Different versions of the rule of law

We have seen that the rule of law embraces a range of ideas which are the subject of much disagreement. In this section, I shall outline three main versions of the rule of law applied in English law developing these in greater detail later. A broad distinction can be made between the rule of law as government *by* law (versions 1 and 2) and the rule of law as government *under* law (version 3). The three versions are as follows:

1. *The 'core' rule of law*. This is the basic rule of law which we discussed earlier. It means government *by* law in the form of general rules as opposed to the discretion of the ruler. All it requires is that the rules are validly made. It does not specify their content. It assumes that general rules, even those may by a tyrant are better than government by the unpredictable whim of a tyrant. It implies 'equality' in the sense that everyone who falls within a given law must be treated the same under it and that government must respect its own laws. This does not amount to much since there can be different laws for different groups of people, for example ethnic minorities. 'Equality' can be said to be satisfied if each individual in the group is treated equality under the laws relating specifically to the group. The core rule of law is therefore consistent with hideously repressive regimes.

2. *The 'amplified' rule of law*. The amplified rule of law claims that certain principles relating to fairness and justice are inherent the notion of law itself as a guide to human conduct and that these at least moderate bad laws, for example a requirement that laws be announced clearly in advance and be applied by independent courts. It is not claimed that these principles cannot be overridden by other factors. The amplified rule of law is primarily procedural. It could conflict with the core rule of law for example a rule which allows a witness in court special protection (see eg *W (Algeria) v Secretary of State for the Home Dept* [2012] 2 All ER 699, Section 24.3.4).

▶ Syrett (2011, 63–65) has pointed out that in *R (Anufrijeva) v Secretary of State for the Home Dept* [2003] 3 All ER 827, different approaches to the rule of law led to judicial disagreement. A statute stated that the entitlement of an asylum seeker to benefit terminated when the Home Office determined that asylum should be refused. A majority of the House of Lords held that this did not apply until the asylum seeker had been informed of the decision, in that case several months later so as the applicant could exercise her right to challenge the decision in the courts. Lord Bingham however dissenting held that the court should follow the plain words of the legislation. Lord Bingham was thus staking out a core rule of law position while the majority followed the amplified approach. They took the view that unless a statute explicitly says otherwise it must be read so as to accommodate basic rights (the *'principle of legality'* below).

3. *The 'extended' rule of law*. This is the most ambitious version. It claims that law encapsulates the overarching political values of the community – assumed to be

liberal, such as freedom of expression and non-discrimination (see Allan, 2006). It claims also to link law with republican ideas of equal citizenship. In as much as this version relies upon vague and contestable concepts, it also conflicts with the core rule of law. It is often claimed that the flexibility of this version of the rule of law allows the courts to respond to the changing values of society. This presupposes that courts are well placed to be in command of these.

Craig (1997) has distinguished between 'formal' and 'substantive' versions of the rule of law. The formal version centres on the shape and application of the law, whether it has been properly made, whether it is clear and fairly applied (thus reflecting the 'core' and 'amplified versions' above). There should be independent courts to interpret and apply the law which should apply equally to those who fall within it. Without independent courts and equality the notion of rules is meaningless (see *R (Cart) v Upper Tribunal* [2010] at [34]–[37]).

The formal version has nothing to say about whether the *content* of the law treats people equally. As John Stuart Mill remarked:

> the justice of giving equal protection to the rights of all is maintained by those who support the most outrageous inequality in the rights themselves (1972, ch 5).

The substantive version opens out to the content of the law, whether it is fair and just and reflects the values of society. The danger of a broad approach is of course that it could reduce the rule of law to a discussion of whether the particular commenta tor likes the law in question.

6.3   The core rule of law

Hayek, the conservative political theorist (see Section 2.3.4), is probably the most enthusiastic champion of the core rule of law. Hayek (1960) asserted of the rule of law:

> stripped of all technicalities this means that government in all its actions is bound by rules fixed and announced beforehand – rules which make it possible to foresee with fair certainty how the authority will use its coercive powers in given circumstances, and to plan one's life accordingly.

It has been claimed that the core rule of law is a universal human good irrespective of the content of any particular law since it favours reason, certainty and equality, acts as a restraint to prevent rulers behaving capriciously or maliciously and prevents officials from picking on individuals. It has been argued that in order to be credible even a bad ruler might act through law thereby behaving better than he or she otherwise might have done. (See Thompson, *Whigs and Hunters* (Allen Lane 1975).) On the other hand the use of rules and regulations could mean that evil laws can be enforced more efficiently.

The core rule of law is a requirement of the ECHR. Under many of its provisions the state can override a right only if it acts 'in accordance with the law' or its action is 'prescribed by law'. This means that the state can act only through definite rules, the application of which is predictable in advance. For example *R (Purdey) v DPP* [2009] UKHL 45 concerned the DPP's discretion whether to prosecute for murder the claimant's husband for assisting her to travel to Switzerland to commit suicide in order to alleviate her suffering from a terminal illness. The House of Lords held that the right to respect for family life under the ECHR can be overridden by a law that is accessible and clear enough to ensure that individuals could foresee, if necessary with legal advice, the consequences of their conduct. The DPP must therefore publish guidelines as to how he would exercise his discretion.

The core rule of law has an underlying political agenda. It appeals primarily to the liberal conservative end of the political spectrum. In common with many economic liberals, Hayek believed that the certainty created by the rule of law would encourage wealth creation through a free market and that the poor would be better off than under alternative regimes. There is no historical evidence either way. However departing from the core idea of the rule of law as rules set out in advance, Hayek favoured the common law as a response to concrete practical problems rather than as being imposed in the abstract by governments that have neither the skills nor the knowledge to plan for the future.

Thus Hayek believed that the core rule of law points to a limited role for government since it prevents government officials having wide discretion. However if we wish government to provide services such as health, education, housing, welfare support and help to business it is sometimes necessary that officials should have wide and flexible discretionary powers in order to target individual needs albeit within a broad legal framework (see Baldwin, *Rules and Government* (Clarendon Press 1995) Chapter 3). Hayek on the other hand suggested that a government which accepted the rule of law would not pick out individuals for special treatment but be restricted to general rules applying equally to everyone. Hayek recognised that his views were likely to lead to economic inequality and perhaps hardship but assumed that these were outweighed by the advantages of individual freedom.

Hayek also thought that the core rule of law automatically supports freedom. This is a mystifying claim compared with the more uncontroversial claim that particular laws may protect some freedoms (those favoured by the lawmakers). For instance my freedom is protected if a law stops you from entering my property, but what the law is doing is transferring freedom from you to me according to what the lawmaker happens to prefer.

A common sense view would assert that laws in their nature restrict freedom. As Hobbes put it, 'freedom lies in the silence of the laws', and in *The Pilgrim's Progress*, Bunyan asks:

> he to whom thou was sent for ease, being by name legality, is the son of the Bond-woman ... how canst thou expect by them to be made free?

However Locke thought that laws did support freedom indeed that freedom means doing what the law allows. Thus Locke said that:

> Law in its true notion is not so much the limitation as the direction of a free and intelligent agent to his proper interest and prescribes no further than is for the general good of those under that law. (Second Treatise of Government (1690) VI, 57)

The explanation of this difference is that Hobbes and Locke were using different senses of freedom, Hobbes the familiar 'negative' version meaning the absence of restrictions. Locke the 'positive' version meaning reason used to expand the possibilities of life (see Section 2.4). Locke's approach makes the large assumption that laws are invariable rational. Indeed Hayek referred to freedom as the absence of *arbitrary* restraint not all restraint. In this sense, by obeying rational laws we are apparently exercising freedom since as rational creatures we are 'obeying laws that we have made ourselves' (Kant). On the other hand, as Berlin pointed out (see Section 2.4), this notion of freedom is trickery. Positive freedom assumes that all rational people would think the same but there are different kinds of reason and unless a law has a specifically freedom-loving content there is no guarantee that it will offer significant life possibilities to anyone except the friends of the lawmaker ... .

Another way of linking law and freedom is to suggest in republican fashion (see Section 2.5) that laws made collectively are objective an argument often used to persuade minorities to obey the law. Hayek claimed that: 'when we obey laws, we are not subject to another's will and are therefore free' (1960, 153–54). However this presupposes that the laws are in fact made by a desirable collective process and do not merely reflect the whims of a ruling group. Parliament is intended to secure this but its members are not independent of the will of the ruling political party.

Hayek might also have meant that we are 'free' to plan our lives around laws and so avoid them, in the sense that outside any law there must be a zone of freedom. The debate therefore seems to be playing on different meanings of freedom. Thus the core rule of law needs to be supplemented by some idea of 'good law' or at least an inclusive law making process to have any serious chance of protecting freedom.

The core rule of law can never fully be realised in practice. The meaning of a rule is rarely clear enough to be applied to every case, so discretion (meaning a choice between alternatives) is unavoidable. To self-styled 'critical' legal scholars this inherent vagueness of law is a fundamental objection to the idea of the rule of law, which they regard as a mask for naked power. The standard liberal reply is that vagueness is a matter of degree and in some circumstances is to be welcomed (see Kutz, 'Just Disagreement: Indeterminacy and Rationality in the Rule of Law' (1994) 103 Yale LJ 997). Most laws in practice have a widely accepted meaning. And even where laws are vague, there are widely accepted standards of 'practical reasoning' such as appeals to consequences, moral values, analogy with precedents widely shared feelings and so on. In order to be legitimate a judge's interpretation must not diverge far from public opinion. Even though there may be no objective 'right' answer it is possible to justify a solution which would be widely accepted. This is how the common law might be reconciled with the rule of law. It claims to conform to widely accepted community standards: 'ordinary notions of what is fit and proper' (*MacFarlane v Tayside Health Board* [2000] at 108; *Invercargill City Council v Hamlin* [1996] at 640–42).

Indeed the core rule of law could be regarded as mechanical and cruel, allowing officials to hide behind rules to avoid personal responsibility, and ignoring sentiments such as compassion, mercy and common sense in favour of ruthless logic (see eg Hutchinson and Monahan (eds), *The Rule of Law: Ideal or Ideology* (University of Toronto Press 1987)). A legalistic perspective is heavily rational, relying on linguistic reasoning turning on verbal definitions and categories, perhaps at the expense of the human feelings involved and making compromise and cooperation difficult. Moreover discretion may be desirable in many legal contexts. The rule of law is not the supreme value. For example the police do not have to prosecute everyone; the Inland Revenue may release a taxpayer from a tax burden.

The courts do not claim that the rule of law is an absolute and recognise that it might be outweighed by other public interests. In *R (Corner House Research) v Director of the Serious Fraud Office* [2008] the House of Lords held that a prosecuting authority could discontinue a prosecution of alleged corruption involving members of the Saudi royal family on the ground that, had the investigation continued, the Saudi government would have withdrawn cooperation with the UK intelligence services, thereby increasing the risk of a terrorist attack. Similarly in *R (Cart) v Upper Tribunal* (2011) the Supreme Court reached a compromise between the rule of law in the sense of access to the ordinary courts and the need for specialised expertise in decision making by limiting the scope of judicial review of certain decisions of the Upper Tribunal (see Section 20.1). There must also be wide emergency powers to some extent outside both law and democracy to deal with unforeseen and exceptional threats. Even the ECHR can be derogated from to meet an emergency (Human Rights Act 1998, s 14). Even here however a limited supervision by a court may be sacrosanct (see Section 23.1).

Thus the rule of law may involve compromises. The law can prescribe broad guidelines within which decisions must be made and in particular lay down procedures policed by the courts that must be followed to ensure that government keeps within the rules it makes and acts fairly and reasonably (Chapters 16–18). Emergency powers can be hedged with legal safeguards, for example a requirement that they lapse after a set period (see Section 23.1).

▶ A scene from Shakespeare's *Merchant of Venice* illustrates some of the above points. Shylock, a member of a disadvantaged minority, asked the court to enforce his bond against Antonio, a member of the ruling elite. The bond required a pound of Antonio's flesh if he defaulted on payment. Portia, posing as a judge, first made an appeal to mercy, which failed. Shylock pointed out that, if mercy were given, people would be less likely to obey the law and disadvantaged minorities would be particularly vulnerable. Portia then opportunistically invoked the core rule of law by interpreting the bond literally so as not to include the shedding of any blood, thus making it impossible to enforce. This crude approach ignores the widely held understanding that laws should be interpreted in their context and according to their purpose or spirit. From this perspective the shedding of blood was an integral part of the bond. It is a different question, outside the scope of the rule of law in its strictest sense, whether a law, based on a free market that enforces such a bond, is good or bad.

6.4 Dicey's version of the rule of law

Dicey (1915, 1958) claimed that constitutional law is based on general rules enforced through the ordinary common law courts and which apply equally to all. It is often suggested that this approach to the rule of law favoured Dicey's own political beliefs, those of a strong supporter of private property rights and an opponent of government intervention (see eg Hibbitts (1994)). In other words Dicey was a founding member of the 'red light' persuasion (Section 1.6).

Although writing between 1875 and 1915, Dicey has been of great influence among English lawyers partly due to the clarity and apparent simplicity of his work but also maybe because the legal profession warms to his politics. In line with the orthodoxy of his time Dicey had faith in science and believed that scientific method could be applied to law so as to produce objective general principles with clear edges. We no longer have such faith and believe that at least some legal ideas, of which the rule of law is an example, are fuzzy, variable and laden with political value judgements (indeed science itself is increasingly recognised as having these features). It is easy to see that Dicey's version of the rule of law has only limited application to modern conditions. Nevertheless it contains some important principles which influence contemporary ideas of the rule of law most notably the principle that officials have only such powers as the law gives them and that their decisions can be challenged in independent courts. Dicey formulated a three-fold version of the rule of law. His three aspects are interrelated but deserve separate treatment since some aspects stand the test of time better than others. They are as follows:

1. The absolute supremacy or predominance of 'regular' law

No man is punishable or can be lawfully made to suffer in body or goods except for a distinct breach of law established in the ordinary legal manner before the ordinary courts. (Dicey, 1915, 183)

This aspect of the rule of law has three branches. Firstly that no official can interfere with individual rights without the backing of a specific law. Officials have no special powers merely because they are agents of the state. This remains important today. In *R v Somerset CC, ex p Fewings* [1995] 1 All ER 513, which concerned an unsuccessful claim by a local authority to ban hunting on its land, Laws J referring to one of the 'sinews' of the rule of law said (at 524) that the principles that govern the application of the rule of law to public bodies and private persons are 'wholly different' in the sense that:

the freedoms of the private citizen are not conditional upon some distinct and affirmative justification for which he must burrow in the law books ... But for public bodies the rule is opposite and so of another character altogether. It is that any action to be taken must be justified by positive law.

Secondly Dicey believed that government should not have wide discretionary powers. For example, in *Rantzen v Mirror Group Newspapers* [1994] QB 670 the Court of Appeal condemned the wide discretion given to juries to fix the amount of damages in libel cases as violating the rule of law. As regards the powers of the executive this must be significantly qualified today. As we have seen Parliament regularly gives wide powers to officials to make discretionary decisions about the provision of public services. These frequently impact on the rights of individuals (eg land use planning decisions). However Dicey did not rule out all discretionary power but only 'wide arbitrary or discretionary power of constraint'. He insisted on limits to and controls over the exercise of discretion. This aspiration is to some extent met by the courts' powers of judicial review of government action. These include principles based on the purposes for which the power is given and standards of reasonableness and fairness.

Thirdly Dicey thought that all punishment should be meted out by the ordinary courts. This is no longer the case. Regulators and local authorities for example have wide powers to issue fines and other civil penalties with only limited rights of appeal to ordinary courts (see Section 5.3.1). The tribunal system is also to some extent outside the ordinary courts (see Section 5.4). Again something of Dicey's belief is preserved by judicial review (see *R (Cart) v Upper Tribunal* [2011]).

2. No one is above the law

Dicey meant that nobody, especially government officials, should be immune from the powers of the ordinary courts. Here every man, whatever his rank or condition, is subject to the ordinary law of the realm and amenable to the jurisdiction of the ordinary [courts]. (Dicey, 1915, 189).

Equality before the law in this sense is essential in the interests of public confidence (see *Sharma v Browne-Antoine* [2007] 1 WLR 780 at [14]) and this aspect of Dicey has stood the test of time. Dicey did not mean that no official has special powers – this would have been obviously untrue. Dicey meant that 'every official, from the Prime Minister down ... , is under the same responsibility for every act done without legal justification as any other citizen' (ibid.). Officials as such enjoy no special protection from legal liability. For example officials and private persons alike are liable if they use excessive force in defending others against criminal acts. And in *M v Home Office* [1993] it was held that a minister cannot refuse to comply with a court order on the basis that he is a servant of the Crown (see also *D v Home Office* [2006] 1 All ER 183). Thus liability is personal to the individual official, who cannot shelter behind the notion of the state (see Section 6.1).

There are exceptions but these require special justification. Judges are immune from personal liability in respect of their actions in court (see Section 7.4), Parliament is immune in relation to its internal proceedings and MPs have certain immunities but not from the ordinary criminal law (see Section 11.6). The Crown has certain immunities (but Dicey's rule of law was influential in removing far more (Crown Proceedings Act 1947 see Section 14.5). In many cases foreign governments and heads of state are immune from the jurisdiction of the UK courts, at least in civil actions (State Immunity Act 1978; see Section 9.5.2). Public bodies are sometimes protected against legal liability in the interests of efficiency, particularly in cases involving discretionary decisions (see eg *D v East Berkshire Community Health NHS Trust* [2005] 2 AC 373: false accusation of child abuse against parents). Dicey's principle can therefore be overcome by showing some justification for an inequality.

Dicey's insistence that the same 'regular law' applies to all does not always work in favour of the citizen. It may be desirable to impose special restrictions on government because its capacity to do harm is often greater than that of the ordinary person. For example, in *Malone v Metropolitan Police Comr* [1979] Ch 344 the police could lawfully intercept telephone calls on the grounds that, at the time, anyone could do so (the law was later changed see Section 23.5). Furthermore, contrary to Dicey's reliance on the ordinary law, where a statute provides a comprehensive set of government powers the government cannot fall back on the general law. For example in *R (Child Poverty Action Group) v Secretary of State for Work and Pensions* [2009] *Times* 22 October) the government could not rely on the general law which would have allowed it to claw back benefits which it had paid out by mistake; it could reclaim only as authorised by statute, that is where there was a false statement or a failure to disclose relevant information. Dicey compared English law where disputes between government and citizen were settled in the ordinary courts favourably with French law, where there is a special system of law dealing with the powers of government (*droit administratif enforced by the* Conseil d'Etat). Dicey thought that special administrative courts would give the government special privileges and shield the individual wrongdoer behind the cloak of the state. This aspect of Dicey's teaching has been particularly influential. As recently as the 1970s, there was resistance to the idea of a distinction between public and private law.

Since 1977, however, there has been a special procedure for challenging government decisions, albeit within the ordinary court system (Chapter 18). However in partial vindication of Dicey, attempts to distinguish between public law and private law have floundered (Sections 19.1, 21.5). There are also numerous special tribunals dealing with disputes between the individual and government (Section 20.1). However they are usually subject to the supervision of the ordinary courts and the rule of law requires that attempts to exclude the ordinary courts be strongly resisted (eg *Anisminic v Foreign Compensation Commission* [1969] 2 AC 147; Section 17.6).

3. The constitution is the 'result' of the ordinary law
[T]he general principles of the constitution are with us the result of judicial decisions determining the rights of private persons in particular cases brought before the courts. (Dicey, 1915, 191)

This derives from the common law tradition. Dicey believed that the UK constitution, not being imposed from above as a written constitution, was embedded in the very fabric of the law, dealing with concrete situations and backed by practical remedies in the hands of the courts. According to Dicey this strengthens the constitution since a written constitution may contain grand but vague abstractions and also can more easily be overturned. Moreover because the common law developed primarily through the medium of private disputes, it biases the constitution against governmental interests by treating private law, with its concentration on individual rights, as the basic perspective.

Dicey's threefold version of the rule of law therefore embodies overlapping ideas. These boil down to Dicey's assumption that private law provides the best legal framework and that governmental intervention is something exceptional and undesirable. Dicey originally believed that Parliament and the electorate would safeguard the individual against attempts by government to claim large powers. However he later became aware that this is not necessarily so and began to consider measures such as constitutional rights more sympathetically.

In his Introduction (1915) Dicey lamented what he saw as a decline in reverence for the rule of law. According to Dicey this was promoted by increasing tendency of legislation to give wide powers to government officials outside the ordinary courts and to attempt to exclude judicial review. He thought that this tendency encourages distrust of the courts and judges and encourages people to break the law in favour of their own private interests such as, according to Dicey, trade unionists, conscientious objectors, suffragettes and over powerful political parties. A century later wide governmental powers are commonplace and private interests such as business and media organisations may influence government at the expense of the law. An enormous increase in statute law enacted by a Parliament that has lost political power to the executive is the main reason why Dicey's analysis is of limited value today.

▶ The early case of *Entick v Carrington* (1765) 19 St Tr 1029, illustrating all three of Dicey's aspects of the rule of law can be contrasted with the modern case of *R v IRC, ex p Rossminister Ltd* [1980] 1 All ER 80. In *Entick* the court held that the Crown had no power to enter and search Entick's premises for books and papers as evidence of sedition. The plea of 'state necessity' was unknown to the common law because there was no precedent from which it could be derived and the practice of issuing general warrants giving officials wide discretion was unlawful. The messengers could therefore be sued in ordinary courts like private citizen. But in *Rossminister* which involved similar search in relation to tax offences, Parliament had given a general power to tax officials to enter and search private premises which the courts upheld, rejecting *Entick v Carrington* as irrelevant antiquarianism. It might be however that modern human rights law provides a compromise solution under which wide powers have to be justified as 'proportionate' in the public interest (see Section 21.5).

> Moreover outside the area of security and intelligence (see Section 23.4) attempts to exclude judicial review have been largely been unsuccessful thus illustrating the core of value promoted by Dicey. (See also Dicey, 'Development of Administrative Law in England' [1915] LQR 31.)

6.5   The 'amplified' rule of law

According to supporters of this wider version of the rule of law, the notion of law as rules necessarily implies certain moral principles. They concern the idea that, in order to guide conduct and be acted on, rules must be clear, look to the future and are applied impartially and publicly. These constitute what is primarily a procedural or formal version of the rule of law in the sense that they have little to say about the content of a law as opposed to how it is made and applied. The fundamental idea is a requirement that there should be access to independent courts and a fair trial, particularly to challenge government action (see Lord Bingham in *A v Secretary of State for the Home Dept* [2005] 2 AC 68 at [42]; Lord Woolf in *M v Secretary of State for the Home Dept* [2004] 2 All ER 863 at 873; *Al Rawi v Secretary of State for the Home Dept* [1012 1 All ER 1: no right to secret trials).

The American legal theorist Lon L. Fuller (*The Morality of Law* (Yale University Press 1969)) includes the following moral principles as embodying the rule of law:

▶ generality: for example officials not exempt from the rules (*M v Home Office* [1993]);
▶ promulgation so that laws can be known in advance (eg *R (Anufrijeva) v Secretary of State for the Home Dept* [2003] 3 All ER 827: decision to refuse asylum-seeker status took effect from the date when the claimant was informed of it);
▶ non-retroactivity: no punishment without a law in force at the time the act was committed (see ECHR, Art 7(1)). The requirements of the amplified rule of law are not absolute. For example retrospective law might occasionally be desirable to deal with a particularly serious social problem or an administrative blunder (eg Housing Corporation Act 2006);
▶ clarity: a law should be sufficiently clear and certain to enable a person to know what conduct was forbidden before he did it (*R v Goldstein* [2006] 2 All ER 257 at [32]–[33]). This is especially important in the context of human rights (see *Gillan and Quinton v UK* [2010] ECHR app No 158/05 [76]);
▶ consistent application: eg *R v Horseferry Road Magistrates Court, ex p Bennett* [1994] 1 All ER 289: fair trial not given to person brought before the court by kidnapping even if court process itself is fair, but evidence can be used in court even if has been obtained unlawfully (see *A-G's Reference (No 3 of 2009)* [2010] 1 All ER 235);
▶ the practical possibility of compliance: eg *R v Secretary of State for Social Services, ex p Joint Council for the Welfare of Immigrants* [1996] 4 All ER 385: regulations which deprived asylum seekers of benefits unless they claimed asylum status at the port of entry would frustrate their right of appeal;
▶ constancy through time: frequent changes in the law might offend this. A conspicuous example is the rapid internet supported changes immigration law that have taken place in recent years (see *R (Alvi) v Secretary of State for the Home Dept* [2012] 1 WLR 2208 [11], *Odelola v Secretary of State for the Home Dept* [2009] 3 All ER 1061, Section 17.9.1).
▶ Raz (1977) adds access to legal assistance: *R v Lord Chancellor, ex p Witham* [1997] 2 All ER 779: increases in legal fees denied access to courts for low-income people); *R v Grant* [2005] 3 WLR 437 at [52]: breach of lawyer–client confidentiality an affront to the rule of law); *R(Evans) v Lord Chancellor* [2012] 1 WLR 38 [25]: Unlawful as contrary to the rule of law to refuse legal aid funding to peace activists on grounds that government defence interests might be harmed. (See also Lord Millett in *Cullen v Chief Constable of the RUC* [2004] at [67].)
▶ Raz also includes 'natural justice': in the sense of a right to a fair hearing in one's own defence (see Section 18.3).
▶ Raz also adds 'openness': for example *R (Middleton) v West Somerset Coroner* [2004] 2 All ER 465: victims of a misuse of state power in relation to the death of prisoners entitled to inquiry in public (see Lord Bingham at [5]). The amplified rule of law includes the principle of open justice not only to protect the parties but also to support the democratic public interest in judicial accountability and the free flow of information through press reporting.

In *R (Mohammed) v Secretary of State (No 1)* [2010] 3 WLR 554 the Court of Appeal emphasised the rule of law in the context of a claim by the government that the content of certain documents from the US government should not be revealed in open court (at [38]–[41]). However the rule of law in this sense is not absolute and might be outweighed by other serious concerns such as national security. (See also *R (Algeria) v Secretary of State for the Home Dept* (2012) [35].)

The amplified rule of law might be criticised as narrow in that by concentrating on procedure rather than substance it favours those who can enlist the support of the legal profession, that is the well-to-do. Its proponents might respond that the rule of law is not meant to address all social problems but is merely one aspect of good government (see Sunstein, 1996).

Related to the amplified rule of law is a political version of the rule of law derived from the republican tradition (see Bellamy, 2007; Chapter 2). From this perspective law is a collective enterprise made by numerous people with many different interests – majorities and minorities alike. Indeed any of us might sometimes be part of a majority and sometimes a minority. The focus is not therefore on courts alone but on ensuring that the laws are made by a regular democratic process in which the representatives of all interests in the community have a voice. English law has not seriously engaged with this idea.

6.6 The extended (liberal) rule of law: 'the principle of legality'

This version of the rule of law overlaps with but goes beyond the amplified rule of law. It claims somewhat extravagantly that law provides the overarching values of the community against which acts of government must be evaluated. Thus when Aristotle pronounced that it is better for the law to rule than for any of the citizens to rule (*Politics* III 16, 1087a), he was probably referring not to rules as we understand them but to the customs of an elite group with common values and traditions designed to bring about their own collective good. The philosopher Ronald Dworkin has put forward an influential American version of this approach based on the idea that law as determined by apparently omnipotent courts should constitute a coherent set of principles, a 'fit' which imposes justice and fairness and gives effect to individual rights against the encroachment of the state (see Section 2.3.2).

The Dworkinian approach has been taken up on this side of the Atlantic. Often called 'the principle of legality', this version of the rule of law claims to restrain 'bad laws' by interpreting legislation and evaluating executive action in the light of common law values. Basic common law rights may be 'curtailed only by clear and express words and then only to the extent reasonably necessary to justify the curtailment' (per Lord Bingham in *R (Daly) v Secretary of State for the Home Dept* [2001] 2 AC 532 at 537–38). In this way the rule of law claims to support liberal democracy. The principle of legality has been reinforced by the Human Rights Act 1998 and often overlaps with it. But the two routes to the protection of rights are distinct.

> In *R v Secretary of State for the Home Dept, ex p Simms* [1999] Lord Hoffmann said:
>
> The principle of legality means that Parliament must squarely confront what it is doing and accept the political cost. Fundamental rights cannot be overridden by general or ambiguous words. This is because there is too great a risk that the full implications of their unqualified meaning may have passed unnoticed in the democratic process. In the absence of express language or necessary implication to the contrary, the courts therefore presume that even the most general words were intended to be subject to the basic rights of the individual. (at 131)
>
> In *R v Lord Chancellor's Dept, ex p Witham* [1997] 2 All ER 779, Laws J asserted that:
>
> In the unwritten legal order of the British State, at a time when the common law continues to accord a legislative supremacy to Parliament, the notion of a constitutional right can in my judgement inhere only in this proposition that the right in question cannot be abrogated by the state save by specific provision in an Act of Parliament ... General words will not suffice. And any such rights will be creatures of the common law, since their existence would not be the consequence of the democratic process but would be logically prior to it. (at 783)

The principle of legality applies both to procedural matters, thus encompassing the amplified rule of law above, and to matters of substance such as freedom of speech and non-discrimination. Examples of the principle of legality include the following:

- personal freedom: *R v Secretary of State, ex p Pierson* [1998] [1998] AC 539; *Roberts v Parole Board* [2006] at [93]; *R (Ullah) v Special Adjudicator* [2004] at [43];
- freedom of expression: *R v Secretary of State for the Home Dept, ex p Simms* [1999] at [131]; *Culnane v Morris* [2006] 2 All ER 149;
- privacy: *R (Daly) v Secretary of State* [2001];
- discrimination against gay couple: *Ghaidan v Mendosa* [2004] at [9];
- access to the courts and fair trial: *R v Lord Chancellors Dept, ex p Witham* [1997] 2 All ER 779; *R (Cart) v Upper Tribunal* [2010], *Al Rawi v Security Service* [2012] 1 All ER 1 (see also Sections 19.7.2, 24.3);
- asset freezing of terrorist suspects with no provision for reasonable suspicion nor a fair right to challenge: *HM Treasury v Ahmed* [2010] 2 AC 534.

The suggested link between liberal values, the rule of law and common law seems to be twofold. Firstly, and echoing Dicey the common law is not merely imposed from the top by a lawmaker but is generated by disputes freely brought before the courts by individuals and requires the exercise of power to be rationally justified. Secondly, there is the idea that the law must be applied according to the understanding of those subject to it as equal citizens. In this respect common law's independence from government means that it can plausibly claim to represent the values of the community. According to Allan:

> The principle that laws will be faithfully applied, according to the tenor in which they would reasonably be understood by those affected, is the most basic tenet of the rule of law: it constitutes that minimal sense of reciprocity between citizen and state that inheres in any form of decent government, where law is a genuine barrier to arbitrary power. (2001, 62)

This brings in a republican dimension but, as we saw in Chapter 1, republican and liberal perspectives may conflict – republicanism stressing the desire for citizen participation as equals in decision making, liberalism stressing the citizen's right to be left alone.

Sir John Laws, a leading contemporary judge, has tried to combine liberal and republican perspectives. He asserted that because the courts derive their powers from common law and have no electoral mandate to pursue any particular policy they must fall back on what he considered to be the only possible moral position, namely individual freedom: 'The true starting point in the quest for the good constitution consists in ... the autonomy of every person in his sovereignty' (Laws, 'The Constitution: Morals and Rights' [1996] PL 622, 623; see also 'Law and Democracy' [1995] PL 72). However such philosophical assumptions are controversial, and concepts such as freedom and equality are inherently vague and applied differently by different groups.

Moreover the common law gets its legitimacy not from abstract philosophy but from community values, whatever they happen to be. The common law is therefore not necessarily liberal. Although confined by the accumulation of precedent, common law arguably tracks the opinions of the dominant group in the legal community at any given time. While legal education and tradition secure a certain conformity, there is no reason to assume that the values of the community sufficiently uniform and stable to form a credible basis for coherent liberal principles. The extended rule of law may therefore be no more than the temporary preferences of a fashionable group of lawyers.

Indeed in *R (Bancoult) v Secretary of State for the Foreign and Commonwealth Office* [2001], Laws LJ held that the extended version of the rule of law based on the underlying rights and values of domestic common law does not apply to British overseas territories. These have to be content with what he called a 'thinner' rule of law, by which he meant something akin to the amplified rule of law in the sense of an obligation to conform to the rules fairly applied (but see Lord Bingham dissenting in *R (Bancoult) v Secretary of State for the Foreign and Commonwealth Office (No 2)* [2008]; Section 9.4).

The extended rule of law may conflict with the ideals behind the core rule of law of certainty and respect for general rules. This is because the nature of fundamental rights and the balance between fundamental rights and other aspects of public interest such as security are inherently uncertain and ultimately depend on a political preference.

The late Lord Bingham (2007), the former Senior Law Lord and probably the foremost judge of the past decade, proposed a version of the rule of law which combines elements of both the amplified and the extended rule of law. His core notion was that 'all persons and authorities within the state, whether public or private, should be bound by and entitled to the benefit of laws publicly and prospectively promulgated and publicly administered in the courts'. Particular elements are that laws should:

- ▶ be intelligible and precise enough to guide conduct;
- ▶ minimise discretion, recognising that discretion cannot be removed completely;
- ▶ apply equally to all unless differences are clearly justified;

▶ give adequate protection to fundamental human rights (Lord Bingham acknowledged the lack of agreement as to whether this is an appropriate rule of law matter as opposed to a matter of politics);
▶ include machinery for resolving disputes without excessive cost or inordinate delay;
▶ provide for judicial review requiring decision makers to act reasonably, in good faith, for the purposes for which powers are granted without exceeding the limits of those powers;
▶ embody fair adjudicative procedures; ensure that the state complies with international law (a controversial proposal; see also Bingham, 2009).

Lord Bingham's general approach probably represents a widely shared view as to what good law should be like in a liberal society. Whether the label 'rule of law' adds anything is questionable. It is sometimes suggested that the rule of law in its extended sense is the foundation of the constitution to the extent that the courts might refuse to apply a statute that conflicted with the rule of law (see Section 8.4).

6.7 The international rule of law

The idea of the rule of law comes under particular stress when there is a clash between different legal regimes, in particular between international and domestic law. International law as such is not automatically part of UK law but international principles can filter into our law by various means (see Section 9.5.1).

The idea of the rule of law is represented in international law by the notion of *ius cogens*, that is certain absolutes that all nations are expected to recognise, such as the prohibition against torture (see *R v Bow Street Stipendiary Magistrate, ex p Pinochet Ugarte (No 3)* [1999] at 198–99). Since the Second World War there have been several attempts to draw up internationally binding codes of basic human rights and to promote liberal values under the banner of the rule of law. However such concepts are vague and are applied in different ways in different cultures. Indeed in order to command support from as many nations as possible treaties are often written in cloudy language so as to avoid clear commitments, thus reflecting the notion of constitutional abeyance (see Section 3.5).

For example the Declaration of Delhi (1959), issued by the International Commission of Jurists, proclaimed that the rule of law is intended to establish 'social, economic, educational and cultural conditions under which [individuals'] legitimate aspirations and dignity may be realised'.

International instruments include the United Nations Universal Declaration of Human Rights (1948), the Refugee Convention (1951) and the Torture Convention (1984). There is an International Criminal Court to deal with war crimes, crimes against humanity and genocide, which has been incorporated into UK law (International Criminal Court Act 2001). Torture is an offence in the UK wherever and by whomever committed (Criminal Justice Act 1988). Of most direct concern to UK law is the ECHR. Individuals have a right to petition the European Court of Human Rights in respect of violations by states. Under the Human Rights Act 1998, most provisions of the Convention have belatedly been made binding in UK law, although they do not override Acts of Parliament.

Summary

▶ The rule of law is an umbrella for assorted ideas about the virtues of law mainly from a liberal perspective. They centre upon law as reason and law as administered by the courts as a means of controlling government. The rule of law in its core sense emphasises the importance of general rules as binding on government and citizen alike. The core sense of the rule of law is morally ambivalent since it can also be regarded as an efficient tool of tyranny.

▶ The rule of law as expounded by Dicey has significantly influenced the UK constitution. Dicey advocated that government discretion should be limited by definite rules of law, that the same law administered by the ordinary courts could in general apply to government and citizen alike, and that Britain does not need a written constitution because the common law provides a firmer foundation for individual rights. This has influenced the thinking of the legal profession but may be unsuited to the circumstances of modern government. It is also difficult to reconcile the rule of law in this sense with the principle that Parliament has unlimited power which can be harnessed by a strong executive. In an amplified sense, the rule of law requires the law to reflect certain basic values derived from the nature of rules as guides to conduct. These centre upon the law being clear and accessible and upon the right to a fair trial. However they are also consistent with repressive laws.

▶ In an 'extended' sense the rule of law is claimed to be the guardian of the liberal values of the community, entrusted to the courts because of their role as sources of impartial reason. It is claimed to be translated into rights such as non-discrimination and, freedom of expression. However there is no reason to believe that these values or reason itself are the prerogative of courts and they have to be accommodated against the social goals of elected governments. Why courts should do this is a theme to be pursued in later chapters.

▶ Other modern ideas of the rule of law include the increasing importance of international treaties which attempt to establish codes of fundamental rights and freedoms that governments should respect.

Exercises

6.1 Do you agree with Thompson that the rule of law is an 'unqualified human good'? Would an evil tyrant favour the rule of law?

6.2 To what extent does Dicey's version of the rule of law advance individual freedom and good government?

6.3 'The Rule of Law functions as a clear check on the flourishing of a vigorous democracy. Attempts to characterise the rule of law as the butler of democracy are false and misleading' (Hutchinson and Monahan). Critically discuss.

6.4 To what extent, if at all, is the rule of law conducive to equality?

6.5 Do the following violate the rule of law?
   (i) Heads of State being exempt from legal liability;
   (ii) a statute banning press criticism of the Prime Minister;
   (iii) a statute which states that an allegation relating to the conduct of the security services cannot be made in the ordinary courts;
   (iv) a statute which gives a discretion to the Education Secretary to decide what courses will be taught in universities;
   (v) a statute requiring that any law concerning the treatment of prisoners must be interpreted literally without any presumption in favour of human rights.

6.6 'The rule of law clearly forms an essential element of liberal democracy and plays its part in providing a theoretical basis for an independent judiciary but it forms only one side of a balanced constitution' (Carol Harlow). Explain and critically discuss.

Further reading

Allan, 'The Rule of Law as Liberal Justice' (2006) 56 U Toronto LR 41

Allan, 'Law, Justice and Integrity: The Paradox of Wicked Laws' (2009) 29 OJLS 705

Bellamy, *Political Constitutionalism* (Cambridge University Press 2007) ch 2

Bingham, 'The Rule of Law' (2007) 66 CLJ 67

Bingham, *The Rule of Law* (Penguin 2009)

Craig, 'Formal and Substantive Concepts of the Rule of Law: An Analytical Framework' [1997]
 PL 467

Dicey, *Law of the Constitution* (Macmillan, 1915), Chs IV, XII, XIII,

Dworkin, 'Political Judges and the Rule of Law' in *A Matter of Principle*, (Clarendon Press 1986).

Endicott, 'The Impossibility of the Rule of Law' (1999) 19 OJLS 1

Hayek, *The Constitution of Liberty* (Henry Regnery 1960) 133–61, 205–19

Hibbitts, 'The Politics of Principle: Albert Venn Dicey and the Rule of Law (1994) 23 Anglo Am LR 1

Horowitz, 'The Rule of Law: An Unqualified Human Good?' (1977) 86 Yale LJ 15

Jennings, 'In praise of Dicey' (1935) 13 *Journal of Public Administration* 123

Jowell, 'The rule of law and its underlying values', in Jowell and Oliver (eds) *The Changing
 Constitution* (7th edn Oxford University Press 2011)

Leoni, *Freedom and the Law,* Chapter 3, Princeton, Van Nostrand, 1961

Loughlin, *Foundations of Public Law* (Oxford University Press 2010) ch 11

Poole, 'Questioning Common Law Constitutionalism' (2005) 25 LS 142

Raz, 'The Rule of Law and Its Virtue' [1977] LQR 93

Sunstein, *Legal Reasoning and Political Conflict* (Oxford University Press 1996) ch 4

Tivey, 'Constitutionalism and the Political Arena' (1999) 70 Pol Q 175

Waldron, 'The Rule of Law in Contemporary Legal Theory' (1989) 2 Ratio Juris 79

Chapter 7

The separation of powers

7.1 Introduction: Montesquieu's doctrine of the separation of powers

The separation of powers is widely regarded as one of the pillars of a liberal constitutional democracy. Its essence is that all power should be divided so that no single person or body can exercise unlimited power and each branch of government requires the cooperation of the others. Article 16 of the (French) Declaration of the Rights of Man (1789) states that 'a society where rights are not secured or the separation of powers established has no constitution'.

The best-known version of the doctrine is that of Montesquieu, *The Spirit of the Laws* (1748). Montesquieu divided government powers into legislative power: which he described as 'that of enacting laws', executive power: 'executing the public resolutions' and judicial power: 'trying the causes of individuals' (Bk XI, ch VI, 174). He based this on the English constitution after the 1688 revolution.

The legislature (Parliament in our case) makes the laws, the judiciary settles disputes and imposes sanctions for breaking the law. The scope of the executive power (the Crown and other bodies created by statute) is more difficult to define. The term means to 'carry out'. The executive carries out the everyday tasks of government which can be anything given to it by the lawmaker. Fundamentally the executive implements the law and therefore commands the resources of the state in particular the use of violence. Going back to the origins of government the executive also represents the state in foreign affairs and has the ultimate responsibility for the well being of the community. A key function of the executive is also to propose and prepare laws to be approved by the legislature. Thus, comprising a threat to the separation of powers, the lawmaking process is actually a combination of executive and legislature.

The doctrine is central to republicanism (Section 2.5). For example the US Constitution with its strong separation of powers was devised primarily to prevent self-interested faction, including democratic majorities from taking over the government. The UK constitution is more ambivalent. All three branches originated with the Crown but gradually evolved into substantially separate institutions. However the same people occupy key positions in the legislature and executive and parliamentary supremacy makes a strict separation of powers problematic. Thus in *R (Jackson) v A-G* (2005) Lord Hope fell back on the truism that the constitution depends on 'mutual respect' between the branches of government [125].

Montesquieu's main aim was to protect liberty. He was no democrat and placed faith in aristocratic government subject to limits. He favoured what he called 'dissonant harmony'. He believed that disagreement was a healthy feature of politics and that the need for different interests to cooperate would prevent any power being used excessively: 'power must be checked by power'. Montesquieu thought that if any two of the three functions fall into the same hands the outcome is likely to be tyranny. Each branch has different functions but each can police the limits of the others. As Nolan J put it:

> The proper constitutional relationship between the executive and the court is that the courts will respect all acts of the executive within its lawful province, and that the executive will respect all decisions of the court as to what its lawful province is. (*M v Home Office* (1992))

However, there must be an understanding as to which branch should have the last word in the event of a stalemate since the separation of powers is capable of producing gridlock. The way this is done depends on the political fears and worries of the day. Montesquieu feared the legislature most and disliked democracy, a view that survives today among supporters of judicial supremacy (Section 8.4)'. He favoured a monarchy as the executive, believing that this gave the constitution stability and continuity. According to Montesquieu, although the executive could not make laws or obtain finance without the support of the legislature, the executive could veto the proposals of the legislature. The executive could also dismiss Parliament and Montesquieu thought that the executive should summon the legislature as and when needed. Montesquieu did not think that the legislature should have the power to remove the executive since government must be continuous. (Today we address the need for continuity by another kind of separation of powers, namely between elected ministers who can be dismissed by Parliament and the permanent civil service which survives changes of government (Section 15.7).)

Similarly at the end of the nineteenth century Mill, influenced by de Toqueville's writing on the emerging American democracy, feared:

> the only despotism of which in the modern world there is real danger – the absolute rule of the head of the executive over a congregation of isolated individuals all equal and all slaves. (*Autobiography* (1873))

Today we usually regard the executive as the most dangerous branch. Parliament can remove the executive but the executive can no longer remove Parliament (Section 11.2).

Although Montesquieu took England as his model it seems clear that he overestimated both the possibility of a separation along his lines and its application in England. In particular he did not accommodate the common law under which the judges as well as Parliament make law. Moreover when Montesquieu was writing (after a visit to England in the early eighteenth century) the conventions which require the Crown to act on the advice of ministers chosen from the legislature had not clearly emerged.

Indeed executive judicial and legislative power inevitably overlap since laws made by Parliament could not cover every conceivable situation faced by government and so the executive often makes rules and decides disputes (see eg Section 5.5). However the separation of powers does not necessarily mean that the three functions are always separate but rather that with each function a separate body has the last word and that the exercise of all power is subject to some kind of external check. This is largely true in the UK.

7.2   The importance of the separation of powers

The separation of powers in Montesquieu's sense has limited but important application in the unwritten UK constitution. As might be expected the UK constitution does not embody the separation of powers systematically but applies it in pragmatic ways in particular contexts. It applies most strongly in relation to the judiciary since judicial independence is an essential feature of the rule of law. There is a weaker separation between executive and legislature since by convention ministers must be members of Parliament. Depending on the political and personal forces of the day, either the executive is subordinate to Parliament or (more likely) the executive dominates Parliament.

There is disagreement among academic writers as to the importance of the separation of powers. Dicey, perhaps the most influential exponent of the 'English' constitution did not rank the separation of powers as one of its basic principles but mentioned it only in passing. Indeed the doctrine of parliamentary supremacy makes a true separation of powers impossible in the UK.

Jennings (*The Law and the Constitution* (University of London Press 1959)) argued that there is no important difference between the three functions, the executive and judicial being essentially a more detailed kind of lawmaking. Marshall (*Constitutional Theory* (Oxford University Press 1971)) argues that the separation of powers is an umbrella for a miscellaneous collection of principles, each of which can be justified in its own right, for example judicial independence. On the other hand Barendt (1995) and Munro (1999) while not claiming that it is universal regard the doctrine as an important organising and critical principle.

The argument may be confused by failing to distinguish between those who think that conventions and trust in our rulers provides a sufficient guarantee of separation and those in republican mode who prefer legal principles. The former are more likely to argue that we have a proper separation of powers. This confusion seems to have affected the discussion about removing the judicial functions of the House of Lords and the Lord Chancellor (Sections 5.4, 7.6.3). Before the creation of the Supreme Court judicial separation was more strongly protected by convention than by law.

7.3 Different kinds of separation of powers

The debate about the separation of powers may also be confused where different protagonists are using the concept of the separation of powers in different senses. In particular separation of powers can mean:

1. separation of function between different units of government (functional separation of powers);
2. separation of personnel in the membership of different units of government;
3. checks and balances between different units of government.

The strictest version of the doctrine, such as that adopted in the US, would aim at all three, although of course practicalities mean that the reality is likely to fall short of the ideal. As with the rule of law, the separation of powers is no more than an underlying set of values.

Moreover if we wish to restrain power it does not follow that this can be done only by dividing powers according to Montesquieu's three abstract kinds. Claus (2005) for example argues that Montesquieu did not go far enough and that it is not the kind of power that matters but the existence of checks and limits on all powers. The essential principle encapsulated by the separation of powers is that power should be divided not that it should be divided in any particular way.

Power can be divided and checked in many ways which might also advance efficiency. For example the division between elected politicians and the professional civil servants who advise them. The civil service constitutes a reservoir of specialist expertise and experience that survives the periodic changes of government characteristic of a democracy. Divisions between central government and local governmental bodies as in a federal system are also a restraining influence and relatively efficient in relating government functions to the wishes of different communities. Even quangos (Section 15.9) may provide a valuable separation of power by focusing on specialist functions albeit those who seek appointment on such bodies are not always conspicuous for their independence. The distinction between the dignified and the 'efficient' parts of the constitution also provides a separation of powers (Section 1.7).

On the other hand the traditional division between legislative, executive and judicial functions is valuable by indicating different kind of procedure for different jobs. For example, law making requires the participation of a wide range of people meeting in public on equal terms, executive functions likely requires decisions by small groups or by individuals with professional expertise, not necessarily in public. Judicial functions above all requires impartiality and also openness and are normally in public. There is no doubt that out of all the aspects of separation of powers judicial independence is paramount (Section 7.4).

7.3.1   The mixed constitution

Montesquieu himself also favoured a different kind of separation of powers, namely the 'mixed constitution' based on Aristotle's three forms of government: monarchy, aristocracy and democracy (Section 1.8). This may be conducive to efficiency as well to the restraint of power. Aristotle believed that any single form of government was unstable, leading to a permanent cycle of disasters. He therefore favoured a blend of democracy and aristocracy: democracy to provide consent, aristocracy to provide stability and wise leadership. Aristocracy meant literally 'rule by the best', by which Aristotle meant an educated group wealthy enough to be independent.

The early Roman republic adopted similar ideas ('power in the people, authority in the Senate' – Cicero) but was later replaced by dictatorship ('what pleases the prince has the force of law'). For Montesquieu, all three elements of the mixed constitution should be represented in the legislature since this was the supreme body. Thus the English legislature had two parts, one (the House of Lords) being aristocratic. Each element would check the others. The monarch could veto legislation but not initiate it: 'prevent wrong but not do wrong'. The aristocratic and the elected elements would have to agree to make changes in the law.

Montesquieu, an aristocrat himself, believed that an aristocracy based on inheritance produced an independent, educated and leisured class who would protect freedom and curb the democratic element ('liberty is the stepchild of privilege') while the other elements of the constitution could prevent the aristocracy from using their powers selfishly.

Blackstone (1723–80), also praised the English mixed constitution:

Herein indeed consists the true excellence of the English government that all the parts of it form a mutual check upon each other. In the legislature the people are a check on the nobility and the nobility a check upon the people ... while the king is a check upon both which preserves the executive power from encroachments. And this very executive power is again checked and kept within due bounds by the two Houses ... For the two Houses naturally drawing in two directions of opposite interest, and the prerogative in another still different from them both, they mutually keep each other from exceeding their proper limits ... like three distinct powers in mechanics, they jointly compel the machine of government in a direction different from what either acting by itself would have done ... a direction which constitutes the true line of the liberty and happiness of the country. (*Commentaries on the Laws of England* (Oxford University Press 1787) 154–55)

The mixed constitution remains a significant element of the formal legal structure in the form of the monarchy and the House of Lords. Originally aristocracy simply meant government by the 'best'. The hereditary principle which was the historical basis of the House of Lords was rationalised on the ground that inherited landholding gave a powerful interest in the government of the country through which the lower classes enjoyed 'virtual representation'. Today the House of Lords is mainly an appointed 'aristocracy' since an automatic link between inheritance and political influence is no longer acceptable, at least openly, although a rump of hereditary peers remain (Section 12.2). Fear of democracy is a significant influence on the constitution many people favouring the continuance of the appointed House of Lords (Section 12.3). This raises the difficulty of whom we can trust to identify the 'best' so as to avoid Aristotle's corruption of aristocracy into an oligarchy of cronies. The mixed constitution is also intimated by contemporary advocates of the supremacy of the judiciary as a kind of aristocratic elite, albeit one not based directly on inheritance.

7.4 Judicial independence

Judicial independence is an aspect of the rule of law in its own right. It has two aspects and goes beyond the separation of powers. Firstly separation of powers concerns the independence of the courts as an institution. Secondly judicial independence requires the independence of individual judges from pressures that threaten not only actual impartiality but also the appearance of impartiality. For example the common law principles of natural justice require that a judge should not be vulnerable to a 'real possibility' of conflict of interest (Section 18.4).

Judicial independence is frail in the UK constitution since, in the absence of a written constitution it depends on a shared understanding that the other two branches which together are dominant will respect it. On the other hand there is a concern for public accountability which requires the involvement of the other branches of government. In particular the Ministry of Justice which is accountable to Parliament funds the courts who must compete for public money with other departments. The Ministry of Justice is also responsible for prisons and sentencing policy. This creates unhealthy competition for resources with the courts. The Lord Chancellor who heads the Ministry of Justice must ensure that the Supreme Court has such resources as the Lord Chancellor 'thinks are appropriate' for the court to carry out its business. (Constitutional Reform Act 2005, s 50 91). This could indirectly threaten judicial independence in favour of taking short cuts in respect, for example to staffing levels and case management.

As part of recent reforms (Section 5.4) a 'concordat' was produced setting out a non-legally binding understanding of the relationship between the judiciary and the other branches (see House of Lords Select Committee on the Constitution 6th Rep 2006–7, *Relations between the Executive, Judiciary and Parliament* (HL Paper 151, 2006–7)). Under the Concordat the Lord Chief Justice must be consulted on budgetary matters (see *Her Majesty's Courts Service Framework Document* (Cm 7350)).

Article 6 of the European Convention on Human Rights (ECHR) includes both elements of judicial independence by requiring 'a fair and public hearing ... by an independent and impartial tribunal established by law' (see Section 18.6). For example in *Millar v Dickson* [2002] 3 All ER 1041 the Privy Council found a violation of Article 6 where the prosecuting authority, the Scottish Lord Advocate, was also responsible for renewing the appointment of a temporary judge even though there was no complaint about the actual impartiality of the judge in question. As Lord Hope stated:

> Central to the rule of law is the principle that the judiciary must be, and must be seen to be independent of the executive (at [41])

Article 6 influenced the Constitutional Reform Act 2005 which removed the judicial roles of the Lord Chancellor and the House of Lords and created a separate Supreme Court to exercise the appellate functions of the House of Lords and also those of the Privy Council in devolution cases (Section 5.4). However Article 6 does not require a formal separation of powers but requires that in the particular circumstances the court is not only independent but also appears to be so (*McGonnell v UK* [2000] 30 EHRR 289). Courts of a 'classic kind' must usually sit in public and be fully independent and impartial, and there must be a full opportunity to give evidence and challenge witnesses (Section 21.4). However sometimes these ideals might be compromised by competing considerations such as security and the desire to protect children.

Statute sometimes acknowledges judicial independence.

The Constitutional Reform Act 2005 (s 3):

1. The Lord Chancellor and other ministers of the Crown with responsibility for matters relating to the judiciary or otherwise to the administration of justice must uphold the continued independence of the judiciary.
2. The Lord Chancellor and other ministers of the Crown must not seek to influence particular judicial decisions through any special access to the judiciary.
3. The Lord Chancellor must have regard to:
   - (i) the need to defend that independence;
   - (ii) the need for the judiciary to have the support necessary to enable them to exercise their functions;
   - (iii) the need for the public interest in regard to matters relating to the judiciary or otherwise to the administration of justice to be properly represented in decisions affecting those matters.

4. Judicial independence is in issue in relation to what have called 'administrative tribunals'; relatively informal bodies set up to adjudicate disputes between citizens and government. The independence of tribunals from the executive has been questioned but recent reforms have related the tribunal system more closely to the judiciary (Section 20.1)

Beyond the separation of powers, judicial independence requires that judges should be protected against attacks on their conduct in court and other participants should be able to speak freely. Judges are immune from personal actions for damages in respect of acts within their powers or done in good faith (*McC v Mullan* [1984] 3 All ER 908; Courts Act 2003, ss 31–35). However superior court judges may enjoy complete immunity (*Anderson v Gorrie* [1895] 1 QB 668). Under section 9.3 of the Human Rights Act 1998, where an action for damages is brought in respect of a judicial act, there is no liability in respect of an act in good faith except for an unlawful arrest or detention. Anything said in court by judges, advocates and witnesses is absolutely privileged against an action in libel and slander but advocates are not protected against liability for negligence (see *Trapp v Mackie* [1979] 1 All ER 489; *Arthur JS Hall v Simons* [2000] 3 All ER 673). There are also restrictions under the law of Contempt of Court in respect of comments on court proceedings which affect the freedom of the press (Section 22.2).

Judicial independence does not mean that judges should not be accountable. Accountability has two main meanings. It means firstly that a decision maker must explain and justify his or her actions and secondly that a decision maker might be corrected or penalised if his or her actions fall short of required standards. Judges are accountable in the first sense. They normally sit in public, disclose all material before them and give reasons for their decisions. Judicial decisions are therefore open to scrutiny by the media. It has been held that only in rare and extreme circumstances should the court's reasoning in a case not be published (*R (Mohammed) v Secretary of State for Foreign Affairs* [2010] 3 WLR 554, Section 23.3). Open justice in this sense is fundamental to democracy and the rule of law.

A three-tier appeal system, access to the European Court of Human Rights, and review by the senior courts of decisions of lower courts and tribunals contribute to accountability, as does the Criminal Cases Review Commission, which deals with miscarriages of justice.

Traditionally judges have not participated in public debate (see McMurdo, 'Should Judges Speak Out?' Judicial Conference of Australia 2001; www.jca.asn.au). However in 1987 the Lord Chancellor relaxed the notorious 'Kilmuir' rules made in 1959 by the then Lord Chancellor which restricted such participation and the matter is now left to the discretion of the individual judge.

The second aspect of accountability is affected by the need for judicial independence but also by the need for some kind of democratic input. A compromise has therefore been made. The Lord Chancellor (LC) (Minister for Justice) and the Lord Chief Justice (LCJ) are jointly responsible for judicial discipline (Constitutional Reform Act 2005, s 108). The Lord Chancellor's disciplinary powers are limited to the removal from office of judges below the rank of High Court judge (Section 7.7.3.1). The LCJ can reprimand and suspend a judge but the agreement of the LC is required. Judges are to a large extent protected against dismissal and judicial salaries are controlled by Parliament (Section 7.7.3.1).

There is a Judicial Appointments and Conduct Ombudsman who can investigate complaints both by and against judges (Constitutional Reform Act 2005, ss 110–14). However the Ombudsman cannot take complaints direct from the public and has power only to investigate whether internal complaints procedures have been handled without maladministration. The Ombudsman reports to the Lord Chancellor and Lord Chief Justice. The report is not published.

7.5 Functional separation of powers

We shall now outline the main concerns of the separation of powers in the UK. Some of these are developed in later chapters. We shall distinguish between separation of functions, separation of personnel, and checks and balances.

The executive function is distinct in that it must be proactive in identifying tasks and taking action whereas the legislature and judiciary are passive in the sense that they are triggered only when specific matters are placed before them. In the case of Parliament this is usually by the executive but also by individual members. Most laws are prepared and drafted by the executive so that Parliament's separate function lies in it having the last word to bring a law into effect.

The judiciary is also passive. A court exercising a judicial function cannot initiate action but must respond to disputes which others bring before it. Thus the judiciary is often claimed to be the 'least dangerous branch', having no weapons at its disposal and having no particular axe to grind. Moreover it is contrary to judicial independence that a judge should be required to advise the executive other than in a case properly brought before the court.

However if, as Montesquieu thought, a judicial function is essentially the resolution of a dispute based on the finding of facts and the application of the existing law to those facts, there is no clear distinction between the judicial and the executive. An executive decision involves a policy choice as to what is the best thing to do but many executive decisions include a judicial component. For example a local authority decision to grant permission for a nightclub in a residential area may well involve a dispute between the owner and local residents as to whether the club is causing a nuisance. A decision by a government minister whether to prohibit a company takeover in the interests of competition has a judicial element but may also raise political considerations which take it into the executive sphere. Decisions of this kind are sometimes called 'quasi judicial' and raise concerns as to the extent to which the minister must be impartial as if he or she were a judge (Section 18.4). The question of what is a judicial function attracting the distinctive features of the judicial process has caused difficulty, notably in connection with the law of contempt of court and until it was circumvented in the 1960s in connection with the common law right to a fair hearing (Section 18.3).

Indeed whether a matter is 'executive' or 'judicial' may depend not on any of its natural quality but on the mechanism chosen to deal with it. For example imposing a penalty by a court is a judicial function but arguably an 'administrative penalty' such as a parking ticket imposed by a local official, is not. Unlike a court, a minister or a traffic warden, can seek out people to penalise by setting up investigations.

7.5.1 Parliament and the executive

The functions of Parliament and the executive are distinct in that Parliament has the last word on legislation and provides checks and balances to hold to executive to account (Section 7.7). The executive cannot make law within the UK (as opposed to some overseas territories (Section 9.6)) without the authority of Parliament. However the overlap of personnel between Parliament and the executive makes the separation of powers fragile (Section 7.6).

There is considerable overlap between the functions of Parliament and executive in that while Parliament has no executive functions (except in relation to its own internal affairs) the executive is involved in lawmaking. Firstly the executive is responsible in practice for most legislative proposals. Secondly the bulk of English legislation consists of delegated or secondary or subordinate legislation (the terms being synonymous) made directly by ministers and other executive bodies under powers conferred by statute

Such statutes typically lay down a general principle conferring power upon a minister to make detailed rules fleshing it sometimes with restrictions protecting basic rights. Delegated lawmaking powers may be very wide, even permitting the minister to alter Acts of Parliament past or future (the 'Henry VIII' clause; eg Regulatory Reform Act 2006). It is also common for a statute to come into effect only when a minister triggers it.

Delegated legislation comes under many names, including regulations, orders, directions, rules and bylaws. Little hinges on the terminology used. However a compendium term, 'statutory instrument', applies to most delegated legislation made by ministers and to Statutory Orders in Council issued by the Privy Council (but in fact made by ministers) (Statutory Instruments Act 1946). Statutory instruments must be formally published, and, in accordance with the rule of law, it is a defence in criminal proceedings to show that an instrument has not been published and that it is not reasonable to expect the accused to be aware of it (s 4). However it seems that failure to publish does not affect validity for other purposes (see *R v Sheer Metalcraft* [1954] 1 All ER 542).

Delegated legislation has often been criticised as an infringement of the separation of powers. It can be made without the public and democratic processes represented, albeit imperfectly, by Parliament. However it is difficult to imagine a complex and highly regulated society that could function effectively if all laws had to be made by Parliament itself (see *Report of the Committee on Ministers' Powers* (Cmd 4060, 1932)). Most delegated legislation is subject to a limited amount of parliamentary scrutiny by means of being laid before the House, although this is usually nominal. There are also committees that scrutinise statutory instruments (see Section 13.5.5).

Unlike a statute the validity of delegated legislation, even if it has been approved by Parliament, can be challenged in the courts as can all executive action.

Delegated legislation must be distinguished from what is often called 'quasi-legislation'. This comprises rules, standards, policies, guidance or advice issued for example in circulars by the government without statutory authority to make rules. Quasi legislation is not strictly binding but must be taken into account and is in practice normally followed.

There is an important separation between Parliament and the executive in that the executive can make and ratify treaties binding in international law but a treaty cannot alter rights and duties in domestic law unless confirmed by statute (Section 9.6).

7.5.2   Parliament and the judiciary

Our common law system means that the judges are also lawmakers and their function is not confined to interpreting laws made by others. There are certain checks and balances, although these depend on the judges restraining themselves. One such check is the judges' duty to follow precedent so as to limit the possibility of making up new law according to a judge's personal preferences. Another is that the judges must make their law only in the context of the particular case before them and must avoid changing the law in matters of large social significance. For example in *Nicklinson v Ministry of Justice* [2012] EWCA (Admin) the court would not extend the law to enable a doctor to assist a sufferer who could not do so himself to commit suicide. The constitutional reason for this was that a radical change in a socially sensitive area that affected many people was outside the powers of the court.

Another limit is the principle that a court must give way to Parliament. In *WH Smith Do It All Ltd v Peterborough City Council* [1991], Mustill LJ remarked that:

> according to the doctrine of the separation of powers as understood in the UK, the legislative acts of the Queen in Parliament are impregnable. (at 196)

Parliament and the courts avoid interfering with each other. A court cannot usually investigate parliamentary proceedings or challenge statements made in Parliament (*Pickin v British Railways Board* [1974] AC 765). However the courts can perhaps decide whether statutory requirements have been complied with even where they relate to parliamentary processes (*R (Jackson) v A-G* [2005] 4 All ER 1253; see Section 8.4.3). In relation to its own composition and internal affairs the House of Commons has exclusive power to decide disputes and punish offenders (see Section 11.6.2).

According to the internal law of Parliament cases in progress should not be discussed except in relation to matters of national importance or the conduct of ministers and there should be no criticism of a judge's personal character, competence or motives except on a substantive motion for his dismissal, although backbenchers but not ministers may criticise individual judgements (Erskine May, *Treatise on the Law, Privilege, Proceedings and Usage of Parliament* (Butterworths 1997) 383–84, 542–43). By convention ministers do not answer questions on cases in progress.

7.5.3 The executive and the judiciary

Although judges are in theory Crown servants, from the seventeenth century it was established that the King cannot act as a judge himself (see *Prohibitions del Roy* [1607]). There is now a strong separation between the courts and the executive which has been endorsed by the judges. As Lord Steyn put it in *R (Anderson) v Secretary of State* (2002): '[o]ur constitution has never embraced a rigid doctrine of separation of powers. The relationship between the legislature and executive is close. On the other hand, the separation of powers between the judiciary and the legislative and executive branches of government is a strong principle of our system of government' (at [39]).

In the same case Lord Bingham emphasised that '[t]he European Court was right to describe the complete functional separation of the judiciary from the executive as "fundamental" since the rule of law depends on it' (at [27]). (See also Lord Templeman in *M v Home Office* [1993] at 540; Lord Hoffmann in *R (Pro-Life Alliance) v BBC* [2003] at 997; Lords Nicholls and Hope in *Wilson v First County Trust* [2003] at 116, 130; Lord Diplock in *Duport Steels v Sirs* [1980] at 157; Sir John Donaldson in *R v HM Treasury, ex p Smedley* [1985] at 593.)

M v Home Office [1993] concerned whether the court could treat the Home Secretary, a minister of the Crown, as being in contempt of court for disobeying a court order. The court rejected the argument that because the courts and ministers were both historically part of the Crown, the Crown would in effect be in contempt of itself. At first instance Simon Brown J ([1992] at 107), citing Montesquieu, pointed out that at least since the seventeenth century the courts had been recognised as an institution separate from the Crown itself and that the Queen had only a symbolic relationship with the three branches of government. Moreover a minister exercising powers conferred on him by law was not to be treated as part of the Crown since to do so, as Lord Templeman remarked (at 540), would undo the consequences of the Civil War. Similarly in *R (Bancoult) v Secretary of State for the Foreign and Commonwealth Office (No 2)* [2008] the House of Lords held that it had jurisdiction to review a Prerogative Order in Council since such an order was in reality made by ministers not the Crown itself.

The executive sometimes makes judicial decisions in the sense of deciding a legal dispute when it decides for example whether a given person is entitled to a welfare payment or a school place. Indeed ministers are often required to decide appeals against government decisions, even those in which their own department has an interest. However this does not violate the right to a fair trial under the ECHR, at least where the decision is one based on policy as opposed to one based on findings of prescribed facts, provided that there is the safeguard of judicial review by the courts (*R (Alconbury Developments) v Secretary of State* [2001] 2 All ER 929 (Section 21.4.2)). What the separation of powers importantly requires is that each body should have the last word in relation to its particular function. Thus by judicial review the courts can review executive action and have the last word as to what a law means.

Before the Constitutional Reform Act 2005 the office of Lord Chancellor violated the separation of functions in respect of all three branches. Often described as a walking contradiction of the separation of powers, the mediaeval office was the nominal head of the judiciary and was responsible for most judicial appointments. The Lord Chancellor was entitled to sit as judge and did so from time to time. The Lord Chancellor also presided over the House of Lords but unlike the Speaker of the Commons had no power to control proceedings since the House regulates itself collectively. More importantly the Lord Chancellor, also known as the Secretary of State for Justice, is the minister responsible for the administration of the courts, legal aid, human rights, constitutional reform and the electoral system. There is a clear conflict of interest in that as a member of the government the Lord Chancellor my be required to place financial restrictions on the courts. Unlike for example the USA, separation of powers does not extend to the courts administering their own budgets.

The 2005 Act which addressed these matters (below) attracted considerable opposition from the legal establishment. It was argued that the overlapping roles of the Lord Chancellor supported rather than infringed the separation of powers by acting as a buffer or lubricant between the three branches. As a member of the House of Lords and therefore unelected, he had a certain independence from party politics. As a spending minister, he could seek to ensure that the courts are properly resourced, and as a judge could defend the judiciary against executive interference. Moreover it was suggested that the antiquity of the office is evidence that it is good and that tradition and continuity should be respected. This kind of argument succeeded in so far as the historic title and ceremonial trappings of the office have been retained.

On the other hand as a member of the government, the Lord Chancellor is bound by collective ministerial responsibility (see Section 15.7.1). Like other ministers the Lord Chancellor is appointed and dismissed by the Prime Minister and has no security of tenure to stand up to the Prime Minister.

The Constitutional Reform Act 2005 removes the Lord Chancellor as Speaker of the House of Lords, which now elects its own Speaker. He also ceases to be head of the judiciary, transferring this role to the Lord Chief Justice as President of the Courts of England and Wales (s 7).

The Lord Chancellor is now primarily an ordinary minister, remaining in charge of the Ministry of Justice, which controls the administrative and financial aspects of the courts. In the absence of a separate budget controlled by the courts this places judicial independence at risk (Section 7.4). The Lord Chancellor retains a role in connection with the appointment of judges (Section 7.7.3). The Lord Chancellor like all ministers must be a member of Parliament but need not be a member of the House of Lords. The office holder must be qualified by experience as a minister or member of either House of Parliament, or practising or academic lawyer (Constitutional Reform Act 2005, s 2). Thus the Lord Chancellor need not have a legal background and can be moved around in ministerial reshuffles or sacked liked any other minister. This is not supportive of judicial independence. The previous Lord Chancellor Keneth Clarke was a barrister and served for two years. The current Lord Chancellor, appointed in 2012, Chris Grayling has no legal experience. As Minister for Justice he is currently piloting measures adversely affecting judicial pensions and legal aid.

The direct access that judges had to Parliament through the Lord Chancellor is replaced by section 5(1), which empowers the Chief Justice of any part of the UK to lay before Parliament or the relevant devolved assembly written representations on matters relating to the judiciary or the administration of justice that appear to him to be of importance. On appointment the Lord Chancellor must swear an oath to protect the rule of law and judicial independence and 'to discharge my duty to ensure the provision of resources for the efficient and effective support of the courts for which I am responsible' (s 17). The Lord Chancellor also has a responsibility to protect judicial independence (Section 7.4).

The Attorney General also has conflicting roles, being a member of the government and of Parliament and the government's chief legal adviser. He plays a part in the judicial process, particularly in relation to decisions to prosecute and is responsible for bringing legal actions against public bodies on behalf of the public interest (Section 15.6). The distinction between the executive advising as to the public interest in relation to a prosecution and bringing pressure to bear is a blurred one (see *R (Corner House Research) v Director General of the Serious Fraud Office* [2008]).

Until recently the separation of powers was violated in that the Home Secretary played a prominent role in the sentencing process. For example the Home Secretary could decide the 'tariff' period that must be served in a life sentence before the prisoner became eligible for release on parole. The Home Secretary could also control the sentences of young persons imprisoned indefinitely 'at Her Majesty's pleasure'. In a series of cases the European Court has held that the involvement of the executive in the sentencing process is normally a violation of the right to a fair trial (ECHR, Art 6; see *R (Anderson) v Secretary of State for the Home Dept* [2002]; *Benjamin v UK* [2002] 13 BHRC 287; *V v UK* [1999] 30 EHRR 121). English law has removed the Home

Secretary's power in most contexts in favour of a judge or the independent Parole Board (eg Criminal Justice and Court Services Act 2000, s 60; Criminal Justice Act 2003, s 269).

However in *R (Black) v Justice Secretary* [2009] UKHL 1 the House of Lords (Lord Phillips dissenting) upheld the power of the Home Secretary to override the Parole Board in the case of a 'determinate' sentence, meaning a sentence for a fixed period. The reason for distinguishing between determinate and indeterminate sentences is that, in the case of a determinate sentence, the sentence has already been decided by a judge. Any later intervention by the Home Secretary can therefore be considered not as part of the sentencing process but a matter of prisoner management. However their Lordships suggested that the involvement of the Home Secretary although lawful was an undesirable anomaly.

A similar distinction can be drawn between fixing a sentence and the royal prerogative of mercy, which allows the executive to release a prisoner, for example on compassionate grounds or where new evidence comes to light throwing doubt on the conviction. It is arguable that the politically accountable executive is the most appropriate body to exercise this kind of power. Thus the executive should periodically review an indefinite sentence, at least in the case of a young person, in order to refer it to the relevant body for possible reduction (*R (Smith) v Secretary of State for the Home Dept* [2006] I All ER 407). The prerogative of mercy remains with the Home Secretary, who can refer the matter to the independent Criminal Appeals Board, which can also directly refer doubtful convictions to the Court of Appeal (Criminal Appeals Act 1995).

Magistrates clerks are members of the civil service (Courts Act 2003) but have certain judicial functions and also advise magistrates on the law, participating in their private deliberations. The Courts Act 2003 makes some concession to their independence by providing that when exercising judicial functions they are not subject to directions from the Lord Chancellor or any other person (s 29). The activities of magistrates clerks do not violate judicial independence provided the clerk advises only on matters of law and procedure and not the actual decision, and any matters that the parties might wish to comment upon are raised in open court (*Clark (Procurator Fiscal Kirkcaldy) v Kelly* [2003] 1 All ER 1106). It is difficult to see how these protections are safeguarded given that the deliberations are in private. In *Kelly* the Privy Council relied on the 'well understood conventions' and the clerk's professional code as safeguards.

Another vital safeguard in the criminal process is that juries should not be vetted by the executive (*R v Crown Court at Sheffield, ex p Brownlow* [1980]) and cannot be required to give reasons for their verdicts or punished for giving or failing to give a verdict (*Bushell's Case* (1670)). It is an offence for anyone to publish information as to what was said in a jury room (Contempt of Court Act 1981, s 8(1)).

It is important for judicial independence that judges have no duty to advise the executive. However judges are sometimes appointed to carry out investigations or inquiries into allegations against government or significant incidents. This carries the risk of compromising the independence of the judiciary by making them appear to be involved in politics (eg the Scott Report into arms sales to Iraq (HC 1995–96, 115) and the Hutton Report into the death of a government adviser in the context of the decision to invade Iraq (HC 2004, 247)). In some countries, such as the US and Australia, the practice of judicial inquiries of this kind is unconstitutional (see Drewry, 'Judicial Inquiries and Public Reassurance' [1996] PL 368; Woodhouse, 2004, 140). As part of the 'concordance' between judges and Parliament entered into in relation to the constitutional reforms of

2005, a senior judge must be consulted on any proposal to appoint a judge of the rank of circuit judge or above to hold an inquiry under section 10(1) of the Inquiries Act 2005 (Section 7.6.3).

Largely for historical reasons (they were once connected with the royal prerogative and the jurisdiction of the Lord Chancellor), some functions are exercised by courts which might be regarded as executive in that they do not necessarily involve disputes. However they are matters requiring impartiality. They include the supervision of charities (shared with the Charity Commission), aspects of the care of children, the winding up of companies and the administration of the estates of deceased persons.

Finally many judicial functions are exercised by special tribunals. These were once called 'administrative tribunals' but are today largely incorporated into the judicial system (Section 20.1).

7.6   Separation of personnel

In view of the risk of bias or conflict of interest, the same individuals should not be members of more than one of the three branches or exercise more than one function. This principle has traditionally been applied pragmatically and not consistently and against a background in which members, all branches of government are usually selected from the same networks of personal associates.

We have already seen that the UK constitution does not comply with this, most importantly by its requirement that ministers must also be members of Parliament. In theory this strengthens executive accountability to Parliament. In practice, due to the subservience of MPs, it enables the executive to dominate Parliament. Ambivalence between the minister's two capacities is most notable in connection with the problems of ministerial responsibility to Parliament and enables the executive to control parliamentary procedure.

7.6.1   Parliament and the executive

The overlap between Parliament and the executive is at the heart of the political constitution. All ministers must also be members of Parliament and executive business has priority in parliamentary procedure. This strengthens the accountability of ministers while ensuring that government business can be achieved without the gridlock that a strict separation between Parliament and the executive could produce. In the nineteenth century Bagehot (1963, 68) described the Cabinet as 'a hyphen which joins, a buckle which fastens the legislative part of the state to the executive part of the state. In its origin it belongs to the one, in its functions it belongs to the other'. However the balance between the two elements is fragile and it is widely believed that the pressures of the modern party system have tipped it in favour of the executive (Section 5.10).

There is some separation of personnel between Parliament and the executive. Not more than 95 ministers can sit and vote in the Commons (House of Commons (Disqualification) Act 1975, s 2(1)), thus preventing the government from packing the Commons with supporters. Other ministers can be members of the House of Lords without apparent limit. However there are limits on the number of ministers who can be paid (Ministerial and Other Salaries Acts 1975, 1997). Nevertheless there seem to be no shortage of MPs willing to be unpaid junior ministers known as parliamentary private secretaries, who under the convention of collective responsibility (Section 15.6) must be loyal to the executive.

Certain officials for whom conflicts of role are especially likely (civil servants, police, regulators, members of the armed forces and so on) cannot be members of the Commons (but there are no such disqualifications from membership of the House of Lords (Section 12.4)).

7.6.2   Parliament and the judiciary

Separation of personnel between Parliament and the judiciary is especially important and has mainly been upheld in the UK. In particular full time judges cannot be members of elected bodies (eg House of Commons (Disqualification) Act 1975). There are however no analogous disqualifications for membership of the House of Lords. The original members of the Supreme Court (Section 7.4) who were formerly law lords remain life peers and so can still sit in the House of Lords but subsequent appointments are unlikely to be given peerages while in office.

7.6.3   The executive and the judiciary

Here the separation of powers is at its strictest. Within the UK (but not necessarily in dependent territories) there is no overlap of personnel between the executive and the judiciary. Such problems as arise concern overlapping functions (above).

7.7   Checks and balances

Checks and balances involve each branch having some control over the others but also require each branch to be protected against interference by the others. The checks and balances concept may therefore conflict with other aspects of the separation of powers. In the UK, in keeping with the 'insider' tradition, but violating republican aspirations to equality and citizenship, many checks and balances, such as the various commissions and committees dealing with standards of government, are not legally enforceable.

Readers should identify examples of checks and balances throughout the book. Some highlights will briefly be discussed here.

7.7.1   Parliament and the executive

The checks and balances between Parliament and the executive are at the heart of the political constitution. They are made uncertain by the overlapping membership of the House of Commons and the domination by the executive of the procedures of the House.

▶ The legislature is protected against the executive by statute and convention (Section 11.3). The legislature can remove the executive but as a result of the Fixed Term Parliaments Act 2011 the executive can no longer remove the legislature. The royal prerogative power to dissolve Parliament has been superseded by the Act, thus what Montesquieu regarded as an essential balance in the constitution no longer exists. For example a government that struggles against a obstructive Parliament would be unable to call for an election so as to put its case to the people.

- Parliament votes funds to the executive to enable the government to carry on.
- The executive must resign if it loses the support of the House of Commons. If an alternative government cannot command the support of the Commons, Parliament must be dissolved (Fixed Term Parliaments Act 2011, Section 11.3).
- Individual ministers must appear before Parliament and explain the conduct of their departments (Section 15.7).
- The House of Lords, the composition of which is not dominated by the executive, could be regarded a partial check over the executive. However under the Parliament Acts 1911 and 1949 the House of Lords cannot veto a bill introduced in the Commons, other than a bill to prolong the life of Parliament and certain other minor exceptions. In *R (Jackson) v A-G* (2005) the House of Lords disagreed but left open whether there might be exceptional cases – for example where the executive was attempting to subvert fundamental democratic principles or abolish judicial review – where the Parliament Acts could not be used (Section 11.4).

7.7.2 Parliament and the judiciary

According to traditional doctrine Parliament has unlimited lawmaking power and an Act of Parliament cannot be overturned in the courts. Thus Parliament can overturn any judicial decision (eg *Burmah Oil Co v Lord Advocate* (1965), War Damage Act 1965). The courts also check Parliament since they have power to interpret statutes independently. On the other hand the intentions of the democratic branch must be respected, so a compromise must be struck based on the limits of interpretation, although these are uncertain. In *Duport Steels Ltd v Sirs* [1980] 1 All ER 529, Lord Scarman said:

> the constitution's separation of powers, or more accurately functions, must be observed if judicial independence is not to be put at risk ... confidence in the judicial system will be replaced by fear of it becoming uncertain and arbitrary in its application. Society will then be ready for Parliament to cut the power of the judges. (at 551)

He meant that judges must observe the separation of powers by sticking to the language of legislation even at the expense of their own views of justice or policy. The orthodox view is that the courts must seek the 'intention of Parliament'. However given that Parliament is a complex assembly of many hundred people, the notion of intention is to some extent a fiction. Parliament is assumed to give words their 'natural' or 'ordinary' meaning and to intend that a statute should be read against the background of basic values associated with rule of law. More controversially the courts may assume, at least where ordinary meaning is unclear, that Parliament intended to comply with international treaty obligations. Furthermore the intention of Parliament must be found primarily by reading the statute not by giving effect to what the government thought it meant (see *R (Q) v Secretary of State for the Home Dept* [2003] 2 All ER 905 [4], [5]).

In relation to statutory interpretation *Pepper v Hart* [1993] 1 All ER 42 presents problems. The traditional approach has been that the courts should not look at what was said in Parliament as an aid to statutory interpretation. The intention of Parliament is assumed to be identified by the objective language of the statute not only to endorse judicial independence but also because the rule of law implies that a statute should be read as understood by a member of the public (see Lord Hoffmann in

Robinson v Secretary of State for Northern Ireland [2002] at [40]). However the courts can consider background material such as official reports as evidence of the policy behind a statute, a distinction that might be regarded as artificial.

In *Pepper v Hart* the House of Lords held that, where the language of an Act is ambiguous, the court can look in *Hansard* (the official record of the proceedings of the House) to discover what the promoters of the Act (usually ministers) intended. Thus if applied liberally *Pepper v Hart* could threaten the separation of powers and the rule of law by putting the executive in a privileged position. A statute is the collective enterprise of Parliament, over which the executive should not have special control.

In *R (Jackson) v A-G* (2005) at [97] Lord Steyn suggested that trying to discover the intentions of government from ministerial statements made in Parliament is constitutionally objectionable and the cases have taken a cautious and reluctant approach to *Pepper v Hart*, emphasising that it is for the courts to decide what a statute means and that the statements of ministers cannot control the meaning (see *R (Public and Commercial Services Union v Minister for the Civil Service* [2010] EWHC (admin) 1027 at [42], [53]–[55]). It has also been stressed that such statements have not generally proved helpful and that *Pepper v Hart* should be applied strictly according to its particular circumstances – namely where the legislation is obscure or ambiguous or would lead to absurd results, and then only if the statements to be used are clear (*R v Secretary of State for Environment, Transport and the Regions, ex p Spath Holme* [2000] 1 All ER 884 at [211]; *Wilson v First County Trust* [2003] 4 All ER 97 at [58], [59], [139], [140]; *R (Jackson) v A-G* (2005) at [40], [98], [172]. In *Spath Holme* a distinction was made between the meaning of a specific provision and the general purpose of an Act. A minister's statement in *Hansard* cannot be used to determine the latter unless the executive attempts to enforce a statute in a way that contradicts a statement made by the minister when promoting the statute in Parliament. Here the executive might be prevented from contradicting what was said. Lords Nicholls and Cook dissenting found this distinction artificial.

In *Wilson* the House of Lords held that, apparently in all cases, *Hansard* can be used to discover factual and policy background to an Act, including its likely impact, but not to evaluate ministerial statements as to its rationale. For example in *Culnane v Morris* (2006) the court was aided by the parliamentary debates in concluding that section 10 of the Defamation Act 1952 was not aimed at altering the general law relating to privilege in defamation (see Section 22.5; see also *Beckett v Midlands Electricity plc* [2001] 1 WLR 281 at [30], [34], [38]).

The Humans Rights Act 1998 attempts to strike a balance between the three branches by requiring the courts to scrutinise acts of all three branches in the light of the main provisions of the ECHR and to interpret legislation if possible to comply with the ECHR. However Parliament can override Convention rights by using very clear language. The court cannot set aside such an Act but can make a non-binding declaration of incompatibility in respect of an Act that it considers to be incompatible with the ECHR (Section 20.3).

The courts cannot interfere with internal parliamentary proceedings, give orders to Parliament or penalise anyone in respect of things said in Parliament. However statements made in Parliament can be used as evidence in court and the courts can decide the limits of Parliament's privileges (Sections 11.6.2, 11.6.3).

7.7.3 The executive and the judiciary

The Lord Chancellor as head of the Ministry of Justice has responsibility for the court system. This requires checks and balances to meet the competing concerns of judicial independence and public accountability (Section 7.4).

7.7.3.1 Security of tenure

Senior judges – that is judges of the High Court and above – have security of tenure designed to protect their independence. As a result of the 1688 revolution they hold office during 'good behaviour' (Act of Settlement 1700, provisions now repealed). In itself this is hardly conducive to independence since what matters is who decides whether they have misbehaved. Today they can be dismissed by the Crown following a resolution of both Houses of Parliament (an important constitutional check in the hands of the House of Lords) and probably then only for misbehaviour (Supreme Court Act 1981, s 11(3); Appellate Jurisdiction Act 1876, s 6). An alternative interpretation of these provisions less sympathetic to the separation of powers is that the Crown (ie the Prime Minister) can dismiss a judge for misbehaviour without an address from Parliament, but on an address a judge can be dismissed irrespective of misbehaviour. Section 33 of the Constitutional Reform Act 2005, which applies similar provisions to the new Supreme Court, continues the ambiguity. No judge has been subjected to these provisions since the nineteenth century, when a judge was dismissed for embezzling court funds.

In the case of judges of Northern Ireland and Scotland there is additional safeguard of a Special Tribunal (Constitutional Reform Act 2005, ss 133, 135; Scotland Act 1998, s 95).

In exceptional circumstances judges can be removed by the Lord Chancellor on medical grounds (Supreme Court Act 1981, s 11(8)). The Lord Chancellor can also suspend a judge pending an address or on grounds of criminality (s 108). Senior judges must retire at 70 (Judicial Pensions and Retirement Act 1993).

Other judges do not have full security of tenure. They hold office under various statutes that make different provisions for dismissal.

▶ Circuit and district judges can be dismissed by the Lord Chancellor for incapacity or misbehaviour (Courts Act 1971, s 17; County Courts Act 1984, s 11; Courts Act 2003, s 22).

▶ Lay magistrates can be removed by the Lord Chancellor for incapacity or misbehaviour, persistent failure to meet standards of competence prescribed by the Lord Chancellor and declining or neglecting their duties (Courts Act 2003, s 11).

▶ Justices' clerks, who advise lay justices, are civil servants and have no security of tenure. They are appointed by the Lord Chancellor (Courts Act 2003, s 27), and can presumably be dismissed on the same basis as other civil servants.

▶ Part-time judges (recorders) who hear criminal cases are appointed for fixed periods renewable by the Lord Chancellor (Courts Act 1971). This could be regarded as threatening judicial independence and the right to a fair trial under Article 6 ECHR (see *Millar v Dickson* (2002), Section 7.4).

▶ Tribunal members (Section 20.1) are usually appointed for fixed terms either by a minister or by the Lord Chancellor and in some cases can be dismissed only with the consent of the Lord Chancellor.

▶ Most judicial salaries can be reduced only by Parliament (Judges' Remuneration Act 1965; Constitutional Reform Act 2005, s 14). However the Lord Chancellor can increase salaries (Supreme Court Act 1981, s 12, Constitutional Reform Act 2005, s 34).

7.7.3.2 Judicial appointments

The executive has an input into judicial appointments on the basis that a democratically accountable element is desirable. A strong democratic input such as the hearings by Congress used in the US would create a risk that judicial appointments and behaviour would be politically partisan. On the other hand since judges make decisions with political consequences and have considerable scope to be influenced by political preferences it is arguable that their political views should be brought into the open.

There are checks and balances to safeguard judicial appointments. These were put in place by the Constitutional Reform Act 2005, replacing a much criticised informal regime for judicial appointments which was in the hands of the Lord Chancellor and, in the case of appointments to the Court of Appeal and House of Lords, the Prime Minister. The centrepiece of the new process is an independent Judicial Appointments Commission, which in substance makes most judicial appointments. However there is still a limited political input by the Lord Chancellor.

Appointments are made either by the Queen on the recommendation of the Lord Chancellor or in the case of lay magistrates and certain other junior judges by the Lord Chancellor directly (Constitutional Reform Act 2005, s 14; Courts Act 2003, s 10). The Lord Chancellor can recommend or appoint only a person selected by the Judicial Appointments Commission or in the case of Supreme Court judges and certain senior judicial officers a special commission or panel.

There are elaborate arrangements to ensure the independence of the Commission. Its 15 members are appointed by the Queen on the recommendation of the Lord Chancellor. It must comprise a lay chair plus five judges, one of each level, one practising solicitor and barrister, one tribunal member, one lay magistrate and five lay members (Constitutional Reform Act 2005, Sch 12). The senior judicial element must be chosen by the Judges' Council, which is a representative body. The lay members must be selected by a panel of four persons. These comprise a lay chair (who must not be a lawyer, judge, MP or member of the Commission or its staff) selected by the Lord Chancellor with the agreement of the Lord Chief Justice, the Lord Chief Justice, a person nominated by the chair and the chair of the Commission. Civil servants are excluded from membership of the Commission. The Lord Chancellor, with the agreement of the Lord Chief Justice and subject to the approval of Parliament, can increase the number of members. Commissioners hold office for a fixed term that is renewable but cannot be more than ten years in total. They can be removed on the recommendation of the Lord Chancellor on the grounds of criminal conviction, bankruptcy, failure to perform duties, unfitness or inability.

The Supreme Court (Section 5.4), is subject to special provisions. Its first members were the existing law lords. Thereafter its members are appointed by the Queen on the recommendation of the Prime Minister, who has no discretion but must recommend the person notified to him by the Lord Chancellor, who in turn must recommend a person selected by a special Selection Commission (ss 26, 28). This Commission comprises the President and Deputy President of the Supreme Court and three member of the Judicial Appointments Commission one from each of England and Wales, Scotland

and Northern Ireland, nominated by the Lord Chancellor on the recommendation of the appropriate body. One member must be a lay person (Sch 8). The Commission must consult the senior judges, the Lord Chancellor and the leaders of the devolved governments.

Appointments of the Lord Chief Justice, Heads of Divisions and Lords Justices of Appeal are made by the Queen on the recommendation of the Lord Chancellor following selection by a special panel of four comprising the chair of the Commission, a lay member of the Commission and two prescribed judges (ss 67, 71, 76, 80). Similar provision applies to the Senior President of Tribunals (s 75(A–G)).

Appointments to the High Court and the lower courts are made by the Queen or the Lord Chancellor, in both cases following a selection by the Commission (s 85). The Lord Chancellor may request an appointment to be made and issue procedural guidance to the Commission (s 65).

All judicial appointments must be made solely on merit (s 63), subject to the appointee being of 'good character' (undefined). Subject to this, 'diversity' must be encouraged. Judges of the main courts and some tribunals have traditionally been appointed from a pool of experienced practising lawyers. Under sections 50 and 51 of the Tribunals Court and Enforcement Act 2007 this pool has been widened in the form of the 'judicial eligibility condition', which enables members of other designated professions such as legal executives and accountants to be eligible for judicial appointment. This contrasts with the position in other European countries where there is a separate judicial profession. The UK system has the advantage of drawing on talented people from outside government who are familiar with the workings of the court process. The disadvantage is to reinforce the perception of the legal system as a closed elite.

In relation to all levels of appointment the powers of the Lord Chancellor are similar (Constitutional Reform Act 2005, ss 29, 73, 82, 90). The commission or panel must submit one name to the Lord Chancellor, who cannot put forward any other name. He can reject a nomination or refer it back for reconsideration but in either case once only. He can reject only on the ground that the candidate is not 'suitable' and require reconsideration on the ground of inadequate evidence of suitability or evidence of unsuitability. He must give reasons. If the Lord Chancellor rejects a nomination, the same name cannot be put forward again for that vacancy. Where a selection has been referred for reconsideration and the same name is put forward the Lord Chancellor must accept it. If a different name is put forward he can reject this. However, where a selection has been referred for reconsideration and not chosen again, the Lord Chancellor can put forward the original name. In the case of the Supreme Court a reconsideration can also be required if the judges between them would not have knowledge or experience in practice of the law of each part of the UK.

These provisions are designed to make it difficult for any interest group to dominate the appointment process. However, given the vagueness of the appointment criteria and the fact that the government system in the UK is pervaded by informal personal networks, it is doubtful whether it is possible to ensure that the appointment process is fully independent or likely to widen the range of candidates.

These provisions do not apply to the appointments of lay magistrates or to tribunal appointments. Although magistrates deal with relatively minor matters they account for the majority of criminal cases. Magistrates are appointed by the Lord Chancellor (Courts Act 2003, s 10), who may seek advice from the Judicial Appointments Commission and must consult locally (Constitutional Reform Act 2005, s 106). Most tribunal members are appointed by the Lord Chancellor on the recommendation of the Commission, in some cases from a pool of specialists in the area of the tribunal's work.

7.7.3.3 Judicial review

The courts provide a check over the executive by means of judicial review in the Administrative Court, where they try to draw a line between the *legality* of government action, which they are entitled to police, and the *merits* of government action, meaning whether a government decision is good or bad, which is a matter for Parliament. However the limits of judicial review are vaguely defined. In some cases the courts will refuse to intervene or intervene only selectively. How this balance is struck is a controversial question (see Section 19.7.1).

▶ In *R v Secretary of State, ex p Fire Brigades Union* [1995] 2 All ER 244, Lord Mustill said:

> It is a feature of the peculiarly British conception of the separation of powers that Parliament, the executive and the courts each have their distinct and largely exclusive domain. Parliament has a legally unchallengeable right to make whatever laws it thinks right. The executive carries on the administration of the country in accordance with the powers conferred on it by law. The courts interpret the laws and see that they are obeyed. This requires the courts to step into the territory which belongs to the executive, not only to verify that the powers asserted accord with the substantive law created by Parliament, but also that the manner in which they are exercised conforms with the standards of fairness which Parliament must have intended. Concurrently with this judicial function Parliament has its own special means of ensuring that the executive in the exercise of delegated functions, performs in a way that Parliament finds appropriate. Ideally it is these latter methods which should be used to check executive errors and excesses; for it is the task of Parliament and the executive in tandem, not of the courts, to govern the country. In recent years however, the employment in practice of these specifically parliamentary remedies has on occasion been perceived as falling short and sometimes well short of what was needed to bring the performance of the executive in line with the law and with the minimum standards of fairness implicit in every parliamentary delegation of a decision making function. To avoid a vacuum in which the citizen would be left without protection against a misuse of executive powers the courts have had no option but to occupy the dead ground in a manner and in areas of public life, which could not have been foreseen 30 years ago. (at 267)

▶ In this case Lord Mustill was in a dissenting minority that refused to intervene in a decision of the Home Secretary not to make an order bringing into force a new Act dealing with criminal injuries compensation, but to introduce another, less generous scheme under royal prerogative powers. He considered that this was a matter for Parliament itself. The majority however considered that the matter was appropriate for the court as a check on executive discretion. They held that although they could not require the Home Secretary to bring the Act into force, they could quash the prerogative scheme and ensure that he kept the matter under review. Thus different aspects of the separation of powers may conflict.

7.7.3.4 Administrative independence

The Supreme Court has some administrative independence. The president may make procedural rules (Constitutional Reform Act 2005, s 45), and has its own staff and budget (s 49). However under the previous regime the House of Lords had special protection against the executive by virtue of parliamentary privilege (Section 11.6).

Summary

▶ The doctrine of the separation of powers means that government power should be divided into legislative, executive and judicial functions, each with its own distinctive personnel and processes, and that each branch of government should be checked so that no one can dominate the others.

▶ In Montesquieu's version, the separation of powers is complemented by the idea of the mixed constitution in which different class interests check and balance each other, particularly in the legislature. There is a vestige of the mixed constitution in the institutions of monarchy and the House of Lords. However the idea of the mixed constitution shorn of its historical association with a hereditary aristocracy might still be valuable as providing a check over crude majoritarian democracy, linking with the idea of deliberative democracy.

▶ The question of judicial independence can be regarded as an aspect of the separation of powers but could be considered an issue in its own right irrespective of other aspects of the doctrine. Judicial independence is safeguarded by the right to a fair trial and public trial under the ECHR. This applies more stringently to ordinary courts than to administrative bodies. There is a tension between judicial independence and ensuring that judges are accountable.

▶ The separation of powers comprises separation of function, institutions and personnel and includes the notion of checks and balances. The particular blend in any given case depends on the preoccupations of the particular country. There is little agreement among writers as to whether the separation of powers is a valuable idea or in what sense it applies in the UK. Separation of powers ideas have influenced our constitutional arrangements but in a pragmatic and unsystematic way.

▶ In the UK there is no strict separation of personnel, particularly between the legislature and the executive. Concern about executive domination is the main driving force.

▶ The Constitutional Reform Act 2005 attempted to strengthen the separation of powers by creating a Supreme Court to replace the Appellate Committee of the House of Lords, injecting an independent element into judicial appointments and removing the Lord Chancellor's roles as head of the judiciary and Speaker of the House of Lords. It could be that aspects of these reforms, particularly in relation to the Lord Chancellor, strengthen institutional separation but weaken checks and balances.

▶ The power of the courts to review government action creates a tension between functional separation of powers and checks and balances.

▶ There are concerns about the relationship between the courts and Parliament, in particular in the context of the use of parliamentary proceedings in the interpretation of statutes.

Exercises

7.1 'The separation of powers is a misleading and irrelevant doctrine'. Discuss.

7.2 'In the government of this commonwealth, the legislative department shall never exercise the executive and judicial powers, or either of them: the executive shall never exercise the legislative and judicial powers, or either of them: the judicial shall never exercise the legislative and executive powers, or either of them: to the end it may be a government of laws and not of men' (Massachusetts Constitution 1780, Art XXX). Does the UK constitution live up to this?

7.3 'The intermingling between the three aspects of the separation of powers in relation to Parliament makes the doctrine futile'. Discuss

Exercises cont'd

7.4 To what extent can the executive interfere with the courts?

7.5 'In some quarters the *Pepper v Hart* principle is currently under something of a judicial cloud ... In part this seems ... to be due to continued misunderstanding of the limited role ministerial statements have in this field' (Lord Nicholls in *R (Jackson) v A-G*, (2005) [65]). Explain and critically discuss.

7.6 The replacement of the Appellate Committee of the House of Lords 'put[s] the relationship between the executive, the legislature and the judiciary on a modern footing, which takes account of people's expectations about the independence and transparency of the judicial system' (Department of Constitutional Affairs, 2003). Discuss in the light of the Constitutional Reform Act 2005.

7.7 To what extent do the reforms made by the Constitutional Reform Act 2005 to the office of Lord Chancellor enhance judicial independence and the separation of powers?

7.8 The government is experiencing a financial crisis. In order to save money the Prime Minister proposes to the Lord Chancellor that no new appointments should be made to the staff of the Supreme Court for five years and that the court should refuse leave to appeal in at least 20 per cent of cases. Advise the Lord Chancellor.

7.9 Julian, a Senior Judge, is alleged to have been sexually harassing the junior staff of the High Court Registry. Parliament is not sitting and the Lord Chancellor advises the Queen to make an example of Julian by dismissing him forthwith. Advise Julian. What would be the position if he was (i) a circuit judge or (ii) a lay justice?

Further reading

Barber, 'Prelude to the Separation of Powers' (2001) 61 CLJ 59
Barendt, 'Separation of Powers and Constitutional Government' [1995] PL 599
Bradley, 'Relations between Executive, Judiciary and Parliament: An Evolving Saga,' [2008] PL 470
Clarke, *The Limits of Judicial Independence* (Cambridge University Press 2011)
Claus, 'Montesquieu's Mistakes and the True Meaning of Separation' (2005) 25 OJLS 419
Cooke, 'The Law Lords: An Endangered Heritage' (2003) 119 LQR 49
Department of Constitutional Affairs, *Constitutional Reform: A Supreme Court for the United Kingdom* (2003)
Ekins, 'The Intention of Parliament' [2010] PL 709
Ewing, 'The Unbalanced Constitution' in Campbell, Ewing and Tompkins (eds), *Sceptical Essays on Human Rights* (Oxford University Press 2001)
Hale, 'A Supreme Judicial Leader' in Andenas and Fairgrieve (eds), *Tom Bingham and the Transformation of the Law* (Oxford University Press 2009)
Kavanagh, '*Pepper v Hart* and Matters of Constitutional Principle' (2005) 121 LQR 98
Keene, 'The Independence of the Judge' in Andenas and Fairgrieve (eds), *Tom Bingham and the Transformation of the Law* (Oxford University Press 2009)
Loughlin, *Foundations of Public Law* (Oxford University Press 2010) ch 15
McHarg, 'What Is Delegated Legislation?' [2006] PL 539
Masterman, *The Separation of powers in the Contemporary Constitution: Judicial Competence and Independence in the United Kingdom* (Cambridge University Press 2011)

Further reading cont'd

Munro, *Studies in Constitutional Law* (2nd edn, Butterworths 1999) ch 9

Sedley, 'The Long Sleep' in Andenas and Fairgrieve (eds) *Tom Bingham and the Transformation of the Law* (Oxford University Press 2009)

Steyn, 'The Weakest and Least Dangerous Department of Government' [1997] PL 84

Steyn, '*Pepper and Hart*: A Re-examination' (2001) 21 OJLS 59

Vogenauer, 'A Retreat from *Pepper v Hart*? A Reply to Lord Steyn' (2005) 25 OJLS 629 (see also Sales, 'A Footnote to Professor Vogenauer's Reply to Lord Steyn' (2006) 26 OJLS 585)

Webber, 'Supreme Courts, Independence and Democratic Agency' (2004) 24 LS 55

Woodhouse, 'The Constitutional and Political Implications of a United Kingdom Supreme Court' (2004) 24 LS 134

Chapter 8

Parliamentary sovereignty

Introduction

The doctrine of parliamentary sovereignty maintains that Parliament has unlimited legal power to enact any law without external restraint. In *R (Jackson) v A-G* [2006] 1 AC 262, [9] Lord Bingham described the doctrine as the bedrock of the British constitution. The classical doctrine of parliamentary sovereignty was most famously stated by Dicey (1915, 37–38):

> Parliament means, in the mouth of a lawyer, ... the [Queen], the House of Lords and the House of Commons; these three bodies acting together may be aptly described as the '[Queen] in Parliament, and constitute Parliament'. The principle of parliamentary sovereignty means neither more nor less than this, namely, that Parliament thus defined has, under the English constitution, the right to make or unmake any law whatever and further that no person or body is recognised by the law of England as having the right to override or set aside the legislation of Parliament.

Parliamentary sovereignty is a legal principle, meaning that a law made by Parliament, in the above sense, must conclusively be accepted as valid by the courts (*Pickin v British Railways Board* [1974] AC 765). Dicey was careful to distinguish legal sovereignty from political sovereignty. He described legal sovereignty as 'the power of law making unrestricted by any legal limit' and contrasted this with political sovereignty, meaning the body 'the will of which is ultimately obeyed by the citizens of the state' (1915, 70). (There is however no reason that there should be a single sovereign in this sense; citizens might obey different bodies in different contexts.)

Dicey recognised both 'internal' and 'external' political limits on the lawmaker. Internal limits are those inherent in the rules and practices of Parliament. Within Parliament a combination of the convention that requires the Queen to assent to all legislation and the law that subordinates the House of Lords to the House of Commons makes the House of Commons the supreme political body. The political and moral pressures imposed by constitutional conventions, patronage and party discipline are also internal limits.

The external limits consist of what those subject to the law are prepared to accept. Parliament cannot in practice pass any law it wishes. Moreover valid laws might be condemned as unconstitutional in a broad sense. Thus in *Madzimbamuto v Lardner-Burke* [1969] 1 AC 645, Lord Reid said:

> [it] is often said that it would be unconstitutional for the UK Parliament to do certain things, meaning that the moral, political and other reasons against doing them are so strong that most people would regard it as highly improper if Parliament did these things. But that does not mean that it is beyond the powers of Parliament to do such things. If Parliament chose to do any of them the courts could not hold Parliament to account (at 723).

Dicey thought that political sovereignty lay in the electorate and that this would make democracy 'self-correcting' (see Craig, *Public Law and Democracy in the UK and the USA* (Oxford University Press 1991) ch 2). Later in life, particularly after the powers of the House of Lords were curbed in 1911, Dicey realised that the executive was increasingly dominating Parliament (1915, 'Introduction'). However we should not take an extreme legalistic position and claim that law and politics are entirely separate. Indeed judges have recognised that at the highest level of the constitution law and politics are inseparable (see *R (Jackson) v A-G* [2005] at [128]). Thus we might be concerned if the law is out of step with political reality.

For example devolution of substantial law making power to the devolved regimes of Scotland, Northern Ireland and Wales has not directly affected the legal principle of Parliamentary sovereignty (Section 16.1). However convention requires that Parliament should not legislate to override the devolved legislatures without their consent and it is possible that in the future the law itself might change as a result of political pressure. The Human Rights Act 1998 cannot strictly be used to override Parliament but a judicial decision that a statute is contrary to a right protected under the Act places strong pressure on Parliament (Section 22.3).

Dicey's version of the doctrine of parliamentary sovereignty is increasingly being questioned. Apart from the above mentioned political pressures challenges to parliamentary sovereignty include external legal requirements, notably those of the EU, and claims that the courts under the common law are the ultimate guardians of the constitution (Section 8.5).

8.2 The basis of parliamentary sovereignty

Since we have no written constitution the basis of parliamentary sovereignty is unclear. There is no logical reason, although it may be practically desirable why there should be a single legal sovereign with unlimited powers. Indeed Dicey himself denied that there was a logical need for an ultimate sovereign (1915, 143), merely pointing out that the evidence suggested that we have in fact adopted the doctrine of parliamentary sovereignty. For example in the US power is carefully divided so that no single entity has unlimited legal power.

It is sometimes argued that the rule of law in the shape of the common law is supreme since the courts voluntarily 'accorded' sovereignty to Parliament (Section 8.5.6). However this solution begs the question of where the common law gets its power. In support of 'common law constitutionalism' it might be argued that historically the common law derives its authority from the values of the community and that it predates Parliamentary sovereignty which emerged only during Tudor times (Section 4.4).

Perhaps the only feasible explanation of Parliamentary sovereignty is a political one, namely that there is sufficient general acceptance of Parliamentary sovereignty by officials including courts and by the public generally to make the doctrine effective (see Lord Hope in *R (Jackson) v A-G* [2005] at [120]). Effectiveness is the only basis of any constitution (Section 1.2). However according to Lakin (2008) the doctrine of parliamentary sovereignty is so uncertain that it is implausible to suppose that officials and the public have accepted it. Lakin argues that the doctrine is a myth and that only the law itself can determine what is legally valid. Lakin sees no need for a concept of sovereignty as such but prefers a network of legal principles in the hands of the courts as champions of political morality. However, Lakin's argument seems vulnerable to the same objection as he makes to the traditional doctrine, namely that political morality is uncertain and also depends ultimately upon widespread acceptance as a political fact. It is doubtful whether public opinion outside that of the legal profession would accept the sovereignty of the judges.

Wade (1955) argues that parliamentary sovereignty derives from a political event widely acknowledged as foundational namely the 1688 revolution, from which Parliament emerged triumphant over the Crown (Section 4.5). According to Wade this makes parliamentary sovereignty a unique kind of rule (a 'grundnorm' or foundational rule) a political principle standing outside and above the ordinary legal system and giving it its validity. Wade accepts that the doctrine of parliamentary sovereignty could be changed but would regard this as another revolution which creates an entirely new basic principle. How will we know whether such a revolution has taken place? Wade would place the matter in the 'keeping of the courts', who can authoritatively signify the 'revolution'. Indeed Wade has argued that the UK's entry to the EU is such a revolution (Section 8.5.4). This seems to make the rule both political and legal.

Wade's approach has several difficulties (see Gordon, 2009 and Section 8.5.3). Most fundamentally why should the courts be the guardians of the unique rule? Wade seems arbitrarily to substitute judicial sovereignty for parliamentary sovereignty. Surely it is for the courts to apply the existing law under the constitution not to declare what is the basis of the constitution. In the USA for example, in the foundational case of *Marbury v Madison* (1803) 1 Cranch 6 the Supreme Court held that it had the power to override unconstitutional legislation. Although the legitimacy of this remains controversial the court purported to find implicit authority for this in the written constitution itself a recourse not available in the UK. It would be equally plausible for Parliament to announce the revolution. Indeed In *Factortame v Secretary of State for Transport* [1991] 1 AC 603, 659 Lord Bridge took the view that parliamentary sovereignty can be altered by statute. If this is so then the doctrine is no more than a provisional working arrangement.

Whatever view is taken the courts have a role since they have to take a view on parliamentary sovereignty. They have to address any uncertainties in the doctrine where relevant to any case before them. However according to the conventional doctrine Parliament could undo any court decision.

8.3 The meaning of 'Act of Parliament'

Parliamentary sovereignty concerns only lawmaking power. Specifically it is concerned only with an Act of Parliament (a statute). An Act of Parliament, as the preamble to every Act reminds us, is an Act of the monarch with the consent of the House of Lords and the House of Commons (subject to the Parliament Acts 1911 and 1949 (below)): the Queen in Parliament (see Lord Steyn in *R (Jackson) v A-G* [2005] at [81]). Dicey's legal sovereign is therefore divided, comprising three bodies. Only in combination can they exercise the lawmaking power of Parliament. Even if we believe that the House of Commons is the political sovereign, a resolution of the House of Commons has no legal force, except in relation to the internal proceedings of the House (*Bowles v Bank of England* [1913] 1 Ch 57; *Stockdale v Hansard* (1839) 9 Ad & E 1).

Two questions arise from this. First, what rules create an Act of Parliament? Second, to what extent can the courts investigate whether these rules have been obeyed? There are complex procedural rules for producing statutes but not all of them affect the validity of a statute.

Three levels of rule can be distinguished:
1. The basic definition of an Act of Parliament (statute) as a document that received the assent of Queen, Lords and Commons. The royal assent signed by the Queen

is usually notified to each House separately as a formality but is sometimes pronounced by commissioners before both Houses assembled in the House of Lords (Royal Assent Act 1967). The preamble to a statute invariably recites that the required assents have been given. A court is not bound by a document that does not appear on its face to have received the necessary assents but conversely must accept the validity of a document that does so appear (*Prince's Case* [1606] 8 Co Rep 1). This is called the 'enrolled Act rule'. It prevents the courts from investigating whether the proper internal procedures have in fact been complied with (*Edinburgh & Dalkeith Rly v Wauchope* [1842] 8 Cl and F 710). The official version of a statute was traditionally enrolled upon the Parliament Roll. Today there is no Parliament Roll as such, but two official copies of the Act are in the House of Lords' Library and the Public Record Office.

2. In two cases the basic requirements have been modified by statute. Most importantly under the Parliament Acts 1911 and 1949, if the Commons so decides and subject to important exceptions, a bill can become law without the consent of the House of Lords after a prescribed delaying period (Section 11.4). The Parliament Act 1911 partly excludes the courts by providing that a certificate given by the Speaker to the effect that the requirements of the Act have been complied with is 'conclusive for all purposes and shall not be questioned in any court of law' (s 3). However this does not prevent the court from deciding the prior question of whether the bill falls within the 1911 Act at all (see *R (Jackson) v A-G* [2005] at [51]). In principle the court can investigate whether statutory requirements have been complied with short of investigating the internal proceedings within either House.

   Secondly the Regency Act 1937 provides that the royal assent can be given by a specified Regent, usually the next in line to the throne, if the monarch is under 18, absent abroad or ill and in certain other events. In this case the court may also be able to investigate whether the Act has been properly applied.

4. There is a complex network of rules concerning the composition and internal procedure of each House. These include the various stages of passage of a bill, voting procedures and the law governing qualifications for membership of either House. They comprise a mixture of statute, convention and the 'law and custom of Parliament' enforced by the House itself that the ordinary courts have no jurisdiction to enquire into any matters related to the internal affairs of the House. Apart from the enrolled Act rule (above), these are matters of parliamentary privilege and are exclusively within the jurisdiction of the House itself (Section 11.6). This is true even if it is alleged that the bill has been introduced fraudulently (*Pickin v British Railways Board* [1974]).

8.4 The three facets of parliamentary sovereignty

Dicey's doctrine has three separate aspects:

1. Parliament has unlimited lawmaking power in the sense that it can make any kind of law.
2. The legal validity of laws made by Parliament cannot be questioned by any other body.
3. A Parliament cannot bind a future Parliament.

8.4.1 Freedom to make any kind of law

Dicey claimed that Parliament can make any laws it wishes irrespective of fairness, justice and practicality. For example the UK courts are bound to obey a statute which concerns anywhere in the world. Whether or not the relevant overseas courts would recognise it is immaterial (eg *Manuel v A-G* [1982] 3 All ER 822: Canada). Parliament can also do the physically impossible. It has been said that Parliament cannot make a man a woman, or a woman a man, but this is misleading. The so-called laws of nature are not rules at all. They are simply recurrent facts. A statute which enacted that all men must be regarded as women and vice versa would be impractical but would be legally valid.

According to Dicey, Parliament can enact laws that are grossly immoral or unjust. Dicey relied on examples of valid statutory provisions that are arguably grossly unjust. However these do not prove that the courts would apply a statute that they considered even more unjust. Nevertheless modern cases support Dicey. They include retrospective legislation (*Burmah Oil Co Ltd v Lord Advocate* [1965]; War Damage Act 1965) and statutes conflicting with international law (*Mortensen v Peters* (1906) 14 SLT 227; *Cheney v Conn* [1968] 1 All ER 779) or with fundamental civil liberties (*R v Jordan* [1967] Crim LR 843).

8.4.2 Parliament cannot be overridden

Firstly, international bodies do not have the power in English law to declare an Act of Parliament invalid. International law can alter legal rights in the UK only if adopted by Parliament (Section 9.5.1). Secondly, in the event of a conflict between a statute and some other kind of law, the statute must always prevail. However this leaves open the possibility that a statute itself might authorise some other lawmaking authority to override statutes. This was probably achieved by the European Communities Act 1972 (Section 8.5.4) but still leaves it open to Parliament to repeal the Act in question, thereby destroying the authority of the other body.

8.4.3 Parliament cannot bind its successors

In a sense this is a limit on Parliament although it also means that Parliament cannot be restricted by a previous statute, so preserving parliamentary sovereignty. This is a vital principle closely associated with democracy in that no generation should be able to tie the hands of the future. For example Edmund Burke argued that the 1688 revolution had permanently enshrined a constitution which included the House of Lords. Thomas Paine answered this as follows:

> Every age and generation must be as free to act for itself, in all cases, as the ages and generations which preceded it. The vanity and presumption of governing beyond the grave is the most ridiculous and insolent of all tyrannies. (1987, 204)

Thus a statute cannot be protected against repeal. Indeed where a later statute conflicts with an earlier one, the later one may 'impliedly repeal' the earlier one. This is so even if the earlier statute states that it cannot be repealed (*Vauxhall Estates Ltd v Liverpool Corp* [1932] 1 KB 733; *Ellen Street Estates Ltd v Minister of Health* [1934] 1 KB 590). However there is a presumption against implied repeal which applies only where the two Acts are necessarily inconsistent (*Henry Boot Ltd v Malmaison Hotel Ltd* [2001] QB 388, 402). The more important the earlier statute the stronger is the presumption (*H v Lord Advocate* [2012] 3 All ER 151 [30]: devolution legislation (Section 16.1). The content of the two statutes must be directly inconsistent. For example in *Thoburn v Sunderland City Council* [2002] 4 All ER 156 (the 'Metric Martyrs' case) a 1985 statute which allowed goods to be sold in pounds and ounces did not impliedly repeal section 2(4) of the European Communities Act 1972, which empowered ministers to make regulations altering Acts of Parliament for the purpose of implementing EU law which required the use of metric measures. Thus the minister could alter the 1985 Act.

It must be stressed that the implied repeal doctrine is not an essential part of parliamentary sovereignty. Although consistent with parliamentary sovereignty, the implied repeal doctrine is merely a particular approach to statutory interpretation. Although Lord Maugham in *Ellen Street Estates (above)* at 597 said that it would be impossible to enact that there shall be no implied repeal this has not turned out to be so. There is nothing to prevent a statute from requiring the courts to interpret legislation as overriding another statute only if express or very clear language is used, thus putting a partial brake on change. For example section 3 of the Human Rights Act 1998 requires all other statutes to be interpreted in accordance with the rights protected by the Act 'if it is possible to do so' (Section 22.3.1). It has also been claimed that under the common law some statutes and some legal rights are so important that they can be repealed only by express words or possibly by necessary implication. In *Thoburn v Sunderland City Council* at [62]–[64], Laws LJ stated that a 'constitutional statute', in the sense of a statute 'which conditions the legal relationships between citizen and state in some general overarching manner, or enlarges or diminishes the scope of what are now regarded as fundamental rights', would be so protected. In this way Parliamentary sovereignty might to some extent be reconciled with the rule of law (Section 8.6).

8.5 Challenging parliamentary sovereignty

There are various arguments that Parliament can after all be legally limited. As we have seen the foundations of the doctrine rest only on general acceptance. In its origins parliamentary sovereignty was a historical response to political circumstances, namely as the focus for rebellion against the Stuart monarchs. It does not follow that the same response is appropriate today. The Victorian period, during which Dicey promoted the doctrine, was one of relative stability and prosperity. The people, or at least the majority, were benefiting from the spoils of empire, and the belief that Parliament, backed by democratic values, could deliver stability and prosperity was still plausible. Popular revolution as experienced elsewhere had been staved off by cautious reforms. Latterly, different forces, both domestic and international, have arisen which have made parliamentary sovereignty appear parochial, politically unreal and intellectually threadbare. These forces include the global economy, devolution, membership of the EU and other international obligations and the increasing powers of the executive over Parliament.

There is no longer a political consensus that Parliament should be legally unlimited and no compelling legal reason why it should be. The main challenges to parliamentary sovereignty are as follows.

8.5.1 Grants of independence

If Parliament were to pass an Act giving independence to a piece of territory currently under UK jurisdiction, such as Scotland, could a later Act revoke that independence? For example the Canada Act 1982 provides that 'no Act of the United Kingdom Parliament passed after the Constitution Act 1982 comes into force shall extend to Canada as part of its law' (s 2). The legal answer is yes as far as the UK courts are concerned (*British Coal Corp v R* [1935] AC 500; *Manuel v A-G* [1982]) although as was pointed out in British coal this has nothing to do with political reality since such a statute would be ignored in its target country. In *Blackburn v A-G* [1971] 2 All ER 1380 Lord Denning remarked that legal theory must give way to practical politics. All his Lordship seems to be saying is that it would be impossible in a practical sense for Parliament to reverse a grant of independence. On the other hand a legal principle that is so out of line with common sense might well be worth reconsidering.

In the early days of the dismantling of the British Empire the statute of Westminster 1931 conferred an ambivalent form of independence which retained a tie with Parliament. This provided that an Act of Parliament shall not extend to the territory in question (eg Australia) unless it has requested and consented to the enactment. This kind of procedural restriction raises special questions (Section 8.5.3)

8.5.2 The devolved countries: Acts of Union. Was Parliament born unfree?

This is a more substantial challenge. The UK Parliament is the result of two treaties. First the Treaty of Union with Scotland in 1706 created the Parliament of Great Britain out of the former Scottish and English Parliaments. The Treaty required among other things that no laws which concern private rights in Scotland shall be altered 'except for the evident utility of the subjects within Scotland'. There were also powers securing the separate Scottish courts and Presbyterian Church 'for all time coming'. The new Parliament was created by separate Acts of the then Scottish and English Parliaments, giving effect to the treaties.

Some Scottish lawyers therefore argue that Parliament was 'born unfree', meaning that the modern Parliament cannot go beyond the terms of the Acts that created it. They suggest that the protected provisions of the Act of Union cannot be altered by Act of Parliament. In effect the Union created a new Parliament combining the qualities of both the old Parliaments. In relation to the protected Scottish provisions, this does not necessarily have the quality of sovereignty inherent in the former English Parliament (see Munro, 1999, 137–42). A contrary argument is that parliamentary sovereignty is an evolving doctrine that developed after the Acts of Union. The current devolution provisions try to endorse parliamentary sovereignty (Section 16.1). Section 37 of the Scotland Act 1998 expressly states that the provisions of the Act are to take priority over the Act of Union.

The case of Northern Ireland is broadly similar. There was a Treaty of Union in 1798 which preserved certain basic rights in Ireland, including the continuance of the Protestant religion and the permanence of the Union itself. The Treaty was confirmed by the Act of Union with Ireland 1800, which created the present UK Parliament. The Act covered the whole of Ireland, but what is now the Republic of Ireland later left the Union. It might be argued that section 1 of the Northern Ireland Act 1998, which provides for the Union to be dissolved if a referendum so votes, would be invalid as contrary to the Act of Union. The 1998 Act makes no express reference to the Act of Union with Ireland, section 2 but provides that the Act overrides 'previous enactments'.

The issue has surfaced in a few cases, in all of which an Act of Parliament was obeyed. In *Ex p Canon Selwyn* [1872] 36 JP 54 (Ireland) the court denied that it possessed the power to override a statute. In two Scottish cases, *MacCormick v Lord Advocate* [1953] SC 369: arguing that Queen Elizabeth 2 of the UK is Elizabeth 1 in Scotland and *Gibson v Lord Advocate* [1975] SLT 134: Scottish fishing rights, the courts avoided the issue by holding that no conflict with the Acts of Union arose. However in both cases the argument in favour of the Acts of Union was regarded as tenable, particularly by Lord Cooper in *MacCormick*. However his Lordship suggested that the issue is 'non-justifiable', that is, outside the jurisdiction of the courts and resolvable only by political means. On this view a statute that flouts the Acts of Union may be unconstitutional but not unlawful. In both cases the courts left open the question whether they could interfere if an Act purported to make drastic inroads into the Act of Union, for example by abolishing the whole of Scottish private law. In *R (Jackson) v A-G* [2006] at [106]: Lord Hope acknowledged that the Acts of Union might not be repealable.

The devolution legislation of 1998 does not directly affect Parliamentary sovereignty. It gives large law making power to bodies in Scotland, Wales and Northern Ireland but does not prevent Parliament from making laws in relation to those countries in respect of matters within the devolved powers or from removing any devolved powers (Section 16.1). Thus the powers of the devolved legislatures are delegated powers and as such can be challenged in the courts by judicial review and overridden by statute. However because the Scottish Parliament is a democratically elected body the court will override an Act of the Scottish Parliament only in extreme circumstances where it violates the requirements of the rule of law (see *AXA General Insurance Ltd v HM Advocate* [2012] 1 AC 868 (where Lord Hope [51] emphasised the dangers of domination of Parliament by a political party) (Section 16.2.1)). Moreover Parliament is restricted by convention from exercising its powers to intervene in the affairs of the devolved countries (Section 16.1) and it is possible that political pressures may lead to legal sovereignty being surrendered in favour of a federal arrangement (see Little, 'Scotland and Parliamentary Sovereignty' (2004) 24 LS 540).

8.5.3   Redefinition theory: entrenchment

Suggested most prominently by Jennings (*The Law and the Constitution* (University of London Press 1959)), the redefinition theory attempts to circumvent the rule that Parliament cannot bind its successors. The argument has various labels, sometimes being called the 'new view', sometimes the 'entrenchment' argument, sometimes the 'manner and form' theory and sometimes the distinction between 'continuing' and 'self-embracing' sovereignty.

The redefinition argument is essentially that if Parliament can do anything, it can 'redesign itself either in general or for particular purpose', as Baroness Hale put it in *R (Jackson) v A-G* ([160]). The core of the argument is that under the idea of the rule of law a lawmaker can only make law in accordance with the procedure laid down (call it P1) even if that procedure is created by itself as Parliament is able to do. Therefore if the lawmaking procedure is changed to P2 the new procedure (P2) must then be followed unless it itself is changed (either to P3 or back to P1 it does not matter). A document which purports to be an Act of Parliament but which has not been passed according to these basic rules has no legal force, so the courts must ignore it.

Suppose for example that a statute enacts a bill of rights and goes on to say that 'no law shall be passed that is inconsistent with the bill of rights nor shall this statute be repealed expressly or impliedly without a referendum of the people'. What Parliament has done is to add to the existing requirement of Queen, Lords and Commons a further requirement of a referendum, thus redefining itself for the particular purpose of the bill of rights. An entrenched statute can still be repealed but not without following the special procedure. However as long as the lawmaker acts within those terms, it can change those terms for the future (ie by holding a referendum as to whether in future the referendum requirement should be repealed). It is of course always important to interpret the measure that creates the entrenched procedure in order to discover what was intended (see *Jackson* case (box below) and *Manuel* case, (below)).

The redefinition argument can be attacked on three fronts:

1. (The argument students usually raise). If Parliament were to ignore the special procedure by passing a statute in the ordinary way, the courts would simply obey the most recent Act of Parliament and thus treat the special procedure as impliedly repealed. However this misses the point, since according to the redefinition argument a document that has not been produced under the special procedure is not a valid statute and so must be ignored, just as an ordinary law would be ignored if it did not have the royal assent. Therefore there are no competing statutes for the implied repeal doctrine to engage with. We have already seen that the implied repeal doctrine can be overridden (Section 8.4.3).

2. It can be argued that any Act which confers lawmaking power subject to a special procedure is in reality delegating power to a subordinate body since, by definition, subordinate legislation is legislation made under the authority of another body and is inherently restricted by the terms of reference given to it. If this is so, then the superior body can always legislate to override the subordinate. However it is equally possible logically to regard what is happening as a body redefining itself.

3. Professor Wade (1955) firmly rejects the redefinition argument. He argues that the meaning of 'Parliament' is 'fixed' by a rule derived from the 1688 revolution which is 'above and beyond the reach of Parliament': a fundamental constitutional principle which he takes to be in the hands of the courts and so a unique rule both 'political' and common law (Section 8.2). Wade argues that because this rule gave Parliament its power, it cannot be altered by Parliament and any attempt to redefine Parliament would at best at best produce delegated legislation.

However, even if we accept the idea of Wade's 'higher rule' why should the higher rule, supposedly made by those in charge of the 1688 revolution, not authorise its creature – Parliament – to alter the rule itself? Indeed In *Factortame v Secretary of State for Transport (No 2)* [1991], 659 Lord Bridge took the view that parliamentary sovereignty can indeed be altered by statute. It is also plausible that the fundamental rule is not fixed at a particular date but, in keeping with the nature of the unwritten constitution, evolves and changes. Indeed the doctrine emerged in its modern form well after 1688 together with the expansion of democracy in the nineteenth century.

In *R (Jackson) v A-G* (2005) (see box), a majority of the House of Lords seemed to support the redefinition theory It was confronted with the redefinition theory when for the first time in a domestic context it was asked to invalidate a statute, namely the Hunting Act 2004 which banned hunting with dogs. This had been enacted without the consent of the House of Lords under the Parliament 1949 which itself had been passed minus the House of Lords. If these Acts were full Acts of Parliament and not mere delegated legislation as Wade would suggest then Parliament has successfully redefined itself. Their Lordships held that a law passed by the Queen and Commons alone under the Parliament Act procedure is indeed a full Act of Parliament as that was the intention of the Parliament Act 1911. Acts made under the Parliament Acts can therefore do anything that an ordinary Act can do. Although their Lordships did not expressly discuss the Wade theory it seems that they recognised that Parliament had indeed chosen to redefine itself for the particular purpose of limiting the power of the House of Lords.

However caution is required. It was stressed in *Jackson* that the 1911 Act did not transfer power to a body other than Parliament or limit the power of the democratic House of Commons. It merely constrained the House of Lords (at [25]). The courts might therefore draw back from accepting a more radical kind of redefinition particularly one that limits democracy. Baroness Hale in particular left 'for another day' the question whether Parliament could redefine itself 'upwards', for example by requiring a referendum for a particular measure in addition to the normal procedure (at [163]).

There is judicial support for the redefinition theory from former UK territories (see *A-G for New South Wales v Trethowen* [1932] AC 526; *Harris v Minister of the Interior* [1952] (2) SA 428: South Africa; *Bribery Comr v Ranasinghe* [1965] AC 172: Sri Lanka). *Trethowen* went so far as to suggest that the court could grant an injunction to prevent a bill being submitted for royal assent if it did not comply with the entrenched procedure. These cases are of limited authority. They have been explained on the basis that the legislatures in these countries were not truly supreme in the same way as the UK Parliament, since a UK Act had established the powers of the legislatures in question. However in *Harris* the Statute of Westminster 1931 had given the South African Parliament unlimited lawmaking power. Moreover the court stressed that its reasoning did not assume that the legislature was subordinate. Indeed in both *Trethowen* and *Ranasinghe* there were dicta that the same arguments might apply to the UK Parliament. Thus it was said in *Ranasinghe* (at 198) that the legislature can alter the very instrument from which its powers derive.

In *Manuel v A-G* [1983] the Canada Act 1982 was claimed to be invalid in that it was enacted without relevant consents as required by section 4 of the Statute of Westminster 1931, which at the time applied to Canada as a former UK dominion. The purpose of the 1982 Act was to free Canada from its constitutional links with the UK. The Court of Appeal was prepared to recognise the possibility of redefinition. However, section 4 merely required that the Act had to *state on its face* that it had received the relevant consents. The 1982 Act did so state and the court could not investigate the internal proceedings of Parliament to see whether the statement was true. Obviously the matter depends on the precise terms of the redefinition in question (a point to watch in any exam question!).

R (Jackson) v A-G [2005] 4 All ER 1253

The Hunting Act 2004, which outlawed hunting with dogs, had been enacted under the Parliament Act 1949 without the consent of the House of Lords The Hunting Act was challenged on two grounds:

▶ The first ground was that Parliament could not redefine itself by changing what counted as an Act of Parliament. Therefore a law passed under the 1911 Act could only be delegated legislation, power being delegated by Parliament in 1911 to the Commons and Queen. Delegated legislation unlike statute can be challenged in the courts. The Hunting Act was passed under the Parliament Act 1949, which shortened the period for which the House of Lords could delay a bill. The 1949 Act was itself enacted without House of Lords' consent under the 1911 Act's procedure. It was assumed to be correct, that, unless there is clear authority to do so from the parent Act, a delegate cannot enlarge its own powers. Therefore on this argument the 1949 Act would be invalid, so that the Hunting Act falls with it.

▶ The second ground was even if laws made under the 1911 Act are Acts of Parliament, nevertheless as a matter of interpretation of the 1911 Act there are implied limits intended by the 1911 Act which prevent the Parliament Act procedure from being used to further reduce the powers of the Lords and perhaps to make other constitutional changes. This would also make the 1949 Act invalid since it would not be properly made under the 1911 Act.

▶ On the first ground nine Law Lords held that Acts passed under the Parliament Acts were not delegated legislation but full statutes. The 1949 Act was therefore a proper Act of Parliament and the Hunting Act was lawful. Thus they endorsed the possibility of Parliament redefining itself. Lord Steyn ([81]–[86], [91]–[93]) treated the definition of Parliament as a matter that Parliament itself could change (see also Lord Bingham at [35]–[36], Lord Carswell [174], Lord Browne [187], Baroness Hale [160]. This raises the possibility of entrenchment (above) (Baroness Hale [163]). It is noteworthy that Lord Hope in particular emphasised that the courts must acknowledge the political reality that laws made under the Parliaments Acts have consistently been regarded as full statuettes [124] [128].

▶ As to the second ground, which depended on the interpretation of the 1911 Act a majority held that there were no limitations to be read into the 1911 Act preventing the Act itself from being altered so as to reduce the delaying period. The 1949 Act and the Hunting Act were therefore valid.

▶ However there was disagreement whether as a matter of interpretation, the Parliament Acts can apply to every bill to alter the Parliament Act 1911. The 1911 Act expressly does not apply to the following (s 2):
  ▶ a bill to prolong the life of Parliament beyond five years. This is a safeguard to prevent a government exploiting a Commons majority to avoid an election;
  ▶ a private bill, which is a bill concerning specific persons or places, and a bill to confirm a provisional order, a largely unused procedure for approving particular projects;
  ▶ a bill introduced in the House of Lords.

▶ A bill which directly violated these limitations would of course be invalid as outside the scope of the Parliament Acts. However, these limitations arguably could be overcome in two stages. First by using the Parliament Acts the Commons might alter the 1911 Act itself so as to remove them. It would then, using the altered Parliament Acts, pass a statute, for example extending Parliament's life to ten years. Lord Bingham [32] and Baroness Hale [164] [166] took this logical view holding that there were no limitations in the Parliament Acts 1911 other than those expressly set out. Therefore the courts could not prevent this, however politically undesirable it might be. However a majority (Lords Nicholls [59], Steyn [79] Hope [118] [122] and Carswell [175] suggested that this manoeuvre would be unlawful as subverting the clear intention of the 1911 Act. Lord Rogers [139] was sympathetic to this view. Lords Walker and Browne did not express a view.

▶ A further issue was discussed. The Court of Appeal had suggested that a bill which made fundamental constitutional changes such as abolishing the House of Lords altogether or violating basic democratic rights could not be passed under the Parliament Acts, which could be read as implicitly limiting such fundamental changes. Their Lordships did not commit themselves on this point but in the main rejected the argument. Lord Bingham [32], Lord Nicholls [61] and Baroness Hale, albeit ambivalently [158] [159] [166]. thought that there are no such limitations although Lord Bingham [41] drew attention to the fact that the Parliament Acts weaken the checks and balances over a powerful executive. Lord Carswell [178] and Lord Browne [194] cautiously left open the possibility. Lord Steyn [102] perhaps endorsed by Lord Hope [107] [120] went furthest, taking the view that fundamental violations of the rule of law might be rejected by the courts – not merely those made under the Parliament Acts but also by the full Parliament (Section 8.5.6).

8.5.4 European Community law

This challenge to parliamentary sovereignty has attracted considerable support, being regarded as politically required realistic. The EU and its powers were created by a series of treaties between the member states. Member states are obliged under the treaties to give effect to those community laws that are intended under the rules of EU law to be binding within domestic law. However, as with all treaties, the law of the EU enters the legal systems of each member state in accordance with the laws of that state.

It is sometimes argued that by enacting the original EU Treaty the UK has therefore surrendered part of parliamentary sovereignty. If this is right then a democratic body has committed the sin of trying to bind the freedom of future generations. We shall discuss the EU law in more detail in Chapter 10 but will outline the position as regards parliamentary sovereignty here.

The European Communities Act 1972 incorporated EU law into UK law. The Act states that 'any enactment, passed or to be passed ... shall be construed and have effect subject to the foregoing provisions of this section' (s 2(4)). The provisions referred to require among other things that the English courts must give effect to certain laws made by the EU (s 2(1)). Section 3 of the Act also requires UK courts to follow the decisions of the European Court of Justice (ECJ), the court of the EU. The effect of the above provisions seems to be that a UK statute, even one passed after the relevant EU law, must give way to EU law. Not surprisingly the ECJ, which is part of the internal

EU system, favours the sovereignty of the EU (see *Costa v ENEL* [1964] CMLR 425). However this in itself is not enough since the matter depends on UK law. (Students often cite *Costa* or other cases of the European Court as if they were conclusive on the issue. The views of EU bodies are irrelevant except in as far as they help to interpret the 1972 Act.)

The courts would try to avoid conflicts between domestic law and EU law by interpreting legislation so as to avoid a conflict with a binding rule of EU law (Section 10.3.2). Conflict between UK law and EU law may arise where a UK statute is clearly inconsistent with an earlier EU law or with the 1972 Act since the implied repeal doctrine would call for the later statute to be followed (Section 8.4.3). Conflicts between a later EU law and an earlier statute would favour the EU rule under the ordinary implied repeal rule.

There are opposing arguments based on differing perspectives to the effect of the 1972 Act. On the one hand it might be argued along traditional lines that since a statute made EU law binding in the UK, a statute can reverse this. According to this argument it might be conceded that, given the importance of EU law and the clear intention in the Act that it should take priority, it should take very clear words in an Act to override an EU law, so that the ordinary implied repeal doctrine is excluded as it can be under ordinary principles (Section 8.4.3). Thus according to Lord Diplock in *Garland v British Rail Engineering Ltd* [1983] 2 AC 751 a statute that unambiguously states that it is to override European law will prevail. Similarly in *Thoburn v Sunderland City Council* [2002] Laws LJ attempted to treat the matter as one of a strong presumption against repeal, regarding the 1972 Act as an example of a 'constitutional statute'(Section 8.4.3). However the case of the EU is possibly even stronger in that in view of the language of the 1972 Act (above) nothing short of an express statement along the lines of 'this Act is to override EU law' would suffice.

On the other hand it could be argued that the 1972 Act had the effect of imposing a European perspective on the UK courts, thus requiring the courts to give priority to EU laws since European law does not recognise our version of parliamentary sovereignty. In *Jackson* Lord Hope (at [105]) and Baroness Hale (at [159]) treated EU law as modifying parliamentary sovereignty. Independently of both arguments it might be conceded that a UK statute could validly expressly repeal the 1972 Act, effectively taking us out of the European Union.

The UK courts have reached an ambivalent solution which is consistent with both the above perspectives, In *R v Secretary of State for Transport, ex p Factortame* [1990] 2 AC 85 there was a clash between Spanish fishermen and the UK government. EU law entitled EU members to fish freely in the seas around member states but the Merchant Shipping Act 1988 which restricted fishing to boats flying the UK flag. Initially the House of Lords refused to grant an injunction to prevent the Act being enforced, holding that it had no power to grant an injunction against the Crown to prevent the enforcement of an Act of Parliament. The matter was referred to the ECJ, which held that the UK court should enforce the EU law. In *R v Secretary of State, ex p Factortame (No 2)* [1991] 1 AC 603 the House of Lords fell into line and 'disapplied' the UK statute. However the precise basis on which it did so remains ambivalent. *Factortame* could be taken as modifying parliamentary sovereignty by requiring EU law to prevail whenever there is a conflict. Indeed Wade ((1991) 107 LQR 1) argued that *Factortame* has signalled his constitutional revolution (Section 8.2.) (See also *Equal Opportunities*

Commission v Secretary of State for Employment [1994] 1 All ER 910, 919–20: provisions of a statute said to be 'invalid'.)

On the other hand *Factortame* could be treated as a matter of interpretation as suggested above. Thus in *Factortame* (1990) Lord Bridge said, 'By virtue of s.2(4) of the Act of 1972, Part II of the 1988 Act is to be construed and take effect subject to directly enforceable community rights ... This has precisely the same effect as if a section were incorporated in ... the 1988 Act ... which enacted that the provisions were to be without prejudice to the directly enforceable community rights of nationals of any member state of the EC' (at 140). This treats the matter as one of interpreting the Act in question so as to conform with the EU rule by requiring nothing short of the clearest language to counter Lord Bridge's presumption. The same approach was taken in *Thoburn* (above). However in *Factortame* No. 2 (1991) (659) Lord Bridge seemed to modify his position by treating EU membership as a voluntary modification of parliamentary sovereignty.

Since the position of EU law derives only from the 1972 Act (Section 10.1) it is clear that a statute could remove EU law from UK law by expressly repealing the 1972 Act so that in the end parliamentary sovereignty is preserved. However this may well be politically difficult.

8.5.5 The Human Rights Act 1998

By virtue of the Human Rights Act a court must interpret a statute, 'if it is possible to do so' so as to comply with rights derived from the European Convention on Human Rights (ECHR). If this is not possible the court can issue a 'Declaration of Incompatibility' (Section 22.3.2). This does not override the statute, and the Act is clear that the court has no power to do so. The effect of a Declaration of Incompatibility is to invite the executive in conjunction with Parliament to change the law so as to comply with the ECHR. Thus the Act does not restrict parliamentary sovereignty. However, along with the EU legislation and the devolution legislation (above) the Human Rights Act has been used as evidence that the position of parliamentary sovereignty is increasingly shaky.

8.5.6 The common law/rule of law

It is sometimes suggested that parliamentary sovereignty may be conditional on compliance with fundamental values embodied in the rule of law so that in extreme cases the court might refuse to apply a statute. Early cases such as *Dr Bonham's Case* [1610] 8 Co Rep 114a possibly suggested that a completely unreasonable statute may be overridden, but at least since Tudor times there has been no serious challenge to parliamentary sovereignty. Nevertheless in the absence of a written constitution we cannot rule out judicial rejection of the doctrine. Indeed the courts themselves inevitably have to decide the limits of their own powers when a case comes before them. Thus it has been said:

> whoever hath an absolute authority to interpret any written or spoken laws, it is he who is truly the lawgiver and not the person who just spoke or wrote them. (Bishop Hoadley's sermon preached before King George I, 1717)

Contemporary judges mainly support parliamentary sovereignty. For example Lord Bingham took the view that the judges did not create parliamentary sovereign and therefore could not change it (*The Rule of Law*, Penguin 2010, 167). Emphasis has been placed on the courts' power to moderate Parliament by interpreting statutes in the light of common law principles. Compromise has been rationalised by claiming that Parliament implicitly recognises this. In *X Ltd v Morgan Grampian Publishers Ltd* [1991] 1 AC 1, Lord Bridge referred to the 'twin foundations' of the rule of law, namely 'the sovereignty of the Queen in Parliament in making the law and the sovereignty of the Queen's courts in interpreting and applying the law' (at 13). In *Hamilton v Al Fayed* [1999], Lord Woolf MR referred to 'the wider constitutional principle of mutuality of respect between two constitutional sovereignties' (at 320).

The courts do not interpret statutes mechanically but apply them in the context of the rule of law, which embodies respect for fundamental values and individual rights. In this way the courts put partial brakes on Parliament's freedom by means of the 'principle of legality' (see Lady Hale in *R (Jackson) v A-G* [2005] at [159]). This relates to the 'extended' rule of law which requires that Parliament must use very clear language if it wishes to override values of fairness and justice developed by the courts. (Section 6.7). The courts therefore act as a check and balance by ensuring that Parliament does not inadvertently or lightly override basic rights.

Some judges have gone further suggesting that parliamentary sovereignty is no longer appropriate and that 'the rule of law' enforced by the courts is the true sovereign. This means that the courts might override a statute that threatens basic principles of the rule of law. For example Lord Steyn in *R (Jackson) v A-G* [2005] at [102] said that 'the Supreme Court might have to consider whether judicial review or the ordinary role of the courts was a constitutional fundamental which even a sovereign Parliament acting at the behest of a compliant House of Commons could not abolish.' In the same case Lord Hope said that '[s]tep by step, gradually but surely the English principle of the absolute legislative sovereignty of Parliament is being qualified' [104] and that 'the rule of law is the ultimate controlling factor on which our constitution is based' [107]. The late Lord Cooke, following Wade's approach (Section 8.5.4), suggested that an attempt by Parliament to override basic rights would be a 'revolution' on which the last word rests with the courts (in Andenas and Fairgrieve (2009) 689–91).

In *AXA General Insurance Ltd v HM Advocate* [2012] (above) the Supreme Court held that the non-sovereign Scottish Parliament is subject to judicial review but only in the most exceptional cases where the rule of law is threatened. Lord Hope [50] said that the position as regards the sovereign UK Parliament is 'still under discussion'. He suggested that, in the light of the dangers of executive domination of Parliament, the court might intervene if Parliament were to abolish judicial review or diminish the powers of the courts in protecting the individual: 'the rule of law requires that judges must retain the power to insist that legislation of this extreme kind is not law which the courts will recognise' [51]. The other members of the court did not raise this issue.

Dicey (1915, ch 13), attempted to reconcile the rule of law and parliamentary sovereignty. He argued that parliamentary sovereignty conforms to the rule of law in that Parliament's will can be expressed only through statutes and there are rules of law defining what a statute is. However this relates only to the core rule of law. Parliamentary sovereignty conflicts with the rule of law in its amplified and extended senses (see Sections 6.6, 6.7). Dicey's view depended on the pivotal role which he thought that the House of Lords played in checking the excesses of the Commons. He also believed that public opinion was a modifying force. Today the House of Lords is subordinate to the Commons. Indeed in his later years Dicey realised that the power of political parties, an increasingly diverse electorate, external threats and the need for governments to provide expensive public services put the traditional place of Parliament as the centre of the constitution into question.

Allan (2001) argues in republican fashion (Section 2.5) that it is inconsistent with the political assumptions of a liberal society on which the rule of law is based that the legislature, or indeed any part of the government, should be all powerful. Allan claims that in the common law tradition the courts have the duty to protect the fundamental values of society. Relying on the fact that the court is concerned not with the statute generally but with its application to the individual case. Allan suggests that the court can legitimately hold that a statute which appears to be grossly unjust in the particular context does not apply to the particular case. This approach could be reconciled with parliamentary sovereignty on the basis that Parliament cannot foresee every implication of the laws it makes and can be assumed to respect the rule of law. In *Cooper v Wandsworth Board of Works* [1863] 14 CB (NS) 175 Byles J said that 'the justice of the common law will supply the omission of the legislature'.

Those supporting the courts might argue in favour of the high level of public reasoned argument practised in the courts and the relative objectivity and independence of judges. A standard argument is that the representative democracy which gives Parliament its legitimacy is an imperfect democracy which carries a risk of overriding minorities. The courts have emphasised in their own favour that Parliament has become dominated by the executive (eg Lord Mustill in *R v Secretary of State, ex p Fire Brigades Union* [1995]; Section 7.7.3.3, Lord Hope in *AXA General Insurance Ltd v HM Advocate* [2012] (above) [49] [50], Lord Bingham in *R (Jackson) v A-G* [2005] [41]. Thus the usual defence of Parliament, namely that it can make laws which are informed by a wider range of opinions than are available to a court and which carry the consent of those subject to them, can be presented as hollow. In AXA (above) Lord Hope emphasised [49] that both sovereign and non-sovereign parliaments share the advantages of democracy which makes them best placed to know what is in the country's best interests but, in view of the dangers of Parliament being dominated by a party majority, 'the non elected judges are best placed to protect the rights of the individual including those who are ignored or despised by the majority'. On the other hand it seems bizarre to remedy a failure of democracy by suggesting an even more undemocratic mechanism.

Arguments in favour of Parliament are also republican. They point to the indignity of political decisions being made on our behalf by people we have not chosen and also to the fact that judges are not accountable. (The latter point is sometimes contested by pointing out that judges sit in public and give reasoned verdicts.) They might also deny that lawyers should have a privileged status, since Parliament comprises a larger cross-section of the community that can make a better-informed decision. The liberal values that the rule of law embraces are not peculiar to law. Ideas such as freedom and equality are the source of much political disagreement which judges may be in no better position to resolve than anyone else (see Section 2.4). Lord Bingham pointed out in *R (Countryside Alliance) v A-G* [2008] AC 719 [45] that the democratic process is liable to be subverted if on a question of political or moral judgement, opponents of an Act achieve through the courts what they could not achieve through Parliament.

Summary

▶ The doctrine of parliamentary sovereignty provides the fundamental legal premise of the UK constitution. The doctrine means that an Act of Parliament must be obeyed by the courts, that later Acts prevail over earlier ones and that rules made by external bodies, for example under international law, cannot override Acts of Parliament. It does not follow that Parliament is supreme politically, although the line between legal and political sovereignty is blurred.

▶ Parliamentary sovereignty rests on frail foundations. Without a written constitution it is impossible to be sure as to its legal basis other than as an evolving practice which is usually said to depend on the 1688 revolution. It is possible to maintain that the common law is really supreme. The question of the ultimate source of power cannot be answered within the legal system alone but depends on public acceptance.

▶ Parliament itself is a creature of the law. The customary and statutory rules which have evolved since medieval times determine that, except in special cases, Parliament for this purpose means the Queen with the assent of the House of Lords and House of Commons. However this can be modified, as in the case of the Parliament Acts 1911 and 1949.

▶ The courts can determine whether any document is an Act of Parliament in this sense but cannot inquire into whether the correct procedure within each House has been followed.

▶ The doctrine has two separate aspects: first that the courts must obey Acts of Parliament in preference to any other kind of legal authority, and second that no body, including Parliament itself, can place legal limits upon the freedom of action of a future Parliament. The first of these principles is generally accepted but the second is open to dispute.

▶ The implied repeal doctrine is sometimes promoted as an aspect of parliamentary sovereignty but is merely a presumption of interpretation. Some statutes can be repealed only by clear language.

▶ The doctrine of parliamentary sovereignty is subject to considerable attack.

▶ Grants of independence to dependent territories can probably be revoked lawfully in the eyes of UK courts.

▶ The possibility that parts of the Acts of Union with Scotland and Ireland are unchangeable is probably outside the courts' jurisdiction.

▶ The 'redefinition' argument proposes that by altering the basic requirements for lawmaking, Parliament can redesign itself to impose restrictions on enacting legislation.

▶ Parliament limited the freedom of future Parliaments in relation to certain laws made by the European communities.

▶ The role of the common law as constituting 'dual sovereignty' through the courts' exclusive power to interpret Acts of Parliament leads to argument that parliamentary sovereignty is conditional upon acceptance by the courts. This links with the extended version of the rule of law (Chapter 7).

▶ Dicey attempted to reconcile parliamentary sovereignty with the rule of law by pointing out that Parliament is defined by law and can act only through the instrument of law, so that independent judges interpret its legislation. This relies on the separation of powers.

Exercises

8.1 Does the doctrine of parliamentary sovereignty have a secure legal basis?

8.2 To what extent can the courts investigate whether an Act of Parliament has complied with the proper procedure?

8.3 'Every age and generation must be as free to act for itself, in all cases, as the ages and generations which preceded it. The vanity and presumption of governing beyond the grave is the most ridiculous and insolent of all tyrannies' (Thomas Paine). Discuss with reference (i) to the implied repeal doctrine and (ii) to the redefinition argument.

8.4 Marshal the arguments for and against the proposition that the UK Parliament cannot legislate inconsistently with EU law.

8.5 Consider the validity and effect of the following provisions contained in (fictitious) Acts of Parliament:
   (i) 'There shall be a bill of rights in the UK and no Act to be enacted at any time in the future shall have effect, in as far as it is inconsistent with the bill of rights, unless it has been assented to by a two-thirds majority of both Houses of Parliament and no Act shall repeal this Act unless it has the same two-thirds majority'.
   (ii) 'The Acts of Union with Scotland and Ireland are hereby repealed'.
   (iii) 'This Act shall apply notwithstanding any contrary rule of European Community law'.

8.6 'The sovereignty of Parliament and the sovereignty of the law of the land – the two principles which pervade the whole of the English constitution – may appear to stand in opposition to each other, or to be at best countervailing forces. But this appearance is delusive' (Dicey). Discuss.

8.7 'The classic account given by Dicey of the doctrine of the sovereignty of Parliament, pure and absolute as it was, can now be seen as out of place in the modern United Kingdom' Lord Steyn in *R (Jackson) v A-G* [2005] at [106]. 'The rule of law enforced by the courts is the ultimate controlling factor on which our constitution is based', Lord Hope *ibid* at [107]. Explain and critically discuss.

8.8 What, if any, limitations are there on the powers exercisable by Parliament under the Parliament Acts 1911 and 1949?

Further reading

Allan, 'In Defence of the Common Law Constitution' (2009) LSE Working Papers 5/2009

Bogdanor, 'Imprisoned by a Doctrine: the Modern Defence of Parliamentary Sovereignty' (2012) 32 OJLS 179

Bradley, 'The Sovereignty of Parliament – Form or Substance?' in Jowell and Oliver (eds), *The Changing Constitution* (7th edn, Oxford University Press 2011)

Craig, 'Constitutional Foundations, the Rule of Law and Sovereignty' [2003] PL 92

Ekins, 'Judicial Sovereignty and the Rule of Law' (2003) 119 LQR 127

Ekins, 'Acts of Parliament and the Parliament Acts' (2007) 123 LQR 91

Elliott, 'Parliamentary Sovereignty and the New Constitutional Order: Legislative Freedom, Political Reality and Convention' (2002) 22 LS 340

Goldsworthy, *The Sovereignty of Parliament: History and Philosophy* (Oxford University Press 1999) chs 1, 2, 9, 10

Further reading cont'd

Goldsworthy, 'Legislative Sovereignty and the Rule of Law' in Campbell, Ewing and Tompkins (eds), *Sceptical Essays on Human Rights* (Oxford University Press 2001)

Goldsworthy, Parliamentary Sovereignty: Contemporary Debates (Cambridge University Press 2010)

Gordon, 'The Conceptual Foundations of Parliamentary Sovereignty: Reconsidering Jennings and Wade' [2009] PL 519

Jowell, 'Parliamentary Sovereignty under the New Constitutional Hypothesis' [2006] PL 562

Knight, 'Striking Down Legislation Under bi- Polar Sovereignty', [2010] PL 90

Lakin, 'Debunking the Idea of Parliamentary Sovereignty: The Controlling Factor of Legality in the British Constitution' (2008) 28 OJLS 709

MacCormick, 'Does the United Kingdom Have a Constitution? Reflections on *MacCormick v Lord Advocate*' (1978) 29 NI LQ 1

Munro, *Studies in Constitutional Law* (2nd edn, Butterworths 1999) chs 5, 6

Tucker, 'Uncertainty in the Rule of Recognition and in the Doctrine of Parliamentary Sovereignty' (2011) 31 OJLS 61

Wade, 'The Basis of Legal Sovereignty' [1955] CLJ 172

Weill, 'Centennial to the Parliament Act 1911: The Manner and Form Fallacy', [2012] PL 105

Part III

International aspects of the constitution

Chapter 9

The state and the outside world

Introduction: the idea of the state

The term 'state' derives from 'status' and originally meant a recognised function in the overall scheme of things. The contemporary idea of the state is that of the 'nation state'. A state is a geographical area with a permanent population and an independent government in control (see McCormick, 2007). There is no necessary connection between the ideas of a nation and of a state, although sometimes the two terms are used interchangeably, for example the National Health Service. A nation is a cultural, political and historical idea but is not a legal concept. It signifies a community marked out by shared cultural traditions. A state is defined by law and based on geographical boundaries drawn up by officials.

However a nation may have a moral claim to be a state with its own laws and government (see Lord Hoffmann in *A v Secretary of State for the Home Dept* [2005] 2 AC 68) and the association of the ideas of nation and state can be used by those in power as a means of inspiring loyalty (eg the Constitution of Ireland, Art 9). As the history of Ireland, the Balkan states, Pakistan and many African states sadly reveals, the artificiality of state boundaries may generate violence and even genocide. The term 'country' has no legal significance and is often used loosely to refer either to a nation or to a state.

The nation state has been the basic unit of political and legal organisation since the Treaty of Westphalia 1688 created the principle that states are equal and independent in their internal affairs. During the eighteenth century, generated by enlightenment ideas of scientific reason, secularism and equality, the state developed as an impersonal command structure. This is broadly the position today. Under the influence of democracy, the state has become an all-purpose organisation with no limitations neither to its functions nor any consensus as to the relationship between citizen and state other than the temporary accommodations produced by the balance of powers within the state.

Today the interdependence of states against shared evils such as terrorism and environmental damage, advances in communications and mobility labelled as 'globalisation' which enable people and money to move swiftly around the world, and also atrocities committed by governments against their own people have placed the Westphalian model in doubt. However state constitutions, including that of the UK, remain geared to the traditional model.

9.2 The UK as a state

We have seen that UK domestic law has no concept of the state as a legal entity (Section 5.1). The UK is a state in international law but it is not a nation. Its legal and cultural basis is complex. The UK comprises England, Scotland, Wales and Northern Ireland each of which with the exception of England has devolved self government (Chapter 16). Before the union with Scotland in 1707, England was a nation state, but now has no legal status. Great Britain, a name coined to represent the union with Scotland means England, Wales and Scotland collectively. Great Britain is not a legal entity although the term is sometimes used in statute to mean the UK (eg 'British Overseas Territory'). The Channel Islands and the Isle of Man are not part of the UK. However they belong to the Crown and have their own systems of law and government. There are various small British overseas territories' scattered around the world.

The Queen is the head of the Commonwealth, which is a loose association of former UK territories. The Commonwealth as such has no legal links with the UK although a few of its members retain the Judicial Committee of the Privy Council as an appeal court (Section 5.8).

England and Wales has a single legal system governed by English law (although there are calls for a distinct Welsh jurisdiction). Scotland and Northern Ireland have their own legal systems, which have much in common with English law, although Scotland has also been influenced by French civil law. In all jurisdictions, other than Scottish criminal cases, the highest appeal court is currently the UK Supreme Court.

9.3 Citizenship

In its general sense citizenship means full membership of a state. In its republican sense (Section 2.5) citizenship is about having equal rights in the community, participating in government and shouldering community responsibilities. The republican idea of citizenship is sometimes used to suggest that human rights are dependent on good behaviour whereas 'liberal' citizenship primarily concerns the rights and entitlements of individuals against the state. However recent citizenship legislation has imposed requirements relating to assimilation into national culture (below) (see Bellamy, 'Constitutive Citizenship vs. Constitutional Rights: Republican Reflections on the EU Charter and the Human Rights Act' in Campbell, Ewing and Tomkins (eds), *Sceptical Essays on Human Rights* (Hart 2001)).

The unpleasant side of citizenship is that it entails 'exclusion', in the sense of an unwelcoming attitude to those regarded as non-citizens, who in UK law are labelled as 'aliens'. Traditionally aliens have fewer rights than citizens. In particular the state has a power to expel aliens, although this is limited by obligations under the ECHR concerning the risk of ill treatment overseas, personal liberty and respect for family life (Sections 9.6.3, 21.4). For example in *A v Secretary of State for the Home Dept* [2005] the House of Lords held that it was contrary to the Human Rights Act 1998 to discriminate between citizens and non-citizens in relation to anti-terrorism measures where there is a risk from both groups (Section 24.7). However citizenship and immigration rights as such are not protected by the ECHR. Moreover Article 16 of the ECHR states that nothing in Articles 10, 11 and 14 (which concern freedom of expression, assembly and association, and discrimination in respect of human rights) shall prevent the imposition of restrictions on the political activity of aliens.

Although there is a status of 'British citizen' (below), those subject to the jurisdiction of English law are strictly speaking not citizens but 'subjects' of the Crown. A subject includes a British citizen anywhere and anyone within the territory of the UK since such a person can claim the protection of the law. Despite the word commonly being associated with subservience, the notion of a 'subject' is sometimes said to give valuable protection in that it presupposes a relationship of mutual respect between ruler and ruled which is safeguarded by law. Thus in return for 'allegiance' (loyalty) the Crown is obliged to protect the rights of the subject and keep the peace (see *Calvin's Case* (1606) 7 Co Rep 2a, *R v Secretary of State for the Home Dept ex parte Thakrar* [1974] 1 QB 684,709). However contemporary UK courts have not been willing to intervene taking the view that matters of diplomatic protection are not suitable for judicial decision except in extreme cases.

Citizenship in its republican sense carries with it the right to participate in government with corresponding obligations to conform to the wishes of the majority. For example Rousseau proclaimed that a citizen must submit to the general will, whatever that might be, and it is sometimes claimed that human rights are conditional upon good behaviour.

In his speech on the scaffold (1649) Charles I announced that:

> I must tell you, that [the people's] liberty and freedom consists in having the government of those laws, by which their life and their goods may be considered most their own; 'tis not for having a share in government that is nothing pertaining to 'em. A subject and a sovereign are clean different things.

In English law citizenship is mainly concerned with the right to reside, rights concerned with political participation and sometimes rights to access to public services and taxation (below). Other legal rights and duties depend on presence in the territory or sometimes, particularly in relation to health and welfare services, a more specific connection such as lawful residence (see eg *R (A) v Secretary of State for Health* [2010] 1 All ER 87: access to health service denied to failed asylum seeker). In the Channel Islands, non-citizens have restricted property rights.

UK citizenship law is complex due to many attempts to restrict immigration following the collapse of the British Empire after World War 2. It can only be sketched here. The British Nationality Act 1981 (BNA) as amended is the main legislation. Although the label is 'British' citizenship there is no citizenship of any other unit within the UK. There is a notion of citizenship of the EU. However this merely endorses certain rights within member states which under European law apply to citizens of all EU states.

The following have 'British' citizenship under the Act:

- Those born or adopted in the UK (s 50). However at least one parent must also be either a citizen or settled in the UK. If the parents are not married then this must be the mother.
- Those descended from a British citizen (s 2). At the time of birth at least one parent must be a citizen other than by descent or be a citizen working abroad for the British government, having been recruited in the UK, or in certain cases working for the EU, having been recruited in a member state.
- Persons who were citizens or who by virtue of specified family connections (patrials) had a right of abode in the UK under the regime that existed before 1983 (s 11).

Citizenship can be acquired by registration or naturalisation:

- Registration is a right available to persons who were born in the UK or who fulfil certain requirements of residence or parentage and who satisfy the Home Secretary that they are of 'good character' (BNA, s 4; Immigration, Asylum and Nationality Act 2006, s 58; Borders, Citizenship and Immigration Act 2009, ss 44, 46, 47). Registration is also available to certain persons who would otherwise be stateless (below).
- Naturalisation (BNA, s 6) is a matter for the discretion of the Secretary of State and is available to anyone, subject to requirements of residence, family association as

prescribed by the Secretary of State, presence in the UK within a qualifying period of years, language, good character and 'knowledge of life in the UK' as prescribed by the Home Secretary (Nationality, Immigration and Asylum Act 2002, s 4; Borders, Citizenship and Immigration Act 2009, ss 39, 40). Thus a communitarian and potentially illiberal element has been injected into the law.

Citizenship can be renounced by registration with the Secretary of State (BNA, s 12). However registration becomes ineffective unless the person in question acquires citizenship of another state within six months.

The Home Secretary can by order remove citizenship (a) on the grounds of public good unless deprivation of citizenship would make the person stateless or (b) where citizenship was acquired by fraud, false representation or concealment of a material fact (BNAs 40 (2), Nationality, Immigration and Asylum Act 2002, s 4; Immigration, Asylum and Nationality Act 2006, s 56). There is a right of appeal in 'public good' cases this is to the Special Immigration Appeals Commission (Section 24.3.4).

Citizenship is legally important mainly in the following respects:

▶ It confers a right to free movement within the UK. There is an ancient common law principle that a citizen cannot be excluded from the territory. However like any other principle this gives way to statute and in the case of some dependent territories to the powers of the executive under the royal prerogative. (See *R (Bancoult v Secretary of State for Foreign and Commonwealth Affairs* (2008 [42]–[45], Section (9.5).) As regards the UK citizens can be expelled in two main cases:
  (i) anyone can be extradited to another country to stand trial for a criminal offence or serve a sentence (Section 9.6.2);
  (ii) under the Terrorism Act 2000 border controls can be exercised over travel between Great Britain and Northern Ireland.
▶ British, Irish and Commonwealth citizens lawfully resident in the UK may vote in parliamentary and local elections (Representation of the People Act 2000) and elections for the devolved governments.
▶ Non-citizens (other than Commonwealth and Irish citizens) cannot be members of either House of Parliament (British Nationality Act 1981, Sch 7).
▶ Honours cannot be conferred upon non-citizens except Commonwealth citizens.
▶ British citizens have a right to call upon the protection of the Crown when abroad, although this is not enforceable in the courts. The main consequence of the Crown's duty to protect British citizens abroad is that the Crown cannot require payment for such protection unless the person concerned voluntarily exposes himself or herself to some special risk (see *China Navigation Co Ltd v A-G* [1932] 2 KB 197; *Mutasa v A-G* [1980] 1 QB 114).
▶ British citizens abroad are subject to special taxation laws.
▶ British citizens owe allegiance to the Crown wherever they are in the world (see *R v Casement* [1917] 1 KB 98). A person who holds a British passport apparently owes allegiance even if he has never visited the UK and even if the passport has been fraudulently obtained (see *Joyce v DPP* [1946] AC 347). Allegiance has two main consequences. Firstly the Crown probably cannot plead the defence of 'act of state' against a person who owes allegiance (Section 9.5.4). Secondly the offence of treason is committed against the duty of allegiance. In addition to citizens anyone resident and perhaps even present in the UK also owe allegiance (*de Jager v A-G of Natal* [1907] AC 326). Apart from renouncing citizenship, allegiance cannot be voluntarily surrendered.

9.3.1 Non-citizens

Certain other categories, although largely obsolete relics of empire, attract privileges mainly in connection with immigration in circumstances too specialised to be discussed here. (See White Paper, *Partnership for Progress and Prosperity: Britain and the Overseas Territories* (Cm 4264, 1999).) Some require registration. These categories include:

- 'British Subjects', which before 1949 included citizens of all British territories but which now applies mainly to persons born in former British territories who would otherwise be stateless. A British Subject has no immigration rights but can be registered as a citizen (above) (BNA, s 31),
- The term 'British National' has no general legal meaning. It is usually used to mean a British citizen.
- Citizens of the United Kingdom and Colonies (abolished).
- British Overseas Citizens which includes citizens of the remaining UK dependent territories (formerly 'British dependent territories citizens'). Many such persons are entitled in certain circumstances to be British citizens (British Overseas Territories Act 2002). In the case of the Falkland Islands (which Argentina claims), this is automatic (British Nationality (Falkland Islands) Act 1983).
- British Nationals (Overseas). A limited group of citizens of Hong Kong, which the UK surrendered to China in 1997, have certain rights to registration as British citizens Others can acquire a British passport, although this in itself carries no legal rights, being essentially an identity document (British Nationality (Hong Kong) Act 1997; Borders Citizenship and Immigration Act 2009, s 44)).
- 'British Protected Person' (BPP), an anomalous category which comprises citizens of countries (including the former Palestine and some African and Gulf states) which were placed under the protection of the UK in respect of their defence under treaties or UN mandates (protectorates). There are no longer any such territories and the status can only be acquired by an Order in Council relating to former protectorates or by children of BPPs would otherwise be stateless (Solomon Islands Act 1978). Although they are not aliens, BPPs have no special immigration rights but unlike aliens can be employed as civil servants.
- Commonwealth Citizens which means citizens of all members of the Commonwealth thus including most of the above groups and also citizens of the former Dominiums, the independent states of Australia, Canada, New Zealand and South Africa. Commonwealth citizens could not originally be excluded from the UK under the royal prerogative (see *R (Munir) v Secretary of State for the Home Dept* [2012] 1 WLR 2192 [23]) but are now treated for most purposes as aliens (below). However commonwealth citizens have certain political rights such as a right to vote or to stand in Parliament (Sections 12.2, 12.4, 12.5.5).
- All other persons are labelled aliens. Their position as regards presence in the UK is discussed below (Section 9.6).

The Channel Islands (Jersey, Guernsey and Sark) and the Isle of Man have special constitutional status, being neither part of the UK nor British overseas territories. They are subjects of the Crown, which makes laws for them in the form of Prerogative Orders in Council. They have their own legislatures, executive and judiciary and can make laws governing their internal affairs. Their status derives from feudal ownership by the Crown as successor to the Duke of Normandy. The common law does not apply in the Channel Islands and their internal law is local customary law. As Crown territories, the protection provided by the judicial review powers of the High Court applies (see *Ex p Brown* [1864] 3 LJ QB 193; *Ex p Anderson* [1861] 3 E&E 487). The Channel Islands are not members of the EU but there are special treaty arrangements. Channel Island citizens are British citizens (British Nationality Act 1981, ss 1, 11, 50(1)).

Parliamentary supremacy was extended to the Channel Islands by a Prerogative Order in Council of 1806. However there is a presumption of interpretation that an Act will not apply to the Channel Islands in the absence of express words or necessary implication.

Sark, with a population of 600, is subject to Guernsey law but retains a feudal structure (the only one in the western world) under which a hereditary ruler, the Seigneur (to whom the Crown granted the right by letters patent of 1565 and 1611), owns the land and appoints the main judicial and executive officers. However under pressure from the European Court of Human Rights a Constitution of 2008 introduced a democratic majority into the legislature, the Chief Pleas (see Reform (Sark Law) Order in Council 2008). The Seigneur can speak in the Chief Pleas but cannot vote. He has a temporary veto over legislation. Contrary to the separation of powers the Chief Judge (the Seneschal) presides over the Parliament. However he can neither speak nor vote.

The position of the Isle of Man is broadly similar to that of the Channel Islands. The Crown's rights seem to derive from an ancient agreement with Norway, confirmed by statute (Isle of Man Purchase Act 1765 (repealed)). Legislation made by its elected legislature, the Tynewald, must be assented to by the Queen in Council. (See generally Royal Commission on the Constitution, 1973, Part XI and Minutes of Evidence VI, 7, 13, 227–34; *X v UK* [1982].)

9.4   British overseas territories

The UK retains some dependent overseas territories. Previously called colonies, they are now 'British overseas territories' (British Overseas Territories Act 2002). They are mainly scattered islands. They include Anguilla, Bermuda, British Indian Ocean Territories (BIOT), British Virgin Islands, Cayman Islands, Falkland Islands, Gibraltar, Montserrat, the Pitcairn Islands, St Helena, South Georgia and South Sandwich Islands (SGSSI), and the Turks and Caicos Islands.

Dependent territories occupy an ambivalent position. They are subject to parliamentary supremacy and the UK courts but lack the protection which the law gives to UK citizens. The rights of their inhabitants depend on the historical accident of how the territory in question came into British hands, often by some unpleasant means. Acts of the UK Parliament do not apply to them unless they specifically so provide. By virtue of section 5 of the Colonial Laws Validity Act 1865, legislatures in overseas territories have full power to make local laws, even if this is inconsistent with a UK statute of general effect or with the common law. This includes altering their own constitution but only in the 'manner and form' required by any UK law applying to the territory at the time (*R v Burah* [1878] 3 App Cas 889).

The application of the common law and the powers of the UK executive depend on how the territory was acquired. There is a distinction between 'settled' colonies and 'ceded and conquered' colonies (see *R (Bancoult) v Secretary of State for the Foreign and Commonwealth Office (No 2)* [2008] 4 All ER 1055). A settled territory is one in which there were no developed political institutions when British settlers first arrived (such as SGSSI). A ceded territory previously had its own governmental institutions and was either ceded (given up) to Britain or conquered by force.

In the case of settled territories the powers of the executive are restricted; English common law as it stood at the time of settlement is deemed to have applied to the territory, which means that the limitations placed on the royal prerogative in England apply in that territory. In effect the settlers took English law with them. Most significant are the restrictions laid down in the *Case of Proclamations* (1611), after which the King could not introduce new laws without the consent of Parliament. In settled colonies therefore as in the UK the Crown does not have the power to make law. Laws can be made only under an Act of Parliament. Under the British Settlement Acts 1837 and 1945 statutory instruments made by ministers can create constitutions for each territory and delegate powers to local officials. Such powers are usually expressed as being for the 'peace, order and good government' of the territory but it is unclear whether this ritual phrase has any specific legal effect (below).

In the case of ceded territories the powers of the Crown are more extensive (*Campbell v Hall* (1774) 1 *Cowp* 204). The reason for the distinction is of course that extended powers were needed to suppress the existing governments in conquered territories. English common law does not automatically extend to the territory, which means that the *Case of Proclamations* does not apply. Thus the Crown has full power to make law under the royal prerogative and to impose its own governmental arrangements and taxation including overriding fundamental rights (see *A-G for Canada v Cain* [1906] AC 542, 545, *Bancoult (No 2) (above)* at [96]–[101]). Governors can be appointed by the Crown ('commissioned') to make laws (in formal 'Royal Instructions' and in subsequent despatches).

Such powers are also usually expressed as being for the 'peace, order and good government of the territory'. However it seems that this requirement does not limit the width of the prerogative lawmaking power and the courts will not inquire into the matter (see *Bancoult (No 2)* at [31], [47]–[50], [109], [127]–[130]). However a similar requirement contained in a statutory instrument in respect of a *settled* territory might limit the executive's power since such power would be only subordinate.

The Crown can deprive itself of the prerogative lawmaking power. Lord Mansfield in *Campbell v Hall* (above) decided that, where there is a local legislature, the power is transferred from the Crown to the colony in question and cannot be recovered except by statute.

In *Campbell* the Crown had issued a proclamation empowering a colonial governor to establish a local legislative assembly, although by the date of the action none had been created. Despite the formally announced intention to decentralise government, the Crown had subsequently attempted to impose a new tax directly on the colony and the court held that this was unlawful. Although the assembly had not actually been established it was held that by promising to create one the Crown had lost its power to pass laws under the prerogative for that colony. The reason for this was that the Crown had sought investment and invited settlers to the colony, who would have relied on the promise to create a local assembly. The quandary for Whitehall was that taxes had to be levied if the colonies were not to be a burden on British taxpayers but, after *Campbell*, unless it continued with direct rule, the Crown had to rely on local assemblies to agree to the required taxation. It is unclear whether *Campbell* – the authority of which has never been doubted – is a decision that is now to be confined to its own facts or whether it establishes a wider principle of constitutional law limiting the crown's prerogative powers (Section 14.6), the boundaries of which remain unclear.

Where a British overseas territory of either kind has its own government, even a rudimentary one, it may be that the Crown is 'divisible', meaning that the Crown in relation to the territory is a separate legal entity from the Crown of the UK (*R v Secretary of State for the Foreign and Commonwealth Office, ex p Indian Association of Alberta* [1982] QB 892; *R v Secretary of State for Foreign and Commonwealth Affairs, ex p Quark Fishing Ltd* [2006] 1 AC 3 [9], [20], [76]). If this is correct the courts will assess the Crown's actions in relation to the interests of the territory in question and not those of the UK. Moreover, unless statute provides otherwise, the Crown should act on the advice only of the government of the territories concerned, not that of UK ministers (see Twomey, 'Responsible Government and the Divisibility of the Crown' [2008] PL 742).

In *Quark* Baroness Hale rejected the divided Crown doctrine as artificial (at [95]). In *Bancoult (No 2)* (which concerned a ceded territory (see below)), the House of Lords also rejected the divided Crown doctrine. Lord Hoffmann, following the eminent eighteenth-century jurist William Blackstone (and changing his mind in relation to what he said in *Quark*), stated that in relation to dependent territories there was a single undivided Crown (at [47]–[50]). The divided Crown doctrine is more plausible in relation to independent states, such as Australia, which have chosen to retain the UK monarch as their head of state.

The divided Crown doctrine is sometimes defended on the basis that it may be politically difficult to separate the interests of the UK government as such from its interests in the dependency and undesirable for a court to try to do so. A formal if artificial distinction is therefore useful (see *Quark*).

The judicial review powers of UK courts apply to overseas territories of both kinds – *Quark* (settled territory) and *R (Bancoult) v Secretary of State for the Foreign and Commonwealth Office (No 1)* [2001] 1 QB 1067 (ceded territory). However Laws LJ has suggested that common law presumptions that protect the individual in domestic law against interference from the state have limited application to overseas territories (*Bancoult (No 1)*; Section 6.6). Moreover the Human Rights Act 1998 does not automatically apply to overseas territories (*Quark* (see below)).

The complexities discussed here are illustrated in the following cases.

R v Secretary of State for Foreign and Commonwealth Affairs, ex p Quark Fishing Ltd (2006) concerned a *settled* territory, South Georgia and South Sandwich Islands (SGSSI), which as such was governed by statute. It comprised mainly a shifting population of scientists and its. 'government' was a part-time civil servant Commissioner. The Secretary of State on behalf of the Crown, acting under the constitution of SGSSI (a statutory instrument made under the British Settlements Act 1837), had ordered the Commissioner to refuse a fishing licence to the claimant. His reason for so doing concerned the UK's relationships with neighbouring countries. The Court of Appeal applied the divided Crown doctrine, holding that the decision was unlawful since it was not made for the benefit of SGSSI but for the purposes of the separate UK government.

The claimant also sought damages under the Human Rights Act 1998, which makes the main human rights under the European Convention on Human Rights binding in domestic law. A majority of the House of Lords (Lord Bingham especially applying the divided Crown doctrine) agreed that the decision was made by the Crown of SGSSI not that of the UK. Therefore the Human Rights Act 1998 did not apply since the Act applies only to the UK government. However Lord Nicholls and Lady Hale thought that the divided Crown doctrine (which Lady Hale at least thought questionable) was irrelevant. Their rationale was that, except in special cases, the Human Rights Act 1998 only applies within the UK itself (Section 22.1.1). The Act might however apply to dependent territories if the ECHR has been extended to them, as the Convention so provides.

R (Bancoult) v Secretary of State for the Foreign and Commonwealth Office (No 1) [2001], involved a *ceded* territory governed under the royal prerogative. The Commissioner of the British Indian Ocean Territories (BIOT), which comprised a group of islands, was delegated power to make law for the territory. On the instructions of the UK government, he made an order (the Immigration Ordinance 1971) expelling the population of the territory from the islands, resettling them elsewhere. The population consisted mainly of plantation workers, some of whose families had lived there for several generations. It was UK government policy to use the territory as a military base jointly with the US and for this purpose it wished to remove the inhabitants, treating them as temporary workers so as to avoid problems with the United Nations. The Divisional Court held that the decision was unlawful since it bore no relationship to the interests of the inhabitants. Envoking Magna Carta Laws J also thought that the prerogative power could not be exercised so as to exile a permanent inhabitant from the territory in which he has a right to live.

Following this decision the Foreign Office announced that the islanders would be compensated and allowed to go home. However subsequently the Crown, under pressure apparently from the US, made a Prerogative Order in Council which purported to change the Constitution of BIOT by denying the exiled inhabitants a right of abode in the territory. In *R (Bancoult) v Secretary of State for the Foreign and Commonwealth Office (No 2)* [2008] the House of Lords held that it had jurisdiction to review a Prerogative Order in Council since such an Order was in reality made by ministers not the Crown itself (an example of convention shaping the law; Section 3.4.2). Although an Order in Council was primary legislation it did not have the democratic credentials that made a statute unchallengeable. However this Order was valid. A majority held that the Order was not an abuse of power since the royal prerogative was not limited by any requirement that the law must be for the benefit of the inhabitants of the territory. There was a single Crown which, provided that the interests of the territory were considered, could prefer the larger interests of the UK as a whole. The common law right of a person no to be expelled from his homeland did not apply to the inhabitants of ceded territories. Any right could be removed by a Prerogative Order in Council since this had full lawmaking powers. Even if the power was to be exercised for the benefit of the inhabitants of the territory this did not limit its scope since the court would not inquire whether the Order was in fact for the peace and good government of the inhabitants because this was a general matter of policy unsuitable for a court [109]. The majority also considered that any rights of the inhabitants' had had been compensated with their agreement and that any statement the government had made was not sufficiently clear and unambiguous to create an enforceable 'legitimate expectation' that they would be allowed to return (Section 17.9). Lord Bingham (in his final case) and Lord Mance strongly dissented. They regarded the right to remain in the territory as a fundamental common law 'constitutional' right which applied to all UK territories They applied the 'principle of legality' (Section 6.6), that only clear words in a statute could take away a constitutional right.

Bancoult (No 2) and *Quark* can be distinguished on the basis that the latter concerned a settled territory the inhabitants of which carry their rights under English law. The divided Crown doctrine is therefore even less plausible in relation to a settled territory. Moreover in a settled territory there is no general power to make law under the prerogative, so the ritual phrase 'peace, order and good government [of the territory]' may have some bite.

9.5 International affairs

It is often argued that the state is no longer appropriate as the basic constitutional unit. It is said that pressures from within towards devolution to areas of regional identity, and pressures from outside towards globalisation, have weakened the legitimacy of the state. It is pointed out that we live in a 'global' economy of interdependent countries supported by electronic communication and dominated by highly mobile organisations. International governmental bodies such as the United Nations, the World Trade Organization, the International Monetary Fund and the European Commission wield considerable influence over national governments. Influential businesses such as banks and media organisations are capable of putting pressure upon state governments. They have assets and operations scattered globally which can readily be moved around. Thus while an international business is subject to state laws, enforcing these may be almost impossible. Contemporary problems require international co-operation and sometimes shared laws. These problems include the environment, terrorism, financial wrongdoing, computer fraud and hacking, refugees, human and drug trafficking, fugitive offenders, international trade and financial regulation.

Constitutional law must identify methods by which principles and rules made internationally can be filtered into domestic law and given effect without sacrificing fundamental constitutional principles, in other words trying to strike a balance between constitutionalism and international requirements.

Specific issues include the following:

▶ To what extent are international treaties and other forms of international law binding in UK law?
▶ To what extent are foreign states and their officials subject to UK law?
▶ What is the role of the law in relation to external matters such as sending forces abroad or expelling people from the country?

9.5.1   International law and domestic law

There are two main kinds of international law, namely customary law and treaties. Other international instruments for example declarations made by meetings of leaders are sometimes called 'soft law' meaning that they are influential but not strictly binding.

Customary international law consists of principles generally accepted and evidenced by the practice of states. Customary international law has traditionally been part of the common law and so can be applied directly by the court. However this principle is not popular today. International custom is difficult to establish and customary law gives way to other common law principles (*R (Al Saadoon) v Secretary of State* [2010] at [58], [59]). In particular customary law cannot create new crimes in the UK since this should done only by the democratic process of Parliament (*R v Jones (Margaret)* [2006]: campaigners who damaged military aircraft contrary to a domestic law had no defence of preventing the international crime of aggression since this was not a crime in English law).

Related to custom are certain fundamental principles which are regarded as generally accepted by the international community. These include duties not to harm other states, for example by pollution or unfair use of common resources such as waterways, and international crimes such as torture, genocide and war crimes. In the case of pollution and resource issues enforcement largely depends on international arbitration but international crimes are increasingly enforced through treaties to which effect is given in domestic law.

Today the main method for imposing constitutional order on an unruly world is through international treaties. A treaty (sometimes called a 'convention' but nothing to do with constitutional conventions) is a binding agreement between states or international organisations such as the UN or the EU and states. After a treaty is agreed by representatives of each party it has to be ratified (confirmed) according to the law of each state involved. Ratification brings the treaty into force at international level but not in domestic law.

In the UK treaties are ratified by ministers under the royal prerogative. However Part 2 of the Constitutional Reform and Government Act 2010 places the ratification of treaties partly on a statutory basis by enacting a convention, the 'Ponsonby Convention', under which a treaty was subject to limited parliamentary scrutiny before ratification. Section 20 applies to all treaties (except certain EU treaties that require statutory approval, certain tax treaties and treaties made by UK dependencies and the Channel Islands and Isle of Man). The main provisions are as follows:

▶ A treaty must be laid before Parliament for 21 days and published in a way that the minister 'thinks appropriate'.
▶ If the House of Commons resolves that the treaty should not be ratified the minister can lay a statement before Parliament that it should be ratified anyway and explaining why.
▶ After another 21 days the treaty can be ratified unless the Commons passes a further resolution that it should not be ratified. This process can be repeated but given the strength of the executive and the lack of background information available to Parliament the executive is likely to prevail.
▶ If the House of Lords but not the Commons resolves not to ratify the treaty it can be ratified anyway.

In cases which in a minister's opinion are exceptional, a treaty can be ratified without complying with the above. Before or as soon as possible after ratification the minister must lay a copy of the treaty before Parliament, publish it and lay a statement before Parliament explaining why the case is exceptional (s 22). Parliament has no power in this situation. A treaty is 'non-justiciable' (Section 19.7.1). A court cannot consider whether a treaty making power has been unlawfully exercised or review the content of a treaty or prevent a minister from ratifying it (See *R v Secretary of State for Foreign and Commonwealth Affairs, ex p Rees-Mogg* [1994] 1 All ER 457). Similarly a domestic court cannot normally determine disputed questions of international law (*R (Gentle) v Prime Minister* [2008] 1 AC 1356). However the common law is an open system which can draw on principles from other jurisdictions including international law as a means of evaluating and improving the law.

In addition to ratification a treaty must be made enforceable in domestic law. In some states, for example Germany and Russia, international law including treaties, is automatically part of domestic law. In the UK, which has a *dualist* system, this is not so. Irrespective of ratification a treaty cannot directly alter rights and duties in domestic law unless it is first enacted by Parliament in a statute, either by adopting the language of the treaty or by setting out the treaty as a Schedule to the Act (see *JH Rayner (Mincing Lane) Ltd v Dept of Trade and Industry* [1990] 2 AC 418). This is separate from any parliamentary scrutiny needed for ratification (below). Thus there is a separation of powers protection against lawmaking by the executive albeit weakened by executive domination of Parliament. Treaties which do not directly affect domestic law require only ratification.

It has been suggested that this dualist approach is too narrow and that general principles of international law embodied in treaties concerning fundamental rights such as freedom from torture and freedom of speech should automatically be part of the common law irrespective of their enactment in statute (see Lord Steyn in *Re McKerr* [2004] 1 WLR 807). However this has not received general support; see *R v Bow Street Metropolitan Stipendiary Magistrate, ex p Ugarte (No 3)* [1999] 2 All ER 97.

The treaties which created the EU are the most outstanding examples of incorporation into domestic law. The *UN Refugee Conventions* (Cmd 9171, 1951; Cmnd 3906, 1967) are also important to the Constitution. They require the UK to give asylum to any person who…owing to well founded fear of being persecuted for reasons of race, religion, nationality, membership of a particular social group or political opinion, is outside the country of his nationality and is unable, or, owing to such fear, is unwilling to avail himself of the protection of that country. These have been incorporated into domestic law by way of the European Convention on Human Rights and the Human Rights Act 1998 and also by the Immigration Rules (Section 9.3). (See eg *R v Secretary of State for the Home Dept ex parte Bugdaycay* [1987] 1 AC 514, *RT (Zimbabwe) v Secretary of State for the Home Dept* [2012] 3 WLR 345.)

Reliance on statutory incorporation may cause problems since there might be gaps in the implementation of important treaties. An example is provided by the various UN Conventions against genocide, war crimes, crimes against humanity, torture, hostage taking and other international crimes. These are intended to ensure that all countries apply these offences, wherever committed, in their domestic law. UK law has done so in some respects but the result is patchy. For example offences are not usually retrospective and apply to different dates where particular acts came into force. Most apply only to

UK citizens or offences committed in the UK (eg International Criminal Court Act 2001 (Section 9.6)), but some apply to anyone anywhere (eg Criminal Justice Act 1988, s 134: torture; Taking of Hostages Act 1982). (See Joint Committee on Human Rights, *Closing the Impunity Gap*, HL 153 HC 553 (2008–9).)

Moreover where a treaty has been incorporated into a statute the courts may interpret the statute in a way that differs from the intention of the original treaty. However the courts should interpret and apply a treaty according to international law principles and not domestic law including having resource to any documentation used in preparing the treaty (*traveux preparatois*) (*R (JS) v Secretary of State for the Home Dept [2010] 3 All ER 881*). Nevertheless in *R (ST)(Eritrea) v Secretary of State for the Home Dept* [2012] 3 All ER 1037: the Supreme Court held that 'lawfully' in the Refugee Convention Article 32 which prevented a state expelling a refugee 'lawfully' on its territory except on prescribed grounds, means lawful in domestic law. Even though the treaty must be interpreted generously according to its humanitarian purpose the court would not assume that a convention would override domestic law unless it stated so explicitly.

Treaties and other forms of international law may also be sucked into domestic law indirectly. For example under the Human Rights Act 1998 decisions of the European Court of Human Rights under the ECHR must be taken into account by UK courts even though the ECHR as such has not been incorporated into UK law (Section 22.1). The European Court in turn sometimes applies other international instruments, all of which must therefore be considered by the UK court. For example in *R (Al-Jedda) v Secretary of State* [2008] 1 AC 332 an Iraqi citizen was interned by the army acting under UK jurisdiction in a British army camp in Iraq. He alleged that his human right to freedom under Article 5 of the ECHR had been violated. The House of Lords held that the claimant's right had not been violated. This was because the European Court took the view that in some circumstances other international obligations, in this case to comply with a UN peacekeeping resolution, could override the protection of the ECHR. The House of Lords, faced with a hard choice, held that the claimant's rights could be overridden only to the extent that was necessary to comply with the UN resolution. This involved a careful examination of the resolution and related principles of international law. See also *Rahmatullah v Secretary of State for the Home Dept* [2012] 1 All ER 1290: court can investigate foreign relations including treaties in order to decide whether prisoner lawfully under control of UK government so as to make *habeas corpus* available.

The UK courts have been divided as to the effect of a treaty that has not been incorporated into English law (see Higgins, 2009; Collins, 2009). On a strict traditional view a court should ignore a treaty that has not been incorporated into domestic law since otherwise it would be allowing the executive to make law (see *JH Rayner v Dept of Trade; Brind v Secretary of State* [1991] at [748]). However a court can take a treaty into account where it is relevant to the issues and can interpret a treaty, although it is reluctant to do so (*Othman v Secretary of State* [2009] 4 All ER 1045 [52], *R (Corner House Research) v Director General of the Serious Frauds Office* [2008] 4 All ER 927 [44] [62] [65]).

However the overriding principle remains that international law as such cannot support any argument for the invalidity of a domestic law (*R (Bancoult) v Secretary of State for Foreign and Commonwealth Affairs* [2008] at [66]).

9.5.2   Acts of foreign governments: state immunity

Once there was general common law immunity for acts of foreign governments but as international transactions have increased this has become more relaxed (see UN Convention on Jurisdictional Immunities of States and Their Property (not yet ratified); *Jones v Ministry of Interior of Saudi Arabia* [2007] 1 All ER 113 per Lord Bingham). Nevertheless the importance of international relations requires a large amount of immunity (*Al Adsani v UK* [2001] 34 EHRR 273).

The position depends primarily on the State Immunity Act 1978. The state itself has complete immunity from civil liability (claims for compensation etc) for the acts of its agents even if carried out outside instructions. This applies to the body exercising sovereign authority, meaning the 'executive organs of the central government', to the head of state and to ambassadors representing the state. The Act's protection for serving governments and their servants is a blanket one and applies also to enforcing judgements of foreign courts It applies to unlawful acts and even to violations of fundamental international principles such as torture.

There are certain exceptions. The main exceptions concern commercial transactions (sales and loans), contracts to be performed within the UK, contracts of employment made in the UK or to be performed there, patents and trademarks, personal injury and property damage within the UK, the ownership, possession and use of property, commercial shipping matters and certain taxation matters. However the property of the state central bank or monetary authority cannot be enforced against (see *AIG Capital Parties Inc v Republic of Kazakhstan* [2006] 1 All ER 284). There is a 'restrictive doctrine of immunity'. For example in *NML Capital Ltd v Republic of Argentina* [2011] 4 All ER 1191 a majority of the Supreme Court held that the enforcement of a foreign judgement concerning a commercial transaction which had no link with the UK was not itself immune as a commercial transaction.

The immunity is more limited in the case of individual officials and separate bodies acting as agents of the state ('separate entities'; State Immunity Act 1978, s 14: see *La Generale des Carriers et de Mines v FG Hemisphere Associates LLC* [2013] 1 All ER 409: separate status not conclusive: test is whether activities are integrated with those of government) and also in the case of former heads of state. These might be personally liable. However the immunity of the state cannot be circumvented by using the individual. The individual servant or separate entity is therefore only liable in respect of actions which are not carried out as 'governmental' functions.

Kuwait Airways v Iraqi Airways (No 1) [1995] 3 All ER 694 concerned the Iraqi invasion of Kuwait in 1990, where Iraq claimed that Kuwait was Iraqi territory. Iraqi forces seized aircraft belonging to Kuwait and took them to Iraq. The Iraqi government later made a law transferring the aircraft to the state-owned Iraqi Airways, which used the aircraft for its business. The aircraft were later destroyed in a UN attack on Iraq and the Kuwaiti airline sued Iraqi Airways for compensation. The House of Lords held that the Iraq government itself was immune under the 1978 Act but that, after the law transferring ownership was issued, Iraqi Airways as a separate entity was not using the aircraft for governmental purposes. There was therefore no immunity. A governmental function therefore seems to mean the basic lawmaking, executive and judicial activities of government.

In *Jones v Minister of the Interior of Saudi Arabia [2007]* the House of Lords held that torture carried out by individual officers under the orders of the Saudi government was a governmental function so that the officers were immune from civil liability even though torture is prohibited by a fundamental principle of international law (see Torture Convention (Cm 1775, 1990)). The state itself had blanket immunity. It was also held that, in the interests of international relations, state immunity in civil proceedings complies with the Human Rights Act 1998 (see Fox, 2006).

However Lord Bingham [19] emphasised the distinction between civil and criminal proceeding. Immunity in criminal cases depends on the Diplomatic Privileges Act 1964 as applied to a head of state by section 20 of the State Immunity Act 1978 (below). This gives a serving head of state complete immunity both from criminal and civil liability.

Other officials of a state and also former heads of state are immune from criminal liability only in relation to the proper functions of the state. In *Pinochet* (below) it was held that the former President of Chile had no immunity since for criminal purposes torture should not be regarded as a proper function of the state. This is because all parties to the Torture Convention 1984 have agreed to make torture wherever committed a crime in their states. It is not clear whether the *Pinochet* principle applies to breaches of international law other than torture.

R v Bow Street Metropolitan Stipendiary Magistrate, ex p Pinochet Ugarte (No 3) [1999] illustrates the difficulties of applying international values. Pinochet was the former head of state of Chile making a private visit to the UK. The Spanish government requested that he be extradited to Spain to stand trial in respect of murders and torture that he was alleged to have organised in Chile during his term of office. The Torture Convention 1984 was put into English law by the Criminal Justice Act 1988. The Convention requires a state either to prosecute or extradite an alleged offender. Pinochet relied on state immunity. The House of Lords, unusually comprising seven judges, held that Pinochet was not entitled to immunity. However their Lordships took different routes to their conclusions.

Lords Browne-Wilkinson, Hutton, Saville and Phillips, forming the majority, held that state-sponsored torture violated fundamental principles of international law that Chile had accepted by signing the Convention. Torture was therefore not to be regarded as a proper state function for the purposes of criminal liability. They held however that Pinochet could only be extradited for offences that were alleged to have taken place after 29 September 1988, when the Act came into force, since treaties as such cannot alter rights in English law (above).

Lord Millett, supported partly by Lord Hope and Lord Hutton, was more radical. He argued that, irrespective of the 1988 Act, torture was an international offence under customary international law and was therefore unlawful at common law whenever and wherever committed. Lord Hutton said that 'certain crimes are so grave and so inhuman that the international community is under a duty to bring to justice a person who commits such crimes' (at 163). (In the end the Home Secretary refused to extradite Pinochet on health grounds.)

A principle of non-justiciability also applies in private law by virtue of an old common law rule that a court has no jurisdiction over claims for damages in relation to property rights overseas. This rule was developed in the context of rights over land and is derived from respect for sovereignty. However in *Lucasfilm Ltd v Ainworth* [2012] 1 AC 228 the Supreme Court held that disputes relating to intellectual property such as copyright (in that case helmets used in *Star Wars*) are justiciable since states have a legitimate interest in protecting their copyrights.

9.5.3 Diplomatic immunity

Under international law (Vienna Convention on Diplomatic Relations 1961, Vienna Convention on Consular Relations 1963), serving heads of state, serving diplomats and consular officials and their households other than UK nationals have complete immunity from criminal prosecution and civil liability. (A consul is a state representative with more limited functions than a full diplomatic representative). The Secretary of State can withdraw diplomatic and consular privileges where the state in question does not offer the same privileges to the UK (Diplomatic Privileges Act 1963, s 3; Consular Relations Act 1968, s 2).

The host state cannot enter diplomatic or consular premises (mission) without permission. Thus an embassy might be resorted by fugitives or asylum seekers or used to commit offences. The Secretary of State can withdraw consent if the premises are not being properly used for diplomatic or consular purposes on certain grounds, for example on security grounds, subject to being satisfied that this complies with international law (Diplomatic and Consular Premises Act 1987, enacted following the shooting of a police officer during a siege of the Libyan Embassy in London).

A diplomat or consular official has complete immunity while in the mission but outside the mission is not immune in respect of his or her personal affairs (see *Wokuri v Kassim* [2012] 2 All ER 1195: no immunity for ill treatment of domestic servant).

9.5.4 Act of State

The doctrine of 'act of state' also gives protection to foreign governments. The term is loosely used but has three main meanings.

Firstly it means that for reasons of mutual respect, UK courts will not normally question the acts of foreign governments within their own territories. This applies not only to actions against the state itself but also in any litigation where the matter arises. However this is not an absolute rule and, although the court will exercise great caution, acts which violate clear principles of international law can be questioned. *In Kuwait Airways v Iraqi Airways (Nos 4 and 5)* [2002] (above) the House of Lords held that by confiscating aircraft the Iraq government had committed a flagrant breach of a fundamental principle of international law and this overrode any claim to act of state. Lord Hope stressed that the reach of the law should evolve in keeping with contemporary circumstances.

Secondly an act of state in a more technical sense is a claim that certain facts as declared by the UK government or by another sovereign government cannot be challenged in any litigation. Such acts are carried out under the royal prerogative and therefore are not subject to approval by Parliament (Section 14.6.3). An act of state in this sense includes claims to territory (eg *Buttes Gas and Oil Co v Hammer (Nos 2 and 3)* [1981] 3 All ER 616); conferring sovereign immunity or diplomatic immunity (eg *Mighell v Sultan of Johore* [1894] 1 QB 149, *Engelke v Musmann* [1928] AC 433); the recognition of a foreign government (*Carl-Zeiss-Stiftung v Rayner & Keeler (No 2)* [1967] 1 AC 853; declaring war which invalidates contracts between the enemies (*R v Bottrill, ex p Kuchenmeister* [1947] KB 41). British subjects or rights within the UK have no special protection. For example in *Cook v Sprigg* [1899] AC 572 the Crown annexed Pondoland and refused to honour railway concessions granted to British subjects by the former government (see also *West Rand Central Gold Mining Co v R* [1905] 2 KB 391). (Current practice seems to be to avoid formal declarations of war. For example the invasion of Iraq in 2002 and the defence of the Falkland Islands against Argentina in 1981 were not formal wars.)

Thirdly the defence of 'act of state' prevents the state being liable for injuries it causes overseas. This version of act of state dates from the days of imperial aggression. The Crown is not liable for injuries caused in connection with bona fide acts of government policy overseas provided that the action is authorised or subsequently ratified by the Crown (again this is under the royal prerogative). It is for the court to decide whether an action is genuinely related to government policy but not to decide whether that policy is good or bad. (See eg *Nissan v A-G* [1970] AC 179: British troops billeted in Cyprus hotel: not an act of policy; *Buron v Denman* [1848] 2 Ex 167: British naval officer set fire to barracks in West Africa in order to liberate slaves: Crown subsequently confirmed the action).

The defence of act of state in this third sense does not apply to acts done within the UK itself, except against 'enemy aliens', that is citizens of countries with which we are formally at war (*Johnstone v Pedlar* [1921] 2 AC 262: US citizen imprisoned: Crown liable). This is because the Crown owes a duty to protect anyone who is even temporarily on British soil. Indeed for the same reason the defence may not be available against a British subject anywhere in the world. In *Nissan* the House of Lords expressed divided views (see also *Walker v Baird* [1892] AC 491). It seems unfair to favour people with no substantial link with the UK merely because they happen to hold British passports.

9.5.5   Other actions abroad

A wider issue overlapping with but not to be confused with act of state is that of *justiciability*. This is a general doctrine (Section 19.7) but applies especially to foreign affairs. We have seen that a treaty is not generally justiciable. Sometimes a policy act of government, will not be investigated by the court on the ground that the court does not consider that it has the expertise, tools or constitutional legitimacy to dig deeper. In *Buttes Gas v Hammer (above)* the doctrine was justified at the international level as applying 'where there are no judicial or manageable standards ... or the court would be in a judicial no-man's land' (at 938). In *R(Gentle) v Prime Minister* [2008] 3 All ER 1 The House of Lords held that the conduct of armed hostilities is essentially non-justiciable.

Even if a governmental act is justiciable the courts may be reluctant to intervene where they regard the particular issues raised unsuitable for the courts in the light of international politics. In particular the executive is given 'deference' or a broad 'margin of discretion' in its dealings with overseas governments so that the court will intervene only in exceptional circumstances (Section 19.7.1). (See *R (Abassi) v Secretary of State for the Foreign and Commonwealth Office* [2002] EWCA Civ 1598, *R (Al Rawi) v Secretary of State for the Foreign and Commonwealth Office* [2007] 2 WLR 1219: diplomatic support for UK citizens imprisoned in Guantanamo Bay (Steyn, 'Guantanamo Bay: The Legal Black Hole" (2004) 53 ICLQ 1)). In *R v Jones (Margaret)* (2006) the House of Lords was influenced by the reluctance of the courts to investigate the deployment of the armed forces in holding that the international crime of aggression was not an offence in domestic law. (See also Section 22.2.)

9.5.6 International co-operation

International relations sometimes involve a tension between the legal and political standards familiar in the UK and those in other countries. This relates in particular to immigration, security and crime. The topic is too large and various to be dealt with in this book and we will confine ourselves to sketching the main constitutional features. The UK has been jealous of its rights in relation to security and law enforcement and has opted out of many EU functions concerned with policing and justice matters. Humanitarian concerns and need for co-operation with other states (comity) have led to important treaties which have been implemented in domestic law. Examples are as follows.

UK criminal law normally applies only within the territory, but some crimes such as torture are regarded as so heinous that they can be prosecuted wherever committed irrespective of nationality (see Torture Convention 1984; Criminal Justice Act 1988, s 134).

Certain UN Conventions, including the power to freeze assets belonging to suspected offenders, can be given effect by Order in Council under the United Nations Act 1947 (Section 24.7.6).

9.6 Removal from the UK

A person can be removed from the UK in three cases, expulsion under immigration law, by deportation and under extradition law. As an aspect of sovereignty States have always had wide powers in international law to control entry and to expel aliens. At common law aliens have no rights to remain in the UK. Since the Immigration Act 1972 which was described by Lord Hope as a constitutional landmark (*R (Alvi) v Secretary of State for the Home Dept* [2012] 1 WLR 2208 [31]), in relation to immigration common law powers under the royal prerogative power have been largely replaced by statute.

Some categories of non-citizen have a right to live in the UK. Those who were ordinarily resident in the UK without restrictions on 1 January 1983 do not need leave to enter and remain (Immigration Act 1971, s 1(2)). Under EU law citizens of the EU and the broader European Economic Area (Norway, Iceland, Liechtenstein: Lisbon Agreement 2004) have freedom of movement within the UK (Immigration Act 1988, s 7). Citizens of the Republic of Ireland, the Channel Islands and the Isle of Man are not subject to immigration control although passport checks have recently been introduced (Immigration Act 1971, ss 1(3), (9)).

Under the Immigration Act 1972 Act (as much amended) the Home Secretary has discretionary powers to give other non-citizens leave to remain either for specific periods or indefinitely (Immigration Act 1972 as amended). A person who is in breach of leave requirements can be expelled. This power is guided by Immigration Rules made by the Home Secretary which comprise a mixture of binding rules and discretionary guidance. The application of these rules is a fertile source of litigation since governments are tempted to push them to their limits. The government cannot impose higher obstacles to immigration than those set out in the rules themselves (*Pankina v Secretary of State* [2011] 1 All ER 1043, *R (Mayaya) v Secretary of State* [2012] 1 All ER 1491). The Home Secretary can revoke indefinite leave on grounds of public good (Immigration, Asylum and Nationality Act 2006, s 57).

9.6.1   Deportation and expulsion

Non-citizens other than those with certain exemptions based on residential status can be expelled on public interest grounds (deportation) notably in connection with public order and security (Immigration Act 1971, s 3(5), s 7). Under the Human Rights Act 1998 this power, in common with the power to expel under immigration law (above), is subject to rights under the ECHR notably respect for family life which could be disrupted by the removal (Section 21.4.3). The court must strike a balance between these rights and the public interest (Section 22.7). It can take into account not only the claimant's family circumstances such as dependents but also the contribution made to the community by the claimant (*UE (Nigeria) v Secretary of State* [2011] 2 All ER 352). Unlike cases where a violation of the right is anticipated in the country to which the claimant is sent this is not limited to *flagrant* violations (see *Norris v Government of the USA (No 2)* [2010] at [29] [30]. Special appeal courts have been established in respect of security issues (Section 24.3.4).

Non-citizens may also be subject to wider powers of exclusion and expulsion under the royal prerogative. Section 33(5) of the Immigration Act 1972 provides: 'This Act shall not be taken to supercede or impair any power exercisable by Her Majesty in relation to aliens by virtue of her prerogative'. If *so* there is no right of appeal and the courts' more limited powers of judicial review provide the only remedy. There is a basic right to a hearing (see *IR (Sri Lanka) v Secretary of State for the Home Dept* [2011] 4 All ER 906).

In *R (G) v Secretary of State for the Home Dept* [2012] 1 All ER 1129: the prerogative power was used to exclude an anti Israeli agitator (following revocation of the claimant's citizenship under statute). However the decision seems doubtful. In *R (Alvi) v Secretary of State for the Home Dept* [2012] Lord Hope suggested that in the light of contemporary human rights standards which require clear legal procedures, the prerogative power no longer has any practical effect. In *R (Munir) v Secretary of State for the Home Dept* (2012) [25] [26] the Supreme Court suggested (obiter) that the prerogative power was confined to times of war.

9.6.2   Extradition

Extradition is a response to a request from another state to send a person to it either to be tried or sentenced for a criminal offence or because that person has escaped from custody. Extradition therefore raises a conflict between mutual co-operation and the question of whether the justice system in the other country is such that serious injustice is being done. There is no general obligation to extradite. Any obligation to do so is based on treaties between the states in question. However as Lord Phillips pointed out in *Norris v Government of the USA (No 2)* [2010] at [5] increasing international co-operation in the fight against crime has generated a number of treaties imposing such an obligation not least with the US.

Extradition law is highly complex and only the main considerations will be sketched here.

Under the Extradition Act 2003 requesting states are graded into two categories:

▶ Firstly there are the trusted *Category 1* countries, mainly other EU members but others can be added by Order in Council. A state which retains the death penalty cannot qualify (s 1). Extraditable offences are offences committed in the requesting state and not the UK, contained on a list of offences specified in the *European Arrest Warrant Framework Decision* of the EU Council (2002/584/HA; Extradition Act 2003, Sch 2) and punishable with at least three years' imprisonment. International crimes such as genocide are also extraditable (s 64(6), (7)). Offences punishable by 12 months' or more imprisonment may also be extraditable even if partly committed in the UK but must be offences both in the UK and in the requesting country.

▶ Where the requesting country issues a warrant to a designated authority in the UK certified as such by the Secretary of State (these are the usual prosecuting agencies) naming the suspect and specifying the offence the offender must be arrested and brought before a senior district judge (lower level criminal judge). A provisional arrest of a suspect in advance of a warrant is permissible. The court's function is limited to checking whether the accused is the right person and the offence is an extraditable offence. The question of guilt or innocence is not investigated. There is an appeal to the High Court and with permission to the Supreme Court, but only if the High Court certifies that a point of law of general public importance is involved.

▶ The accused must be extradited unless certain 'extraneous considerations' apply, in which case the accused cannot be extradited. These include double jeopardy (s 12), lapse of time where extradition would be unjust or oppressive (s 14), discrimination (s 13), age (below the age of criminal responsibility in the UK, which is ten years), human rights (s 21) and 'Speciality', meaning the absence of an agreement between the UK and the requesting state that the suspect will be dealt with only in relation to the matters specified in the warrant. There are provisions relating to the offence of hostage taking under which a person cannot be extradited if his trial would be prejudiced because he cannot communicate with the authorities.

▶ In respect of Category 2 states, which include all other states, the main differences are as follows:

(i) There must be an extradition treaty between the requesting state and the UK.

(ii) The extradition request is made to the Home Secretary.

(iii) The warrant is a UK warrant issued by a court.

(iv) The offence must be an offence in UK law if it were committed in the UK.

(v) The court must be satisfied that there is sufficient evidence to justify the extradition, namely a prima facie case, that is evidence that if proved would mean guilt. However in the case of requests from the US the treaty dispenses with this safeguard (Extradition Treaty 2003, Cm 5821). There is no reciprocal provision on the US side and the arrangements are widely regarded as unfair.

(vi) After rights of appeal have been exhausted the final decision is taken by the Home Secretary, who has a limited discretion (s 93). She can consider whether on the grounds of physical or mental condition extradition would be unjust or oppressive. She must also take into account whether the death penalty is involved and the Speciality issue (above). The Home Secretary is not involved with Category 1 cases.

The former exclusion for 'political offences' was abolished by the 2003 Act. However the UK can refuse to extradite a person who was acting as an agent for the UK government, on national security grounds, if the conduct in question was not criminal in the UK due to authority given by the Secretary of State (s 203; Sections 23.4, 23.5).

The International Criminal Court Act 2001 gives effect to the Statute of the International Criminal Court (ICC). This makes provision for states to extradite suspects to the International Criminal Court in the Hague. The Act covers offences of genocide, war crimes and crimes against humanity. (The latter includes enslavement, expulsion, torture, rape, forcible transfer of property, enforced prostitution, apartheid, and other' inhuman acts of a similar character which intentionally cause great suffering or serious injury to the body or to mental or physical health.) The crime of Aggression which covers attacks upon other countries has not been included to date because of difficulties of definition. The ICC can designate the UK as the state where a sentence of imprisonment is to be served.

The ICC has jurisdiction where the domestic jurisdiction is unable or unwilling to investigate. There is no state immunity. A UK court must deliver a suspect for extradition to ICC on production of a properly issued warrant. The slowness of ICC procedure has been criticised. So far there has been only one conviction that of a former African Head of State.

The Act also creates offences in domestic law of genocide, crimes against humanity and war crimes committed in England and Wales by anyone or outside the UK by a British national. The UK has therefore rejected a wider principle of international law that of universal jurisdiction which would have given the courts jurisdiction over these crimes committed anywhere. It applies the 'active personality principle' based on the nationality of the offender. Moreover crimes committed abroad before 2001 when the Act came into force are immune. It is however possible that heinous offence might be subject to customary international law (above).

9.6.3   Human rights restrictions on removal

Under the UN Refugee Conventions 1951 and 1967 a person cannot be removed to a country where he or she would be at risk of torture or inhumane or degrading treatment contrary to Article 3 of the ECHR (*Chahal v UK* (1997) 23 EHRR 413). In *R (Ullah) v Special Adjudicator* [2004] 3 All ER 785 the House of Lords extended this principle to the risk of serious violations of other right under the ECHR in that case religious freedom (Art 9). The same applies to the right to a fair trial (Art 6, Section 21.4.2), and privacy and respect for family life (Art 8, Section 21.4.3). However in these cases there must be a real risk of a flagrant breach of the Convention (*EM (Lebanon) v Secretary of State for the Home Dept* [2009] 1 AC 1198).

This raises problems concerning respect for international relations given the cultural and social differences involved. For example in *HJ (Iran) v Secretary of State for the Home Dept* [2010] 3 WLR 386 the House of Lords held that a person could not be expelled to a country where he or she would be unable openly to live as a homosexual. However it was emphasised that UK is not entitled to impose its own values on other countries but only to protect the core entitlements recognised by the international community. (See also *EM (Lebanon) v Secretary of State* (above): separation of mother and child was a flagrant violation but the arbitrary and discriminatory nature of Lebanese family law was not sufficient in itself.)

In *Chahal v UK* (1996) (above) the European court required an effective remedy in the form of 'independent scrutiny' to protect rights under Article 3 but held that this does not require a full judicial hearing compliant with the right to a fair trial under Article 6. Thus in *RB (Algeria) v Secretary of State for the Home Dept* [2010] 2 AC 110 the claimants could not resist deportation to Jordon on the ground that a trial in Jordan would not be independent of the government. The House of Lords held that even though in a English case the arrangements in the Jordanian court would violate the right to a fair trial, in relation to a foreign trial the court would intervene only if there was evidence of a 'flagrant denial of justice'. There was a risk that evidence obtained by torture of witnesses might be used but it was held that this would not necessarily be a flagrant denial of justice and the court was entitled to rely on assurances from the overseas government that a person would not be mistreated.

However in *Othman (Abu Quatada) v UK* (ECHR App No 8139/09 (2012)) the European Court of Human Rights held that it would be a 'flagrant denial of justice' to deport the claimant, a long standing terrorist suspect, to stand trial in Jordan where there was a 'real risk' that evidence obtained by torture might be used. Assurances from the Jordon government could be taken into account. Satisfactory assurances were given that the claimant himself would not be tortured and the court took into account the historical strong relations between the UK and Jordon and the high levels of the Jordon government at which the assurances were approved. However no assurances had been given about witnesses. Despite further discussions between the UK and Jordan governments, the Special Immigration Appeals Tribunal (SIAC) refused to permit the claimant's deportation on the ground that adequate assurances have not been given (*Times* 13 November 2012).

Where the death penalty is involved removal is never justified. However in cases where a harsh penalty such as life without the possibility of parole is involved the court must take into account the proportionality of the sentence in relation for example to any mitigating factors such as age or mental health problems. (See *Harkins and Edwards v UK*, ECHR App Nos. 9146/07, 32650/07, 17 January 2012, *R (Wellington) v Secretary of State for the Home Dept* [2009] 1 AC 335).)

There is also human rights protection where removal would violate rights within the UK notably the right to family life and especially the interests of children which the removal would disrupt. In expulsion, deportation and extradition cases these rights are balanced against the public interest under the doctrine of proportionality (Section 22.7). The same general principles apply in all cases. All the circumstances are examined. For example in *ZH (Tanzania) v Secretary of State for the Home Dept* [2011] 2 AC 166 the Supreme Court upheld an appeal against the removal of a mother under immigration control in the interests of the stability of the children's lives (see also *AA v UK* (2011) App 8000/08: deportation of a child who had been convicted of rape was excessive given that there were strong family and community links and a previous record of good behaviour.

However in *extradition* cases respect for international relations carries great weight and so may change the balance (*H v Lord Advocate* [2012] 3 WLR 151). Thus in *Norris v USA (No 2)* (2010) where no children were involved, the offence, obstructing justice, was of significant gravity and the importance of co-operating with the US outweighed the health effects on the claimant and his wife. By contrast in *H v Deputy Prosecutor of the Italian Republic Genoa* [2012] 3 WLR 90 an appeal was allowed where an unwell husband would be left as sole carer for young children and the offence of importing drugs was regarded as 'of no great gravity'. But in *H v Lord Advocate* (2012) a husband and wife lost their appeal against extradition to the USA to face a much larger scale commercial drug trafficking charge even though the children were at risk of being put into care. The importance of combating crime and the desirability of a trial in the US was held to be overwhelming. Thus the matter is one of subjective judgement.

Summary

▶ The UK constitution has no unified concept of the state. This leads to a fragmented system of government but may protect individual freedom.

▶ Citizenship entitles a person to reside in the UK and has certain other miscellaneous consequences. There is no legal concept of the citizen corresponding to the republican notion of equal and responsible membership of the community.

▶ The UK constitution does not distribute power geographically so as to limit the power of the state. The UK is therefore not a federal state. The UK has devolved governments subordinate to the centre (see Chapter 16).

▶ British overseas territories are subject to the jurisdiction of the UK courts but not generally to the Human Rights Act 1998. The lawmaking power of the UK government depends on whether the territory in question is a settled territory. The powers of the executive are wider in the case of a ceded territory.

▶ The traditional 'divided Crown' doctrine is questionable and the cases conflict.

▶ The Queen is head of the Commonwealth. This has no constitutional connection with the UK.

▶ International law does not automatically apply in domestic law but is filtered into UK law by Parliament and the courts. Customary international law is to a limited extent recognised by the common law. A treaty must be ratified by the Crown, normally with the consent of Parliament.

▶ The courts have recently become more liberal in their use of treaties in domestic law but a treaty cannot directly alter legal rights and duties unless incorporated into a statute. Treaties can be used to help the interpretation of statutes. The practice of incorporation by statute has made it difficult for universal principles of international law to be applied systematically.

▶ Substantial immunity from control by the courts is given to foreign governments and heads of state by statute but this only applies to individual officials and separate public bodies in respect of government functions as such.

▶ Foreign governments, and sometimes the UK government exercising functions in relation to foreign affairs, are also protected by the overlapping concepts of 'act of state'. This has at least three different meanings: conclusive evidence of a state of affairs, an act of high policy that is non-justiciable and a defence to an action against the Crown for causing injury or damage abroad. However important international standards have made some inroads into this.

▶ There are arrangements for co-operation with other states in relation to criminal jurisdiction. There are different levels of extradition arrangements depending upon the relationship with the other state. There are special arrangements regarding the International Criminal Court.

Exercises

9.1 To what extent does UK law recognise the concept of the state? Is the concept of the Crown an adequate substitute? (See also Section 14.1.)

9.2 What is a federation? Outline the advantages and disadvantages of a federal structure compared with a devolved structure.

9.3 To what extent does the UK constitution provide satisfactory means of giving effect to international treaties?

9.4 Explain and illustrate the different meanings of 'act of state'.

9.5 The UK government decides to recognise Cornwall as an independent state. In order to help the new Cornish government to get established, the Prime Minister sends an army platoon to Cornwall as a peacekeeping force. Bill, a UK citizen, and Hilary, a US citizen, each own a hotel in Cornwall. Bill also runs a taxi business from his hotel. Hilary's hotel is damaged by British troops during a birthday party for their corporal. The Cornish head of state uses Bill's hotel as his office while a new palace is being built. He has not paid his bill for several weeks. Also, on the instructions of the Cornish government, Cornish soldiers commandeered Bill's fleet of taxis for use in military operations.
  (i) Advise Bill and Hilary as to any remedies available to them in the English courts.
  (ii) The UK government learns that officials in the Cornish Mission in London are holding a group of English nationalists against their will and are possibly torturing them. Advise the UK government. Suppose that the group are released. Advise them of any legal remedies available to them.

9.6 The (imaginary) island of Stark was settled by the UK in the seventeenth century. It has a population of 600. It is governed by a Commissioner employed by the Foreign Office, who is advised by an elected Council. The UK government makes an Order requiring all the inhabitants to leave the island. The reason it gives is that it fears the island will soon be devastated by a volcano. George, whose family has lived on Stark for many years, is told by an American friend that the government's real motive is to hand the island over to the US for a naval base. Advise George as to whether he can successfully challenge the Order in the English courts. Would it make any difference if Stark had originally been seized by Britain from France?

9.7 The Government of Carribia, an independent Commonwealth country, is overthrown by a rebel force, The People's Front. Cane, the displaced Prime Minister of Carribia, requests the aid of the British government. British troops are sent to Carribia and are authorised under an agreement between the British government and Cane to 'use all necessary measures to restore the lawful government of Carribia'. During the British troops' campaign on the island they requisition buildings owned by Ford, an American citizen, for use as a military depot, and destroy the home of Austin, a British citizen, in the belief that it is being used as a base by the rebels. Ford and Austin sue the British government for compensation. Discuss. Would your answer differ if Carribia was a British overseas territory?

9.8 Suppose that a new government recognised by the UK has been installed in Ruritania (above) and Toby the former Governor General has fled to the UK together with his wife. His children are already at school in the UK. Toby devotes himself to charitable fund raising. Two years later the Ruritanian government requests the UK to extradite Toby on charges of fraud. There is a possible sentence of life without parole for this offence. Advise the UK government. Would it make any difference if the alleged fraud related only to Toby's private affairs?

9.9 Jack and Jill are mercenary soldiers who are suspected of being involved in torture and hostage taking during conflicts in several states. The dates when these crimes were allegedly committed are unclear. Jack is a UK citizen, Jill is not. The ICC has issued a warrant for their arrest. Advise the UK authorities as to what matters they should consider as to whether they should be prosecuted in the UK or surrendered to the ICC.

Further reading

Brown, 'Moving from Cosmopolitan Legal Theory to Legal Practice: Models of Cosmopolitan Law' (2008) 28 LS 430

Collins, 'Aspects of Justiciability in International Law' in Andenas and Fairgrieve (eds), *Tom Bingham and the Transformation of the Law* (Oxford University Press 2009)

Dober and Loughlin, eds, *The Twilight of Constitutionalism* (Oxford University Press 2010)

Dyson, *The State Tradition in Western Europe* (Martin Robertson 1980) chs 1, 4

Feldman, 'The Internationalization of Public Law and Its Impact on the UK ' in Jowell and Oliver (eds), *The Changing Constitution* (7th edn, Oxford University Press 2011)

Fox, 'In Defence of State Immunity' (2006) 55 ICLQ 399

Higgins, 'National Courts and the International Court of Justice' in Andenas and Fairgrieve (eds), *Tom Bingham and the Transformation of the Law* (Oxford University Press 2009)

Ladeur (ed), *Public Governance in the Age of Globalisation* (Ashgate 2004) chs 2, 3, 5, 7, 8

Lester, 'Citizenship and the Constitution', in *Halsbury's Laws of England Centenary Essays 2007* (Lexis Nexis Butterworths 2007)

Loughlin, *Foundations of Public Law* (Oxford University Press 2010) chs 7–9

Lowe, 'Rules of International Law in English Courts' in Andenas and Fairgrieve (eds), *Tom Bingham and the Transformation of the Law* (Oxford University Press 2009)

Malkani, 'Human Rights Treaties in the English Legal System,' [2011] PL 554

Murray, 'In the Shadow of Lord Haw: Guantanamo Bay,' Diplomatic Protection and Allegiance [2011] PL 115

Walker, 'The Idea of Constitutional Pluralism' (2002) 65 MLR 317

Chapter 10

The European Union

In this chapter, we shall discuss the main legal principles relating to the European Union as they affect the UK constitution. We shall not discuss the internal workings of the EU except from this perspective. Readers should also refer to Section 8.5.4, which discusses the impact of the EU on parliamentary supremacy.

10.1 Introduction: the nature of the European Union

The legal basis of the EU comprises treaties which authorise the making of laws which are directly enforceable under the law of the member states as well as at the European level. However despite claims made by EU bodies that the EU Treaty is a 'basic constitutional charter' (see *Parti Ecologiste 'Les Verts' v European Parliament* [1986] ECR 1339), as far as the UK constitution is concerned, the EU is part of UK law by neither more nor less than the normal process for enacting a treaty into domestic law (Section 9.5.1). EU law was made effective in the UK by the European Communities Act 1972. The courts of other member states have made it clear that EU law is valid domestically only by virtue of their own constitutions (see *Brunner v EU Treaty* [1994] 1 CMLR 57 [55], Germany; *Carlsen v Rasmussen* (1999) 23 CMLR 854, Denmark). In that sense there is nothing constitutionally peculiar about the EU.

This is not to deny the importance of EU law which was famously described by Lord Denning as an 'incoming tide' (*Bulmer Ltd v Bollinger SA* [1974] 2 All ER 1226). Laws made by EU bodies permeate many areas of law and EU principles and reasoning methods have infiltrated into the general law. Some EU laws can override UK statutes but while this modifies the practical application of parliamentary sovereignty this is by virtue of the 1972 Act and does not override parliamentary sovereignty (Section 8.5.4).

The main constitutional problem arising out of the relationship between the EU and the UK is the weakness of democratic accountability of EU decisions. Unlike the UK the main EU lawmakers, the European Commission and Council of ministers are unelected. (Members of the Council may or may not have been elected under their own countries' constitutions.)

What was originally called the Common Market was created after World War 2 as an aspiration to prevent further wars in Europe and to regenerate the European economies. The prototype was the European Coal and Steel Community created by the Treaty of Paris (1951). This was intended as an international control over the resources of war and is now abolished. Two other communities were created in 1957 by two Treaties of Rome. They were the European Community (formerly called the European Economic Community) and the European Atomic Energy Community. The communities shared the same institutions.

The founder members were France, Germany, Italy, Luxembourg, Belgium and the Netherlands. Membership has steadily increased. The UK became a member in 1972 (European Communities Act 1972), membership being endorsed by a referendum in 1975. There are now 27 members, including former communist countries, thereby altering the original balance and introducing a wide range of economic, political, cultural and religious perspectives that challenge the old-fashioned blend of republicanism and liberalism of the founder members. Members who joined at later dates are Austria, Denmark, Finland, Greece, Ireland, Portugal, Spain and Sweden. The following joined in 2004 under the Nice Treaty (2003): Cyprus, the Czech Republic, Estonia, Hungary, Latvia, Lithuania, Malta, Poland, Slovakia and Slovenia. Bulgaria and Romania joined in 2007. Turkey, Serbia and Iceland have applied for membership.

The objectives of the communities were originally economic, primarily to encourage free movement of people, services, goods and capital between member states. However the organisation was heavily influenced by a desire to protect agricultural interests, espoused principally by France. This has left the EU with a substantial financial burden in that about a third of its budget is still devoted to agricultural subsidies. The interests of the EU have steadily widened, partly by a process of interpreting the existing objectives liberally and partly by the member states formally agreeing to extend its areas of competence. For example the Single European Act 1987 made environmental protection a separate area of competence and the Lisbon Treaty (2009) has added space, policy, energy, tourism, civil protection and administrative cooperation. The EU has also developed substantial security, justice, policing and foreign policy objectives in an attempt to increase its influence on the world stage. However there is provision for states to take competencies back and indeed to leave the EU. This requires the agreement of the European Council and the Parliament (Section 10.2).

A series of treaties broadened the scope of the EU but also introduced measures under which individual states could participate to different extents:

▶ *The Single European Act 1987* was intended to strengthen community institutions and widen the scope of community powers. It created the European Council of heads of state and strengthened the role of the European Parliament. It broadened the scope of EU law, in particular to include environmental protection. It also initiated a gradual process of reducing the power of individual states to veto community proposals.

▶ *The Maastricht Treaty* (1992) created the EU as an umbrella political organisation but at the time without its own legal identity. Maastricht also instigated progress towards monetary union, including the creation of an independent European Central Bank and single European currency, the euro, which has been adopted by 17 of the member states but not by the UK. The Euro is currently in trouble because of the disparate economic strengths of its subscribers. A single currency usually presupposes a strong central political authority which is lacking in the EU. There is also freedom of movement between the mainland EU states under the *Schengen Agreement*. The UK is not a party to this. Thus the Maastricht Treaty enabled participation in the EU at different levels.

▶ *The Amsterdam Treaty* (1997) introduced further safeguards and flexibility arrangements in favour of national governments, which can opt in or out of some provisions. Involvement in the European enterprise is therefore sometimes described as 'variable geometry'.

▶ *The Nice Treaty* (2003) made some reforms to cater for the larger membership of the community. These included the creation of the Court of First Instance and enlarging the membership of the European Parliament.

▶ *The Lisbon Treaty* (Cm 7294, 2009) is an attempt to rationalise and consolidate the European Union as a supranational organisation. It replaces the so-called Constitutional Treaty which was rejected in 2005 by referenda in France and

Germany. Illustrating the political sensitivity of the idea of a written constitution, the Lisbon Treaty reproduces the main provisions of the abortive constitution minus its constitutional rhetoric. Instead it is drafted as a complex amending treaty overlaying previous treaties. The Lisbon Treaty is intended to strengthen the European Union as an international organisation, a role the EU has so far failed to achieve, and to streamline its decision-making processes (see House of Lords Select Committee on the European Union, Tenth Report (HL 2007–08, 62)). The Lisbon Treaty extends the 'variable geometry' of the EU by introducing arrangements for 'enhanced cooperation' under which at least nine states may apply to the Council of Ministers to 'opt in' to exercise extra powers. This must be a last resort and must not undermine the internal market or economic, social or territorial cohesion. Thus the aspiration towards universal abstract rules and ideals cutting across cultural differences is far from achieved. The current treaties as revised by the Lisbon Treaty are the *Treaty on European Union* (TEU) and the *EC Treaty*, now to be called *The Treaty on the Functioning of the European Union* (TFEU). The TEU deals with general political principles and the basic structure and functions of the institutions. The TFEU deals with the specific powers and functions of the EU, its legal machinery and the detailed composition, powers and processes of the institutions. It also deals with the Charter of Fundamental Rights. In 1991 the European Court of Justice (ECJ), which is charged not only with securing compliance with the law but also with advancing the aims of the communities, described the EC Treaty as a 'constitutional charter' based on the rule of law. It emphasised that individuals as well as states are the subjects of community law, although in fact individuals other than those employed by the EU have only limited rights to instigate proceedings in the Court (see *Opinion on the Draft Agreement on a European Economic Area* [1991] ECR I-6084).

The rule of law is a primary concern. All EU laws and decisions must fall within the powers conferred by the treaties and cannot go beyond what is necessary for achieving the objectives of the treaties. As with all treaties, an alteration to the EU treaties requires the consent and ratification of member states. To this end there is an elaborate procedure for consultation involving the EU institutions and national Parliaments and an intergovernmental conference (TEU, Art 48).

The following are the broad areas of competence of the EU (TFEU). They are ordered historically. They overlap, and some (notably the internal market) have a higher priority than others, acting as a general theme. The same is true to a lesser extent of the environment, which must be integrated into all policies. There are sometimes provisions for states to opt out or take individual measures.

- the internal market: free movement of goods within the EU;
- free movement of export and imports (customs union);
- agriculture and fisheries;
- free movement of persons, services and capital;
- establishment (setting up businesses etc);
- providing services within member states;
- movements of capital;
- freedom (mainly immigration), security (policing) and justice (cooperation between court systems); this is a sensitive area due to different legal cultures within the Union (the UK has opted out of much of this);
- transport;

- competition, taxation and 'approximation' (harmonisation) of national laws in order to achieve the single market;
- economic and monetary policy (the UK has opted out of the single currency, the euro);
- employment;
- social policies: living and working conditions, social security, high employment, labour relations;
- European Social Fund: employment in deprived areas (eg Cornwall);
- education, vocational training, youth and sport;
- culture;
- public health;
- 'trans-Europe networks': transport, telecommunications, energy infrastructure;
- industry (competitiveness);
- economic, social and territorial cohesion (reducing regional disparities);
- environment;
- energy;
- tourism;
- civil protection;
- administrative cooperation;
- external relationships.

Before the Lisbon Treaty the powers of the EU bodies were grouped into three main policy areas, or 'pillars': economic development, common foreign and security policy, and cooperation in justice and home affairs. Only the first pillar, which of course is very large, together with immigration, was regulated by law. The Lisbon Treaty enables all areas of EC concern in principle to be legally enforceable. The EU now has three kinds of power (TFEU, Arts 3–6):

- *Exclusive power* concerns customs, competition in relation to the internal market, the euro, the common fisheries policy and common commercial policy. In these cases, member states cannot legislate independently at all.
- In most other cases there is *shared power*. Here member states can legislate, at least until the EC has decided to intervene (see *Commission v UK* [1981]).
- *Supporting, co-ordinating or complementary functions* are primarily for the member states but the EU can exercise funding powers. This category includes health, industry, culture, tourism, education, vocational training, youth and sport, civil protection and administrative cooperation.

The EU generates its values mainly from individualistic and economic liberalism (Section 2.3). Its values are declared to be respect for human dignity, freedom, democracy, equality, the rule of law and human rights. In certain circumstances the Council of Ministers can suspend membership rights of states which are judged to have seriously violated these values (TEU, Art 7).

There is some republican element (Section 2.5). For example it is made clear that every citizen has an equal right to participate in the democratic life of the Union (TEU, Arts 9, 10). However this is realised only by limited voting rights for political parties in the European Parliament (below) and various opportunities to make requests of officials. There is a concept of citizenship of the EU that is conferred automatically on citizens of the member states (TEU, Art 9; TFEU, Arts 20–22). This is additional to state citizenship and gives certain rights. These are free movement and residence within the EU, the right to stand or vote in local government and devolved government elections and in elections to the European Parliament on the same terms as nationals, and various rights of access to EU institutions. Democracy has not been the highest value of either the original or the revised union. Democratic government is a requirement of membership and the EU claims to act on the principle of representative democracy. By this it means the right to vote for representatives in the European Parliament and the fact that the European Council and the Council of Ministers (below) are made up of representatives of the member states, albeit not necessarily elected ones (see TEU, Art 10). The EU is a paternalistic concept intended to impose a particular vision of the good life built around a combination of welfare and market liberalism. The various unelected European institutions therefore have a larger share of power than the elected European Parliament. However the democratic element in EU processes has been strengthened by the Lisbon Treaty, mainly by improving links with national Parliaments (Section 10.4).

The historian Tony Judt doubted the democratic credentials of the EU. He characterised the EU as similar to the enlightened European despots of the eighteenth century with their 'ideal of efficient, universal administration, shorn of particularisms and driven by rational calculation and the rule of law' (*New York Review of Books* 1995, quoted by Wheatcroft, *Guardian*, 9 August 2010).

10.2   Institutions

The main EU institutions are as follows:

▶ Council of Ministers;
▶ European Council;
▶ European Commission;
▶ European Parliament;
▶ European Court of Justice.

Other important community institutions include the Court of Auditors and the Committee of Permanent Representatives (COREPER), comprising senior officials who prepare the Council's business and are very influential, and the European Central Bank. There are also advisory and consultative bodies, notably the Economic and Social Committee and the Committee of the Regions. These are outside the scope of this book.

The EU has lawmaking, executive and judicial powers which are blended in a unique way that does not correspond to traditional notions of the separation of powers or liberal democracy. There are no clear lines of accountability. Power is divided between institutions, some of which share the same functions. The primary concern is to provide a balance between the interests of the Community and those of the member states. Thus lawmaking is divided between the Commission which represents the community and the Council of Ministers which comprises representatives from the member states. The directly elected Parliament also has a role in lawmaking but not a primary one. Such democratic accountability as there is takes the forms of a limited degree of accountability to the Parliament and arrangements under the constitutions of the individual states. The balance between the different bodies varies according to the treaty provision under which a particular issue arises. It might be said that the primary distribution of power creates a tension between a centralising rationalist element represented by the Commission and the Court and a negotiating cooperative element represented by the Council and the Parliament.

10.2.1 The Council of Ministers

This is the primary lawmaking body, in conjunction in many cases with the Parliament. The Council's main function is to approve or amend laws proposed by the European Commission, although in some cases it can ask the Commission to make a proposal. It also decides the budget, adopts international treaties and is responsible for ensuring that the objectives of the Treaties are attained. The Council comprises a minister representing each member state who must be authorised to commit the government. The membership fluctuates according to the business in hand. A President holds office for six months, each member state holding the office in turn.

The Council is biased towards national interests rather than towards an overall 'community view'. The way in which Council decisions are made is therefore all important. When it considers draft legislation it must meet in public (TFEU, Art 15). Certain decisions (albeit a shrinking category) must be unanimous, thus permitting any state to impose a veto. An increasing number of decisions are made by a qualified majority, whereby votes are weighted according to the population of each state. From 2014 under the Lisbon Treaty a 'double weighting' will be applied. This will require a majority of 55 per cent of states (at least 15, and with a blocking minority of 4), together with 65 per cent of the population, thus reflecting the more varied membership of the EU (TEU, Art 16(4)). Sometimes a simple majority suffices.

10.2.2 The European Council

The European Council is a twice-yearly meeting of heads of state, together with the President of the Commission. It 'provide[s] the Union with the necessary impetus for its development and shall define the general political guidelines thereof' (Single European Act 1987). The Council as such has no lawmaking power but is the most important political influence on the European Union. It appoints the Commission (below). It is particularly important in relation to foreign and security policies. It seems to tip the balance of power away from the supranational elements of Commission and Parliament towards the intergovernmental element. It makes reports to the European Parliament after its meetings and also a yearly written report on the progress of the Union. The Lisbon Treaty has created the office of President of the Council, whom it elects for two-and-a-half years (TEU, Art 15(2)). The President is chair of the Council but has no executive powers. The President cannot hold any national elected office. The purpose of this office is apparently to strengthen the public profile of the EU.

Under the Lisbon Treaty there is also an office of High Representative for Foreign Affairs, appointed and dismissed by the European Council with the agreement of the President of the Commission and working with the Council to develop foreign policy and to represent the EU abroad (TEU, Art 18).

10.2.3 The European Commission

The Commission is the executive of the EU (TEU, Art 17). It represents the interests of the EU as such. It is required to be independent 'beyond doubt' of the member governments. It is responsible to the European Parliament.

The main functions of the Commission are:

▶ to propose laws or political initiatives for adoption by the Council. The Council or the Parliament can request the Commission to submit proposals;

▶ to make laws itself, either directly under powers conferred by the Treaty or under powers delegated to it by the Council;
▶ to enforce EC law against member states and the other EC institutions. The EC has no police or law enforcement agencies; it enforces the law by issuing a 'reasoned opinion', negotiating with the body concerned and if necessary initiating proceedings in the ECJ (Art 226);
▶ to administer the EU budget;
▶ to negotiate with international bodies and other countries.

Because membership of the Council of Ministers fluctuates, it is vulnerable to being dominated by the permanent officials of the Commission. The Commission is driven by an abstract rationalist ideology reflecting the rule of law in its narrow sense, as opposed to the politically driven negotiating character of the Council. The political legitimacy of the Commission is weak. The number of commissioners is determined by the European Council, which also fixes their salaries. The Commission currently comprises 27 members, one member from each state irrespective of its size. There is however provision to reduce the number of commissioners from 2014 to comprise two-thirds of the member states on a revolving basis (TEU, Art 17(5); TFEU, Art 244). Whether this can be achieved is controversial.

The President of the Commission is chosen by the European Council with the approval of the Parliament. The Vice President is the High Representative for Foreign Affairs (above). The European Council appoints the other commissioners with the agreement of the President, the candidates being nominated by the member states. Each commissioner is appointed for a renewable term of five years. The appointment of the Commission as a body must be approved by the Parliament. The appointment process takes place within six months of the elections to the Parliament, thereby strengthening democratic input. However the Parliament cannot veto individual candidates, so accountability is weak.

The whole Commission can be dismissed by the Parliament. The President can be dismissed by the European Council for serious misconduct. Individual commissioners have limited independence. The President assigns departmental responsibilities (directorates-general) to the other commissioners, who are required to conform to the political direction of the President. Members of the Commission cannot formally be dismissed during their terms of office but can be 'compulsorily retired' by the European Court on the ground of inability to perform their duties. Moreover individual commissioners must resign at the President's request. Individual commissioners can it seems also be withdrawn by their governments, thus placing doubt on the independence of the Commission.

10.2.4 The European Parliament

The European Parliament is the only elected institution. It does not initiate law and was originally created as an 'advisory and supervisory' body. However it increasingly participates in the lawmaking process. It has a maximum of 751 seats (temporarily raised by treaty amendment to 754). These are allocated in proportion to the population of each member state, ranging from 6 to 96. Elections are held every five years. Since 1979 members of the European Parliament (MEPs) have been directly elected by residents of the member states, the detailed electoral arrangements being left to each country.

Elections to the EU Parliament in Britain are on the basis of a 'closed party list' (Section 12.7.1) (European Parliamentary Elections Act 2002). There are 87 seats, divided into electoral regions (nine for England, one each for Scotland, Wales and Northern Ireland, with 71, 8, 5 and 3 members respectively).

A Parliament lasts for five years and is required to meet at least once a year. It meets roughly once each month, alternating expensively between Strasbourg and Luxembourg. Its members vote in political groupings and not in national units. It meets in public. Freedom of speech and proceedings within the Parliament are protected but, unlike the UK Parliament, the European Parliament does not enjoy privilege against interference from the courts, and the ECJ can review the legality of its activities (*Grand Duchy of Luxembourg v Parliament* [1983] 2 CMLR 726).

The Parliament's main functions are as follows:

▶ As a result of a gradual extension of the Parliament's powers, culminating in the Lisbon Treaty, most areas of lawmaking require the consent both of the Council of Ministers and the Parliament (Ordinary Legislative Procedure). Under the Special Legislative Procedure in certain cases regarded as especially sensitive, such as competition law and exemptions from the internal market, the Parliament need only be consulted, while in other cases, including discrimination law and the admission and withdrawal of member states, the Parliament can veto a measure but cannot amend it. Some provisions concerning external trade are made by the Council alone.

▶ The Parliament approves the EU budget jointly with the European Council. It can veto only the whole budget – a sanction too extreme to be of practical use.

▶ It approves treaties, the appointment of the Commission and its President, the admission of new member states and certain other important matters. It must be consulted on the appointment of certain other senior officials.

▶ By a two-thirds majority that is also an absolute majority of all members, it can dismiss the entire Commission but not individual members of it. Again this sanction is too extreme to be of much use.

▶ It can question members of the Commission orally or in writing. Commissioners often appear before its committees, although it has no legal power to compel this.

▶ It can hold committees of inquiry into misconduct or maladministration by other EC bodies.

▶ It appoints an Ombudsman to investigate complaints by citizens, residents or companies based in member states against EC institutions (other than the ECJ).

▶ Any citizen, resident or company based in a member state can petition it on a matter that comes within the EC's field of competence and affects him, her or it directly. (Apart from the Parliament's limited powers, the fragmented nature of community decision making makes parliamentary accountability weak, a problem compounded by the fact that the implementation of EC laws and policies is carried out by national governments. The accountability of MEPs is itself weak since elections are in large constituencies and there is little relationship between an individual member and the voter. It is not surprising that the turnout for elections to the Parliament is usually low (around 25%).)

10.2.5   The European Court of Justice

The ECJ comprises judges appointed by agreement between the governments of the member states. Unlike national judges they have little security of tenure, being appointed for a renewable term of six years and dismissible by the unanimous opinion of the other judges and advocates-general (Statutes of the Court, Art 6). As well as the judges there are eight advocates-general, who provide the ECJ with an independent opinion on the issues in each case. The opinion of the advocates-general is not binding on the ECJ but is highly influential.

There is one judge from each member state. Appointments must be made from those eligible for the highest judicial office in each member state and also from 'juris consults of recognised competence'. This permits such persons as academic lawyers or social scientists to be appointed. The judges elect a President for a renewable period of three years. The ECJ sits as a Grand Chamber of 11. There is also a Court of First Instance, sitting in panels of three or five. This hears cases of kinds designated by the Council (unanimity is required). There are no specific qualifications for appointment to the Court of First Instance other than being a person 'whose independence is beyond doubt and who possesses the ability required for judicial office'. The Court of Justice hears appeals on a point of law from the Court of First Instance.

The ECJ's task is to ensure that 'in the interpretation and application of the EC treaty the law is observed'. The 'law' consists of the treaties themselves, the legislation adopted in their implementation, general principles developed by the Court, the *acquis communautaire*, which is the accumulated inheritance of community values, and general principles of law common to the member states, including the European Convention on Human Rights (ECHR). There is also 'soft law' comprising governmental agreements, declarations, resolutions etc. These are not binding but in a way threatening to the rule of law must be taken into account (see Stefan, 'Hybridity before the Court: a Hard look at Soft Law in the EU Competition and State Aid Case Law' (2012) 37 ELR 49).

The main jurisdiction of the ECJ is as follows:

▶ enforcement action against member states who are accused of violating or refusing to implement European law. These proceedings are usually brought by the Commission but can be brought by other member states, subject to their having raised the matter before the Commission. The Court can award a lump sum or penalty payment against a member state which fails to comply with a judgement of the Court that the state concerned has failed to fulfil a treaty obligation. The EC has no enforcement agencies of its own. The Court therefore depends on national law to enforce its rulings;

▶ judicial review of the acts or the failure to act of community institutions. Such actions can be brought by other institutions and by member states. An individual or private body can bring an action only in special circumstances where the community act in question is directed to the individual in person or is of 'direct and individual concern to him or her' (eg *Salamander v European Parliament* [2000] All ER (EC) 754). In contrast to its reluctance to permit individuals to sue the EC, the Court has been liberal in supporting individual rights against national governments;

▶ preliminary rulings on matters referred by national courts. This is the linchpin of the ECJ's role as a constitutional court. Any national court, where it considers that a decision on the question is necessary to enable it to give judgement, may request the ECJ to give a ruling on a question of community law. The role of the European

Court is confined to ruling upon the question of law referred to it. It then sends the matter back to the national court for a decision on the facts in the light of the Court's ruling. A court against whose decision there is no judicial remedy in national law (ie the highest appeal court or any other court against which there is no right of appeal or review) must make such a request. UK courts are required to follow decisions of the ECJ (European Communities Act 1972, s 3(1)). The power to give preliminary rulings does not apply to the Court of First Instance.

It may be difficult to decide whether a reference can or should be made. The parties have no say in the matter (*Bulmer v Bollinger* (1974)). A court need not make a reference if it thinks the point is irrelevant or 'reasonably clear and free from doubt' (the *acte-claire* doctrine) or if 'substantially' the same point has already been decided by the ECJ (see *CILFIT Srl v Ministro della Sanita* [1983] 1 CMLR 472). In *R v International Stock Exchange, ex p Else (1982) Ltd* [1993] 1 All ER 420, Bingham LJ said that 'if community law is critical to the decision the court should refer it if it has any real doubt' (at 422). The court can take into account the convenience of the parties, the expense of the action and the workload of the European Court (ibid; *Van Duyn v Home Office* [1974] 3 All ER 178; *Customs and Excise Comrs v Aps Samex* [1983] 1 All ER 1042).

It may also be difficult to decide whether the law is sufficiently clear to entitle the UK court to decide for itself. Much depends upon how English legal culture responds to the different reasoning methods of the ECJ, that is whether the UK court approaches the problem by way of our traditional 'literal' approach to questions of interpretation or takes a broader approach, focusing on the 'spirit' as opposed to the letter of the law, in the continental manner (below). The same applies to the question of whether a decision in the matter is 'necessary' for the resolution of the case. We may not know this until we know what the relevant community law means.

The ECJ's jurisdiction over criminal and security matters depends on the consent of the state concerned. It has no jurisdiction in respect of the operations of the police and other law enforcement agencies. However in other areas, for example policing demonstrations, the ECJ can require the police to give priority to EC aims such as freedom of trade (see *R v Chief Constable of Sussex, ex p International Traders Ferry* [1999] 1 All ER 129).

The Treaty itself is not explicit as to the relationship between the ECJ and the law of the member states, but the ECJ has developed principles that have enabled it to favour EC law. According to some commentators the ECJ has, in defiance of the normal values of judicial impartiality and democracy, taken upon itself the political agenda of promoting the European enterprise. It has attempted to enlist national courts by requiring them to defer to EC law and by conferring on individuals European law rights that are enforceable in national courts. On the other hand it has injected some democratic principles into EC law, albeit in a sporadic fashion.

10.3 Community law and national law

Although the EU is not strictly a federal system (Section 10.6), issues arise as to the boundaries between EU law and the domestic laws of the member states that are similar to federal issues. It will be recalled that section 2 of the European Communities Act 1972 makes UK statutes subject to EU law and that section 3 requires all courts to decide questions as to the meaning validity or effect of EU law in accordance with principles and decisions of the European Court.

There are different ways of approaching the relationship between EC law and national law. One is to regard EC law as a distinct system in which the UK courts must participate by applying European methods as if they were federal courts. On this basis the UK court dealing with an EC matter is effectively a European court. Another would be to regard EC law as 'processed' into English law by the European Communities Act 1972, to be approached in much the same way as other legislation in the light of the strict reasoning methods of English law. The choice between these two approaches influences the extent to which the courts are willing to subordinate UK law to EC ideas.

There seems to be no consistent practice among the English judges and examples of both approaches can be found. In *Mayne v Ministry of Agriculture, Fisheries and Food* [2001] EHLR 5 it was held that UK regulations implementing an EC Directive do not apply to future amendments of the Directive unless they are clearly worded as doing so. However in *Berkeley v Secretary of State for the Environment* [2000] 3 All ER 897 Lord Hoffmann emphasised the importance of giving effect to EC law's environmental purposes.

There is also a 'spillover effect' whereby rights initially established for European purposes are later extended to domestic contexts on the basis that it would be unjust for domestic law to be more restrictive than EC law (eg *M v Home Office* [1993]: interim relief against the Crown). More generally it has been said that involvement with Europe has accelerated the tendency to approach the interpretation of legislation from a broad purposive perspective as opposed to the narrow linguistic perspective traditionally favoured by the English courts (Lord Steyn in *R (Quintavalle) v Secretary of State for Health* [2003] 2 All ER 113).

Some EC measures take effect in domestic law 'without further enactment' (European Communities Act 1972, s 2(1)) and are automatically part of UK law. This is determined by EC law itself (below). In other cases there must be a conversion to UK law, usually in the form of a statutory instrument (s 2(2)). Certain measures, including taxation, the creation of new criminal offences and retrospective laws, can only be implemented by an Act of Parliament (Sch 2).

The main kinds of EC legal instrument are as follows (TFEU, Art 288):

▶ *The Treaty.* Treaty provisions are sometimes directly enforceable in the UK courts (below).
▶ *Regulations.* These are general rules which apply to all member states and persons. All regulations are 'directly applicable' and as such are automatically binding on UK courts except where a particular regulation is of a character that is inherently unsuitable for judicial enforcement.
▶ *Directives.* A Directive as such is not automatically binding but is sometimes so (below). It is a requirement to achieve a given objective but leaves to the individual states the choice of forms and methods to implement the Directive. A Directive may be addressed to all states or particular states. A time limit is usually specified for implementing the Directive.
▶ *Decisions.* A Decision is 'binding in its entirety' but if it specifies those to whom it is addressed it is binding only on them.
▶ *Opinions and recommendations.* These do not have binding force. However the ECJ has power under Article 228(6) of the TFEU to give an opinion at an early stage of a matter, for example in relation to a proposed treaty.

10.3.1   Direct applicability and direct effect

'Direct effect' must be distinguished from 'direct applicability', which applies only to EC regulations. Regulations are always binding whereas 'direct effect' depends upon the quality of the particular EC instrument. Where the direct effect doctrine applies, the national court must give a remedy which as far as possible puts the plaintiff in the same position as if the Directive had been properly implemented. This might for example require national restrictions to be set aside, national taxes to be ignored or national rules that are stricter than a Directive covering the same ground to be set aside (eg *Defrenne v SABENA* [1976] ECR 455: retirement restrictions; *Pubblico Ministero v Ratti* [1979] ECR 1–1629: excessive labelling requirements). It has been suggested that the ECJ developed the direct effect doctrine in order to make use of domestic law enforcement agencies as a means of compensating for the weak enforcement provision offered at EC level through the Commission (see Weatherill, *Law and Integration in the European Union* (Oxford University Press 1995) 101ff). Direct effect applies to the Treaty, to general principles of Union Law and to Directives. A Treaty provision and a general principle that has direct effect is enforceable against anyone (see *Mangold,* Case C-1440 [2005] ECR 1–9981). Directives can be enforced only 'vertically', that is against a public authority or 'emanation of the state', and not 'horizontally' against a private person (*Marshall v Southampton AHA (No 1)* [1986] 2 All ER 584; *Faccini Dori v Recreb* [1995] 1 CMLR 665). The reason for this limitation on a directive seems to be that the state, which has the primary duty to implement a Directive, cannot rely on its failure to do so, an argument that it would be unfair to apply to a private body (*Pubblico Ministero v Ratti* (1979)). For the purpose of direct effect, any public body seems to be regarded as an emanation of the state (*Marshall v Southampton AHA (No 1) [1986]*). The meaning of 'public body' varies with the context (Section 5.1). For this purpose a public body must (i) exercise functions in the public interest subject to the control of the state and (ii) have special legal powers not available to individuals or ordinary companies (see *Foster v British Gas* [1990] 3 All ER 897). The privatised utilities of gas, electricity and water are probably emanations of the state but it is unlikely that the privatised railway companies would be since, although they are subject to state regulation and receive state subsidy, they have no statutory obligation to perform public duties or significant special powers (see *Doughty v Rolls-Royce* [1992] IRC 538).

To have direct effect an instrument must be 'justiciable', meaning that it is of a kind that is capable of being interpreted and enforced by a court without trespassing outside its proper judicial role. In essence the legal obligation created by the instrument must be certain enough for a court to handle.

The tests usually applied are as follows (see *Van Duyn v Home Office* [1974]):

1. The instrument must be 'clear, precise and unconditional'. It must not give the member state substantial discretion as to how to give effect to it. For example in *Francovich v Italy* [1993] 2 CMLR 66 a Directive concerning the treatment of employees in an insolvency was not unconditional because it left it to member states to decide which bodies should guarantee the payments required by the directive (see also *Gibson v East Riding of Yorkshire DC* [2000] ICR 890): directive about paid leave did not make clear what counted as working time). The European Court interprets the precision test liberally, bearing in mind that apparent uncertainty could be cured by a reference to the Court.

2. The instrument must be intended to confer 'rights'. A problem arises here in respect of purely 'public' interests, for example some environmental concerns such as wildlife conservation. It is arguable that a body with a public law right sufficient to give standing in national law to challenge the government's action, such as a pressure group (Section 19.4), could rely on the direct effect doctrine. In other words the 'rights' requirement is no more than an aspect of the general principle that the claimant must have a genuine interest.

3. The time limit prescribed by a Directive for its implementation must have expired. However even a correctly implemented directive might be directly relied on if the way in which it is applied does not give its full effect (Case C-62/00 *Marks and Spencer* [2002] ECR I-6325).

10.3.2 Indirect effect

Even where a European law lacks direct effect, the courts must still take account of it. Member states are required to 'take all appropriate measures' to fulfil European obligations and the objectives of Directives must be given effect. In *Marleasing v La Comercial Internacional de Alimentacion* [1992] 1 CMLR 305 the ECJ held that all domestic law, whether passed before or after the relevant community law, must be interpreted 'so far as possible' in order to achieve the result pursued by the directive However *Marleasing* involved a law (in the Spanish civil code) that could be interpreted in different ways. It is therefore uncertain whether clear, unambiguous domestic law must give way to a European rule. This raises the difference between the narrower traditional approach of English law and the more liberal European approach. In *Webb v EMO Cargo (UK) Ltd* [1992] 4 All ER 929 Lord Keith said that *Marleasing* applies to laws passed at any time provided that their language is not distorted. In *Ghaidan v Mendoza* [2004], which concerned analogous similar words in the Human Rights Act 1998 (Section 22.3), Lord Steyn accepted that *Marleasing* created a strong obligation. Sympathetic interpretation of EC law may avoid confrontation between EC law and the domestic principle of parliamentary supremacy.

10.3.3 State liability

Even where a Directive does not have direct effect, an individual may be able to sue the government in a domestic court for damages for failing to implement it. This was established by the ECJ in *Francovich v Italy [1993]*, where the Directive was too vague to have direct effect. Nevertheless the Court held that damages could be awarded against the Italian government in an Italian court. The Court's reasoning was based upon the principle of giving full effect to EC rights. This is a powerful and far-reaching notion. In domestic law damages cannot normally be obtained against the government for misusing its statutory powers and duties (Section 19.2).

In order to obtain damages:

1. The Directive must confer rights for the benefit of individuals.
2. The content of those rights must be determined from the provisions of the Directive (a degree of certainty is therefore needed).
3. There must be a causal link between breach of the Directive and the damage suffered (see also *R v Secretary of State for Transport, ex p Factortame (No 4)* [1996]

QB 404 *(No 5)* [2000] 1 AC 524), *Kirklees MBC v Wickes Building Supplies* [1992] 3 All ER 717).

Francovich leaves the procedures for recovering damages to national courts but any conditions must not make recovery impossible or excessively difficult. The *Francovich* principle avoids the 'vertical' enforcement rule (Section 10.3.1) since failure to implement a Directive against a private person would entitle the plaintiff to sue the government.

10.3.4 Effective remedies

There is a general obligation to give effective remedies to protect rights in EC law. The courts originally took the view that this obligation merely required that the remedies available in European cases should not be worse than those in equivalent domestic cases. However it now appears that the courts must sometimes provide better remedies in relation to European rights than would be available domestically. For example in *R v Secretary of State, ex p Factortame (No 2)* [1991] the House of Lords granted an injunction to prevent a statute being enforced in order to protect an EC right (see also *Johnston v Chief Constable of Royal Ulster Constabulary* [1986] ECR 1651).

It remains to be seen how much freedom a member state has in adjusting its remedies to its own circumstances. For example in *Factortame (No 2)* the court still had a discretion whether to issue the injunction based upon the justice and convenience of the circumstances. The English courts are very cautious about issuing interim injunctions and will do so only as a last resort. The governing principle is that the remedy must be adequate and effective, but member states can choose among different possible ways of achieving the object of a Directive.

It is also controversial how far European rights attached to 'citizenship' (Section 10.1) such as that of freedom of movement apply in purely domestic situations, where there is no cross border element (see Adam and Van Elsuwege, 'Citizenship Rights and the Federal Balance between the European Union and its Member States: Comment on Dereci' (2012) 37 ELR 176).

10.3.5 Fundamental Rights

It is important to be clear that the ECHR is separate from the European Union. The ECHR is under the auspices of the Council of Europe, which is a different organisation with its own court, the European Court of Human Rights (Section 21.3). The ECJ is not therefore currently bound by the ECHR. However the court takes the Convention into account as a source of general principles of law. The European Court of Human Rights can consider whether an EU measure which is binding within a member state complies with the Convention (*Matthews v UK* (Appl No 24833/94), ECHR 1999–1). The EU is required to accede to the ECHR (TEU, Art 6) and negotiations are in progress.

The EU has its own Charter of Fundamental Rights. This is a source of general principles of law. It is also directly enforceable by the ECJ against EU bodies and member states when implementing EU law. In this respect the Charter has the same status as the treaties themselves (TEU, Art 6). The Charter overlaps with but goes beyond the ECHR. In particular it includes social rights such as workers' rights and rights of the elderly and children, data protection and bioethics, and is structured on the basis of the nebulous concepts of dignity, freedom, equality, solidarity, citizenship and justice. Its protection must not fall below that provided by the ECHR (Art 5 (3)).

However political tendency in the UK is to object the notion of fundamental rights (Section 21.1). In the Lisbon Treaty the UK opted out of making the Charter directly enforceable by the ECLJ or by our domestic courts at least in respect of new rights as opposed to existing general principles of law (TEU Protocol 30). (The relevant wording is perhaps deliberately obscure. The UK has also opted out of the Charter in respect of asylum and immigration matters and can pick and choose which rights to accept in the areas of justice and home affairs.

There are also many provisions relating to discrimination in EU law. Most generally Article 19 of the TFEU requires that member states must control discrimination based on sex, racial or ethnic origin, religion or belief, disability, age or sexual orientation (see also TEU, Art 2). Discrimination on the ground of nationality is not included. Indeed the EU could be regarded as a highly nationalistic enterprise, a club of relatively wealthy nations.

10.4 Democracy and the European Union

A democratic government is a requirement of membership. The Union claims to function on the basis of representative democracy and respect for equality, freedom, the rule of law, democracy and human rights (TEU, Art 2; TFEU, Art 10). Nevertheless a fundamental constitutional problem of the EU is the 'democratic deficit'. As we have seen, powers are fragmented between the non-elected Council and Commission, with the latter as the driving force. The Commission is accountable to a limited extent to the Parliament. The Council of Ministers is representative of the member states, so its members are responsible to their own legislatures. The European Parliament has an increasingly significant role but cannot initiate legislation. Some of the founders of the European communities, such as Jean Monnet (1888–1979), a businessman, were paternalistic idealists who had little interest in democratic processes, assuming perhaps that the 'European spirit' could gradually be infused into public opinion by example and propaganda. Not surprisingly this has not materialised.

Indeed the treaties may not be compatible with the premise that democracy is about governing with the consent of the people and cannot be tied to any particular substantive goals. For example Article 4(3) of the TEU provides that:

> member states shall take all appropriate measures, whether general or particular, to ensure fulfilment of the obligations arising out of this Treaty or resulting from actions taken by the institutions of the Community. They shall facilitate the achievement of the Community's tasks. They shall abstain from any measure that could jeopardise the attainment of the objectives of the Treaty.

This seems to impose an obligation to place EU goals above democracy (see *Internationale Handelsgesellschaft* [1970] ECR 1125 at 1135). On the other hand the member states, acting collectively within procedures prescribed by Article 48 of the TEU, have the ultimate power to change the treaties.

The EU relies mainly on the democratic processes of the member states and the Lisbon Treaty has increased the role of national Parliaments.

▶ National Parliaments have increased rights to information and draft legislation from EU bodies. Draft legislation must be submitted 8 weeks before the Council begins to consider it (TEU, Art 11; *Protocol on the Role of National Parliaments in the EU* [2004] OJ C310/204).

▶ A national Parliament can veto Council proposals to change voting arrangements by means of the so-called *Passerelle* principle (TEU, Art 48). The *Passerelle* principle applies to all EU policies except defence and enables the Council of Ministers by unanimous vote to alter requirements for unanimous voting to qualified majority voting and to change the Special Legislative Procedure in the Parliament to Ordinary Legislative Procedure.

▶ A national Parliament can veto proposals in the areas of 'freedom, justice and security' (which deal with immigration, courts and police matters). These matters are subject to enhanced scrutiny by Parliament and it can pick and choose which measures to accept (see House of Lords Select Committee on the European Union, Second Report (HL 2008–09, 25)).

▶ There are special provisions concerning 'subsidiarity' (Section 10.5).

▶ There is a bizarre provision in the Lisbon Treaty for a 'citizen's initiative'. One million citizens from at least one-third of member states with the signatories distributed in proportion to the size of the country can 'invite' the Commission to consider a proposal (TEU, Art 11(4); TFEU, Art 24). Detailed arrangements have not been prescribed and the Commission is not bound by the invitation.

In the UK proposed EC legislation is scrutinised by Parliament, although it may not have any power of veto or amendment. Council and Commission documents are made available to both Houses, ministerial statements are made after Council meetings, questions can be asked, and in addition to the ordinary departmental committees there are select committees in each House to monitor EU activity. The House of Lords Select Committee is particularly well regarded and its reports are a valuable resource. In addition to scrutinising new legislation it makes wide-ranging general reports on the EU. However Parliamentary scrutiny is patchy. This is due to the limited information available to Parliament from EU institutions and to time pressures.

The government must place proposals for changes in EU law before select committees of the Commons and the Lords, together with an explanatory memorandum. The committees report to their respective Houses. There may be a convention that no UK minister should consent in the Council to an EC legislative proposal before Parliament has considered the matter unless there are special reasons, which must be explained to the House as soon as possible. However this is not consistently followed. The volume of EC legislation is greater than the time available and much European business is conducted without MPs having the opportunity to consider it in advance.

There are four specific legal constraints:

1. By virtue of the European Parliamentary Elections Act 1978, no treaty which provides for an increase in the powers of the European Parliament can be ratified by the UK without the approval of an Act of Parliament (s 6). It is perhaps ironic that this provides protection only against the elected element of the EC.
2. A treaty that alters the founding treaties of the European Union must be ratified by statute (European Union (Amendment) Act 2008, s 5).
3. A minister of the Crown may not support a decision in the Council of Ministers to alter its voting arrangements without the approval of Parliament (European Union (Amendment) Act 2008, s 6).

4. The European Union Act 2011 is intended to strengthen democratic control over changes to the EU law in politically sensitive areas. There is a sliding scale of controls. Depending on the subject matter and its importance such changes cannot take effect or ministers may not support such changes in the Council without:

▶ Approval by Act of Parliament and by a majority of those voting in a referendum (ss 2,3,4)
▶ Approval by statute
▶ Approval by statute or in urgent cases parliamentary approval meaning an affirmative resolution of both Houses of Parliament (s.8).
▶ Parliamentary approval meaning in some cases an affirmative resolution of both Houses of Parliament.

As regards the executive, accountability is weak in that there is no minister specifically dealing with the EU. However the main departments have European sections and there are numerous committees liaising between UK and EU institutions. The Foreign Office acts as a co-ordinating body and a junior minister is responsible for 'Europe'. Thus there is a complex network of negotiating machinery involving the competing interests of the UK and the EU, the UK and other member states, and interdepartmental rivalries, with Parliament on the sidelines. In keeping with the ethos of UK government, the operation of EU matters relies on informal contacts between unelected officials.

Within their allocated subject areas the devolved governments of Scotland and Wales are responsible for implementing EC law. The devolved governments are represented in the Council of Ministers by UK ministers. Although having no right to do so, Scottish and Welsh ministers have sometimes attended Council meetings on behalf of the UK government. Scottish and Welsh ministers have direct representation at lower levels, for example on the Committee of the Regions. Both devolved legislatures have European committees (see Mather, 'The Impact of European Integration', in O'Neill, 2004).

Democracy depends on open decision making and wide access to information about governmental activity. Openness is claimed to be a principle of the EU (TFEU, Art 15). Council proceedings on legislative matters must be in public and its decisions must be made public. Citizens have a right to communicate with EU institutions and to a written reply in the same language. There are general provisions for access to documents held by EU bodies (see Regulation 1049/2001). Documents must be disclosed to any citizen of the EU and to any person residing in or having a registered office in a member state. This includes documents both drawn up by them and received

There are however many exceptions relating to most important community activities. (These include data protection for individuals (TFEU, Art 16), security, defence and military matters, international relations, financial, monetary or economic policy, privacy and the integrity of the individual. Commercial interests, legal matters, inspections, investigations and audits are also excepted, subject to a public interest test. Internal documents are excepted if disclosure would seriously undermine the decision-making process, again subject to a public interest test.) No specific enforcement measures are provided. (See Adamski, 'Approximating a Workable Compromise on Access to Official Documents: the 2011 Developments in the European Courts' (2012) 49 CMLR 521.)

The Court has taken a more vigorous attitude to the right to information. In *World Wildlife Fund for Nature v Commission* [1997] All ER (EC) 300, which concerned information about Commission policy on environmental protection, the Court of First Instance held that, although at the time there was only a voluntary undertaking to disclose information, having adopted it the Commission is bound to respect it. The Court also held that exceptions should be interpreted restrictively so as not to inhibit the aim of transparency and that the Commission must give reasons for refusing to disclose information. The Court has also refused to accept blanket immunity for particular kinds of information and required the Commission to balance the public right to know against a clear public interest in secrecy in the particular case (see *JT's Corp v Commission* [2000] Times 18 Oct ; *Van der Val v Netherlands* [2000] *Times* 22 Feb).

10.5 Federalism and the European Union: subsidiarity

The EU is difficult to fit into a coherent constitutional structure. In particular there is a conflict between the ideal of European integration and that of national identity. This tension suggests the possibility of a federal model since federalism is intended to reconcile this kind of tension by marking out spheres of independence for each unit. While some idealists, notably Jean Monnet, pursued the agenda of a federal Europe, the thrust of the original initiative evolution towards what the treaties call 'ever closer union' but with no agreed final destination.

At present the EU has an important feature of federalism in that the powers of the EU are itemised and limited by the treaties, with the member states having residual independence (TEU, Arts 4, 5). The principle of 'proportionality' is stressed, namely that EU powers shall not exceed what is necessary to secure the objectives of the treaties. The 'conferral principle' (TEU, Art 5(2)) states that the powers of the EU are conferred on it by the member states. Thus fears that the EU is a 'superstate' are ill founded. Furthermore, major increases in the powers and competences of EU institutions require the consent of member states in the Council of Ministers. As we have seen there are also several ways in which individual states can opt into or opt out of particular EU powers (Sections 10.1, 10.4). It has been suggested that parts of the EU system are 'entrenched' in the sense that not even the Treaty itself could be altered in defiance of them. However in *Grau Gromis* [1995] All ER EC 688 the ECJ accepted that 'the Member States remain free to alter even the most fundamental parts of the Treaty'.

The tension between the interests of member states and those of the EU is expressed through the concept of subsidiarity. Introduced by the Maastricht Treaty (1992), subsidiarity is a vague term with no agreed meaning. It can therefore be enlisted to serve different political interests. Historically subsidiarity is an authoritarian doctrine used by the Catholic Church to legitimise a hierarchical power structure but it can also be a pluralist liberal principle that decisions should be made at a level as close as possible to those whom they affect. Subsidiarity enables the EU to make decisions that cannot effectively be made by the member states, and on the other hand it enables the member states to act for themselves where this is more appropriate.

Subsidiarity was formally introduced into EU law by the Maastricht Treaty and, together with the principle of proportionality, is embodied in Article 5 of the TEU:

> In areas that do not fall within its exclusive competence, the Community shall take action, in accordance with the principle of subsidiarity, only if and insofar as the objectives of the proposed action cannot be sufficiently achieved by the Member States either at central level or at regional level but can rather, by reason of the scale or effects of the proposed action, be better achieved at Union level ... Any action by the Community shall not go beyond what is necessary to achieve the objects of this Treaty.

Article 10 announces that 'decisions shall be taken as openly and as closely as possible to the citizen', thereby giving a republican flavour to the EU.

These provisions are characteristically vague and are unlikely to be directly enforceable in law but may operate at a political level, thereby indirectly influencing the law.

The Lisbon Treaty gives an important role to national Parliaments in connection with subsidiarity. If one-third of member states raise an objection to a Commission proposal on subsidiarity grounds the Commission must reconsider it and must give reasons for continuing with it. If a majority do, the Council of Ministers by a 55 per cent majority or the Parliament must vote for it to proceed (see Protocol on the Role of National Parliaments in the EU).

On the whole the Lisbon Treaty has maintained a balance between national and EU institutions and is not the charter for EU supremacy that was sometimes feared. Unlike the usual form of federation the EU is dependent on its powers being channelled through the laws of the member states and has no enforcement mechanisms of its own. The EU is arguably more like a confederation or an intergovernmental body than a genuine supranational body but is perhaps best regarded as a unique legal order not reducible to other forms.

Summary

- The EU (EC) exists to integrate key economic and increasingly social and security policies of member states, with the primary aims of providing an internal market and creating a powerful European political unit. The constitution of the EU is an evolving one aimed at increasing integration between its member states. Some functions are exclusive to the EU while others are shared with member states. However there is substantial provision for individual states to opt out of certain European powers, although not the core areas of the single market. The UK has opted out of several areas of EU activity, and the EU Charter of Fundamental Rights (not to be confused with the ECHR) is not enforceable in UK courts.

- EC law has been incorporated into UK law by the European Communities Act 1972, which makes certain EC laws automatically binding in the UK, requires other laws to be enacted in UK law either by statute or by regulations made under the 1972 Act, and obliges UK courts to decide cases consistently with principles laid down by the European Court of Justice. In some cases questions of law must be referred to the ECJ. The ECJ has developed the role of constitutional court and is sometimes regarded as being a driving force for integrationist policies that enlist national courts in the project of giving primacy to European law.

- The main policy and lawmaking bodies are the Council of Ministers, which is the main lawmaking body; the European Council of heads of state, responsible for policy direction and making key appointments; the appointed European Commission, which is the executive of the EU; and the elected European Parliament, which participates in the lawmaking process and has powers to control the Commission and the EU budget. Taken together these bodies are meant to balance the interests of national governments and those of the EU as such, but not to follow strict separation of power ideas.

- There is only limited democratic input into the EC lawmaking process but the role of national Parliaments has recently been strengthened and there is provision, albeit limited, for direct input by 'citizens' initiative'.

- Lawmaking and policy-making power are divided between the Council and the Commission, with the Commission as the driving force but the Council having the ultimate control. Voting sometimes has to be unanimous but there is increasing use of qualified majorities, where voting is weighed in favour of the more populous states. The Parliament does not initiate laws but has certain powers of veto and can sometimes suggest amendments.

Summary cont'd

▶ Not all EC law is directly binding on member states. Regulations are binding. Other laws, including the Treaty itself, are binding if they satisfy the criteria of 'direct effect' created by the ECJ. Directives must also satisfy the criteria of direct effectiveness and can have direct effect against public bodies (vertical direct effect) but not against private bodies (horizontal direct effect). However the concept of 'indirect effect', which requires domestic law to be interpreted so as to conform to EC law, may alleviate this. The government may also be liable for damages if its failure properly to implement an EC law damages an individual in relation to rights created by the EC law in question.

▶ The doctrine of 'subsidiarity' is ambivalent. It seems to have little concrete legal content and can be applied in favour of giving greater power to the member states or reinforcing the power of central European Union bodies. National Parliaments may require proposed EU laws to be reconsidered on subsidiarity grounds.

▶ Membership of the EU may not have fundamentally altered the doctrine of parliamentary supremacy, but the UK courts have accepted that a statute which conflicts with a binding EC rule must be 'disapplied'. There is a general political principle – perhaps an emerging convention – in favour of the supremacy of EU law.

Exercises

10.1 Explain the constitutional structure of the European Union. To what extent is it federal? Does it conform to the separation of powers?

10.2 It is a requirement of membership of the EU that the member state have a democratic form of government, but it has often been remarked that the EU would not satisfy the conditions for membership of itself. Do you agree?

10.3 What powers does the UK Parliament possess in relation to the EU?

10.4 To what extent is the European Commission accountable for its actions?

10.5 Explain the relationship between UK courts and the European Court of Justice. To what extent is the ECJ a constitutional court?

10.6 What is the purpose of the direct effect doctrine and what are its main limitations?

10.7 An EU Directive requires member states to ensure that compensation is paid to part-time workers who are made redundant. The compensation must be paid by the employer. The UK has not implemented the Directive. Jeff, a part-time employee of Dodgy Burgers plc, is made redundant. His employer refuses to pay him compensation. Advise Jeff as to his legal rights, if any.

10.8 AN EU Directive requires all decisions of public authorities which may affect the rights of nature to made only after consulting significant interest groups. The UK government implements the Directive in the same terms. The government later decides to build an airport in an area of beautiful countryside. A local residents association request to be consulted but are refused o n the ground that 'rights of nature' was intended by the Directive to include only animals. The Association challenges the refusal in the High Court, Fossil J rejects their application on the ground that the Directive has been implemented and they cannot therefore directly enforce it and that in any case the Directive is not of direct effect. The group also claims that the decision violates their property rights under the EU Charter of Fundamental Rights. Advise the Association.

Further reading

Bast, 'New Categories of Acts after the Lisbon Reform: Dynamics of Parliamentarianization in EU Law' (2012) 49 CMLR 885

Craig, 'Directives: Direct Effect, Indirect Effect and the Construction of National Legislation' (1997) ELR 519

Craig, 'Britain in the European Union' in Jowell and Oliver (eds), *The Changing Constitution* (7th edn, Oxford University Press 2011)

Dashwood, Dougan, Rodger, Spaventa, Wyatt, *European Union Law* (6th edn, Hart Publishing 2011) chs 1, 2, 3, 4 (IV, C), 5 (III), 8, 9, 10, (III), 11, 12

Gordon and Dougan, 'The United Kingdom's European Union Act 2011: "Who Won the Bloody War Anyway?"' (2012) 37 ELR 3

Harlow, 'European Governance and Accountability' in Bamforth and Leyland (eds), *Public Law in a Multi-Layered Constitution* (Hart 2003)

Hartley, 'The European Court, Judicial Objectivity and the Constitution of the European Union' (1996) 112 LQR 411

O'Neill (ed), *Devolution and British Politics* (Pearson 2004) ch 11

Peers, 'European Integration and the European Union Act 2011:An Irresistible Force Meets an Immovable Object?' [2013] PL 119

Walter, 'European Constitutionalism and European Integration' [1995] PL 266

Part IV

Government institutions

Chapter 11
Parliament: constitutional position

Introduction

In this chapter we will discuss Parliament generally. In the following two chapters the composition and procedures of Parliament will be discussed more closely. Parliament comprises two Houses, the appointed House of Lords and the elected House of Commons. As a result of the seventeenth century conflict between the monarchy and Parliament, it was established that the monarch could not make law or raise taxes without the consent of Parliament and that Parliament should be free from royal interference (Section 4.4). These powers formed the platform for the subsequent development of Parliament's roles of maintaining the executive and holding it to account. Together with the court centred rule of law this forms the basis of modern constitutionalism.

Parliament's functions are:

▶ to enact legislation; apart from the limited powers of the Crown under the royal prerogative no other body can do so without the power being specifically conferred by Parliament.

▶ to 'sustain' the government by choosing and removing it and providing it with money by voting for taxation. Parliament is ultimately responsible for ensuring that government carries on. (This may require it to pull its punches).

▶ to hold the government to account by scrutinising government action and to redress the grievances of the people.

▶ to debate in public matters of public concern as a focus for the nation.

▶ a recruiting ground for ministers. Parliament acts as a mechanical but distorted way of translating the popular vote into the appointment of an executive, since by convention whichever party or coalition of parties commands a majority in the House of Commons is entitled to form a government. Owing to the distortions of the electoral system, a popular majority does not necessarily translate into a parliamentary majority (Section 12.5).

A dominant feature of the UK constitution is its extreme parliamentary character. This is derived from conventions under which the leader of the government (the Prime Minister) is chosen by the House of Commons, the executive depends on the support of the Commons, and all ministers, although chosen by the Prime Minister, must be members of Parliament. The Prime Minister and all Treasury ministers (finance ministers) must be members of the House of Commons. Other ministers could be appointed as members of the House of Lords, thus enabling the Prime Minister, on whose advice the Queen must appoint both ministers and members of the Lords, to appoint his friends.

Most laws are proposed by the executive and many laws are directly made by the executive as delegated legislation. Thus in practice Parliament does not make law itself but scrutinises proposals from the executive, amends them and gives consent. Individual MPs can propose legislation but the time available for this is so limited that such attempts rarely succeed. Control of parliamentary business and the timetable in the House of Commons is largely in the hands of the government party, although this has recently been slightly modified (Section 13.1).

A strong two-party adversarial system developed in the UK Parliament since the early twentieth century during which highly disciplined parties funded by private interests emerged. One reason for this is that most MPs are paid professional politicians dependent on party conformity. Each party has a highly organised 'whip' system dedicated to enforcing party discipline and persuading members to vote in the required way. Thus Parliament is the setting of a party/market democracy (Section 2.8.3).

The political power and prestige of Parliament has declined in recent years. It is widely acknowledged that the executive has become dominant over a largely subservient Parliament and recent scandals such as the misuse of expenses claims and the alleged receipt of payments for access have weakened public confidence (Sections 4.9, 5.11). Two factors in particular strengthen the power of the executive over Parliament.

Firstly, under the procedural rules of the Commons, government business has priority and a government minister organises the business of the House. Recent reforms have to some extent increased the influence of backbench MPs (Section 13.1) but this is insignificant in relation to the government's power to control the extent to which proposed laws are discussed. The House of Lords is not dominated by the government but its proposals can be rejected by the Commons.

Secondly, there is the first past the post (FPP) voting system for Parliament and therefore the executive which is normally formed out of members of the majority party. Coalition government such as exists at present are unusual (Section 5.2). This contrasts with systems of proportional representation (PR) used in many countries under which seats are distributed among the parties according to their share of the total vote (Section 12.7.1). PR is likely to weaken the power of the larger parties, allowing members of Parliament greater independence. The present system has been justified on the basis that it usually produces a strong government.

However, executive domination of Parliament must not be overstated. Reflecting the separation of powers, Parliament is a separate institution with large powers and distinctive functions, and it could overcome the executive were it so minded.

- Apart from about 100 ministers, public officials and the judiciary cannot be members of the House of Commons thus reinforcing the separation of powers (Section 12.4). There are no such limitations on membership of the Upper House although in practice other officials and serving judges are not appointed.
- Government proposals must be publicly explained in Parliament and ministers must justify their decisions in public if required to do so by Parliament. The dual role of ministers as MPs means that a minister must have regard to the voters as well as to the authority of the government thus providing a check on executive power.
- The independent Speaker, who chairs the Commons, is responsible for ensuring fair and focused debate and that ministers answer questions properly and for protecting the interests of minorities.
- The Opposition, the second largest party in the Commons, is a formal institution protected by the law of parliamentary procedure – a government and Prime Minister in waiting. It has a duty to oppose government policy, short of frustrating the governmental process, and forms a 'shadow Cabinet' ready to take office. There is funding designated by the House of Commons ('Short Money', named after the MP who proposed it) for the parliamentary work of opposition parties. This is determined by a formula based on the number of seats and votes the party received in the previous election. There is also funding for the Opposition leader's office.

▶ The House of Lords is less subject to party discipline than the Commons and may not have a government majority.

While there is no law to this effect, it is often claimed that an MP has a duty to exercise independent judgement on behalf of all his or her constituents and not merely those who voted for him or her. However in practice many MPs mechanically support the party that sponsors them, although there are a few independent voices. Occasionally an MP changes parties. Once elected, unless he or she becomes disqualified to sit in Parliament (Section 12.4), an MP cannot be removed until the next election. However the main parties have proposed the introduction of 'recall' machinery which would enable a proportion of the electorate, so far unspecified, to trigger a special election to remove a sitting member.

11.2 The meeting of Parliament

Reflecting its early history as an assembly of advisors to the monarch, Parliament cannot convene itself must be summoned by the monarch originally under the royal prerogative. The abuse of this power was a major contribution to the seventeenth-century revolution. This resulted in statutory intervention. Under the Septennial Act 1715 as amended by section 7 of the Parliament Act 1911 (now replaced (below)), a Parliament could last for not more than five years after which a general election must be held. Moreover 'Parliament ought to be held frequently' (Bill of Rights 1688, Art 13) and must meet at least once every three years (Meeting of Parliament Act 1694). By convention Parliament meets annually, backed by administrative necessity, for example to authorise taxation and public spending. In practice Parliament is in session for about eight months in the year with a long recess over the summer.

The termination (dissolution) of a Parliament was radically reformed by the Fixed Term Parliaments Act 2011. Described as 'constitution making at its worst' (Brazier (2012) 128 LQR 315). This was enacted with little public discussion (see Political and Constitutional Reform Committee Report HC 436, 2010–11). The Act removed or at least suspended the longstanding royal prerogative power to dissolve Parliament at any time (exercised on the advice of the Prime Minister which must usually be accepted). The power to dissolve Parliament was an important weapon in the hands of a prime minister and could be used to time an election to the advantage of the ruling party. The act is intended to remove this possibility and to reinforce stability.

The Act imposes a statutory timetable for dissolution and subsequent general elections as follows. Parliament can be dissolved only by this process.

▶ A general election must be held on *7 May 2015* and thereafter on the *first Thursday in May* every five years after the previous general election (s 1).
▶ An 'early general election' must be held in either of the following cases (s 2):
  1. If a motion for an early general election is passed by two thirds of the whole number of seats of the House of Commons, including any vacancies, or
  2. If the House of Commons passes a vote of no confidence in the government of 51 per cent of those actually voting and there is no motion of confidence passed in an alternative government within 14 days.
▶ The date for the 'early general election' is set by royal proclamation on the recommendation of the Prime Minister (s 2(7)). This allows time for any outstanding parliamentary business to be completed. However no time limit is set.

▶ Where the previous election was an 'early general election' the next regular election is held in the fourth year after that election if it was held before the first Thursday in May (s 1(4)). Thus a government cannot last beyond five years between elections. However, subject to the approval of both Houses of Parliament, the Prime Minister can extend the polling date of any general election by not more than 2 months. This allows for an unexpected crisis.

▶ Parliament is automatically dissolved at the beginning of the 25th working day before the date set for the election whether normal or early. 'Parliament cannot otherwise be dissolved' (s 3(2), Electoral Registration and Administration Act 2013, s14).

▶ The Act does not make clear the position in the unlikely event of the Prime Minister refusing to make a recommendation as to date of an early general election. This would prevent dissolution. The monarch seems to have no discretion independently of a recommendation from the Prime Minister. It is arguable that in an extreme case the courts might require the Prime Minister to make a recommendation (below).

▶ 'Once Parliament dissolves' the monarch may issue a proclamation summoning the new Parliament and appointing the date for its first meeting (s 3(4)). This will be presumably be on the advice of the existing Prime Minister who will remain in office unless and until the Queen appoints a successor (Section 14.1). At the same time the Lord Chancellor issues the writs which call upon the election officers to start the election process (Section 12.5.3). There are no statutory provisions relating to the date for the new Parliament to meet other than the three year requirement (above). Usually a new Parliament meets within a few days of the election.

▶ The different matter of 'proroguing' Parliament is not affected by the 2011 Act and is governed by the royal prerogative (below) (s 6(1)).

▶ The 2011 Act arguably does not abolish the royal prerogative power to dissolve Parliament but it certainly suspends it while the Act remains in force (Section 14.6). Between June and November 2020 the Prime Minister must set up a committee with a majority being members of the Commons to review the operation of the Act with a view to amending or repealing it (s 7). This is in response to concerns that the Act was rushed through without full consideration so as to protect the current coalition government and that its relative rigidity may harm the democratic process for example if a weak government wishes to get public support against an obstructive House of Commons. There are also concerns that the five year fixed term is too long (see *Hansard*, HC Vol. 515 col 625, 672–3, 682).

▶ It has been suggested that because the Act places the dissolution of Parliament on a statutory basis the courts might become involved (see Hansard HC Vol 515 Sept 13 2010). However this seems unlikely. Those aspects of the process concerned with the resolutions of the Commons are subject to parliamentary privilege (Section 11.6.2). The powers of the Prime Minster under the Act are not subject to privilege since they are not within the internal affairs of the House. For example should a prime minister refuse to set an election date the courts might interfere (see *R v Secretary of State for the Home Office ex parte Fire Brigades Union* (1985)). However the courts refuse to intervene in matters which they consider to be non-justiciable in the sense that they raise political issues more suitable for the democratic branch of government (Section 19.7).

The Act therefore removes a significant 'check and balance' of the traditional separation of powers in that the executive can no longer dismiss the legislature.

Montesquieu thought that the executive should be able to dismiss an obstructive legislature since the continuity of the government was paramount. Writing in the eighteenth century he praised the British system as a balance of equal constitutional forces (Sections 7.1, 7.2). However Montequieu did not anticipate the extent to which executive power and party control would increase over the following centuries. His fear was the power of the elected mob over the aristocracy. By contrast prime ministers have used the power of dissolution as a threat to keep the House of Commons subservient or for political advantage to call an election at a time favourable to themselves.

The 2011 Act can of course be altered or repealed. However the life of Parliament cannot be extended without the consent of the House of Lords since a provision that does so is excepted from the procedures of the Parliament Acts 1911 and 1949 which enable statutes to be passed without the consent of the Lords. Thus to some extent there is protection against an attempt by the executive to keep itself in power. It is arguable however that this safeguard can be removed in two stages first by using the Parliament Act procedure to repeal section 2(1) itself, and then by-passing the House of Lords under the Parliament Acts (Section 11.5.1).

During the election period, the meeting of Parliament can be postponed by the monarch by 'prorogation' under the royal prerogative (see Prorogation Act 1867). The effect of prorogation is to suspend Parliament until recalled by the monarch. The power of Prorogation is not affected by the 2011 Act (s 6(1)). This might be appropriate for example if the election does not produce a clear winner to form or continue the government. Sometimes Parliament is prorogued a few days before it is dissolved but there is no legal or constitutional reason for this.

A Parliament is divided into 'sessions'. These are working periods usually of a year, but there is no fixed timetable, running from November (about 170 sitting days). Sessions are ended by being prorogued by the monarch under the royal prerogative, thus being under the control of the Prime Minister on whose advice the monarch by convention must act. A new Session is summoned by the Monarch by Proclamation. Again there is no fixed time but in practice pressure of business means that the new Session starts a few days after the old one has ended. Although there is no constitutional requirement for this, each session is opened by the monarch, with an address from the throne which is written by the government and outlines its legislative proposals. A general debate on government policy takes place over the following week. Within a session, each House can be adjourned at any time by resolution of the House. Adjournments apply to daily sittings and the breaks for holidays and over the summer. The rump of the session following the summer break is used to finish outstanding business. The Speaker can suspend individual daily sittings of the Commons for disciplinary reasons.

There is machinery for recalling each House by proclamation while it stands prorogued (Parliament (Elections and Meetings) Act 1943, s 34) and also under emergency legislation (Civil Contingencies Act 2004). As usual this is on the advice of the Prime Minister. An adjourned Parliament can be summoned by proclamation (Meeting of Parliament Act 1870) and also by the Speakers of both Houses at the request of the Prime Minister or perhaps at the request of the leader of the Opposition. However it does not seem to be possible for ordinary MPs to recall Parliament in order to debate any crisis that may arise while Parliament is not sitting. This again illustrates the subservience of Parliament to the executive.

11.3   The House of Lords

The purpose of the Upper House is to act as a check on the House of Commons by scrutinising bills (its members claim special expertise) and providing an opportunity for second thoughts. In the UK the appointed House of Lords is subordinate to the elected House of Commons. This is secured by the Parliament Acts 1911 and 1949 and by conventions, notably the 'Salisbury Convention', which requires the Lords to accept proposals contained in the government's election manifesto. The House of Lords should also defer to the Commons on matters of government finance since this is a matter between the Crown, who asks for money, and the Commons, who supply it.

The House of Lords is unusual among second chambers in the following respects:

▶ Its members are not elected. Most of them are appointed by the Crown (by convention the Prime Minister). There are also 26 senior Church of England bishops. Until the House of Lords Act 1999, the bulk of members were hereditary peers whose descendants enjoyed permanent seats. As the first stage of a reform programme, the 1999 Act removed all but 92 hereditary peers. Substantial further reform is unlikely (below).

▶ The House is one of the world's largest legislative chambers having about 831 members compared with 650 in the Commons. However attendance is on average less than 50 per cent. Members other than the bishops sit for life. Membership is a legal right on appointment and can be removed only by statute (Section 12.2). The absence of any provision for retirement or expulsion means that the size of the House is inexorably increasing (Section 12.2).

▶ Members receive no payment other than expenses. As a result of allegations about misuse of expenses it is proposed that this should consist of a flat rate of £300 per day's actual attendance.

▶ Members have no constituencies and are accountable to no one. About 25 per cent of the members are 'cross benchers' independent of political parties.

▶ By longstanding practice, the proceedings of the House are regulated by the House itself without formal rules or disciplinary sanctions, members being treated as bound by 'personal honour'. This has not prevented some peers from abusing their position and there is a now a Code of Conduct (2009, amended 2010). This is policed by a Commissioner for Standards, who reports to the House through its Standards and Privileges Committee. In 2010 three peers were suspended for false expense claims.

11.3.1   The functions of the House of Lords

Being undemocratic, the position of the House is controversial. It could be variously depicted as a constitutional abomination, a valuable ingredient of a mixed constitution or a historical survival that, from a pragmatic perspective, might nevertheless have some useful functions. The Parliament Act 1911 removed the power of the House of Lords to veto most legislation. Its preamble stated that this was a precursor to replacing it by a second chamber 'constituted on a popular basis' and 'limiting and defining' its powers. However there has been no agreement as to how that should be done. In 2000 the Wakeham Report (Royal Commission on the House of Lords, *A House for the Future* (Cm 4534, 2000)) endorsed the Conservative view that the House of Lords should remain subordinate to the Commons (thus ensuring the clear democratic accountability of the government), that it should provide constitutional checks and balances and that it should provide a parliamentary voice for the 'nations and regions of the United Kingdom'. Despite numerous consultations, government papers and parliamentary debates and reports (see White Paper, *House of Lords Reform* (Cm 7027, 2007) for a useful history) no agreed proposals for further reform of the House of Lords have emerged – a pattern that has been repeated since 1911 (Section 12.3).

The conventional justification for the existence of a second chamber in the UK is that it acts as a revising chamber to scrutinise the detail of legislation proposed by the Commons and to allow time for second thoughts, thus acting as a constitutional safeguard against the possible excesses of majoritarianism and party politics. According to the Wakeham Report (above), the functions of the second chamber include, and should continue to include, the following:

▶ to provide advice on public policy, bringing a range of perspectives to bear that should be broadly representative of British society and in particular to provide a voice for the nations and regions of the UK and ethnic minorities and interest groups. The present composition of the Lords obviously does not reflect this aspiration;

▶ to act as a revising chamber, scrutinising the details of proposed legislation within the overall polices laid down by the Commons. By convention, supported by the Parliament Acts 1911 and 1949 (Chapter 13), the House of Lords does not discuss matters of government finance, this being a prerogative of the Commons;

▶ to provide a forum for general debate on matters of public concern without party political pressures;

▶ to introduce relatively uncontroversial legislation or private bills as a method of relieving the workload of the Commons. Any bill other than a financial measure can be introduced in the Lords;

▶ to provide ministers; thus unelected persons can be appointed as ministers. However by convention the Prime Minister and the Chancellor of the Exchequer must be members of the Commons;

▶ to provide committees on general topics, such as the European Communities Committee and the Science and Technology Committee. These are highly respected;

▶ to enable persons who have made a contribution to public life, other than party politicians, to participate in government. It is often claimed that the House of Lords is a valuable source of expertise in that outstanding persons from all walks of life can be appointed. The reports of its specialist committees such as the European Union committee are highly regarded.

However its expertise may be patchy and skewed in favour of persons who have been subservient to government. Membership is dominated by former officials, politicians and leading members of the elite professions and business interests. There have been allegations that seats in the Lords can be bought (Section 12.2). Moreover appointment to the Lords is likely to be towards the end of a career, thus risking out-of-date expertise. Conversely those with active expertise may be infrequent attenders. (For example attendance on average is about 50 per cent). During 2009–10, 148 members attended for less than 10 sittings out of 68 and 40 per cent for less than half the sittings (see www.parliament.uk). Moreover it has been suggested that the House of Commons may command greater expertise (see Bochel and Defty, 'A Question of expertise: The House of Lords and Welfare Policy' (2010) 63 (1) *Parliamentary Affairs* 66).

▶ to act as a constitutional check by preventing a government from prolonging its own life, in respect of which the Lords has a veto (Parliament Act 1911(below)). The consent of the Lords is also needed for the dismissal of senior judges (Section 7.7.3.1);
▶ to act as a constitutional watchdog. The House has no specific powers for this purpose but has a Constitutional Committee which examines the constitutional implications of bills brought before the House.

These functions can be pursued in the House of Lords partly because its procedure and culture differ significantly from those of the Commons. In particular, party discipline is less rigorous and the House of Lords is less partisan than the Commons. Members of the House of Lords other than bishops are removable only by statute and are therefore less susceptible to political pressures than MPs. The House as a whole controls its own procedure, making it relatively free from party constraints, and is subject to less time pressure than the Commons. Its members have a considerable accumulation of experience and knowledge. The House of Lords cannot therefore easily be manipulated by the government, is attractive to external lobbyists and can ventilate moral and social issues in a non partisan way.

11.4 The Parliament Acts

Under the Parliament Acts 1911 and 1949, subject to a delaying period intended to give time for the Commons to reconsider, most public bills (Section 13.3) can be enacted without the consent of the House of Lords thus ensuring that the democratic will prevails. There are two exceptions (Parliament Act 1911, s 2(1)). They are a bill to prolong the life of a Parliament beyond five years thus ensuring that a government cannot use its majority to keep itself in office and a bill introduced in the Lords itself. The 1949 Act reduced the period during which the Lords can a delay a bill from about two years to one year.

The Lords can reject a bill in two parliamentary sessions provided it is sent to them at least one month before the end of each session and no more than one year elapses between the second reading in the first session and the date the bill passes the Commons in the second session (Parliament Act 1911, s 2 as modified by 1949 Act). After the second session the bill can receive the royal assent without the consent of the Lords. (However if the Commons amends a bill after it has come back from the Lords in the first session, then it may not count as the same bill unless the amendments were suggested by the Lords.)

In the case of a 'money bill' the Lords can delay only for one month, provided the bill is sent to them at least one month before the end of a session (Parliament Act 1911, s 1). A money bill is a public bill that in the opinion of the Speaker deals exclusively either with central government taxation or central government spending, borrowing or accounts. This definition is narrow since few bills deal exclusively with these matters. The Speaker must certify that the Parliament Act's procedure has been followed and his certificate cannot be questioned in a court (Parliament Act 1911, ss 2(2), 3). However irrespective of the Speaker's certificate a court can decide whether a bill falls within the limits of the Parliament Act in the first place (*R (Jackson) v A-G* [2005] at [116]).

Before 1991, the 1911 Act was used only three times (Government of Ireland Act 1914; Welsh Church Act 1914; Parliament Act 1949). Since then it has been used four times for relatively minor purposes (War Crimes Act 1991; European Parliamentary Elections Act 1999; Sexual Offences (Amendment) Act 2000; Hunting Act 2004). The Parliament Acts do not apply to delegated legislation, which sometimes requires the approval of Parliament.

The conventional view is that subject to the limits specifically mentioned in the 1911 Act any statute can be enacted under the Parliament Acts. It is not clear how far this applies to an alteration to the Parliament Acts themselves so to remove the limitations. In *R (Jackson) v A-G* [2005] (Section 8.4.3) the House of Lords held that the changes made to the 1911 Act by the Parliament Act 1949 which was enacted without the consent of the House of Lords were effective. Although there was disagreement a majority also considered that other limitations on the Parliament Act procedure could similarly be removed since there was no implication in the 1911 Act preventing it from being applied to itself. Thus the limits currently contained in the 1911 Act concerning extending the life of a Parliament could be removed in two stages, first by repealing that part of the Act, and then by legislating free of those limitations. It seems clear moreover that the House of Lords could be abolished under the Parliament Acts. (See Pannick [2012] PL 230.)

11.5 The functions of the House of Commons

The main functions of the Commons are as follows:

▶ choosing the government indirectly by virtue of the convention that the person who commands a majority of the Commons is entitled to form a government. The Commons has no veto over individual appointments nor can it dismiss individual members of the government (another prime ministerial power);

▶ sustaining the government by supplying it with funds and authorising taxation. The size and complexity of modern government means that parliamentary control over finance cannot be exercised directly. Parliamentary approval of the executive's budget and accounts is largely a formality. Detailed scrutiny and control over government spending takes place mainly within the government itself through the medium of the Treasury (Chapter 15). However a substantial parliamentary safeguard is provided by the National Audit Office, headed by the Comptroller and Auditor-General (Section 13.5.4);

▶ legislating. Any member can propose a bill but in practice the parliamentary timetable is dominated by government business and legislation is usually presented to Parliament ready drafted by the executive. This is why Bagehot thought that the absence of a strict separation of powers made the UK constitution an effective machine for ensuring government by experts. There are certain opportunities for private members' bills but these rarely become law (Section 13.3.1);

▶ supervising the executive by scrutinising its activities. By convention ministers are accountable to Parliament and must appear in Parliament to participate in debates, make statements, answer questions and appear before committees (Section 15.7). Policy announcements should be made to Parliament before releasing them to the media although there is no clear convention to this effect and the principle is often ignored. The House of Commons can require a government to resign by a vote of no confidence or it can trigger a dissolution of Parliament under the Fixed Term Parliaments Act 2011 (Section 11.2). These sanctions are rarely used since the resignation of the government is likely to result in a general election, putting the jobs of MPs at risk;

▶ redressing grievances raised by individual MPs on behalf of their constituents. There are certain opportunities to raise grievances in debates but they are usually pursued by correspondence with ministers or by the Parliamentary Ombudsman. By convention every constituent has a right of access to his or her MP, which can be exercised by visiting Parliament if necessary. Individuals may also petition Parliament (Section 13.7);

▶ debating matters of public concern. Again there are limited procedural opportunities for such debates.

11.6 Parliamentary privilege

In *R (Chaytor) v A-G* [2010] EWCA Crim 1910 the Court of Appeal said that 'properly understood the privileges of Parliament are the privileges of the nation and the bedrock of our constitutional democracy' (at [5]–[7]). It is important as part of the separation of powers that a legislature can control its own affairs and that its members be protected against outside interference. Interference by the Crown with parliamentary business was an ingredient of the seventeenth-century revolution (see *R v Elliot* [1629] Cro Car 181, reversed (1668) Cro Car 182n: King forcibly dismissed Parliament, Elliot holding the Speaker down in an attempt to prevent this). As a result at the beginning of every Parliament the Speaker symbolically asserts the 'ancient and undoubted privileges' of the House of Commons against the Crown. The House of Lords also has privileges, but does not have the power to punish. The devolved legislatures of Scotland, Wales and Northern Ireland do not have parliamentary privilege but are protected against liability for defamation (eg Scotland Act 1998, s 41).

Some parliamentary privileges are mainly of historical or symbolic interest. These include the collective right of access of the Commons to the monarch. Members of the Commons also enjoy immunity from civil, as opposed to criminal, arrest during a period from 40 days before to 40 days after every session. In the case of peers the immunity is permanent and seems to be based on their status as peers rather than membership of the House (*Stourton v Stourton* (1963)). Now that debtors are no longer imprisoned, civil arrest is virtually obsolete, being concerned mainly with disobedience to court orders. Members and officers of both Houses have automatic exemption from jury service (Juries Act 1974) and the House can exempt members from giving evidence in court.

The two most important privileges overlap. They are:

(i) the collective privilege of each House to control its own composition and procedure and

(ii) the freedom of speech both of Parliament as such and of individual members (Art 9 Bill of Rights 1688).

We shall discuss these below. The courts accept that Parliament has the exclusive power to regulate its own internal affairs but claim the right to determine the limits of parliamentary privilege (see *R (Chaytor) v A-G* [2011] 1 AC 684: Supreme Court).

Parliamentary privilege in relation to the freedom of speech of an MP has been upheld by the European Court of Human Rights as a proportionate way of securing the independence of the legislature (*A v UK* (2003)).

11.6.1   Contempt of Parliament

Breach of a specific parliamentary privilege is one kind of 'contempt' of Parliament. A parliamentary privilege is a special right or immunity available either to the House collectively (eg to control its own composition and procedure) or to individual members (eg freedom of speech). Contempt is a general term embracing any conduct, whether by MPs or outsiders:

> which obstructs or impedes either House of Parliament in the performance of its functions or which obstructs or impedes any member or officer of the House in the execution of his duty or which has a tendency directly or indirectly to produce such results. (May, *Parliamentary Practice* (Butterworths 1997) 108)

This is very wide. It includes for example abuses by MPs of parliamentary procedure, breaching confidences, refusing to obey a committee, causing disruption in the House, improper or dishonest behaviour by MPs, and harassment of, or allegations against, MPs in newspapers. Contempt not only protects the 'efficiency' of the House but also its 'authority and dignity'.

Perhaps the most striking feature of contempt of Parliament is that Parliament accuses, tries and punishes offenders itself. This is an aspect of the wider principle that Parliament claims to look after its own affairs without outside interference. The ordinary courts have no jurisdiction over the internal affairs of Parliament (below) and there are no independent safeguards for the individual. This is a violation both of the separation of powers (in its functional sense) and the rule of law concerning the right to be judged by an independent court (see *Demicola v Malta* [1992] 14 EHRR 47). The immunity of Parliament from interference by the courts is reinforced by the Human Rights Act 1998, which provides that Parliament is not a public body for the purpose of the Act (s 6(3); Section 21.3). This prevents an action being brought against Parliament.

The procedure for dealing with a contempt of Parliament, or a breach of privilege, is as follows (see Committee of Privileges, Third Report (HC 1976–77, 417)):

1. Any member can give written notice of a complaint to the Speaker.
2. The Speaker decides whether to give priority over other business.
3. If the Speaker decides not to do so, the member may then use the ordinary procedure of the House to get the matter discussed. This would be difficult in practice.
4. If the Speaker decides to take up the matter, the complaining member can propose that the matter be referred to the Committee on Standards and Privileges or that some other action be taken, for example an immediate debate. A select committee can in certain cases refer a contempt against itself direct to the Committee (HC Deb 18 March 1986, vol 94, cols 763–64).
5. The Committee (currently 10 senior members chaired by an Opposition MP) investigates the complaint. The Committee reports back to the House, which decides what action to take. This could range from a reprimand, through suspension or expulsion from the House, to imprisonment for the rest of the

session, renewable indefinitely. The House of Lords can imprison for a fixed term and can also impose a fine. The procedure is entirely up to the Committee and has been widely criticised as archaic and unfair. Witnesses are examined but there is no right to legal representation. The accused has no legal right to a hearing or to summon or cross-examine witnesses. The Sixth Report of the Committee on Standards in Public Life (*Reinforcing Standards* (Cm 4557, 2000)), recommended that a panel containing independent persons be used and that there should be legal representation and a right of appeal (see also Eighth Report (*Standards of Conduct in the House of Commons* (Cm 5663, 2002)). So far these suggestions have no been fully implemented. However it is now proposed that external members be included on the Standards and Privileges Committee (see HC Procedure Committee, *3rd Special Report*, 2010–12, HC 1869). Parliament is not subject to the Human Rights Act 1998 (Section 22.4.1) so the right to a fair trial cannot be invoked.

6. The Speaker also has summary powers to deal with disruptive behaviour in the House or breaches of the rules of debate. He or she can exclude MPs and others from the Chamber until the end of the session (HC Standing Orders 24–26) and make rulings on matters of procedure. The Speaker of the House of Lords has no procedural or disciplinary powers.

The conduct of MPs and the justice and effectiveness of the internal disciplinary process came into the public spotlight during the 1990s when several MPs were accused of accepting payments to give favours to outside interests. Further problems arose during 2008–09 when it was revealed by the press that many MPs had been abusing their expense allowance claims, some grotesquely so, and that there was no effective way to police this. There was considerable public concern on the theme of distrust of government in general. Perhaps as an overreaction, machinery was introduced which for the first time brings an external element into policing the behaviour of MPs (below).

11.6.2 'Exclusive cognisance'

Each House of Parliament claims exclusive control over its internal affairs both against the other House and outside bodies. It was originally based on the premise that Parliament has its own peculiar law which was not known to the courts but issues also arise in connection with ordinary legal wrongs committed in a parliamentary setting. For example, although the qualifications for being a member of Parliament are fixed by statute, each House has the exclusive right to decide who will actually sit, to regulate all internal proceedings and to expel members (*Bradlaugh v Gossett* [1884] 12 QBD 271: refusal to let atheist take his seat even where court had ruled in his favour in *Clarke v Bradlaugh* [1881] 7 QBD 38)). No one can be prevented from placing a matter before Parliament even where they have contracted not to do so (*Bilston Corp v Wolverhampton Corp* [1942] Ch 391). The courts cannot order a minister to present a matter to Parliament even where a change in the law is required by European law (*R v Secretary of State for Employment, ex p Equal Opportunities Commission* [1992] 1 All ER 545). Nor can the courts decide whether the procedures for enacting legislation under the internal rules of each House of Parliament have been properly followed (*Pickin v British Railways*

Board [1974], cf *R (Jackson) v A-G* [2005] 4 All ER 1253, Section 8.2). In some cases, notably in connection with elections Parliament has handed over a matter by statute to the ordinary law and so can no longer claim privilege.

The exclusive cognisance privilege only applies to the internal affairs of the House. Resolutions of the House of Commons cannot alter the general law. This requires a statute (*Stockdale v Hansard* (1839); *Bowles v Bank of England* [1913]). Similarly, approval by the House of subordinate legislation or a government decision cannot make valid something unlawful under the general law (*Hoffman La Roche v Trade and Industry Secretary* [1974] 2 All ER 1128). However in considering whether government action is unreasonable the court will be especially deferential to decisions that have been approved by Parliament (Section 19.7.1).

The Ombudsman who investigates citizens' complaints against the executive and reports to Parliament is not protected by privilege because he deals with external matters (Section 20.3). By contrast the Parliamentary Commissioner for Standards, who polices the conduct of MPs and so is concerned with matters internal to the House, is subject to privilege and so is not subject to review by the courts (Section 11.7.1). The position as regards the Independent Parliamentary Standards Authority which polices salaries and expenses arrangements (Section 11.7.2) is unclear since IPSA has both external and internal aspects.

Exclusive cogniscence has two aspects. Firstly it includes the management and administration of Parliament such as control over the premises (precincts), arrangements for salaries and expenses, libraries, catering etc all of which support Parliament as an independent institution. Secondly it ensures that MPs are not impeded from performing their duties, namely lawmaking, scrutinising the government and representing constituents in the House. This second aspect overlaps with the separate privilege of freedom of speech (below).

On a wide view, the first aspect has sometimes been thought to include anything that happens within the precincts of the Houses of Parliament (the Palace of Westminister). Parliament has control over the precincts in the sense that permission is required to enter even by the police. Thus in 2008 the police searched the parliamentary office of Damian Green, then a shadow immigration minister, in connection with an investigation into a leak of information from the Home Office. This may have been politically unwise and an overreaction but since the Speaker had apparently given permission it was not a contempt of the House (see Bradley, 'The Damian Green Affair-All's Well that Ends Well?' [2012] PL 396). In *R v Grahame-Campbell, ex p Herbert* [1935] 1 KB 594 the Divisional Court held that the House of Commons bar was exempt from the liquor licensing laws and so could sell drinks without restriction. However another explanation of this case is that a statute might apply only to the Palace of Westminister only if it expressly say so. Moreover the decision is probably wrong (see below).

It has become clear that not all matters relating to the House fall within the privilege. The privilege applies (i) to decisions made by Parliamentary bodies and (ii) to MPs in the performance of their 'core' or essential functions of legislating, holding government to account and representing constituents but not to ordinary management matters, activities that might take place in any institution for example theft or fraud or the treatment of staff. In some cases such as use of research facilities in the House the distinction may be difficult to make.

In *R (Chaytor) v A-G* [2011] 1 AC 684 (which contains a useful review of the authorities) three MPs claimed to be protected by the exclusive cogniscence privilege against prosecution in the ordinary courts for making fraudulent claims for parliamentary expenses. The Supreme Court held that parliamentary privilege is subject to the rule of law and so for the Court to determine its limit. The Court was not bound by decisions made by parliamentary bodies, although it would treat them with respect. For example it may sometimes be more suitable or fairer for an MP to be dealt with by Parliament itself.

The Court held that the exclusive cogniscence privilege was not available in respect of the expenses claims. Lord Phillips said that Parliament can waive (give up) its exclusive cognisance privilege and has done so for many years in respect of the administrative management of the two Houses including statutory interventions. [74, 89–92]. There is a distinction between the making of administrative rules of the House including decisions by parliamentary committees on such matters as expenses and salaries. These rules remain subject to privilege and cannot be reviewed by the courts. However in respect of matters relating to the *application* of the rules to individuals, Parliament has permitted the ordinary authorities to act and where there is an overlapping jurisdiction will co operate with outside authorities [89]–[92]. Ordinary civil actions and criminal matters against individuals are not therefore protected. Thus the prosecution of the MPs in question was lawful. Moreover according to Lord Clarke, although the point remains open, the individual cannot invoke a privilege which Parliament has waived and except by statute Parliament cannot withdraw this long standing waiver [131–2], cf Lord Rodgers [124]. It was also left open whether a statute only applies to activities within the Palace of Westminister if it expressly states as much [78].

Lord Rodgers held that even without waiver the privilege applied only to matters directly related to the core functions of an MP and there was nothing in the allegations which related in any way to these. The other members of the court agreed with both Lord Phillips and Lord Rodgers. Therefore Lord Rodgers would exclude most administrative matters and questions of ordinary legal liability from the privilege. See also *Corporate Officer of the House of Commons v Information Comr* [2009] 3 All ER 403: expense claims are subject to Freedom of Information Act (Section 23.2.1); *Re McGuinness* [1997]: Speaker's decisions not reviewable by the courts.

11.6.3   Freedom of speech

Freedom of speech is the central privilege of an individual MP, who must be at liberty to speak and write freely and frankly without pressure from outside bodies, whether participating in a debate, asking questions of ministers, acting in a committee or raising the problems of his or her constituents. Moreover people who communicate with MPs about concerns with public officials also deserve protection against retaliation from the executive or police.

Article 9 of the Bill of Rights 1688 (part of the revolution settlement for the purpose of protecting MPs against the Crown) states that:

> 'The Freedom of Speech or Debates or Proceedings in Parliament ought not to be impeached or questioned in any court or place out of Parliament'.

Article 9 overlaps with the exclusive cognisance privilege discussed above although the latter goes beyond speech to all matters relating to the control of parliamentary business. In *R v Chaytor* (above) the Supreme Court explained that the two are separate in that exclusive cognisance is a privilege belonging to the House as a whole and can be waived by it. Neither the House nor the individual MP can waive Article 9 [63]. Only a statute can do so. Thus the Defamation Act 1996 amended Article 9 in order to accommodate Neil Hamilton, a Conservative MP who wished to sue a newspaper for defamation, relying upon parliamentary material for the purpose. Section 13 permits an MP to use things said in Parliament in evidence provided that the MP waives his or her own immunity. This illustrates the frailty of constitutional principle against party politics.

There are conflicting approaches to the interpretation of Article 9. Thus two constitutional principles both important to democracy conflict. On the one hand Article 9 protects a vital constitutional interest namely that MPs should not be subject to pressures from outside which might prevent them from performing their duties properly. This calls for a broad reading of Article 9 (see *Pepper v Hart* [1993] AC 593, 638). On the other hand in *Chaytor* (above) the Supreme Court held that since Article 9 violates the rule of law (in its wide sense) and restricts ordinary legal rights, in particular freedom of speech it should not be construed broadly (See also *A-G for Ceylon v De Livera* [1963] AC 103, 162; *Prebble v Television New Zealand* [1995] 1 AC 321 at 340.)

The main limit on the scope of Article 9 is what is meant by 'proceedings in Parliament'. In 1688 it was probably thought that the phrase was self-explanatory. It certainly includes speeches and written or oral questions by an MP in the House or in committee proceedings. The work of a modern MP goes beyond this. Much of an MP's time is spent in communicating with constituents and attending meetings in the UK and abroad with ministers, officials, pressure groups, local authorities, business organisations, and so on. In *R v Chaytor* (above) the Supreme Court took a narrow approach. It held that Article 9 applies only to the 'core' or essential business of Parliament [62]. The false expense claims made by the MPs did not relate to this and scrutiny of expense claims by the courts would not inhibit an MP from performing his essential duties [48]. Lord Rodgers with whom the others agreed said that Article 9 could not cover matters outside the scope of the exclusive cognisance privilege (above).

Anything said in the Chamber as part of the business of the House and in committees or reports related to the business of the House is certainly protected. Parliamentary committees often visit places around the country, and interference with their proceedings wherever they take place is a contempt of Parliament (eg a disturbance at Essex University in 1969 (HC 1968–69, 308)). On the other hand, even within the House itself, speech unrelated to parliamentary business enjoys no privilege (see *Re Parliamentary Privileges Act 1770*). In *Rivlin v Bilankin* [1953] 1 QB 485, for example libellous letter about a private matter posted within the precincts were not protected.

There are many borderline cases since the limits of an MP's duties are vague. However the onus is on the MP to show that he falls within the immunity since this is an exception from the basic assumption of equality before the law (see *Chaytor* at [41], [42]). It is clear that statements by an MP to the media including TV and radio interviews are not covered by parliamentary privilege, although they may be covered by 'qualified privilege' (Section 11.6.4). In *Buchanan v Jennings [2005] 1 AC 115* the Privy Council held that an MP who in a television interview endorsed a defamatory statement he had made in the New Zealand Parliament could not claim parliamentary privilege for the interview since this was not part of his parliamentary functions. Thus an MP could be liable if he or she repeats in the media or anywhere else anything said in Parliament. Statements made by MPs in election campaigns or at public meetings are similarly not protected (*Culnane v Morris* [2006] 2 All ER 149).

The main area of uncertainty about Article 9 concerns things said or written to or by MPs as part of their wider duties on behalf of their constituents, for example a letter complaining to the Secretary of State about an NHS hospital. In the case of *Strauss* [1956] the House of Commons by a tiny majority (218 to 213) rejected a recommendation by the Committee of Privileges that such letters should be protected by parliamentary privilege. *Strauss* concerned a complaint about the activities of the London Electricity Board. It is not clear what the reasons for the Commons resolutions were, and the vote may have been on party lines. On the basis of a narrow view of *Strauss*, a letter from an MP is privileged only if it is to do with a matter currently being debated in the House or is the subject of an official parliamentary question. One way of distinguishing Strauss is that the LEB was not a government department, so the minister to whom Strauss wrote was not directly responsible to Parliament for its activities.

In 1967 a Select Committee on Parliamentary Privilege (HC 1967–68, 34) recommended that privilege should include all official communications by and to an MP. This seems to be consistent with *Chaytor* (above) at least if the matter is intended to be raised in Parliament. Thus the alleged conduct of Damian Green (above) to use in Parliament information given to him unlawfully by a civil servant could fall within Article 9.

A narrow view of Article 9 was taken in earlier cases. In *R v Greenaway* [1992], unreported, see [1998] PL 356, the court held that parliamentary privilege did not apply because the offence occurred when the bribe was received and therefore the court did not need to investigate what went on in Parliament. Moreover the ordinary courts were best equipped to deal with the matter. However protection could apply where an MP acts on a bribe for example in a debate. (*Greenaway* was doubted in *Chaytor* [42] (see *US v Brewster* (1972) 408 US 501,524–5.) In *Rost v Edwards* [1990] 2 All ER 641 the Register of Members' Interests was held not to be protected on the basis that it was a public document; compare *R v Comr for Standards ex parte Al Fayed* [1998] 1 WLR 689: report of Commissioner to Parliament protected. See also Report of the Joint Committee on Parliamentary Privilege (1998–99, HL 43–1, HC 214–1).

It is also important to decide what is meant by 'impeached or questioned'. Article 9 prevents civil and criminal proceedings against an MP and also prevents parliamentary materials from being used as evidence against an MP in court proceedings (*Church of Scientology of California v Johnson-Smith* [1972] 1 QB 522 (below). Article 9 is not restricted to legal proceedings but prevents interference with the freedom of speech of MPs by any outside body. This could include publishing MPs' home telephone numbers (*Daily Graphic Case* (HC 1956–57, 27)), accusing MPs of drunkenness (*Duffy's Case* (HC 1964–65, 129)) or making press allegations of conflict of interest by MPs.

However Article 9 has not been used against media criticism of speeches by MPs. In this context the Human Rights Act 1998 might restrain an expansive interpretation of Article 9. The court is required to interpret all legislation, including Article 9, 'if it is possible to do so', in a way that conforms to the rights set out in the Act, one of which is freedom of expression (s 3). Nor does Article 9 prevent courts or other bodies from looking into matters which are also before Parliament.

However Article 9 does not exclude the use of parliamentary material in court to establish what was said in Parliament provided that the parliamentary processes or things said in them are not criticised (see *Hamilton v Al Fayed* [1999] 3 All ER317): MP accused of misleading Parliament. For example, although evidence of something a minister said in Parliament cannot be used to determine whether he is acting honestly (*R v Secretary of State for Trade, ex p Anderson Strathclyde* [1983] at 238–39), it can be used as evidence of the reasons for executive action (*Toussaint v A-G of St Vincent and the Grenadines* [2008]). privilege Under the *Pepper v Hart* rule statements in Parliament can sometimes be used as an aid to statutory interpretation (Section 7.6.2). In *Pepper v Hart* [1993] the House of Lords took the view that the purpose of Article 9 was only to prevent MPs from being penalised for what they said in the House. However in *R v Forsythe* [2011] 2 AC 69 the Supreme Court refused to look at Parliamentary debates in order to decide whether a statute which gave power to the government to penalise funding the Iraq government had an implied time limit. The Court took the view that, unless fundamental rights were in issue when a clear parliamentary intention would be required, there would be a 'real risk' of breaching parliamentary privilege.

As with any liberty, the price to be paid is that an MP might abuse privilege to make untrue allegations against persons who cannot answer back or to violate privacy. (See the *Child Z* case (HC 1995–96, vol 252, paras 9, 10), where a child was named in defiance of an order of the Court of Appeal.) Thus the limits of freedom of speech have to be defined. There are therefore limitations placed upon members' freedom of speech by Parliament itself, for example by rules of procedure or possibly by party discipline within the House. Indeed these restrictions are themselves immune from control by the courts because of the exclusive cognisance privilege (Section 11.6.2). The Speaker, who presides over the House of Commons, has a duty to control procedure impartially. Internal rules exist to prevent MPs misusing their privilege of freedom of speech, for example by attacking people who cannot answer back or by commenting upon pending legal proceedings. For example 'the invidious use of a person's name in a question should be resorted to only if to do so is strictly necessary to render the question intelligible and the protection of parliamentary privilege should be used only as a last resort' and 'in a way that does not damage the good name of the House' (see HC Deb 17 March 1986, vol 94, col 26).

11.6.4   Qualified privilege

Independently of parliamentary privilege, an MP performing his official duties may be protected by 'qualified privilege'. Qualified privilege is not confined to MPs. It available to anyone who has a legal or moral duty to make the statement in question and where the recipient has a corresponding interest in hearing it (Section 22.5). Qualified privilege is much narrower than parliamentary privilege. It does give complete immunity but covers only statements made in good faith and taking proper care. It applies only to defamation (the law relating to statements that damage reputation) whereas full or 'absolute' parliamentary privilege covers every kind of legal action. It is a defence to an action, so the MP must subject herself or himself to the burden of legal proceedings. Even if she or he eventually wins, the expense and uncertainty of litigation may discourage an MP from speaking freely.

Qualified privilege could apply to cases such as *Strauss (above)*. In *R v Rule* [1937] 2 All ER 772 it was held that a constituent's letter to an MP has qualified privilege. It could also apply to a media interview or press statement (*Church of Scientology v Johnson-Smith (above)*, or to a statement made in an election campaign (*Culnane v Morris (above)*: anti-BNP leaflets). Political freedom of expression is regarded as of the highest importance, and the scope of qualified privilege is correspondingly generous (*Culnane*). The public have a general interest in a democracy of receiving information and opinions from MPs. However it is doubtful whether an MP who merely repeated what he had said in the House could claim qualified privilege because the statement would already be accessible to the public. An MP who makes a defamatory statement which is not related to his parliamentary duties would not have qualified privilege. Nor perhaps would a message on social media such as Twitter since these are arguably not sufficiently public in character.

11.6.5 Publication of parliamentary proceedings

A controversial aspect of contempt of Parliament concerns public access to parliamentary information, which arguably should be unrestricted except where the disclosure would harm the public interest. However parliamentary committees often sit in private and 'leaks' of reports of select committees have been prohibited since 1837, although action is only likely to be taken if the leak causes substantial interference with the function of a committee. The House of Commons has waived any more general right to restrain publication of its proceedings and has authorised the broadcasting of its proceedings, subject to a power to give directions. It has also undertaken generally to use its contempt powers sparingly (HC 1967–68, 34, para 15).

There is also statutory protection Documents published by order of Parliament or correct copies, such as *Hansard*, have full parliamentary privilege (Parliamentary Papers Act 1840, ss 1, 2). The publication by the press of fair and accurate extracts or abstracts from authorised reports of parliamentary proceedings are also protected if the publisher shows that they are published in good faith without malice (s 3), as are broadcasts of parliamentary proceedings (Defamation Act 1952, s 9; Broadcasting Act 1990, s 203(1)).

Other press reports including parliamentary sketches and probably broadcasts and Internet reports are protected by the general law of qualified privilege provided that they are honest and fair (*Wason v Walter* [1868] 4 QB 73; *Cook v Alexander* [1974] QB 297). Section 15 of the Defamation Act 1996 protects fair and accurate reports of legislative proceedings and other public meetings anywhere. Here it is for the claimant to show that the publication was not in good faith. Qualified privilege applies only to defamation.

Where a report is embellished with additional material which may flesh it out or comment on it, the privilege is lost unless the ordinary reader can clearly distinguish the reportage from the other material (see *Curiston v Times Newspapers* [2007]). The privilege does not in any case apply to the additional material, although this may be protected by the more general defence of 'responsible journalism' (Section 22.5.3). As we have seen above, if an MP repeats in the media a statement he has made in Parliament probably neither he nor the broadcasters are protected even by qualified privilege.

11.6.6   The courts and Parliament

As we have seen, the courts do not intervene in the internal affairs of the House. On the other hand, where parliamentary activity involves the rights of persons outside the House, the courts have intervened at least to the extent of deciding whether the privilege asserted by Parliament exists. Both the rule of law and the separation of powers are engaged in this context. In a famous eighteenth-century controversy that asserted basic rule of law values the courts held that parliamentary officers have no power to deprive citizens of voting rights: 'where there is a right there is a remedy' (*Ashby v White* [1703] 2 Ld R 938; see also *Paty's Case* [1704] 2 Ld R 1105). In *Stockdale v Hansard* (1839) it was held that parliamentary privilege did not protect reports published by order of the House from being the subject of libel actions. The subject matter of these disputes is only of historical interest. Parliament no longer controls elections and *Stockdale v Hansard* was soon reversed by statute (Parliamentary Papers Act 1840). Nevertheless the general principle about the power of the courts remains relevant.

Parliament has never accepted that *Stockdale v Hansard* was correctly decided and has never withdrawn the claim to be the exclusive judge of its own privileges. Thus in the *Sheriff of Middlesex* case [1840] Parliament imprisoned the two holders of the office of sheriff for enforcing the court's judgment in *Stockdale v Hansard*. Not surprisingly the sheriffs applied to the court for release but the court, including Lord Denman, who had decided *Stockdale v Hansard* itself, held that it was powerless to intervene. Parliament had the undoubted right to commit to prison for contempt and it did not have to give reasons. Unless some improper reason was disclosed on the face of the committal warrant, the court must assume that Parliament was acting lawfully even though the judges knew otherwise.

Whether this principle will be taken advantage of in modern times rests with Parliament's – or the courts' – political sense. The courts are unwilling to take action that might be considered as trespassing on Parliament's preserves. Parliament too has shown restraint in asserting claims to privilege. This standoff could be regarded as an example of the dual sovereignty which it is claimed that the separation of powers requires and of the reliance upon voluntary restraint in support of the separation of powers. Thus it has been claimed that there is a voluntary, mutual respect between the two institutions (*Hamilton v Al Fayed* [1999] 3 All ER 317 at 333–34). In *R (Chaytor) v A-G* [2010] (Section 11.6.2) the Supreme Court held that it was settled that the court can decide the limits of parliamentary privilege. In that case no challenge was made to the court's jurisdiction.

There is also the wider question of whether the courts can review matters related to Parliament under its judicial review jurisdiction. The court will not generally do so, not only because of Parliamentary privilege as such but also under the wider principle of respect due to a co-equal branch of government (Section 19.7). Thus the question whether the proceedings of the Select Committee on Standards satisfy normal principles of fairness and due process Section 11.6.1) is probably outside the ambit of the courts. Moreover the Human Rights Act 1998 does not apply to Parliament (Section 21.4.1).

11.6.7 Reform of parliamentary privilege

The Nicholls Report (Report of the Joint Committee on Parliamentary Privilege (1998–99, HL 43–1, HC 214–1)) recommended reforms. These have yet to be implemented although *Chaytor* has overtaken several of them (see Consultation paper, *Parliamentary Privilege* Cm 8318, 12 April 2012). The Nicholls Report suggested the enactment of a code of parliamentary privilege to include modest reforms largely intended to clarify the relationship between Parliament and the courts. They include the following:

- 'Place out of Parliament' for the purposes of Article 9 should be defined to include courts and tribunals empowered to take evidence on oath but not tribunals of inquiry if both Houses so resolve.
- The offence of abuse of public office should include MPs.
- MPs should be subject to the criminal law relating to corruption (see *Chaytor*).
- Members of the Lords should be compellable before Commons' committees.
- Parliament's 'exclusive cognisance' should be confined to 'activities directly and closely related to the business of the House' (see *Chaytor*).
- Contempt by non-members should be dealt with by the ordinary courts and limited to a fine.
- Freedom from arrest should be abolished.

11.7 Standards in the Commons

Following the recommendations of the First Report of the Committee on Standards in Public Life (Cm 2850, 1995) there is a Code of Conduct for MPs (2005). In keeping with parliamentary privilege, this is policed by the House itself.

The primary duty of an MP is to be an independent representative of his or her constituents. There are obstacles to the independence of MPs. First and foremost there are party loyalties. Secondly many MPs are sponsored by outside bodies, including trade unions and business interests, who may contribute towards their expenses. Some MPs accept employment as paid or unpaid 'consultants' to businesses and interest groups, such as the Police Federation, or hold company directorships. MPs are also frequently offered 'hospitality', or gifts, or invited on expenses-paid 'fact-finding' trips. There are also 'all-party' subject groups of MPs which involve relationships with outside bodies (see HC 1984–85, 408). Except in the case of a private bill, a member is free to vote on a matter in which she or he has a personal interest. There is therefore a risk that MPs are susceptible to lobbying by private interests.

It is often said that sponsorships and consultancies enable MPs to keep in touch with informed opinion outside Westminister and to develop specialised knowledge. They also enable MPs without private means to supplement their parliamentary salaries. The process of enacting legislation is also helped by consultation with interested parties. There is much 'lobbying' of civil servants and it is desirable that this should be counterbalanced by MPs having their own access to outside interests. On the other hand, apart from the risk of corruption, MPs might also spend time in company boardrooms that may generate little understanding of social problems and would be better spent helping their constituents. Compromises are therefore made.

In the *Brown* case [1947] an MP sponsored by a trade union was dismissed by the union for not advocating its interests in Parliament. The Committee of Privileges voted that a contract could not require an MP to support or represent his or her sponsor's interests in Parliament, nor could the sponsor punish the MP for not doing so. However it was not contempt to dismiss a consultant if for whatever reason the employer or sponsor was unhappy with his or her services. This somewhat evasive compromise does not seem to take the matter much further. It would be a contempt to threaten to dismiss an MP unless she or he took a certain line in Parliament but not, apparently, to dismiss her or him after the event. Arguably pressures from local constituency parties would also be contemptuous.

Since the seventeenth century, resolutions of the House have declared that certain kinds of external influences are in contempt of Parliament. The latest distinction seems to be between promoting a specific matter for gain, which is forbidden, and acting as a consultant generally, which is acceptable. There have been many resolutions attempting to capture this elusive matter.

For example a resolution of 1995 which amends a resolution of 1947 (HC 1994–95, 816 (see HC Deb 6 November 1995, cols 604, 661) states that:

> It is inconsistent with the dignity of the House, with the duty of a Member to his constituents, and with the maintenance of the privilege of freedom of speech for any Member of this House to enter into any contractual agreement with an outside body, controlling or limiting the Member's complete independence and freedom of action in Parliament or stipulating that he shall act in any way as the representative of such outside body in regard to any matter to be transacted in Parliament; the duty of a Member being to his constituents and to the country as a whole, rather than to any particular section thereof: and that in particular no Members of the House shall, in consideration of any remuneration, fee, payment or reward or benefit in kind, direct or indirect, which the Member or any member of his or her family has received, is receiving or expects to receive –
>
> (a) advocate or initiate any cause or matter on behalf of any outside body or individual, or
> (b) urge any other Member of either House of Parliament, including Ministers, to do so by means of any speech, Question, motion, introduction of a bill, or amendment to a Motion or a Bill.

A further resolution restricts the extent to which a member may participate in a delegation to ministers or public officials; see Code of Conduct for MPs (HC 2009–10, 735):

> A member should not initiate, participate in or attend any such delegation where the problem to be addressed affects only the body with which the member has a relevant paid interest except when that problem relates primarily to a constituency matter.

The MPs' Code of Conduct (2009) forbids paid advocacy, prohibits payment for promoting or opposing any matter in Parliament, requires openness and frankness and forbids the use for gain of information received in confidence for the purpose of parliamentary duties.

There are also criminal offences involving members of public bodies. Misuse of public office is a common law offence and there are also offences under the Public

Bodies (Corrupt Practices) Act 1889 and the Prevention of Corruption Act 1916. These offences may include cases where MPs are offered bribes. It is arguable that an MP is not a 'public servant' and does not hold a public office as such, so is outside these offences (see *A-G's Reference (No 3 of 2003) [2004] EWCA 868*).

MPs must enter information about their financial interests in a Register of Members' Interests (see Code of Conduct for MPs (2009)). The register itself has been held not to be protected by parliamentary privilege on the ground that it is a public document (*Rost v Edwards* [1990]). The categories of interest required by the register have been strengthened to include full details of an employment contract, the provision of services such as consultancy, company directorships, employment or offices, professions and trades, names of clients, financial sponsorships, overseas visits as an MP, payments received from abroad, land or property, shareholdings and 'any interest or benefit received which might reasonably be thought by others to influence the member's actions in Parliament'. However the precise value of such payments need not be entered. According to the register, only one in five MPs is without an external source of income.

As a result of allegations concerning tax avoidance members of both Houses of Parliament are deemed to be resident, ordinarily resident or domiciled in the UK for tax purposes and so are fully liable for UK tax (Constitutional Reform and Governance Act 2010, s 41).

11.7.1 The Parliamentary Commissioner for Standards

Following the First Report of the Committee on Standards in Public Life (Cm 2850, 1995) the House of Commons appointed a Parliamentary Commissioner for Standards empowered to investigate complaints of misuse of the Commons register and to report to the Standards and Privileges Committee of the House of Commons (HC Standing Orders (Public Business) (1995) No 150). The Commissioner can also investigate complaints by MPs and the public concerning the Code of Conduct and give advice to MPs. The decisions of the Commissioner are subject to parliamentary privilege and are not subject to judicial review (*R v Parliamentary Comr for Standards* [1998] 1 WLR 689).

Parliament can appoint and dismiss the Commissioner. In 2001 Elizabeth Filkin did not have her contract renewed. She had attracted a reputation as an assiduous investigator. In its Eighth Report (Cm 5663, 2002) the Committee on Standards in Public Life recommended that the independence of the Commissioner be strengthened. The Commissioner should be appointed for a non-renewable term of five to seven years, should have the power to call for witnesses and documents and should not be an employee of the House. This has not been implemented.

The Commissioner cannot investigate the interests of ministers acting as such, thus reflecting the separation of powers. There is no independent mechanism to regulate ministers. Compliance with the Ministerial Code is a matter for the Prime Minister. Independent inquiries in the form of a Royal Commission or under the Inquiries Act 2005 can be held into ministerial misconduct (Chapter 5). However these are set up by ministers. The Tribunals of Inquiry (Evidence) Act 1921, under which Parliament could order an inquiry, was repealed by the 2005 Act.

11.7.2   The Independent Parliamentary Standards Authority

IPSA is responsible for the salaries and expenses of MPs and has a role in the administration of MPs' pensions. Revelations in the press during 2008–09 that many MPs had been abusing their expenses claims caused considerable public concern. This led to legislation which for the first time introduced an element of outside policing into the affairs of Parliament. MPs' expenses had previously been dealt with relatively informally within the House (see Committee on Standards in Public Life, Twelfth Report (*MPs' Expenses and Allowances: Supporting Parliament, Safeguarding the Taxpayer* (Cm 7724, 2009)); Standards and Privileges Committee Second Report (HC 2009–10, 67)).

IPSA is a statutory body (Parliamentary Standards Act 2009 modified by the Constitutional Reform and Governance Act 2010). It has no jurisdiction over the House of Lords. The Acts go to considerable lengths to make IPSA independent. The members of IPSA must comprise a Chairman (currently Sir Ian Kennedy, a lawyer and seasoned recipient of government patronage), a former senior judge, a qualified auditor and a former MP. Apart from this no MP or former MP may serve. Members hold office for five years, non-renewable, and can be removed only on an Address from both Houses of Parliament. Thus they have similar status to a senior judge.

The members of IPSA are appointed by the Queen on an Address from the Commons on the nomination of the Speaker on the recommendation of the Speaker's Committee (below), subject to the usual mantra of appointment on merit by fair and open competition ('OMFOC'). The Act does not prescribe how the appointment process should be conducted. In fact MPs play no part in the selection of the nominee and the appointment process is subject to the Code for Public Appointments made by the Public Appointments Commissioner. An independent panel is used.

IPSA determines the salaries and expenses of MPs and polices the expenses system. There is a Compliance Officer appointed by IPSA for five years, non-renewable (OMFOC). The Compliance Officer reviews the rejection of an expenses claim by IPSA and investigates misuses of the expenses scheme. An investigation can be carried out on the Compliance Officer's initiative or at the request of the MP concerned or at the request of any individual, including therefore a member of the public. There is a right of appeal from the Compliance Officer to the ordinary tribunal system. IPSA can recover improper payments through the ordinary courts. There is a penalty of up to £1,000 for failing to provide information to IPSA. MPs' expenses claims must be published, containing such information as IPSA considers appropriate.

IPSA must make an annual report to the House of Commons.

The Speaker's Committee approves appointments to IPSA and that of the Compliance Officer. This Committee comprises the Speaker, the Leader of the House (a government minister), the Chair of the Committee on Standards and Privileges, five backbench MPs, who are nominated by and can be replaced by the House, and three laypersons who have never been MPs. The latter are appointed by resolution of the House (OMFOC).

In *R (Chaytor) v A-G* [2011] (Section 11.6.2), it was conceded that the expenses scheme as it was before the introduction of IPSA was protected by parliamentary privilege. However IPSA may not be protected by parliamentary privilege. The 2009 Act states that nothing in it affects Article 9 of the Bill of Rights 1688 (s 1) but this in itself does not determine the matter since the question is what Article 9 covers (Section 11.6.3). It is arguable that IPSA is not covered by privilege given its statutory basis and the fact that the expenses system is linked into the general legal system and publicised. IPSA may be vulnerable to accusations of interfering with proceedings in Parliament under Article 9. For example an MP might complain to the Standards and Privileges Committee that the expenses scheme is so mean that it prevents him from performing his functions. IPSA has already attracted criticism from MPs as being overly bureaucratic, and its staff have been subjected to abuse from some MPs (see *Guardian* 26 August 2010). Its hasty creation and immediate modification may illustrate how constitutional reform can be driven by panic reaction to short-term problems.

11.7.3 Standards in the House of Lords

There is a 'custom' that the House of Lords should not be subject to formal regulation. It is said by its members that it should rely on their 'personal honour' (Seventh Report of the Committee on Standards in Public Life (Cm 4903, 2000)). However no reason has been offered as to why members of the Lords are more honourable than members of the Commons. With the possible exception of treason, a member could not be deprived of a peerage or expelled for misconduct without statutory authority. Nor can a member resign, although a member can take a leave of absence. The Letters Patent from the Crown that create a peerage confer a legal right to sit in the House of Lords. There is however a power to suspend a member from sitting (see Reports of the Committee for Privileges (HL 2008–09, 87, 88)). It is customary for membership not to be regarded as a full-time commitment and many members have outside interests, including full-time jobs. The present government proposes to introduce a power to remove members of the House of Lords.

There is a House of Lords Code of Conduct (2009) embodying the Nolan Principles of Public Life. This includes a Register of Members' Interests. The register was originally voluntary in respect of non-financial interests. However as a result of the Seventh Report of the Committee on Standards in Public Life (Cm 4903, 2000) it was made compulsory (see HL 1994–95, 90, 98). It is however less stringent than the Commons register.

The Code also provides for an independent House of Lords Commissioner for Standards who investigations allegations against members involving misuse of their position or undisclosed financial interests. A complaint can be made by anyone, including a member of the public. The Commissioner reports to the House of Lords Committee for Privileges, which after a hearing reports to the House. The first Commissioner appointed in May 2010 is a former Chief Constable. IPSA does not apply to the House of Lords, which polices its own expenses claims. Peers now receive a flat rate of £300 per day's attendance.

Summary

▶ Parliament has developed primarily through the party system. It has the competing functions of sustaining the government and holding the government to account. It scrutinises legislation, provides the executive with finance, debates matters of public concern and redresses grievances. The executive is usually too powerful and complex for Parliament to be effective. However at least Parliament is a public forum in which the executive can be forced to justify its actions.

▶ There is a network of laws and conventions to ensure that Parliament lasts no more than five years, that it meets annually and that it can remove the government. However the Prime Minister can dissolve Parliament subject to the possibility of the overriding powers of the Crown, and MPs cannot hold the government to account during the periods when Parliament is not sitting.

▶ After the 1688 settlement the House of Lords was regarded as holding the constitutional balance of power, but by the twentieth century it had become subordinate to the elected House of Commons. The Lords was given a new lease of life by the introduction of life peers in the 1960s but the constitutional role of the House remains controversial. By convention and law the Lords must ultimately defer to the Commons. It is primarily a delaying and revising chamber. Since the bulk of the hereditary peers were removed in 1999 the House of Lords has become more aggressive in resisting the executive. The House of Lords is less subject to party pressures than the House of Commons. The rules of procedure and party discipline in the House of Lords are more relaxed than is the case with the Commons. Because of the control over the Commons exercised by the executive, a second chamber is desirable but there is no agreement as to how the hereditary element in the Lords should be replaced. At present the House of Lords is accountable to no one.

▶ Parliament can protect itself against interference from without and within through the law of parliamentary privilege and its powers to punish for contempt. Parliament can enforce its own privileges free from interference by the ordinary courts. The Committee on Standards and Privileges, which adjudicates on matters referred to it by the House, has been criticised on the grounds of lack of independence and a low standard of procedural fairness.

▶ The main parliamentary privileges are Parliament's exclusive control over its own affairs and freedom of speech. There are difficulties in terms of what counts as parliamentary proceedings for these purposes. These are probably confined to matters related to the core business of the House and to purely internal matters within the precincts of the House. MPs and the media also have qualified privilege in the law of defamation but this is limited.

▶ There are safeguards against conflicts of interest for MPs, including the Register of Interests and the Parliamentary Commissioner for Standards. There are similar but less stringent safeguards in the House of Lords. There is no independent mechanism to enforce standards against ministers. IPSA was recently created to determine and police MPs' salaries and expenses but has already run into problems. IPSA does not apply to the House of Lords.

▶ There has been conflict between the courts and Parliament as to who decides whether a claimed privilege or contempt exists. It is probably recognised that the courts have the power to do so.

Exercises

11.1 'It has been a source of concern to some constitutionalists that the effect of the 1911 Act and more particularly the 1949 Act has been to erode the checks and balances inherent in the British Constitution' (Lord Bingham in *R (Jackson) v A-G* [2005] at 41). Explain and discuss.

11.2 'The virtue, spirit and essence of a House of Commons consist in its being the express image of the feelings of the nation. It was not instituted to be a control on the people. It was designed as a control for the people' (Edmund Burke). 'Parliament really has no control over the executive. It is a pure fiction' (David Lloyd George). To what extent do these statements represent the contemporary constitution?

11.3 The routes to the dissolution of Parliament provided by the Fixed Term Parliaments Act 2011 have been described by Professor Hazell (in evidence to the Commons Political and Constitutional Reform Committee) as 'a change of driver' or a 'change of car.' Explain and discuss.

11.4 The government has just been defeated in a vote of confidence in the House of Commons. The Prime Minister enters into discussions with the leaders of various minority parties with a view to forming a new government. Two weeks later it is clear he cannot do so. However he becomes aware of a report due to be published by an important international organisation in the following month that he believes will increase the government's popularity with the voters. He therefore refuses to set the date for a general election until the report has been published. Advise the Leader of the Opposition as to the legal position and any legal remedy available to her.

Suppose the government was defeated on the vote of confidence on 1 March 2013 and the Prime Minister recommends to the Queen that an election be held on 1 April. What is the likely date of the following general election?

11.5 'It is not unduly idealistic to regard the integrity of Members' judgement, however constrained it may be by the party system, and the devotion of their time to the job to which they have been elected, as fundamental values worth not only protecting but insisted on' (Sedley). Discuss in relation to the outside interests of MPs and peers.

11.6 Dave is an MP. Sam, a constituent, steals documents from a government office which suggest that officials working there have been systematically deceiving the public. Sam sends these documents to Dave by E mail. Dave saves the documents on his computer and also sends them to the relevant minister. Dave plans to ask a question in the House relating to the documents but before he can do so the police raid his office in Parliament and remove his computer. Dave is arrested on a charge of aiding and abetting a theft. An official working at the government office in question commences an action against Dave for libel. Advise Dave as the extent, if at all, he is protected by Parliamentary privilege.

11.7 George an MP is accused by the Officers of the House of refusing to cooperate in revealing information about his associates in the business world in connection with an expenses claim. He is denied access to facilities in Parliament including the library, bars and restaurants. He claims that the parliamentary rules relating to expenses claims have been improperly approved by the relevant committee of the House to favour members who have family connections to ministers and that the meanness of the expense allowance prevents him from performing his duties properly since he has to seek outside work from 'business contacts'. He also claims that Nick a member of the committee has been bribed by a firm of accountants to recommend them. To what extent can these matters be considered by the courts?

11.8 Bulldog, an MP, asks Fox, the Minister of Health, in the House of Commons a question in which he strongly criticises Quangoman the head of the National Health Board for allegedly taking bribes from drug companies. Bulldog is later asked in a television interview whether he stands by the allegation. He replies, 'You must refer to my speech.' Bulldog also announces on Twitter that 'what I said in the House needed to be said'. Quangoman issues a writ for libel against Bulldog. Contending that this is a matter of parliamentary privilege over which the court has no jurisdiction, Bulldog refuses to enter an appearance or to defend the action. Meanwhile the House of Commons resolves that any judge, counsel or party who takes part in such proceedings will be guilty of contempt. Discuss the position of Bulldog and any possible action that may be taken against Quangoman, and any solicitor or counsel who proceeds with the libel.

11.9 i) Tessa, an MP is accused by a colleague Tony of sexual harassment in her office in Parliament. Advise Tony as to any legal obstacles to bringing an action in the courts.

(ii) Jack an MP is prosecuted for buying alcohol in the House of Commons bar to give to a person who is under age (his son). Advise him whether he can claim Parliamentary privilege.

Further reading

Archer, 'The House of Lords, Past, Present and Future' (2000) 70 Pol Q 396

Blackburn, 'The Summoning and Meeting of New Parliaments in the United Kingdom' (1989) 9 LS 165

Brazier, 'The Constitutional Role of the Opposition' (1989) 40 Northern Ireland LQ 131

Brazier, 'The Financial Powers of the House of Lords' (1998) 17 Anglo-American L Rev 131

Joseph, 'Parliament's Attenuated Privilege of Freedom of Speech' (2010) 126 LQR 568

Lock, 'Parliamentary Privilege and the Courts' [1985] PL 64

Munro, *Studies in Constitutional Law* (2nd edn, Butterworths 2000) ch 7

Oliver and Drewry (eds), *The Law and Parliament* (Butterworths 1998)

Riddall, 'The Second Chamber: In Search of a Complementary Role' (2000) 70 Pol Q 404

Royal Commission on the House of Lords, *A House for the Future* (Cm 4534, 2000) [Wakeham Report]

Ryan, 'The Fixed Term Parliaments Act 2011' [2012] PL 213

Tomkins, *Public Law* (Clarendon Press 2003) ch 4

Chapter 12

The composition of Parliament and Parliamentary elections

12.1 Introduction

The composition of Parliament raises questions about the legitimacy of the constitution. Which of the different kinds of democracy (Section 2.7) if any, best captures the UK's arrangements? Can a non-elected element in the legislature be justified? Do the voting rules give fair representation and cater for the different functions of Parliament? What restrictions should there be on the right to vote, stand for election or participate in an election campaign? Liberal freedoms such as freedom of expression may conflict with the aspiration of equality.

12.2 The House of Lords

The dominant feature of the House of Lords is that none of its members is elected, all being chosen by the executive in one form or another. Apart from senior Church of England bishops who sit *ex officio* and 92 hereditary members, its members are appointed by the Queen on the advice of the Prime Minister. Once appointed a member is entitled to remain for life irrespective of attendance. There are certain disqualifications. These are as follows:

1. non-citizens other than Commonwealth and Irish citizens. A non-resident Commonwealth citizen can sit in the Lords but not in the Commons (see Act of Settlement 1700, s 3 as amended by the Constitutional Reform and Governance Act 2010, s 47);
2. persons under the age of 21 (SO2 – Standing Order);
3. undischarged bankrupts (Insolvency Act 1986, s 426(A));
4. persons convicted of treason until their sentence is served or pardoned (Forfeiture Act 1870, s 2).

Unlike the position with the Commons (Section 12.4) in defiance of the separation of powers there are no disqualifications of the judiciary and executive. Thus the independence of the Lords depends only on convention. (The creation of the Supreme Court is irrelevant in this context since this removes appeal jurisdiction from the House of Lords but says nothing about its membership (Sections 5.4, 7.7.2).)

A member of the House of Lords can apparently be removed only by statute. It has often been proposed that those convicted of a serious criminal offence should be expelled but no measures have been taken. However the House can suspend a member if he or she abuses his or her position, for example by selling favours (three peers were recently suspended for this; see *Independent* 7 October 2010).

Apart from the hereditary peers and the bishops, members of the House of Lords are appointed by the Queen on the advice of the Prime Minister. Small upper chambers could be justified on the basis that they can be more cohesive and more focused. However there is no legal limit on the size of the House of Lords and no legal regulation over appointments. With about 792 serving members (831 in all) the House of Lords is one of the largest second chambers in the world. (Germany's *Bundesrat* has 69 members and the US Senate 104.) Its membership is expanding since the rate of appointments (currently about 128 per annum) outnumbers that of deaths (about 18 per annum), see Maer and Brocklehurst, *Peerage Creation since 1997*, House of Commons Library 2011). However attendance in the House of Lords is far from assiduous. About 45% attend less than half the sittings and there are currently 78 persistent absentees.

Protocol 3 of the European Convention on Human Rights (ECHR) requires states to hold free elections to the legislature. In *Matthieu-Mohun v Belgium* [1988] 10 EHRR 1 the ECHR held that this requires at least one chamber to be elected. However one of the judges stated that the elected element must comprise a majority of the legislature and the non-elected element must not have greater powers than the elected element. The present House of Lords violates the majority requirement, there being currently 650 seats in the House of Commons.

The membership of the House of Lords comprises the following three categories:

1. *The Lords Spiritual.* These are the Archbishops of Canterbury and York, the Bishops of London, Durham and Winchester, and 21 other diocesan bishops of the Church of England, these being the senior bishops in order of appointment. Bishops are appointed by the Queen on the advice of the Prime Minister, the practice being that the Prime Minister chooses one from a list of nominations provided by the Church authorities. The bishops vacate their seats in the Lords on ceasing to hold office. They are not peers and can vote in parliamentary elections. (Dignitaries from other faiths may of course be appointed to the House of Lords as ordinary peers.) Other than on historical grounds it is difficult to see why the Church of England should be so privileged.

2. *Hereditary peers* – dukes, marquises, earls, viscounts and barons. Until the House of Lords Act 1999 the hereditary peers formed a majority, thereby biasing the House of Lords in favour of Conservative interests and being difficult to justify rationally. The notion of the 'mixed constitution' could be raised in this context (see Section 7.2). However this presupposes that the peerage is a powerful economic or political force, neither being the case today, particularly as the historical link between peerage and landholding no longer exists (although some peers, such as the Duke of Westminster, are among the largest landowners in the UK).

   At common law a peer cannot surrender his or her peerage. However under the Peerage Act 1963, a hereditary peerage can be disclaimed for life. This would enable the former peer to vote and to stand for election to the Commons. The peerage must be disclaimed within 12 months of succeeding to it (1 month if the new peer is an MP) or within 12 months of coming of age. The succession to the peerage is not affected. A peer who disclaims his or her title cannot again become a hereditary peer but could be appointed a life peer (below).

   The House of Lords Act 1999 (intended as part of a larger reform (which has now stalled (below)) provides that no one shall be a member of the House of Lords by virtue of a hereditary peerage. This is subject to an exception, negotiated to prevent the peers from rejecting the Act. Under the exception the House can retain 90 peers, together with the Earl Marshall and the Lord Chamberlain, who are royal officials. Under the relevant Standing Orders a vacancy can be filled by an election by the remaining hereditary members. The elected peers sit for life. They comprise 75 peers elected on the basis of party balance, together with 15 elected as deputy speakers and committee chairs. Peers who are not members of the House of Lords can stand for and vote in elections to the House of Commons (s 4). As a result of the 1999 Act, no single party is likely to command an overall majority in the House.

3. *Life peers.* Life peers (about 600) are appointed by the Crown on the advice of the Prime Minister, with the rank of baron. Originally life peers could not sit in the House of Lords but under the Life Peerages Act 1958, which was enacted in order to regenerate the House of Lords, they can now do so. A life peerage cannot be disclaimed. Life peerages are intended to enable hand-picked people to play a part in public life.

No reason need be given for the conferring of a peerage and it is unlikely that the conferring of honours or titles is subject to judicial review (see Section 19.7.1). By convention appointments are normally made on particular occasions including the New Year, the Queen's official birthday and the dissolution of Parliament. Appointments usually include the following categories: retiring ministers and MPs, a limited number of outstanding contributors to public life, and an unspecified number of 'working' party political peers. The proportion of party political peers is negotiated between the parties. Individuals are also appointed to the Lords so that they can be ministers without having to stand for election. This raises a problem of legitimacy (see Yong and Hazell, *Putting Goats Among the Wolves: Appointing Ministers from Outside Parliament* (The Constitution Unit UCL 2011)) Leading business people and associates of the Prime Minister have commonly joined government by this route.

The Prime Minister's conventional power to appoint life peers is subject to a non-statutory House of Lords Appointments Commission (see White Paper, *Modernising Parliament: Reforming the House of Lords* (Cm 4183, 1999)). The Commission is appointed by and reports to the Prime Minister and is only advisory. It is composed of insiders namely a cross-bench peer as chair, three peers nominated by the main parties and three 'independent' persons who can be politicians.

The Commission vets proposals for political appointments on the ground of propriety mainly by examining their application forms for evidence of misconduct. It also administers a process for a small number (about 6 per year) of non-party political appointments. Any British or Commonwealth citizen over 21 can apply for appointment. The criteria for appointment are a record of 'significant achievement', 'independence of political parties' and 'an ability to contribute to the work of the House'. The last of these criteria invites preference to be given in the manner of a private club to those with whom the existing members feel personally comfortable.

In 2007 there was a police investigation into allegations that the Labour Party then in government was selling peerages to party donors. However, although there was a strong statistical correlation there was no evidence of any specific agreement as required by the Honours (Prevention of Corruption) Act 1925 (enacted following the sale of peerages on behalf of the Prime Minister Lloyd George). (See also Sale of Offices Act' 1809, and the common law offence of Misconduct in Public Office amounting to an abuse of the public's trust.) The systematic unspoken misuse of power that is possible within the informal part of the Constitution is almost impossible to prove to a legal standard. (See Peston, *Who Runs Britain?* (Hodder 2008).)

There is no correlation between the composition of the Lords and the distribution of votes at a general election. Because a member stays until death the pattern of appointments made by previous governments is a controlling factor. For example there are currently 243 Labour members, 231 Tories, 93 Liberal Democrats and 27 'others'. There are 184 cross benchers forming a recognised group without party affiliations. Some small parties including Scottish Nationalists are not represented. The members of the House of Lords are overwhelmingly white and male and 54% live or work in London or the south east of England. Reforms have often been advocated including compulsory retirement, a cap on numbers and disqualification of wrongdoers (see Russell, *House Full: Time to Get a Grip on Lords Appointments*, The Constitution Unit UCL 2011).

12.3 Reform of the House of Lords

There is substantial agreement among politicians and academic commentators that the House of Lords should be reformed. This is partly because an appointed House is regarded as out of place in a democracy and also because of the increasing size of the House and the belief that some of its members are inactive or disreputable. However there is no consensus on the shape of any reform and most attempts at reform since the Parliament Act 1911, which claimed to herald further 'popular' reform, have failed. The House of Lords itself is likely to resist reform but there is no doubt that any reforms can be enacted under the Parliament Acts (see *R (Jackson) v AG* [2005]).

The issue of Lords reform is worth discussion because it exemplifies some fundamental features of the UK constitution. These include firstly its conservative evolutionary nature which resists fundamental change, secondly the absence of any special machinery for constitutional reform so that reform proposals are usually mixed up with ordinary party politics and therefore dominated by the immediate concerns of the government in power, thirdly a distrust of democracy and fourthly a concern with the pre-eminence of the executive. It is also worth remembering that it is difficult to address particular reforms in isolation since the various aspects of the constitution are often interdependent.

On the one hand there is a body of opinion, probably a majority, that the House should be at least elected but with no agreement as to the details of this. On the other hand there is substantial opinion in favour of a House made up of ' experts' chosen by other experts. However there is a consensus that the second chamber should remain subservient to the House of Commons with the latter sustaining the government and having the last word on legislation. This preserves a clear line of accountability and also the power of the executive which would be threatened by a stronger Upper House.

After the Parliament Act 1911 (Section 11.4) which was a response to a crisis, only three reforms have been successful. These were the Parliament Act 1949 which modified the 1911 Act to meet the needs of the post war reforming government, the Life Peerages Act 1958 (Section 12.2) which was relatively uncontroversial and the Peerage Act 1963 which enabled peeresses in their own right to sit and enabled a peer to disclaim his or her peerage so as to stand for election to the Commons. The most recent reform, the House of Lords Act 1999, which removed most of the hereditary element is uncompleted business leading to the present chaos.

There are several reasons why House of Lords reform has proved intractable: 'a roll call of pointless constitutional seminars and stillborn proposals' (*Guardian* 28 June 2012). Firstly Lords reform is not urgent nor does it command significant interest among voters to be a priority nor is it in the personal interest of existing politicians and their acolytes in the media, business and academia. This means that reforms have been stalled by arguments over detail or delaying tactics or mixed up with other issues. For example, the most recent proposal in 2012 was withdrawn because of a combination of Conservatives who objected to various aspects of the proposed electoral arrangements and Labour who objected to the limited time available for discussion possibly hoping to displace other government measures.

Secondly, reform crosses party boundaries making party discipline weak. This disagreement reflects profound differences between those who favour the evolutionary pragmatic nature of the UK constitution and so prefer marginal if any change and those of a more rationalist bent who favour radical change. Thus arguments in favour of the status quo claim that the House of Lords has 'worked' subject to interventions from time to time to deal with particular problems. It is argued along the lines of the mixed constitution (Section 7.2) that the present appointed House mainly comprises the best people, aristocracy in its original sense, who modify the excesses of democracy. As a result when moderate proposals are introduced both groups object to them. This was the fate of the reform bill in 1968 which was defeated by a combination of conservatives to whom the status quo was untouchable and socialists for whom the bill was too limited. The conservative politician Enoch Powell is reputed to have said at the time that the House of Lords should no more be questioned than should an oak tree.

Thirdly and most importantly there is a fear that an elected House might either duplicate or rival the House of Commons, thereby weakening the accountability (or power) of the executive and threatening the Parliament Acts. It is argued that attempts to codify the relationship between the two Houses by statute so as to protect the dominance of the Commons risk bringing the Courts into the political arena (Section 3.4.6). However the relationship could be regulated by the internal rules of each House and so outside the jurisdiction of the courts (Section 11.6).

On the other hand an entirely appointed chamber may lack public credibility and reinforce the patronage that currently undermines the constitution. A mix of the two elements risks the unelected element being marginalised. Moreover there is no agreement as to the pool from which any appointed element should be made. One possibility would from representatives of major community interests such as regional legislatures, business, charities, churches, ethnic groups, the professions and local communities. However it could prove impossibly complex and controversial to achieve an acceptable balance of interests.

Finally it is argued that reform is expensive and time consuming and that there is little public interest in the matter (see eg *Times* 24 April 2012).

However Lord Bingham, a former senior judge, suggested that a second chamber be purely advisory, with no lawmaking powers but designed as a senate of experts to give independent advice to the House of Commons (see Bingham 2010). He proposed that the composition of the House be similar to its present composition and that it should select its own membership. It is questionable whether such a body would be able to establish public confidence in its political impartiality and, as with the current House, its membership would be likely to be dominated by persons who conform to the interests of those in power. The notion of unbiased expertise is highly questionable.

Mill (1972, ch 13) argued that a second chamber should primarily act as a partial check on the majority and should ideally embody 'the greatest number of elements exempt from the class interests and prejudices of the majority, but having in themselves nothing offensive to democratic feeling'. He thought that in every constitution there should be a centre of resistance to the predominant power 'and in a democratic constitution, therefore, a nucleus of resistance to the democracy'. He recommended including experts in a second chamber, recruited primarily from persons distinguished in the public professions, such as the judiciary, armed forces and civil service. However, although he thought that the question of a second chamber was relatively unimportant, it could be justified (in both liberal and republican terms) on the basis of the corrupting effect of absolute power and as a mechanism for producing compromise. Mill's preferred solution was proportional representation in the *House of Commons* (below), which would make it more difficult for any majority faction to be dominant.

A democratic possibility would be random selection from the whole adult community, as is currently the case with jury service. However, this raises many practical and economic problems and is probably unrealistic (see Phillipson, 2004). Another possibility would be a House made up of representatives of major community interests such as business, charities, churches, ethnic groups, the professions and local communities. However it could prove impossibly complex and controversial to achieve an acceptable choice of interests and balance between them.

There is no significant support among politicians for abolishing the House of Lords altogether. This might be a rational and cheap solution although the essential functions of the Lord, namely scrutinising proposed legislation and acting as a check on constitutional abuse would have to be provided for. The former function could be dealt with by advisory committees, but the latter would seem to point towards a written constitution with an enhanced role for the courts.

The following is a brief chronicle of the various attempts at reform. The Parliament Act 1911 began the process of reform by removing the power of the House of Lords to veto most public bills introduced in the Commons (Section 11.4). The Bryce Conference of 1917–18 (*Conference on the Reform of the Second Chamber* (Cd 9038, 1918)) attempted to tackle the problem of the composition of the House of Lords but was unable to agree. The Parliament Act 1949 further reduced the delaying power of the Lords (Section 11.4). In 1958 the introduction of life peers reinvigorated the House to a certain extent. In 1968 an all-party conference proposed removing voting rights from most of the hereditary element and introducing the concept of 'working peers', mainly life peers, who would form a permanent nucleus of the House. The bill to introduce these reforms was abandoned because of opposition from both sides of the House of Commons (above).

The Labour government of 1997–2010 intended to reform the House of Lords in two stages. Stage one comprised the House of Lords Act 1999 (above), the main result of which was to remove most of the hereditary element. Stage two has not taken place.

Subsequent attempts at reform have come to nothing and there is little common ground other than a desire to retain the present functions of the Lords (See Russell, 'House of Lords Reform: Are we Nearly There Yet?' (2009) 80 *Political Quartery* 119.)

A Royal Commission on the House of Lords (*A House for the Future* (Cm 4534, 2000), the Wakeham Report) examined the composition of the House of Lords superficially in isolation from wider questions of constitutional reform and therefore did not question the role and powers of the House of Commons or those of the executive. Wakeham endorsed the existing roles of the House of Lords as subordinate to the Commons, providing limited checks on the executive, a revising mechanism for legislation and a 'constitutional long-stop' to force the government to have second thoughts.

Wakeham's governing principles seem to be:

> the capacity to offer counsel from a range of sources ... broadly representative of society in the UK at the beginning of the 21st century ... It should give the UK's constituent nations and regions, for the first time, a formally constituted voice in the Westminster Parliament. (31)

The electorate is not to be trusted to produce these outcomes but must be paternalistically protected from itself.

Wakeham rejected the extremes of an all-elected second chamber and one made up of 'experts'. Wakeham thought that a wholly elected second chamber might produce the 'wrong sort of people', reinforce party political control, result in 'voter fatigue' and either gridlock or rubber stamp the Commons, thus weakening governmental accountability. Wakeham rejected random selection, apparently because of the risk of appointing persons who would not 'fit in'. Wakeham also rejected the notion of a 'council of the wise', recognising that government is about accommodating disagreement and is necessarily political. Perhaps updating the classical 'mixed constitution', Wakeham proposed a balance of representatives from the main interests in the community with about one-third elected. Elections would be on a 15-year cycle, with one-third being elected every five years to ensure that the outcome did not duplicate elections to the Commons. An independent statutory commission would appoint all other members, taking account of regional, ethnic, gender and religious concerns.

A White Paper (*The House of Lords: Completing the Reforms* (Cm 5291, 2001)) broadly adopted Wakeham's proposals but weakened them in favour of a larger element of government control over the House of Lords. This was not well received and was followed by proposals from the Public Administration Committee (Fifth Report, HC 2001–02, 494–1), the House of Commons and the political parties for different permutations of elected and appointed members. In 2002 a joint committee of both Houses set out seven options ranging from complete election to complete appointment. None of these was approved by the Commons, while the Lords voted for an all-appointed House (2002–03, HL 17, HC 171).

Revised proposals were set out in a White Paper which remains of value for its historical summary and references (*House of Lords Reform* (Cm 7027, 2007)). These proposals were not well received. This was superseded by the White Paper *An Elected Second Chamber* (Cm 7438, 2008) which favoured an elected House with the same functions and powers as now. However it left open the most contentious matters, namely whether there should be an appointed element and the voting system to be used. For example a form of proportional representation would ensure a different distribution of seats from the House of Commons (Section 12.7.1). In order to avoid the political balance of the upper house reflecting that of the Commons, its members would sit for terms of 12–15 years, with staggered elections.

A more radical proposal in the White Paper was that of 'recall'. This allows a proportion of the electorate to sign a petition which triggers a special election to remove a sitting member. The recall device has a reactionary tendency against the principle of representative democracy in that opinion can most easily be generated against voices for change.

Following proposals by a Joint Committee of both Houses the present government introduced a Bill in 2012. This provided for a House of 450 members paid £300 per day. It comprised an elected element of 80% elected in eight regions by the 'open' party list system (Section 12.5.7), every 15 years on a five year cycle coupled to general elections. (This device of relatively long periods of membership seems to be widely accepted and might reinforce the different roles of Lords and Commons). The remainder would mainly be appointed on a non-party basis as 'experts' by an independent commission but there would be 12 Bishops. There would be provision for expelling non-attenders and criminals. The Bill was withdrawn in August 2012 as a result of resistance by Conservative MPs and lack of support from the Opposition. It was argued that the bill was a botched unprincipled compromise.

A more modest Private Members Bill, the House of Lords (Cessation of Membership) Bill, promoted by Lord Steele, a former leader of the Liberal Party, tackles the most immediate problems of the ballooning size of the House and its reputation. The Bill includes compulsory retirement, removal of members who are absent for six months, expelling criminals and making the Appointments Commission a statutory body. There is no indication that this Bill will succeed and further reforms are unlikely in the next few years.

12.4 Membership of the House of Commons

Anyone can be a member of the House of Commons, other than the following:

- ▶ non-citizens other than Commonwealth citizens with indefinite leave to reside in the UK or citizens of the Irish Republic (Act of Settlement 1700, s 3 as modified by Electoral Administration Act 2006, s 18). Resident EU citizens can sit in the devolved legislatures but not the Commons;
- ▶ people under the age of 18 (Election Administration Act 2006, s 17);
- ▶ persons detained as mental patients (Mental Health Act 1983; there are special provisions for removing sitting MPs under this Act, involving two medical reports at six-month intervals);
- ▶ peers who are members of the House of Lords (peers can sit in the devolved legislatures);
- ▶ bishops who sit in the House of Lords (House of Commons (Removal of Clergy Disqualification) Act 2001);
- ▶ bankrupts, until five years after discharge unless the discharge certifies that the bankruptcy was not caused by the debtor's misconduct (Insolvency Act 1986, s 426(A));
- ▶ persons convicted of election offences (below);
- ▶ persons convicted of treason, until expiry of the sentence or pardon (Forfeiture Act 1870);
- ▶ persons convicted of an offence and sentenced to prison for more than one year while actually in prison or unlawfully at large (Representation of the People Act 1981, designed to prevent convicted terrorists in Northern Ireland from standing);
- ▶ persons holding certain public offices (House of Commons (Disqualification) Act 1975).

The last of these disqualifications is an example of the separation of powers. One element of the seventeenth-century conflict between Crown and Parliament was the Commons' fear that the Crown might bribe members by giving them jobs. The Act of Settlement 1700 therefore provided that nobody who held Crown office or a place of profit under the Crown could sit in the Commons (the Lords was not affected, and there are no formal separation of powers disqualification from membership of the Lords (Sections 7.7, 12.2)).

This would of course have prevented ministers from sitting and the constitution would have had a stricter separation of powers. This part of the Act was repealed by the Succession to the Crown Act 1707. However there are limits upon the number of ministers who can be MPs, thus giving the Commons a degree of independence. These are as follows:

1. Under the House of Commons (Disqualification) Act 1975, not more than 95 ministers may sit and vote. There are usually about 20 ministers in the House of Lords.
2. The Ministerial and Other Salaries Act 1975 (as amended) fixed the salaries of the various grades of minister and limits the number of paid ministers of the government to 83, plus about 30 other specialised political office holders such as whips and also four law officers. However a government can increase its loyalists in the House by appointing unpaid parliamentary secretaries.
3. The House of Commons (Disqualification) Act 1975 debars certain other holders of public office from sitting in the Commons. The main examples are as follows:
    ▶ full-time judges of various kinds;
    ▶ regulators of privatised undertakings;
    ▶ civil servants;
    ▶ members of the regular armed services and police (other than specialised forces such as railway police);
    ▶ members of foreign legislatures. However by virtue of the Disqualifications Act 2000 a member of the Irish legislature (the Oireachtas) can be a member of the Commons;
    ▶ members of certain public boards and undertakings;
    ▶ holders of the offices of Steward or Bailiff of the Chiltern Hundreds or the Manor of Northstead. These are meaningless titles in the gift of the Chancellor of the Exchequer. There are no specific rules entitling MPs to resign or retire but a successful application for one of these offices has the same effect.

In the event of a dispute about a disqualification, the Judicial Committee of the Privy Council may make a declaration on the application of any person (1975 Act, s 7). The House may also refer a matter to the Privy Council for an opinion (Judicial Committee Act 1833, s 4).

12.5 The electoral system

Election law is found primarily in the Representation of the People Acts 1983 and 1985 and the Parliamentary Constituencies Act 1986. Important changes were made by the Representation of the People Act 2000, the Political Parties, Elections and Referendums Act 2000, the Electoral Administration Act 2006 and the Electoral Registration and administration Act 2013.

12.5.1 The purpose of elections

We can assess the electoral system only in relation to its aims. Is it intended (i) to secure fair democratic representation, (ii) to produce effective government, (iii) to produce 'accountable' governments or (iv) to provide a local representative? No electoral system has yet been thought up that successfully combines all these. Underlying these conflicting aims is the difference between 'representative democracy' and 'market democracy' (Section 2.7). Protocol 1, Article 3 of the ECHR provides a general and vague standard, limited to representative democracy:

> Free elections at reasonable intervals by secret ballot, under conditions which will ensure the free expression of the opinion of the people in the choice of the legislature.

There is no requirement that the people choose the executive government or that each vote should have equal weight. In the case of a market democracy the voter chooses a party from the range on offer in the same way that he or she might buy a car.

Until well into the nineteenth century, the prevalent belief was that only landowners had a sufficient stake in the realm to vote, the majority of the population enjoying 'virtual representation' through the property owners (Section 4.7). There is a conflict between the law of the electoral process and practical politics. The legal basis of democracy in the UK is that the electorate in each constituency chooses an individual to represent the constituency in the House of Commons. However this is distorted by the convention that the executive government must be supported by the House of Commons and is usually drawn from the majority political party. Thus election candidates are overwhelmingly members of and chosen by political parties. (Exceptionally in the 2010 election the Conservative Party let the whole local community choose one of its candidates.) Elections are fought and funded between the parties on a national battlefield and one vote has to serve three not necessarily compatible purposes, namely choosing a local representative, choosing the governing party and choosing a Prime Minister.

The ECHR (Protocol 1, Art 3) requires free elections but does not require any particular kind of electoral system, thus endorsing the principle that elections may have different aims. An electoral system must not discriminate against particular groups of citizens, although a political party cannot apparently challenge the electoral system on the basis that it is at a disadvantage (see *Lindsey v UK* [1979] 3 CMLR 166; *Matthieu-Mohun v Belgium* [1987] 10 EHRR 1; *Liberal Party v UK* [1982] 4 EHRR 106). The courts are likely to adopt a low level of review in relation to electoral machinery because of sensitivity to interfering with the province of Parliament (*R v Boundary Commission for England, ex p Foot* [1983] 1 All ER 1099).

12.5.2 The Electoral Commission

The Electoral Commission is a quango (Section 15.9) established as an independent public body to regulate the electoral system and the conduct of elections. Created by the Political Parties, Elections and Referendums Act 2000 with wide-ranging functions it was a response to the concerns of the Fifth Report of the Committee on Standards in Public Life (*The Funding of Political Parties in the United Kingdom* (Cm 4057, 1998)). This was against a background of reduced public confidence as a result of worries about the funding of political parties by wealthy business interests.

The Commission has had mixed success and was the subject of the Eleventh Report of the Committee on Standards in Public Life (*Review of the Electoral Commission* (Cm 7006, 2007)). The Committee found that the Electoral Commission was unclear about its role as regulator and was passive and timid in investigating abuses. The report pointed out that the Commission's staff lacked relevant expertise and experience, this being due to the requirement that the Commission be independent, thus raising a familiar tension between efficiency and the appearance of fairness. The report recommended that the Commission's structure and processes should focus more strongly on regulation. In particular its statutory remit as a regulator, as opposed to a monitor, should be clarified.

These recommendations have been implemented by the Political Parties and Elections Act 2009, which has extensively amended the 2000 Act.

The main functions of the Electoral Commission are as follows:

1. It reviews and reports to the Secretary of State such matters relating to elections and referendums as it may determine from time to time.
2. It registers political parties and keeps records of their accounts and of donations to them, thereby bringing what had previously been regarded as private concerns into the open.
3. It has powers to investigate infringements of election requirements and to impose penalties (Political Parties and Elections Act 2009).
4. It provides for public access to information relating to the financial affairs of political parties.
5. It is responsible for periodic reviews of constituency boundaries.
6. It must be consulted on changes in electoral law.
7. It prescribes performance standards for the local authorities who administer elections (Electoral Administration Act 2006).
8. It advises broadcasters in relation to party political broadcasts.
9. It promotes understanding of electoral systems in the UK (Political Parties and Elections Act 2009, s 8).
10. It is involved, together with local authorities, in pilot schemes for alternative methods of voting such as electronic and postal ballots, making voting facilities available in shops or extending voting times.
11. Subject to modifications by the Secretary of State, it can make 'policy development grants' to registered political parties with at least two sitting MPs for the purpose of preparing their election manifestos.

The Electoral Commission has nine or ten members. It is appointed by the Queen on an Address from the House of Commons on a nomination by the Speaker in consultation with the party leaders. The Speaker's Committee, which comprises relevant ministers and backbench MPs (Political Parties, Elections and Referendums Act 2000, Sch 2), must determine the appointment process. A member can be dismissed on an Address from the House of Commons on various grounds of incapacity, misbehaviour or failing to perform duties (Sch 1). Members can be reappointed on the recommendation of the Speaker's Committee.

The Commission's members must not be members, officers or employees of political parties or holders of elective office. Nor must they have had such connections or been registered party donors (below) within the last five years. A member ceases to hold office if he or she becomes an election candidate. However four commissioners are nominated by the political parties from persons with political experience, one of whom must be from a party other than the three largest parties (Political Parties and Elections Act 2009, s 4).

The Electoral Commission reports to the Secretary of State and is accountable to the Speaker's Committee and an advisory Parliamentary Parties Panel comprising persons appointed by the parties, who must include at least two MPs.

12.5.3   General elections and by-elections

A general election occurs when a Parliament is dissolved. It must normally be held on the First Thursday in May every five years commencing 7th May 2015 (Fixed Term Parliaments Act 2011, s 1). An early general election can be triggered only by resolutions of the House of Commons (Section 11.2). The election process is triggered by writs issued by the Lord Chancellor and Secretaries of State for Scotland and Northern Ireland when the previous Parliament dissolves (Fixed Term Parliaments Act 2011, s 3(3)).

A by-election takes place when there is an individual vacancy in the House. The House itself decides the election date and by convention the motion is proposed by the party to which the former member belonged. Unfortunately there is no time limit for this. When the House is not sitting, the Speaker can issue the writ for a by election (Recess Elections Act 1975).

The timetable and other procedural matters for an election are set out in 'Parliamentary Election Rules' (Representation of the People Act 1983 (RPA) Schedule 1). The writs are sent to Returning Officers in each constituency. The Returning Officer is either the Sherriff in a county constituency (otherwise a largely ceremonial Crown officer) or in other cases a mayor or council chairman (RPA 1983, s 24). The returning officers are responsible for the conduct of the election including decisions as to qualifications of voters and candidates. Registration officers, who are normally local authority chief executives, make the detailed arrangements.

Section 48 of the Constitutional Reform and Governance Act 2010 deals with slack local officials. It requires the returning officer to take reasonable steps to begin the count of votes as soon as practicable within four hours of the poll closing at 10 pm. The constitutional tradition of the UK is that power should be handed over with brutal speed. Assuming that a clear majority in favour of another leader emerges, the Prime Minister is expected to resign on the following day.

It is important that the law does not violate the principle of free elections. The law is therefore concerned with fairness between candidates and with preventing fraud, disruption or confusion. To this end it requires clear lines of accountability for the conduct and spending of the parties and candidates. Elections also raise questions of freedom of speech. This might conflict with fairness, for example by enabling well-financed candidates to dominate the media. This is especially important now that elections are largely fought through print and electronic media rather than personally within local communities.

12.5.4 Candidates

A candidate must provide a deposit of £500 (forfeited if 5 per cent of the vote is not won) and be supported by ten signatures (RPA 1983, Sch 1). The nomination paper must state either that the candidate stands in the name of a qualifying registered party or that they do not purport to represent any party (s 22). The latter applies to candidates standing as independents, to the Speaker seeking re-election or if the nomination paper provides no description. A party is any organisation or person that puts up at least one candidate, so a one-person party is possible (s 40). Each political party must be registered with the Electoral Commission under the Political Parties, Elections and Referendums Act 2000. In order to qualify for registration, the party must provide its name, its headquarters address and the names of its leader, treasurer and nominating officer. These can be the same person. It can also provide the name of its campaign officer and if it does so the campaign officer will have some of the responsibilities of the treasurer (s 25). It must also have a scheme approved by the Commission for regulating its financial affairs. It can also provide up to 12 descriptions of itself. The Commission can refuse to register a name or description on the following grounds: having more than six words, being obscene or offensive or where publication would be an offence, being misleading, contradictory or confusing, being in a script other than roman or containing words prohibited by the Secretary of State (Electoral Administration Act 2006, s 28, ss 48, 49). This seems to create a significant possibility of executive censorship. Similar rules apply to party emblems (s 29).

A registered political party is subject to accounting and audit requirements (Political Parties, Elections and Referendums Act 2000, Part III; Electoral Administration Act 2006). Accounts must be lodged with the Electoral Commission and must be available for public inspection (s 46). For the first time the law has acknowledged that political parties are more than private clubs and should be subject to external financial controls. However this creates a risk of state interference with political freedom.

12.5.5   Eligibility to vote

Under section 1 of the Representation of the People Act 2000, to be eligible to vote a person must be:

1. 18 years of age on the date of the poll;
2. a British citizen, a citizen of Ireland or a 'qualifying' Commonwealth citizen (ie one who is entitled to reside in the UK). (EU citizens can vote in local elections and in elections in the devolved regimes);
3. registered on the electoral register for the constituency. To qualify for registration, a person must be 18 years of age or due to be so within 12 months beginning on 1st December following the date of the application for registration and resident in a dwelling in the constituency on the date of the application for registration: 'rolling registration' (see RPA 2000, ss 3–7 replacing RPA 1983, s 5, s 7).

'Residence' means the person is normally living at the address in question as his or her home. It is a question of fact and seems to focus on whether the dwelling is the applicant's home for a substantial period as opposed to his being a guest or a lodger for some particular purpose. The fact a person may have more than one home is important but not conclusive:

> regard shall be had in particular to the purpose and other circumstances, as well as to the fact of his presence at or absence from the address on that date ... for example, where at any particular time a person is staying at any place other than on a permanent basis he may in all the circumstances be taken to be at that time (a) resident there if he has no home elsewhere, or (b) not resident there if he does have a home elsewhere (RPA 2000, s 3; see eg *Fox v Stirk* [1970] 2 QB 46 1060: student resident in college entitled to registration; *Hipperson v Newbury Electoral Registration Officer* [1985] QB 1060,1073: protesters camping outside airforce base entitled to registration; *Scott v Phillips* [1974] SLT 32: holiday home does not qualify). A person may therefore be validly registered in more than one constituency but can vote only once.

Temporary absence at work or attendance on a college course does not interrupt residence if either the applicant intends to return to the actual residence within six months and will not be prevented from doing so by performance of that duty or the dwelling would otherwise be his or her permanent residence and he or she would be in actual residence (RPA 2000, s 3).

There are special provisions for the benefit of certain people who may be absent for long periods. Detained persons are not resident where they are detained. However remand prisoners and mental patients who are not offenders are deemed to be resident where they are detained if they are likely to be there long enough to satisfy the residence requirement. Alternatively they can make a 'declaration of local connection'. Members of the armed forces who make a 'service declaration', and merchant seamen can be registered in the place where they would otherwise live (RPA 1983, s 15, Electoral Administration Act 2006, s 13). People living overseas who would otherwise qualify to vote can make an 'overseas electors declaration' (RPA 1985, s 1). They must either have been registered in the constituency during the last 15 years or if they were too young a parent or guardian must have been so registered.

A problem with the registration arrangements was that registration depended on the householder providing the names of eligible voters living in the house. The Eleventh Report of the Committee on Standards in Public Life (Cm 7006, 2007) proposed that registration by households be replaced by individual registration. This is designed to combat fraudulent postal voting whereby one member of a household can return votes on behalf of others. This was implemented by the Electoral Registration and Administration Act 2013. However this could mean many fewer people voting especially among the young, the poor and ethnic minorities. (See *Individual Electoral Registration*, Commons Library, SN05995, 16 Feb. 2012.)

Even if they are on the register, the following have no right to vote:

▶ members of the House of Lords, other than bishops sitting *ex officio*;
▶ convicted prisoners and persons detained in mental hospitals as offenders (except for contempt of court or refusing to pay a fine), including persons unlawfully at large (Representation of the People Act 2000, s 2). A common law mental capacity test was abolished by the Electoral Administration Act 2006;
▶ persons convicted of election offences (corrupt practices – for five years; illegal practices – for five years in the particular constituency);
▶ illegal immigrants and asylum seekers waiting for a decision (Political Parties, Elections and Referendums Act 2000, s 2).

In *Hirst v UK (No 2)* [2006] 42 EHRR 41 the European Court of Human Rights held that the blanket exclusion for prisoners violates the right to free elections (above), by depriving some 850,000 people of the right to vote. The Court held that an automatic absolute bar was not acceptable, there being no legitimate policy reason for excluding all convicted prisoners irrespective of such matters as the nature of the offence or length of sentence. In *Frodl v Austria* [2010] App No 20201/04 prisoners serving sentences of more than one year for intentional crimes were denied the vote. The ECtHR held that a decision to deny the franchise should be made by a judge, must take account of the particular circumstances and there must in accordance with proportionality (Section 21.5) be a link between the offence committed and issues relating to elections and democratic institutions [34]. In March 2010 the Committee of Ministers of the Council of Europe required the UK government to comply with *Hirst*. The government has not changed the law and appears to be defying the European Court.

12.5.6 The voting system

There are problems with the workings of all voting systems. Firstly a system that always produces a genuine majority may be impossible to achieve. For example in an election where there are three candidates, different majorities might prefer A to B, B to C and C to A. In the 2010 UK general election no party had an overall majority, although this is relatively rare in the UK, having previously happened in 1973. The electoral system for Parliament is that of 'first past the post' (FPP), or 'relative majority'. This gives the seat to the candidate with the largest number of votes. This is rarely an overall majority. FPP is particularly defective in terms of democratic representation in that it ignores the votes for all but the winning candidate. Moreover the outcome usually depends only on a limited number of marginal seats.

For example in 2005 Labour won an overall majority of 356 seats with 36.9 per cent of the vote, the Conservatives won 198 seats with 33.9 per cent and the Liberal Democrats won 62 seats with 23 per cent of the vote. In England the Conservatives, with 600,000 more votes than Labour, won 90 fewer seats. Thus most voters voted against Labour. In some years the winning party had a smaller share of the overall than the runner up.

In Parliament itself the members always vote by simple majority in a straight yes/no way between two propositions. The combination of these two forms of voting means that any particular law may command the support of only about 20 per cent of the public.

However the first past the post system is simple and transparent, offering voters a clear choice. It encourages accountable governments that are supported by substantial numbers of voters. A party stands or falls as such at an election and it must answer on its own record. It cannot blame any minority parties and, unlike in systems with proportional representation (below), governments cannot change without the consent of the electorate (below). It also produces a direct link between the constituency and the individual MP, reinforcing accountability.

12.5.7   Other voting systems

The choice between voting systems is between the incommensurables of strong government, fairness, reflecting the majority will and protecting minorities. No voting system has yet been devised that reconciles the competing demands on it. Complex systems of proportional representation (PR) are widely used in an attempt to achieve fairness and protect minorities. They rely on mathematical formulae to make the outcome correspond more closely to the distribution of the vote (see Farrell, *Electoral Systems: A Comparative Introduction* (Macmillan 2000) ch 4; Bogdanor and Butler, *Democracy and Elections* (Cambridge University Press 1983)).

PR systems favour negotiations between political parties and could produce unstable governments held together by shifting alliances between small and large parties, thus weakening accountability. However Germany and the Scandinavian countries which use PR systems are at least as stable as the UK. Arguably a degree of instability is desirable in a liberal society where there is no agreement as to the right answer to social and political problems. The main forms are as follows:

▶ *The party list.* Under the 'closed list system', the voter chooses only the party, individual seats being allocated by the party in accordance with the party's share of the vote. Various formulae can be used to calculate the precise share required. The party list system has been said to destroy the principle of local representation and to put excessive power into the hands of party leaders. This method is used for elections to the European Parliament. Under an 'open party list' system, the voter can choose between the names on the list, sometimes subject to a preset ranking In Germany a party must achieve at least 5 per cent of the votes or three seats.

▶ *The additional member system*. This system combines FPP and the party list system. It has the advantage of retaining a connection between the MP and the constituency while ensuring representation for minorities. It is used for elections to the Scottish Parliament, the Welsh Assembly and the London Assembly (Section 16.2.1, Greater London Authority Act 1999, s 4). A proportion of candidates are elected on the first past the post principle in local constituencies. This is topped up by a second vote in a larger regional constituency either for an individual candidate or from an open party list. Each region is allocated the same number of seats (eg five in the Welsh regions, seven in the Scottish) and an 'electoral region figure' is produced. The electoral region figure is the number of votes won by that party divided by the number of seats won by the party's candidates in the local constituency elections plus one. The candidate or party with the highest electoral region figure wins the first seat. The second and subsequent seats are awarded on the same basis, in each case after a recalculation to take account of seats already won. Thus the fewer the seats won by a party in the local constituency elections, the better the chances of winning a seat in the regional election. A person cannot of course take a seat in more than one constituency.

▶ *The single transferable vote*. This is probably the method that most reflects voting preferences. It is used for elections in Northern Ireland, where the desire to neutralise conflicting political forces dominates the constitutional arrangements (Section 16.3; see Northern Ireland Act 1998, ss 8, 28, 34). Each constituency can elect a given number of members. Votes are cast for candidates in order of preference. There is an 'electoral quota' for each constituency, calculated according to a formula based on the number of voters divided by the number of seats plus one. The quota is the winning post. A candidate who obtains the quota based on first preferences is elected. Any surplus votes over the quota are transferred to other candidates according to the second preference on the winning candidate's voting slips. This may produce more winners who reach the quota. The process is repeated until all the seats are filled. If no candidate reaches the quota, the candidate with the lowest number of votes is eliminated and his or her votes distributed among the other candidates. This system enables voters to choose between different candidates within the same party since all seats within a constituency could be fought by each party. It also prevents wasted votes and protects minorities. On the other hand it weakens the direct link between constituency and member.

▶ The *alternative vote (AV) system* is a compromise non-PR system that attempts to produce a single candidate with majority support. The candidates are voted for in order of preference and there are several rounds. After each round the candidate with the lowest vote is eliminated and his or her votes distributed among the others until a winner with a clear overall majority emerges. If there is still a deadlock, a winner might then be chosen by lot. This system seems unfair in that it takes account of the second preferences only of those who supported losing candidates. On the other hand it keeps a strong link between the member and the constituency. It is the system used for elections for the Mayor of London (Greater London Authority Act 1999, s 4 and some local authorities).

- AV was recommended for the UK in 1910 by the Royal Commission on Electoral Systems. In 1998 the Independent Commission on the Voting System (Cm 4090) recommended the introduction of the *AV Plus* voting system. This combines the alternative vote in single-member constituencies with a system of topping-up from a party list. Under the Parliamentary Voting Systems and Constituencies Act 2011 a referendum was held whether AV should be used for parliamentary elections. The proposal which had little support from the larger parties was rejected.
- Finally the *double-ballot system* is used in France. A candidate who gets an overall majority in round one is elected. Failing that there is a second ballot which only those who achieved a certain proportion of the vote can enter (in France 12.5 per cent). The candidate with the most votes in the second round wins.

12.5.8   The constituencies

In an ideal election system there would be the same number of voters in each constituency. This is not the case in the UK. The population is not evenly distributed across the country, so each vote does not carry equal weight. Constituency boundaries and voting patterns are significantly influenced by geography. For example the largest constituency, the Isle of Wight, has about 108,000 potential voters; the smallest, Na h-Eileanan (Western Isles), 21,600. It is tempting for a government to gerrymander, that is to alter the constituency boundaries in favour of its own party. The natural tendency over time is for traditional boundaries to favour right-wing parties since the old industrial conurbations which formed the basis of many constituencies are losing population in favour of suburbs and rural areas.

Under the Parliamentary Voting System and Constituencies Act 2011 it is proposed to reduce the number of seats from the present 650 to 600 (an arbitrary figure) with broadly equal numbers of voters in each constituency. (This reform is part of a deal made between the Conservative and Liberal Democrat partners in the coalition government in exchange for holding a referendum on the AV voting system, Section 12.5.7.) This would increase the influence of the executive in that the number of ministers in the House unchanged same. It may also weaken the link between an MP and a local community since equalization might override traditional community boundaries.

However the change must be triggered by Parliament approving the report of a Boundary Review (below). At the time of writing the Liberal Democrat members of the coalition government may refuse to support the review in retaliation for the Conservative party's refusal to support House of Lords reform. This is another example of the dependence of constitutional reform on ordinary party politics.

There is semi-independent machinery for fixing electoral boundaries (Parliamentary Constituencies Act 1986). This is currently the responsibility of the Secretary of State for Justice, subject to four independent Boundary Commissions for England, Wales, Scotland and Northern Ireland (Parliamentary Constituencies Act 1986). A range of criteria including the number of voters and local community boundaries are applied and there is substantial discretion. The dilemma is the conflict between fairness in the sense of equality of votes and the desire that an MP should represent a genuine geographical community.

There must be a review of the number and boundaries of constituencies. Previously this was at intervals of between 8 and 12 years, including provision for public hearings.

The last review was in 2007. A review may take several years to complete and once made could well be out of date. However the Parliamentary Elections and Constituencies Act 2011 introduces a requirement for a five-yearly review commencing before 1 October 2013. The Commission consults in the local area and must considers any representations but there is no requirement for a formal public hearing.

A report of the review is submitted to the Secretary of State, who is required 'as soon as may be' to lay the report before both Houses of Parliament, together with a draft Order in Council giving effect to it (s 3(5)). Each House must approve the Order, which is then submitted to the Queen in Council. It then becomes law.

The main criteria are as follows (Sch 2 as amended by the Parliamentary Voting Systems and Constituencies Act 2011):

1. Currently there are 650 constituencies. The Parliamentary Voting Systems and Constituencies Act 2011 reduces the number of constituencies to 600.
2. There must be a separate City of London constituency.
3. Each country has an 'electoral quota'. This is a rough average of voters per constituency. It is calculated by dividing the total electorate by the number of constituencies on the date when the Commission begins its review. It cannot be updated during the course of a review. For England the quota is roughly 70,000. At present few constituencies correspond to the quota. However the Parliamentary Voting Systems and Constituencies Act 2011 require that the number of voters in each constituency should vary only between 95 per cent and 105 per cent of the electoral quota, thus favouring equality over community. There are however special provisions for the Isle of Wight and Western Isles of Scotland and for exceptionally low-population areas. No constituency should be larger than 13,000 square kilometres.
4. Other factors to be taken into account, as amended by the 2011 Act, include:
   ▶ existing constituency boundaries and European Parliament constituency boundaries;
   ▶ local ties;
   ▶ the inconvenience involved in altering boundaries;
   ▶ special geographical considerations. These include the size, shape and accessibility of a constituency.

The report and the Order in Council can be challenged in the courts but the chances of success are small. The time factor is important. As we have seen, no court can interfere with parliamentary procedure, so that the Secretary of State could not be prevented from laying an order before the House nor required to lay an Order (*Harper v Home Secretary* [1955] Ch 238, see Section 11.6.2). Moreover by virtue of section 4(7) the validity of any Order in Council which purports to be made under the Act and which recites that approval was given by each House 'shall not be questioned in any legal proceedings' (but see Section 19.7.2).

A report must therefore be challenged before it is submitted to the Secretary of State. Even here the chances of success are slim. There is no statutory mechanism for challenging a review but judicial review would apply. Even though the matter concerns a human right the court will respect the subjective judgment of the Commission and would interfere only if the review was arbitrary made in bad faith, or seriously disproportionate or a statute was violated. Moreover out of respect for Parliament a court would not normally make an order that prevents the report from going to Parliament. At most it would make a declaration (a non-binding opinion, *see R v Boundary Commission for England, ex p Foot* [1983] 1 All ER 1099).

12.5.9 Voting procedures

Voting is traditionally in person at a designated polling station. However any person otherwise qualified to vote can have a postal vote. 'Absent voters' are permitted to vote by post or proxy (Representation of the People Act 2000, Sch 4). A person on the register for that year but no longer resident in the constituency can have an absent vote. Absent voters must provide a signature and date of birth as a protection against fraud (Electoral Administration Act 2006, s 14). A proxy vote also applies in special cases. These include service and overseas voters, disabled people, people with work or education commitments and people who have to make a long journey. A proxy must be a registered voter (Electoral Registration and Administration Act 2013). The government is currently encouraging the use of postal and electronic voting.

The ballot is secret in the sense that the vote itself is cast in privacy. However there is no protection for postal votes and, by comparing the registration number on the voting slip with the register of electors, it is possible for officials to discover how a voter cast his or her vote. Indeed this is necessary to prevent multiple voting. There are provisions intended to prevent ballot papers being examined except for the purpose of detecting election offences (Representation of the People Act 2000, Sch 1). Offences of stealing votes were created by the Electoral Administration Act 2006 (s 40).

12.6 Election campaigns

For most purposes the election period begins with the date of the proclamation announcing the dissolution of Parliament and ends with the date of the poll (Political Parties, Elections and Referendums Act 2000, Sch 10) but an election campaign may start well before that (s 72). This chapter is concerned with parliamentary elections but similar principles apply to other elections.

The election campaign at constituency level has long been regulated by laws designed to ensure fairness between the candidates campaigning in their local areas. The law was open to the charge that it did not allow for national party politics with its massive financial backing from private donors or for modern methods of campaigning, including the intensive use of the media. The Political Parties, Elections and Referendums Act 2000 attempts to bring the law up to date by addressing this reality (see *The Funding of Political Parties in the United Kingdom* (Cm 4443, 1999)).

12.6.1 Campaign expenses

UK law concentrates on regulating campaign spending but does not put a limit on donations to political parties (see Webber (2012)). The controls are intended to ensure that expenditure is open to public scrutiny and that no candidate has an unfair advantage or can buy votes (see *R v Jones* [1999] 2 Crim App Rep 253). In the US restrictions upon election expenses have been held to violate freedom of speech (see *Citizens United v Federal Election Commission [2010] 558 US 50*). A counter argument is that equality of resources is a better safeguard of democracy in the long run.

The main controls over election expenses are as follows (Representation of the People Act 1983 applies unless otherwise stated):

1. Every candidate must have an election agent who is accountable for the conduct of the candidate's campaign. A candidate can appoint himself as agent. There are controls over receipts and expenses out of the candidate's own pocket (ss 73, 74).

2. There is a maximum limit upon the amount that can be spent on behalf of any individual candidate in respect of 'the conduct or management of an election' (s 75; Political Parties, Elections and Referendums Act 2000, s 132). This can be varied by statutory instrument in line with inflation. It depends primarily on the size of the constituency and number of voters and currently amounts to about £x,000 (SI 2009/186). There is no fixed definition of an election expense. Some expenditure, for example to canvassers, on posters (except to advertising agents), on hiring vehicles to take people to vote and on broadcasting from abroad, is banned completely (ss 101–12). Reasonable personal expenses can also be incurred (s 18).

3. Candidates are entitled to free use of schools and public buildings for meetings (ss 95, 96). Each candidate can send one election address to each voter post-free (s 91).

4. The Political Parties, Elections and Referendums Act 2000 Part V extended controls over 'campaign expenditure' by registered political parties at national level. Thus the artificiality of distinguishing between promoting the party and promoting the candidate no longer arises. This applies during the 'campaign period', which is 365 days, ending with polling day (Sch 9 para 3 (7). Campaign expenditure includes party political broadcasts, advertising, market research, rallies, press conferences and transport (Sch 8). It also includes the provision of property, services to facilities to a party either free or at more than 10% below the commercial rate (s 73). There are overall limits on expenditure based on the number of constituencies contested, amounting to about £30,000 for each constituency (s 79). All campaign expenditure must be authorised by the party treasurer who must deliver a return of expenditure to the Electoral Commission (ss 75, 80, 82). This must be made available for public inspection (s 84).

5. Third parties such as pressure groups are restricted in promoting candidates during the campaign period. No expenditure over £500 can be incurred with a view to promoting a candidate without the authority of the candidate or agent, thus counting as part of the candidate's expenses (Representation of the People Act 1983, s 75; Political Parties, Elections and Referendums Act 2000, s 131; c.f. *Bowman v UK* [1998]: earlier limit of £5 held to be restriction on freedom of expression: does a higher limit make a difference?).

Indirect support is also restricted. It is an offence to incur 'controlled expenditure' above certain limits unless it is made by a 'recognised third party' (s 94). The limits are about £10,000 for England and £5,000 for the other regions. Controlled expenditure is the production or publication of material which is made available to the public and which can reasonably be regarded as intended to promote any candidate (including prejudicing another candidate) even if the material serves some other purpose as well (s 85). For example a leaflet put out by an animal rights pressure group might be controlled expenditure if the concerns of the group feature in the election campaign. Problems might arise however where a pressure group publicises a cause such as reducing poverty by issuing factual material which might be incidental to the election but where no specific intention to influence the election can be shown.

A 'recognised third party' registered with the Electoral Commission has higher limits (£793,500 for England, £108,000 for Scotland, £60,000 for Wales, £27,000 for Northern Ireland; Sch 10). A recognised third party must be an individual resident in the UK or on the electoral register, or a registered political party, company, trade union, building society, friendly society, partnership or unincorporated association. This could include a pressure group (s 88).

There are certain exceptions to these limits on payments by third parties. These include newspaper editorial matter, broadcasts, personal expenses and the value of services provided free by individuals (s 87).

12.6.2 Donations to political parties

There are no general restrictions on donations to a political party. Attempts to impose such restrictions could fall foul of the right to freedom of expression. Party donations have been a subject of serious concern, mainly in respect of the possibility that wealthy individuals, some resident overseas and non-taxpayers, are in a position to influence political parties by means of gifts and loans which may be anonymous. The Power Commission (2006) suggested that political parties should be funded by the state so as to avoid being unduly influenced by wealthy individuals. On the other hand state funding attracts state control, which may also be undesirable. Moreover it is not easy to produce a formula for payments that would be democratically fair and would not favour the status quo.

There is currently no general state funding for political parties. However policy development grants of up to £2 million are available from the Electoral Commission to parties with at least two MPs and money is provided by each House of Parliament to opposition parties for their parliamentary duties ('Short Money', after the proposer). (See White Paper, *Party Finance and Expenditure in the UK* (Cm 7329, 2008).) The Committee on Standards in Public Life is currently investigating the general issue of party finance.

Controls have been progressively increased but methods of evading them have been exploited. Introduced by the Political Parties, Elections and Referendums Act 2000 (PPERA) controls were tightened by the Electoral Administration Act 2006 and the Political Parties and Elections Act 2009. The controls are not intended to outlaw payments but to bring them into the open and ensure accountability.

Controls apply to donations, loans and credit facilities of more than £200 to political parties. They are not confined to the election campaign. 'Donation' is widely defined to include gifts, sponsorship, subscriptions, fees, expenses and the provision of non-commercial services (PPERA, s 50). A registered party cannot accept a payment if it is not made by a 'permissible donor' or if it is anonymous (PPERA, s 54(2); Electoral Administration Act 2006, s 61). A permissible donor must be registered to vote in the UK or be a business, trade union or registered political party based in the UK. In the case of a company, the shareholders must have approved the donation and the amount must be disclosed in the directors' report (PPERA, s 140, Sch 19).

There are particular disclosure requirements. These were imposed as a result of failure by political parties to check adequately the sources of donations. In the case of a donation of more than £7,500 there must be a written declaration of its source, including whether the donor is an agent for someone else (Political Parties and Elections Act 2009, s 9). Exceptions to the duty of disclosure include voluntary services provided by an individual, various payments made under statute, payments to MPs by the European Parliament and the hire of stands at party conferences for a payment deemed reasonable by the Commission.

It is arguable that non-taxpayers should not participate in government. For example members of Parliament are deemed to be domiciled or resident in the UK for tax purposes (Section 11.7). No donations or loans amounting to more than £7500 in a single calendar year can be made to a political party unless the donor makes a declaration that he or she is resident or domiciled in the UK for tax purposes (Political Parties and Elections Act 2009, s 10). However this provision comes into force by a ministerial order and has not yet done so. A substantial number of 'tax exiles' give money to political parties (see *Times* 20 September 2012).

A party must report relevant donations or loans of more than £5,000 regularly to the Electoral Commission (ss 63, 65, 68, 96; Electoral Administration Act 2006, ss 56, 57). This has caused problems since the person responsible for reporting is not clearly identified. The Commission keeps a public register but this must not include the address of a donor who is an individual (s 69). Impermissible payments must be returned or, if the donor or lender cannot be identified, given to the Commission (s 56). The court can order a payment to be forfeited (s 58) (see *R (Electoral Commission) v City of Westminster Magistrates Court* [2010] 1 All ER 1167).

12.6.3 Broadcasting and the press: freedom of expression

Rules which attempt to ensure that the parties are treated fairly must be balanced against freedom of expression under Article 10 of EHCR (Section 20.4.3). Campaign publicity has qualified privilege in the law of defamation, so there is no liability if it is published in good faith (*Culnane v Morris* [2006]). The same applies to the press and broadcasting (Section 22.5). There are further controls over the broadcast media, reflecting its power to influence a campaign:

▶ Political advertising by commercial broadcasters is unlawful except for party political broadcasts made by agreement between the BBC, OFCOM (the Office of Communications) and the main parties (see Communications Act 2003, ss 319–21; *R v Radio Authority, ex p Bull* [1997] 2 All ER 561). This prevents the worst excesses of wealthy parties. Only registered political parties can make party political broadcasts (Political Parties, Elections and Referendums Act 2000, s 37). Political broadcast programmes do not count as election expenses (Representation of the People Act 1983, s 75(1)).

▶ There is a general duty on OFCOM to preserve good taste and balance and impartiality in all political broadcasting (Communications Act 2003, s 6). The BBC is not governed by statute but operates under a royal charter and an agreement with the Home Office. However OFCOM can regulate the BBC in accordance with the charter and agreement (Communications Act 2003, s 198). OFCOM forbids the expression of editorial opinion about matters of public policy, excluding broadcasting matters. The independent broadcasters are protected by the Human rights Act 1998 in respect of the right of freedom of expression (Section 20.4.3). However as a public body the BBC may not be entitled to such protection (Section 21.5).

▶ In principle the broadcasters' duties are enforceable by the courts. However the idea of political impartiality is both vague and complex and the courts are reluctant to interfere in party political matters. For example must there be balance within the context of every specific subject? How much coverage should minority parties enjoy? The court will not intervene with the broadcasting authority's decision except in a case of bad faith or complete irrationality (see *R v Broadcasting Complaints Commission, ex p Owen* [1985] QB 1153; *R (Pro-Life Alliance) v BBC* [2003] 2 All ER 977. Each broadcasting authority in consultation with the parties must adopt a code of practice concerning the participation of the parties in items about the constituency (Representation of the People Act 1983, s 93 as amended).

▶ It is an illegal practice (Section 12.6.5) for a person to 'use or aid, abet, counsel or procure' the use of broadcasting stations outside the UK for electoral purposes except where the matter is to be retransmitted by one of the domestic broadcasting companies (Representation of the People Act 1983, s 93 as amended). However this may not prevent overseas stations from directly broadcasting to voters and does not control the Internet. Indeed considerable political propaganda is now disseminated over the Internet and there seem to be no relevant controls other than the general limits on election expenditure.

▶ Under RPA, s 106 it is an illegal practice (below) for any person to make a false statement of fact for the purpose of affecting the election result in relation to a candidate's personal character or conduct unless the person making the statement had reasonable grounds to believe and did believe that it was true. Section 106 risks involving the judiciary in politics. A balance must be struck between the right to respect for privacy and family life under Article 8 which includes personal integrity and freedom of expression under Article 10 including the public's entitlement to truth (*Lingens v Austria* (1986) 8 EHRR 407 [42], *Lindon v France* (2007) ECHR 836.

In *Watkins v Woolas* [2010] EWHC 2702 (upheld in *R (Woolas) v Parliamentary Election Court for Oldham East and Saddleworth* [2010] EWHC 3169) an MP was convicted for making a false statement that an opponent encouraged support from Muslim extremists. Even though this had large political implications, it was held to be a matter of personal character or conduct because its basic meaning was that the candidate condoned violence. The court distinguished between the personal and the political holding that a statement cannot be both personal and political.

This distinction can be artificial since personal matters, such as family, religion, business or finance, and political matters may overlap. For example dishonesty in personal affairs may be evidence that an MP is untrustworthy. It was held that a political statement falling outside s 106 is a statement relating to the candidate's official position. Even if a political statement also has personal implications it is will not fall within s 106 if the personal aspects are 'insubstantial', for example a statement that a candidate does not live in the constituency as required. However a serious political allegation such as corruption in Parliament which also seriously reflects on the candidate's personal character becomes personal and so falls within s 106 (see Hoar (2011), 74 (4) MLR 607). A primarily personal allegation such as, according to the court, the one about Muslim extremists seems to be always within s 106 however strong the political implications. Thus freedom of expression is constrained.

12.6.4 Election disputes

There is an Election Court comprising two judges. Either a voter or a candidate may within three months of the election lodge a petition to the court. The court can disqualify a candidate, order a recount or scrutiny of the votes, declare the result, invalidate it and order a fresh election (Representation of the People Act 1983, s 159). The decision takes the form of a report to the Speaker which the House is bound to accept (s 144(7)). Even though it comprises High Court judges the Election court is subject to judicial review by the High Court (see *R (Woolas) v Parliamentary Election Court for Oldham East and Saddleworth* (2010).

Election offences involve the offender being disqualified as a candidate or prevented from sitting in Parliament. The extent of the disqualification depends upon whether it is a 'corrupt practice' (ten years everywhere) or an 'illegal practice' (five years in a particular constituency). 'Innocent' illegal practices can be overlooked (s 167). A corrupt practice involves dishonesty, improper pressure on voters or improper expenditure. Illegal practices concern breaches of various statutory requirements and raise questions of freedom of expression (above).

There are also offences concerning misuse of the voting process which are prosecuted in the ordinary courts (Electoral Administration Act 2006).

Summary

▶ The House of Lords is unelected and with nearly 700 members is one of the largest legislatures in the world. This is thought to be inappropriate to its functions. The composition of the House of Lords is to be further reformed. The government has proposed that the House remain mainly unelected but with an elected element of one-fifth. A further one-fifth should be chosen by an independent commission but most of the House should be nominated by the political parties and appointed by the Prime Minister. As yet no further reforms have been made.

▶ The voting system for parliamentary elections is currently the simple plurality, first past the post system. Voting systems must cater for the incommensurables of effective government, accountable government and democratic representation. It is questionable whether the electoral system is adapted to its modern task of choosing governments, whether it is truly representative of public opinion and whether it is fair to all candidates. We briefly compared different kinds of voting system, including the alternative vote and proportional representation.

▶ Variations of PR are used in elections to the regional legislatures and the European Parliament. This is likely to create political tensions within the UK.

▶ The machinery for regulating constituency boundaries gives a certain amount of protection against political interference but proposals for changes must be approved by the House of Commons. It is difficult to challenge decisions made by this process in the courts.

▶ The law governing the conduct of elections, which had previously ignored national politics in favour of the individual election at local level, has been reformed to regulate campaign expenditure at national level, including spending by third parties on election campaigns and sponsorship of political parties. The independent Electoral Commission has wide responsibilities in relation to the finances of political parties and the conduct of elections. This is intended to bring greater openness and accountability to political parties.

▶ Controls over election broadcasting are designed to ensure fairness between the parties in accordance with their popular support and are more stringent than are restrictions over the press.

Exercises

12.1 'In a democracy there is no point in an upper house of the legislature. If both houses are elected, there is a problem of duplication. If the upper house is not elected then it is not legitimate.' Discuss.

12.2 The Prime Minister makes the following recommendations to the Queen for elevation to the peerage.
   1. George a banker who has made large donations to the Prime Minister's party and who was told by an advisor to the Prime Minister that his donations should be worth a peerage.
   2. Clara an artist whose application was rejected by the House of Lords Appointment Commission on the ground that she would not 'fit in' to the culture of the House of Lords because she had been conceited of drug related offences.
   3. 'Benjy' the Prime Minister's brother-in-law who has recently been rejected in an election to the House of Commons.

   Advise the Queen as to the legality of these proposals and as to the constitutional implications if any. What are her powers in the matter?

12.3 To what extent can common ground be found in the attempts to reform the House of Lords that have been made since 1911? What reforms would you suggest?

12.4 Do the present arrangements for designating parliamentary constituencies contain adequate safeguards against gerrymandering?

12.5 Jack who is 18 has been thrown out his parents' home in Bangor where he has lived all his life. He now divides his time between his girlfriend's home in London, a holiday cottage belonging to his girlfriend's parents in Devon and a squatters' commune in Newcastle where he is a part time student at the University. In which place if any is Jack entitled to vote? He would like to vote in Bangor. What would be the position if Jack had been a voluntary patient in a mental hospital in Edinburgh for the last 6 months?

12.6 To what extent has the law successfully regulated the funding of political parties? Should there be legal restrictions on the amount of all private donations to political parties?

12.7 A general election is expected to take place within the next year.
   i. The Campaign for Free University Education proposes to distribute leaflets and hold meetings during the election campaign in various university towns.
   ii. Jerry, a wealthy businessman resident in the US, wishes to make an anonymous loan of £5 million to any political party that will campaign to withdraw the UK from the EU. He also proposes to advertise in the national press and on TV in favour of repealing the Anti hunting law in the UK.
   iii. Clive, who is resident in the Channel Islands, wishes to donate £8000 to the Get Out of Europe! Party.

   Discuss the legality of these proposals.

12.8 During an election campaign Clive a supporter of one of the candidates wrote to a newspaper stating falsely that Joanna, a candidate for a rival party, did not live in the constituency, was a member of an animal rights group that advocated violence and in a previous job as an accountant had often made false expenses claims.

12.9 'Reforms of the electoral system through the introduction of a single transferable vote ... would revitalise the operation of political processes and make a major contribution to the development of a more accountable, effective system and a more influential citizenry' (Oliver). Discuss.

Further reading

Bingham, 'The House of Lords: Its Future' [2010] PL 261

Bogdanor, *The New British Constitution* (Hart 2009) ch 6

Committee on Standards in Public Life, Fifth Report, *The Funding of Political Parties in the United Kingdom* (Cm 4057, 1998)

Committee on Standards in Public Life, Thirteenth Report, *Political party Finance: Ending the Big Donor Culture* (Cm 8208, 2011)

Phillips, *Strengthening Democracy: Fair and Sustainable Funding of Political Parties* (HMSO 2007)

Hansard Society, *The Future of Parliament: Reform of the Second Chamber* (Hansard Society 1999)

Independent Commission on the Voting System, *Report of the Independent Commission on the Voting System* (Cm 4090, 1998) [Jenkins Report]

Lardy, 'Democracy by Default: The Representation of the People Act 2000' (2000) 64 MLR 63

Marriot, 'Alarmist or Relaxed: Election Expenditure Limits and Freedom of Speech' [2005] PL 764

Phillipson, 'The "Greatest Quango of Them All" ' [2004] PL 352

Power Commission, *Power to the People: An Independent Inquiry into Britain's Democracy* (Rowntree Trust 2006)

Royal Commission on the Reform of the House of Lords, *A House for the Future* (Cm 4534, 2000) [Wakeham Report]

Russell, *Reforming the House of Lords: Lessons from Overseas* (Oxford University Press 2000)

Russell and Cornes, 'The Royal Commission on the House of Lords: A House for the Future?' (2000) 64 MLR 82

Webb, 'Parties and Party Systems: Modernisation, Regulation and Diversity' (2001) 54 Parl Aff 308

Webber, 'The Polycentricity of Political Financing' [2012] PL 311

Weill, 'We the British People' [2004] PL 380

Chapter 13

Parliamentary procedure

Introduction

Parliamentary procedure may seem to be a dry topic but it is of great importance. It is only through procedures for debating, questioning and voting that the voice of Parliament as a collective institution can make itself known. It will be recalled that there is no strict separation of powers between the executive and the legislature in that all ministers must also be members of Parliament and the most important ministers must be members of the elected House of Commons. This has democratic strengths, ensuring that ministers are directly answerable to Parliament, but where the government has a strong majority it weakens the independence of Parliament. The procedural rules attempt to ensure that Parliament as representative of the people can perform its four sometimes conflicting tasks. These are:

1. making legislation;
2. sustaining the government by providing it with funds and ensuring that government business can be adequately dealt with;
3. holding the executive to account;
4. redressing individual grievances.

It is widely acknowledged that the voice of Parliament is to some extent stifled by executive dominance (Section 5.11). One reason for this is that the government controls the day-to-day procedures of the House of Commons. Under Standing Order (SO) 14 (HC 2009–10, 539), government business has priority. Twenty days per year are set aside for Opposition business. Private members' bills, that is bills promoted by individual MPs, have priority on 13 Fridays (the House does not otherwise sit on Fridays, so few MPs are likely to be present).

The government also controls the timetable for debating legislation and can invoke procedures which enable a bill to be passed with little discussion. Time pressures and its majority mean that much business gets through without proper scrutiny. The government through its whips (party managers) attempts to ensure the party members vote loyally and the Chief Whip advises the Prime Minister upon the careers of ministers and MPs. It is for the House collectively to control its own procedures, so it could, if it so wished, radically transform itself. In some countries, influenced by the doctrine of separation of powers, there are provisions which prevent the procedure from being controlled by the executive.

Parliamentary procedure is based upon Standing Orders made by each House, customs and conventions, and rulings by the Speaker of the Commons. The authoritative manual of parliamentary procedure is Erskine May, *Parliamentary Practice* (Butterworths 2004). The finance, administration and staffing of the House of Commons are supervised by the House of Commons Commission, which comprises a group of MPs chaired by the Speaker (House of Commons (Administration) Act 1978). It does not have a government majority and is therefore independent of the executive.

Parliamentary procedure is adversarial, presupposing a government and Opposition constantly in conflict. The rectangular layout of the chamber reflects this. Government and Opposition confront each other on either side and the seats are symbolically arranged two sword lengths from each other. Other European legislative chambers are characteristically semicircular in layout, representing a more conciliatory ethos, with the parties, usually elected by proportional representation, merging into each other. The adversarial nature of parliamentary procedure is mitigated by what are known as 'usual channels'. These involve informal cooperation between the parties so as to ensure that the procedures operate smoothly and fairly. For example absences from votes may be arranged in 'pairs' so as to maintain party balance. Whips have the responsibility of liaising between the government and backbench MPs. The Selection Committee on the Modernisation of the House of Commons has proposed a range of measures to improve the processes of Parliament (see *Modernisation of the House of Commons: A Reform Programme* (HC 2001–02, 1168)). These will be mentioned in context. Some of them, in particular the streamlining of the timetable for debating legislation, seem to enhance governmental control. The *Power Report* (Rowntree Trust 2006) recommended that select committees should get enhanced powers, that there should be limits on the powers of the whips and that Parliament should have greater freedom to initiate legislation, petitions and inquiries independently of the executive.

A Select Committee on Reform of the House of Commons (the Wright Committee) reported in March 2010 (*Rebuilding the House* (HC 2008–09, 1117)). It made several recommendations. These were designed to strengthen the collective power of the Commons, to give individual members greater influence and to make the proceedings of the House more transparent so as to increase public ability to influence and understand parliamentary business.

The Committee's most important recommendations were accepted by the government and the House and implemented by Standing Order. These were:

1. that a backbench business committee should timetable business in the House of Commons. This would initially apply only to non-government business but would eventually extend to most government business;
2. that backbench members should have greater control over the membership of select committees of the House (Section 13.5.3);
3. that more time should be made available to debate select committee reports;
4. that backbenchers should have greater opportunity to initiate debates.

The Wright Committee also recommended that the Opposition should have greater control over the timetabling of the 20 'Opposition days' available for debating subjects of its choosing, that the government should not decide for how long its business should be debated without reference to the House, that aspects of the 'estimates' (Section 13.4) should be more thoroughly debated and that backbenchers' motions should be voted on. These recommendations have not been formally implemented.

13.2 The Speaker of the Commons

The office of Speaker, 'the first commoner', symbolises the historical development of the House of Commons. The Speaker presides over meetings of the Commons and is the intermediary between the House and the Crown. Originally the Speaker was a Crown servant but since the seventeenth century has asserted independence from the Crown. When Charles I entered the chamber to arrest the Five Members (1642), Speaker Lenthall replied: 'I have neither eyes to see nor tongue to speak in this place but as the

House is pleased to direct me, whose servant I am here.' Thus the Speaker represents the rights of the House against the Crown.

Since the nineteenth century it has become established that the Speaker is independent of party, cannot hold ministerial office and takes no part in debate. The Speaker is required to be impartial between the political parties. The Speaker controls the procedure, keeps order and is responsible for protecting the rights of all groups within the House, particularly those of minorities. He or she has considerable discretion. The Speaker makes procedural rulings, decides who shall speak and has summary powers to suspend members or terminate a sitting. In terms of the conduct of particular proceedings, the Speaker need not normally give reasons for decisions. The Sergeant at Arms is the enforcement agency responsible to the Speaker. There is also a Deputy Speaker and deputies to him or her. One of these presides when the whole House is sitting as a committee, as it does in relation to financial matters (Section 13.4).

The Speaker is elected by secret ballot from among its members by the House at the beginning of each Parliament. The 'Father of the House', the longest-serving member, runs the election. Traditionally a newly elected Speaker has to be dragged to the chair, a reminder that this was once a dangerous post. The Speaker can be removed by the House. Removal of a Speaker is rare but happened in 2009 when Speaker Martin resigned amid allegations that his conduct was overprotective to MPs accused of excessive expense claims. He unsuccessfully resisted publication of MPs' expense claims.

13.3 Legislative procedure

Parliament debates each bill in a process that distinguishes between general principles and detail. Parliamentary debates consist of a motion and a question proposed by the chair in the same form as the motion. Following debate the question is put and voted upon, the result being expressed as a resolution or order. At any stage there may be amendments proposed, but in all cases issues are presented to the House one at a time for a yes or no vote by a simple majority. Given that the electoral system may produce a government with the support of around a third of the popular vote this means that a given law may be supported by no more than 25 per cent of the people. The main distinctions are between public bills and private bills. There are also special arrangements for financial measures.

13.3.1 Public bills

A public bill is a bill intended to alter the general law. The formal procedures in the House are only the tip of the iceberg. Any member can propose a bill (a private member's bill) but almost all public bills are promoted by the government and introduced by ministers. Private members' bills are unlikely to succeed without government support. As we have seen, 13 Fridays are provided in each session on which precedence is given to private members' bills (SO 14(4)). Priority is determined by a ballot held annually, for which only backbenchers are eligible. Only the first six in the ballot have a realistic chance of success because, of the Fridays, five are devoted to bills in their later stages. A private member can also get a bill debated under the 'ten minute rule' (SO 23). This involves a motion twice a week that leave be given to present a bill. A short debate takes place. There is little prospect of the matter going any further, the essential aim being to publicise an issue. Nevertheless some important social reforms have been made by private members' bills, including abortion legislation, the abolition of the death penalty and divorce reform. However all had government support in the form of time allocation and drafting assistance.

Before their formal introduction, public bills go through various processes within the administration involving the formulation of policy and principles and consultation with outside bodies although there is no legal requirement of consultation or probably even a convention. The bill is then sent to the Parliamentary Counsel for drafting. Some bills, particularly those dealing with commercial matters, are drafted with the aid of outside lawyers. The relationship between the draftsmen and the government is similar to that of lawyer and client. The draftsmen work under considerable pressure of time and there is continuous consultation with government departments. Some bills relating to reform of the general law are prepared by the Law Commission. Important bills may be foreshadowed by Green Papers, which are consultation documents, or White Papers, which state the government's concluded opinions, albeit sometimes leaving matters open for further discussion. Both are published. Recently, as part of the modernisation programme, important bills have been published as draft bills for 'pre-legislative' discussion by Parliament and with public consultation before the formal process is started. Draft bills are considered by a select or standing committee.

The final version of a bill is approved by the Cabinet and then introduced into Parliament. Except for financial measures, which must be introduced by a minister in the Commons, a bill can be introduced into either House. The same stages apply in each House. Relatively uncontroversial bills are likely to be introduced in the House of Lords.

The stages of a public bill are as follows:

- *First reading*. A formality which ensures that the bill is printed and published.
- *Second reading*. At which the main principles of the bill are discussed. In theory, once a bill has passed this stage, its principles cannot later be challenged. Occasionally the second reading is dealt with by a special committee. After second reading there is a 'programme motion' timetabling the bill and there may be a vote authorising any expenditure concerning the bill.
- *Committee stage*. The bill is examined usually by a standing committee, with a view to suggesting detailed amendments. Unlike a select committee, which exists for the whole of a Parliament, a standing committee is set up only for the purpose of a particular bill. Its membership of around 50 is based upon the strength of each party in the House, so it is difficult for amendments to be made against the wishes of the government. Opponents of a bill sometimes deliberately cause delays by discussing matters at length in committee. However the chairman has the power to decide which amendments should be discussed and a business subcommittee allocates time for discussion. The parliamentary draftsman may be present and civil servants or experts might be called to give evidence.
- Sometimes a bill is referred to a committee of the whole House. This might happen for example when the bill is uncontroversial or, at the opposite extreme, where it is urgent, highly controversial or a 'major bill of first-class constitutional significance', although the meaning of this is unclear. For example the Bank of England Bill 1997, which transfers power to fix interest rates to the Bank, went to an ordinary standing

committee. A government can effectively neutralise the committee stage by obtaining a resolution that a committee of the whole House shall deal with a bill. This means that the bill is unlikely to be examined in detail. This device was used in 2010 for the Academies Bill, which allows qualifying schools to remove themselves from local authority into central control. Occasionally a specialised bill is referred to one of the permanent select committees.

▶ *Report stage.* The bill is returned to the House, which can then vote upon the committee amendments and consider further amendments. The Speaker can select the amendments to be debated. The report stage can be dispensed with where the bill has been discussed by a committee of the whole House.

▶ *Third reading.* This is the final vote on the bill. Only verbal amendments are usually possible at this stage (SO 77) but the bill as a whole can be opposed.

▶ The bill is then sent to the other House. If the Lords veto the bill or make amendments, it is returned to the Commons. If there is continuing disagreement between the two Houses, the Parliament Act procedure can be triggered (Section 11.4) Otherwise the bill is sent for royal assent. This is usually notified by commissioners at the prorogation ceremony that ends each session (Royal Assent Act 1967). By convention the monarch must always assent, except possibly in the unlikely event of the Prime Minister advising to the contrary. In this case however the government would be at odds with the Commons and so required to resign.

▶ Once a bill has received the royal assent it becomes law. However it is often provided that an Act or parts of it shall take effect only when a minister so orders. A minister's decision whether or not to bring an Act into effect can be subject to judicial review (see *R v Secretary of State for the Home Dept, ex p Fire Brigades Union* [1995]). It is also common for an Act to confer power on ministers to make regulations without which the Act itself cannot operate. These might include a 'Henry VIII clause' under which a minister is empowered to alter the Act or other statutes.

▶ If a public bill has not become law by the end of a session, it lapses. However some bills can be carried over into the next session (SO 80A (HC 1997–98, 543)). This must be authorised by a resolution of the House, which is of course usually under the control of the governing party.

Some bills can be passed without debate but with scrutiny by a joint committee of both Houses. These are bills of a largely formal nature to consolidate other legislation without making significant changes or to repeal redundant statutes. The Law Commission prepares these bills.

13.3.2 Private bills

A private bill is one directed to particular persons or places, for example a bill to build a new section of railway line. It is not subject to the Parliament Acts. Private bill procedure allows both local and national perspectives to be examined and is therefore suitable for very important private schemes. The procedure includes a special committee stage involving an inquiry open to the interests concerned, who can be legally represented. Although private bill procedure involves outside elements, it is still wholly within parliamentary privilege. Therefore the courts cannot intervene on the ground that the procedure has not been properly followed or even that there has been fraud (*Pickin v British Railways Board* [1974]).

A public bill with a private element is called a 'hybrid bill'. For example the Aircraft and Shipbuilding Bill 1976 nationalised these industries and was, as such, a public bill but it exempted certain named firms from its proposals. A hybrid bill is subject to the public bill procedure until the committee stage, when it is examined by a select committee in the same manner as a private bill.

Private bill procedure has been much criticised, not only because it is slow and antiquated but also because it fails to provide opportunities for the public to be directly involved in debating schemes that may have serious environmental impact, for example new railway lines. There are however a range of alternative procedures. The main examples involving Parliament are as follows:

▶ *The Transport and Works Act 1992* applies primarily to large rail and waterway projects. A Secretary of State authorises projects after consulting local authorities and affected parties and after an environmental assessment. A public inquiry must be held into objections. The Secretary of State can refer proposals of national importance to Parliament for debate.

▶ *Provisional orders* made by ministers, again following a public local inquiry, are confirmed by a provisional order confirmation bill, the committee stage of which involves a select committee at which interested parties can be heard. It is not subject to the Parliament Acts. This procedure is rarely used.

▶ *Special parliamentary procedure* involves a ministerial order which is subject to a public inquiry and also to a hearing before a special parliamentary committee. It can be debated on the floor of the House. This procedure is less cumbersome than the procedure for private bills or provisional order confirmation bills. It gives the authority of Parliament to sensitive proposals but is rarely used.

13.3.3 Government control over procedure: cutting short debate

By virtue of its majority and the submissiveness of its supporters, the government is usually in a position to control the timing of debate. Moreover the parliamentary timetable is usually crowded, with the result that many, if not most, clauses of a bill are not discussed at all. As part of the 'modernisation' agenda, the passage of a bill can be timetabled in advance under a 'programme motion' by the government (SO 83A–83I; for background see *Modernisation Select Committee Report* (HC 1997–98, 190); Procedure Committee Report, *Timetabling Legislation* (HC 2003–04, 325): government's response (HC 2003–04, 1169)). This applies to most government bills and increases the government's control over Parliament. There are other procedural devices to cut short the time spent on debate. The main devices are:

▶ *Closure*. A motion in the House or in a committee that the question now be put. This must be supported by at least 100 members and means that the matter must immediately be voted on (SOs 36, 37). The Speaker can also cut short debate when she or he thinks there has been adequate discussion. Except in the case of private members' bills, closure motions are rare but are important as a last resort.

▶ *Guillotine*. A minister may propose a timetable for a bill, a motion that cannot be debated for more than three hours (SO 83).

▶ There is a limited safeguard in that a *business committee* or *programme committee* appointed by the Speaker and chaired by the chair of the Committee of Ways and

Means (a senior committee concerned with overseeing the government budget) divides up the time allocated to bills that have been subject to a programme motion (SO 83B) or guillotine (SO 82) in relation to a committee of the whole House or at report or third reading stage.

▶ *Kangaroo*. The Speaker at report stage or the chairman of a committee selects clauses or amendments for discussion.

13.4 Financial procedure

Financial controls generally have developed pragmatically over the centuries. They are a confusing mixture of statute, convention, parliamentary customs and administrative practice based possibly on royal prerogative powers to control the civil service. They reveal the untidiness of the UK constitution at its worst.

The dependence of the executive on money voted by the people is an essential feature of a democratic constitution. It is a fundamental principle embodied in both law and convention that the House of Commons controls public finance and that proposals for public spending can be initiated only by the Crown: 'The Crown demands money, the Commons grant and the Lords assent to the grant' (May, *Parliamentary Practice* (Butterworths 1997), 732–36). On the other hand modern government finance is so large and complex that parliamentary control may be unrealistic. It is widely accepted that, particularly in relation to advance scrutiny of government demands for money, parliamentary control is ineffective. The Commons can only scrutinise taxation and expenditure proposals very superficially, relying heavily on what the government tells it and having limited resources to carry out independent scrutiny. In practice the most substantial control over government finance is exercised internally by the Treasury (Chapter 15). The independent National Audit Office is effective in relation to scrutiny of past expenditure.

Financial procedure is based on an ancient distinction between 'ways and means' – raising money – and 'supply' – allocating money to the purposes of the executive. This is somewhat artificial since the two are closely related. By virtue of the Bill of Rights 1688 the Crown cannot raise taxation without the consent of Parliament. The basis of the principle that the Crown cannot spend money without the consent of Parliament is partly long-standing custom endorsed by the common law (*Auckland Harbour Board v R* [1924] AC 318) and partly statute, in that payments out of the Consolidated Fund, the government's bank account, require statutory authority (Exchequer and Audit Departments Act 1866, s 11).

The Crown comes to the Commons to ask for money in the form of the 'estimates' for each government department. Financial measures can be proposed only by a minister. The Commons can reduce the estimates but not increase them. The survival of a government depends upon the Commons voting it funds, and the refusal of the Commons to do so is equivalent to a vote of no confidence so that the government must resign. By convention the House of Lords cannot amend measures relating to central government finance and, under the Parliament Act 1911 can delay bills that are exclusively concerned with raising or allocating central government money only for one month.

Taxation and expenditure must first be authorised by resolutions of the House of Commons. Amendments cannot be made outside the terms of the resolution, thus strengthening the government's hand. The enactment of the legislation is a formality, any serious discussion, itself limited, having taken place months earlier when the government presented its public spending proposals according to a timetable of its choosing.

There are three main financial measures (see Brazier and Ram, 2004, chs 1 and 2 for a clear account). Firstly the Finance Act raises taxation. The royal assent to a taxation measure is expressed in the words *La Reyne remercie ses bons sujets, accepte leur benevolence et ainsi le veult* ('the Queen thanks her good subjects, accepts their kindness and thus assents'), as opposed to the normal *La Reyne le veult*. Secondly an Appropriation Act, usually in May, allocates amounts out of the Consolidated Fund to the Crown according to the estimates ('votes') presented for each government department for the current financial year, that is until the following April. It also confirms spending that has been authorised provisionally by other legislation for the current and previous years. Thirdly Consolidated Fund Acts authorise interim spending until the following Appropriation Act and may also authorise additional spending from time to time. These bills have no committee or report stage but go straight from second to third reading.

Central government money does not come exclusively from taxation. Governments borrow large sums of money in the form of bonds and on the international money market. Money is also raised from landholding, from investments both in the UK and overseas and from trading activities. These sources of finance are not subject to detailed parliamentary scrutiny, although statutory authority is required in general terms for borrowing (National Loans Fund Act 1968).

13.4.1 Taxation procedure

The key taxation event is the annual 'budget' resolution proposed by the Chancellor, usually in March. The budget speech sets the general economic framework of government policy and proposals for tax changes. The budget resolution is followed by the annual Finance Bill. This includes taxes (notably income tax) that must be authorised afresh each year albeit enforced and administered under permanent legislation (Income and Corporation Taxes Act 1988). Some taxes, mainly indirect taxes such as customs duties, are authorised by permanent legislation although their rates can be changed at any time. Constitutional principle is preserved in the case of EU law by the requirement in the European Communities Act 1972 that laws affecting taxation, for example VAT, must be implemented by a statute.

The effect of the budget resolution is that the tax proposals become law with immediate effect, but lapse unless embodied in a Finance Act that becomes law by a specified time. This is 5 August if the speech is in March or April, otherwise within four months (Provisional Collection of Taxes Act 1968). The main parts of the Finance Bill are considered by a committee of the whole House. This procedure illustrates the constitutional principle that resolutions of the Commons cannot by themselves change the law but need statutory backing (*Bowles v Bank of England* (1913)). However unless an aspect of the Finance Bill is especially controversial it is subject to little scrutiny. For example ministers inserted provisions into the Finance Act 1984 which exempted MPs' expense claims from normal taxation (see Little and Stopworth (2013) 76 (1) MLR 83).

13.4.2 Supply procedure

Most public expenditure must be authorised annually by the Appropriation Act which approves the government's estimates. These estimates are made under the supervision of the Treasury. They include 'votes' setting out the government's proposed allocation of funds between departments. Thus the Commons approves both the global sum and the executive's broad priorities. However the Appropriation Act is very short and general, merely listing the broad functions of each department to be financed, allocating a global amount, designating a grant from the Consolidated Fund (the government's main bank account) and setting a limit to 'appropriations in aid', that is money that can be raised from fees and charges and so on. Moreover the Act deals only in cash, so contemporary methods of 'resource accounting', which includes other government assets, may not fall properly within parliamentary controls (see Daintith and Page, 1999, 166).

The Public Accounts Committee admitted in 1987 that parliamentary control over the estimates is largely a formality (HC 1986–87, 98, para 2). The Appropriation Act and Consolidated Fund Acts are usually passed without debate. Debates on the estimates have been replaced by 20 'Opposition days', which allow the Opposition parties to raise anything they wish, and by special 'adjournment debates' following the passage of the Acts. The latter allow issues to be discussed without a vote.

The Act appears to authorise payment to the Crown rather than to the individual department, thus reinforcing the Treasury's power to control other departments by presiding over the internal allocation of funds. However in *R v Lords Comrs of the Treasury* [1872] LR 7 QB 387 it was said that the Treasury is obliged to pay the sums in question.

There is an arcane debate as to whether the Appropriation Act alone is sufficient to make lawful particular items of expenditure that fall within its general provisions. This is worth briefly considering as it raises wider concerns as to the role of internal understandings and influences as against legal constraints in the constitution (see Daintith and Page, 1999, 35, 174, 203–06). One view is that in addition to the Appropriation Act, specific powers must be conferred either by statute or under the royal prerogative. In other words the Appropriation Act authorises the Crown to use the government's bank account for purposes that are lawful but does not in itself make any purpose lawful. On the other hand if an act of the Crown does not involve interfering with the legal rights of others, why should the Crown require specific powers since as a person it can do anything that the law does not forbid, including, presumably, spending its money? On this argument the Appropriation Act that puts the money into the Crown's hands should be a sufficient legal basis for spending.

Where a statute confers specific spending powers, this cuts down any general power derived from the Appropriation Act (eg *R v Secretary of State for Foreign and Commonwealth Affairs, ex p World Development Movement* [1995] 1 All ER 611; *R v Secretary of State for the Home Dept, ex p Fire Brigades Union* [1995] 2 All ER 244). However a later Appropriation Act could possibly validate past unlawful expenditure. A concordat in 1932 between the Treasury and the Public Accounts Committee (see Treasury, Government Accounting, 1989, Annex 2.1) assumed that an Appropriation Act could override limits in other statutes but stated that it was 'proper' that permanent spending powers and duties should be defined by particular statutes. Other government statements are inconsistent (see Daintith and Page, 1999, 205). It may be that the courts would be reluctant to read general provisions in an Appropriation Act as overriding specific provisions in other Acts (see *Fisher v R* [1903] AC 158).

Some items of expenditure are permanently authorised by particular statutes. These are called 'Consolidated Fund Services'. They include judicial salaries, royal expenses, EC payments and interest on the national debt. The Government Trading Act 1990 gives permanent authority to the financing of certain commercial services such as the Post Office by means of a Trading Fund. In practice most government spending is the subject of long-term commitments (eg pensions), thus leaving little flexibility.

13.5 Supervision of the executive

Supervision of the executive depends upon the doctrine of ministerial responsibility and relies in the last resort upon the convention that the House of Commons can require the government to resign. In modern times the role of Parliament has been weakened by the party system and the difficulty of obtaining information from the government. It should also be remembered that not all government activity requires formal parliamentary authority. This includes royal prerogative powers such as going to war and other matters concerning foreign affairs (and also commercial and property transactions carried out under ordinary private law powers such as buying and selling weapons). Parliamentary scrutiny is also limited by the practice of transferring government functions to bodies outside the central government. The main procedures for scrutiny of the executive are discussed in this chapter. Particular issues of ministerial responsibility are discussed in Chapter 15.

13.5.1 Questions to ministers

Questions can be written or oral and must be about something for which the minister is responsible. About one hour each day is allowed for oral questions to ministers, the departments being on a fortnightly rota. Questions are selected at random by the Speaker. The Prime Minister has one oral session of 30 minutes each week for which any MP can put down a question. In other cases there is a rota of three ministers per day but members must ballot for the privilege of asking an oral question. Except in the case of Prime Minister's Questions, two weeks' advance notice must be given but a member may ask one unscheduled supplementary question. Civil servants who brief ministers, although required by the Civil Service Code to be as open as possible with Parliament, are skilled in anticipating possible supplementaries, which need only bear a tenuous relationship to the main question. Sycophantic questions by government supporters are frequently asked.

There is provision for an urgent question to be asked without prior warning as a 'private notice' question (SO 8(3)). This must be of an urgent character and relate either to matters of public importance or to the arrangement of business. The Speaker's permission is required and the minister must attend on the same day. For example on 6 September 2010 a question was asked concerning allegations that the Prime Minister's Press Officer had connived in telephone hacking in his previous post as editor of the *News of the World*. There are usually less than a dozen permitted urgent questions per session.

Oral questions are probably of value mainly as a means of ensuring that ministers present themselves in public to acknowledge their personal responsibility for their departments and of assessing the personality and parliamentary skills of the minister. They are of limited value as a means of obtaining information. Written questions, of which there are many thousand per session, can be asked without limit and the answers are recorded in *Hansard*, the official parliamentary journal.

The Ministerial Code (2010) requires that ministers must be as open as possible with Parliament and give accurate and truthful information to Parliament, correcting any inadvertent error at the earliest opportunity (see also Cabinet Office, *Guidance to Officials on Answering Parliamentary Questions; HC 1996–97, 671, annex C*). However, given the government's in-built majority in Parliament, this may carry little weight. The Ministerial Code is enforceable only by the Prime Minister. Moreover ministers can refuse to answer on various grounds, including cost, government efficiency, commercial sensitivity, confidentiality and the 'public interest', and cannot be pressed upon a refusal to answer. Some specific matters are excluded. These include matters relating to the monarchy and personal criticism of a judge. Matters subject to litigation in UK courts cannot be discussed subject to exceptions ruled on by the Speaker in connection with civil litigation relating to ministerial decisions or matters of national importance. Exemptions in the Freedom of Information Act 2000 (Section 23.2.1) also apply. Reasons must be given for refusing to answer. However answers might be perfunctory or incomplete, although under the Ministerial Code ministers must not 'knowingly' mislead Parliament.

MPs have often expressed frustration that ministers are not always prepared to provide full and timely answers to parliamentary questions. The Public Administration Committee monitors the government's responses to questions. There is no coercive machinery to compel a minister to offer a prompt, relevant and full answer in Parliament and it is unlikely that Parliament would use its contempt powers to compel ministers to answer questions.

13.5.2 Debates

There are various opportunities for debates; all involve limited time. However ministers must respond if required and thus debates require government to present itself in public. The different kinds of debates include:

▶ *Adjournment debates*. These can be on any matter for which a minister is responsible. The most common is a half-hour daily adjournment debate which can be initiated by a backbencher. There is a weekly ballot (SO 9). There can also be adjournment debates following passage of a Consolidated Fund or Appropriation Act (Section 13.4), emergency adjournment debates (which are rarely permitted) and 'recess' debates, in which miscellaneous topics can be debated for up to three hours. Amendments cannot be moved to adjournment motions, so adjournment motions can be used by the government to restrict the Opposition. Adjournment debates do not result in a formal vote and a minister's response cannot be questioned.
▶ *Opposition days*. Twenty Opposition days are dispersed through the session which allow the Opposition parties to raise anything they wish.
▶ *Emergency debates*. The Speaker must hold that the matter is urgent, specific and important and should have urgent consideration. Only three minutes are allowed for

the application. If permission is granted there can be a three-hour debate. Urgency debates are rare but could concern such matters as a hospital closure.

▶ *The debate following the Queen's Speech at the opening of a session.*

▶ *Censure motions.* By convention a government is expected to resign if defeated on a censure motion (also called a no confidence motion). The government must provide time to debate the motion. Until the 1970s the convention also seemed to include other government defeats on important matters, but the latter seem no longer to require resignation. The possibility that a government can be defeated on a major part of its programme but also remain in office strengthens a weak government by providing a safety valve for dissidents within its party. Since 1964 a government has resigned only once following a censure motion (1979). On that occasion the government was a minority government, again a rare event. A no confidence motion has no particular form. Either government or Opposition can declare any vote to be one of confidence. In today's conditions the procedure seems to be essentially a publicity stunt. However such a vote does require the government to publicly defend itself.

▶ *The budget debate* (Section 13.4.1).

▶ *Early day motions.* This procedure allows an MP to put down a matter for debate without a fixed date. Early day motions are hardly ever debated. Their function is to draw public attention to a particular issue. They may be supported by a large number of members across parties, amounting in effect to a petition.

▶ *Procedural debates such as points of order.* These must nominally relate to the practices of the House but might be used ingeniously to raise a broader issue.

▶ *Ministerial statements which can be followed by questions and discussion.* The Speaker can require a minister to attend and make a statement.

▶ *Westminster Hall.* Part of the 'modernisation' programme, this sits in a large committee room on three weekdays. It is a supplement to the main chamber as a forum for debates initiated by backbenchers on less contentious business for which time might not otherwise be easily found. Decisions must be unanimous and otherwise are referred to the main House. Ministers must be available to respond every other week, whereas in the main chamber they must respond if required to any debate.

13.5.3 Select committees

A select committee is appointed from backbenchers for the whole of a Parliament. A select committee must be distinguished from a standing committee, the function of the latter being to scrutinise bills at the committee stage. A select committee is supposed to be independent of government but there is the possibility that committee members would try to curry favour with ministers, for example by discussing proposed committee reports with them.

There are four main kinds of select committee:

1. committees charged with investigating the expenditure, administration and policy of the main departments and reporting to the House (SO 130). There is no Prime Minister's committee as such but the Prime Minister voluntarily appears twice per year before the Liaison Committee, which is composed of the chairs of the other committees. The Security and Intelligence Committee is made up of MPs but is appointed by and reports to the Prime Minister;

2. committees dealing with important general concerns. These include broadcasting, environmental audit, food standards, European scrutiny, public accounts, public administration and regulatory reform;
3. The Backbench Business Committee is chosen by backbenchers and can designate matters for debate. It has a limited time allocation given by government of about 1 hour per week but part from that is free of government control.
4. committees dealing with matters internal to the House such as standards and privileges, modernisation and procedure. There is also the Speaker's Committee, which deals with electoral matters (Political Parties, Elections and Referendums Act 2000). Some select committees are joint committees of the Lords and Commons. These include human rights, statutory instruments, financial services and markets, and reform of the House of Lords.

The work of the departmental select committees is coordinated by the Liaison Committee, elected by the House. Previously committees were appointed mainly by party managers. However a result of the recommendations of the Wright Committee (Section 13.1) chairs of departmental and other important select committees are now elected by the House (although the *distribution* of chairs between the parties is still be decided by party managers). Members of select committees are chosen by secret ballot within party groups according to the strength of their representation in the House. Select committees may also recruit outside advisers such as academics.

Committee proceedings are open to the public unless the committee resolves to meet in closed session. Decisions are made in private. Strictly speaking, evidence taken by a select committee cannot be published without the consent of the committee, unless and until it becomes part of the formal record of Parliament. However evidence given in public can be published (SOs 135, 136). Select committees have little ability to probe deeply. Time, party discipline, the doctrine of ministerial responsibility and the rules of parliamentary procedure combine to frustrate their activities (see Liaison Committee, *Shifting the Balance: Select Committees and the Executive* (HC 2000–01, 321)). Relatively minor reforms were made in 2002 to strengthen select committees as a response to a more ambitious agenda from the Modernisation Committee (HC 2001–02, 224). These included paying committee chairs and encouraging committees to monitor the government's response to their reports.

A select committee can issue a report which is published. The government may make a published response, after which nothing is required to happen. A committee has limited powers since enforcement of its report (which the press often misleadingly calls that of a 'powerful' committee) depends on a vote of the whole House. Parliamentary Committees can take evidence on oath (Parliamentary Witnesses Act 1871). However they rarely do so and this would raise questions about the jurisdiction of the ordinary courts (Section 11.6.2).

In principle a select committee has power under Standing Orders to send for 'persons, papers and records' at any time, even when Parliament is not sitting, and failure to attend or refusal to answer questions could be a contempt of the House. As with questions, exemptions in the Freedom of Information Act 2000 apply (Section 23.2.1). The scope of these powers is unclear and enforcement would require a resolution of the House:

▶ MPs as such can be compelled to attend and produce evidence. This is explicit as regards the Committee on Standards and Privileges (SO 149(6)). Members of the

House of Lords, being protected by their own privilege, cannot be required to attend. It is not clear whether ministers as part of the Crown can be compelled to attend. In practice, because of the government's majority, compulsion is unlikely. However assurances have been given that ministers will attend and give information to committees.

▶ Civil servants attend only with the permission of ministers and cannot be compelled to speak. Their evidence is also significantly limited (Section 15.8.3).

▶ Committees have no power to demand papers from government departments. An Address to the Queen (in respect of a Secretary of State) or a formal order from the House may be required.

▶ Other persons, for example former MPs and the heads of public or private bodies, may be compellable. However this raises the unresolved issue of whether the House has power outside its own internal affairs (Section 11.6.2).

Ministers have relied on these obscurities as a means of shielding the inner workings of government from publicity, slightly tempered by a general undertaking by ministers to cooperate with committees, for example by explaining why evidence cannot be given. However the backbench composition of select committees and their practice of seeking consensus have given them a certain independent status. They have drawn public attention to important issues and have exposed weaknesses in governmental policies and procedures. Their capacity to do this may have a deterrent effect on government departments. However their reports do not necessarily lead to action or even to debate in Parliament.

13.5.4 Supervising expenditure

As we have seen, money raised by central government goes into the Consolidated Fund. The control of spending from the Consolidated Fund is the responsibility of the Commons but given the size and complexity of modern government this is clearly an impossible task for an elected assembly. In practice direct parliamentary control over expenditure is very limited. More substantial if less independent controls are imposed within the government machine itself (Section 15.6.1). These are based on a mixture of statute, royal prerogative, convention, insider networking and the inherent power of any employer to administer its workforce.

In medieval times the Court of Exchequer supervised government spending but the modern courts have relinquished this responsibility in favour of Parliament.

The courts are therefore reluctant to interfere with central government spending decisions which are subject to parliamentary scrutiny (see *Nottinghamshire CC v Secretary of State for the Environment* [1986] AC 240). However in *R v Secretary of State for Foreign and Commonwealth Affairs, ex p World Development Movement* (1995) a Foreign Office decision to give a large grant to the Malaysian government for the Pergau Dam project was set aside by the Court of Appeal on the basis that the project had no economic justification. The governing legislation required that the decision be based on economic grounds, which, crucially, the court equated with 'sound' economic grounds. This has the potential to give the courts a wide and possibly undesirable power of review. On the other hand the matter only came to light because of the intensive, adversarial process of the court. The internal process of control had not revealed the misapplication of public funds.

Spending by central departments and other public bodies related to the centre is scrutinised on behalf of Parliament by the Comptroller and Auditor-General, who reports to the Public Accounts Committee of the House of Commons. With characteristically British equivocation the Comptroller is semi-independent of the executive being an officer of the House of Commons but appointed by the Crown on a motion from the House of Commons proposed by the Prime Minister with the agreement of the chair of the Public Accounts Committee (Budget Responsibility and National Audit Act 2011, s 11). The Comptroller holds office for 10 years and cannot be reappointed. He or she can be removed only on an Address from both Houses of Parliament (s 14). The Comptroller is not directly concerned with the merits of government policy but only with the efficient and economical use of money (National Audit Act 1983, ss 6, 7). However it is difficult to separate these two concerns.

The Comptroller is supported by the National Audit Office (NAO), structured on a broadly similar independent basis (Sch 2). The NAO scrutinises the accounts of central government departments and those of some outside bodies dependent on government money, such as universities. The NAO carries out two kinds of audit. 'Certification audit' is based on financial accounting practice. 'Value for money audit' is based on the wider concerns of the 'economy, efficiency and effectiveness' of government expenditure (National Audit Act 1983, s 6). This is not meant to include the substantive merits of government policy, although the line between them may be difficult to draw. The NAO is also concerned with matters of 'regularity, legality, propriety and probity'.

The Budget Responsibility and National Audit Act 2011 puts the Office for Budget Responsibility (OBR) on a statutory basis. The OBR is intended to provide an objective assessment as to how far the government is achieving its fiscal goals (tax and public spending) and its policies for managing the National Debt. It is required to report at least twice yearly on the sustainability of the public finances. This includes making fiscal and economic forecasts and assessing whether the 'fiscal mandate' has been achieved (the fiscal mandate is the means by which the Treasury will attain its fiscal objects as set out in a 'Charter for Budget Responsibility' prepared by it (s 1)). The report must be published and laid before Parliament. Its members are semi independent being appointed and dismissed by the Chancellor of the Exchequer. The appointment and dismissal of the Chair and two other members (the Budget Responsibility Committee) requires the consent of the Treasury Committee of the Commons. At least two other members, (the Non-executive Committee) can be nominated by the Office itself. The Constitutional Reform and Governance Act 2010 Part V has introduced a technical but useful reform intended to make government accounts more transparent. The Act gives the Treasury power to direct that information be included in government accounts coordinating and aligning the different accounting methods used by government departments and designated quangos. (See House of Commons Liaison Committee, *Financial Scrutiny: Parliamentary Control over Government Budgets* (HC 2008–09, 804); Chief Secretary to the Treasury, *Alignment (Clear Line of Sight) Project* (Cm 7567, 2009).)

13.5.5 Scrutiny of delegated legislation

Most delegated legislation is detailed and y technical. It would be impracticable to subject all delegated legislation to detailed democratic scrutiny. Delegated legislation is subject to a limited degree of parliamentary control by being laid before one or both Houses for approval. Unlike a bill, the House of Commons cannot usually amend delegated legislation.

Originally the laying process was haphazard but as a result of public concern about 'bureaucratic tyranny' (see *Report of Committee on Ministers' Powers* (Cmd 4060, 1932)), limited reforms were made by the Statutory Instruments Act 1946. A statutory instrument made after the 1946 Act came into force is defined as such either if it is made by Order in Council or if the parent Act expressly provides. Thus there is no legal obligation on governments to comply with the controls in the 1946 Act. However in practice most delegated legislation takes the form of a statutory instrument.

A statutory instrument has to be laid before the House only if its parent Act so requires. The laying procedures typically require only that the statutory instrument be 'laid on the table' of the House in draft or in final form for 40 days subject to annulment by a vote of the House – the 'negative' procedure. The fate of the instrument therefore depends upon the chance of a member seeing the document and securing a debate. Some important statutory instruments are subject to an 'affirmative' procedure under which there must be a positive vote in order to bring them into effect. Such instruments are usually referred to a standing committee. There are also 'super-affirmative' forms, used occasionally, notably in connection with Quangos (Section 15.10). These require advance scrutiny by a committee and enable the House to propose amendments.

The 1946 Act requires that statutory instruments be published 'as soon as may be' unless there is a special excuse for not doing so (s 3). Failure to publish may not make the instrument invalid but provides a defence to prosecution, provided that the accused was unaware of the instrument and that no reasonable steps had been taken to publicise it (s 3(2); see *R v Sheer Metalcraft Ltd* [1954] 1 All ER 542). Failure to lay a statutory instrument before Parliament does it seems invalidate the instrument (See *R (Alvi) v Secretary of State for the Home Dept* [2012] 1 WLR 2248: code of practice under Immigration Rules (not statutory instruments but required to be laid in a similar way). Compare *R (Munir) v Secretary of State for the Home Dept* [2012] 1 WLR 2192: non-binding aspects of immigration rules not within laying requirement).

The Joint Committee on Statutory Instruments is responsible for scrutinising statutory instruments laid before Parliament. The Scrutiny Committee is not concerned with the political merits of the instrument but is required to draw the attention of Parliament to specified constitutional matters. These are as follows:

- Does the instrument impose taxation or other forms of charge?
- Does it exclude control by the courts?
- Is it retrospective without the express authority of the parent Act?
- Has there been unjustifiable delay in laying or publishing it?
- Is there doubt as to its legal validity or does it appear to make some unusual or unexpected use of the powers under which it was made?
- For any special reason does its form or purport call for elucidation?
- Does its drafting appear to be defective?
- Any other ground other than those relating to policy or merits.

There is also a House of Lords Scrutiny Committee which looks at the merits of statutory instruments laid before the House.

13.6 Redress of grievances

Members of Parliament have a duty, and Parliament collectively has a right to seek the redress of the grievances of subjects of the Crown. This flow historically from the Crown's need to ask Parliament for money, which request is granted in return for the redress of grievances.

No parliamentary time is reserved for the redress of grievances as such. An MP is able to give publicity to a grievance by placing it on the parliamentary record. Apart from that, the process is haphazard. The main procedures available are questions, adjournment debates, early day motions and, perhaps most effective, informal communications with ministers, although the latter are not always protected by parliamentary privilege (Section 11.6.3). All these suffer from the inability of an individual MP to force disclosure of information. There are other opportunities by way of the debates and motions which we discussed above but these suffer from limited time and the absence of voting. An MP can also refer a matter to the Parliamentary Ombudsman (Section 20.2).

Finally there are public petitions that members can present on behalf of their constituents (SO 153). In 2009–10, 393 such petitions were presented. The right of the subject to petition Parliament dates from the thirteenth century, reflecting the history of the Commons as a means of raising grievances with the monarch. On receipt (each petitioner's name and address must be supplied) petitions can be formally presented to the House or, most commonly, are placed in a green bag behind the Speaker's chair and read out before close of business each day. A petition can be about any subject and is published in *Hansard*. There is no formal machinery for giving effect to petitions, although they are referred for comment to the relevant department and may *provide publicity for a cause*. A petition can also be presented to the House of Lords but this is very rare, the last such occasion being in 2000. There is also provision for *E Petitions* (see HC 2006–07, 513; HC 2007–08, 136). A petition which has 100000 supporters is eligible for a Commons debate scheduled by the Backbench Business Committee albeit this may be in 'Westminster Hall' (Section 13.5.2).

These examples suggest that a sophisticated knowledge of the procedures of the House can be used tactically to some effect. However it is easy for an MP to avoid following up a complaint from a constituent by passing it to another agency. Members habitually deal with grievances outside the formal parliamentary framework, acting in effect as generalist welfare offices. A letter from an MP is likely to be dealt with at a higher level in the civil service hierarchy than would otherwise be the case.

An MP can also refer a grievance to the Parliamentary Ombudsman (Section 20.2).

13.7 House of Lords procedure

The House of Lords regulates its own procedure, which is less adversarial and party dominated than the Commons. There is also less reliance on formal procedural rules. The Speaker is elected by the House but does not have the disciplinary powers available to the Speaker of the Commons, the only power being to put a question to the vote (SO 18). The House of Lords has no power to expel a member but can suspend a member for a limited time.

Any bill other than one involving government taxation or expenditure can be introduced in the House of Lords. Such a bill is not subject to the Parliament Acts

(Section 11.4). A bill introduced in the House of Commons and passing all its stages then goes to the House of Lords. The procedure in the House of Lords is broadly similar except that the committee stage usually takes place before a committee of the whole House. The House can call upon considerable specialist expertise from among its membership even if some of it may be out of date. This is often regarded as a justification for an appointed upper house.

According to the 'Salisbury Convention' the House of Lords must respect the 'mandate' which the electorate is assumed to have given to the government in its election manifesto. The Salisbury Convention was articulated by Lord Salisbury in 1964 when the House of Lords had an inbuilt Conservative majority. However now that most of hereditary element has been ejected (Section 12.2), this is no longer the case. (See Griffiths and Ryle, *Parliament: Functions, Practice and Procedures* (2nd edn, 2003, 12–123.) The scope of the convention is therefore unclear particularly as the Parliament Acts protect the power of the Lords to delay legislation.

The Parliament Acts do not apply to delegated legislation so the House of Lords can veto a statutory instrument. However it has done so only on one occasion in the last 30 years, when it vetoed two measures relating to the election for the Mayor of Greater London, one of which would have denied free mailing to candidates (HL Deb 20 February 2000, cols 184–85). Nevertheless the House has asserted the existence of the power (see Griffiths and Ryle (above), 121–61).

Except for committees of the whole House and some minor committees, all committees in the House of Lords are select committees existing for the whole Parliament, which can therefore accumulate expertise. Select committees in the House of Lords deal with subjects rather than departments, reflecting the role of the upper house as a forum for the detailed discussion of important issues free of immediate party pressures. Reports of select committees of the House of Lords, notably those of the European Union Committee, the Science and Technology Committee and the Environment Committee, command considerable respect. On the other hand, as a consequence of the senior judges no longer being members of the House of Lords (Section 7.7.2), substantial legal expertise over a wide variety of subjects has been lost.

Ministerial accountability in the House of Lords is limited since only a minority of ministers none of them at the most senior levels sit in the upper house. Questions are normally addressed to 'Her Majesty's Government' rather than to individual ministers.

Summary

▶ Parliament does not embody a strict separation of powers, the executive being in practice the dominant force in Parliament. Parliamentary procedure is designed to ensure that government business goes through but subject to Parliament's duty to control the executive. Recent reforms have attempted to strengthen the independence of Parliament as against the executive.

▶ We outlined the lawmaking procedure as it applies to public bills and private bills. We then looked at the procedural framework within which the Commons attempts to make legislation, hold the government to account, control public finance and redress citizens' grievances.
  The timetable is largely under the control of the government, as are procedural devices for cutting short debate. However there are opportunities for backbenchers and the Opposition to intervene.

Summary cont'd

▶ There are mechanisms for approving government spending and taxation proposals and scrutinising government expenditure, notably the office of Comptroller and Auditor-General and the Public Accounts Committee. In general however the House of Commons is not equipped for detailed control of government expenditure. In recent years the emphasis has switched to internal controls over expenditure through the Treasury (Chapter 15).

▶ Other devices for parliamentary control of the executive include specialist select committees and the Parliamentary Commissioner for Administration. These devices have implications for ministerial responsibility (Section 15.7). This is because they involve investigating the activities of civil servants and they raise questions about the relationship between ministers, civil servants and the House of Commons. Select committees provide a valuable means of publicising issues but have weak powers and are subject to influence by the executive.

▶ Delegated legislation is often required to be laid before the House, although unless the affirmative procedure is used it may not get serious scrutiny. The Joint Committee on Statutory Instruments monitors delegated legislation on constitutional grounds.

▶ Procedure in the Commons is dominated by the government through its power to propose business and its control of a majority of votes. Government proposals take up most of the available time. Members of Parliament have no privileged access to government information, so their debate is not especially well informed.

▶ The House of Lords regulates its own procedure. The presiding officer does not have the disciplinary powers available to the Speaker. Its committees are valued for their expertise.

▶ The conventional assessment of Parliament is that it has become subservient to the executive, primarily because its members have capitulated to party loyalty, reinforced by the electoral system and the dual role of ministers as members of both executive and Parliament. Parliament, according to this view, is at its worst as a method of controlling government finance, poor at supervising the executive and lawmaking but better at redressing individual grievances, although this owes a lot to the work of members outside the formal parliamentary procedures. On the other hand Parliament provides a forum where the executive must defend itself in public and expose the strengths and weaknesses of its leaders. The possibility of defeat in an election may encourage members to distance themselves from an unpopular government and act as a limited constitutional check.

Exercises

13.1 'The role of Parliament is not to run the country but to hold to account those who do' Gladstone. Is this correct? To what extent does the procedure of Parliament perform this role successfully?

13.2 'As no government is more just in the constitution than that of parliaments, having its foundation in the free choice of the people ... yet such have been the wicked policies of those who from time to time have endeavoured to bring this nation into bondage that they have in all times, either by disuse or abuse of parliaments, deprived the people of their hopes. (The Large Petition, 1647). To what extent is this true today? Discuss.

13.3 'The key to democracy is the power to control public finance'. Are the powers of Parliament adequate in this sense?

13.4 A group of Opposition MPs believe that a senior government minister has been holding secret discussions with a defence equipment company concerning the possibility of engineering a uprising by anti-Western elements in an African state so as to sell weapons to the government of that state. In an answer to a question in the House, the minister denies that the government has any involvement with the state in question. Advise the group as to their chances of obtaining a thorough investigation into the matter.

13.5 Compare the strengths and weaknesses of parliamentary questions and select committees as a means of controlling the executive.

13.6 'Parliament in principle can do what it likes but lacks a mechanism independent of the party system controlled by government, in particular to initiate independent inquiries.' Explain and critically discuss.

13.8 Compare the procedures of the House of Commons and House of Lords. To what extent do these reflect the different constitutional functions of the two Houses?

13.9 To what extent can backbench MPs play an effective role in Parliament?

Further reading

Blackburn and Kennon, *Parliament: Functions, Practice and Procedures* (2nd edn, Sweet & Maxwell 2003)

Brazier, *Parliament, Politics and Law Making* (Hansard Society 2004) chs 1–6, 13

Brazier and Ram, *Inside the Counting House* (Hansard Society 2004)

Brazier, Flinders and McHugh, *New Politics, New Parliament? A Review of Parliamentary Modernisation since 1997* (Hansard Society 2005)

Daintith and Page, *The Executive in the Constitution* (Oxford University Press 1999) ch 4

Davies, 'The Significance of Parliamentary Procedures in Control of the Executive: A Case Study: The Passage of Part 1 of the Regulatory Reform Act 2006' [2007] PL 677

Flinders, 'Shifting the Balance: Parliament, the Executive and the British Constitution' [2002] Pol Stud 50

Howarth, 'The House of Commons Backbench Business Committee' [2011] PL 490

Judge, 'Whatever Happened to Parliamentary Democracy in the United Kingdom?' (2004) 57 Parl Aff 682

Maer and Sandford, *Select Committees under Scrutiny* (The Constitution Unit UCL 2004)

Nicol, 'Professor Tomkin's House of Mavericks' [2006] PL 467

Oliver, 'Improving the Scrutiny of Bills: The Case for Standards and Checklists' [2006] PL 219

Oliver 'Reforming the United Kingdom Parliament' in Jowell and Oliver (eds), *The Changing Constitution* (7th edn, Oxford University Press 2011)

Rogers and Walters, *How Parliament Works* (5th edn, Pearson 2004) chs 6–11, 13

Tomkins, 'Professor Tomkin's House of Mavericks: A Reply' [2007] PL 33

Tomkins, 'What Is Parliament For?' in Bamforth and Leyland (eds), *Public Law in a Multi-Layered Constitution* (Hart 2003)

14.1 Introduction: the nature of the Crown

We saw in Chapter 5 that UK law has no concept of the state as such and sometimes uses the notion of the Crown as a substitute. The Crown is an ambivalent concept. The ambivalence derives from the gradual evolution of the constitution from a position where the monarch personally headed the government hierarchy to one where the monarch exercises power only through others. Nevertheless the fiction persists that this power is still monarchical. The term 'Queen' is normally used to refer to the Queen acting personally, whereas the term 'Crown' is used as shorthand for the central government, for example in 'Crown property' or 'Crown immunity'.

As head of state, the Queen has the undefined responsibility of being the ultimate guardian of the constitution. No minister appears to have this responsibility. The fundamental problem about the monarchy is therefore that it is difficult to see how there can be legitimacy and public confidence in the important role of head of state where it is held by a person who is neither elected nor appointed on merit. Furthermore, as we shall see, the monarch inherits the role subject to conditions of religion and blood ties based on the controversies of the seventeenth century.

By convention the Queen must act on the advice of ministers, thereby separating the 'dignified' from the 'efficient' constitution and preventing the Prime Minister from pretensions to the role of head of state and ministers from sheltering behind the dignities and privileges of the Crown. Sir Robert Armstrong, the then Cabinet Secretary, said that 'for all practical purposes, the Crown is represented by the government of the day' (Hennessy, 1995, 346).

Thus a minister exercising powers conferred on him by statute was not to be treated as part of the Crown since to do so, as Lord Templeman remarked in *M v Home Office* (1983) at 540, would undo the consequences of the Civil War. Similarly in *R (Bancoult) v Secretary of State for the Foreign and Commonwealth Office (No 2)* [2008] the House of Lords held that it had jurisdiction to review a Prerogative Order in Council since such an order was in reality made by ministers and not the Crown itself.

The Queen is:

▶ part of the legislature, albeit by convention with no substantive powers. Her formal consent is required for an Act of Parliament and she summons and dissolves Parliament. It has been settled since the Bill of Rights that, apart from a residue of special royal prerogative powers (Section 14.6), the monarch has no independent lawmaking powers;

▶ as the Crown, formal head of the executive for the UK, the devolved governments and dependent territories. In relation to each government, the Crown has traditionally been regarded as a separate entity (cf Section 9.4);

▶ source of the authority of the judiciary, although since *Prohibitions del Roy* (1607) it has been clear that the Queen cannot participate in or interfere with judicial proceedings;

▶ as the Crown, prosecutor of criminal offences. By statute, the independent Crown Prosecution Service carries out this role under the Director of Public

Prosecutions, who is accountable to the Attorney General (Prosecution of Offences Act 1985);
- head of the Church of England;
- head of the armed forces;
- head of the Commonwealth, which is a loose association of former UK territories. The role has symbolic importance no longer especially connected with the UK but carries no legal powers.

Thus, although historically the source of all power was the Crown, a separation of powers has evolved according to which the Crown is mainly the executive arm of government.

The historical process of removing power from the monarch (Chapter 4) has left us with ambiguities and confusions concerning the legal nature of the Crown and its relationship with the executive. There is no generally accepted view (see McLean, 2004). It is not clear whether the Crown as the executive means:

- the Queen as an individual;
- or a corporate body with one member, namely the Queen – a corporation sole akin, for example to a bishop. In *Calvin's Case* [1608] 7 Co Rep 1a it was said that the Crown has two inseparable capacities, one being a 'natural' person, the other a mystical 'body politic' which is immortal (see also *Duchy of Lancaster Case* [1567] 1 Plow 325 at 327). Hence the maxim 'the monarch never dies'.
- Neither the individual nor the corporation sole theory explains the modern principle that the Crown as the executive acts through ministers. However the corporation sole theory seems to fit the Queen in her role as head of state, separating her from her private capacity;
- a kind of company together with ministers (corporation aggregate); see Maitland, 'The Crown as Corporation' (1901) 17 LQR 131, 140;
- or merely a 'brand name' with no legal identity as such. For example for purposes of civil liability the defendant is a designated government department (Section 14.5). Maitland (1931, 418) regarded the Crown (as opposed to the monarch) as a fiction, a cover for ignorance; Munro (1999, 255) as a convenient abstraction.

In *Town Investments Ltd v Dept of the Environment* [1977] 1 All ER 813 the House of Lords disagreed as to the legal nature of the Crown. The question was whether an office lease taken by a minister, using the standard formula 'for and on behalf of Her Majesty', was vested in the minister or the Crown, since in the latter case it would be immune from taxation. The House of Lords held that the lease was vested in the Crown. Lord Diplock thought that the Crown was a fiction, a legal shell overlaid by conventions. He seemed to favour the corporation sole model. Lord Simon of Glaisdale said that the expression 'the Crown' symbolises the powers of government that were formerly wielded by the wearer of the crown and reflects the historical development of the executive as that of offices hived off from the royal household. He stated that the legal concept best fitted to the contemporary situation was to consider the Crown as a corporation aggregate headed by the Queen and made up of 'the departments of state including ministers at their heads'. His Lordship added two riders (the second of which may be questionable):

'First the legal concept still does not correspond to the political reality. The Queen does not command those legally her servants. On the contrary she acts on the formally tendered collective advice of the Cabinet.' Secondly, 'when the Queen is referred to by the symbolic title of "Her Majesty" it is the whole corporation aggregate which is generally indicated. This distinction between "the Queen" and "Her Majesty" reflects the ancient distinction between "the King's two bodies", the "natural" and the "politic".'

The 'corporate aggregate' explanation may be plausible according to which the Crown is akin to a company acting through many members designated by the law, in this case through ministers (this explains not only why the Queen must act on the advice of ministers but also why the powers of the Crown are exercised automatically by ministers). (For a useful critical account see Weait and Lester, 'The Use of Ministerial Powers without Parliamentary Authority' [2003] PL 415.)

Thus it has been said that the powers of the Crown are 'channelled' through ministers, who for this purpose *are* the Crown (see *R v Secretary of State for Foreign Affairs, ex p Quark Fishing Ltd* (2006) at [12], [19], [78]–[79]). However, in *R (Bancoult) v Secretary of State for the Foreign and Commonwealth Office* (2008) at [114] the Court of Appeal turned this on its head, suggesting that ministers govern through the instrumentality of the Crown, thereby making the Crown into a kind of power drill but reflecting the reality rather better. Thus the Crown may be a redundant concept, mysticism obscuring political reality. On the other hand, in the absence of a legal concept of the state (Section 5.1), this is all we have.

Statutory powers are usually conferred directly on ministers, who cannot then claim to be acting on behalf of the Crown. In *M v Home Office* (1993) the Home Secretary attempted to rely on Crown immunity in order to deport an immigrant in defiance of a court order. The House of Lords held that he was liable in his official capacity for contempt of court. He was separate from the Crown and was not protected by any Crown immunity. In that case Parliament had conferred the power in question directly upon the Secretary of State. Sometimes however statutory powers are conferred on the Crown as such (eg Bank of England Act 1998, s 1(2): appointment of Governor of Bank). Property is often vested in the Crown as such, since not all government departments have their own legal personality.

If we were to abolish the monarchy, a different explanation would have to be found as to the basis of legal power. This could lead to a written constitution. Thus even though the role of the monarch herself is relatively insignificant, the monarchy remains the keystone of the constitution.

14.2 Succession to the monarchy

Under the 1688 settlement Parliament obtained the power to designate who shall be the monarch. The Act of Settlement is primarily concerned to ensure that Catholics are excluded from the monarchy. It provides that the Crown is to be held by the direct descendants of Princess Sophia (the granddaughter of the deposed James II). The monarch does not apparently have to be a British citizen. However there are provisions designed to prevent a monarch dragging the country into foreign disputes. If the monarch is not 'a native of this kingdom of England', any war for the defence of a foreign country needs the consent of Parliament (s 3). The holder of the crown must be or become a communicating member of the Church of England and must not be or marry a Catholic (s 3). Under the Royal Marriages Act 1772, a member of the British royal family directly descended from George II cannot marry without the consent of the monarch, subject, if over the age of 25, to an appeal to Parliament.

The rules of descent are based upon the medieval law governing succession to land. Preference is given to males over females and to the older over the younger. The land law rules required sisters to hold land equally (co-parcenaries). However in the case of the Crown the first-born prevails (although the matter has not been litigated).

The Act of Settlement 1700 might violate the Human Rights Act 1998 since it is discriminatory in relation to sex, religious freedom and the exercise of property rights (the succession being arguably a property right). The present government proposes to repeal the Act of Settlement at least to the extent of giving females equal rights to inherit the Crown.

The succession was last altered when Edward VIII abdicated in 1936 and his brother, the next in line, succeeded (His Majesty's Declaration of Abdication Act 1936). It is not clear whether the monarch has the power to abdicate without an Act of Parliament. Since monarchy is a status conferred by law and without a voluntary act, the answer is probably not. The Crown's titles are also determined by statute (Royal Titles Act 1953).

When the monarch dies, the successor immediately and automatically becomes monarch. A special Accession Council, composed mainly of members of the House of Lords, proclaims the successor. This is confirmed by the Privy Council. Whether these bodies have a power of veto is unclear. One view is that the Accession Council reflects the mythical 'ancient constitution', according to which the monarch was appointed with the consent of the 'people'. The monarch is also required to swear a coronation oath of loyalty (Act of Settlement 1700), although the Coronation Ceremony has no legal significance. It is not clear who resolves the question of a dispute to the succession. Possibly it should be Parliament in its capacity as a court or the Privy Council advising the putative monarch.

In order for succession to take place smoothly the demise (death) of the Crown does not affect the arrangements for the meeting of Parliament or an election unless the demise occurs between 7 days before the date of the dissolution of Parliament and the date fixed for the election (Section 11.2). In these circumstances the election is postponed for 14 days (Fixed Term Parliaments Act 2011 Schedule). If the monarch is a minor, ill or absent abroad, the royal functions are exercised by a regent or councillors of state. These are the persons next in line to the throne (see Regency Acts 1937–53). In such cases certain bills cannot be assented to – most importantly a bill for altering the succession to the Crown.

14.3 Financing the monarchy

The official expenses of the monarchy and of those members of the royal family who perform public duties were traditionally funded from the Civil List in return for the monarch surrendering to Parliament the hereditary income from Crown property (the

Crown Estate). The Civil List was an amount granted by Parliament at the beginning of each reign. Under the Sovereign Grant Act 2011 the Civil list is replaced by a more streamlined and transparent arrangement. This comprises a grant from the Treasury (£31 million for 2012–13) to cover the Queen's official duties: the Sovereign Grant. In subsequent years the amount of the grant is to be decided by the Royal Trustees according to a formula based on 15 per cent of the net surplus from the Crown Estate or the previous years grant, whichever is the greater. There are provisions for the grant to be renewed six months after the end of each reign. There is also a reserve fund which, if used, is deducted from the next year's grant. Income from the Duchy of Cornwall which is owned by the Prince of Wales is also deducted. The revenues of the Crown Estate are still surrendered to Parliament under the Civil List Act 1952. The accounts of the royal household are audited by the government and laid before Parliament.

Many of the royal expenses are funded directly by government departments, such as the upkeep of some Crown buildings, security, travel and entertaining political dignitaries. However, sections 11 and 13(8) of the 2011 Act clarify that the government is not responsible for the upkeep of the royal palaces. The Queen has considerable personal wealth, there being no clear line between this and assets derived from the monarchy as an institution. Even in her private capacity the Queen is exempt from taxes unless statute specifically provides otherwise. However the Queen has entered into a voluntary agreement to pay tax on current income and personal capital.

14.4 The functions of the monarch

The modern functions of the monarchy can be outlined as follows:

1. *to represent the nation*. For this purpose the monarch participates in ceremonies and public entertainments. It is often said that the popularity and public acceptance of the monarchy is directly related to the fact that the monarch has little political power and is primarily an entertainer. It is not clear why a modern democracy requires a personalised 'leader'. There is a strong element of superstition inherent in the notion of monarchy, hence the importance of the link between the monarch and the Established Church;

2. *to 'advise, encourage and to warn'*. The monarch has access to all government documents and regularly meets the Prime Minister. The monarch is entitled to express views in private to the government but there is no convention as to the weight to be given to them;

3. *certain formal acts*. These include:
   - ▶ assent to statutes;
   - ▶ Orders in Council made in the Privy Council (Section 5.7) which give effect to important decisions, laws under the royal prerogative and some statutory instruments regarded as especially important;
   - ▶ appointments of ministers, ambassadors, bishops and judges;
   - ▶ proclamations, for example dissolving and summoning Parliament or declaring a state of emergency (where the presence of the Privy Council is required);
   - ▶ ratifying certain solemn treaties;
   - ▶ awarding peerages, honours and medals.

14.4.1 Personal powers of the monarch

Apart from the award of certain honours, the monarch must exercise all her powers on the advice of or through ministers. Until after the reign of George V (1910–34), monarchs occasionally intervened in connection with ministerial appointments and policy issues. The abdication of Edward VIII (1936) probably spelt the end of any political role for the monarch. However it has been suggested that in certain special cases the monarch can and indeed must exercise personal power. There is little precedent and no principles as to whose advice she should take. Although the monarch must as far as possible avoid intervening in politics, as head of state the monarchy is the ultimate guardian of the constitution and must intervene where the normal machinery of government has broken down (see Brazier, *Constitutional Practice* (3rd edn, Oxford University Press 1999)). The most basic principle is that the government must have the support of the House of Commons.

However most of these special cases have depended on the monarch's ultimate power to dismiss the executive and dissolve Parliament, regarded by Montesquieu as an essential check and balance in the constitution (Section 7.1). This power has been abolished or at least suspended by section 3(2) of the Fixed Term Parliaments Act 2011 (Section 11.2). The monarch might however retain some power in respect of the appointment of a Prime Minister (Section 15.2). She might also refuse to appoint peers to the House of Lords if the Prime Minister asked her to do so in order to flood the Lords with his supporters. However the exercise of these powers ultimately depends on endorsement in a general election which under the 2011 Act only the House of Commons can bring about.

It has also been suggested that the royal assent to a bill might be refused. The monarch has not refused assent since 1709. However the Queen might conceivably refuse assent where the refusal is on the advice of the Prime Minister, for example, in the unlikely event of a private member's bill being approved by Parliament against the wishes of the government. Here two conventions clash. It is submitted that the better view is that she must still give assent because the will of Parliament has a higher constitutional status than that of the executive. It has also been suggested that the Queen has a residual discretion to refuse consent to a statute that violates fundamental constitutional principles (see Twomey, 'The Refusal or Deferral of Royal Assent' [2006] PL 580; Blackburn, 'The Royal Assent to legislation and the monarch's fundamental human rights' [2003] PL 205). This turns the monarchy into a Supreme Court, which seems unlikely. An internal manual required to be published by 25 September 2012 under the Freedom of Information Act, sets out a practice under which the consent of the Crown and the Duchy of Cornwall (which provides income to Prince Charles) is obtained in respect of any bill that affects their private interests (*Guardian* 1 September 2012).

14.5 Crown immunities

The Crown has special privileges in litigation. The monarch cannot be made personally liable in any court. More importantly at common law no legal action would lie against the Crown in nay of its capacities in respect of its property rights and contracts, or in respect of damage or injuries caused by the Crown (torts). This gap in the rule of law was avoided by the Crown's practice of voluntarily submitting to the jurisdiction of the courts. In the case of actions involving property and contract, this was through a procedure called a 'petition of right'. In the case of a tort, the individual Crown servant who committed the tort could be made liable and the Crown would pay the damages.

There is also the obscure maxim 'the King can do no wrong'. This means that wrongdoing or bad faith cannot be attributed to the Crown. For example the Crown at common law could not be liable for wrongs committed by its employees because unlawful acts of its employees were necessarily committed without its authority. However the maxim has never prevented the courts from deciding whether a particular action falls within the lawful powers of the Crown. Invalid acts as such are not wrongful acts (see *Dunlop v Woollahra Municipal Council* [1982] AC 158). Moreover individual Crown officers can be accused of any kind of wrongdoing.

The Crown Proceedings Act 1947 subjected the Crown to legal liability as if it were a private person for breaches of contract, for the wrongs of its servants and for injuries caused by defective Crown property. Section 1 permits action for breach of contact against the Crown; section 2 permits action in tort but only where a private person would be liable in the same circumstances. However the Act still leaves the Crown with several special privileges. The most important are as follows:

▶ No court order can be enforced against the Crown, so the claimant's right to damages depends upon the Crown voluntarily paying up. Similarly no injunction lies against the Crown or against a Crown servant acting on behalf of the Crown (Crown Proceedings Act 1947, s 21). However this applies only in civil law cases involving private rights. In judicial review cases where the legality of government action is in issue and in cases involving the enforcement of EC law ministers cannot claim Crown immunity (*M v Home Office* [1993]; *R v Secretary of State for Transport, ex p Factortame (No 2)* [1991]).

▶ In an action for breach of contract the Crown can plead 'executive necessity'. This means that it can refuse to comply with a contract where it has an overriding power to take some action in the public interest (*Amphitrite v The King* [1921] 3 KB 500; *Comrs of Crown Lands v Page* [1960] 2 QB 274). Either there must be some definite prerogative power that overrides the contract or the contract must conflict with a statutory duty. Governments cannot cancel contracts without compensation merely because of policy changes.

▶ The Crown is not liable in tort for the acts of its 'officers' unless the individual officer was appointed directly or indirectly by the Crown and paid wholly from central government funds (s 2(6)). (The term 'officer' includes all Crown servants and ministers.)

▶ The Crown is not liable for wrongs committed by 'judicial' officers (s 2(5)), that is, judges or members of tribunals. A person exercising judicial functions also enjoys considerable personal immunity (Section 8.4).

▶ Until 1987 a member of the armed forces injured on duty by another member of the armed forces or while on military property could not sue the Crown if the injury was pensionable under military regulations (s 10). This caused injustice because it was irrelevant whether or not the victim actually qualified for a pension. The Crown Proceedings (Armed Forces) Act 1987 abolished this rule but the Secretary of State can restore it in times of war or national emergency (see *Matthews v Ministry of Defence* [2003] 1 AC 1153: immunity does not violate right to a fair trial because it is a matter of substantive law not procedure).

▶ The Crown is not bound by an Act of Parliament unless it expressly or by necessary implication binds the Crown. Necessary implication is a strict notion. It is not sufficient to show that the Crown is likely to cause unfairness and inconvenience or even that the exemption is against the public interest (*Lord Advocate v Dumbarton DC* [1990] 2 AC 580). It has to be established that the statute would be unworkable unless the Crown were bound (*Cooper v Hawkins* [1904] 2 KB 164: 2 mph speed limit for tractors did not bind Crown). It is debatable whether the Crown can take the benefit of statutes where it is not bound by them. For example, the Crown can evict a tenant free of statutory restrictions, but could the Crown as a tenant resist eviction by a private landlord by relying on the same statutory rights that it can ignore as a landlord?

14.6 The royal prerogative

The royal prerogative comprises special powers, rights and immunities vested in the Crown at common law. Identifying each of these powers and their scope is problematic since there is no authoritative source. This uncertainty is a concern because as a matter of constitutional principle those exercising power should be able to identify authority justifying its exercise. The prerogative can be explained historically as the residue of the special rights and powers conferred on the monarch by medieval common law. Some aspects might also be justified in Hobbesian terms (Section 2.3.1) on the basis that a residue of discretionary power is always needed to protect the community against unexpected dangers.

Lord Denning in *Laker Airways Ltd v Dept of Trade* [1977] QB 643 considered that the Crown had a general discretionary power to act for the public good in certain spheres of governmental activity for which the law had otherwise made no provision. This interpretation is however inconsistent with the rule of law as famously invoked in *Entick v Carrington* (1765). Here the court emphatically rejected a claim of 'executive necessity' that officers of the state had a general power to enter and search private property. The better view is that although the Crown has certain discretionary powers in relation to emergencies, such as the requisitioning of property (Section 24.6.1), the prerogative comprises a finite number of miscellaneous powers rather than one general power to act for the public good.

Some prerogative powers were based upon the position of the monarch as chief landowner within the medieval feudal system. Others are inherent in the notion of sovereignty, derived from the responsibility of the monarch to keep the peace and defend the realm. This duality may have corresponded to the distinction drawn in seventeenth-century cases between the 'ordinary' and the 'absolute' prerogatives, the latter being discretionary powers vested in the King and arguably beyond the reach of the courts.

From the sixteenth century, theories of absolute monarchy became dominant in Europe but were less influential in England. Thus in 1611 it was made clear that the King could legislate only within areas of prerogative allowed to him by the existing law (*Case of Proclamations* (1611)). The debate therefore shifted to exploring the limits of the prerogative. The Stuarts attempted to extend the prerogative and to impose taxes, imprison without trial and override the ordinary law. However, even they submitted themselves to the courts and in a series of famous cases punctuating the political conflicts of the time the scope of the prerogative was inconclusively argued (Section 4.5). An issue pervading these cases was whether the king or the court decides whether the state of affairs exists that triggers the prerogative power, for example an emergency. This issue has echoes even today (eg *Nissan v A-G* [1970] Section 9.6.4). The outcome was revolution culminating in the 1688 settlement (which provides the framework of the modern law). This can be summarised as follows:

▶ In principle the royal prerogative remains but must give way to statute.
▶ No new prerogatives can be created (*BBC v Johns (Inspector of Taxes)* [1965] Ch 32).
▶ The prerogative can be controlled by the courts, although the extent of such control depends upon the type of prerogative power in question and the context (Section 14.6.4).
▶ The Bill of Rights 1688 outlawed certain aspects of the prerogative, including the power to suspend laws without parliamentary consent. The Bill of Rights also banned taxation under the royal prerogative. Modern judges have taken this further by refusing to imply a power to raise money in any way unless clear statutory language is used (see *A-G v Wilts United Dairies* [1921] 37 TLR 844: tax on milk; *Congreve v Home Office* [1976] QB 629: increase in TV licence fee *Macarthy & Stone (Developments) Ltd v Richmond upon Thames LBC* [1991] 4 All ER 897: charge for giving advice).

14.6.1   The scope of modern prerogative powers

There is no authoritative list of prerogative powers. Only the courts or Parliament can determine the scope of the prerogative. Prerogatives embrace a variety of subjects, most of the important ones concerning foreign affairs.

The main prerogative powers are as follows. (Those marked * are traditionally performed by the Queen personally, usually on the advice of ministers and sometimes in the Privy Council. Others are exercised directly by ministers.) Many domestic prerogative powers have been wholly or partly superseded by statute (Section 14.6.5).
In relation to domestic affairs:

▶ the appointment and dismissal of ministers;*
▶ the summoning, prorogation and dissolution of Parliament* (the latter superseded by statute (Section 11.2);
▶ royal assent to bills;*
▶ grant of peerages, honours and titles* (some being in the Queen's personal gift);
▶ the appointment and regulation of the civil service. A general framework for the civil service was enacted by the Constitutional Reform and Governance Act 2010 (Section 15.7);
▶ the commissioning of officers in the armed forces;
▶ security:
  (i) the Crown has a residual power to keep the peace within the realm, for example, by deploying the military or issuing the police with weapons (*R v Secretary of State for the Home Dept, ex p Northumbria Police Authority* [1989] QB 26; *Chandler v DPP* [1964] AC 763). In relation to emergencies the prerogative has largely been superseded by statute (see Section 24.6);
  (ii) to control entry to the UK (*A-G for Canada v Cain* [1906] AC 542). Recognised as one of the oldest powers of a sovereign state this has mainly been superseded by statute but may still apply in wartime (see *R (Alvi) v Secretary of State for the Home Dept* [2012] 3 WLR 2208 [27–31] (Section 14.6.5).

- the appointment of Queen's Counsel (senior barristers);
- the prerogative of mercy: releasing convicted persons from punishment (Section 7.5.3).
- the granting by the Privy Council of a royal charter to bodies such as universities, learned societies, charities or professional associations that gives the body the status of a legal person and signifies state approval of its activities (see e.g. Section 23.3). A royal charter cannot confer powers other than those possessed by private persons;
- the regulation of charities; mainly superseded by statute;
- the care of the vulnerable: children and the mentally ill; superseded by statute;
- the Attorney General's power to institute legal proceedings in the public interest and to stop criminal proceedings.

In relation to foreign affairs:
- the making of treaties;
- the declaration of war (formal declarations of war are not currently made (Section 9.6.4).
- the deployment of the armed forces on operations overseas;
- the recognition of foreign states;
- the accreditation and reception of diplomats;
- the governance of some overseas territories (Section 6.6);
- the granting and revoking of passports.

Finally there are prerogatives based on feudal landholding. The most important of these are the Crown's ownership of the seashore and tidal waters, rights to bona vacantia, that is property without any other owner, and rights over certain living creatures, notably swans.

On the whole the government apparently prefers to leave reform of the prerogative to the traditional evolutionary process. The main reforms proposed included increasing parliamentary oversight of treaties, the management of the civil service, war powers and reform of the office of Attorney General. Only the first two have so far been implemented (Sections 15.7, 9.6.1). The Public Administration Committee (above) took the view that some prerogative powers, for example, a power to press men into the navy, may have lapsed through disuse. Similarly the ancient writ of *ne exeat regno*, which prevents persons from leaving the country, is sometimes regarded as obsolete. However there is no doctrine of obsolescence in English law.

14.6.2   Two kinds of prerogative power?

There is ambiguity as to what a prerogative power is. Blackstone (1723–80), whose view seems to be technically correct, regarded the prerogative as confined to the special powers of the Crown which we have outlined above. However Dicey (1915, 429) described the prerogative as including all the non-statutory powers of the Crown, including the 'private law' powers of ownership, employment, contracting and so on apparently possessed by the Crown as a legal person in common with everyone else. These are sometimes called 'ordinary' powers, sometimes 'third source' powers or 'residual' powers (eg *Shrewsbury and Atcham BC v Secretary of State* [2008] EWCA Civ 148).

Blackstone's distinction seems unreal inasmuch as all Crown powers are important politically, and in the way they are exercised are indistinguishable from powers that Blackstone would regard as genuine examples of the prerogative. For example, the Crown has enormous economic power (sometimes called dominium power); a defence contract or health service contract made with the Crown could affect the livelihoods of millions. The Crown may be a property owner in common with others but its economic and political power surely put it in a special position and call for additional controls. There is much to be said for Dicey's view and for treating all common powers alike. It is true that the residual powers cannot directly violate individual rights but they can nevertheless have serious consequences, for example in terms of livelihood or reputation (eg *R v Secretary of State for Health, ex p C* [2000] FLR 471: creating sex offenders register).

The cases seem to support Dicey. In *Council of Civil Service Unions (CCSU) v Minister for the Civil Service* [1985] AC 374 (*CCSU*; also known as the GCHQ case) the House of Lords treated the control of the civil service as part of the royal prerogative, holding that they could review the validity of an Order in Council varying the terms of employment of certain civil servants. Lord Diplock expressed the view that the distinction between special and ordinary powers of the Crown is artificial and would regard all common law powers of the Crown as part of the prerogative. In *R v Criminal Injuries Compensation Board, ex p Lain* [1967] 2 QB 864 a government scheme to pay compensation to the victims of crime was treated as a matter of prerogative, thus enabling the court to review errors of law made by the board set up to run the scheme. The scheme was financed out of money provided by Parliament but was not statutory. Since anyone can give away money, this scheme would arguably not count as royal prerogative under the Blackstone definition.

14.6.3 Political control over the prerogative

Most prerogative powers are exercised by ministers. These powers include some that are among the most significant powers possessed by government, for example a decision to deploy troops and the power to make a treaty. The constitutional problem concerns a lack of democratic control over officials claiming to act under the prerogative. As common law powers, prerogative powers do not need to be approved by Parliament, so there is a gap in democratic accountability. Decisions taken under the prerogative are essentially decrees with no formal accountability other than the limited possibility of judicial review.

There was for instance no legal requirement for the government to gain parliamentary approval to send British troops to Iraq in 2003. However since approval was in fact sought on that occasion there may now be a convention requiring this. Whether the convention extends to the deployment of troops in a peacekeeping role as opposed to armed conflict is unclear. Similarly until the enactment of the Constitutional Reform and Governance Act 2010 there were few democratic safeguards in relation to the treaty-making power: a ministerial signature, without parliamentary approval, is all that is legally required to make a treaty (Section 9.6.1).

The absence of any statutory requirement for parliamentary approval thus raises profound questions in a modern democracy (see Public Administration Committee, *Taming the Prerogative* (HC 2003–04, 422)). The UK constitution is perhaps unique in allowing government such extensive and imprecise powers that are not granted by the legislature. In some cases however the exercise of a prerogative power must be confirmed by statute. These cases include treaties that alter the existing law and certain EU treaties (Sections 9.6.1, 10.4).

Some parliamentary control is possible, firstly because all government functions depend on money which must be authorised by Parliament and secondly through the doctrine of ministerial responsibility, although this may be after the event. These methods of control are weak since Parliament has insufficient resources adequately to investigate government spending and there is in any case normally an automatic majority for the executive. Moreover, government spending is usually authorised by a blanket departmental allocation or met out of a general contingency fund or a retrospective vote. Although conventionally ministers are responsible to Parliament, at least one Prime Minister has expressed the view that 'it is for individual Ministers to decide on a particular occasion whether and how to report to Parliament on the exercise of prerogative powers' (HC Deb 1 March 1993, col 19W).

By convention the Prime Minister cannot be questioned about advice given to the sovereign concerning certain prerogative powers, such as the granting of honours and appointments and the dissolution of Parliament. The reason is that these powers are exercised personally by the monarch even though the monarch must usually act on the advice of the Prime Minister. In addition ministers sometimes refuse to be questioned about prerogative powers relating to foreign relationships, national security matters and the prerogative of mercy. However Parliament, if it wished, could insist on investigating these. Whether their exclusion is justifiable upon any basis other than the mystique that has traditionally attached to the prerogative is debatable. They involve wide discretionary powers, but that in itself could be an argument for rather than against political accountability.

14.6.4   Judicial control

The courts have developed sophisticated rules for judicial review of the exercise of statutory powers. These do not (in theory at any rate) entitle the courts to make the government's decisions for them but are designed to ensure that government keeps within the limits of its powers and complies with basic standards of fairness, reasonableness and relevance. Is there any reason why the same should not apply to the prerogative?

Historically the courts exercised only limited control over the prerogative. If a prerogative power was disputed, a court could determine whether it existed and (if it existed) what it empowered the executive to do, but the monarch was the only judge of how to exercise the power. For example, in the *Saltpetre Case* [1607] 12 Co Rep 12 the King had the power in an emergency to enter private land and was held to be the sole judge both of whether an emergency existed and what measures to take (see *A-G v De Keyser's Royal Hotel Ltd [1920] AC 508*). Accordingly, before the speeches in the House of Lords in *Council of Civil Service Unions (CCSU) v Minister for the Civil Service* [1985] it was assumed that the courts could determine the existence and limits of a prerogative power but could not interfere with how it was exercised.

However, in *CCSU* the House of Lords held that decisions made under prerogative powers are in principle reviewable on the same basis as decisions made under a statutory power. But this does not mean that this jurisdiction will always be exercised. The power must be of a 'justiciable' nature, which means that it must be suitable for the courts' scrutiny. This is no longer resolved by looking at the source of the power (statute or prerogative) but at its subject matter and its suitability in the context of the facts of the case, the particular grounds of review and the political role, expertise and knowledge appropriate to the court.

The courts seem to be increasingly reluctant to treat any power as wholly non-justiciable and to take the view that the matter is one of judicial restraint in relation to the particular issue (Section 19.7.1). For example, in *R (Bancoult) v Secretary of State* [2008], the House of Lords held that it had jurisdiction to review a Prerogative Order in Council even though this was primary legislation made by the Queen in Council. Their Lordships were influenced by political reality in the sense firstly that such an Order was in fact made by ministers and secondly that unlike a statute it was not subject to a democratic process. However, a majority went on to hold that the Order was valid partly because its particular subject matter was not suitable for the courts to assess (Section 9.5). The majority also seemed to suggest that a clearly worded Order in Council can override a fundamental right, whereas Lord Bingham's and Lord Mance's dissenting speeches suggested that only statute can do so.

Justiciability will be considered in more detail in the context of judicial review generally (Section 19.7.1). In summary, in cases where there is a high level of political discretion without guidelines, or where there are considerations outside the proper functions or expertise of the courts the threshold of successful challenge is likely to be high. Thus a characteristically non-justiciable power is likely be a royal prerogative power, such as the power to deploy the armed forces or make treaties. Powers relating to the dissolution of Parliament and the appointment and dismissal of ministers, whether statutory or prerogative, are central to the democratic process and are unlikely to be justiciable in order to respect the separation of powers. At the other extreme a more intensive standard of review is likely in respect of routine administrative decisions (*R v Secretary of State for Foreign Affairs, ex p Everett* [1989] 1 All ER 655: granting passports).

> Other prerogative powers have been held to be reviewable. These include the powers to make *ex gratia* payments to the victims of crime (*R v Criminal Injuries Compensation Board, ex p P* [1995]), to compensate farmers affected by the foot and mouth epidemic (*National Farmers Union v Secretary of State for the Environment, Food and Rural Affairs* [2003]), to issue warrants for telephone tapping (*R v Secretary of State for the Home Dept, ex p Ruddock* [1987]) and the policy of discharging gay men from the armed services (*R v Ministry of Defence, ex p Smith* [1996]).

14.6.5 Prerogative and statute

Since Parliament is sovereign, statute can abolish a prerogative power. How easily can this be achieved in the light of the courts' approach to interpretation? Express words or necessary implication certainly do so. Problems arise where Parliament has enacted statutory provisions dealing with the same subject matter as the prerogative without clearly abolishing the prerogative powers. Where an area of governmental activity is subject both to a statutory and a prerogative power, the statutory power may supersede the prerogative power. Whether or not it does so is a matter of interpretation of the statute. Firstly it depends on whether the statute is intended to bind the Crown (Section 14.5) and secondly whether the statute is intended to replace the prerogative.

There is uncertainty as to when the statute is regarded as prevailing. In *A-G v De Keyser's Royal Hotel Ltd* (1920) the House of Lords took a wide view. It was held that where a statute comprehensively covers the same ground as a prerogative power the prerogative power cannot be exercised. The Crown took possession of the hotel ostensibly under a statute that conferred a right to compensation. It was nevertheless argued that the Crown had a prerogative power to take possession of land during an emergency and that no compensation was payable under this prerogative power. The House of Lords upheld the property owner's claim, holding that the occupation of the hotel had taken place under statutory powers. The prerogative had been superseded by a comprehensive statute regulating this field of governmental activity and it would be meaningless for the legislature to have imposed limitations on the exercise of governmental power if these could merely be bypassed under the prerogative.

However in *R v Secretary of State for the Home Dept ex parte Northumbria Police Authority* [1989] the prerogative was not overridden. The Court of Appeal held that the Home Secretary could use the prerogative power to keep the peace to supply the police with weapons even though statute gave local authorities the power to provide the police with resources. The court said that the prerogative power was overridden only when its exercise was actually inconsistent with a statutory power (see pp 44, 45).

On this basis *De Keyser's* could be regarded as an example of inconsistency. On the other hand, in support of the wide view, *Northumbria* can be explained as one where the statute did not intend to provide a comprehensive regime.

The recent decisions of the Supreme Court in *R (Munir) v Secretary of State for the Home Dept* [2012] 1 All ER 2192, [23]–[26] and *R (Alvi) v Secretary of State for the Home Dept* [2012] 1 WLR 2208 seem to support the wide view. It was held that the Immigration Act 1971 has created a comprehensive regime governing immigration so that any prerogative powers no longer apply. (The government had failed to lay statutory rules before Parliament as the Immigration Act 1972 required.)

However dicta of Lord Hope in *Alvi* [28] with whom the others agreed are ambivalent. Consistent with the wide view Lord Hope said that 'Where a complete and exhaustive power is to be found in the statute, any powers under the prerogative which would otherwise have applied are excluded entirely'. However he went on to say: '(A)ny exercise of a prerogative power in a manner or for a purpose inconsistent with the statute will be an abuse of power'(ibid).

In any case prerogative power must not be exercised in a manner which, in substance, conflicts with the intention of Parliament. In *R v Secretary of State for the Home Dept, ex p Fire Brigades Union* [1995] the Secretary of State had power to make a commencement order bringing legislation into force intended to establish a particular regime for compensation for victims of crime. It was held that he could not refuse to bring the statute into effect in order to establish a different scheme under the prerogative. However, as their Lordships remarked, the case is not strictly an example of a conflict between statute and prerogative. The statute was not yet in force and the gist of their Lordships' reasoning was that by committing himself to the prerogative scheme the minister had disabled himself from bringing the statute into force (see also *Laker Airways Ltd v Dept of Trade* [1977] QB 643: inconsistency).

It has been argued that the common law powers which the Crown shares with ordinary people (Section 14.6.2) can be extinguished only by clear statutory language, (*R(Hooper) v Secretary of State for Work and Pensions* [2006] 1 All ER 487 [46], [47] but leaving the point open; cf *Shrewsbury and Atcham BC v Secretary of State* [2008] EWCA Civ 148 suggesting the wider approach).

It is not clear whether repeal of the statute revives the prerogative power. In other words is the prerogative power abolished or merely suspended while the Act is in force? (see *A-G v De Keyser's Royal Hotel Ltd* at 539; *Burmah Oil Co v Lord Advocate [1965]* at 143), *R (Munir) v Secretary of State for the Home Dept* [2012] [33]. The point has not so far arisen. It seems to depend on the intention of the particular statute (see Section 11.2 for an example).

Summary

▶ In this chapter we first discussed the meaning of the term 'Crown'. The Queen as head of state, the monarchy, must be distinguished from the Crown as the executive. The legal nature of the Crown is unclear but the dominant view is that the Crown is analogous to a company (corporation aggregate), its members being ministers. Ministers exercise the powers of the Crown directly (see also Section 6.6).

▶ Succession to the monarchy depends on statute, thus reinforcing the subordinate nature of the monarchy.

▶ The monarch has certain personal political powers which should be exercised in times of constitutional crisis. These include the appointment of a Prime Minister, the dissolution of Parliament and the appointment of peers.

▶ At common law the Crown was immune from legal action. Some of this immunity has been reduced by the Crown Proceedings Act 1947, but the Crown is still immune from enforcement and has certain special defences. There is however no general doctrine of state necessity as justifying interference with private rights. Certain acts of the Crown give rise to immunity from legal liability.

▶ The Crown's executive powers derive from three sources:
  (i) statutes;
  (ii) the royal prerogative, that is, the residue of special common law powers peculiar to the monarch;
  (iii) powers possessed by virtue of the fact that the Crown is a legal person with basically the same rights and duties as an adult human being. The Crown can therefore make contracts, own property, distribute money and so on. There is a dispute as to whether this kind of power is part of the royal prerogative.

▶ The prerogative cannot be used to make law or raise taxation.

▶ No new prerogative powers can be created.

Summary cont'd

▶ Prerogative powers can be reviewed by the courts unless they concern a 'non-justiciable' subject matter or issue such as foreign relationships.

▶ While prerogative powers are subject to some parliamentary scrutiny, in practice political control over prerogative power is limited.

▶ The prerogative must give way to statute, although the scope and extent of this is unclear. The matter depends on the interpretation of the particular statute.

Exercises

14.1 Compare the royal prerogative with parliamentary privilege (Chapter 11), with reference to (i) its purposes, (ii) its history and sources and (iii) the extent to which it can be controlled by the courts.

14.2 Which analysis of the nature of the Crown best fits the law?

14.3 The UK has a constitutional monarchy. Explain and critically discuss.

14.4 'For all practical purposes, the Crown is represented by the government of the day' (Sir Robert Armstrong, former Cabinet Secretary). Is this a correct statement of the law?

14.5 To what extent are royal prerogative powers subject to control by Parliament?

14.6 The Railways (Suspicious Persons) Act 2012 (imaginary) gives the operators of railway stations in the UK power to remove any person from any railway premises in the UK. The Home Secretary requests Network Rail, who operates many railway stations, to ban all photographers from railway premises in the interests of 'national security'. Network Rail refuses to do so. The Home Secretary seeks your advice as to whether she can use powers under the royal prerogative to impose such a ban. Advise her.

14.7 Advise the Queen in the following cases:

　(i) There has just been a general election in the UK. The existing government has obtained the largest number of seats in the Commons but without an overall majority. The Opposition is negotiating with a minority party to form a government. The Prime Minister refuses to resign.

　(ii) What would be the position if the Opposition had obtained the largest number of seats in the Commons and the government was negotiating with the minority party?

　(iii) The government is defeated in a vote on the annual Finance Act. The Prime Minister refuses to resign.

　(iv) The Prime Minister has just been sacked as party leader. However due to an agreement with the Opposition and a minority party, he could still command a small majority in the Commons.

14.8 The Queen's birthday honours list has just been published. It includes 10 Knighthoods for retiring senior civil servants whose careers have included no recorded achievements and three of whom are related to the chair of the Honours Committee (a civil servant). There were no honours for the winners of gold medals in the recent Olympic Games. A spokesperson for the Honours Committee explains to the press that 'they were just doing their jobs'. Discuss whether there are any methods of challenging these awards.

Further reading

Blackburn, 'Monarchy and the Royal Prerogative', in Blackburn and Plant (eds), *Constitutional Reform* (Longman 1999)

Bogdanor, *The Monarchy and the Constitution* (Oxford Clarendon Press 1995)

Harris, 'The Third Source of Authority for Government Action Revisited' (2007) 123 LQR 225

Loughlin, *Foundations of Public Law* (Oxford University Press 2010) ch 13

Maitland, *The Constitutional History of England* (Cambridge University Press 1931)

McLean, 'The Crown in Contract and Administrative Law' [2004] OJLS 129

Ministry of Justice (2009), *The Governance of Britain: Review of the Executive Royal Prerogative Powers*

Public Administration Committee, *Taming the Prerogative: Strengthening Ministerial Accountability to Parliament* (HC 2003–04, 422)

Sunkin and Payne (eds), *The Nature of the Crown: A Legal and Political Analysis* (Clarendon Press 1999)

Tomkins, *Public Law* (Clarendon Press 2003) ch 3

Twomey, 'Challenging the Rules of Succession to the Throne' [2011] PL 378

Vincenzi, *Crown Powers, Subjects, Citizens* (Pinter 1998)

Chapter 15

Ministers and departments

15.1 Introduction

This chapter concerns one of the central issues of the constitution, namely the accountability of government. We shall be concerned with conventions more than with law in the strict sense. The structure and powers of the central executive depend on powers being channelled from Parliament and the Crown, usually to ministers, and upon the general principle, which combines law and convention, that ministers can exercise power through civil servants.

There are few legal controls over the organisation of government departments or the relationship between ministers, civil servants and Parliament. The size and structure of the executive has not normally been regarded as a matter of constitutional significance, although it is of course central to the role of government. The most important matters are governed by convention. This aspect of the constitution has been relatively untouched by reform, and the problems raised during the 1990s remain largely unresolved.

The Constitutional Reform and Governance Act 2010 has finally given statutory effect to the basic principles of the civil service but without changes of substance. Some general principles are published in the Ministerial Code (revised 2010) and the Civil Service Code (revised 2006). The Ministerial Code, having no legal basis, is not enforceable in the courts (*R (Hemmings) v Prime Minister* [2006] EWHC Admin 293). However the Civil Service Code is statutory and may therefore be enforceable.

The relationship between ministers, civil servants and Parliament is governed by the conventions of collective and individual ministerial responsibility but there is no consensus as to what these mean and no method of enforcing them other than by Parliament itself. While Parliament has the power, for example to call civil servants to account, it does not have the will to do so, preferring to defer to ministers, who in practice control its proceedings.

15.2 Appointment of the Prime Minister

The office of the Prime Minister, which dates from the early eighteenth century, was originally that of acting as an intermediary between the monarch and the government and chairing the Cabinet. The main principles relating to the office are matters of convention. Today the powers and influence of the Prime Minister have enormously increased so that the office is effectively that of head of the government and perhaps eclipses the Cabinet (below) as a policy maker. This reflects what appears to be a universal human desire for a personal authority figure.

The Prime Minister is appointed by the Queen subject to the following conventions:

▶ The Prime Minister must be a member of and have the support of the House of Commons. The size of the popular vote is constitutionally irrelevant but may be politically influential.

▶ As far as possible the Queen must take no initiative and must not influence the outcome. The monarch normally acts on the advice of the outgoing Prime Minister.

Although this is not a constitutional rule as such the Prime Minister is usually the leader of the political party with the largest number of seats in the Commons as determined by a general election. In the unusual case of a 'hung Parliament', where no single party has an overall majority, a leader might gain the support of the Commons by forming a coalition between two or more parties, as is presently the case with the Conservative and Liberal Democrat parties. Alternatively a minority government might be possible with the looser support of other parties.

The usual process is as follows. If the existing government has won the election the existing Prime Minister continues in office. Otherwise the existing Prime Minister approaches the Queen and advises her as to the succession, that is to appoint the candidate with majority support in the Commons. The same applies in cases where there is no general election but where the office becomes vacant owing to resignation or death or where the existing Prime Minister's party is no longer the largest party as a result of by-election defeats. The successor then approaches the Queen, who requests him or her to form the government. If there is no clear-cut successor it appears that the existing Prime Minister has the first right to try to form a government. Failing this, as in the 2010 election, informal discussions between political leaders supported administratively by civil servants, including the Queen's officials, seem to be the only mechanism for gauging Parliament's support.

In the event of deadlock it seems that the monarch must exercise her legal power to make the appointment. Unlike the position in the devolved regimes (Section 16.2.2) Parliament has no formal role in appointing the Prime Minister. However, if the new Prime Minister however appointed is defeated on a vote of confidence in the Commons then, unless by the end of 14 days there is a vote of confidence in a new government, Parliament must be dissolved and a new election called (Fixed Term Parliaments Act 2011, Section 11.2).

After an election a new Parliament meets on the date already fixed by proclamation (ibid) although the meeting could be prorogued (postponed) under the royal prerogative. There is no formal timetable for forming a government, although the practice is to act quickly. Where there is a clear election winner, any change of government is dramatically quick, taking place immediately after the election results are known. In 2010, when there was no overall majority, the process took five days.

15.3   The powers of the Prime Minister

The powers of the Prime Minister are mainly derived from convention. They are also scattered in statute, custom and practice, royal prerogatives and 'nods and winks' derived from the British culture of sycophancy. The Prime Minister exercises the most important prerogative powers. Apart from political powers (below) these include overall responsibility for security, control of the civil service and the mobilisation of the armed forces. The Prime Minister also has statutory powers in sensitive political areas (eg Police Act 1997, s 9; Intelligence Services Act 1994, s 2; National Minimum Wages Act 1998; National Audit Act 1983, s 1). In recent years Prime Ministers have also assumed control over foreign policy, which has the attraction of providing opportunities for self-promotion without the chore of detailed administration.

The main conventions that secure the pre-eminent power of a Prime Minister are as follows:

- The Prime Minister appoints and dismisses all government ministers and determines their status and pecking order. She or he also has powers of appointment in relation to many other important public posts (a mixture of statute and convention).
- By convention the Prime Minister controls the Cabinet agenda, formulates its decisions and allocates government business. In this way Cabinet discussion can be bypassed and matters entrusted to selected prime ministerial supporters, smaller groups of ministers or advisers, or indeed anyone since there are no controls over a Prime Minister taking advice. Ministers' energies are centred upon their own departmental interests. Few have the time or knowledge to concentrate upon issues outside their departmental concerns.
- Except for the unlikely event of intervention by the monarch, impeachment by Parliament or removal by his or her party under its rules, there is no formal machinery to get rid of a Prime Minister. A vote of no confidence in the House of Commons can only bring down the government as a whole.
- The Prime Minister is head of the internal security services.
- The Prime Minister is the channel of communication between Queen and government.
- The Prime Minister is the main spokesperson for the nation and in many contexts such as international meetings acts on behalf of the head of state. As such he has unique access to the media. The Prime Minister's press office holds a key position. There is a danger that, in terms of public perception the Prime Minister is perceived as a head of state, thereby eclipsing the monarchy.

There are limited checks and balances that prevent the Prime Minister using powers arbitrarily. In the main they rely on the unlikely event of the Prime Minister's supporters turning against him. Their inadequacy can be illustrated by the then Prime Minister's decision to invade Iraq in 2003, where, despite limited information being given both to the Cabinet and Parliament, a vote in the Commons endorsed the decision. The checks and balances include:

- defeat of the government in a vote of confidence in the Commons;
- the Queen's legal power to dismiss the Prime Minister as occurred in Australia in 1975. If she were to dismiss the Prime Minister she would then appoint a replacement who would be subject to a vote of confidence in the Commons (Section 15.2);
- the risk of dismissing Cabinet ministers who may enjoy political support in their own right. In practice, a Prime Minister's freedom to appoint ministers may be limited by party considerations.
- The Cabinet is full of rivals for power. the absence of a separate prime ministerial department (apart from a Private Office). However Prime Ministers may have a substantial staff of political special advisers;
- the possibility of a Prime Minister being deposed as party leader and therefore losing the support of the Commons. The influence of senior backbench MPs may be significant. The resignation of Margaret Thatcher in 1989 provides an example.

15.4   The Cabinet

The Cabinet is the policy-making body which formally coordinates the work of government departments. It comprises all Secretaries of State and includes other ministers chosen by the Prime Minister some of whom attend without membership as such. Its proceedings are confidential.

The Cabinet originated in the seventeenth century as a group of trusted Privy Counsellors called together to give confidential advice to Charles II. The term was originally one of abuse and referred to the King's 'closet' or anteroom. An attempt was made in the Act of Settlement 1700 to prevent 'inner caucuses' from usurping the functions of the Privy Council, but the provisions were never implemented and were later repealed. George I (1714–27) leaned particularly heavily on party leaders and from his reign onwards the monarch ceased to attend Cabinet meetings, substituting the Prime Minister. During the reign of George III (1760–1820) the convention emerged that the monarch should generally consult the Cabinet. The eighteenth-century Cabinets served the vital purposes of ensuring that the executive could command the support of the Commons and presenting the monarch with a united front. From a mid-nineteenth-century perspective, Bagehot regarded the Cabinet as the 'buckle' that held the government together.

The Cabinet has no legal powers as such. However statute law recognises the status of the Cabinet by protecting Cabinet secrecy (Health Service Commissioners Act 1983, s 12; Parliamentary Commissioner Act 1967, s 8(4)), and sometimes powers can be exercised only by a minister of Cabinet rank (eg Data Protection Act 1998, s 28(10)).

According to the Ministerial Code (2010) the business of the Cabinet and ministerial committees consists in the main of (i) questions which significantly engage the collective responsibility of the government because they raise major issues of policy or are of critical importance to the public and (ii) questions on which there is an unresolved argument between departments. Cabinets usually comprise between 20 and 30 ministers, including the heads of the main government departments and certain other senior office holders. Other ministers and civil servants often attend Cabinet meetings for particular purposes, notably the Chief Whip, who forms a link between the government and its backbench supporters.

Cabinet business is frequently delegated to committees and subcommittees or informal groups of ministers and other persons such as civil servants and political advisers. This is an inevitable consequence of the complexity of modern government and is an important method by which the Prime Minister can control the decision-making process. There are two kinds of formal Cabinet committees: (i) ad hoc committees set up on a temporary basis to deal with particular problems and (ii) named permanent committees, for example defence and overseas policy, economic strategy and legislation. The names and membership of these committees are published (www.cabinetoffice.gov.uk). The Butler Report (Section 15.7.1) criticised the contemporary practice of policy making by informal groups and individuals selected by the Prime Minister without written records and without the Cabinet being fully informed. Indeed the tendency to bypass the Cabinet raises the question whether the Cabinet is a convention of the Constitution or only a working practice (Section 3.4.3).

Collective Cabinet responsibility (Section 15.7.1) ensures that every member of the government is bound by decisions approved by the Cabinet whether or not the full Cabinet has discussed them. Thus it is sometimes said that the Cabinet has become merely a rubber stamp or 'dignified' part of the constitution. The secrecy surrounding the workings of the Cabinet is also an aspect of collective responsibility and makes objective analysis difficult. Other practical limits upon Cabinet power are that its meetings are relatively short (about two hours per week), its members have departmental loyalties and its agenda and procedure are controlled by the Prime Minister.

The Cabinet Office services and coordinates the work of the Cabinet and records its decisions for implementation by departments. It comprises about 100 civil servants headed by the Cabinet Secretary, who also coordinates other Whitehall committees, designates most of their chairmen and, as head of the civil service, reports to the Prime Minister. Arguably these three roles create fundamental conflicts of duty. The Ministerial Code (2010) issued by the Cabinet Office provides a general framework for the conduct of ministers which we shall draw upon in context.

15.5 Ministers

A minister is defined by section 8 of the Ministers of the Crown Act 1975 as an office holder under Her Majesty. It is for the Queen on the advice of the Prime Minister to designate the number and titles of ministers and to appoint and dismiss ministers. Some ministers have separate legal personality as corporations sole. By convention a minister must be a member of Parliament and most ministers, particularly those in major spending departments and the Treasury, must be members of the House of Commons. In principle any number of ministers can be appointed. However there are statutory limits on the number of ministers who can sit in the Commons and also the number of paid ministers in either House (Section 12.4). There are about 100 ministers, ranked as follows:

- *Cabinet ministers.* Most Cabinet ministers head departments but some offices are traditionally without departments and can be assigned to special or coordinating work by the Prime Minister. These include the Chancellor of the Duchy of Lancaster and the Lord President of the (Privy) Council. The Leader of the House of Commons is responsible for managing government business in the House. The most important departments are traditionally headed by Secretaries of State. These are the successors of the powerful officials created by Henry VIII to control the central government.
- *Ministers of state and parliamentary under-secretaries of state* (where the head of the department is a Secretary of State). The two law officers, the Attorney General and the Solicitor General, who deals primarily with internal matters, are also of this rank.
- *Parliamentary secretaries.* These are mainly recruited from the House of Commons and assist more senior ministers with political and administrative work.
- *Parliamentary private secretaries.* These are members of Parliament who act as unpaid assistants to individual ministers.
- *Whips.* The whips control party discipline and provide a channel of communication between government and backbenches. They are formally officers of the royal household. The Chief Whip is not a member of the Cabinet but attends Cabinet meetings and consults with the Prime Minister on matters such as the appointment of ministers.

By convention a minister must head each government department in order to ensure ministerial responsibility to Parliament. Ministers are often appointed for their political or parliamentary skills or for reasons of political balance and reward for loyalty. They do not necessarily have the skills, interest or experience to run complex departments. Unlike the position with most other parliamentary systems there is a practice in the UK of 'reshuffling' ministers at roughly two-yearly intervals so that only exceptionally does the same person hold office for the duration of a Parliament. During a reshuffle ministers may be sacked or reallocated and junior ministers or backbench MPs promoted. This is a prime ministerial tool to enforce party loyalty and perhaps to deflect public attention from policy failures. It also underpins incompetent government by inexperienced politicians who are likely to leave office without taking responsibility for the consequences of their failings.

15.6 Government departments

There are no constitutional requirements relating to the organisation of government departments. Most can be freely created, abolished or amalgamated by the Prime Minister. For example the Ministry of Justice was created in 2007 taking over the functions of the Department of Constitutional Affairs (created in 2003) and parts of the Home Office. This has implications for the separation of powers (Section 7.5, see *Relations between the Executive Judiciary and Parliament* HL Paper 151, para 19). The only statutory limitations concern restrictions upon the number of ministers who can sit in the House of Commons (Section 12.4) and provisions relating to particular offices, notably the Lord Chancellor (Constitutional Reform Act 2005). The Treasury also has a special position.

The organisation of departments is sometimes regarded as one of royal prerogative but could also be the right of the Crown, as of any private organisation, to organise itself as it wishes, thus illustrating a possible weakness in our non-statist constitution. In the nineteenth century committees of the Privy Council or special bodies were set up to deal with new governmental responsibilities but as the work of government increased separate permanent departments headed by ministers were created. These have been expanded, abolished, split up or combined as circumstances dictated without apparent constitutional constraints.

Some government departments and ministers, notably the Treasury and the Lord Chancellor, trace their origins back to medieval times. The other 'great offices of state' the Home Office and the Foreign Office are nineteenth-century creations of the royal prerogative. Other departments are either statutory or more commonly set up by using the prerogative to create a Secretary of State, at least in relation to his statutory powers over them. Some departments, such as the Revenue and Customs Department, have substantial administrative and financial independence, with powers conferred directly upon them. They are known as non-ministerial departments. However a minister remains constitutionally responsible for them, at least in relation to any statutory powers he possesses in respect of them.

Because English law has no umbrella concept of the state (Section 9.1), government property is sometimes held by the Crown, often through the Crown Estates Commission, and sometimes by ministers and sometimes by departments created with legal personality. This has caused problems in deciding in what capacity a given asset is held (eg *Town Investments v Dept of the Environment* (1977); Section 14.1). Provision must also be made for transferring rights and liabilities between ministers and from ministers to other agencies. Under the *Carltona* principle (Section 15.8.3) functions entrusted to a minister can be exercised by a civil servant in his own department but not transferred to other ministers or to anyone else. These matters are dealt with by standardised legislation (eg Ministers of the Crown Act 1975; Deregulation and Contracting Out Act 1994). Under the Civil Service (Management Functions) Act 2002 a minister can transfer the management of civil servants to any other Crown servant. This is intended to allow ministers to create semi-independent 'executive agencies' (Section 5.2.7). There is a curiosity that since the office of Secretary of State is in law a single office, the various Secretaries of State can interchange functions and assets without the need for legislation.

For the purposes of litigation a list of appropriate departments is maintained by the Treasury. In cases of doubt the Attorney General represents the Crown (Crown Proceedings Act 1947, s 17). Criminal cases are prosecuted in the name of the Queen.

15.6.1   The Treasury

The Prime Minister is the First Lord of the Board of the Treasury, a body that never meets. By convention the Chancellor of the Exchequer is the responsible minister. The Treasury is an overlord and coordinating department in that it is responsible for the economy as a whole, allocates finance to government departments, supervises their spending and is responsible for the tax-gathering agencies and the Bank of England.

The Treasury has special constitutional significance and its activities provide a good illustration of the mix of legal and informal controls that typify the UK constitution and make the exercise of power obscure. There is a general 'understanding', the basis of which lies in internal practices based on 'ancient authority', that the Treasury both authorises and polices departmental expenditure (see Daintith and Page, 1999, 109–26). The support of the Public Accounts and Public Administration Committees of the House of Commons also authorises Treasury power. Article 10 of the Ministerial Code requires government departments to consult the Treasury in relation to spending proposals. Thus the Treasury can strongly influence if not control the spending priorities of other departments.

The Treasury also plays the role of gatekeeper to Parliament, in which it authorises and presents government spending and taxation proposals. Parliament depends on an initiative from the Treasury since (by convention) the Crown's recommendation is required for all taxation and public expenditure. Moreover it is arguable that Parliament votes money to the Crown rather than to any particular department (Chapter 13). This gives the Treasury a powerful lever since it can approve allocations to individual departments. The Treasury fixes the overall levels of expenditure for each department and can set objectives against which the effectiveness of spending is measured. It approves spending proposals by departments either in general or in relation to especially sensitive items. Thus a strong Chancellor can concern himself with the business of every government department as a rival power centre to the Prime Minister. This was apparently the case during the Labour government led by Tony Blair, leading to confusion and hostility within the government organisation.

Treasury pre-eminence is backed by specific legal powers. Firstly the Treasury has statutory power to approve payments from the Consolidated Fund and the National Loans Fund (the government's main bank accounts) and to place limits on other sources of income such as fees and charges (Government Resources and Accounts Act 2000, ss 2, 3). Secondly the Treasury approves the form and method of the accounts of government departments (ss 5, 7). Under these powers the Treasury is in a position to decide what count as public assets and expenditure and thereby to determine the extent to which public bodies can raise private money. Thirdly the Treasury can authorise additional payments to departments (s 6) and many items of expenditure require Treasury consent under particular statutes. It is unlikely that in the absence of a plain violation of statute, matters of economic policy would be subject to judicial review (see *R v HM Treasury*, ex p Smedley [1985]: payments contrary to statute).

The Treasury appoints an Accounting Officer for each department who is responsible for the management of the department (Exchequer and Audit Department Act 1866, s 22). This is usually the head (Permanent Secretary) of the department and in the case of an executive agency, its chief executive. The Comptroller and Auditor General examines departmental accounts and reports unauthorised expenditure to the Treasury, which can either authorise it or report the matter to Parliament (Exchequer and Audit Departments Act 1921, s 1).

Under the Fiscal Responsibility Act 2010 the Treasury has certain duties to control public finances. It must ensure that the level of government borrowing is reduced year by year. After 2016 it must make an Order imposing on itself a duty to ensure 'sound public finance' (until 2016 it may do this). It must report annually to Parliament but its performance or non-performance of these duties 'does not affect the lawfulness of anything done by any person' (s 4). This formula would prevent judicial review of a failure to perform the duty, although the court is unlikely to decide what counts as sound public finance (Section 19.7.1).

The Bank of England has some independence. A statutory body, it administers the government's bank account and in conjunction with the Treasury and the Financial Services Authority regulates other banks (Bank of England Act 1998). Subject to the statutory objectives of maintaining price stability, supporting the economic policies of the government and complying with inflation targets set by the Treasury, it is responsible for monetary policy (primarily fixing interest rates) and for issuing currency. Its directors are appointed by the Crown and can be dismissed on prescribed grounds with the consent of the Chancellor of the Exchequer, and 'in extreme economic circumstances' it is subject to directions from the Treasury. The Bank is also subject to scrutiny by the Treasury Select Committee and is required to publish the minutes of its Monetary Policy Committee, an annual report and an annual inflation report.

15.6.2 The law officers

As members of the executive, members of parliament but also connected with the legal process the law officers infringe the separation of powers in respect of all three branches of government. Governed mainly by convention they occupy a vague area of dubious independence, lack of accountability and conflict of interest characteristic of the UK constitution.

The Attorney General is the chief law officer. He is assisted by the Solicitor General to whom he can delegate his functions (Law Officers Act 1997). The Attorney and Solicitor are ministers and therefore members of Parliament. Like all ministers they are appointed and dismissed on the advice of the Prime Minister. By convention if he is not a member of the Cabinet, the Attorney attends Cabinet meetings. The Attorney General has the following main functions:

▶ representing the government in legal proceedings, including intervening in any legal proceedings to put the government's view;

- giving confidential legal advice to the government. The government has no obligation to obtain independent legal advice;
- legal adviser to the House of Lords and House of Commons: another potential conflict of interest;
- political responsibility for the Crown Prosecution Service, the Serious Fraud Office and powers under various statutes to consent to the prosecution of certain offences and under the prerogative power to interfere to prevent a prosecution (*nole prosequi*);
- bringing legal proceedings on behalf of the general 'public interest', either on his or her own initiative or on the application of any member of the public (a relator action). This might include an action against a public authority including the government of which he is a member. No Attorney General has challenged his own government although there have been many proceedings against local authorities whose decisions have been contrary to central policy;
- referring questions of law to the Court of Appeal where an accused person has been acquitted of a criminal offence or requesting a more severe sentence for a convicted person'
- by tradition the Attorney is also Leader of the Bar, even though it is important that the legal profession should be seen to be independent of government.
- The law officers are entitled to consult other ministers but by convention act independently. Their claim to independence does not fit easily with their collective responsibility for government policy. The law officers may make statements but are not required to answer questions in Parliament. The Attorney's advice to ministers is confidential, a convention that has been defended by the inappropriate analogy of a lawyer's advice to a private client. Moreover the Scott Report (*Report of the Inquiry into the Export of Defence Equipment and Dual Use Goods to Iraq and Related Prosecution* (HC 1995–96, 115)) revealed an official culture in which the advice of the A-G was treated as if it had legal force, a practice condemned by the court in *R v Brown* [1993] 2 All ER 75. The Attorney General's decision whether or not to intervene in legal proceedings cannot be challenged in the courts (*Gouriet v Union of Post Office Workers* [1978] AC 435). However the Privy Council has hinted that this might be reconsidered (*Jeewan Mohit v DPP of Mauritius* [2006] UKPC 20 [21]). Thus the law officers are uniquely unaccountable.

The A-G's two roles as government lawyer and representative of the public interest are sometimes in conflict. For example in 2007 the A-G was required to obtain an injunction preventing the BBC from reporting allegations relating to the Prime Minister's Office selling peerages. We have only the predictable assertions of successive A-Gs that they can be trusted – a notion offensive at least to republicans (Section 2.5) but a recurring theme in the UK constitution.

In 1924 the government fell because the A-G acted on instructions from the government in relation to a prosecution of an anti-government journalist (see 177 HC Deb., 5s, c 10, 598–629). In 2002 the government claimed that it was lawfully entitled to invade Iraq in 2002 on the basis of advice from the A-G over which he changed his mind. His reports were never fully disclosed. Lord Bingham, a former senior Law Lord, argued that the invasion of Iraq was clearly unlawful and that the A-G's advice was fundamentally flawed (*Grotius Lecture*, British Institute of International and Comparative Law, 17 November 2008).

Recent reform proposals to make the law officers compliant with the separation of powers have not been implemented (see Select Committee on the Constitution, *Reform of the Office of A-G* (HC 2007–08, 93)).

15.7   Ministerial responsibility

Ministerial responsibility defines both the relationship between ministers and Parliament and that between ministers and civil servants. Ministerial responsibility has two aspects:

▶ Firstly all members of the government are collectively responsible to Parliament for the conduct of the government.
▶ Secondly each minister is individually responsible to Parliament for the conduct of his or her department.

Ministerial responsibility developed during the eighteenth and nineteenth centuries, corresponding to the rise of the House of Commons and the decline in the power of the Crown. Its original purpose was as a weapon against the monarch by achieving coherence among politicians with divergent views. Ministerial responsibility is a matter of convention, although it is recognised by the law (eg Freedom of Information Act 2000, s 36(2)(a)(i); Section 23.2.1).

While the rule of law might be the cornerstone of the legal constitution, ministerial responsibility is the cornerstone of the political constitution. Ministerial responsibility in a broad sense gives the constitution a republican element (Section 2.5). However it is arguable that the doctrine is so nebulous and so damaged by executive domination of Parliament that it currently has little value as a constitutional principle.

Parliament may from time to time make grand pronouncements in favour of ministerial responsibility but these are seldom translated into action (see Tomkins, 2003, 134, who is more optimistic). In particular Tomkins identifies three 'fault lines' in the doctrine. These are firstly a lack of openness in government; secondly 'ownership', in the sense that the government itself can influence the meaning and enforcement of the doctrine; and thirdly, and most importantly, the pressures of party domination. These work together to weaken Parliament.

'Responsibility' is sometimes used interchangeably with 'accountability'. Both terms have a range of meanings (see Public Service Committee, Second Report (HC 1995–96, 313) paras 14–21, 32). They include obligations to provide explanation, information, acknowledgement, review and redress. Sometimes resignation may also be expected. The particular combination appropriate to any given case depends on the circumstances. In addition to ministerial responsibility as such, there are instruments such as the Freedom of Information Act 2000, the Codes of Conduct for MPs and civil servants and the *Guidance to Officials on Drafting Answers to Parliamentary Questions* which inform the notion of openness and accountability. More generally the openness and accountability of government is required by the fourth and fifth Principles of Public Life, namely accountability and openness, set out by the Committee on Standards in Public Life (Section 5.9).

Ministerial responsibility does not mean that Parliament (except through a statute) can give orders to ministers or lay down policies. Parliament does not itself govern and to this extent there is a separation of powers. Ministerial responsibility means only that ministers must discharge their duties in a manner that has the continued support of the Commons and they must give an account of their actions and decisions. If the Commons so votes on a motion of confidence, the government collectively must resign.

Opposition MPs as well as those of the minister's own party influence ministers in their decisions and exert pressure for changes in government policy. Ministerial responsibility also provides information to arm opponents in the adversarial conduct of British political debate. Indeed it is a characteristic of the parliamentary system of government that there is a continuing struggle on the part of MPs to gain more information than ministers are willing to provide.

On its face the convention can be acclaimed as a device to ensure accountable government. An alternative view is that the convention favours 'strong' government because it allows ministers to govern with little effective parliamentary supervision or interference since Parliament has neither the will nor the resources to hold ministers effectively to account (see Flinders, 2000). Ministerial responsibility may also be out of line with the practices of modern government, in particular the techniques of privatisation and devolved public management. In this context the convention actually shields government from public accountability because the impugned decision may have been taken in an agency that has been hived off from central government. Although in principle the minister remains fully responsible, the vague meaning of responsibility enables ministers more easily to evade blame the further away they are from the location of decision making. The party system and the tradition of secrecy within the civil service have also played a part in breaking the chain of accountability through Parliament to the electorate.

15.7.1 Collective responsibility

Collective responsibility applies to all government ministers. It was developed originally so that government and Parliament could put up a solid front against the King. It suggests collegial government that is at odds with the legal basis of government with powers given to individual ministers. Collective responsibility has four aspects:

1. It requires all ministers to be loyal to the policies of the government whether or not they are personally concerned with them (solidarity). Collective responsibility therefore applies even though many important decisions are made elsewhere and are not fully discussed by the Cabinet as a whole. Resignation is required before a minister can speak out on a particular issue. Nevertheless as a convention collective responsibility may be adapted to new circumstances. The Prime Minister can apparently modify it over a particular issue (such as membership of the EEC in 1975).
2. It requires the government as a whole to resign if it is defeated on a vote of confidence in the House of Commons or if the Prime Minister resigns.
3. It requires that Cabinet and government business be confidential (see Ministerial Code (2005) para 6.17).
4. It protects ministers against personal responsibility since collective responsibility can be used to justify individuals' avoiding blame. For example the Butler Report into intelligence failures relating to Iraq (*Review of Intelligence on Weapons of Mass Destruction: Report of a Committee of Privy Counsellors* (HC 2004, 898)) absolved all

ministers and civil servants from blame for misleading the public on the basis that the various falsehoods were 'collective'. (Butler himself was a former head of the civil service.) Collective responsibility and individual responsibility (Section 15.7.2) are therefore in conflict.

The drastic sanction of a vote of confidence is the only method by which Parliament can enforce collective responsibility but governments have rarely been defeated in this way in modern times. In 1924 Ramsay MacDonald's Labour government resigned, and in 1979 so did James Callaghan's Labour government. Both were minority governments.

The relationship between Prime Minister and Cabinet has an important impact on how well collective responsibility works in practice. The collegial model of government, which emphasises the participation of all Cabinet ministers in decision making, disguises the dominance of the Prime Minister in the formulation of policy, which tends to blur the difference between a parliamentary and a presidential system. There are no formal checks and balances. The extent to which the Prime Minister can exercise an authoritarian style depends on the composition and mood of the Cabinet, the attitude and cohesion of the party and of the Commons, the temper of the electorate and not least the personal style of the Prime Minister. If undue reliance is placed on a select group of senior ministers (the 'inner cabinet') or unelected 'cronies', if too many 'private deals' are struck with individual ministers or if too many controversial policies are effectively formulated in Cabinet subcommittees, ministers may feel less inclined to loyalty. Serious embarrassment can result where senior ministers resign, having concluded that the workings of the Cabinet have strayed unacceptably far from the collegial model. Michael Heseltine resigned during the Westland affair in 1986. Similarly Geoffrey Howe's resignation over EC policy in 1990 resulted from his concern about the Prime Minister's apparent distaste for collective decision making. This resignation played a pivotal role in ending Mrs Thatcher's tenure of No 10 Downing Street in 1990.

It could be argued that collective responsibility is no different from the solidarity expected within any organisation. Ministers can discuss policy differences in private, confident that all will support the decision which is eventually reached. The presentation of a single view also adds authority to the government's position because it disguises the coalition nature of many governments. This argument begs the question whether government can be compared with, say, a large private sector company. Given that an important value of democratic government is to manage disagreement without suppressing it, it may be desirable for government not to speak with a single voice but to recognise the provisional nature of any decision reached. It can also be argued that the doctrine of collective responsibility could contribute to a general public disenchantment with politics if ministers were seen to vote in support of policies they were believed not to support.

15.7.2   Individual responsibility

Sir Edward Bridges, the Permanent Secretary to the Treasury, expressed the classical interpretation of the doctrine of individual responsibility in 1954, after the Crichel Down affair (see Public Service Committee, Second Report (HC 1995–96, 313) para 8). He stated that a minister is responsible to Parliament for the exercise of all executive powers and every action taken in pursuance of those powers. This emphasises that a minister must always answer questions and give a full account of the actions of his or her department. This is so whether or not the minister is personally at fault for what has gone wrong and has been subject to only limited exceptions, related among other things to commercial confidence, national security and some macroeconomic issues.

Individual ministerial responsibility is concerned with a chain of accountability from Parliament through ministers to civil servants. Ministerial responsibility protects civil servants from direct public responsibility since they owe their loyalty to the government and especially to the minister in charge of their department. Thus civil servants appear before Parliament only with the permission of ministers and on terms set by ministers.

Beyond that, its meaning and scope are unclear: firstly in respect of what 'responsibility' entails and secondly in respect of what actions the minister is responsible for. Ministerial responsibility is primarily enforced by Parliament. Most specifically it requires that ministers provide information to Parliament by means of answers to parliamentary questions, evidence to select committees, formal ministerial statements and letters to MPs. Within the executive the Prime Minister is responsible for enforcing ministerial responsibility and therefore, indirectly, for defining it.

Ministers are certainly responsible for their departments, less clearly so in relation to executive agencies sponsored by their departments. There does not seem to be direct responsibility for non-ministerial government departments or for quangos, although in both cases ministers are responsible for their specific functions in relation to these bodies (Sections 5.7, 5.8).

Ministers have attempted to limit their responsibility by making various distinctions and by seeking to ensure that their civil servants are not subject to direct scrutiny by Parliament. On the whole Parliament has pandered to ministers in these respects rather than asserting its undoubted right to have the last word.

Firstly it has been claimed that responsibility applies only to 'policy' matters as opposed to 'operational' matters, which are deemed to be failures properly to implement policy. This has been particularly evident following the radical restructuring of government in the 1990s, with the majority of civil servants working in semi-detached executive agencies under the day-to-day direction of chief executives with only limited departmental control (Section 15.8). This restructuring has tended to confuse lines of accountability. In *Williams v Home Office (No 2)* [1981] 1 All ER 1151 the court drew a distinction between acts done by civil servants in the exercise of statutory functions conferred on ministers and routine management matters, saying that the latter are not to be regarded as the act of ministers. This is questionable in terms of the traditional doctrine of ministerial responsibility but perhaps represents a more realistic view of the nature of modern government.

Similar problems arise where a quango (Section 15.9) stands between the minister in charge of policy formulation and the delivery of a service. It seems however that ministers do not always escape blame where serious errors occur in such cases (see McCaig, 'School Exams: Leavers in Panic' (2003) 56 Parl Aff 471).

The policy/operational dichotomy is a vague one. Indeed the two are often inextricably interconnected. The effect has been to make it more difficult for Parliament to find out who is to blame when problems arise. For example is prison overcrowding policy or operation? Thus ministers can exploit confusion by intervening where they perceive electoral gains, as in the events leading up to the dismissal of Derek Lewis, the head of the prison service, following allegations of interference by the Home Secretary in the detailed administration of the service (see *Review of Prison Service Security in England and Wales and the Escape from Parkhurst Prison on Tuesday 3rd January 1995*

(Cm 3020, 1995) (the Learmont Report); Report of the House of Lords Public Service Committee (HL 1997–98, 55) para 341).

Ministers may also interfere in 'operational' matters while declining to answer questions about them, claiming that such matters fall within the responsibility of the chief executive. Moreover, since it is the minister who decides what is policy and what is operation, ministers can effectively determine the extent of their constitutional responsibilities. The House of Lords Public Service Select Committee concluded that it was not possible effectively to separate policy from operations and that such a division was not desirable (HL 1997–98, 55, para 348).

Secondly ministers have distinguished between 'accountability' and 'responsibility'. This seems to divorce the circumstances in which a minister must give to the House an explanation of the actions of his department (accountability) from cases in which a minister must accept the blame for departmental mistakes and resign (responsibility). In *Taking Forward Continuity and Change* (Cm 2718, 1995, 27–28) the government stated that Parliament can always call a minister to account for all that goes on in his department but it added that a minister cannot be responsible in the sense of having personal knowledge and control of every action taken and cannot be personally blameworthy when delegated tasks are carried out incompetently or errors of judgement are made at an operational level. Coupled with this is a reluctance by ministers to subject civil servants to independent scrutiny, thereby creating an 'accountability gap' (Section 15.8.3).

The accountability/responsibility distinction was rejected in 1996 by the Public Service Committee of the Commons (above) but accepted by the Scott Report on the Arms to Iraq affair (HC 1995–96, 115). It demands that ministers be prepared to offer a complete explanation of any error to Parliament but not to take the blame. The duty embraces an obligation to offer reasons by way of justification in the face of criticism. Experience reveals however that ministers have not always been willing to give a full account of their actions. Notoriously the conclusion of the Scott Inquiry was that there were numerous examples of ministers failing to give full information about the policies, decisions and actions of government regarding arms sales to Iraq (HC 1995–96, 115, K8.1, para 27) and that this had undermined the democratic process (D4.56–D4.58). Answers to parliamentary questions in the affair had been 'designedly uninformative' because of a fear of adverse political consequences if the truth were revealed (D3.107).

Following revelations of this kind, it became clear that there should be a renewed commitment to the doctrine of individual responsibility combined with a need to clarify the obligations entailed by it, and in particular to ascertain the matters about which ministers must answer questions. This led to resolutions of the House of Commons and House of Lords on ministerial accountability (HC Deb 19 March 1997, vol 292, cols 1046–47; HL Deb 20 March 1997, cols 1055–62).

These resolutions led to the adoption by the government of the Ministerial Code (2010), which now incorporates a 'Ministerial Code of Ethics'. The Code sets out the following principles of ministerial conduct (which are mostly in the terms of the resolutions):

1. Ministers must uphold the principle of collective responsibility.
2. Ministers have a duty to Parliament to account, and be held to account, for the policies, decisions and actions of their departments and Next Steps agencies.

3. It is of paramount importance that ministers give accurate and truthful information to Parliament, correcting any inadvertent error at the earliest opportunity. Ministers who knowingly mislead Parliament will be expected to offer their resignation to the Prime Minister.
4. Ministers should be as open as possible with Parliament and the public, refusing to provide information only when disclosure would not be in the public interest, which should be decided in accordance with the relevant statutes and the Freedom of Information Act 2000.
5. Ministers should similarly require civil servants who give evidence before parliamentary committees on their behalf and under their direction to be as helpful as possible in providing accurate, truthful and full information in accordance with the duties and responsibilities of civil servants as set out in the Civil Service Code.

However there is no independent method of enforcing the Code, which has no legal force. It states that it is not an enforceable rule book (para 1.3). It is not policed by the Cabinet Secretary or by the Parliamentary Committee on Standards since this has jurisdiction only over MPs as such. Part 1 of the Code reminds ministers that they can only continue to hold office for as long as they have the support of the Prime Minister. The Code states that the Prime Minister 'is the ultimate judge of the standards of behaviour expected of a Minister and the appropriate consequences of a breach of those standards'. This suggests that the Code envisages that the Prime Minister is both a setter of standards and responsible for their enforcement. For that reason the statement reads rather oddly in the light of the resolutions.

The respective resolutions of each House are of fundamental importance because ministerial responsibility is no longer an unwritten convention which can be varied at will by the government of the day; ministerial responsibility is now a rule of Parliament. The terms of the resolutions are not however without difficulty. As Woodhouse (1997) observes, satisfying them may not be unduly burdensome. Ministerial judgement will still govern what it means to be 'as open as possible' and when disclosure 'would not be in the public interest'. This means that the problems of interpretation remain and that the doctrine of ministerial responsibility is still somewhat elusive. However, subject to substantial exceptions, the Freedom of Information Act 2000 gives legal backing to requests for information from ministers (Section 23.2.1).

15.7.3 Ministerial resignation

Ministerial resignation engages both collective and individual responsibility. This is because where resignation takes place it saves fellow ministers from having to offer support for the beleaguered minister under the principle of collective responsibility. One interpretation of the convention is that resignation is required for every serious departmental error regardless of the personal blame of the minister. Characteristically of conventions, such a convention if it ever existed seems to have been destroyed by disuse. The Crichel Down affair (Cmd 9220, 1954), which involved serious civil service misconduct in relation to government confiscation of land, was once thought to have required resignation. However, Sir Thomas Dugdale's resignation in that case probably owed more to political misjudgement and a lack of parliamentary support. Lord Carrington resigned as Foreign Secretary in 1982 when his department failed to spot the invasion of the Falkland islands by Argentinia.

It seems that resignation is only constitutionally required in three categories of cases:

1. where a minister has knowingly misled Parliament (except in the very limited cases where this is justified: Public Service Committee, Second Report (HC 1995–96, 313) para 32). However an honest even though unreasonable belief in the accuracy of information given to Parliament can be a lifeline to beleaguered ministers. The Scott Inquiry found that William Waldegrave unreasonably clung to the view that government policy governing the sale of arms to Iraq had not changed (HC 1995–96, 115, D4.1–D4.7) but Waldegrave did not resign. Similar questions arose after Lord Falconer's refusal in 2001 to resign in respect of the funding and sale of the Millennium Dome;

2. where the minister is personally to blame for a serious departmental error (Sir Richard Butler in evidence to the Scott Inquiry, 9 February 1994, Transcript 23–24);

3. in the case of personal dishonesty or wrongdoing, at least when the minister is politically vulnerable. Examples include David Laws in 2010 for breaching rules on MPs' expenses at a time when the matter was the subject of considerable public agitation. Private misconduct unrelated to a minister's duties might also lead to resignation but perhaps only where the minister becomes politically vulnerable. Woodhouse argues that personal indiscretions are relevant because they affect the public credibility of the minister concerned ('Ministerial Responsibility in the 1990s: When Do Ministers Resign?' (1993) 46 Parl Aff 277).

However, raw politics including the support of the Prime Minister and media attention rather than constitutional obligation may be the best explanation of ministerial resignations. For example David Laws' resignation in 2010 involved a technical breach of expenses rules but in circumstances of massive public anger at MPs' conduct generally.

15.8 The civil service

The civil service is a professional, permanent and independent part of the executive. Its purpose is to assist the government in formulating its policies, to carry out decisions of the government and to administer services for which the government is responsible. More broadly the civil service being an institution independent of changing governments gives the constitution continuity and stability and is a source of expert advice and 'institutional memory'. In the last resort where ministers fail the civil service must keep the government functioning.

The civil service might also be regarded as another form of separation of powers, providing a check and balance against politicians. However civil servants have no constitutional status or independent powers of their own but can exercise powers only channelled from ministers. In some countries notably the USA the senior civil service is overtly political its leaders being appointed in accordance with the preferences of the President. In the UK attempts are made to protect the independence of the civil service. However in accordance with UK constitutional culture these have not until recently been backed by law.

There is no meaningful legal definition of a civil servant. The Constitutional Reform and Governance Act 2010 following the Tomlin Commission on the Civil Service (1931) (Cmnd 3909) unhelpfully refers to 'the civil service of the State'. This may include every person who serves the Crown other than the military, ministers holding political offices and holders of judicial offices. The armed forces are of course also Crown servants but are subject to a distinctive legal regime. The police are not civil servants because they are not employed by the Crown. Thus the definition of a civil servant is partly negative, meaning a Crown servant other than those falling into special categories (see Sandberg, 'A Whitehall Farce? Defining and Conceptualising the British Civil Service', 2006, *Public Law* 653). About 3000 civil servants (5% of the whole: the Senior Civil Service) are responsible for policy making. The remainder are responsible for service delivery either in executive agencies or non-ministerial departments (Section 15.9).

Management of the civil service is currently vested in the Minister for the Civil Service, currently Sir Bob Kerslake who also heads the Department of Communities and Local Government. The Treasury also has powers over the civil service. Each department is managed by its Accounting Officer usually of the highest rank of Permanent Secretary. The Accounting Officer's activities can be examined by Parliament by means of the Public Accounts Committee and the Comptroller and Auditor-General. According to the Ministerial Code (Art 5.4) the accounting officer is personally responsible for the department thus raising the question of ministerial responsibility (below).

There is tension from two directions. On the one hand the civil service must offer impartial advice and expertise to governments of all political colours (Civil Service Code 2006, paras 1, 13). On the other hand it is required loyally to carry out government instructions. The argument that UK civil servants should have wider duties to the Crown as distinct from duties to the government of the day has not succeeded (see House of Commons Public Services Committee, Ministerial Accountability and Responsibility, HC 313, 1995–6, para 169).

Ministers (perhaps weak ones) may therefore complain that they are dominated or subverted by their civil servants. Civil servants may complain about political interference with the impartiality and influence of the civil service. These tensions are particularly acute in connection with a kind of civil servant known as a Special Adviser. Special advisers are party political advisers appointed directly by ministers and working closely with them. They were formally recognised by a government announcement in 1974 but have probably always existed. They are temporary civil servants appointed for the purpose of providing 'assistance' to ministers, a purpose which goes beyond advice (Constitutional Reform and Governance Act 2010, s 15). Unlike other civil servants they are not required to be impartial or objective and they need not be appointed on merit by fair and open competition. There is no legal limit on the number of special advisers. In June 2010 there were 68 posts attached to UK government ministers, 14 of them in the Prime Minister's office. Special advisers lose their posts when their minister does so or after a general election.

Special advisers are therefore a link between the political and the permanent parts of the government. There has been concern that their activities, particularly in relation to communication with the media, may threaten the reputation of the civil service for impartiality. There is also a concern that permanent civil servants may be denied access to ministers and their role will be reduced to carrying out orders from special advisers (see Report of Select Committee on Public Administration (2001) HC 293 and HL Deb 7 Nov 2005 col 482–98, Sixth and Ninth Reports of the Committee on Standards in Public Life (2000, Cm 1817, 2003 Cm 5964).

The position of special adviser has been put on a statutory basis by section 15 of the Constitutional Reform and Governance Act 2010, which applies to the UK government and to the devolved governments of Scotland and Wales. The powers of special advisers have been constrained (below). However accountability has not been increased other than by requiring an annual report to Parliament concerning the number and cost of special advisers (s 16).

15.8.1 The statutory framework

Following persistent recommendations by the Committee on Standards in Public Life (see Ninth Report, 2003, Cm 5775) the Constitutional Reform and Governance Act 2010 enacted the a framework of principles regulating the civil service. This replaces the previous mixture of royal prerogative rules and conventions. The Act does not however remove the royal prerogative power to regulate the civil service (see *Civil Service Order in Council* 1995, as amended; *Civil Service Management Code*; *Civil Service Code*, revised 2006). The 2010 Act does not apply to the Security Services, the Northern Ireland Civil Service nor to civil servants serving wholly outside the UK.

Most importantly the Act has nothing to say about the detailed relationship between civil servants, ministers and Parliament so that the disagreements surrounding these conventions remain (see Institute for Public Policy Research (2006), recommending a statutory framework).

The main provisions of the Act are as follows:

▶ The Civil Service Commission previously existing under the royal prerogative is established as a corporate body with its own legal identity. The Commission hears complaints relating to violations of the Civil Service Code, disciplinary and recruitment matters but has no enforcement powers. It also monitors recruitment practices (ss 2, 9, 11, 12, 14). It is directly involved with senior civil service appointments.

▶ Managers must have regard to the need to ensure that civil servants who advise ministers are aware of the constitutional significance of Parliament and of the conventions governing the relationship between Parliament and Government (s 3). Unfortunately the Act does not state what these are.

▶ The Civil Service Code must be published and laid before Parliament (s 5). The code must require civil servants to carry out their duties with integrity, honesty, objectivity and impartiality. However special advisers need not be objective or impartial (s 7). In addition the *Ministerial Code* (2010) which is not statutory, requires ministers to uphold the impartiality of the civil service and to give due consideration to its advice.

▶ The Minister for the Civil Service must publish a Special Adviser's Code which must be laid before Parliament (s 8). Special advisers cannot authorise expenditure from public funds nor manage other civil servants, except other special advisers, nor exercise statutory or prerogative power (s 8(5)). This of course raises the question whether the 'ordinary' common law powers of the Crown such as contractual powers should be regarded as prerogative powers (Section 14.6.2). A special adviser must be appointed by the minister personally, subject to the approval of the Prime Minister (s 15). The terms of the appointment require the consent of the Minister for the Civil Service.

15.8.2 Recruitment

Civil servants, other than special advisers, short term appointments and statutory Crown appointments such as the Governor of the Bank of England, must be appointed by a fair and open competition (Constitutional Reform and Governance Act 2010, s 10). Specific qualifications for appointment are prescribed by a Recruitment Code made under the Civil Service Order in Council and published in the Management Code (above). Normally only a Commonwealth citizen, a British Protected Person or a citizen of the Republic of Ireland can be appointed.

The recruitment process is supervised by the Civil Service Commission which must publish 'recruitment principles' (s 11). These can create further exemptions from the open competition requirement, for example when someone with a particular expertise or experience is needed. In such cases the Commission must approve the appointment and can participate in the appointment process. In the case of senior appointments ministers can be consulted but by convention do not make the decision. Senior appointments must be approved by the Civil Service Commission. However some senior appointments are approved by the Prime Minister and the head of a department (Permanent Secretary) is appointed by the Prime Minister in all cases on the advice of the Head of the Home Civil Service.

Ministers can appoint anyone they wish to advise them outside the civil service, there being no safeguards in place. For example in 2010 Lord Browne, a former chairman of BP, was asked to advise the Prime Minister in relation to reducing the costs of running the executive. There was no formal appointment process nor apparently any element of competition. It is arguable that business persons are unlikely to be successful government appointees often being unfamiliar with the practices of consultation, openness and detailed accountability that are desirable in a democracy.

15.8.3 Legal status

According to one view, a civil servant being subject to the royal prerogative has no contract of employment and cannot enforce the terms of his employment other than those laid down by statute. At common law the Crown can dismiss a civil servant 'at pleasure', that is, without notice and without giving reasons (*Dunn v R* [1896] 1 QB 116). This is consistent with the view that there is no contract. On the other hand it has been held that there can be a contract between the Crown and a civil servant but that as a matter of public policy the contract can be overridden by the Crown's power to dismiss the civil servant at pleasure (*Riordan v War Office* [1959], 3 All ER 552). On this second analysis other terms of employment such as pay and conditions are enforceable against the Crown.

Modern cases have stressed that there is no inherent reason why the relationship cannot be contractual (see *Kodeeswaren v A-G for Ceylon* [1970] AC 1111; *R v Civil Service Appeals Board ex parte Bruce* [1988] 3 All ER 686; *R v Lord Chancellor's Dept ex parte Nangle* [1992] 1 All ER 897). The Employment Act 1988 deems there to be a contract between the Crown and a civil servant for the purpose of making a civil servant liable for industrial action (s 30). Indeed senior civil servants are required on appointment to enter into a written contract with specified periods of notice (*Civil Service Management Code*). However the Crown can probably still dismiss at pleasure and a contractual term which says otherwise is not enforceable. This can be regarded as a matter of public policy.

15.8.4   Discipline

Civil servants like other citizens may be protected by judicial review. However in *Nangle* (above) it was held that judicial review did not apply to internal disciplinary decisions unless a formal adjudicative process is involved (but see *Bruce* (above) and *R v Civil Service Appeals Board ex parte Cunningham* [1991] 4 All ER 310). Moreover internal remedies must be used before resorting to the courts. Most civil servants are also protected by statutory unfair dismissal rules administered by industrial tribunals (Employment Rights Act 1996 s 191).

Special machinery applies to security issues. A minister can, by issuing a certificate, remove any category of Crown employee from the employment protection legislation on grounds of national security (Employment Rights Act 1996, s 193). A civil servant who is suspected of being a security risk is given a special hearing, but without the normal rights of cross examination and legal representation, before a panel of 'three advisers'. These usually comprise two retired senior officials and a High Court judge.

Problems arise when a civil servant considers that his or her integrity is compromised, for example by being required to act for politically partisan purposes or possibly to break the law. Obeying the orders of a superior is not a defence in English law. The orthodox doctrine is that civil servants owe an absolute duty of loyalty to ministers (above) and the Civil Service Code imposes a lifelong duty not to disclose official information without authority.

There are internal mechanisms to enable civil servants to express issues of conscience. These include a right of appeal to the independent Civil Service Commission (above) and special provisions relating to the Official Secrets Act (Chapter 21). Judicial review may also be available.

Civil servants cannot be members of Parliament (House of Commons (Disqualification) Act 1978). The political activity of civil servants is also restricted according to the level of the individual in the policy making hierarchy. The majority are unrestricted except while on duty or in uniform or on official premises. An 'intermediate' group can take part in political activities with the consent of their head of department. This includes clerks, typists and officials performing specialist non-political jobs. A 'restricted' group of senior officials directly involved in policy making cannot take part in national politics at all but can indulge in local politics with the consent of their head of department. However whole departments can be exempted. Civil servants are also prohibited from taking gifts or doing other things that could create a conflict between their private interests and their official duties. A retired civil servant requires government approval before accepting employment with private sector organisations that are likely to have dealings with the government (see *Civil Service Pay and Conditions Code*, Fifth Report of Treasury and Civil Service Committee, HC 1989–90).

15.8.5   Civil servants and ministerial responsibility

Under the *Carltona* doctrine (*Carltona v Comr for Works* [1943] 2 All ER 560) a minister can lawfully exercise any of his statutory powers through a civil servant in his department and need not personally exercise any power unless statute specifically so requires (eg Immigration Act 1971, s 13(5); Regulation of Investigatory Powers Act 2000, s 59). The decision remains that of the minister – the civil servant and the minister being indivisible in law (see also *Bushell v Secretary of State for the Environment* [1981] AC

75; *R (Alconbury Developments Ltd) v Secretary of State for the Environment, Transport and the Regions* [2001]). The *Carltona* principle does not apply to delegation to other departments nor outside the civil service. Thus statute is required to give a minister wider powers of delegation (eg Extradition Act 2003, s 101: decisions to senior officials in civil and diplomatic services).

The classical doctrine has been that as civil servants have no powers of their own and so cannot take decisions or do anything except and insofar as they are subject to the direction and control of ministers, a civil servant has no direct responsibility to Parliament and cannot be called to account by Parliament. Civil servants are therefore accountable to ministers, and ministers accountable to Parliament. In particular advice given to ministers by civil servants cannot be disclosed without the permission of ministers (see Freedom of Information Act 2000, s 35). According to the government, civil servants appear before parliamentary committees only with the consent of their ministers. Ministers therefore shield civil servants from outside scrutiny. In return civil servants are loyal to ministers and owe no other allegiance, thus emphasising the minister's own accountability to Parliament.

Their evidence before Select Committees (Section 13.5.3) has been limited to describing their actions taken on behalf of ministers as opposed to their conduct generally. Thus civil servants cannot give evidence about the merits of government policy, or the consultation process within government or the advice they gave to government. Indeed ministers have sometimes forbidden civil servants from appearing, in particular on the grounds of national security, 'good government' and 'excessive cost'. There are also conventions that civil servants should not give evidence about the conduct of other officials or matters before the courts and evidence from papers of a previous government or of a different political party (see Cabinet Office, *Departmental Evidence and Response to Select Committees* (2004)).

The relationship between ministers and civil servants can cause an 'accountability gap'. This is because accountability can break down where a minister blames a civil servant for some failure and subsequently directs that individual not to appear before a select committee. Notoriously the Secretary of State for Trade and Industry refused to allow the civil servants involved in aspects of the Westland affair to appear before the Commons Defence Select Committee (see HC 519, 1985–6, 1986, Cmnd 9916). This problem has in part been addressed in the parliamentary resolutions. Although civil servants still give evidence to select committees under the direction of ministers, the minister must insist that civil servants be as helpful as possible in providing accurate, truthful and full information (HC resolution para iv). However, Parliament still lacks power to compel ministers to answer questions and cannot require civil servants to give evidence to select committees (see Section 13.6.3).

The Scott Inquiry (above) revealed how civil servants have sometimes acted independently of ministers or in the expectation of subsequent ministerial ratification of their actions (Scott, 1996, HC 115, para D3.40). This exposed the constitutional fiction that civil servants only give advice to ministers. Civil servants concealed important questions from ministers and may even have defied ministerial instructions. Moreover as we saw above, ministers have attempted to pass responsibility to civil servants, first by distinguishing between policy and operational matters and secondly by distinguishing between 'accountability' as a duty to explain and 'responsibility' as liability to take the blame (Fifth Report of Treasury and Civil Service Select Committee, *The Role of the Civil Service*, HC 27, 1993–4, para 120). It has long been accepted that as Accounting Officer the permanent head of a department must appear before the relevant parliamentary committee. It has never been settled whether select committees can require other civil servants to attend to answer questions. In 1986 the Defence Select Committee claimed the absolute right to secure attendance from civil servants (HC 519, 1985–86). However, a compromise has been arrived at whereby ministers are enjoined to permit civil servants to appear but subject to restrictions (see para 37, Departmental Evidence and Response to Select Committees, Cabinet Office, January 1997, replacing the so-called Osmotherly Rules). This document exhorts civil servants to be as forthcoming as possible in providing information. Moreover civil servants cannot disclose or discuss the advice they gave to ministers, only the action they took on behalf of ministers. However the Ministerial Code provides some protection to the civil service. If the accounting officer considers that a minister's action breaches requirements of propriety, regularity or value for money he or she may set out objections in writing and, if the minister decides to override the objections, the Accounting Officer may 'seek' written instructions and the Comptroller and Auditor General must be notified (Art 5.4).

15.9 Executive agencies and non-ministerial government departments

Since the 1980s, many government functions have been removed from the traditional civil service structure of a pyramid topped by ministers and transferred to semi separate 'executive agencies' (originally called 'Next Steps' agencies), sometimes competing for work with private bodies, for example to run prisons.

Executive agencies are part of the civil service and remain subject to control by ministers. Each agency has a sponsoring government department and most departments have several agencies. Examples include the Courts Service, the Border Agency, the Benefits Agency, the Driver and Vehicle Licensing Agency, the Prison Service and the Met Office.

There are about 48000 civil servants in agencies. The division between an agency and its sponsoring department is that responsibility for 'service delivery' should reside with the agency, while policy matters should be reserved for the department acting under direct ministerial control (see *Building on Progress: The Role of the State* (Prime Minister's Strategy Unit (2007) para 7.2))). 'Framework agreements' made between the agency and the sponsoring department (sometimes with the Treasury as a party) constitute the relationship between the two. The framework agreement contains the strategy and financial arrangements under which the agency will work. It sets out the objectives of the agency and the division of responsibility between the agency and the department.

Agencies are permitted to run themselves semi-independently from their sponsoring government department, recruiting their own staff and managing themselves by copying the practices of private businesses. A chief executive for each agency is appointed by the minister, usually for a fixed period, to be responsible for the day-to-day management of the agency.

The chief executive is responsible to the minister but as accounting officer also appears before select committees of Parliament to answer MPs' questions about the functioning of the agency but not policy matters. Controversially this suggests that a convention may have been emerging under which agency chief executives are directly responsible to Parliament in their own right. MPs have also been encouraged to approach chief executives directly on behalf of their constituents and chief executives answer written parliamentary questions. The answers are published in *Hansard* (the official record of parliamentary proceedings) in order to avoid the bypassing of Parliament which might occur if chief executives responded directly to individual MPs.

Executive Agencies are distinct from non-ministerial government departments. These have long existed. They are departments which carry out basic governmental functions but in the interests of stability and impartiality are not subject to direct political control. They are normally created by statute and have a separate legal identity. They are however servants of the Crown and their staff are civil servants. They include among others HM Revenue and Customs, the Crown Prosecution Service, the Serious Fraud Office, the Charity Commission, and the regulators of rail, media and energy companies are non-ministerial departments.

Non-ministerial departments are headed by a civil servant who, unlike the case of a ministerial department, is directly accountable to Parliament. A minister has powers over it which depend on the particular statute. Normally a minister appoints the chair or board. Dismissal powers vary according to the extent of independence and security desired. Sometimes a minister has power to give non-binding 'guidance' or binding 'directions'.

15.9.1 Executive agencies and non-ministerial departments and ministerial responsibility

The fragmentation of government departments coupled with the privatisation of some governmental activities (the 'hollowing out' of the state), has placed the classical model of accountability under strain. In principle ministerial responsibility applies in full to executive agencies (*Ministerial Code* para 1.2) but the policy/operational distinction discussed above complicates the matter. The House of Commons Public Service Committee has stated that ministers remain accountable for what goes on in agencies just as in their departments (see Public Service Committee, Second Report (HC 1995–96, 313) paras 84–91, 109–23; Cabinet Office, *Modernising Government* (Cm 4310, 2002)).

The *Carltona* principle (Section 15.8.3) applies to executive agencies when they are exercising functions delegated by a minister by means of the normal framework agreement (see *R v Secretary of State, ex p Sherwin* [1996] 32 BMLR 1; cf Freedland, 'The Rule against Delegation and the *Carltona* Doctrine in an Agency Context' [1996] PL 19, arguing that this should only be the case where there is a clear line of decision making from the minister). In *Sherwin* Brightman J thought that there might be activities of an executive agency which no one would reasonably connect with the minister but gave no example.

It seems that ministerial responsibility is limited in the case of a non-ministerial government department to circumstances where a minister possesses specific statutory powers in relation to the department. This is appropriate since bodies of this kind frequently exercise quasi-judicial powers akin to those of courts or tribunals so that it is important that politicians maintain a separation.

15.10 Non-departmental public bodies: quangos

The UK constitution has no general concept of government or the state and there are no constitutional limitations on the kind of bodies that that be created to act on behalf of government. Thus there is a bewildering profusion of specialised bodies created at different times for particular political purposes. Functions are conferred, on many miscellaneous specialised bodies outside the central government usually created by statute but sometimes informally (see Cabinet Office, *Public Bodies* (2009). For example the Environment Agency controlling waterways and regulating pollution, Natural England regulating nature conservation, the Charity Commission, the Arts Council which funds the arts and the Higher Education Funding Council). These bodies (currently about 650, but their numbers are constantly changing) are often called 'quangos' (quasi-autonomous non-governmental agencies) but there is no legal significance in these labels.

Quangos are not part of the Crown so that their members and staff are not civil servants and they are not directly headed by a minister. Thus they fall outside the traditional chain of accountability between Parliament, ministers and civil servants. However depending on the particular statute ministers have certain important functions in relation to them which usually enable a minister to dominate what is characteristically an anxiety to please membership based on patronage (below).

Quangos enable selected functions to be exercised outside the constraints of central government, giving at least an appearance of greater independence than in the case of a government department. This might be because a function is specialised or is regarded as uncontroversial or requires impartiality akin to the judicial or is a problem that minister prefers to dump on someone else. Quangos therefore embody a fundamental constitutional dilemma arising out of clashing incommensurable values (Section 1.9) in that the aspiration towards independence from political pressure conflicts with the need for accountability.

Some functions which might be expected to call for impartial expertise retain at least some involvement by ministers presumably because they are politically sensitive, for example the approval of company takeovers or mergers. To add to the complexity some specialist bodies whose functions are similar to those of quangos are within the central government as non-ministerial departments (above). Being part of the Crown non-ministerial departments are responsible to Parliament for all their activities. The existence of quangos is therefore a pragmatic matter without a coherent constitutional basis.

Loughlin (2010) classifies quangos into five main functions. Many bodies have more than one function raising questions about conflicts of interest.

(i) Service providers such as the Bank of England (monetary policy), the BBC and the Homes and Communities Agency.

(ii) Risk assessors who provide government with specialist information and who may also have enforcement powers, for example the Environment Agency.

(iii) Boundary watchers: who ensure that powerful businesses such as the utility companies pay regard to the public interest and do not abuse their powers.

(iv) Auditors concerned with ensuring the public money is properly spent.

(v) Adjudicators such as tribunals and ombudsmen who resolve disputes. These provide accountability but also raise questions about their own accountability (Section 20.1, 20.3).

Tribunals (Section 20.1) are also regarded as non-departmental public bodies but are best regarded as part of the judicial system.

Quangos are usually managed by boards appointed by ministers. They provide a useful source of patronage whereby a minister can give posts on the boards of quangos to persons he or she wishes to favour or keep quiet. The same people are often recycled between several quangos. Some include representatives of particular interests or local councillors.

The main quangos can be divided into advisory bodies and executive bodies although many have both functions. Advisory bodies, such as various health, education, trade, scientific and agricultural authorities and committees, have no decision-making power but give independent advice to ministers, thus legitimising government policy. Advisory bodies can be created by ministers, or indeed anyone else, without statutory authorisation.

Executive bodies such as the Environment Agency require statutory powers. Their powers include granting licences and permits, requiring registration, enforcing compliance with standards and procedures by means, for example of inspections and auditing accounts and other documents, giving finance. They might also carry out operations, such as flood relief work. *The numerous regulators with powers over many welfare, business and professional activities include both quangos and non-ministerial government departments,* carried out by the Environment Agency (Section 20.4).

There are also a few statutory 'public corporations' which run operational services. During the 1980s many public corporations were converted into private companies supervised by a new breed of regulators (Section 5.6). The surviving public corporations are constituted either by statute or under company law on the model of private companies. These may be wholly or partly owned by the government in the form of shareholdings or under statute, for example the BBC and the Independent Broadcasting Authority, the Post Office and, as a result of the recent financial crisis, some banks. This kind of body may be subject to the commercial pressures of a private company, so that public accountability is even more blurred.

The Bank of England is a special type of Quango of central importance to government. It was, created after the seventeenth-century revolution in order to support loans to the Crown and as such was crucial to development of a powerful state. Nationalised after World War 2 its activities are interrelated with those of the Treasury. Its independence is safeguarded by statute (Bank of England Acts 1946, 1964, 1998). It administers the government's bank account. It has responsibilities relating to the stability of the economy including the money supply and determining the basic interest rate. It lends to other banks and is the lender of last resort on behalf of Parliament. It also regulates the financial services industry in relation to governance and financial security (Financial Services Act 2012). Its Governor appears before Parliament in his own right.

Quangos are formally independent of government. Setting up a quango therefore enables a minister to avoid direct responsibility. However ministers are likely to have substantial powers of control, including sometimes power to give general directions for which they are accountable to Parliament. Board members are usually appointed by a minister and funding is mainly provided by ministers from funds voted by Parliament to the minister's department. In addition ministers may produce non-statutory 'advice', 'guidance' or 'concordats' regulating the relationship between the quango and government departments or informally exercise influence over compliant members of quango boards.

In theory quangos might provide a vehicle for diverse democracy where independent opinions can be publicly expressed. This may however be more apparent than real. Independently minded persons are unlikely to be appointed to the boards of quangos. Members of quangos are usually appointed for fixed periods and quangos can be created or dissolved either by statute or by ministers at any time.

The constitutional accountability of a quango is unclear and indirect since they are not government departments but yet are normally funded, mainly by Parliament.

Other constitutional issues are first whether a body is part of the Crown so as to enjoy legal immunities (in the case of statutory bodies the statute will usually make this clear; most quangos are not part of the Crown); secondly whether it has any democratic element, this being unlikely; thirdly the extent to which it is accountable to Parliament (Section 15.7.3) and fourthly whether it is a public body for particular purposes such as the Human Rights Act 1998 as it usually will be (Section 21.3). Bodies with powers conferred by statute may also be immune from liability for damages provided that they do not exceed their statutory powers (see eg *Marcic v Thames Water Utilities* [2004]; *X (Minors) v Bedfordshire CC* [1995]).

The appointment of members of quangos has been subject to concerns that members are chosen from a pool of persons linked by personal, professional, business or political relationships. This problem of patronage is not confined to quangos and is inherent in the political side of the constitution (Section 5.9). As a result of the work of the Committee on Standards in Public Life the process for ministerial appointments of members of the main quangos and also of some non-ministerial government departments and public corporations is subject to general regulation, monitoring and audit by an independent Commissioner for Public Appointments, who is appointed by the Prime Minister under the royal prerogative (Public Appointments Orders in Council 1995, 2002). However the Commissioner has advisory powers only and does not take part in individual appointments.

The Commissioner has issued a code of practice which includes a requirement to advertise vacancies and to ensure that the selection is on merit and that the process is open, transparent and fair and encourages diversity. The appointment principles include independent assessors and 'proportionality', which enables simplified procedures to be used in the case of less important appointments (see Public Administration Select Committee, *Government by Appointment: Opening Up the Patronage State* (HC 2002–03, 135); Committee on Standards in Public Life, *Getting the Balance Right* (Cm 6407, 2005)). However the Code does not prevent reappointments or recycling and, without positive attempts to identify suitable candidates, no code can fully address the problem that the pool of applicants is likely to be dominated by insiders.

There is a National Health Services Appointments Commission with a similar role. The NHS is not itself a quango but comprises a complex network of bodies governed by statute. Some are directly part of the Crown, some are quangos, and others such as doctors are linked to government by contracts.

Quangos have limited protection against interference by ministers. Under the Public Bodies Act 2011 a minister can abolish, modify or alter the funding arrangement of many quangos. However the minister cannot exercise these powers so as to prevent the quango from acting independently of ministers in cases where the quango exercises judicial powers or has enforcement activities in relation to obligations imposed on a minister or which exercises oversight or scrutiny of the actions of a minister (s 7). An Order made by a minister under the Act is subject to parliamentary scrutiny by the 'special affirmative procedure' (Section 13.5).

Since Quangos are normally funded by Parliament and their accounts are laid before Parliament, in principle quangos are accountable to Parliament. A Select Committee might summon the Chief Executive or Chair of a Quango to appear before it and disclose documents. The extent to which this could be enforced at best depends on a resolution of the Commons (Section 13.5). However, the parliamentary process is geared towards the hierarchy of ministers and their departments so that in practice accountability may be sporadic. Ministers may be accountable to Parliament for their own involvement, in relation to appointments, funding and general oversight and policy. Some quangos closely related to government departments are subject to the Parliamentary Ombudsman (Section 20.3).

There are also numerous voluntary bodies and private companies, for example charities such as the National Trust, housing associations and the Royal Society for the Prevention of Cruelty to Animals, that carry out functions for the public good, sometimes under contract on behalf of the government with state funding and occasionally subject to special statutory provisions (eg National Trust Act 1907). It must be established in each context whether the body itself or a particular function of the body is regarded as public or private (Section 19.5). These bodies are not subject to direct political accountability but are accountable only to their own members.

Comparison between quangos, executive agencies and non-ministerial government departments (NMDs)

- ▶ Executive agencies are not separate legal entities but are part of the Crown. Their staff are therefore civil servants. Quangos are separate legal entities or committees of individuals. Their staff are not civil servants. NMDs are separate legal entities but part of the Crown.
- ▶ Ministers are responsible for the acts of executive agencies. Ministers are only responsible for the acts of quangos and NMDs in relation to the actual involvement of the minister.
- ▶ Executive agencies may exercise powers on behalf of ministers under statute or the royal prerogative. Quangos may freely give advice to anyone who will listen but have no legal powers unless conferred specifically by statute. NMDs have direct statutory powers.
- ▶ An executive agency is required to carry out instructions from ministers as to any of its activities. A quango is nominally independent of ministers except where the minister has statutory power to intervene. However this difference may be unreal given the desire of those chosen to be members of quangos to please their patrons. Ministers may have specific statutory powers in relation to NMDs.
- ▶ As Accounting Officer, the chief executive of an executive agency must appear before parliamentary select committees but on behalf of the minister. The leaders of quangos and NMDs appear in their own right (Section 15.7).

> ▶ Executive agency appointments, in common with most civil service appointments, are subject to regulation by the statutory Civil Service Commission with a view to preventing political involvement (Constitutional Reform and Governance Act 2010, ss 11–14). Quangos and NMDs are subject to regulation by the non-statutory Commissioner for Public Appointments.

Summary

- ▶ The Prime Minister has large powers under the royal prerogative, pre-eminently to dissolve Parliament, appoint and dismiss ministers and control the government agenda. However these are largely convention, and determined political opposition could control a Prime Minister.

- ▶ As a body the Cabinet has been reduced in power in recent years, with decisions effectively being made by smaller groups within and outside the Cabinet and by departments of the executive.

- ▶ There are few constitutional laws or conventions concerning the detailed distribution of functions between departments. Political and administrative considerations rather than constitutional principle determine the number, size, shape and interrelationship of government departments. The creation of bodies outside the framework of the Crown is of greater constitutional and legal significance.

- ▶ The convention of ministerial responsibility is central to the UK constitution. Collective responsibility means that all members of the government must loyally support government policy and decisions and must not disclose internal disagreements. Individual responsibility means that each minister is answerable to Parliament for all the activities of the department under his control. It also means that civil servants are not personally accountable. From these principles follow (i) the traditional notion of the civil service as anonymous and politically neutral, having a duty to serve with unquestioning loyalty governments of any political complexion, and (ii) the secrecy that pervades the British system of government.

- ▶ The traditional doctrine of ministerial responsibility may be out of line with the practices of modern government and effectively shields the government from accountability. In particular (i) Cabinet decisions are rarely made collectively; (ii) many government bodies are not directly controlled by ministers, the creation of executive agencies reinforcing this; (iii) civil servants are increasingly expected to make political decisions and to be responsible for the financial management of their allotted activities; (iv) public functions are increasingly being given to special bodies or private bodies (below). Thus the traditional chain of accountability between Parliament, ministers and civil servants is weakened.

- ▶ In law civil servants are servants of the Crown. They can be dismissed 'at pleasure', that is without notice and without reason being given. However the modern cases suggest that there can be a contractual relationship between the Crown and a civil servant and that a civil servant can be protected by the law of judicial review.

- ▶ In the light of the convention relating to ministerial responsibility civil servants are regarded as servants of the government of the day with an absolute duty of loyalty to ministers. Their advice to ministers is secret and they appear before Parliament only with the consent of ministers. They are supposed to be non-political and neutral, responsible for giving ministers objective advice and for carrying out ministerial orders. However 'special advisers' need not be neutral or appointed on merit. Their existence creates tensions within the civil service.

Summary cont'd

▶ The internal arrangements for the carrying out of government business involve entrusting individual civil servants with considerable decision-making responsibility and in recent years with financial accountability within the government machine. Many civil servants work in executive agencies, hived off from the central departmental structure and outside the direct control of ministers. This has led to tensions between traditional ideas of ministerial responsibility and the actual channels of accountability and has raised problems in connection with the supposed distinction between policy and operational matters.

Exercises

15.1 Consider whether the relevant laws and conventions support Bagehot's view that the Cabinet is the central institution of the UK constitution.

15.2 A general election has just been held. The Prime Minister's party has won the largest number of votes but has only 45 per cent of the seats in the Commons. The Solidarity Party, with 10 per cent of the seats is willing to support the Prime Minister's party but only if he resigns in favour of a candidate supported by the Solidarity Party. Advise the Queen as to the constitutional position.

What would be the position if the Opposition party had won the election with 40 per cent of the seats and minority parties had agreed provisionally to support amounting to another 15 per cent of seats.

15.3 Although it has a substantial majority in the House of Commons, the government has difficulties in getting Parliament to approve its policies mainly because many of its backbenchers are discontented claiming that the voters are unhappy. Green the Prime Minister is unpopular and behaving increasingly eccentrically but refuses to resign. Advise the Queen as to the constitutional position. Advise Tina the Leader of the Opposition whether a legal action to remove Green might succeed.

15.4 'Ministerial responsibility is, in practice, an obstacle to the availability of information and to the holding of government to account' (Oliver). Discuss.

15.5 To what extent can Parliament and the public scrutinise the activities of a civil servant?

15.6 When should a minister resign?

15.7 Critically evaluate the constitutional significance of special advisers.

15.8 The government creates an executive agency to regulate motorway service areas. The Secretary of State for Consumption delegates to the agency his statutory powers to ensure the 'adequate provision of motorway services'. Under a contract made with the Secretary of State the agency promises to achieve certain targets, including a clean environment. The agency employs Grasper plc to run the Crusty Group of service areas. Due to cuts in its funding from the Secretary of State the agency does not check Grasper's performance but increases its chief executive's annual bonus by 100 per cent. A newspaper subsequently discovers that many of the catering staff employed by the Crusty Group are illegal immigrants and several of them have contracted food poisoning. In response to a parliamentary question, the Secretary of State asserts that the matter is no concern of his and he knows nothing about it. He also refuses to permit the agency chief executive to appear before the Select Committee for Consumption. Discuss.

Further reading

Benn, 'The Case for a Constitutional Premiership' (1980) 33 Parl Aff 7

Brazier, *Constitutional Practice: The Foundations of British Government* (3rd edn, Oxford University Press 1999) chs 2–7

Burnham and Piper, *Britain's Modernised Civil Service* (Palgrave Macmillan 2008)

Daintith and Page, *The Executive in the Constitution* (Oxford University Press 1999) chs 1–6

Flinders, 'The Enduring Centrality of Individual Ministerial Responsibility within the British Constitution' (2000) 6 JLS 73

Greer, *Transforming Central Government: The Next Steps Initiative* (Open University Press 1994)

Harden, 'Money and the Constitution, Financial Control, Reporting and Audit' (1993) 13 LS 16

Hennessy, *The Hidden Wiring* (Gollancz 1995) chs 3–5, 8

Hough, 'Ministerial Responses to Parliamentary Questions: Some Recent Concerns' [2003] PL 211

Institute for Public Policy Research, *Whitehall's Black Box: Accountability and Performance in the Senior Civil Service* (2006)

Jowell and Oliver (eds), *The Changing Constitution* (7th edn, Oxford University Press 2011) chs 7, 13

Sampson, *Who Runs This Place?* (John Murray 2004) chs 1–4, 7, 8

Vennard, 'Prime Ministerial Succession' [2008] PL 302

Chapter 16

Devolution

The general nature of devolution in the UK

This chapter discusses the devolution provisions for Scotland, Northern Ireland and Wales. In relation to Scotland the Supreme Court has called the devolution legislation a fundamental constitutional settlement (*H v Lord Advocate* (2012) [30]). It is not appropriate in a general book to discuss the internal systems of government within those countries in-depth. We shall concentrate on two general themes: (i) a comparison of the devolved regimes with the constitutional arrangements for the UK as a whole; (ii) a comparison of the extent of the powers conferred on the three regimes. The main aim is to introduce readers to the role which devolution plays in the wider UK constitution.

The UK is a union of what were the separate states of England, parts of Ireland and Scotland. Wales is a nation within the UK but was assimilated with England. Before the introduction of devolved government in 2000, the internal affairs of Scotland, Northern Ireland and Wales were governed by the UK central executive. This took the form of 'administrative devolution' to ministers for each territory. There was no specific democratic power base or accountability mechanism linking the ministers to their regions since the relevant minister might have an English constituency. Scotland and Northern Ireland have separate legal systems but the Supreme Court is the final court of appeal for all the UK jurisdictions except Scottish criminal cases.

In 1973 the Royal Commission on the Constitution (Cmnd 5460) asserted that government in the UK was overcentralised and recommended devolved government. Referendums were subsequently held in Scotland and Wales which foundered because they failed to obtain the required two-thirds majorities in favour of change. The Labour government that took office in 1997 was supportive of devolved government as part of an agenda of constitutional reform in favour of dispersing power. Further referendums (this time requiring only a 51% majority) produced considerable public support for devolution in Scotland and significant but less support for devolution in Wales. Legislation was then enacted to give devolved powers to a Scottish Parliament (Scotland Act 1998), a Northern Ireland Assembly (Northern Ireland Act 1998) and, to a lesser extent, a Welsh Assembly (Government of Wales Act 1998). The powers of the Welsh Assembly were later expanded (Government of Wales Act 2006) but are still less than those of Scotland and Northern Ireland.

The devolution statutes could be regarded as embodying a constitution for the territory in question. The basic devolution arrangements are entrenched in statute so that they cannot be altered by the devolved regimes. On the other hand the devolution arrangements are not stable in that they can be altered by Parliament at any time. The Welsh provisions in particular have been substantially altered, so Welsh devolution has the appearance of an experiment.

The devolution arrangements for the three territories have many features in common but there are important differences in relation to each region. This is sometimes called 'asymmetric devolution'. Scotland, with its history as an independent state with its own legal system, has the greatest devolved power. The devolved structures are modeled broadly on the UK parliamentary system but with different voting systems which make strong executive governments less likely. In Northern Ireland there are substantial restriction on the composition of the executive government. In the cases of Scotland and Northern Ireland the Acts do not specify the powers of the devolved governments but specify what they cannot do. They can legislate on any other matter. Wales by contrast can legislate only on matters specifically assigned to it in the legislation. Provisions for ensuring that the devolved regimes keep within their powers are similar in all three cases, relying heavily on the courts. To this extent devolution has 'juridified' the constitution. The devolved governments have very limited tax-raising powers. They are funded mainly by block grants from the UK Parliament. The Scotland and Northern Ireland governments have certain limited tax-raising powers and only the Northern Ireland government has borrowing powers other than from the UK government. Thus there is incomplete accountability to voters. However, the Scotland Act 2012 (not yet in force) increases the taxation and borrowing powers of the Scottish government.

There is no federal element. The devolution arrangements do not affect the unlimited legal power of the UK Parliament to make laws for the devolved regions and to override laws made by the devolved regimes (eg Scotland Act 1998, s 28(7)). The UK government retains ministers responsible for each of the devolved regimes. The devolved arrangements, including the structure of the executive and the proceedings of the legislative assemblies, cannot be changed by the devolved bodies. Thus there is limited room for evolution generated by the wishes of people in the devolved areas, the progress of devolution remaining centralised in the UK.

Although the law is not federal there are political mechanisms which give protection to the devolved governments. Under the 'Sewel Convention' (1999), the UK Parliament does not legislate for a devolved territory without the consent of its legislature (see HL Deb 1998, vol 592, col 791). There are also non-legally binding 'concordats' between each UK government department and the devolved administrations. These put in place principles for coordinating the activities of the governments, for example through a joint ministerial committee, and may buttress the kind of secretive informality characteristic of the UK constitution (see *Memorandum of Understanding and Supplementary Agreements* (Cm 4444, 2001; Cm 4806, Cm 5420, 1999); Poivier, 'The Function of Intergovernmental Agreements' [2001] PL 134; Rawlings, 'Concordats of the Constitution' (2000) 116 LQR 257).

The courts are responsible for ensuring that the limits of the devolved powers are respected. The devolution legislation therefore marks a change in our constitutional arrangements away from reliance upon informal and political methods and towards juridification, although devices such as the Sewel Convention make this far from complete. This leads to the question of whether the devolution arrangements can be regarded as 'constitutional' and so subject to a special approach to interpretation (Chapter 1). We might invoke matters such as the importance of the devolved arrangements with respect to the fundamental concerns of the particular community. On this basis the Northern Ireland arrangements have a particularly strong claim to be regarded as constitutional. Indeed in *Robinson v Secretary of State for Northern Ireland* [2002], Lord Hoffmann asserted (at [33]) that the Northern Ireland Act 1998 is to be construed:

> against the background of the political situation in Northern Ireland and the principles laid down by the Belfast Agreement for a new start. These facts and background form part of the admissible background to the construction of the Act just as much as the Revolution, the Convention and the federalist papers are the background to construing the Constitution of the USA.

It is important that there are provisions for dealing with issues that cross boundaries and for settling disputes between the different layers of government. Characteristic of the UK constitution these tend to be political rather than strictly legal, although some are formal in the sense that they are contained in published documents such as concordats (above). There are also legal arrangements for interaction between the different levels. These allow functions to be shared or transferred in both directions between the UK government and the devolved regimes (see, eg Scotland Act 1998, ss 63, 108, 109).

The following sections discuss the main features of each regime. Unless stated otherwise the relevant provisions in Wales and Northern Ireland are similar to those in Scotland. The detailed matters that are devolved to each regime are significantly different but will not be discussed here. They are set out in schedules to the statutes.

16.2 Scotland

Scotland was a separate nation state from 1010 until 1706, although after 1603 the Crowns of England and Scotland were united. Since the sixteenth-century Reformation there had been some cultural assimilation between the two countries but also quarrels between Catholics and Protestants. In 1689 Scotland offered its Crown to William and Mary on the same revolutionary terms as in England (Chapter 4). After quarrels between the two Parliaments, the Treaty of Union 1706 agreed to abolish the separate Scottish and English Parliaments and to create a Parliament of Great Britain.

The Union was unpopular but was brought about by economic interest in Scotland and fear of invasion in England. The treaty was confirmed by separate Acts of each Parliament (Act of Union with England 1706; Act of Union with Scotland 1706). Scottish rebellion on behalf of the Stuarts' claim to the throne continued until defeat at Culloden in 1746. The Acts of Union are still in force. They preserve the separate Scottish legal system and Church and safeguard the private rights of Scottish subjects. Scotland has its own judicial system, and its Church, although not 'established' in the sense that the Crown and Parliament are not part of its governance, enjoys independence by statute (Church of Scotland Act 1921). There is an argument that the UK Parliament cannot override these aspects of the Acts of Union, although section 37 of the Scotland Act 1998, which makes the Acts of Union subject to the 1998 Act, assumes that the UK Parliament can do so (Section 8.4.2).

The Scotland Act 1998 creates the greatest freedom of the three regimes. It is modelled on the UK's parliamentary system giving legal force to provisions akin to those which in the UK constitution are conventions. There is a Scottish Parliament and a Scottish government responsible to it. The Scottish government has somewhat less power in relation to the Parliament than its UK counterpart.

Scottish devolution claims to uphold four basic aspirations (*Shaping Scotland's Parliament* (HMSO 1999); see Procedures Committee, *The Founding Principles of the Scottish Parliament* (Third Report 2003, SP Paper 818)). These are political guidances rather than legally enforceable provisions. They are:

▶ sharing of power between the people, Parliament and the executive (but there is no legal provision other than periodic general elections to enable the people to exercise power);

▶ accountability of the executive to the Parliament and the Parliament to the people;

- access and participation;
- equal opportunities.

However, the structure of the devolution legislation like that of the UK parliamentary system relies on a central executive responsible to Parliament and with no direct involvement of the people other than voting in party-oriented elections. On the other hand the introduction of proportional representation and the relatively stronger powers of the Parliament in relation to government appointments may marginally alter the balance in favour of Parliament.

16.2.1 The Scottish Parliament

The Scottish Parliament can enact Acts on any matter other than those specified in the 1998 Act (below). Acts of the Scottish Parliament require royal assent (Scotland Act 1998, s 28). The validity of the procedure leading to an enactment does not affect the Act's validity (s 28(5)) but otherwise Acts of the Scottish Parliament that are outside its competence 'are not law' (s 28). Where a measure is ambiguous it must be interpreted narrowly in favour of its validity (s 101).

The UK Parliament retains its full power to legislate for Scotland, thus overriding the devolution provisions (s 28(7)). However this may be politically unreal. Indeed, according to the Sewel Convention (Section 16.1), the UK Parliament will not intervene in a devolved area without the consent of the Scottish Parliament (the normal procedure is a 'Sewel Resolution'). UK statutes apply in Scotland only expressly or by necessary implication. Moreover, it seems that the Scotland Act itself as fundamental constitutional legislation can be altered only by express language (*H v Lord Advocate* (2012) [30]).

Although sometimes called 'primary' legislation, Acts of the Scottish Parliament are strictly subordinate legislation, owing their validity only to the Scotland Act 1998 (see Human Rights Act 1998, s 21: not primary legislation under Act). They can be set aside by the courts if they are outside the devolution provisions and also under the domestic law of judicial review. However the courts are unwilling to review a decision made by a high level democratic body and will review the Scottish Parliament on judicial review grounds only in exceptional circumstances.

AXA General Insurance Ltd v HM Advocate (2012) concerned a challenge to a Scottish Act which reversed recent case law which had removed employers liability for certain asbestos related illnesses. It was held that the Act did not violate the insurers property rights under the ECHR since as an elected body the Scottish Parliament was entitled to a wide margin of discretion in relation to questions of social justice such as this. As a creation of statute the Scottish Parliament was a subordinate body and therefore was subject to judicial review under domestic law. The court would ensure that the Parliament complied with the statutory limits on its power. Other than that in view of the democratic credentials of the Scottish Parliament, judicial review would apply only in exceptional circumstances, not present here namely where the Parliament violates the rule of law. The ordinary judicial review standards of irrationality, unreasonableness or arbitrariness (Section 18.1) would not apply [51] Lord Hope [51]. suggested that, in the light of the dangers of executive domination of Parliament, the court might intervene if Parliament were to abolish judicial review or diminish the powers of the courts in protecting the individual: the rule of law requires that judges must retain the power to insist that legislation of this extreme kind is not law which the courts will recognise. (We have seen (Section 8.5.6) that the same argument might apply to the UK Parliament.)

The following are the main limits on the power of the Scottish Parliament (s 29):

▶ Although it can alter UK statutes it cannot, except in minor respects, amend the Scotland Act 1998 itself or various UK statutes, including the parts of the Act of Union dealing with free trade (Sch 4). (Possibly neither the Scottish nor the UK Parliament can amend the Act of Union in as far as it includes certain basic rights; Section 8.4.2.)
▶ It cannot alter any law which 'would form part of the law of a country or territory other than Scotland, or confer or remove functions exercisable otherwise than in or as regards Scotland'. The UK government can specify these functions (s 30(3)). This is of particular significance in relation to fishing.
▶ It cannot override European law (s 29(2)d). UK ministers have the exclusive power to bring EC law into effect (ss 52, 54, 57(2)).
▶ It cannot override Convention Rights (s 29(2)d) meaning rights under the European Convention on Human Rights specified in the Human Rights Act 1998 (Section 22.1).
▶ It cannot remove the powers of the Lord Advocate as head of the criminal prosecution system and investigator of deaths (s 29(2)e).

Most of the Scottish government's finance is derived from the UK government. It currently has taxation powers limited to altering the basic rate of income tax by three pence in the pound (s 73). However the Scotland Act 2012 Part 3 (not yet in force) substantially increases both taxation and borrowing powers. This gives the Scottish regime enhanced political legitimacy.

There are 'reserved matters' on which only the UK Parliament can legislate (s 30, Sch 5). They include the most basic functions of government and important constitutional matters. The main reserved matters are matters affecting the Crown (but not the exercise of the royal prerogative which in principle can be exercised by Scottish ministers); the civil service; certain aspects of electoral arrangements (Scotland Act 2012, s 1)); the registration and funding of political parties; the Union with England; the UK Parliament; the higher Scottish courts; international relations; defence and national security; treason; fiscal, economic and monetary policy; currency; financial services and markets; money laundering; border controls; transport safety and regulation; media policy; employment regulation; certain health matters; the regulation of key professions; and social security. Drug control drink driving limits and certain speed limits are to become devolved matters (Scotland Act 2012 ss 19, 20, 21). Reserved matters can be altered by Order in Council (s 30(2) but without affecting things already done (Scotland Act 2012 s 9). There are provisions for guarding against ultra vires legislation. A person in charge of a bill must, on or before the introduction of the bill in Parliament, state that in his view the provisions of the bill would be within the legislative competence of Parliament (s 31(1); Scotland Act 2012, s 6). The Presiding Officer, who submits bills for royal assent (s 32), must on or before its introduction 'decide whether or not in his view' the bill is within the powers of the Parliament (s 31(2)). This statement does not block the bill. These provisions generate political accountability but have no legal effect on the bill since only a court can decide what a law means. The Advocate General, the Lord Advocate or the UK Attorney General can require a bill to be referred to the Supreme Court (s 33).

Somewhat controversially due to the 'colonial' flavour of such a power, the Secretary of State can prohibit a bill from being sent for royal assent where she or he 'has reasonable ground to believe' that the bill would be incompatible with international obligations or the interests of national security or defence or would have an adverse effect on the law relating to reserved matters (s 35). (See also section 58 in relation to the Scottish government.)

The UK government can make subordinate legislation remedying ultra vires Acts of the Scottish Parliament and the Scottish government (s 107). The court can protect people who may have relied on invalid laws by removing the retrospective effect of the invalidity or suspending the invalidity to allow the defect to be corrected (s 102).

The Parliament comprises 129 members elected by *the 'additional member system'* (Scotland Act 1998, ss 6–8 (Section 12.5.7)). Seventy-three candidates are elected on the 'first past the post' basis in local constituencies. This is topped up by a second vote on the 'open party list' basis for 56 candidates in eight regions. There is therefore more likely to be a coalition government involving more than one party in Scotland than is the case in the UK, where the present coalition is relatively unusual.

Entitlement to vote is based on that for local government elections (s 11). It includes adult resident citizens of the UK and EU citizens (EU citizens cannot vote in UK parliamentary elections).

Before 1998 Scotland was entitled to at least 71 seats in the UK Parliament, thus making it overrepresented in terms of its population. Section 86(1) of the Scotland Act 1998 abolishes this entitlement and places Scotland under the same regime as England in terms of the criteria for defining constituencies (Chapter 12). This has reduced the number of Scottish MPs to 59. Originally the constituencies for the Scottish Parliament were the same as those for the UK Parliament. However, by virtue of the Scottish Parliament (Constituencies) Act 2004, the link between the two has been severed.

Membership of the Scottish Parliament is subject to similar disqualifications to those applying to the UK Parliament, mainly the holding of certain public offices (s 15; Section 12.4). There is no residence requirement in either case. However, unlike in the UK Parliament, a citizen of an EU country can be a member of the Scottish Parliament (MSP) (s 16). The same person cannot be a candidate in more than one constituency but, unlike the case in Wales, can stand in both a regional election and a local constituency election in the same region (s 5). The constituency election has priority. If the candidate wins the constituency he or she must be excluded from the regional count. The same person can be a member of the Scottish Parliament and the UK Parliament.

The Presiding Officer, elected by the House for the duration of the Parliament (s 19), has a larger role than is the case with the UK Parliament. This includes submitting bills for royal assent (below), recommending the appointment of the First Minister, advising a dissolution (below) and proposing the date of the general election.

The Scottish Parliament sits for four years, after which it is automatically dissolved. A general election must be held on the first Thursday in May in the fourth year after the previous ordinary general election, after which the Parliament must meet within seven days (s 2). (The Presiding Officer may vary this by up to one month (s 2). The date for the election must not be the same as for a UK General election (Fixed Term Parliaments Act 2011, s 4).

The Parliament can be dissolved earlier by the Queen in two cases (s 3). In both cases the power to dissolve is triggered by the Presiding Officer fixing a date for an 'extraordinary general election'. The first case is following a two-thirds majority resolution of the Parliament and the second is where the Parliament fails to designate a First Minister within 28 days of the post becoming vacant. This could arise where the government is defeated on a vote of confidence requiring the First Minister to resign (Section 16.2.2). As with the UK Parliament there is no time limit specified for this election). However the new Parliament must meet within 7 days after the election. In the UK there is no fixed date (Section 11.2).

The Parliament and its members do not enjoy parliamentary privilege, although its members do have absolute privilege in defamation (s 41; Section 11.6). Parliament's power to control its own procedure is limited by the Act (s 22) but it does have the right to require any person, including ministers, to attend, give information and disclose documents in relation to matters for which the Scottish government has responsibility (ss 23–25). This contrasts with the murkiness of the practices surrounding ministerial responsibility in the UK. In practice however the Scottish Parliament seems to have followed the Westminster model, according to which the executive dominates parliamentary processes and decides what information to disclose.

There have been innovations in practice which have made the Scottish Parliament more proactive than the UK Parliament. Scottish committees not only scrutinise the executive and revise legislation but may initiate legislation and conduct inquiries that involve direct engagement with the people. A public petitions system has been introduced and there are Internet-based information and discussion mechanisms.

The Scottish Parliament has enacted a substantial amount of legislation, particularly concerning social matters and public services, which has markedly distinguished the regime from its English counterpart. These include free personal care for the elderly, greater support for students, rescue packages for fisheries and the victims of foot and mouth disease, land reform, mental health and freedom of information.

16.2.2 The Scottish government/executive

The Scottish executive to be renamed 'government' (Scotland Act 2012, s 12) comprises a First Minister, ministers, junior ministers and law officers (Lord Advocate and Solicitor General (Scotland Act 1998, ss 44–50)). The Crown is the formal head of the Scottish government. The Crown in relation to Scotland is separated from the Crown in relation to the UK, so that they can enter into property transactions with each other, for example (s 99).

Within the devolved areas the Scottish Parliament can confer functions on Scottish ministers either individually or collectively (s 52). Statutory and royal prerogative powers previously exercised by UK ministers are automatically transferred to Scottish ministers (s 53). In order to provide flexibility additional functions outside devolved matters can be given to Scottish ministers either alone or jointly with UK ministers by Order in Council (s 63).

In *H v Lord Advocate* (2012) the Supreme Court stressed that Scottish Ministers have no powers other than those conferred by the Act (UK ministers also have common law powers (Section 14.6)). In particular ministers cannot act incompatibly with Convention Rights within the meaning of the Human Rights Act whatever the source of the power in question, that is, whether a Scottish Act or a UK Act (s 57(2). This is a devolution issue (Section 16.2.4)) and as such is independent of the Human Rights Act itself (*Somerville v Scottish Ministers* [2007] 1 WLR 2734: time limits on applications under HRA not applicable, cf Scotland Act 2012, ss 34–37). Thus provisions of the Human Rights Act which allow the government to override a convention right when enforcing a statute may not apply (Section 22.4) and a litigant can choose which way to proceed (see Beatson *et al*, 2008, ch 8) (s 57(2)). There is an exception where the Human Rights Act itself must apply. This concerns the prosecuting and criminal investigation role of the Lord Advocate under UK statutes so as to ensure that these powers are the same throughout the UK (s 57(3)).

The principles for forming and dismissing the Scottish government are broadly similar to the conventions applying to the UK government (Section 14.1). The Scottish rules however are wholly statutory thus in theory permitting intervention by the courts. The Scottish rules give significant roles to the Presiding Officer and to Parliament, whereas no office holder except the monarch has a formal role in the UK.

- ▶ The monarch appoints the First Minister on the nomination of the Parliament (s 46). The Presiding Officer recommends the nomination to the Queen (s 46(4)). Presumably she must accept.
- ▶ The Parliament must nominate the First Minister within 28 days of a 'triggering' event (s 46). This means:
    - (i) a general election or extraordinary general election (above);
    - (ii) the resignation of the First Minister. The First Minister can resign at any time and must do so if the government is defeated on a vote of confidence. The First Minister remains in office until a successor is appointed (s 45(3)).
    - (iii) the First Minister ceases to be a member of the Scottish Parliament, except on dissolution, when the trigger event is (i).
- ▶ If there has been no nomination after 28 days the Parliament is dissolved, leading to an extraordinary general election and thus starting the process again. If the First Minister cannot act or the office is vacant, the Presiding Officer appoints an acting First Minister from among MSPs (or former MSPs in the event of a dissolution; s 45(4), (5)). (There is no UK equivalent; the Cabinet makes the arrangements.)
- ▶ The monarch appoints other ministers and law officers (the Lord Advocate and Solicitor General) on the nomination of the First Minister with the agreement of the Parliament (ss 47–49). All ministers but not the law officers must be MSPs (ss 47, 48). (The UK convention is that the monarch appoints all ministers and law officers on the advice of the Prime Minister. All must be MPs or members of the House of Lords.)
- ▶ The First Minister can dismiss ministers (ss 47(3), 49(4)). The First Minister can dismiss law officers only with the approval of the Parliament (s 48(1)). (Under the UK convention the monarch can dismiss ministers and law officers on the advice of the Prime Minister.)
- ▶ Ministers and law officers can resign at any time and must resign if they are defeated in a vote of confidence (ss 47(3), 48(2), 49(4)). They lose office immediately, except that the Advocate General continues in office for essential functions until a replacement

is appointed (ss 47(3)(d), 49(4)(d), 48(3)). (The UK has a similar convention but after a vote of confidence ministers and law officers do not lose office until they are replaced.)

▶ Ministers lose office if they cease to be MSPs, except on dissolution, when they stay in office until the election (ss 47(2)(e), 49(4)(e)). (The UK convention is that ministers must resign if they cease to be MPs, except on dissolution.)

▶ The law officers are the Lord Advocate and the Solicitor General for Scotland. They can be but need not be MSPs. They can participate but cannot vote in the Parliament (s 27). Unlike ministers they cannot be dismissed without the agreement of the Parliament (s 48(1)). The Parliament cannot interfere with the independence of the Lord Advocate as head of the criminal prosecution and investigation of death systems (ss 29(2)(e), 48(5)). (The UK law officers are ministers and members of Parliament and dismissible by the Prime Minister (Section 15.6). There is also an Advocate General for Scotland, who is responsible for giving advice on Scottish matters to the UK government (s 87).)

▶ Ministers in the UK government cannot hold office in the Scottish government (s 44(3)). However MSPs can sit in the UK Parliament and be UK ministers.

The civil service is part of the UK civil service and subject to the UK law regulating the civil service. Management of the civil service is not a devolved matter. Civil servants are however appointed by and presumably responsible to Scottish ministers (s 51). Thus there may be a conflict of loyalty. However since the Crown in relation to the Scottish government is a different entity from the Crown in relation to the UK government (s 91), their primary loyalty is to Scottish ministers. They are however responsible to Scottish ministers only in relation to functions exercised by those ministers. Conflicts of loyalty might therefore still arise in relation to functions exercised jointly by Scottish and UK ministers.

In relation to the continuing role of the UK government in respect of Scotland, there are special committees in Parliament to examine Scottish affairs and a Secretary of State for Scotland accountable to the UK Parliament.

16.2.3 The courts

Scotland has its own legal system with separate courts and separate substantive law which has been influenced by continental civil law as well as by English common law. Final civil appeals are decided by the Supreme Court, which has jurisdiction over the whole of the UK while criminal appeals are decided wholly within the Scottish courts However under the Scotland Act 2012 ss 35–36 (not yet in force) issues of compatibility with Convention rights under the ECHR are decided by the Supreme Court. The Supreme Court is unbalanced in relation to the devolved legal systems in that there are only two Scottish members and one from Northern Ireland (Section 5.4).

English and Scottish civil law have much in common although property law has many differences. Scottish criminal law and procedure is markedly different from that in England which has the potential to create problems of cooperation. In *Stuart v Marquis of Bute* (1861) 9 HL Cas 440, 454, Lord Campbell LC said 'as to judicial jurisdiction, Scotland and England, although politically under the same Crown and under the supreme sway of one united legislature, are to be considered as independent foreign countries, unconnected with each other' (see *R v Manchester Stipendiary Magistrate, ex p Granada Television Ltd* [2000] 1 All ER 135).

The most senior Scottish judges (the Lord President of the Court of Session and the Lord Justice Clerk) are appointed by the monarch on a recommendation from the Prime Minister on the nomination of the First Minister (s 95). Other judges are appointed on the recommendation of the First Minister.

In some respects Scottish judges appear to have stronger protection against political interference than their UK counterparts (Chapter 8). Senior judges can be dismissed for inability, neglect of duty or misbehaviour only on a recommendation by the First Minister following a resolution of the Parliament (s 95). The resolution can be made only on the basis of a written report from a tribunal, chaired by a member of the Privy Council who has held a high judicial office, concluding that the judge is unfit for office on one of these grounds. In the case of the Lord President and the Lord Justice Clerk, the Prime Minister must be consulted.

16.2.4   Devolution issues (Sch 6)

The courts have a special role in relation to 'devolution issues'. These are:

▶ whether the Parliament has exceeded its powers;
▶ whether a member of the government has acted outside his or her devolved competence or violated rights under the Human Rights Act 1998 or European Community law;
▶ any other question about whether a function is within devolved competence;
▶ any other question arising by virtue of the Act about reserved matters.

Devolution issues can arise in any legal proceedings. A devolution issue is ultimately decided by the Supreme Court, either on appeal or by way of a reference from a lower court or directly if referred by the Lord Advocate or the Advocate General. This has been said to be an essential part of the constitutional settlement ensuring that the rule of law is respected throughout the entire range of the activities of the Scottish government (*H v Lord Advocate* (2012) [31]), a safeguard denied against the UK executive. In English and Welsh courts the UK Attorney General can also bring devolution proceedings and in Northern Ireland courts the Advocate General for Northern Ireland.

16.2.5   Independence

There is a proposal to hold a referendum in Scotland as whether Scotland should become an independent state. This requires UK legislation since changes in the relationship between Scotland and the UK are not devolved matters. At the time of writing it is proposed by way of an agreement between the political parties to allow some people from the age of 16 to vote. This is another example of an important constitutional change resulting from private party negotiations.

If Scotland is to retain sterling as its currency independence may in practice be limited. Apart from arrangements concerning immigration and political rights of Scottish citizens such as membership of Parliament and voting rights (analogous to questions which arose when Ireland left the Union), and subject to the recherché debate about the Act of Union (Section 8.5), the question of Scottish independence does not pose major constitutional issues in English law. It does of course raise major economic questions and questions about Scotland's position in international law and membership of the EU.

16.3   Northern Ireland

Devolved powers are more limited in Northern Ireland than in Scotland. This is intended to cater to problems arising out of an entrenched historical divide. The history of Ireland is complex and raises fundamental political issues about the sharing of political power. Disagreements centre on divisions between the Catholic and Protestant communities and on a history of imposed settlement from England and Scotland. Broadly speaking the majority Protestant community prefers to remain an integral part of the UK, while the Catholic community would prefer union with the Republic of Ireland.

Ireland had been nominally subject to the English Crown from the tenth century. According to the English story, laws made by the Irish Parliament had been subject to English statutes and approval by the King in Council since 1494 ('Poyning's Law'). However until Tudor times England effectively controlled only an area around Dublin called the Pale. Henry VIII and Elizabeth I attempted to extend English administration to the whole of Ireland, precipitating rebellion followed by confiscation of land and extensive settlement by English and Scots Protestants in what is now Northern Ireland. Cromwell's regime during the 1650s consolidated this policy with large-scale massacres. The conquest of Ireland was completed in 1690 when William III, in alliance with France and supported by the Pope, defeated the deposed Catholic King of England, James II, at the Battle of the Boyne.

After a series of violent rebellions against Protestant supremacy, the Acts of Union of 1800 joined Britain and Ireland into the UK, thus creating the UK Parliament. The Irish Parliament was abolished in favour of Irish representation in the UK Parliament. The Acts of Union declared that the Union was to last 'forever'. They also protected the United Church of England and Ireland, but the repeal of this provision by the Irish Church Act 1879 has been upheld (*Ex p Canon Selwyn* (1872)).

Unrest punctuated by periods of violence continued throughout the nineteenth and twentieth centuries. In the late nineteenth and early twentieth centuries the question of 'Irish home rule' was among the most important questions in UK politics. It had profound constitutional implications. It weakened the personal authority of the monarch, who unwisely took sides in the dispute and generated disputes about the authority of Parliament. It was one reason for the enactment of the Parliament Act 1911 (Section 11.3), which removed the House of Lord's power to veto a bill approved by the Commons.

The Government of Ireland Act 1914 gave internal home rule to Ireland. This was not widely acceptable and from 1916 there was a period of violent rebellion in favour of independence from the UK. The UK attempted to impose a compromise in the form of the Government of Ireland Act 1920. This partitioned Ireland between what is now the Republic of Ireland and the six counties of Northern Ireland. The Act introduced a devolved government in Northern Ireland. The Irish Free State (Constitution) Act 1922 purported to give the rest of Ireland internal self-government.

Both measures were ignored in the Republic of Ireland, which created its own constitution based upon the sovereignty of the people. This constitution applied to the whole of Ireland, although it was ineffective in the north. As a result there were conflicting legal orders, each being valid from its internal viewpoint. Eventually the UK recognised the independence of the Republic (Ireland Act 1949) but provided that 'in no event will Northern Ireland cease to be part of the UK without the consent of the Parliament of Northern Ireland' (s 1(2)).

From 1972, following continuing violence resulting from perceived discrimination against Catholics, direct rule from Westminster was imposed and, characteristic of UK government, stringent emergency legislation was introduced. A series of agreements attempted to engineer a compromise by creating machinery for inter-community negotiations (Anglo-Irish Agreement 1985; 'Downing Street Declaration' (Cm 2422, 1994)). These led to the Belfast, or Good Friday, Agreement (Cm 3883, 1998) between the two governments and the main political parties in Northern Ireland. This is the basis of the current arrangements.

The Good Friday agreement provides for the restoration of devolved government, the amendment of the Irish constitution to accept that Northern Ireland is currently controlled by the UK, and the creation of various consultative bodies representing the interests of the UK, Northern Ireland and the Republic of Ireland (North/South Ministerial Council, British–Irish Council, British–Irish Intergovernmental Conference). The Good Friday Agreement was endorsed by 71 per cent of voters in Northern Ireland and 94 per cent in the Republic of Ireland in separate referendums.

The Northern Ireland Act 1998 attempts to ensure a balance between the competing communities. It is sometimes characterised as an example of deliberative democracy and liberal pluralism (Sections 2.7, 2.3.6). It restricts the political freedom of the legislature and executive to a greater extent than is the case in the rest of the UK. Ministers are directly elected by the Assembly in accordance with the balance of the parties within it. Thus the system is very different from the UK's traditional system, which concentrates power in the leader of the largest party. The Northern Ireland devolution settlement also provides for the people to vote in a referendum to leave the UK and for the Republic of Ireland to participate in the affairs of Northern Ireland. The Assembly's powers are more limited than is the case with Scotland, and the UK Secretary of State has stronger powers.

The following are the main provisions of the Act:

- Northern Ireland remains part of the UK and the status of Northern Ireland will be altered only with the consent of a majority of its electorate (s 1). If a referendum favours a united Ireland, the Secretary of State is required to 'make proposals' to implement this by agreement with the Irish government (s 1).
- The overriding power of Parliament to make law for Northern Ireland is not affected by the Act (s 5(6)). UK statutes apply in Northern Ireland only expressly or by necessary implication.
- The Northern Ireland Assembly is elected by a single transferable vote (Section 12.7.1).
- The Assembly sits for a fixed four-year term but can be dissolved on a resolution supported by two-thirds of its members, or by the monarch on the advice of the Secretary of State, or if a Chief Minister or Deputy Chief Minister cannot be elected within six weeks of the first meeting of the Assembly (ss 16, 32). (See *Robinson v Secretary of State for Northern Ireland* [2002].)
- If 30 members petition the Assembly in relation to any matter to be voted on, the vote shall require cross-community support (s 42).
- The Assembly can legislate generally in relation to matters exclusively within Northern Ireland except in relation to matters which are excluded (s 6). As in Scotland the Assembly's powers are subject to EC law and to the rights protected by the Human Rights Act 1998. It can raise certain taxes but not the main taxes that

apply generally throughout the UK. Unlike in Scotland excluded matters are of two kinds: 'excepted' matters and 'reserved' matters, listed in Schedules 2 and 3. The Assembly cannot legislate on excepted matters unless ancillary to other matters. It can legislate on reserved matters and on ancillary matters with the consent of the Secretary of State (ss 6, 8, 10). Policing and justice finally became devolved matters in 2010. Discrimination on the grounds of religious belief or political opinion is outside the competence of the Assembly, and certain statutes (European Communities Act 1972; Human Rights Act 1998; parts of the Justice (Northern Ireland) Act 2002) cannot be altered (s 7).

- The Presiding Officer introduces bills to the Assembly. If the Presiding Officer decides that a bill is outside the powers of the Assembly he must refuse to introduce it (s 10) (cf Scotland, where the bill is not blocked).

- Acts of the Assembly require royal assent (s 5). Unlike the case in Scotland, where this is a matter for the Presiding Officer, the Secretary of State submits bills for royal assent (s 14). He can refuse to submit a bill if he thinks it is outside the competence of the Assembly or contains provisions incompatible with international obligations, the interests of defence or national security, or the protection of public safety or public order, or would have an adverse effect on the operation of the single market within the UK.

- The First Minister lacks the discretionary power of a UK Prime Minister to appoint or dismiss other ministers or dissolve the legislature. Instead there is a bipartisan arrangement for power sharing, ensuring that both unionists and nationalists play a part. The First Minister and Deputy First Minister are elected jointly by the Assembly from its members. This requires a majority of the Assembly and also separate majorities of unionists and nationalists (s 16). The First and Deputy First Ministers must both lose office if either resigns or ceases to be a member of the Assembly. Subject to a maximum of ten, which can be increased by the Secretary of State (s 17(4)), and to the approval of the Assembly, the First and Deputy First Ministers jointly decide on the number of Northern Ireland ministers heading departments and forming a Cabinet. Ministers are then nominated by the political parties from members of the Assembly in accordance with a formula designed to reflect the balance of parties in the Assembly (s 18). Assembly committees must also reflect party strengths.

- A minister can be dismissed by his or her party's nominating officer and loses office on ceasing to be a member of the Assembly other than after a dissolution (s 18). Ministers collectively lose office when a new Assembly is elected, where a party is excluded on a vote of confidence, where a new determination as to the number of ministers is made or as prescribed by Standing Order (s 18).

- Ministers and political parties can be excluded for up to 12 months (renewable) by the Assembly on the grounds that they are not committed to peace or have otherwise broken their oath of office (s 30). The motion must have the support of at least 30 members (from a total of between 96 and 108) and must be moved by the First and Deputy First Ministers jointly or by the Presiding Officer of the Assembly if required to do so by the Secretary of State. The Secretary of State must take into account the propensity to violence and cooperation with the authorities of the excluded person. The resolution must have cross-party support.

- Ministers must take a pledge of office which includes a Ministerial Code of Conduct (s 16(10), Sch 4). The Code requires the 'strictest standards of propriety, accountability, openness, good community relations and equality and avoiding or declaring conflicts of interest'. Any direct or indirect pecuniary interests that members of the public might reasonably think could influence ministers' judgement must be registered. The Code is similar to the Ministerial Code for UK ministers and requires compliance with the Nolan Principles of Public Life (Chapter 5). In Northern Ireland, unlike the rest of the UK, it might therefore be enforceable in the courts.

▶ The Attorney General for Northern Ireland is the government's principle legal adviser and representative. Although the Attorney General cannot be a member of the Assembly, he or she can participate in its debates but cannot vote. The Attorney is appointed for a single term of five years, and dismissed, by the First Minister and Deputy First Minister jointly. The office has greater security than its Scottish equivalent in that dismissal is only on the ground of misbehaviour or inability and requires a proposal from a special tribunal (s 24). There is also an Advocate General for Northern Ireland, who shares certain functions with the Attorney General. The post of Advocate General must be held by the UK Attorney General (Justice (Northern Ireland) Act 2002, s 27, Sch 7). Thus governmental legal arrangements are less independent than is the case in Scotland since the Advocate is appointed and dismissed by the UK Prime Minister without safeguards.

▶ Northern Ireland has its own legal system but the substantive law is closely related to English Common law.

▶ As in Scotland, devolution issues can arise in any legal proceedings and can also be referred directly to the Supreme Court. In Northern Ireland courts the power to do so and to defend legal proceedings lies with the Attorney General and Advocate General for Northern Ireland.

▶ There is a separate civil service for Northern Ireland but the functions of the Civil Service Commissioners (dealing with appointments and standards) are reserved matters (Sch 3).

▶ There are human rights and equal opportunities commissioners with powers to advise government and support legal proceedings.

16.4 Wales

Wales was never a separate state but consisted of a number of principalities which were gradually assimilated by the English. Until Tudor times there was continuing hostility between the English Kings and the Welsh rulers. The largest of the principalities passed into English rule in 1084 (Statute of Wales) and the English local government system was imposed by the Statute of Rhuddlan (1284), when much of north Wales had been conquered by Edward I. England claimed control over the whole of Wales by the sixteenth century and imposed the English language and administration (Act of the Union of Wales 1536). In 1543 a system of Welsh courts was introduced to apply English law. There were Welsh representatives in the English Parliament and a separate Welsh Assembly was abolished in 1689. A single court system for England and Wales was introduced in 1830.

Although there have always been voices in favour of Welsh independence the political pressures are less clear than in the case of Scotland, and in economic terms Wales and England are more closely assimilated. Earlier proposals for Welsh devolution in the Wales Act 1978 were defeated by a referendum and the current proposals were only narrowly approved.

The system of devolution created by the Government of Wales Act 1998 is a weaker form of devolution than those in Scotland and Northern Ireland. Unlike the Scottish Parliament and the Northern Ireland Assembly, the Welsh Assembly can legislate only on prescribed subjects. Thus it requires a positive power to make law as opposed to being able to do anything that is not forbidden. Unlike the case in the other devolved territories UK statutes apply in Wales unless excluded expressly or by necessary implication. Wales has no separate judicial system. Wales and England have a common legal system.

Originally all powers, both lawmaking and executive, were vested in the Welsh National Assembly with flexible powers for delegation to committees and secretaries. The Welsh system was a hybrid of a local government model based on committees formed out of an elected assembly, a parliamentary model and an administrative model based on the former Welsh Office of the UK government. The Assembly was confined to making subordinate legislation under powers that were previously exercised by UK ministers under particular statutes or were subsequently conferred on it by statute.

However the Government of Wales Act 2006 substantially increased the powers of the Assembly but still less than in Scotland. It also created a system of ministers responsible to the Assembly on a similar basis to that in Scotland. The Act therefore introduced a separation of powers between legislature and executive. It replaced most of the 1998 Act. The new powers of the Assembly were triggered following a referendum held in 2011.

Under the 2006 Act the Welsh Assembly can do anything that could be done by an Act of Parliament but only on the particular subjects (fields) designated by the Act. Thus unlike the position in Scotland and Northern Ireland the need for a positive power to make a law still applies. The fields currently include agriculture, ancient monuments, economic development, education, environment, food, fisheries, health, highways and transport, housing, local government, the National Assembly, public administration, social welfare, sport, tourism, town and country planning, water supply and sewage and the Welsh language.

Legislation must take effect exclusively within Wales, or in the case of enforcement and incidental matters in England and Wales (s 94). As in Scotland the powers of assembly are subject to EC law and to Convention rights under the Human Rights Act 1998 and also to restrictions limiting the creation of criminal offences and the alteration of certain statutes.

Section 114 empowers the Secretary of State to veto an Assembly Act on public interest grounds, including interference with the English water supply. In *A-G's Reference Re Local Government By Laws (Wales) Bill 2012* [2013] 1 All ER 1013 the Supreme Court upheld an Assembly Bill intended to increase the powers of the Welsh government by removing a statutory requirement for the consent of the Secretary of State to changes in certain local government bylaws. In the light of the wide legislative powers given to the Assembly Lord Hope took the view that within the prescribed fields the powers of the Assembly were to be treated as similar to those of the Scottish Parliament. Acts of the Assembly are therefore subject to limited judicial review (Section 16.2.1). However, although it was of constitutional significance, the 2006 Act should be interpreted in the same way as ordinary legislation.

The system created by the 2006 Act is closer to the parliamentary system than was previously the case. The Welsh Assembly of 60 members is elected by a method similar to that in Scotland, with 20 members elected in five regions and 40 in local constituencies (Section 12.7.1). However, unlike in Scotland, a person cannot stand in both regional and local constituency elections (ss 7, 17). The Assembly sits for a fixed term of four years but, unlike the position under the 1998 Act, can be dissolved earlier by a two-thirds majority or if a First Minister is not nominated within 28 days, as in Scotland (ss 5, 47) (Section 16.2.2).

A First Minister is chosen by the Assembly and appoints and dismisses other ministers and deputy ministers from Assembly members (ss 46–51). However the approval of the Assembly is not required for ministerial appointments. Instead the total number of ministers and deputy ministers is limited to 12.

A Council General, responsible for giving legal advice to the government, must also be appointed and can be removed by the First Minister with the agreement of the Assembly. The Council General loses offices when a new First Minister is appointed (s 49). Safeguards for the independence of the law officer are therefore less than in Scotland and Northern Ireland. She or he can be but need not be an Assembly member.

Welsh ministers are financially responsible to the Assembly, for which purpose there is an Auditor General (ss 143, 145). However, unlike the position in Scotland, their accounts are regulated by the UK Treasury and can be examined by the UK Comptroller and Auditor General. The UK Secretary of State for Wales represents Welsh affairs at national level and in the Council of Ministers of the EU.

As regards accountability, the Committee on Standards of Conduct receives and investigates complaints referred to it by the Presiding Officer relating to the conduct of any member of the National Assembly for Wales. If the complaint is substantiated, in its report to the Assembly the Committee may 'recommend' action in appropriate cases. In addition the Code of Practice on Members' Access to Information (2004) confers on members of the National Assembly for Wales more extensive rights of access to information than those available under the UK Freedom of Information Act 2000. The National Assembly Commissioner for Standards can investigate complaints that any Code of the Assembly has been breached.

The 2006 Act has a communitarian edge. Welsh ministers are empowered to promote or improve the economic, social and environmental well-being of Wales (s 60) and under the rubric of 'inclusiveness' must consult widely, advance various social and cultural concerns and prepare strategies dealing with sustainable development, the voluntary sector, equal opportunities and the Welsh language. There must also be a 'Partnership Council' comprising ministers and local authority representatives (s 72).

There is no separate Welsh legal system England and Wales being a single jurisdiction system, although there is a division of the Administrative Court in Cardiff dealing with Welsh governmental issues. This could develop distinctive constitutional principles in the Welsh context. In R (Deepdock) v Welsh Ministers [2007] EWHC 3347 [20] it was suggested that there should be a presumption that public law cases involving Welsh public authorities should normally be heard in Wales. Indeed, given the wider law making powers now exercised by the Welsh Assembly, it is arguable that there should be separate Welsh courts. On the other hand a distinctive Welsh legal regime might evolve pragmatically (see Gardner, 'Public Law Challenges in Wales:the Past and the Present' [2013] PL 1; Justice outside London Report: Cardiff and Wales (2007), Dept of Justice). There are provisions similar to those in Scotland and Northern Ireland for the Supreme Court to deal with devolution matters but there is no provision for the court to include a Welsh member. The Council General is responsible for referring devolution issues to the Supreme Court and for defending challenges to Welsh enactments, the provisions being similar to those for Scotland (s 96).

There is a Public Services Ombudsman (Public Services Ombudsman (Wales) Act 2005). This is a stronger version of the Ombudsman mechanism than the English and UK equivalents. The Ombudsman can receive complaints directly from the public and has jurisdiction over the Assembly and government, local authorities, health authorities and social landlords. The Ombudsman's report may be published and the authority concerned must also do so unless the Ombudsman excludes publication in certain circumstances on public interest grounds (s 21). In the event of non-compliance, the Ombudsman can refer the matter to the High Court.

The Commission on Devolution in Wales (the Silk Commission) was established by the UK government in October 2011 to report on the accountability and powers of the Welsh government. The first part of its report published in November 3012 recommended that the Welsh Assembly should have tax raising powers subject to a referendum. popowerpowerssubjectota referendum.

16.5　England

England, comprising 85 per cent of the population of the UK, has neither elected institutions of its own nor indeed a legal identity. England is governed by the central UK government. Therefore Scottish, Welsh and Northern Ireland members of the UK Parliament are entitled to vote in debates affecting exclusively English matters for which they are not accountable to their own voters. Similarly a UK government might be kept in power on the strength of Scottish votes. For example in 2004, by a majority of five, the Labour government won the vote in favour of increasing university tuition fees in England by virtue of its Scottish supporters.

This problem (often called 'West Lothian question' after the constituency formerly represented by Tam Dalyell, a relentless pursuer of the matter) is an inevitable result of the UK Parliament having exclusive jurisdiction over English affairs. It can be resolved adequately only by creating a separate lawmaker for England, a proposal for which there is little public interest. Indeed the same problem arose without solution in relation to the Irish Home Rule Bills between 1886 and 1914.

A possible compromise solution of creating a procedure under which Scottish MPs cannot vote on 'English' matters is fraught with problems relating to how English matters are to be identified and disentangled from UK matters, particularly in relation to finance (see Hazell, 2006). Moreover Scottish, Welsh and Northern Ireland voters are represented in the UK Parliament roughly in proportion to their population. This means that the UK Parliament is dominated by English MPs who can vote on Scottish matters, including devolved matters such as the amount of money to be given to Scotland from the UK government. A more limited compromise would be a 'Grand Committee' comprising English MPs to scrutinise English Bills.

A sketchy proposal for an elected regional assembly for northeastern England was defeated by 78 per cent in a referendum in 2004 (see Regional Assemblies (Preparations) Act 2003, *Your Region, Your Choice: Revitalising the English Regions* (Cm 5511, 2002)).

There is a limited form of regional devolution for the London region in the form of an elected Mayor and Assembly (Greater London Authority Act 1999). The Assembly is elected on the basis of 'first past the post' (Chapter 12), together with an 'additional member' from a party list in accordance with the party's share of the vote, thereby reflecting public opinion to a greater extent than is the case with local government and Parliament. The Mayor and Assembly have certain executive powers in relation mainly to transport, policing, land use planning, housing and local amenities.

Summary

▶ Legislative and executive power has been devolved to elected bodies in Scotland and Northern Ireland but without significant tax-raising powers. The UK Parliament has reserved the power to legislate in respect of many matters and has a general power to override the devolved assemblies. Their legislation is subordinate legislation, which is invalid if it exceeds the limits prescribed by the devolution statutes and also on judicial review grounds, although the courts will be circumspect in reviewing the acts of an elected body (Section 19.6.1). In particular, unlike a UK statute, legislation violating the rights protected by the Human Rights Act 1998 is invalid.

▶ A more limited devolution applies to Wales. The Welsh Assembly can legislate only on matters specifically assigned to it, whereas Scotland and Northern Ireland can legislate on any subject other than those specifically excluded.

▶ Elections to the devolved bodies are partly by proportional representation. Citizens of EU countries resident in the UK can be candidates for and vote in elections to the devolved bodies.

▶ The Scottish and Welsh executives are structured according to the UK parliamentary system. However the balance of power is more in favour of the Parliament than is the case in the UK system. The Northern Ireland system is primarily concerned to achieve a balance between different political factions and is more restrictive than is the case with Scotland.

▶ There is no devolved government in England. Representatives from the devolved countries can therefore vote in the UK Parliament on purely English matters.

Exercises

16.1 To what extent is Wales a 'poor relation' in relation to devolution?

16.2 '…Scotland and England, although politically under the same Crown and under the supreme sway of one united legislature, are to be considered as independent foreign countries, unconnected with each other.' Lord Campbell in *Stuart v Marquis of Bute* (1861) 9 HL Cas 440, 454. To what extent is this true today?

16.3 Compare the rules governing the appointment and removal of the Scottish and Northern Ireland First Ministers. Which is the more democratic?

16.4 Compare the methods in the UK and Scotland, (i) for dealing with a hung Parliament and (ii) for choosing the leader of the government.

16.5 Compare the positions of the law officers in the devolved governments from the point of view of their independence.

16.6 To what extent can a majority in the Northern Ireland Assembly control the executive?

16.7 What are the constitutional problems, if any, of Scottish devolution in respect of England? How would you address them?

16.8 What safeguards are there in the devolved regimes (i) for ensuring that the devolved lawmakers do not exceed their powers and (ii) for ensuring that the UK government respects the independence of the devolved governments?

16.9 On 4 May, elections take place in Scotland. The Socialist Party gets the largest number of seats in the Scottish Parliament (40%). The Freedom Party, which came third with 15 per cent, agrees to support the Socialists in order to nominate Cherie, the leader of the Socialists, as the

Exercises cont'd

next First Minister. The Socialists and the Freedom Party together hold 55 per cent of the seats of the Parliament. In response to its support, Cherie promises to appoint two members of the Freedom Party as ministers.

On 4 June, the Parliament nominates Cherie for appointment as First Minister. The Conservatives, who came second in the election, oppose the nomination. The General Secretary of the Socialist Party, on behalf of the Scottish Parliament, submits the nomination to the UK Prime Minister, who advises the Queen to accept it.

Once Cherie is appointed as the First Minister, she decides to appoint as ministers exclusively members of her political party, irrespective of whether they have been elected as members of the Scottish Parliament. Nick, the leader of the Freedom Party, claims that the First Minister has breached her promise and warns her that she will face severe consequences and that he will use the most drastic measures at his disposal.

After this controversial commencement, the Socialist government declares that it is going to develop an extremely ambitious programme for Scotland. In its electoral programme, the Socialist Party had promised a stronger voice for Scotland in both the UK and Europe, and therefore the government announces a bill concerning legally binding international agreements between Scotland and other European States. This bill will be introduced in the Scottish Parliament by Dave, a Scottish Minister. The Secretary of State for Scotland informs Edinburgh that he will block this bill if they decide to put it forward.

Discuss the constitutional position in respect of each of these events.

16.10 Elections in Wales are to be held on the first Thursday of May. Huw is very pleased because this is the first time he is entitled to vote. In his polling station in the local constituency of Ynys Môn he is planning to cast two votes for two different political parties, Hope for Wales and Welsh People Together. In Huw's opinion both offer what the Welsh nation needs for further political development and he hopes that they will govern together.

Catrin, an enthusiastic woman who is a personal friend of Huw's, is standing to be the Assembly member for Ynys Môn, a local constituency. She lives in London and is a member of the party Welsh People Together. Catrin also wishes to be a candidate in the regional constituency in Wales where she spent her childhood.

Dyfed, who is standing to be the Assembly member for the local constituency of Caernarfon, is a member of the political party United Celtic Nations, which aims to unify Scotland, Wales and Northern Ireland and secure their independence from the United Kingdom. His Italian friend Fabrizio and his American friend Ron, both of whom are very keen on Dyfed's political ideas, have decided to vote for him.

Comment on any legal issues which arise.

Further reading

Beatson, Grosz, Hickman, Singh, *Human Rights: Judicial Protection in the United Kingdom* (Sweet & Maxwell 2008) ch 8 [devolution cases]

Bogdanor, *The New British Constitution* (Hart 2009) ch 4

Cornes, 'Devolution and England: What Is on Offer?' in Bamforth and Leyland (eds), *Public Law in a Multi-Layered Constitution* (Hart 2003)

Hadfield, 'Devolution, Westminster and the English Question' [2005] PL 286

Further reading cont'd

Hadfield, 'Devolution: A National Conversation?' in Jowell and Oliver (eds), (7th edn, Oxford University Press 2011)

Hazell, *The English Question* (Manchester University Press 2006)

Hazell and Rawlings (eds), *Devolution, Law Making and the Constitution* (Imprint Academic 2005)

Himsworth, 'The Domesticated Executive in Scotland' in Craig and Tomkins (eds), *The Executive and Public Law* (Oxford University Press 2005)

Himsworth and O'Neill, *Scotland's Constitution: Law and Practice* (LexisNexis 2003)

House of Lords Select Committee on the Constitution Committee, *Devolution: Inter-Institutional Relations in the United Kingdom* (HL 2002–03, 147)

Jones, 'The Laws of England and Wales', in *Halsbury's Laws of England Centenary Essays 2007* (LexisNexis Butterworths 2007)

Jowell and Oliver (eds), *The Changing Constitution* (6th edn, Oxford University Press 2007) chs 9–11

Merinos, 'Democracy, Governance and Governmentality: Civic Public Space and Constitutional Renewal in Northern Ireland' (2001) 21 OJLS 287

Rawlings, 'Hastening Slowly: The Next Phase of Welsh Devolution' [2005] PL 824

Tierney, *Constitutional Law and National Pluralism* (Oxford University Press 2004)

Trench, 'The Government of Wales Act 2006: The Next Steps in Devolution for Wales' [2006] PL 687

Winetrobe, 'Collective Responsibility in Devolved Scotland' [2003] PL 24

Part V

Administrative law

Chapter 17

The grounds of judicial review, I: illegality and ultra vires

Introduction: the constitutional basis of judicial review

Judicial review has ancient origins (see *Keighly Case* [1609] 10 Co Rep 139). Sometimes called the 'supervisory jurisdiction', judicial review is the High Court's power to police the legality of decisions made by public bodies. Judicial review cases are decided by the Administrative Court, part of the Queen's Bench Division of the High Court (the *Upper Tribunal* also has certain judicial review powers (Section 20.1)). Judicial review applies to all public bodies, including courts and tribunals other than Parliament which is protected by privilege (Section 11.6) and the High Court itself. Judicial review applies to government decisions and actions that affect individual rights and interests and also to general statements of government policy (eg *Gillick v West Yorkshire CC* [1986] AC 162: guidance on contraception).

Although partly regulated by statute, judicial review is a creation of the common law so that the courts themselves control its scope and limits. It is an essential aspect of the rule of law (see *R (Alconbury Developments Ltd) v Secretary of State for the Environment, Transport and the Regions* [2001] 2 All ER 929 at 981; *R (Cart) v Upper Tribunal* [2011] at [71]–[73]).

Judicial review strikes an accommodation between competing aspects of the separation of powers. On the one hand the principle of checks and balances require that government action be subject to review by independent and impartial tribunals. On the other hand judicial review operates within the context of the parliamentary accountability of the executive. From this perspective the functional separation of powers pulls in the other direction by requiring the court to avoid trespassing into the political territory of Parliament.

The courts strike this accommodation mainly by claiming not to be concerned with the 'merits' of government action, that is whether it is good or bad, but only with whether governmental decisions fall within their authorising legislation and meet legal standards of fairness and 'reasonableness'. However these principles are vague, shading into questions of merit, and there is considerable room for debate as to the proper limits of the courts' powers. The courts may also make a particular matter off limits or 'non-justiciable', meaning that for various reasons it is not appropriate for investigation by the courts. A clear example is a decision to invade another country (*R (Gentle) v Prime Minister* [2008]). Justiciability will be discussed later (Section 19.7, see also Section 14.6).

Moreover the judicial review principles are flexible in that the intensity of review, the range of grounds available and the selection of remedies vary with the context. While not excluding review entirely the courts may allow a wide discretion to the government decision maker in relation to a particular issue. This is often called 'deference' but is really an application of the separation of powers (Section 19.7). In particular courts respect the sphere of democratic bodies especially Parliament, albeit they have long been alive to the dangers of a dominant executive (see *Dyson v A-G* [1911] 1 KB 410,

R v Secretary of State, ex p Fire Brigades Union (19950, Section 7.8.1; *AXA General Insurance Ltd v HM Advocate* (2012), Section 8.5.2). The Human Rights Act 1998 (HRA) has added a further dimension to judicial review by creating additional grounds for challenge (although some of them overlap).

Judicial review is a last-resort method of challenge and there are procedural barriers intended to prevent it being too easily taken up (Section 19.3). Other and cheaper methods of challenging government decisions exist, for example through tribunals, statutory regulators, ombudsmen and MPs. However these may be questionable either because of the absence of enforcement or investigatory powers or because of a lack of independence (see *R v Secretary of State for the Home Dept, ex p Fire Brigades Union* [1995], Lord Mustill at 267).

17.2 The legal basis of judicial review

The legal basis of judicial review is disputed, reflecting the wider debate as to the nature of our constitution. There is a large and repetitive literature on this issue (the main viewpoints are collected in Forsythe, 2000). One perspective bases judicial review on freestanding common law principles, according to which powerful bodies must act in accordance with rule of law values of fairness and rationality (*Dr Bonham's Case* [1610] 8 co Rep 114a; *Bagg's Case* [1615] 11 Co Rep 936; *Cooper v Wandsworth Board of Works* [1863] 14 CB (NS) 175). This draws inspiration primarily from liberal ideas and from the history of the common law as claiming to be the embodiment of community-based values of fairness and justice.

The other perspective gives greater emphasis to parliamentary supremacy, democracy and the separation of powers. It is republican in tone (Section 2.5). It assumes that because most government powers are created by Act of Parliament, the courts' job is to ensure that powers do not exceed the limits set out by Parliament: the ultra vires doctrine. The underlying principle is that of parliamentary supremacy. The courts must obey a statute. Conversely acts outside a statute have no legal effect. To its supporters this provides a more substantial and democratic basis for judicial review than does the common law. Rather tediously, both approaches can be made to fit the facts, and the historical evidence is inconclusive.

Both approaches conform to possible meanings of the separation of powers and the rule of law. The ultra vires approach is biased towards the functional aspect of the separation of powers (Section 7.5); the common law approach towards checks and balances. One difference between the two approaches is that the ultra vires approach would not permit the courts to override an Act of Parliament. The common law approach is in itself neutral on this issue. However some of its adherents claim that the courts might be able to override a statute in an extreme case (Section 8.4.5).

Another difference between the two approaches is that the common law approach has less difficulty with freeing up judicial review to apply to bodies whose powers do not derive from statute. For example royal prerogative powers and other non-statutory powers exercised by public bodies are subject to judicial review (*CCSU v Minister for the Civil Service* [1985]; *R v Panel on Takeovers and Mergers, ex p Datafin plc* [1987] QB 815). The common law might also be the basis for extending judicial review principles, similar to those applied to government, to powerful private bodies (eg sports regulatory bodies and powerful commercial companies) which exercise control over aspects of public life. Proponents of the ultra vires doctrine accommodate this possibility by suggesting that there need not be a single basis for judicial review. Thus the extent of judicial review depends on political choice rather than an abstract conceptual theory.

Even the ultra vires approach accepts that the judges are developing their own principles in accordance with the 'amplified' or 'extended' versions of the rule of law and the principle of legality according to which basic rights cannot be infringed unless Parliament uses very clear language (Sections 6.5, 6.6). The ultra vires approach claims that judge made rules are part of Parliament's 'constructive intention' by which is meant that Parliament is assumed to intend that these principles be implied into the exercise of every statutory power because Parliament is taken to respect the rule of law. There are many presumptions of statutory interpretation which require courts to assume that Parliament intended to act fairly while allowing the court considerable room to decide what this means. Judicial review may be regarded as an application of this. The difference between the two approaches is that according to the common law view Parliament *tolerates* judicial review, whereas on the ultra vires view Parliament somehow *authorises* judicial review.

Forsythe (1996) suggests that the ultra vires doctrine is a useful 'fig leaf' which gives constitutional respectability to what is happening and at least reminds us that Parliament has the last word. Forsythe's fig leaf could be taken to hide something we would prefer not to see, namely that the ultra vires doctrine is an empty vessel for whatever happens to be the prevailing judicial fashion. The common law version claims to be more honest. It does not ignore the intention of Parliament. Firstly a decision which is ultra vires in the sense that it violates a statute is invalid under both theories albeit from the common law perspective this is part of a larger picture. Secondly the common law approach is perfectly consistent with the view that Parliament can exclude any ground of judicial review just as Parliament can change any other common law rule. There is therefore no inconsistency with parliamentary supremacy.

There is substantial judicial support for the ultra vires doctrine as the basis of judicial review (eg *Boddington v British Transport Police* [1998] 2 WLR 639; *Credit Suisse v Allerdale BC* [1996] 4 All ER 129 at 167; *Page v Hull University Visitor* [1993] 1 All ER 97 at 107). On the other hand in *CCSU v Minister for the Civil Service* (1985) Lord Diplock famously abandoned the ultra vires doctrine by classifying the grounds of judicial review under the three broad heads of 'illegality, irrationality and procedural impropriety', claiming that the law should not pursue 'fairy tales'.

In *R v Secretary of State for Education ex parte Begbie* [2000] 1 WLR 1115 (1129) Laws LJ suggested that the root concept behind judicial review is 'abuse of power'. However this seems too vague to be helpful.

17.3 Appeal and review

Judicial review must not be confused with an appeal. An appeal is a procedure which exists only under a particular statute or, in the case of a voluntary body, by agreement. An appeal allows the appellate body to decide the whole matter again unless the particular statute or agreement limits the grounds of appeal, for example to questions of law only. An appeal therefore may involve a thorough reconsideration of the whole decision, whereas judicial review is concerned only with ensuring that legal standards are complied with. Depending on the particular statute, an appellate body might be a court, tribunal, minister or indeed anyone. A claim for judicial review is possible only in the High Court or the Upper Tribunal.

An appellate body can usually substitute its decision for the first instance decision, although in some cases its powers are limited to sending the matter back to be decided again by the lower body. In judicial review proceedings, unless there is no doubt as to the right decision, the court cannot make the decision itself but must send the matter back to the decision maker with instructions as to its legal duties.

Unlike a right of appeal, which can be raised only in the body specified, the invalidity of government action can be raised not only in the Administrative Court but also, by way of 'collateral challenge', in any proceedings where the rights of a citizen are affected by the validity of government action (eg *Boddington v British Transport Police* (1998): defence to prosecution for smoking contrary to railway bylaws alleged to be ultra vires). This is because an unlawful government decision is of no effect in law (void/nullity) and can be ignored, thus vindicating the rule of law (*Entick v Carrington* (1765). In the case of an appeal, the offending decision is fully valid until the appeal body changes it.

17.4 Nullity: void and voidable decisions

According to the rule of law and also the ultra vires doctrine, an invalid government act should be a nullity (*void*) and have no legal consequences. Indeed this has been emphasised by the courts (eg Lord Reid in *Ridge v Baldwin* [1964] AC 40 and *Anisminic Ltd v Foreign Compensation Commission* [1969] 2 AC 147 at 171, 195, 207; *Secretary of State for the Home Dept v JJ* [2008] 1 All ER 613 at [27]). On the other hand it may be impractical simply to ignore a decision since its invalidity can be exposed only once a court has ruled as much. In that sense a decision is only *voidable*: valid until set aside by a court. This is reinforced by the fact that all the judicial review remedies are discretionary, so in judicial review proceedings the court does not have to set aside even an ultra vires decision. By contrast, where a decision is challenged collaterally, for example as a defence to a prosecution, the court has no discretion (so a different outcome is possible depending solely on which route is taken for the challenge *(see Credit Suisse v Allerdale BC* (1996) at 167).

If a decision is held in judicial review proceedings to be a nullity then in principle it will be treated as never having had legal effect and its consequences will be unwound. For example in *Ridge v Baldwin* [1964] a Chief Constable dismissed without a hearing was held still to be in office and so entitled to his pension rights. In *Secretary of State v JJ (2008)* it was held that a void Control Order made by the Home Secretary under anti-terrorist legislation could not be amended to make it lawful. Similarly in *R (Lumba) v Secretary of State for the Home Dept* [2012] 1 AC 245 the Supreme Court rejected the government's contention that the government was not liable for false imprisonment on the basis of an unlawful decision validated because the same decision could have lawfully been made (however this prevented the claimant getting substantial compensation).

The concept of nullity does not always do justice. In *DPP v Head* [1959] AC 83 a woman was improperly confined in a mental hospital as a result of an invalid medical procedure. A man charged with having sexual relations with a patient 'detained' under the Mental Health Acts successfully argued that, due to the invalidity, the patient was not 'detained' under the relevant Acts. On the same analysis the officials who administered the hospital would have made numerous decisions affecting the detainee on the assumption that the initial order was valid. If, due to the initial infection of the invalid decision, all consequential acts had to be unpicked the result would be chaos. In *Credit Suisse v Allerdale BC* [1996] a local authority successfully argued that a guarantee which it had given was ultra vires so that it could not be enforced against it (see Local Government (Contracts) Act 1997 reversing this). Similarly, would everyone granted a driving licence under a regulation which later turned out to be invalid for some procedural reason find themselves guilty of an offence?

There are various ways of attacking this problem, none of them entirely satisfactory.

1. to argue that only the most serious defects make a decision void, while others make it only voidable in the sense that it might be set aside for the future only (see *Bugg v DPP* [1993] QB 473 at 493). This was rejected by the House of Lords in *Anisminic (1965)*, who took the view that all defects make the decision a nullity (cf Lords Browne Wilkinson and Slynn in *Boddington (1998)*);
2. to claim that there is a 'presumption of validity', meaning that until it is set aside a decision must be treated as valid but if successfully challenged it can be set aside retrospectively, that is, treated as if it never existed (see *Hoffmann-La Roche v Secretary of State* [1974] 2 All ER 1128). In that sense all decisions would be voidable. This does not address the problem of third parties who rely on a decision before it is set aside;
3. using judicial discretion. This sits uncomfortably with the rule of law;
4. treating the matter as one of statutory interpretation in the particular context (see *Seal v Chief Constable of South Wales Police* [2007] 4 All ER 177). Of course a statute can prevent a decision being treated as void but this approach abandons any general principle. It was favoured by Lord Hoffman (dissenting) in *Secretary of State v JJ (2008)*;
5. Professor Wade deals with the conundrum by using the concept of 'relative nullity', meaning that an invalid decision is indeed a nullity but only if challenged in the right court by the right person in the right way ('Unlawful Administrative Action: Void or Voidable?' (1968) 84 LQR 95). For example a claimant may be out of time, in which case the decision must stand and a third party can rely on it (See *Agricultural Training Board v Aylesbury Mushrooms Ltd* [1972] 1 WLR 190 regulation invalid only against those who had no been consulted as required by statute.);
6. Forsythe (1998) suggests a distinction between an act valid in law and an act that exists in fact. This refers to the situation where an invalid decision has a chain of consequences where it is relied upon by other officials or citizens – the 'domino effect' and 'the theory of the second actor', that is an official who makes a decision on the assumption that a previous decision is valid (see also Beatson and Matthews, *Administrative Law: Text and Materials* (3rd edn, Oxford University Press 2005) 94–101). The crucial question which depends on interpreting the particular statute and so gives the court a discretion is whether the validity *in law* of the first act is a precondition to the validity of the second decision or whether a decision *in fact* is sufficient. For example in *R v Wicks* [1998] AC 92 the House of Lords held that a developer could be prosecuted for disobeying a planning enforcement notice even though the notice was invalid since the statutory requirement was only for a notice that existed in fact, that is, one that appeared to be valid;
7. distinguishing between the decision itself and the preliminary steps leading to it. These are not necessarily void and so the whole process need not be unpicked (see *Shrewsbury and Atcham BC v Secretary of State* (2008) at [57]–[58]).

17.5 Classification of the grounds of review

Unfortunately there is no general agreement on how to classify the grounds of judicial review, and textbooks take different approaches. I shall organise the grounds of judicial review on the basis of Lord Diplock's classification in *CCSU v Minister for the Civil Service* (1985), that is, under the three heads of 'illegality, irrationality and procedural impropriety'. However the Diplock categories tell us little in themselves and do not avoid overlaps. Indeed the House of Lords has emphasised that the heads of challenge are not watertight compartments but run together (*Boddington v British Transport Police* (1999), eg *Wheeler v Leicester City Council* [1985] 2 All ER 1106 (Section 18.1)). In this chapter, we shall discuss illegality. The other grounds are discussed in Chapter 18.

It might be helpful at this point to provide a checklist:

1. *Illegality*
   - ▶ 'narrow' ultra vires, or lack of jurisdiction, in the sense of straying beyond the limits defined by the statute;
   - ▶ errors of law and (in certain cases) errors of fact;
   - ▶ 'wide' ultra vires, or acting for an ulterior purpose, taking irrelevant factors into account or failing to take relevant factors into account; fettering discretion.

2. *Irrationality*
   - ▶ *Wednesbury* unreasonableness. This could stand alone or be the outcome of taking an irrelevant factor into account;
   - ▶ proportionality, at least under the Human Rights Act 1998.

3. *Procedural impropriety*
   - ▶ violating important statutory procedures;
   - ▶ bias;
   - ▶ lack of a fair hearing;
   - ▶ failure to give reasons for a decision.

17.6 Illegality: 'narrow' ultra vires

Illegality concerns ultra vires in its basic sense, namely a requirement that the decision falls within the statute that confers the power. The doctrine is based on the principle of the rule of law that a public authority can interfere with the freedom of others only if specifically authorised by law to do so. Thus in *R v Somerset CC ex parte Fewings* (1995) a local authority attempted to ban stag hunting on land that it owned. The Court of Appeal upholding Laws J on this point held that the Council was not entitled to rely on its ownership of the land as a private landowner might but must justify the ban by reference to a statutory power (Section 17.9.2).

The focus is therefore upon statutory interpretation. Most government bodies are statutory; for example local authorities and tribunals and most central government powers are conferred by statute on individual ministers. In the case of courts and judicial tribunals, the terminology of 'lack' or 'excess' of jurisdiction is often used. (Jurisdiction means 'area of power' and 'lack' or 'excess' of jurisdiction means here the same as ultra vires).

Here are some famous examples of ultra vires. In *A-G v Fulham Corp* [1921] 1 Ch 440 a local authority had power to provide a 'wash house' for local people. It interpreted this as authorising the provision of a laundry service for working people, who could leave washing to be done by staff and delivered to their homes. This was held to be unlawful in that 'wash house', according to the court, meant a place where a person can do their own washing. This raises the possibility of political bias in interpreting statutes. For example the court might have been influenced by a prejudice against local bodies spending taxpayers' money on welfare services. If the court had read the statute against an assumption of democratic freedom, the outcome might have been different. More recently in *Bromley LBC v GLC* [1983] 1 AC 768 the House of Lords held that an obligation to provide an 'efficient and economic' public transport service meant that the Council could not subsidise the London Underground for social purposes. Among other lines of reasoning, it was held that 'economic' meant that there was an obligation to break even financially (see also *Prescott v Birmingham Corp* [1955] Ch. 210: free transport for pensioners held ultra vires under a power to charge such fares as the Council thought fit since no 'fare' was charged), *Roberts v Hopwood* [1925] AC 578: 'wages' should not include a social welfare element). These cases suggest that the courts take a narrow approach and are reluctant to read a statute as authorising a local authority to be guided by radical political ideologies

Where the scope of a statute is unclear, the courts rely on presumptions of interpretation. They will read a statute as overriding certain principles only if it uses clear words. Examples include *R v Secretary of State for the Home Dept, ex p Simms* (1999) at 412 (freedom of expression); *Congreve v Home Office* [1976] QB 629 and *MaCarthy & Stone v Richmond upon Thames LBC* [1991] 4 All ER 897 (no taxation without statutory authority); *R v Secretary of State for the Home Dept, ex p Pierson* [1998] AC 539 (retrospective use of powers); *Raymond v Honey* [1983] 1 AC 1 (prisoner's rights); *Anisminic Ltd v Foreign Compensation Commission* [1969] 2 AC 147 and R v *Lord Chancellor's Dept, ex p Witham* (1997) (access to the courts). These presumptions embody the amplified and extended versions of the rule of law (Sections 6.6, 6.7). They have been reinforced by the Human Rights Act 1998, which imposes a strong obligation to interpret all legislation so as to conform with rights embodied in the European Convention on Human Rights (ECHR). Many of these presumptions appeal to individualistic liberals (red light) have been criticised by 'welfare liberals' as attempts to counter policies based on the collective public interest (green light) (Section 1.6).

There is some leeway in the ultra vires doctrine in favour of the government. The courts will permit an activity which, although not expressly authorised by the statute, is 'reasonably incidental' to something that is expressly authorised. For example in *Akumah v Hackney LBC* [2005] 2 All ER 148 the House of Lords held that it was lawful to clamp cars in a car park attached to a block of local authority flats under a scheme which required tenants to obtain parking permits at a cost of £2. The Council had statutory power of 'management, regulation and control' over the 'dwelling houses' and this should be interpreted broadly to include the regulation of car parking since this affects the quality of life of the residents. This was the case even though the Council could have made parking regulations under other, more specific legislation. However the House of Lords was not asked to rule on the legality of the particular scheme, thus leaving it open whether making a charge or clamping was lawful.

A narrow approach was taken in *Macarthy & Stone* (above), where a charge for giving advice in connection with planning applications was held not to be incidental to the authority's planning powers. Giving advice was not expressly authorised and was itself an incidental function. The House of Lords took the view that something cannot be incidental to the incidental. Moreover there is a presumption dating from the Bill of Rights 1688 that taxation cannot be imposed without clear statutory authority (but is a charge for a service taxation?). (See also *A-G v Crayford UDC* [1962] Ch 575: voluntary household insurance scheme reasonably incidental to the power to manage council housing because it helped tenants to pay the rent; *Hazell v Hammersmith and Fulham LBC* [1992] 2 AC 1: interest swap arrangements – made by several local councils to spread the risk of future changes in interest rates – were not incidental to the Council's borrowing powers because they concerned debt management rather than borrowing as such.)

17.7　Errors of law and fact

By 'error' or 'wrong' in this context I mean a mistake. A typical error of law would be to misunderstand the meaning of a legal term (eg what is meant by 'residence' in a dwelling). Errors of law must be contrasted with errors of *fact* (Section 17.8). A typical error of fact is a mistake about something happening in the real world (eg whether a person was actually in the dwelling). Sometimes the term 'error' is used loosely to mean any unlawful act. This broad meaning should be avoided here.

The question of whether the court can review decisions on the ground of legal or factual errors has caused problems. There is a clash of principle. On the one hand if the court could intervene merely because it considered that a mistake had been made, it would be trespassing into the merits of the case, showing disrespect for the deciding body and violating the separation of powers. Thus it has been said that if a body has jurisdiction to go right it has jurisdiction to go wrong (Lord Reid in *R v Governor of Brixton Prison, ex p Armah* [1968] AC 192 at 234).

In other words the question is not whether there was a mistake but who should have the last word in deciding whether a mistake has been made. It is not obvious that a reviewing court is in a better position than the original decision maker to decide what the facts are (see *R v Nat Bell Liquors* [1922] 2 AC 128: false evidence not reviewable). On the other hand the rule of law surely calls for a remedy if a decision maker makes a clear mistake. The courts have therefore adopted a compromise. Almost all errors of law and some errors of fact can be challenged. However they have reached this position only after much technical wrangling.

A rationale that was popular in the nineteenth century and still exists is the doctrine of the 'jurisdictional' or 'collateral' or 'preliminary' question. According to this doctrine, if a mistake relates to a state of affairs which the court thinks that Parliament intended should exist objectively as a condition of the official having power to make the decision, then the court will interfere if it thinks that the required state of affairs does not exist. The decision is ultra vires, or outside jurisdiction. This applies both to mistakes of law and to mistakes of fact. For example in *White and Collins v Minister of Health* [1939] 2 KB 838 the Secretary of State had power to acquire land 'other than a garden or parkland'. It was held that the court could interfere if it thought that the minister had wrongly decided whether the claimant's land was parkland. The doctrine can be justified on the rule of law ground that a minister should not be allowed to expand his own powers (see Farwell J in *R v Shoreditch Assessment Committee, ex p Morgan* [1910] 2 KB 859 at 880). However there seems to be no logical way of deciding which of many issues that a decision maker has to decide are 'preliminary' in this sense.

17.7.1 Errors of law

A second device, which flourished during the 1960s but has largely been superseded, is the doctrine of 'error of law on the face of the record', or patent error (*R v Northumberland Compensation Appeal Tribunal, ex p Shaw* [1952] 1 KB 338). This allows the court to quash a decision if a mistake of law can be discovered from the written record of the decision without using other evidence. This could not be squeezed into the ultra vires doctrine and decisions tainted by patent error may only be 'voidable', that is valid unless and until formally quashed by the court (Section 17.3). The face of the record principle provides a practical compromise by allowing obvious mistakes to be rectified without reopening the whole matter. Many bodies are required to give written reasons for their decisions as part of the record (eg Tribunals and Inquiries Act 1992, s 10) and the courts were liberal in what material they regarded as part of the record. However mistakes of fact could not be challenged at all.

Most importantly, as a result of *Anisminic Ltd v Foreign Compensation Commission* (1969), the older doctrines have been made largely redundant in relation to errors of law. *Anisminic* appears to have made all errors of law reviewable, at least in principle. Before *Anisminic* it was widely believed that a jurisdictional error was an error committed at the beginning of its decision-making process which made the tribunal go entirely outside its allotted sphere ('excess of jurisdiction') and that errors committed subsequently (errors within jurisdiction) could not be reviewed unless they were 'on the record'. For example suppose a tribunal has power to fix the rent for a 'furnished dwelling'; in order to decide whether it had jurisdiction it must first decide whether the dwelling in front of it is 'furnished'. A mistake about this would go to its jurisdiction. Mistakes which it committed later, for example in calculating the rent, would not. In *Anisminic* a majority of their Lordships rejected this approach as arbitrary and held that defects at any stage in the process could go to jurisdiction.

▶ The Foreign Compensation Commission (FCC) was established to adjudicate on claims to compensation for war damage in connection with an Arab–Israeli war. Under the complex regulations it had to decide many questions, one of which was that the owner of the damaged property and the owner's successor in title must be British subjects. The FCC had interpreted the term 'successor in title' as including a purchaser. This led it to refuse compensation to Anisminic, a British company which had sold its property to an Egyptian company. The House of Lords held that as a matter of law a purchaser was not a successor in title because the term 'successor in title' in this context was intended to mean only someone who succeeds to property on the death or winding up of its original owner. Therefore an irrelevant matter had been taken into account that Parliament did not intend, namely the nationality of the Egyptian company. According to a majority of their Lordships, this made the decision not just wrong but outside the FCC's jurisdiction.

Anisminic has been widely taken as deciding that any mistake of law affecting a decision makes the decision ultra vires *and the issue is probably closed* (see *Re Racal Communications* [1981] AC 374; *O'Reilly v Mackman* [1982] 3 All ER 1124; *Page v Hull University Visitor* (1993); *Boddington v BTC* (1999) at 158), *R (Cart) v Upper Tribunal* (2012), [17], [18], [39], [40], [110]. The reason for this seems to be the loose way in which the majority characterised a jurisdictional error as taking an irrelevant matter into account, failing to take a relevant matter into account or 'asking the wrong question'.

All mistakes could logically be presented under those heads. Nevertheless there are dicta in *Anisminic* itself denying that all errors of law are jurisdictional, and Lord Morris strongly dissented (see 174, 189, 195, 209; see also *Pearlman v Governors and Keepers of Harrow School* [1979] QB 56; *South East Asia Fire Brick Sdn Bhd v Non-Metallic Mineral Products Manufacturing Employees Union* [1981] AC 363).

The courts have to some extent drawn back from *Anisminic*. They have recognised that some matters raise specialised issues which the expert tribunal or government decision maker is better equipped to decide than the court. For example in *Re Racal Communications* (1981) Lord Diplock suggested that *Anisminic* did not apply to decisions of lower courts where questions of law and questions of fact were inextricably mixed up. In *Page v Hull University Visitor* (1993) it was held that the specialised rules of universities should be conclusively interpreted by the university visitor. In both these cases it was recognised that unfair or unreasonable decisions could be reviewed.

17.7.2 Errors of fact

Anisminic has not been applied to mistakes of *fact*, Errors of fact are not normally reviewable since the courts regard the initial decision-making body as in the best position to find the facts. There are exceptions. However these might best be explained on the basis that the particular error falls within another head of review:

▶ The doctrine of the jurisdictional/preliminary question (Section 17.7) applies both to errors of law and errors of fact, where it is sometimes called the 'precedent fact' doctrine. This allows the court to decide the question of fact itself. For example in *Khawaja v Secretary of State for the Home Dept* [1983] 1 All ER 765 the Home Secretary could deport an 'illegal immigrant'. The House of Lords held that the court could decide whether the appellant was in fact an illegal immigrant and was not limited to deciding whether the minister's decision was unreasonable. The problem is to decide what kind of case falls within the doctrine. This depends upon the statutory context. In *Khawaja* the court was influenced by the fact that the decision involved personal freedom, so that a high level of judicial control was required. By contrast in *R v Secretary of State for the Home Dept ex parte Bugdaycay* [1987] 1 AC 514 the question was whether the applicant was a 'refugee' (Section 9.6.1) This question was only one of several given to an immigration officer to decide under immigration rules and could not be regarded as a precedent fact (522–3). In *R (A) v Croydon LBC* [2009] 1 WLR 2577 a refugee was eligible for housing only if there was a child in need. It was held that the court could interfere where there was an objectively right or wrong answer (ie whether there was a child) but not on the question of need which was a subjective value judgement. It was also held that the court would look at the quality of the initial decision-making process: the better it was, the less willing the court would be to interfere. This is an important feature of judicial review which emphasises the way a decision is reached rather than the outcome in isolation.

▶ A finding of fact which is completely unreasonable in the sense that it has no evidential basis is reviewable (*Ashbridge Investments v Minister of Housing and Local Government* [1965] 1 WLR 1320 at 1326).

▶ In *R v Criminal Injuries Compensation Board, ex p A* [1999] 2 AC 330 at 344 Lord Slynn said that 'misunderstanding or ignorance of an established and relevant fact' is reviewable but emphasised that this is no more than an application of ordinary review principles (see also *Secretary of State for Education and Science v Tameside Metropolitan BC* [1977] at 1017). By contrast judicial review does not include a reinvestigation of disputed facts unless the decision is perverse (*Adan v Newham LBC [2002] 1 All ER 931*). In other words the courts will not attempt to investigate factual disagreements or to weigh evidence but will intervene in clear cases. It may be that the level of review for error of fact is insufficient to satisfy the ECHR Article 6: right to a fair trial (Section 21.4).

▶ In general it might be preferable in cases both of law and of fact to allow judicial review only where the decision is an *unreasonable* one, for example where proper consideration was not given to the matter. This provides a safeguard without infringing the competence of the decision maker. A right of appeal can be provided by statute where a more detailed scrutiny is required. Indeed in *R (A) v Croydon LBC* (2009), (above) it was remarked that the court would look at the quality of the initial decision-making process: the better it was, the less willing the court would be to interfere. This is an important feature of judicial review which emphasises the way a decision is reached rather than the outcome in isolation.

17.8 'Wide' ultra vires: improper purposes and relevance

These aspects of illegality arise in the context of discretionary powers where the governing statute does not define the extent of the powers precisely. They are sometimes labelled 'abuse of discretion'. Even though the decision maker keeps within the express language of the statute:

▶ it may act for an improper purpose; or
▶ it may be influenced by irrelevant factors; or
▶ it may fail to take relevant factors into account.

These grounds apply even where the statute appears to give the decision maker an unrestricted, subjective discretion, using such expressions as 'if the minister thinks fit', since even the widest discretionary power is in principle reviewable. It is for the court to decide what factors are relevant and what are the purposes of the Act (*Padfield v Minister of Agriculture, Fisheries and Food* [1968] AC 997: a minister who had a wide subjective discretionary power to refer an issue to a committee of investigation must not be influenced by considerations that do not advance the policy and objects of the particular Act).

17.8.1 Improper purpose

This is where a decision maker acts for a purpose of his own outside the statute. In *R v Secretary of State for Foreign and Commonwealth Affairs, ex p World Development Movement* [1995] 1 All ER 611 the government had statutory power to give financial aid to other countries for 'economic' purposes. It decided to give a grant to Malaysia for the Pergau Dam project. The Court of Appeal held that Parliament must have intended the word 'economic' to include only 'sound' economic decisions, so the court was entitled to infer that the decision had been made primarily for an ulterior purpose (perhaps of facilitating an arms sale arrangement). This seems to come near to the courts trespassing on forbidden territory by interfering with the merits of the decision since the court could deepen its investigation into any statutory function by saying that Parliament must have intended that function to be carried out 'soundly' (see Irvine [1996] PL 59). On the other hand parliamentary scrutiny had been ineffective, so the court's role may be justifiable as the only available constitutional check.

In *Porter v Magill* [2002] 1 All ER 465 the leader of a local authority had embarked upon a policy of selling off the authority's housing. This in itself was a lawful policy. However sales were concentrated in marginal electoral wards with a view to attracting votes for the Conservative Party. The House of Lords held that the policy could not be justified on the basis of legitimate housing purposes. A democratic body can hope for an electoral advantage as the incidental outcome of its policies (and probably choose between alternative legitimate policies for electoral reasons) but it cannot distort policies in order to seek electoral advantage. In other words a matter may lawfully be taken into account along with other relevant matters but cannot be the predominant purpose of the decision.

17.8.2   Relevant considerations

The decision maker may be broadly acting for the proper purpose but may take an improper route to achieving by taking into account an irrelevant matter or failing to take into account a relevant matter. As usual the starting point is the language of the statute but where wide discretionary powers are concerned this may not be helpful and the courts have leeway to impose their own view as to what is relevant. Thus the concept of relevance sets out conditions of proper decision making and the courts are policing the boundaries of the democratic process. For example in *R v Secretary of State for the Home Dept, ex p Venables* [1997] 3 All ER 97 public opinion, in the shape of an opinion poll in the *Sun* newspaper, was not relevant where the Secretary of State reviewed the sentence in a notorious child murderer case, since his judicial function must be exercised using his independent judgement. Moreover factors which are relevant must be clearly explained. For example if a policy refers to 'exceptional circumstances' the authority must be able to indicate as far as possible what these might be (*R (Rogers) v Swindon Primary Health Care Trust* [2006] EWCA Civ 392: refusal to provide drug).

In deciding what factors are relevant, the court can look at background evidence, for example official reports that influenced the legislation in question and also things said in Parliament as to government policy. However statements made in Parliament cannot be used as evidence that a minister has acted in bad faith since this would violate parliamentary privilege (Section 11.6). An unequivocal statement as to the scope of a provision might however prevent a minister subsequently from attempting a different explanation (*R v Secretary of State for the Environment, Transport and the Regions, ex p Spath Holme* [2001] 1 All ER 884: were rent control powers limited to anti-inflation measures or of wider scope?).

A decision maker must take into account all relevant government policies and guidance, including international obligations, even though these do not necessarily have the force of law. In *R (Bulger) v Secretary of State for the Home Dept* [2001] 3 All ER 449 the court, drawing on international obligations, held that in fixing the length of time a convicted child offender must serve, the Secretary of State must take into account the welfare of the child and keep the child's progress and rehabilitation under review. The courts have also held that local authorities should concern themselves with local issues as opposed to general issues of national or international politics (*R v Lewisham LBC, ex p Shell UK Ltd* [1988] 1 All ER 938).

The courts will protect individual interests against bureaucratic zeal. In *R v City of Westminster Housing Benefit Review Board, ex p Mehanne* [2001] 2 All ER 690 legislation required the Board to reduce a claim when it considered that the rent was unreasonably high, 'having regard in particular to the cost of suitable accommodation elsewhere'. The board interpreted this as preventing it from taking into account the claimant's personal circumstances, including his wife's pregnancy and his reduced income as a refugee. The House of Lords held that personal circumstances were relevant, pointing out that the phrase 'in particular' invited other factors to be considered. Lord Bingham said that 'in the absence of very clear language I would be very reluctant to conclude that the board were precluded from considering matters which could affect the mind of a reasonable and fair minded person' (at 617).

In *R v Somerset CC, ex p Fewings* (1995) the Council had banned hunting on its land for ethical reasons. The Court of Appeal held that under the governing statute which gave them power to 'manage' land, the moral question of cruelty was a relevant consideration. However it was not open to a Council merely to impose the individual moral views of its members. In that case the Council had correctly canvassed public opinion.

In earlier cases the courts appeared to restrict the powers of local authorities to innovate in order to compel them to conserve taxpayers' money by adopting 'business principles' in fixing wages, fares and prices at the expense of local democratic freedom (see *Roberts v Hopwood* (1925); *Prescott v Birmingham Corp* (1955); *Bromley LBC v GLC* (1983), Section 17.5). However, it has been stressed that the scope of what is relevant should be responsive to changing community values (see *Pickwell v Camden LBC* [1983] QB 962).

In relation to general factors such as hardship or expense, or political or moral considerations (as in *Fewings* above), unless the statute plainly requires otherwise, the decision maker may have discretion to decide what is relevant in the particular circumstances. The court will interfere only where the authority exercises its discretion unfairly or unreasonably. (See *Ashby v Minister of Immigration* [1981] NZLR 222 at 224: 'obligatory' and 'permissible' considerations, *R (FDA) v Secretary of State for Work and Pensions* [2012] 3 All ER 301: effect of changes to public sector pensions on national economy.)

An important instance of this issue arises where it has had to be decided whether a decision maker is entitled to take financial cost into account. This is especially important today when financial cuts mean that public services are under pressure. For example in *R (Condliffe) v North Staffordshire Primary Health Care Trust* [2012] 1 All ER 629 it was held that a hospital could decide to provide treatment outside its normal guidelines on the basis of clinical factors alone without taking into account the personal circumstances of the patient since this was a reasonable and fair way of allocating scarce resources (Section 21.4). In *HSE v Wolverhampton City Council* [2012] UKSC 34 the Supreme Court held that in deciding whether to revoke a planning permission a local authority could take into account the cost to the public of the compensation involved.

There is a dilemma where a local authority refuses to provide a welfare benefit to which a person may be entitled on the ground that it does not have sufficient resources. If the court were to order the authority to provide the benefit, it could be accused of interfering with democratic choice. If it were not to do so there may be unfairness if different standards are applied in different local areas. In *Southwark LBC v Tanner* [2001] 1 AC 1 at 9–10, Lord Hoffmann warned against judicial intervention in a field which is so very much a matter of the allocation of resources in accordance with democratically determined priorities.

In this kind of case the court interprets the particular statute in order to determine whether the duty to provide the benefit is intended to be absolute (mandatory) or permissive which would allow the authority to take its resources into account. Words such as 'shall' or 'may' are indicative but not conclusive and the whole statutory context must be examined. The importance of the matter, the desirability of uniformity and resource implications are taken into account.

In *R v Gloucestershire CC, ex p Barry* [1997] a majority of the House of Lords held that a statutory duty to give such assistance as was 'necessary' to meet the 'needs' of a disabled person allowed the authority to take into account its resources as part of the meaning of 'necessary'. However an authority should provide an explanation of how it prioritises competing needs. (See *R(KM) v Cambridgeshire CC* [2012] 3 All ER 1222.)

In *R (G) v Barnet LBC* [2004]1 All ER 97 the House of Lords held that the duty imposed on local authorities by the Children Act 1989 to 'safeguard and promote' the welfare of children in need provided only broad aims which the authority should bear in mind. The Act therefore gave the authority a discretion to choose between competing demands and to take cost into account, and the court will interfere only if the discretion is exercised unreasonably. This is sometimes labelled a 'target duty', reflecting the fact that not all needs can realistically be met in full.

In *R (Conville) v Richmond on Thames LBC* [2006] EWCA Civ 718 the Court of Appeal held that a statute which required the Council to give a tenant a 'reasonable opportunity' to secure other accommodation did not allow it to take its own circumstances into account in deciding what was reasonable. (See also *R (M) v Gateshead Council* [2007] 1 All ER 1262, *R v East Sussex CC, ex p Tandy* [1998] 2 All ER 769; *R v Sefton Metropolitan BC, ex p Help the Aged* [1997] 4 All ER 532; *R v Newham LBC, ex p Begum* [2000] 2 All ER 72).

The relevance principle does not require the decision maker to give any particular weight to a given matter. In general the appropriate weight to be given to a factor is a political matter that is not for the court. The decision maker can choose which of the competing factors to prefer, provided that a relevant consideration is not completely ignored. For example in *Tesco Stores v Secretary of State [1995] 2 All ER 636* the House of Lords held that in accordance with a government circular, a planning authority must take into account an offer from Tesco to contribute to the building of a new road in the area in return for planning permission. However it could give the offer 'nil' weight in influencing its decision.

The court is not entirely excluded from matters of weighting.

▶ A statute might expressly or implicitly indicate that special weight be given to some factors.

▶ According to the 'principle of legality' special weight must be given to the fundamental rights of the individual (Section 6.7).

- Similarly matters falling within the Human Rights Act 1998 attract the 'proportionality' principle, which is essentially one of weighting, requiring as it does a strong reason to override a human right (Section 22.5).
- A 'legitimate expectation' might be given special weight (Section 17.9).
- The court can interfere if the decision maker has acted irrationally in relation to matters of weighting (Section 18.1).

An improper purpose or an irrelevant consideration is not automatically fatal. Firstly the court will not set aside a decision if the factor in question would not objectively have made any difference to the outcome. In this sense the line between legality and merits is blurred. In the context of improper purposes, this is sometimes expressed as the 'dominant purpose' test. The following are illustrations:

- In *Westminster Corp v London and North Western Railway* [1905] AC 426 the local authority had power to construct public lavatories. It incorporated a subway into the design of its lavatories and it was objected that this was its real purpose. This was held to be lawful on the basis that the subway was merely incidental. Although it could be used by people to cross the street, it was also an appropriate method of reaching the lavatories. By contrast in *Webb v Minister of Housing and Local Government* [1965] the local authority had power to construct coast protection works. It incorporated a promenade into a scheme, compulsorily acquiring a number of houses for the purpose. This was held to be unlawful on the ground that more land was acquired than was needed for a coastal protection barrier. The whole scheme was invalid and the good part could not be separated from the bad.
- In *R v Lewisham LBC, ex p Shell UK Ltd* (1988) the Council decided to boycott Shell's products on the ground that Shell had interests in South Africa, which at the time was subject to apartheid. It was held that the policy could have been lawfully justified on the ground of promoting good race relations in the borough. However as the Council had tried to persuade other local authorities to adopt a similar policy, it had gone too far, its purpose being to put pressure on Shell.
- In *R v Secretary of State for Social Services, ex p Wellcome Foundation* [1987] 2 All ER 1025: irrelevant commercial factors were taken into account but decision could be justified on proper health grounds.

17.8.3 Failure to take relevant factors into account: fettering discretion

Officials fetter their discretion by binding themselves in advance to decide in a particular way, without being prepared to consider all the circumstances of an individual case on its merits. Thus this is an extreme example of a failure to take relevant factors into account.

Discretion can be fettered in many ways since administrators may find this is an attractive method of disposing of cases without too much effort or responsibility. Examples of unlawful fetters include the following:

- rigid application of rules, 'guidance' or policies made within the government. Unless the rule is made legally binding by a statute or subordinate legislation, it is unlawful to treat it as binding (*R v Port of London Authority, ex p Kynoch* [1919] 1 KB 176). An official can of course take into account guidelines drawn up within the government. Indeed government would be impracticable without them. Moreover fairness and certainty require policies to be published and followed (see eg *R (Purdy) v DPP* [2009] 4 All ER 1147: prosecution policy in cases of assisted suicide). No more is required by the rule against fettering than that the decision maker must keep an open mind by considering whether in any given case an exception to the policy should be made. This is a vital protection for the individual against official intransigence. In *British Oxygen Co v Ministry of Technology* [1971] AC 610 there was a valid policy that grants would be payable only in respect of products above a certain size. Nevertheless the possibility of making an exception should have been considered. As Lord Reid put it:

> a Ministry or large authority may have had already to deal with a multitude of similar applications and then they will almost certainly have evolved a policy so precise that it could well be called a rule. There can be no objection to that, provided that the authority is always willing to listen to anyone with something new to say (at 625).

For example in *R v Secretary of State for the Home Dept, ex p Hindley* [2001] 1 AC 387 a 'whole life tariff' set by the Home Secretary for a convicted murderer was lawful, provided that it was open to periodic review. In *R (Lumba) v Secretary of State for the Home Dept* [2012]: the Supreme Court held that a blanket policy to detain all foreign nationals' prisoners on completion of sentence pending deportation was unlawful unless individual cases were considered as possible exceptions. Administrative convenience is no excuse.

In policy cases therefore two distinct issues arise. Firstly is the policy itself lawful? Under this head, apart from questions of ultra vires (above), the policy must not be inconsistent with any relevant published policy. (See *Lumba* (above) [34]–[39], *R (Mayaya) v Secretary of State for the Home Dept* [2012] 1 All ER 1491.) Secondly has the policy been applied too inflexibly so as to fetter discretion?

- rigid application of party political policies, without making an independent
- judgment (*R v Waltham Forest LBC, ex p Baxter* [1988] QB 419);
- electoral mandates (*Bromley LBC v GLC* (1983)). These can of course be given great weight (*Secretary of State for Education and Science v Tameside Metropolitan BC* [1977] AC 1014;
- agreements and contracts that contradict a statutory obligation (*Ayr Harbour Trustees v Oswald* [1883] 8 App Cas 623; *Stringer v Minister of Housing and Local Government* [1971] 1 All ER 65). Contracts are always binding and so inevitably fetter the future exercise of a discretion. However the principle seems to be that a contract is invalid only if it is inconsistent with a clear statutory obligation (see *R v Hammersmith and Fulham LBC, ex p Beddowes* [1987] 1 All ER 369);
- statements made by officials (*Western Fish Products v Penwith DC* [1981] 2 All ER 204: developer wrongly told that he would not need planning permission). Thus the doctrine of estoppel familiar in private law areas such as contract, under which in certain circumstances a person is bound by a promise or statement on which another relies, does not apply in public law (*R (Reprotech (Pebsham) Ltd) v East Sussex CC* [2003] 1 WLR 348: Council subcommittee resolution recommending grant of planning permission for waste treatment plant not binding.

The justification for this harsh principle is the public interest that government decisions should be made according to law. On the other hand a citizen who is misled by an official is the victim of unfairness. As Lord Hoffmann pointed out in *Reprotech* (above)

[33]–[35], the more flexible concept of a 'legitimate expectation' attempts to compromise between these competing considerations by giving special weight to cases where a citizen has relied upon an official statement (Section 17.9).

There is of course no unlawful fetter where the decision-making power has been validly delegated to the official in question (Section 18.2). Here the decision will be binding. However it may be difficult for the citizen to discover whether this is in fact the case. It is not enough (as it would be in private law) that the official reasonably appears to be authorized ('ostensible authority'). However in *South Buckinghamshire DC v Flanagan* [2002] 1 WLR 2601 where the Council's solicitor made a decision it was held that ostensible authority can validate a decision provided that the official *could* under statute have made it although he had not in fact been authorised to do so. In other words the decision would not be ultra vires the statute.

▶ acting under the dictation of another body (*Lavender & Son Ltd v Minister of Housing and Local Government* [1970] 3 All ER 871). But consulting another body and even relying on the decision of another body unless an objection is raised is lawful (see *R v GLC, ex p Blackburn* [1976] 3 All ER 184).

17.9 Legitimate expectations

By ensuring that the decision maker takes all relevant factors into account, the fettering discretion doctrine sometimes protects the citizen. It also protects the general public interest by allowing a public body to change its mind or put right a mistake if the public interest so requires. This is one of the most important democratic principles. On the other hand it may be unjust to the individual if the decision maker disregards a previous promise or announced policy, particularly where the individual has re-arranged his or her affairs in reliance on the undertaking. Suppose, for example a student gives up a job or pays fees for a course on the strength of a government announcement that a student of her category will be given a grant. The government later withdraws the announcement. Thus the law creates a dilemma in which fairness to the individual and legal certainty are in conflict with the public interest.

The concept of 'legitimate expectation' confronts this dilemma. There is much uncertainty about its rationale and limits. First expressed by Lord Denning in *Schmidt v Secretary of State for Home Affairs* [1969] 2 Ch 149, a legitimate expectation arises where the citizen has been led to believe by a statement or other conduct of the government that he is singled out for some benefit or advantage of which it would be unfair to deprive him. The expectation might be generated by a promise or assurance either announced generally or given specifically to an individual (eg *R v Secretary of State for the Home Dept, ex p Khan* [1985] 1 All ER 40: Home Office circular stated that adoptions of children from abroad would be allowed in certain circumstances; *Preston v IRC* [1985] 2 All ER 327: letter concerning tax affairs). A legitimate expectation might also be generated by a consistent practice whereby people in the same position as the applicant have been given a benefit in the past (*CCSU v Minister for the Civil Service* [1985].

A legitimate expectation must single out the claimant or a group including the claimant. The statement must be an official one made by a person with power to make the decision. Unofficial statements such as an election address or media interviews cannot create a legitimate expectation (*R v Secretary of State for Education, ex p Begbie*

(2000). There may be a legitimate expectation that the government will honour an international treaty obligation which it has ratified (*R (Abassi) v Secretary of State* [2002] EWCA Civ 169, but cf *R v DPP, ex p Kebeline* [1999] 2 AC 326).

Although Article 9 of the Bill of Rights 1688 prevents the courts from holding a minister liable for anything said in Parliament, a statement in Parliament might be used as evidence in judicial review proceedings and might create a legitimate expectation (see *Wilson v First County Trust* [2003] 4 All ER 97 at [140]). Article 9 does not seem to be violated since the minister is not being *penalised* for anything said in Parliament (Section 11.6.2).

Where an assurance is given to an individual, the individual must have disclosed all relevant information (*R v IRC, ex p MFK Underwriting Agents Ltd* [1990] 1 WLR 1545). The statement that gives rise to the expectation must be clear and unambiguous and it must be reasonable for the claimant to rely upon it (see *Preston v IRC (1985)*: letter not sufficiently clear; see also *R (Bancoult) v Secretary of State for the Foreign and Commonwealth Office (No 2) (2008)*). *Abassi (above)* shows the need to define exactly what the legitimate expectation is. Lord Phillips explained that a legitimate expectation can be of 'a regular practice that the claimant can reasonably expect to continue' (at [82], [92]). However, the expectation in that case was only that the Foreign Office would *consider* making diplomatic representations about the treatment of prisoners in Guantanamo Bay not that it would actually do so.

A legitimate expectation cannot arise if the decision in question would be ultra vires *or contrary to statute*. In other words the legitimate expectation doctrine is about a *valid* government statement or practice which the government subsequently withdraws. For example in *R (Bloggs61) v Secretary of State for the Home Dept* [2003] 1 WLR 2724 a prisoner was given an assurance by the police that he would be put on a witness protection scheme. However since the scheme was the responsibility of the Home Office the police had no power to give such an assurance which could not therefore give rise to a legitimate expectation.

In *Rowland v Environment Agency* [2004] 3 WLR 249 an assurance was given to a purchaser of land that a stretch of river was private but public rights existed over it under statute. It was held that there was no legitimate expectation since statute cannot be overcome. However this might violate the wider principles of the ECHR since it is clearly unfair that that public body should be able to rely on its own illegality so as to override the interests of the individual (see *Stretch v UK* (2004) 38 EHRR 12). In *Rowland* the Court of Appeal reached its conclusion reluctantly, being constrained by the ultra vires doctrine. It required the authority to do what it could within the law to mitigate the injustice to the claimant.

17.9.1 Reliance

It is sometimes suggested that the individual must rely on the statement that creates the legitimate expectation by incurring expense or other detriment in a way very similar to the doctrine of estoppels (Section 17.8.3). In practice this will often be the case. It must certainly be *reasonable* to rely on the statement. For example in *Odelola v Secretary of State* [2009] 3 All ER 1061 the claimants were Nigerian doctors who had applied to work in the UK. While their applications were in progress the government changed immigration policy. The change meant that only doctors with UK qualifications would now be admitted. The court rejected the claimants' argument that the application should be assessed under the rules as they were when the application was made. There was no legitimate expectation that the policy would not change because the claimants should have realised that immigration policy frequently does so. It would however be irrational and 'conspicuously unfair' not to return the claimants' application fees.

Where the individual is relying on a general government policy, the statutory context might exclude a legitimate expectation if it is directed to concerns inconsistent with the interests of the claimant (eg *Findlay v Secretary of State for the Home Dept* [1985] 1 AC 318: change in parole policy intended to protect the public interest).

However the need for actual reliance has been denied (see *R v Minister of Agriculture, Fisheries and Food, ex p Hamble (Offshore) Fisheries* [1995] 2 All ER 714). Indeed in the Australian case of *Minister of State for Immigration, ex p Teoh* [1995] 183 CLR 273 it was suggested that the individual need not even know of the statement. This was the case in *R (Rashid) v Secretary of State* [2005] EWCA Civ 744, where the Court of Appeal condemned as 'conspicuous unfairness' (at [52]) a refusal to give asylum to a group of Kurds fleeing Iraq. Neither the officials concerned nor the asylum seekers knew about a government policy that relocation to an apparently safe part of Iraq should not defeat an asylum claim. However in *R v MoD, ex p Walker* [2000] 1 WLR 806 a compensation scheme for soldiers injured by crimes of violence when serving overseas was subsequently changed. The House of Lords held that there was no legitimate expectation other than that the ministry would apply whatever its policy was, because there had been no reliance on the original scheme (813) (816). In *R (Bancoult) v Secretary of State (No 2) [2008]*, Lord Bingham suggested (at [73]) that *detriment* was required but not reliance.

This raises the question of what the purpose of the legitimate expectation doctrine is. In support of *Teoh* and *Rashid* it might be suggested that it is to ensure good administration and consistency. It is wrong for government to disregard serious assurances that it has given. On the other hand as suggested in *Walker* the purpose of the doctrine could be to redress injustice suffered by the individual as an aspect of a broad principle of 'fairness'. On this basis the principle of equality indicates that the individual should not get special treatment unless he or she has suffered in some exceptional way.

Perhaps a distinction can be drawn as suggested in *Walker* (813) and *Begbie* (2000) (1113) between statements made to particular individuals and general statements of policy. Where a specific undertaking is given it is arguable that reliance is not required. However where an announcement or practice is directed to the public at large, the claimant must show that she or he can be distinguished from the public at large by acting on the expectation so as to incur expense or other detriment (see *R v Jockey Club, ex p RAM Racecourses* [1993] 2 All ER 225 at 236–40).

Perhaps detrimental reliance may be one aspect of a wider principle of *abuse of power and un*fairness, something to be taken into account but not conclusive (see *Begbie (2000)*, 1131; *R (Bibi) v Newnham LBC* [2002] 1 WLR 237).

17.9.2   Consequences: procedural or substantive

The legitimate expectation doctrine does not prevent a policy from being changed for the future. It concerns only the possible injustice to those who have already been affected by it. It is clear that a legitimate expectation does not create a fully enforceable right (*O'Reilly v Mackman* [1982] 3 All ER 1124: prisoners' expectation of early release). What then are its consequences?

In *R v North and East Devon HA, ex p Coughlan* [2000] 2 WLR 622, 644–46 three kinds of outcome were identified.

1. At the very least a legitimate expectation is a relevant consideration which must be taken into account in making a decision (*R (Theophilus) v Lewisham BC* [2002] 3 All ER 851: student grant to study abroad). In *R (A) v Secretary of State for the Home Dept* [2006] EWHC 526 Collins J said: 'Legitimate expectation is grounded in fairness. The courts expect government departments and indeed all officials who make decisions affecting members of the public to honour statements of policy. To fail to do so will…mean that the decision maker has failed to have regard to a material consideration' [29]. On this basis, as long as the expectation is taken into account, the court will interfere only if the decision is completely unreasonable (see *R v North and East Devon HA, ex p Coughlan* [2000] 2 WLR 622 [57]).

2. At least where the claimant has relied on it a legitimate expectation may also entitle the claimant to a fair hearing and perhaps require reasons to be given before the benefit is refused or withdrawn (*R v Secretary of State for the Home Dept, ex p Khan* [1985]). Indeed the expectation itself may be only of a hearing (eg *A-G for Hong Kong v Shiu* [1983] 2 AC 629: to consider applications for citizenship on their individual merits; *R v Liverpool City Council, ex p Liverpool Taxi Fleet Operators Association* [1975] 1 All ER 379: undertaking to consult). This is called a 'procedural' expectation.

3. Where the expectation is that of an actual benefit (a 'substantive' expectation), the court may go further and in certain cases require the authority to give the citizen the benefit itself (substantive protection). However the circumstances where this will be so are unclear since this would restrict the government`s democratic freedom to change its policy. In other cases like the second category the only outcome would be a hearing (procedural protection). In *Khan (above)*, where the government stated by letter that certain policies concerning overseas adoptions would be followed, Lord Parker CJ suggested that 'vis-à-vis the recipient of such a letter, a new policy can only be implemented after such recipient has been given a full and serious consideration whether there is some overriding public interest which justifies a departure from the procedures stated in the letter' (at 48).

The circumstances in which substantive protection will be given are unclear. The Supreme Court has not yet decided the issue. The main principles seem to be firstly that it would be unfair or an abuse of power to deny the expectation; secondly that to give effect to the expectation would not harm the public interest.

Initially the notion of substantive protection was strongly resisted. In *R v Secretary of State for Health, ex p US Tobacco International Inc* [1992] 1 All ER 212 the government had encouraged the company to manufacture snuff in the UK. After the company had incurred expense on its investment, the government withdrew its permission on medical advice. It was held that a legitimate expectation could not override a statutory discretion so that the government could withdraw its invitation. The company was entitled only to a hearing on the health issue giving it an opportunity to persuade the government to change its mind. However in *R v Minister of Agriculture, Fisheries and Food, ex p Hamble (Offshore) Fisheries* [1995] Sedley J suggested that a legitimate expectation created a binding obligation that could be overridden only if in the court's view it was necessary to do so to achieve the objectives of the statute. However in *R v Secretary of State, ex p Hargreaves* [1997] 1 All ER 397 (at 412) this approach was described as heresy as it went beyond the normal limits of judicial review.

However in *R v Secretary of State, ex p Hargreaves* [1997] 1 All ER 397 (at 412) this approach was described as heresy as it went beyond the normal limits of judicial review. In that case a prisoner's only legitimate expectation was that policies should be fairly applied to his case.

In *R v North and East Devon HA, ex p Coughlan* [2000] 2 WLR 622, which remains the only case where substantive protection was unequivocally given, the Court of Appeal held that a severely disabled resident of a local authority nursing home could hold the local authority to a previous assurance that it would be her home for life. The authority proposed to close the home in order to transfer nursing care to the local authority. It was held that the assurance created an enforceable legitimate expectation that only an overriding public interest could displace. The scope of this is not clear. Lord Woolf formulated a vague test, namely where 'to frustrate the expectation is so unfair that to take a new and different course will amount to an abuse of power'. In particular the human right to respect for home and family life (ECHR, Art 8) was in issue, thereby raising the threshold of review. Moreover, although the decision to close the home had financial consequences, it did not raise general policy issues. Lord Woolf suggested that the court should weigh the expectation against any overriding interest required by the change of policy. This balancing exercise invites the court to scrutinise the merits of the decision beyond the usual limits of judicial review. Lord Woolf also distinguished between statements made to a few individuals or to a group with a common interest and statements made to large numbers of people or to diverse groups. Substantive protection may be less appropriate in the second kind of case.

▶ In *R v Minister of Agriculture, Fisheries and Food, ex p Hamble (Offshore) Fisheries* (1995) (above) there was a claim to retain a fishing licence on the basis of a previous announcement, in the face of a change in a policy designed to conserve fishing stocks. However this would seriously have disrupted government fishing policy, so the expectation was not honoured.

▶ In *Begbie* (2000) (1130–31) Laws LJ treated the matter as one of abuse of power. The court should not usually interfere where the matter raised issues in the 'macro-political field' that affected large numbers of people or had wide-ranging or 'multi layered' consequences or where the effect of the court's order was not clear. See also *R (Rashid) v Secretary of State* (2005) [50]).

▶ In *R (Wheeler) v Office of the Prime Minister* [2008] EWCA 936 it was claimed that government announcements gave rise to a legitimate expectation that the Lisbon Treaty, which increased EU powers, would not be ratified without a referendum. The court refused to give effect to any expectation on the ground that this was a macro-political matter appropriate only to Parliament and would involve improper interference by the judiciary with Parliament.

The cases are inconclusive. The legitimate expectation debate sets the individual claim to respect against the public good takes the court very near to the forbidden territory of 'merits'. The law can reach untidy accommodation, by offering the individual a hearing that might persuade the authority to change its mind. Another compromise solution would be to pay compensation to the victim. Unfortunately there is no right to compensation in UK law for unlawful administrative action as such.

R v Secretary of State for Education, ex p Begbie (2000) provides an illustration of the ingredients and operation of a legitimate expectation.

▶ The Education (Schools) Act 1997, introduced after the general election of 1997, abolished the 'assisted places' scheme, which funded children from low-income families in private schools. Children already in the scheme would be funded only until the end of primary education unless the minister decided otherwise at his discretion.

▶ The position of children at 'all-through' schools was in doubt. There was a pre-election announcement by the Opposition leader and letters from MPs saying that funding would continue. These were not government statements, so they could not create a legitimate expectation.

▶ There was also a newspaper article by the Prime Minister stating that the funding would continue. This could not create a legitimate expectation because it was contrary to the statute and was also unclear.

▶ There was an official letter from the minister to a grandparent. This also contradicted the statute and was unclear. Moreover it was corrected later, so there was no reliance upon it.

▶ If there had been a legitimate expectation the court might have given it substantive protection since there would be no effect on broader policy issues and relatively few people were involved.

Summary

▶ Judicial review is constitutionally ambivalent. On the one hand it supports the rule of law, parliamentary supremacy and democracy by enabling the courts to police the limits of government power. On the other hand the courts are open to the complaint based on the separation of powers that they are interfering with the decisions of democratically elected bodies. The basis of this complaint is that the courts interpret the legislation in question in the light of their own values and presumptions of interpretation which are not necessarily democratic.

▶ Judicial review is not concerned with the merits of a government decision but with whether the decision maker has kept within legal limits and followed broad principles of fairness and rationality. The grounds of judicial review are loosely classified under the heads of illegality, irrationality and procedural impropriety.

▶ The constitutional basis of judicial review is contested. According to one view, it depends on the ultra vires doctrine. The alternative view is that judicial review is a freestanding part of the common law but subject to parliamentary supremacy. Proponents of the ultra vires doctrine cater to the fact that much of the law is actually judge made by claiming that Parliament intends and so implicitly authorises legislation to be interpreted according to principles of judicial review

▶ A statutory decision maker must act within the limits of the statute, including what is 'reasonably incidental' to the statute. The courts apply presumptions of statutory interpretation, notably 'the principle of legality', in policing the limits of statutory powers.

Summary cont'd

▶ Review for mistakes of fact is limited since this might involve a reviewing court going outside its proper sphere. Clear errors of fact may be reviewable and an error of fact might also fall within one of the other grounds, for example irrationality (Chapter 17). The interpretation of broad subjective terms in a statute may be classified as mixed questions of law and fact to limit review. Limitations on review for mistakes of fact may raise the question of the right to a fair trial under the ECHR, which in cases where civil rights or obligations are in issue requires an independent decision on factual matters.

▶ A decision maker also acts ultra vires by acting for an improper purpose, taking an irrelevant factor into account or failing to take a relevant factor into account where this affects the outcome of the decision. Matters directly related to the statute must always be taken into account. Broader factors can be taken into account.

▶ Fettering discretion concerns the application of a self-created rigid rule, policy or undertaking in a case where, under a statute, the decision maker must exercise a discretion. A decision maker can adopt guidelines but cannot treat them as absolutely binding.

▶ The doctrine of 'legitimate expectation' attempts to deal with the injustice arising where a decision maker departs from a lawful undertaking, policy statement or practice which it is reasonable for the citizen to rely upon. It is not settled how far an individual must actually rely on the expectation. Basically a legitimate expectation does no more than entitle the individual to a hearing to persuade the decision maker to give effect to its previous statement. In some cases the court may require the authority to honour its previous statement by weighing the interests of the individual against the public interest. Matters of general policy are unlikely to be so restricted.

Exercises

17.1 'The simple proposition that a public authority may not act outside its powers (ultra vires) might fitly be called the central principle of administrative law' (Wade and Forsythe, *Administrative Law*). Discuss.

17.2 Dumbo City Council owns and manages the Dumbo Leisure Centre which by statute must be accessible to the public at all reasonable times. It has statutory power to make regulations for the purpose of 'good order' within the Centre. One such regulation provides that no person may sell or buy goods from any stall or vehicle within the precincts of the Centre unless the seller displays a permit in a prominent place on the stall or vehicle. A fee is payable for the issue of a permit. The Council places notices around the centre advertising the opinions of councillors on the issue of using live animals for medical experiments. George operates a burger bar from a van in the Centre's car park without a permit. Mary objects to the Council's advertisements. Advise them.

Another regulation made by the Council requires all users of the Centre to purchase accident insurance from the Council. Advise Dave who refuses to do so and is banned from entering the Centre.

17.3 When can mistakes of law and fact be challenged in the courts? To what extent has the Human Rights Act 1998 affected the position?

17.4 The (imaginary) Higher Education Act 2012 provides that local councils 'shall award grants to university students such as are necessary to meet their reasonable needs'. In March 2013 the Secretary of State issues guidance in a circular sent to all schools stating that grants will be awarded to anyone whose family income is less than £15,000 or if there is evidence of hardship. Peter, who has read the guidance, and Wendy, who has not, decided to leave their current employment to take up university places in September 2013. Their family incomes are £10,000 and £12,000 respectively. Fi wishes to take a university course in Surfing Studies from September 2013. Her family income is in excess of £15,000 but her family refuses to support her as they want her to study Law. An official from the council writes to Fi informing her that this constitutes hardship and that she is eligible for a grant.

In June 2013 the Secretary of State issues new guidance. This states that 'due to a funding shortfall, grants will be awarded only where family income is less than £8000'. The same official now writes to Fi telling her that she will not receive a grant. Peter and Wendy are also refused grants. In Wendy's case the local authority tells her that they will only give a grant in cases of extreme hardship.

Advise Peter, Wendy and Fi as to the likelihood of a successful challenge to these decisions in the courts and whether they are entitled to grants.

Would your advice to Fi differ if the Council had power to authorize its officials to make the decision concerning grants in cases such as Fi's but had not in fact done so?

17.5 Under the Sports Act 2002 (fictitious) the Minister of Sport has power 'where he considers it necessary in the interest of public safety and good order, to require the admission of paid spectators to any sporting event to be subject to showing membership cards at the entrance'. The minister, interpreting 'sport' as including any activity that is competitive, has made an order requiring entrance to chess competitions to be subject to the showing of membership cards. The minister has been advised that chess events are an important source of the Opposition party's finances. In another case the minister has revoked the membership cards of all the members of a football club because the club has failed to provide adequate refreshment facilities for visitors. Discuss.

17.6 Assume that the Welsh Assembly government has statutory power to control the disposal of household waste within Wales. The Assembly makes the following regulation: 'Each household must produce, if required to do so by an authorised officer, a standard sized bin containing a reasonable amount of recyclable waste. Failure to do so will incur a penalty at the discretion of the authorised officer'.
(a) Alf fails to produce a bin. He claims that his bin was recently stolen. The authorised officer tells him that he has no choice but to impose a penalty.
(b) Bill produces a bin containing only a small amount of waste. He explains that he has recently been absent abroad. The officer who considers that Bill is lying and who has fallen behind with his performance target imposes a penalty on Bill.
(c) Clara's bin is filled to overflowing. The officer imposes a penalty on her on the ground that the amount of waste produced will impose an excessive financial burden on the government.

Advise Alf, Bill and Clara as to any grounds on which they can challenge the regulations and the decisions in their individual cases.

Further reading

Allan, 'Constitutional Dialogue and the Justification for Judicial Review' (2003) 23 OJLS 129
Atrill, 'The End of Estoppel in Public Law?' [2003] CLJ 3
Barber, 'The Academic Mythologians' (2001) 21 OJLS 369
Craig, 'The Common Law, Shared Power and Judicial Review' (2004) 24 OJLS 237

Further reading cont'd

Craig and Bamforth, 'Constitutional Principle, Constitutional Analysis and Judicial Review' [2001] PL 763

Craig and Tomkins (eds), *The Executive and Public Law* (Oxford University Press 2006)

Forsythe, 'Of Fig Leaves and Fairy Tales: The Ultra Vires Doctrine, the Sovereignty of Parliament and Judicial Review' (1996) 55 CLJ 122

Forsythe (ed), *Judicial Review and the Constitution* (Hart 2000) [includes articles cited here]

Forsythe and Elliot, 'The Legitimacy of Judicial Review' [2003] PL 286

Forsythe *et al* (eds), *Effective Judicial Review: A Cornerstone of Good Governance* (Oxford University Press 2010)

Halpin, 'The Theoretical Controversy concerning Judicial Review' (2001) 64 MLR 500

Hannett and Busch, 'Ultra Vires Representations and Legitimate Expectations' [2005] PL 729

Hare, 'Separation of Powers and Error of Law', in Forsythe and Hare (eds), *The Golden Metwand and the Crooked Cord* (Clarendon Press 1998)

Harlow and Pearson, *Administrative Law in a Changing State* (Hart 2008)

Jowell, 'Of Vires and Vacuums: The Constitutional Context of Judicial Review' [1999] PL 448

Knight, 'Expectations in Transition: Recent Developments in Legitimate Expectations' [2009] PL 519

Poole, 'Legitimacy, Rights and Judicial Review' (2005) 25 OJLS 697

Reynolds, 'Legitimate Expectations and the Protection of Trust in Public Officials' [2011] PL 330

Sales and Steyn, 'Legitimate Expectations in English Public Law: An Analysis' [2004] PL 564

Steele, 'Substantive Legitimate Expectations: Striking the Right Balance' (2005) 121 LQR 300

Tomkins, 'The Role of the Courts in the Political Constitution' (2010) 60 U Toronto LJ 1

Tucker, 'Legitimate Expectations and the Separation of Powers' (2009) 125 LQR 233

Vandeman, 'Ultra Vires Legitimate Expectations: An Argument for Compensation' [2012] PL 84

Williams, 'When Is an Error Not an Error? Reform of Jurisdictional Review of Errors of Law' [2007] PL 793

Woolf, 'Judicial Review: The Tensions between the Executive and the Judiciary' (1998) 114 LQR 579

Chapter 18

The grounds of judicial review, II: beyond ultra vires

This chapter continues the discussion in Chapter 17. It concentrates on grounds of review that are less directly linked to the notion of *ultra vires* and which therefore especially raise issues of the proper limits of the courts' role. It is important to bear in mind that the level of review, in other words the depth of the court's intrusiveness, varies with the context. The court will scrutinise a decision more rigorously according to the seriousness of its impact on the individual (see *R(KM) v Cambridgeshire CC* (2012) [36]: community care for the disabled). On the other hand the court will show respect for a democratic decision maker or an expert body and be less intrusive in such cases (Section 19.6.1). As so often an accommodation must be struck between competing concerns.

18.1 Irrationality/unreasonableness

Irrationality or 'unreasonableness' is an overriding ground of review. It can be used to challenge the exercise of discretion or findings of law and fact (Section 17.7). Although the question of what is reasonable must, as always, be decided in the context of the particular statutory power, this ground of review operates as an external control in that it draws on values not directly derived from the statute. Indeed the notion of 'unreasonableness' is so vague that it seems to invite the court to impose its own opinion of the merits in place of that of the decision maker.

Against this, the separation of powers coupled with practical considerations suggests that the courts should be cautious in interfering with the decisions of the executive on vague grounds such as unreasonableness. The former Lord Chancellor Lord Irvine (1996) suggested that three broad reasons lay behind this: firstly respect for Parliament, which had conferred decision-making power on the body in question; secondly limited judicial expertise in matters of policy concerning the general public interest; thirdly what he called the 'democratic imperative', namely that government is judged by the electorate every few years. Lord Irvine's third rationale seems ludicrous since the electorate cannot vote in respect of individual decisions. The courts have struggled to give the notion of unreasonableness a limited meaning. The starting point and baseline is usually called 'Wednesbury unreasonableness' after Lord Greene's speech in *Associated Provincial Picture Houses Ltd v Wednesbury Corp* [1948] 1 KB 223. Lord Greene said obscurely that the court will interfere only where a decision is 'so unreasonable that no reasonable authority could have made it'. In that case the court upheld a condition that no child should attend a cinema in the town on a Sunday. (Of course perceptions of what is unreasonable may change over time.)

Other attempts have been made to capture this elusive idea. For example the decision must be 'beyond the range of responses open to a reasonable decision maker' (*R v Ministry of Defence, ex p Smith* [1996] QB 517, *R v Chief Constable of Sussex, ex p International Trader's Ferry Ltd* [1999] 1 All ER 129 at 157). In *CCSU v Minister for the Civil Service* (1985) Lord Diplock said that the courts will interfere only where a decision has no rational basis or 'is so outrageous in its denial of accepted moral standards that no sensible person who has applied his mind to the question to be decided could have arrived at it' (951). Significant errors of reasoning make a decision *Wednesbury* unreasonable (eg *R (AB) v Secretary of State for Justice* [2010] 2 All ER 151: refusal to transfer transgender prisoner to woman's prison: misunderstanding of expert advice [82]–[85] contrast *R(KM) v Cambridgeshire CC* (2012): errors made but not material).

Lord Diplock's formulation is often used to justify not interfering with a decision. For example in *Brind v Secretary of State for the Home Dept* [1991] 1 AC 696 the government banned live media interviews with supporters of the Irish Republican Army (IRA). The House of Lords held that although the ban was probably misguided it had some rational basis as a means of denying publicity to terrorists and was therefore valid (see also *R v Radio Authority, ex p Bull* [1997] 2 All ER 561 at 577).

On the other hand although successful challenges for unreasonableness are rare, they seem to fall short of irrationality in the extreme sense suggested above. For example in *Hall & Co Ltd v Shoreham-by-Sea UDC* [1964] 1 All ER 1 a local authority planning condition required the plaintiff to dedicate a road to the public. This was held to be 'unreasonable' because it amounted to the confiscation of property without compensation. However, the condition was hardly perverse or irrational, given that the plaintiff stood to make considerable profit out of the permission. Indeed such arrangements are nowadays commonplace.

In *R v Secretary of State for the Home Dept, ex p Daly* [2001] 2 AC 532 Lord Cooke described *Wednesbury* as 'an unfortunately retrogressive decision in English administrative law, in so far as it suggested that only a very extreme degree [of unreasonableness] can bring an administrative decision within the scope of judicial invalidation' ([32]). He emphasised that the level of interference should vary with the subject matter: 'It may well be, however, that the law can never be satisfied in any administrative field merely by a finding that the decision under review is not capricious or absurd'.

A more flexible formula is to ask whether a reasonable decision maker *in the light of the material properly before him* could reasonably justify his decision, or whether a decision shows 'conduct which no sensible authority acting with *due appreciation of its responsibilities* would have decided to adopt' (*Secretary of State for Education and Science v Tameside MBC* [1977] AC 1014, 1064, see Lord Cook in *International Trader's Ferry* (above) at 157). This formula enables the court to apply different levels of scrutiny in different contexts and to evaluate the quality of the decision maker's reasoning. However, it comes perilously close to enabling the court to interfere merely because it disagrees with the decision.

Where important interests of the individual are at stake, the level of review is sometimes called 'heightened *Wednesbury*'. It requires the decision maker to show that it has placed particularly close attention – 'anxious scrutiny' – to the interests in question (see *Bugdaycay v Secretary of State for the Home Dept* [1987] AC 514 at 952; *R v Ministry of Defence, ex p Smith; R v Lord Saville of Newdigate* [1999] 4 All ER 860).). Heightened *Wednesbury* may however give way to other concerns. In *R v Ministry of Defence, ex p Smith* (1996) the Court of Appeal refused to interfere with a decision to ban practising homosexuals from serving in the army. The court recognised that the decision affected fundamental rights and therefore called for 'anxious scrutiny' but also thought that the court was not in a position to assess the specialist needs of military service and should therefore defer to the views of the military establishment. The decision of the UK courts was later held to violate the European Convention on Human Rights (ECHR) (Section 18.2).

At the other end of the scale, where a decision depends on broad social, economic or political factors or matters remote from ordinary judicial experience, the court has been cautious in interfering. In cases of this kind, at least where human rights interests are not an issue, the courts may apply a standard even lower than Lord Diplock's rationality test, interfering only where a decision is entirely capricious – an approach sometimes called 'super-*Wednesbury*'. This also applies where separation of powers issues are at stake, in particular where the decision in question is one that has been approved after a debate in Parliament.

Thus in *Hammersmith and Fulham LBC v Secretary of State for the Environment* [1990] 3 All ER 14 (central grants to local government), Lord Bridge said:

> since the statute has conferred a power on the Secretary of State which involves the formulation and implementation of national economic policy and which can only take effect with the approval of the House of Commons, it is not open to challenge on the ground of irrationality short of the extremes of bad faith, improper motive or manifest absurdity. Both the constitutional propriety and the good sense of this restriction seem to me to be clear enough. The formulation and implementation of national economic policy are matters depending essentially on political judgment. The decisions which shape them are for politicians to take and it is in the political forum of the House of Commons that they are properly to be debated and approved or disapproved on their merits. If the decisions have been taken in good faith within the four corners of the Act, the merits of the policy underlying the decisions are not susceptible to judicial review by the courts and the courts would be exceeding their proper function if they presumed to condemn the policy as unreasonable. (at 637)

(See also *Nottinghamshire CC v Secretary of State for the Environment* [1986] AC 240.)

It must be emphasised that Lord Bridge's remarks apply only to unreasonableness. Where a decision is *ultra vires* on some other ground, then approval by Parliament (other than in the form of a statute) does not validate it or prevent the court scrutinising it in the ordinary way. Thus the separation of powers works in both directions. It must also be emphasised that the fact that a matter may be controversial is not in itself a reason for deference.

Sometimes the statute itself may require that a decision maker act 'reasonably' or 'have reasonable cause' to believe or do something. In this kind of case the court may decide for itself what is reasonable in the ordinary, non-*Wednesbury* sense (see eg *Nakkuda Ali v Jayaratne* [1951] AC 66). On the other hand if a wide political discretion is involved the court may apply the *Wednesbury* approach even here. The matter depends on the particular context (see eg *Secretary of State for Education and Science v Tameside MBC* (1977): Secretary of State could interfere with local school decisions on reasonable grounds: *Wednesbury* applied).

Unreasonableness may overlap with other grounds of review. In *Wheeler v Leicester City Council* [1985] 2 All ER 1106 a local authority refused to allow a rugby club to use its playing field. This was because the club had not prevented certain of its members from touring in South Africa during the apartheid era. The House of Lords held that the Council had acted unlawfully. This could be regarded as an unreasonable infringement of individual freedom, as a decision based upon an improper political purpose or as an unfair decision in that the matter had been prejudged. Today *Wheeler* would probably be explained on human rights grounds, a perspective that was raised in the Court of Appeal but which the House of Lords avoided.

18.1.1   Proportionality

At least in cases subject to the Human Rights Act 1998 and in EC law, a more stringent standard of review than *Wednesbury* unreasonableness applies in the form of the doctrine of 'proportionality'. Proportionality will be discussed more fully later in the context of human rights (Section 22.7). Broadly speaking a decision is proportionate only if it meets an important public goal (a 'pressing social need') and in doing so violates the right in question as little as possible. As Lord Diplock ponderously put it in *R v Goldsmith* [1983] 1 LR 151, proportionality 'prohibits the use of a steam hammer to crack a nut if a nutcracker would do' (at 155).

In *CCSU* (1983) Lord Diplock suggested (950) that proportionality might at a future date become a distinct ground of domestic judicial review. This has not yet been fully realised, although proportionality is closely related to unreasonableness and often overlaps with it.

Proportionality overlaps with unreasonableness but will sometimes produce a different outcome, as in *Smith and Grady (above)*. In many cases however the two produce the same outcome. For example in *R v Barnsley Metropolitan BC, ex p Hook* [1976] 3 All ER 452 a market trader was dismissed by the market manager for the relatively minor wrong of urinating in the street. This was held to be an unreasonably severe penalty. In *R v Secretary of State ex parte Daly* (2001) it was government policy that a prisoner's confidential correspondence with his lawyer could be examined in the prisoner's absence. Lord Bingham based his reasoning firstly on the common law, 'heightened *Wednesbury*' approach appropriate where important rights are in issue. A reasonable minister could not have concluded that the policy was necessary for the legitimate goal of keeping order in prisons. However, the policy was also contrary to Article 8 of the ECHR (respect for correspondence) and Lord Bingham also said that under the Human Rights Act 1998 'domestic courts must go beyond the ordinary standard and themselves form a judgment whether a Convention right has been breached, conducting such an inquiry as is necessary to form that judgment' (at 455). In that case keeping of order could have been achieved by less intrusive albeit more inconvenient means. Lord Steyn applied the proportionality test, emphasising that it went beyond *Wednesbury* by requiring the court itself to decide whether the right 'balance' had been struck between the conflicting interests.

Before the Human Rights Act 1998 English judges had objected to proportionality on the ground that it takes the court too far into the political merits (*Hone v Maze Board of Prison Visitors* [1988] 1 All ER 321 at 327–29; *Brind v Secretary of State for the Home Dept* [1991]). Therefore English law sometimes fell foul of the ECHR because it failed to reach the standard of necessity required by the proportionality doctrine. For example *Smith*

(Section 18.1) was condemned by the European Court of Human Rights in *Smith and Grady v UK* [2000] 29 EHRR 493. It was held that even heightened *Wednesbury* failed to satisfy the ECHR because it excluded any consideration of whether the interference with the applicant's rights answered a pressing social need or was proportionate to the military aims pursued.

It is sometimes suggested that proportionality should not be confined to human rights cases but should be treated as an aspect of unreasonableness. However the two approaches, although overlapping, have not merged. A decision can be disproportionate but pass the *Wednesbury* test. For example in *Aguila Quila v Secretary of State for the Home Dept* (2011): immigration restriction on young adults to combat forced marriages was not *Wednesbury* unreasonable but was too wide to be proportionate since less intrusive measures could have achieved the policy. Conversely a decision might be irrational due to an error of logic or lack of evidence but not disproportionate.

In other words proportionality is concerned with the outcome of a decision while irrationality includes the decision-making process. In *R (Alconbury Developments Ltd) v Secretary of State for the Environment, Transport and the Regions* (2001) Lord Slynn emphasised that 'the difference in practice is not as great as is sometimes supposed' (at 976). He thought that proportionality and *Wednesbury* should not be kept in separate compartments and that 'even without reference to the 1998 Act the time has come to recognise that this principle is part of English administrative law, not only when judges are dealing with Community acts but also when they are dealing with acts subject to domestic law'.

In *R (Association of British Civilian Internees; Far East Region) v Secretary of State* [2003] QB 1397 [35]–[37] it was suggested that *Wednesbury* be replaced by proportionality but the court was bound by authority to apply *Wednesbury* meanwhile. In that case a policy to pay compensation to people interned by the Japanese in World War II was limited to those with close connections with the UK. It was held that this was not *Wednesbury* unreasonable and that proportionality could not be applied.

18.2 Procedural impropriety: statutory procedural requirements

This topic illustrates the elastic nature of contemporary judicial review. Failure to comply with a procedural requirement laid down by statute (such as time limits, consultation or giving required information or notice) could make a decision *ultra vires* and so void. However the courts are reluctant to set aside a decision on purely technical grounds. Traditionally the courts have tried to rationalise this by distinguishing between 'mandatory' (important) and 'directory' (unimportant) procedural requirements by reference to the language of the governing statute (see eg *R v Clarke and McDaid* [2008] 1 WLR 338). They also take a flexible response to the particular context. Using their discretionary power to withhold a remedy, the courts will set a decision aside for procedural irregularity only if the harm or injustice caused to the applicant by the procedural flaw outweighs the harm to the government or to innocent third parties in setting the decision aside (see eg *Coney v Choyce* [1975] 1 All ER 979; *London and Clydeside Estates Ltd v Aberdeen DC* [1979] 3 All ER 876; *Wang v IRC* [1995] 1 All ER 367; *R v Immigration Appeal Tribunal, ex p Jeyeanthan* [1999] 3 All ER 231).

On the other hand the courts will not allow administrative convenience to override a statutory right of the public to be consulted. In *Berkeley v Secretary of State for the Environment* [2000] 3 All ER 897 the House of Lords held that a local authority was required to make environmental information relating to a planning application for a football stadium available to the public even though the Council successfully argued that it already had adequate evidence to enable it to make a proper decision. Lord Hoffmann in particular, reflecting the broad concept of democracy, suggested that public consultation was an end in itself and not merely an instrument of effective decision making (see also *R (Boyejo) v Barnet LBC* [2009] EWHC 3261: consultation must be genuinely interactive: providing an opportunity for questions not sufficient).

Another important statutory procedural requirement is the rule against delegation. An official (or indeed anyone) who is entrusted with power to make a decision affecting the rights of individuals should not transfer that power to someone else (*delegatus non potest delegare*; *Barnard v National Dock Labour Board* [1953] 2 QB 18). However applying this principle strictly would cause administrative breakdown and many exceptions have been made. Nevertheless public bodies have sometimes ignored the requirement. For example the Housing Corporation (now abolished) had done so for more than 40 years without anyone complaining until the matter was put right by retrospective legislation (Housing Corporation Act 2006).

Exceptions to the rule against delegation are as follows:

▶ Under the *Carltona* doctrine a minister can act through a civil servant in her or his department (Section 15.8.3). This can be rationalised as not being a true exception in that constitutionally the minister and civil servant are one, the minister being responsible to Parliament for the act of the civil servant (see *R (Alconbury Developments Ltd) v Secretary of State for the Environment, Transport and the Regions* (2001)). On the other hand why should political responsibility affect the legal position, particularly as we have seen that ministerial responsibility is weak and uncertain. Nevertheless unless possibly the method of delegation is *Wednesbury* unreasonable it seems that the courts cannot interfere (in *R v Secretary of State for the Home Dept, ex p Olahinde* [1991] 1 AC 254 the House of Lords held that a deportation decision could be made by an immigration officer on behalf of the Secretary of State. However Lord Templeman remarked (at 397) that the person exercising the power must be 'of suitable seniority in the Home Office for whom the minister accepts responsibility'. In *R v Minister of Agriculture ex parte Hamble Fisheries* (1995), 732, Sedley J suggested that the *Carltona* principle does not apply to the making of policy. However, in *Re Golden Chemical Products Ltd* (1976) the court rejected any distinction between powers that a minister must exercise personally and those that can be delegated).

▶ *Carltona* does not apply to government agencies outside the central civil service such as the police or the local government or statutory bodies (but see *R (Chief Constable of the West Midlands Police) v Birmingham City Justices* [2002] EWHC 1087: basing the rule on a wider rationale of implied statutory authority and distinguishing between normal decision making within the organisational hierarchy and cases where the statute requires a named official to act personally).

▶ Many local authority functions can be delegated by statute to committees, subcommittees, officers and other authorities but not to individual councillors or outside bodies unless authorised by statute (see Local Government Act 1972, s 101; *R v Port Talbot BC, ex p Jones* [1988] 2 All ER 207). A committee cannot comprise one person.

▶ Many governmental functions can be transferred to private bodies (Deregulation and Contracting Out Act 1994, ss 61, 69).

▶ Functions involving little independent discretion can be delegated. Indeed the courts seem ready to imply statutory authority to delegate in cases where it would be inconvenient for the decision maker to do everything her or himself (*Provident Mutual Life Assurance Association v Derby City Council* [1981] 1 WLR 173). Fact finding, making recommendations and giving advice can be delegated but the decision maker must not merely 'rubber stamp' the advice she or he is given. The decision maker must have enough information before him or her, for example a summary of evidence, to make a genuine decision (*Jeffs v New Zealand Dairy Production and Marketing Board* [1967] 1 AC 551).

18.3 Procedural impropriety: the right to a fair hearing

This ground of review is of ancient common law origin and is central to the idea of the rule of law. It is called in aid by those who claim that judicial review is based on a freestanding common law (Section 17.1). Until the early twentieth century the courts applied a broad principle with biblical origins and usually labelled 'natural justice', namely that anyone whose rights were affected by an official decision was entitled to advance notice and a fair hearing before an unbiased judge (eg *Bagg's Case* (1615); *Dr Bonham's Case* (1610); *Cooper v Wandsworth Board of Works* (1863)).

The advance of the democratically supported administrative state produced a more cautious judicial approach. *Local Government Board v Arlidge* [1915] AC 120 marks a turning point where Dicey felt that the rule of law itself was at risk. In *Arlidge* the House of Lords held that in the case of administrative decisions (in that case a house closure order), provided that the government can decide for itself what procedures to follow, the citizen's protection lying not in the courts but in ministerial responsibility to Parliament (see also *Board of Education v Rice* [1911] AC 179).

The courts then refused to apply natural justice to decisions other than those which they deemed 'judicial'. For this purpose 'judicial' means the impartial application of rules to settle a dispute about the parties' existing rights, narrowly defined – essentially what a court does. Thus the courts removed natural justice from political, discretionary and policy-oriented decisions, which the court labelled 'administrative'. This excluded much of the welfare state from natural justice since the conferring of benefits such as education and housing does not strictly affect existing rights. It also excluded government powers such as planning, compulsory purchase and other forms of licensing which, although they affect rights, are usually discretionary. The main area left for natural justice was where a formal tribunal or inquiry determined a specific dispute, but even this caused problems in the case of public inquiries held as part of a larger discretionary process leading to a political decision, for example to build a new road. These were labelled 'quasi judicial' with a right to be heard only at the judicial stage of the inquiry itself thereby raising suspicions that the real decision was taken behind closed doors in characteristically English fashion (see eg *Franklin v Minister of Town and Country Planning* (1948).

However in *Ridge v Baldwin* [1964] AC 40, a landmark case that marks the beginning of the contemporary renaissance of judicial review, the House of Lords returned the law to its older rationale. The Chief Constable of Brighton had been dismissed by the local police authority without a hearing. The authority had statutory power to deprive him of his position for incapacity or misconduct but not otherwise. The House of Lords held that he was entitled to a hearing for two reasons: (i) he had been deprived of an important right; (ii) the power to dismiss was limited by statute, so the authority did not have a complete discretion. Lord Reid emphasised that irrespective of whether it is judicial in the above sense a government decision that causes serious harm to an individual ought in principle to attract the right to be heard. Moreover it was emphasised that the right to be heard applies irrespective of how clear-cut the outcome appears to be. Indeed the protection of a hearing may be most necessary in what seems to be an open-and-shut case.

Since *Ridge v Baldwin* the right to a hearing is no longer limited to judicial functions. The courts have extended the right to a hearing into most areas of government, including, for example immigration and prison management (*R v Hull Prison Visitors, ex p St Germain* [1979] QB 425; *Leech v Parkhurst Prison Deputy Governor* [1988] 1 All ER 485). Although the expression 'natural justice' is still occasionally used it has become interchangeable with 'fairness' (*Re HK* [1967] 2 QB 617). The concept of 'judicial' is still relevant since a judicial decision will certainly attract a right to a hearing and this may be of a higher procedural standard than in the case of an administrative decision. A legitimate expectation (Section 17.9) is also ground for a right to be heard in order to persuade the decision maker to honour the expectation (*A-G for Hong Kong v Ng Yuen Shiu* (1983); *R v Secretary of State for the Home Dept, ex p Khan* (1985).

However the courts have introduced limits to the right to be heard. These are based on pragmatic factors. They include the following:

▶ 'Fairness' concerns the protection of persons who are adversely affected by government action and not the idea of democratic participation in government. Thus the right to be heard may not include access to policy information (see *Bushell v Secretary of State for the Environment* (1981); *Hammersmith and Fulham LBC v Secretary of State for the Environment* [1990] 3 All ER 14).

▶ Advisory or preliminary governmental decisions do not attract a right to be heard unless the decision has direct adverse consequences for the individual's rights (*Norwest Holst v Trade Secretary* [1978] Ch 201: decision to start an investigation, no right to be heard; cf *Furnell v Whangarie High Schools Board* [1973] AC 660: suspension of teacher pending investigation, hearing required).

▶ A judicial decision to remove existing legal rights usually attracts a hearing but the refusal of a discretionary benefit in the public interest and where the claimant has no specific entitlement may not do so; *McInnes v Onslow-Fane* [1978] 3 All ER 211: refusing a referee's licence; *Findlay v Secretary of State for the Home Dept* (1985): parole, change in policy). However, a decision to refuse a benefit that can only be made on limited grounds or involves accusations of misconduct or bad character or affects a legitimate expectation will attract a hearing (see *R v Gaming Board, ex p Benaim and Khaida* [1970] 2 QB 417; *R v Secretary of State for the Home Dept, ex p Fayed* [1997] 1 All ER 228).

▶ Other factors might override or limit the right to a hearing, in particular national security considerations (*CCSU v Minister for the Civil Service* (1985). The need to act quickly in an emergency will also exclude at least a prior hearing (*R v Secretary of State for Transport, ex p Pegasus Holidays* Ltd [1989] 2 all ER 481: air safety; *Calvin v Carr* [1980] AC 574 (below)). A hearing might be excluded where large numbers compete for scarce resources, for example applications for university places, or in respect of general decisions such as school closures. On the other hand where a policy decision, for example to close an old people's home, directly affects the existing rights of the persons concerned there may be a collective right to be consulted, although not necessarily a hearing in individual cases (*R v Devon CC, ex p Baker* [1995] 1 All ER 73).

▶ Although the courts have warned against this (eg *Ridge v Baldwin (1964)*; *John v Rees* [1969] 2 All ER 274) a hearing may be excluded when the court thinks that the outcome of the decision was not affected, so that a hearing would be futile (*Cheall v Apex* [1983] 1 All ER 1130). In *Cinnamond v British Airports Authority* [1980] 2 All ER 368, the Court of Appeal upheld a decision to withdraw licences without a hearing from a group of Heathrow Airport taxi drivers who had been repeatedly warned about allegations of misconduct but had not responded.

▶ The same flexible concept of 'fairness' also determines the ingredients of a hearing. There are no fixed requirements. Subject to any statutory requirements, a decision maker can decide its own procedure provided that they are 'fair' in the circumstances of the particular case (see *Lloyd v McMahon* [1987] 1 All ER 118). Fairness means knowledge of the case against the person and a chance to answer any allegations (*Board of Education v Rice* (1911). Thus where a decision involves the application of a government policy the policy must be published and transparent so that informed and meaningful representations can be made (*R (Lumba) v Secretary of State for the Home Dept* [(2011)).

▶ The more serious the consequences for the individual, the higher the standard of hearing that is required. To this extent the notion of a judicial decision remains important. At one end of the scale preliminary investigations at best entitle a person to be told only an outline of any accusations against him or her and answer them (*Maxwell v Dept of Trade and Industry and ors* [1974] 2 All ER 122). At the other end of the scale a person accused of misconduct or whose rights are in issue is normally entitled to see all the evidence and cross-examine witnesses (*R v Army Board, ex p Anderson* [1992] QB 169). Administrative convenience cannot justify refusing to permit a person to call witnesses, although the tribunal does have a residual discretion in the matter (*R v Hull Prison Visitors, ex p St Germain (No 2)* [1979]1 WLR 1401).

▶ Fairness is a minimum standard to be balanced against the government's right to decide its own procedure. An oral hearing is not necessarily required although an absolute rule excluding an oral hearing is not permitted (*Lloyd v McMahon* (1987). The importance of the matter and the nature of the particular issues should be taken into account to decide whether the matter can be fairly determined without an oral hearing (see *R (Smith) v Parole Board* [2005] 1 All ER 755; *R (Dudson) v Secretary of State for the Home Dept* [2006] 1 All ER 421). Formal rules of evidence are not required.

▶ Fairness demands only that the evidence be relevant and that the parties have a chance to comment on it (*Mahon v Air New Zealand* [1984] 3 All ER 321). There is no automatic right to legal representation but the decision maker must not adopt an absolute rule on the matter and must allow representation where a person cannot effectively present his or her own case (*Hone v Maze Prison Board of Visitors* (1988); However under the ECHR Article 6 a person subject to a severe penalty is entitled to legal representation (Section 21.4).

▶ Problems arise where an individual is confronted with those who claim inside knowledge but are reluctant to have this challenged. An expert decision maker can rely on his own accumulated experience without having to disclose this to the parties. Expert assessors are sometimes used to help judges and other decision makers; they need not disclose their advice in advance. However, where the judge disagrees with an assessor on an important matter he should give the parties a chance to comment (*Ahmed v Governing Body of Oxford University* [2003] 1 All ER 917). If an inquiry is held the decision maker cannot subsequently take new evidence or advice received from an outside source into account without giving the parties an opportunity to comment (*Elmbridge BC v Secretary of State for the Environment, Transport and the Regions* [2002] Envir LR 1; *AMEC Ltd v Whitefriars City Estates* [2005] 1 All ER 723). However, advice given to a minister by a civil servant in his or her department does not count as outside advice and by virtue of the doctrine of ministerial responsibility need not be disclosed (*Bushell v Secretary of State for the Environment* [198]).

18.4 ▶ Procedural impropriety: bias

An impartial and independent judge is a fundamental aspect of the rule of law. However complete impartiality is impossible to realise. Not only is bias inherent in human nature but many kinds of decision-making processes inevitably involve conflicts of interest. The problem is especially acute in the UK with its culture of personal connections within the governing elite. The law therefore has to compromise, and has done so by distinguishing between different kinds of decisions and different kinds of biases.

The decision maker need not actually be biased – this would fall under the head of irrelevant considerations (Section 17.7). The bias rule is importantly concerned with the risk or appearance of bias, hence the dictum of Lord Hewart in *R v Sussex Justices, ex p McCarthy* [1924] 1 KB 256 that 'justice must not only be done but must manifestly and undoubtedly be seen to be done' (at 259). The rationale is not only that of fairness to the parties but also that of public confidence in the integrity of the decision-making process. A decision maker who becomes aware that he or she is subject to a biasing factor must disqualify him or herself, irrespective of the cost, delay or inconvenience that may result (*AWG Group v Morrison* [2006] 1 All ER 967). However the parties can consent to the bias in question (waiver) (see *Smith v Kvaener Cementation Foundations Ltd* [2006] 3 All ER 593).

The main principles are as follows:

▶ *financial interests*. A direct personal financial interest, however small, will automatically disqualify the decision maker, the law conclusively presuming bias (*Dimes v Grand Junction Canal Co* [1852] 3 HLC 759: Lord Chancellor held shares in company appearing before him; *R v Hendon RDC, ex p Chorley* [1933] 2 KB 696: local councillor had financial interest in development for which planning permission was sought; see also *R v Camborne Justices, ex p Pearce* [1955] 1 QB 41 at 47);

▶ *parties to the case*. In *R v Bow Street Stipendiary Magistrate, ex p Pinochet (No 2)* [1999] 1 All ER 577 the House of Lords extended automatic disqualification to a case where a judge is a member of an organisation that is party to the case even though there is no financial interest. Lord Hoffmann, a Law Lord, was an unpaid director of a charitable subsidiary of Amnesty International, a human rights pressure group, which was a party to an appeal concerning whether to extradite the former

President of Chile to Spain to face charges of torture and genocide. *Pinochet* has been criticised on the ground that there is an important distinction between 'interest', where the judge stands to gain personally, so he is a judge in his own case and should automatically be disqualified, and 'favour', where the judge might prefer a particular outcome, where a more flexible approach is appropriate (Olowofoyeku, 2000). Other common law jurisdictions have confined automatic disqualification to strictly financial interests and, bearing in mind that *Pinochet* was a case of special political significance, it is unlikely that its rationale will be extended beyond the case where a party directly controls an organistion of which the judge is an active member (*R (Kaur) v Institute of Legal Executives (ILEX) Appeal Tribunal [2012] 1 All ER 1435 (see below), Meerabux v A-G of Belize [2005] 2 AC 513 [21], [22], [30]*: mere membership does not disqualify, active involvement needed.)

▶ *other personal connections* such as social, family or professional relationships with the parties, previous involvement with the same decision-making process, the holding of opinions or the membership of groups related to the issues. These do not automatically disqualify and a more flexible approach is taken. The courts have tried to find a formula which on the one hand reflects the interest of public confidence in the impartiality of the decision maker and on the other hand blocks challenges for flimsy or ill-informed suspicions. The current formula asks whether in the view of a 'fair-minded and informed observer' taken as knowing all the circumstances there is a 'real possibility' or 'real danger' of bias (*Porter v Magill* [2002] 1 All ER 465).

This formula emerged from *R v Gough* [1993] AC 646, which replaced two earlier tests (albeit often producing the same outcome). These were firstly a strict 'reasonable suspicion' test according to which any suspicious factor as it appeared to a reasonable hypothetical observer might disqualify the judge, even though if all the circumstances were known the observer might be reassured; secondly the more liberal 'real likelihood' test allowed the reviewing court to decide for itself whether in all the circumstances bias was likely. *Gough* tried to compromise between the two. It did not include the device of the hypothetical outsider but neither did it require an overall balance, only a 'real danger' of bias. However *Gough* seemed to be out of line with the ECHR and the practice in other English-speaking countries (see Olowofoyeku, 2000). In particular the court might be too trusting of other decision makers, sharing the 'insider' view of public life which is endemic among the clannish professional and official elite.

The Gough test was modified by *Re Medicaments (No 2)* [2001] 1 WLR 700, which reintroduced the imagined standpoint of a hypothetical reasonable outsider. It is questionable whether this makes any difference since the outsider who knows all and is fair-minded seems to be no more than an idealised avatar for the judge (*Virdi v Law Society* [2010] 3 All ER 653).

Each case depends on its particular circumstances. There seems to be a large element of subjective guesswork and some indulgence towards fellow professionals. Generally speaking a conflict of interest disqualifies only if it is focused on the specific type of case. The following are examples.

▶ In *R v Gough* (1993) the accused's brother was a neighbour of a jury member, who did not however recognise him. The jury was not disqualified.

- In *R v Abdrocar* [2005] 4 All ER 869 it was held that the presence of a policeman and a prosecuting solicitor on a jury was acceptable in the light of the normal understandings of what citizenship entailed.
- In *Re Medicaments (No 2)* (2001) a lay member of the Restrictive Practices Court was applying for a job with a firm one of whose members often appeared as an expert witness before the court. The Court of Appeal held that she was disqualified even though she had taken steps to minimise the conflict of interest.
- In *Locobail (UK) v Bayfield Properties* [2000] QB 451 the Court of Appeal stressed that *general* objections based on religious, racial, ethnic or national characteristics, gender, age, class, political views, membership of organisations, income and sexual orientation would not normally disqualify. *Specific* connections might include personal friendships or animosity but making adverse remarks on a previous occasion would not in itself be sufficient. The court disqualified a judge who had written polemical articles in legal journals attacking the practices of insurance companies in circumstances similar to those in the case before him. However it did not disqualify a judge who had been a member of a solicitors' firm acting for one of the parties since he had not been personally involved, or a decision to give a licence to a betting shop where the judge was a director of a company of which the shop was a tenant. Nor did the court disqualify the chair of a tribunal that had decided both a preliminary application to proceed in a sexual harassment case and the full case later.
- In *AMEC Ltd v Whitefriars City Estates* [2005] the reappointment of the same adjudicator to re-determine a previous flawed arbitration constituted bias.
- In *Gillies v Secretary of State for Work and Pensions* [2006] 1 All ER 967 prior experience and specialist knowledge were not a disqualification.
- In *R v L* [2011] 1 Cri App Rep 338 it was held that a juror who was an employee of the Crown Prosecution Service carrying out general administrative duties was disqualified.

Allegations of bias have been successfully met by the claim that professional practices ensure integrity; in other words we should trust those in power. For example in *Porter v Magill* [2002] a local government auditor investigating allegations of bribery had made a provisional press announcement endorsing the allegations. His later formal report confirmed his findings. The House of Lords held that he was not disqualified since the reasonable observer could assume that an experienced professional was impartial. Similarly in *Helow v Secretary of State for the Home Dept* [2009] 2 All ER 1031 a judge who was a member of the International Association of Jewish Lawyers was presiding over an asylum application by a supporter of the Palestine Liberation Front. The House of Lords held that the fair-minded and informed person would not conclude that there would be a real possibility of bias. It would require extreme words or conduct identifying with a partisan cause to justify such a conclusion. Even though this was a campaigning organisation it could be assumed that when he put his judicial hat on the judge would put any private views aside.

Similarly in *Taylor v Lawrence* [2002] 3 All ER 353 it was held that a judge was not disqualified where a solicitor appearing before him had recently transacted family business on his behalf. Lord Woolf remarked that an informed observer can be expected to be aware of 'the legal traditions and culture of this jurisdiction' (at [61–64]), with the implication that this would be reassuring. In *Virdi v Law Society (2010)*, in a disciplinary hearing by the Law Society, the clerk, who was a Law Society employee, retired with the tribunal and drafted its report. The Court of Appeal held that there was no danger of bias because the 'well-informed reasonable person' would know that there was no impropriety.

Lawal v Northern Spirit [2004] 1 All ER 187 suggests a less complacent approach. The claimant appealed to the Employment Appeal Tribunal in respect of an allegation of racial discrimination by his employer. The senior counsel for the employer had previously sat as a part-time judge with one of the lay members of the Tribunal. The House of Lords held that the reasonable outsider might well suspect that the relationship could bias the lay member. Lord Steyn warned against complacent assumptions of professional integrity, pointing out that:

> the indispensable requirement of public confidence in the administration of justice requires higher standards today than was the case even a decade or two ago. The informed observer of today could perhaps be expected to be aware of the legal traditions and culture of this jurisdiction … But he might not be wholly uncritical of that culture. (at [22])

Moreover in *R (Kaur) v ILEX Appeal Tribunal* [2012] the Court of Appeal held that the Vice President of the Institute of Legal Executives was disqualified from sitting on its Appeal Tribunal in a case where a student was accused of cheating. The hypothetical fair-minded, all-knowing observer could well believe that the Vice President's concern with the reputation of the organisation would make him less than impartial. The court also discussed whether this was an example of automatic disqualification as in *Pinochet* (above). It was suggested that the automatic disqualification test which applies to financial interests and some cases where a judge is linked with a party (above) was not a separate doctrine but merely a clear example of the reasonable observer test. This means that a financial interest could sometimes be disregarded.

The bias rule is overridden where there is an unavoidable conflict of interest, in which case Parliament must be taken to have impliedly authorised the bias (see also Supreme Court Act 1981, s 11: judges as taxpayers). In the case of administrative decisions taken by politicians, conflicts of interest arising out of political policies or competing responsibilities may be built into the system by statute (*eg Franklin v Minister of Town and Country Planning [1948]*, a case which is discredited on wider grounds but remains relevant in this context), *R v Secretary of State for the Environment, ex p Kirkstall Valley Campaign Ltd* [1996] 3 All ER 304: local authority had interest in developing land for which it also had to decide whether to grant planning permission.

The same applies in organisations, such as prisons and universities, where officials have a mixture of administrative and disciplinary functions (*eg R v Frankland Prison Board of Visitors, ex p Lewis* [1986] 1 All ER 272: prison visitors having both judicial and investigatory roles. Of course an avoidable bias disqualifies (*R (Al-Hasan) v Secretary of State for the Home Dept* [2005] 1 All ER 927 a deputy prison governor who had been present while the governor gave an allegedly unlawful order to carry out an intimate body search on a prisoner). Similarly a decision may be upheld if there is no possible unbiased decision maker (*R v Barnsley Licensing Justices* [1960] 2 QB 167: all justices members of the local Co-op).

18.5 Procedural impropriety: reasons for decisions

There is no general duty to give reasons for decisions, although many statutes impose such a duty (see *R v Criminal Injuries Compensation Board, ex p Moore* [1999] 2 All ER 90; *Stefan v GMC* [1999] 1 WLR 1293). The absence of a duty to give reasons has been justified on the grounds of cost, excessive formality, the difficulties of expressing subjective reasons and because in the case of collective decisions it may be difficult to identify specific reasons (see *McInnes v Onslow-Fane* (1978); *R v Higher Education Funding Council, ex p Institute of Dental Surgery* [1994] 1 All ER 651; *Stefan v GMC* (1999)).

The main justification for the giving of reasons is respect for human dignity and equality so that those who purport to exercise power must be accountable. Even an admission that a decision is based on subjective judgement fulfils this requirement. The giving of reasons also strengthens public confidence in the decision-making process, concentrates the mind of the decision maker and helps identify problems.

The courts have required reasons to be given in certain cases based on the principle of fairness which allows the court to take all the circumstances into account. In *R v Secretary of State for the Home Dept, ex p Doody* [1993] 3 All ER 92 Lord Mustill referred to 'a perceptible trend towards an insistence upon greater openness in the making of administrative decisions' (at 107). The dominant view seems to be that a duty to give reasons must either be expressed or implied in the relevant statute or there must be some special justification for giving reasons. In *R v Higher Education Funding Council, ex p Institute of Dental Surgery* [1994] Sedley J held that arguments which applied to all cases were not sufficient, for example the difficulty of challenging a decision in the absence of reasons.

Examples of cases where there is a duty to give reasons include the following:

- judicial decisions analogous to those of a court;
- cases that involve very important interests where if reasons were not given the individual would be at a disadvantage (eg *Doody (1993)*: fixing of minimum sentence for life prisoner; *Stefan v GMC (1999)*: risk of loss of livelihood, unrepresented defendant);
- cases where the particular decision is unusual or a severe penalty is involved (eg *R v Civil Service Appeals Board, ex p Cunningham* [1991]: compensation award out of line with that given in analogous cases by industrial tribunal; *R v DPP, ex p Manning* [2000] 3 WLR 463: decision not to prosecute after coroner's finding of unlawful killing);
- a legitimate expectation (Section 17.9) might also generate a duty to give reasons for overriding the expectation (*R v Secretary of State for Transport, ex p Richmond upon Thames BC (No 4)* [1996] 4 All ER 903);
- if an appeal is provided this may point to a duty to give reasons where the appeal would otherwise be pointless (*Stefan v GMC [1999]*). On the other hand a comprehensive appeal that reopens the whole case may point against a duty to give reasons at first instance;
- in *Padfield v Minister of Agriculture, Fisheries and Food* (1968) the House of Lords suggested that if a minister refuses to give reasons, the court can infer that he has no proper reasons for his decision. However, in *Lonrho v Secretary of State for Trade and Industry* [1989] 2 All ER 609 the House held that a failure to give reasons does not in itself justify the drawing of an adverse inference but is at most supportive of other evidence that the decision is improper.

In answer to the complaint that a duty to give reasons would overburden officials, reasons need not be detailed or comprehensive, provided that they enable the parties to understand the basis of the decision (see *South Bucks DC v Porter* [2004] 4 All ER 705).

A duty to give reasons arises after the decision is made and should be distinguished from failing before the decision is made to disclose *grounds* in the sense of allegations against the applicant. Failure to disclose such grounds would normally be unfair as a breach of the right to a hearing. Moreover, once an applicant has obtained leave to apply for judicial review there is a duty of full and frank disclosure. The authority 'owes a duty to the court to cooperate and make candid disclosure of the relevant facts and the reasoning behind the decision challenged' (Lord Walker in *Belize Alliance of Conservation NGOs v Dept of the Environment* [2003] UKPC 63 [86]; *R v Lancashire CC, ex p Huddlestone* [1986] 2 All ER 941). However this is of no help in finding grounds for challenge in the first place.

18.6   The European Convention on Human Rights

The Human Rights Act 1998 requires all public authorities to comply with the 'Convention Rights' incorporated into UK law by the Act unless primary legislation makes this impossible (Section 22.4). The Act provides a freestanding basis for challenge in addition to the domestic ground of judicial review thus providing an additional and more direct remedy. The human rights perspective differs from that of domestic judicial review in that its primary focus is on the outcome in the sense of the impact of the decision on the individual. Although the distinction is not an absolute one, judicial review is mainly concerned with the *process* of decision making. Thus in a human rights case the court itself will investigate the facts and merits and although it will give appropriate weight to the views of other experts, is not confined to ensuring that the decision maker has properly considered the human rights aspects (*R (Begum) v Head Teacher of Denbigh High School* (2007), *Manchester City Council v Pinnock* [2010] 3 WLR1441; *Thomas v Bridgend CBC* [2012] JPEL 25).

The Human Rights Act also affects particular domestic grounds of review in several ways:

▶ The flexibility of notions such as unreasonableness and legitimate expectation means that the courts will review more intensively where a human right is engaged (eg *R v North and East Devon HA, ex p Coughlan* (2000), *Rowland v Environment Agency* [2003] EWCA Civ 1885, *R (Reprotech (Pebsham) Ltd.) v East Sussex CC* [2003] 1 WLR 348 per Lord Hoffmann). In particular 'proportionality' rather than *Wednesbury* unreasonableness applies to human rights cases (Section 18.3). The court can decide directly what is proportionate. However in some contexts the court will show deference to a decision which the court regards as outside its proper competence. In this kind of case provided that the decision maker has properly considered the human rights aspects, the court is effectively reverting to the Wednesbury level of review (Section 19.7.1).

▶ Article 6 of the ECHR, confers a right to a fair trial where 'civil rights and obligations' are in issue (Section 21.4.2). This includes a right to challenge an administrative decision before a body with 'full jurisdiction'. The meaning of 'civil rights' for Article 6 purposes is narrower than the range of interests protected by the common law doctrine of fairness. For example an alien has no civil right in relation to expulsion from the UK but is entitled only to a basic hearing, which must however be before an independent tribunal, to enable him to answer accusations against him (*IR (Sri Lanka) v Secretary of State for the Home Dept* [2011]).

In deciding whether there has been a fair trial, the court will look at the process as a whole, including any right of judicial review (*Albert v Belgium* (1983) 5 EHRR 583). A question which especially arises here is whether the limited review on questions of fact in English law satisfies Article 6 (Section 21.4.2).

The common law has been said to accord with the 'spirit' of Article 6 (*Secretary of State for the Home Dept v MB* [24]). However, although Article 6 does require a balance between the rights of the individual and the public interest there is an irreducible minimum of fairness whereas the common law duty is less strict, involving a broader balance between fairness and the public interest (*Re Officer L* [2007] 4 All ER 965; *Secretary of State for the Home Dept v MB* [2008]). Thus, except in connection with the right to a hearing in public, which can be excluded in certain circumstances (Art 6(1)), the right to a fair trial cannot be overridden by other factors, although particular aspects might be modified to deal, for example with security matters (Section 24.3). The common law does not require a public hearing.

As regards both the bias rule and the giving of reasons English law seems to be compliant with the ECHR. The European Court has confined itself to holding that the courts, as the citizen's last protection, must give reasons for their decisions but has not required administrative bodies to do so (*Van de Hurk v The Netherlands* [1984] 18 EHRR 481; see also *Helle v Finland* (1998) 26 EHRR 159: detailed reasons not necessary).

Summary

▶ The doctrine of *Wednesbury* unreasonableness comes near to interfering with the merits of a decision. The threshold of unreasonableness varies with the context on a sliding scale determined by the impact of the decision on the individual and whether the decision involves political factors with which a court should not interfere. At one extreme a bare 'rationality' test is applied. At the other extreme where the Human Rights Act 1998 applies the court itself may weigh the competing considerations, exercising what is effectively an appeal function. Between these extremes the test appears to be whether the outcome is within the range of reasonable responses to the particular context. In effect the court is drawing upon widely shared social and moral values.

▶ The principle of proportionality is applied in the human rights context and may extend to other contexts such as legitimate expectations. This requires the court to weigh the competing factors on the basis that the interference with the right must be no greater than is necessary to achieve a legitimate objective (in the case of some rights protected by the ECHR 'a pressing social need').

▶ Natural justice or fairness requires that a person adversely affected by a decision be entitled to a hearing. The requirements of a hearing are flexible and depend on the circumstances.

▶ In order to respect the interests of government efficiency, fairness is regarded as the minimum necessary to do justice. The courts are increasingly requiring reasons to be given for decisions.

▶ A decision maker must also be free from the appearance of improper bias. This too depends on the circumstances. A direct financial interest automatically disqualifies the decision maker, as perhaps does membership of an organisation which is a party to the case. In other cases the test is whether a hypothetical, reasonable and fully informed observer would consider there to be real danger of bias.

▶ The rules of natural justice or procedural fairness are underpinned by the Human Rights Act 1998, although what amounts to a fair trial depends on the context and in particular the extent to which the decision is a policy-oriented political decision.

Exercises

18.1 'I think the day will come when it will be more widely recognised that the *Wednesbury* case was an unfortunately retrogressive decision in English administrative law' (Lord Cooke). What does he mean and do you agree?

18.2 'The difference in practice [between *Wednesbury* unreasonableness and proportionality] is not as great as is sometimes supposed … even without reference to the 1998 Act the time has come to recognise that this principle is part of English administrative law, not only when judges are dealing with Community acts but also when they are dealing with acts subject to domestic law' (Lord Slynn). Do you agree?

18.3 'Judicial review is mainly concerned with the way in which a decision is reached rather than with its outcome.' Do you agree?

18.4 There is a statutory scheme to decide whether elderly persons should be entitled to free bus passes. An applicant must satisfy a local tribunal that he or she has a special need for a bus pass due to infirmity, low income or other special circumstances. The tribunal consists of a local magistrate, a manager of a bus company and an assessor who is a medically qualified. The tribunal does not hold an oral hearing but decides applications by e mail from the applicant and e mails between the tribunal members. Jones who has a heart complaint and breathing difficulties applies for a bus pass. He has no access to a computer and makes his application by letter. His application is rejected without giving reasons. Jones sends a further letter requesting to see any medical evidence in his case and to appear in person before the tribunal assisted by his lawyer. This letter is ignored. Advise Jones.

18.5 The local Council is given statutory power to 'regulate the operation of cinemas'. The Council introduces a system of licences for cinemas. It imposes the following conditions:
  (i) Children are prohibited from attending any performance on a Sunday.
  (ii) No refreshments are to be sold at the cinema.

  The Chairman of the Council owns a fast food shop next to the cinema and is a well-known Evangelical preacher.
  (a) A local cinema wishes to challenge conditions (i) and (ii). Advise it.
  (b) Another local cinema is accused of breaching condition (i), and without giving it a hearing the Council orders it to close. Advise the Council. What would be the position if a councillor had said to the cinema manager, 'Between ourselves, we are not likely to enforce the condition where a child is accompanied by a parent,' and the manager had followed that advice?

18.6 Does the bias rule strike a reasonable balance between efficiency and justice?

18.7 Dan is accused of plagiarism in his dissertation at the University of Business Enterprise. His Head of Department holds a hearing into the matter and recommends to the University Best Practice Committee that Dan be expelled from the University. Dan appeals to the Committee and is invited to a hearing. Before the hearing Dan discovers that the Chair of the committee is a business studies professor who has recently sold internet programmes on 'how to detect plagiarism'. Dan's head of department is also a member of the Committee. Dan writes to the committee stating that he does not believe that he would get a fair hearing from 'this gang of cronies'. The Chair replies that the professional integrity of colleagues is absolute. Dan appears before the committee which confirms his expulsion from the university.

  Would your answer differ if the committee had refused to permit Dan to appear in person before it but invited him to make a written statement?

Further reading

Allan, 'Procedural Fairness and the Duty of Respect' (1998) 18 OJLS 497

Craig, 'Substance and Procedure in Judicial Review', in Andenas and Fairgrieve (eds), *Tom Bingham and the Transformation of the Law* (Oxford University Press 2009)

Daly, '*Wednesbury's* Reason and Structure' [2011] PL 238

Elliot, 'Has the Common Law Duty to Give Reasons Come of Age Yet?' [2011] PL 56

Goodwin, 'The Last Defence of Wednesbury' [2012] PL 445

Hickman, 'The Reasonableness Principle: Reassessing Its Place in the Public Sphere' (2004) 63 CLJ 166

Hunt, 'Sovereignty's Blight: Why Contemporary Public Law Needs the Concept of Due Deference', in Bamforth and Leyland (eds), *Public Law in a Multi-Layered Constitution* (Hart 2003)

Irvine, 'Judges and Decision Makers: The Theory and Practice of *Wednesbury* Review' [1996] PL 59

Jowell, 'Beyond the Rule of Law: Towards Constitutional Judicial Review' [2000] PL 671

Jowell, 'Judicial Deference: Servility, Civility or Institutional Capacity' [2003] PL 592

Olowofoyeku, 'The *Nemo Judex* Rule: The Case against Automatic Disqualification' [2000] PL 456

Poole, 'The Reformation of English Administrative Law' [2008] CLJ 67

Rivers, 'Proportionality and Variable Intensity of Review' [2006] CLJ 174

Taggart, 'Reinventing Administrative Law', in Bamforth and Leyland (eds), *Public Law in a Multi-Layered Constitution* (Hart 2003)

Taggart, 'Proportionality, Deference, *Wednesbury*' [2008] New Zealand LJ 423

Walker, 'What's Wrong with Irrationality?' [1995] PL 556

Wong, 'Towards the Nutcracker Principle: Reconsidering the Objections to Proportionality' [2000] PL 92

Chapter 19

Judicial review remedies

19.1 Introduction

It could be argued that the courts provide the only open and universal means by which the individual can challenge government action. Ministerial responsibility to Parliament is of little use to the citizen directly in that it can be called upon only by members of Parliament, who are unlikely to be independent and cannot force minsters to disclose information. The Committee on Standards in Public Life plays a valuable monitoring role but has no enforcement powers. The 'ombudsman' which investigates citizens' complaints against government is free to complainants and its powers of investigation into facts are extensive. However its jurisdiction is limited to maladministration and many public bodies are excluded, it has no enforcement powers and it does not hold public hearings (Section 20.2). The courts have the advantage of sitting in public and have unlimited power to require the disclosure of information.

Until 1977 there was no distinctive legal process for judicial review. The powers of the courts to review government action developed historically in different courts through a variety of remedies, some of which were general remedies applying also to private disputes. As we saw (Section 6.4) one aspect of the 'rule of law' emphasised by Dicey was that the common law does not distinguish between public law and private law but applies the same principles to government and citizen alike, so that an official is in no better position than a private individual. However, since Dicey's day the powers of government have expanded enormously and this approach has become inadequate both to protect the citizen and to reflect the democratic interest in the effective delivery of government policy. Since 1977 the various remedies have been concentrated in a single jurisdiction, part of the Queen's Bench Division of the High Court and now called the Administrative Court. Originally the Administrative Court sat only in London. However in order to enhance access to justice it now also sits in regional centres (Cardiif, Birmingham, Manchester, Leeds), the venue normally depending on the claimant's connection (see Practice Direction 54D-Administrative Court (Venue)). It is sometimes suggested that a shortage of specialist lawyers outside London might weaken the court.

The workload of the Administrative Court is substantial. Further flexibility is added by the Tribunals, Courts and Enforcement Act 2007, under which the Upper Tribunal, which also hears appeals from the main tribunals, has a judicial review jurisdiction in types of case (other than those concerning the Crown Court) designated by the Lord Chief Justice or another judge designated by him or her (ss 15, 18). The Upper Tribunal has the same status as the High Court but includes other senior judicial officers (Section 20.1).

The law is governed by section 31 of the Senior Courts Act 1981 and Part 54 of the Civil Procedure Rules 1998 (CPR) (*Practice Direction* [2000] 1 WLR 1654). There is a unified procedure for all the remedies. This replaces numerous technical rules which had developed over the years in relation to individual remedies. These had made challenge to government action complex and sometimes unjust, with litigants having to traverse a minefield of procedural niceties and sometimes being frustrated by choosing an inappropriate remedy in the wrong court. A Law Commission Report in 1976 (Law Com No 6407) led to the main reforms. A further Law Commission Report (No 226, 1994) led to further, relatively minor changes.

A claim for judicial review means a claim to review the lawfulness of (i) an enactment or (ii) a decision, action or failure to act in relation to the exercise of a public function (CPR 54.1). The procedure as a whole is characterised by wide discretionary powers which allow the court to choose the most appropriate remedy from the whole range. It also embodies principles concerned with the special nature of disputes between government and citizen.

These principles are of three kinds:

1. The remedies are designed to set aside unlawful government action and to send the matter back to the decision maker or to restrain an unlawful act but not, normally, to allow the court to make a new decision itself, thus complying with the separation of powers. However, where there is only one possible decision that could lawfully be made the court can make it itself (CPR 54.19). Moreover, the court might exceptionally correct a mistake made, for example in a statutory instrument where it is plain that the mistake was inadvertent and when the purpose of the instrument is clear (*R (Confederation of Passenger Transport (UK)) v Humber Bridge Board* [2004] 4 All ER 533).
2. The procedure reflects the limited role of the courts. In particular the procedure is normally based on written statements since the court is not primarily concerned with factual disputes. However there is power to hear witnesses if justice so requires.
3. The procedure contains barriers designed to safeguard the public interest in protecting government against improper challenges (Section 19.3). To a certain extent judicial review could be regarded as part of the political process since it provides a public platform for grievances against the government so that, to a well-funded partisan, even hopeless litigation might be attractive as a means of publicising a cause. On the other hand any restriction on the right to go to court might be seen as an affront to the rule of law. However in cases where a person's ordinary private rights are at stake, for example if a public authority interferes with private property, an action or defence can be brought in any court, thus reflecting the traditional idea of the rule of law.

19.2   The range of remedies

Historically there are two groups of remedies suitable for judicial review. Firstly from the seventeenth century the courts developed the 'prerogative orders' (so-called because in theory they issue on the application of the Crown). These were *certiorari, prohibition and mandamus,* and they enabled the High Court to police the powers and duties of 'inferior bodies', that is, lower courts and government officials. *Certiorari* summoned up the record of an inferior body to be examined by the court and the decision was set aside and sent back if it was invalid. *Prohibition* was issued in advance to prevent a body from exceeding its jurisdiction. *Mandamus* ordered a body to perform its duty. These orders remain the basis of the modern law of judicial review but are now called quashing orders, prohibiting orders and mandatory orders, respectively (CPR 54.1). They are available only in the Administrative Court (CPR 54.2). A quashing order sets aside the offending decision and is the most common remedy.

The second group of remedies comprises declarations, injunctions and damages (Senior Courts Act 1981, s 31(2)). These are also available in other courts and are primarily private law remedies. A claimant may apply for these in the Administrative Court and must do so if he or she is seeking these remedies in addition to a prerogative order (CPR 54.3). A declaration is a statement of the legal position which declares the rights of parties (eg 'X is entitled to a tax repayment'). Declarations are not enforceable but a public authority is unlikely to disobey one. Indeed a declaration is useful where an enforceable order would be undesirable, for example in the case of a draft government order before it is considered by Parliament or an advisory government opinion. It might, for example be used to avoid offending Parliament (see *R v Boundary Commission, ex p Foot* [1983]). The former prerogative orders do not lie against the Crown as such but the declaration does. However, this is relatively unimportant because most statutory powers are conferred on ministers and the prerogative orders lie against individual ministers.

An injunction restrains a person from breaking the law or orders a person to undo something done unlawfully (a mandatory injunction). An interim injunction can restrain government action pending a full trial. In *M v Home Office* [1993] the House of Lords held that an injunction can be enforced against a minister of the Crown (see also *R v Minister of Agriculture, Fisheries and Food, ex p Monsanto plc* [1998] 4 All ER 321). This overturns a long tradition that the Crown and its servants cannot be the subject of enforceable orders which still applies to ordinary civil law actions involving contract, tort or property issues (Crown Proceedings Act 1947, s 21). However it was stressed that injunctions should be granted against ministers only as a last resort. Injunctions cannot be granted against the Crown itself.

Claimants often apply for more than one of the remedies, which may well overlap. For example a quashing order has the same effect as a declaration that the offending decision is void. The court can issue any of the remedies in any combination and is not limited to those for which the claimant has applied (Senior Courts Act 1981, s 31(5)).

A claimant cannot seek a financial remedy, damages, restitution or the recovery of a debt alone in judicial review proceedings but must attach it to a claim for at least one of the other remedies (CPR 54.3(2)). Moreover, damages are not available in respect of unlawful government action as such but can be awarded only in respect of conduct and losses which are not authorised by statute and which would be actionable in an ordinary civil action (Senior Courts Act 1981, s 31(4); Tribunals, Courts and Enforcement Act 2007, s 16(6)). In other cases damages must be sought in an ordinary civil action.

The law relating to the liability for damages of public authorities is complex and cannot usefully be discussed without prior knowledge of the law of tort. We will not attempt to discuss the matter here other than to remark that the courts are reluctant to impose liability in damages upon bodies exercising statutory powers in respect of purely public functions on the basis of negligence or a failure of a public duty (see, eg *X (Minors) v Bedfordshire CC* [1995] 2 AC 633; *Marcic v Thames Water Utilities Ltd* [2004] 1 All ER 135; *Cullen v Chief Constable of the RUC* [2004] 2 All ER 247; *Anufrijeva v Southwark LBC* [2004] 1 All ER 833). This is because the risk of paying damages might inhibit the decision maker from exercising its powers independently (but see *Connor v Surrey CC* [2010] 3 All ER 905: existing duty in private law, public law duties should conform to this).

In four kinds of case, however, damages may be awarded on the basis of unlawful government action:

1. under the *Francovich* principle in EC law (Section 10.3.3);
2. under the tort of 'misfeasance in public office' where an authority has a specific intention to injure or knowingly acts outside its powers, being reckless as to the consequences, and causes material damage (see *Dunlop v Woollahra Municipal Council* [1982] AC 158; *Calverley v Chief Constable of Merseyside Police* [1989] 1 AC 1228); *Racz v Home Office* [1994] 1 All ER 97; *Three Rivers DC v Bank of England (No 3)* [2003] 2 AC 1; *Watkins v Secretary of State for the Home Dept* [2006] 2 All ER 353);
3. where a right protected by the Human Rights Act 1998 is infringed (see *D v East Berkshire Community Health NHS Trust* [2005] 2 AC 373);
4. where there has been a breach of a duty specifically intended to be enforced by the person to whom it is owed. However the courts are reluctant to interpret statutes as imposing such enforceable duties on a public authority (*Marcic v Thames Water Utilities Ltd [2004]*).

When it quashes a decision the court may remit the matter to the original decision maker to decide again in accordance with the court's findings. It is fundamental to judicial review that the court's role is secondary. It cannot normally substitute its own decision for that of the designated decision maker. However by virtue of section 35(5) b as modified by section 141 of the Tribunals, Courts and Enforcement Act 2007 the court can substitute its own decision if the original decision was made by a court or tribunal, that is, not the executive, and was quashed on the ground of error of law and without the error there could only be one decision which the tribunal could have reached.

19.2.1   Habeas corpus

There is also the ancient prerogative writ of *habeas corpus* ('produce the body'). It is not part of the judicial review procedure. *Habeas corpus* is applied for in the High Court and has priority over other business. It requires anyone detaining a person (other than a convicted prisoner) to bring the prisoner immediately before a judge to justify the detention. It provides a swift emergency remedy. Unlike judicial review the court has no discretion whether to hear the case and there is no time limit. Habeas corpus probably issues on the same grounds as those for judicial review (*R v Secretary of State for the Home Dept, ex p Khwaja [1991]*). However, there is authority that habeas corpus applies only where a decision is ultra vires in the narrow sense (*R v Secretary of State for the Home Dept ex parte Cheblak* [1991] 1 WLR 890, 894).

Habeas corpus was described as 'perhaps the most important writ known to the constitutional law of England, affording as it does a swift and imperative remedy in all cases of illegal constraint or confinement' (*Ex Parte O' Brian* [1924] AC 603, 609, *Rahmatullah v Secretary of State for the Home Dept* [2012] 1 All ER 1290 [43]. According to Dicey (1959, 199) habeas corpus is 'worth a hundred constitutional articles guaranteeing civil liberty' (even though it can be excluded by statute, eg *Re Hilali* [2008] 2 All ER 207 and has several times been suspended).

Habeas corpus may be of little practical importance today, when judicial review can provide a speedy way of challenging unlawful detention. Indeed because it cannot be used to challenge facts, habeas corpus has been held not to provide an effective remedy under Article 5 of the European Convention on Human Rights (ECHR): right to liberty (*X v UK* [1982] 4 EHRR 188). (See Le Sueur, 'Should We Abolish the Writ of Habeas Corpus?' [1992] PL 13; Shrimpton, 'In Defence of Habeas Corpus' [1993] PL 24; Law Com No 226, 1994, Part XI.)

19.3 The judicial review procedure: public interest safeguards

The judicial review process contains mechanisms designed to protect the public interest against improper challenges. In attempting to do this, it is vulnerable to objections relating to the right of access to the courts and the right to a fair trial under Article 6 of the ECHR.

The judicial review process must also be set in the wider context of the 'Woolf' reforms in civil procedure introduced in 1999 (Woolf, *Access to Justice: A Final Report to the Lord Chancellor* (HMSO 1996)). These reforms include the following general aspirations in respect of which the parties are under an obligation to assist the court (CPR 1.1):

(a) ensuring that the parties are on an equal footing;
(b) saving expense. In this connection 'a protected costs order' can put limits on the exposure of the parties in cases involving the public interest (see, eg *R (Boggis) v Natural England* [2010] 1 All ER 159);
(c) dealing with the case in ways which are proportionate
   (i) to the amount of money involved;
   (ii) to the importance of the case;
   (iii) to the complexity of the issues;
   (iv) to the financial position of each party;
(d) ensuring that the case is dealt with expeditiously and fairly;
(e) allocating to the case an appropriate share of the court's resources while taking into account the need to allot resources to other cases.

The main distinctive features of the judicial review procedure are as follows:

▶ Permission to apply is required from a judge before proceedings can be commenced in or transferred to the Administrative Court (Senior Courts Act 1981, s 31(3); CPR 54.4). The procedure is *ex parte*; that is the government side need not appear, although it must be given the opportunity to do so. At this stage the applicant merely shows that she or he has a chance of success, so as to discourage spurious challenges and help the court to manage an ever-increasing caseload by filtering out hopeless cases. There is a right to renew the application for permission before another judge in open court, and in the case of a refusal in open court, before the Court of Appeal, and then with leave to the Supreme Court. If the Court of Appeal gives permission it often then proceeds to deal with the whole matter. After permission has been granted, interim relief preventing the implementation of the government action in question can be granted pending the full hearing either by injunction (Section 19.2) or under section 31 of the Senior Courts Act 1981.

▶ At the full hearing the court has a discretion in relation to procedural matters. The case is normally decided on the basis of affidavits (sworn written statements) but the court may order discovery of documents, witnesses and cross-examination 'where the justice of the case so demands' (CPR 54.16(1)). In *Tweed v Parade Commission for Northern Ireland* [2007] 2 All ER 273 it was held that this was a broad principle which should take account of all the circumstances and that there may be a greater need to examine evidence in cases where the doctrine of proportionality applies. Moreover the government is obliged to make full and frank disclosure of all relevant material (see *R v Secretary of State for Foreign and Commonwealth Affairs, ex p Quark Fishing Ltd* [2006]; Lord Walker in *Belize Alliance of Conservation NGOs v Dept of the Environment* (2003)). With the agreement of the parties, the court can decide the whole matter without a hearing (CPR 54.18). It is arguable that in view of the broad policy issues that may arise in judicial review cases, particularly under the Human Rights Act 1998, it would be desirable that a more expansive process be used, at least in cases of major importance. One suggestion has been to appoint an Advocate General or Director of Civil Proceedings with the duty of representing the public interest before the court.

▶ Procedural flexibility is enhanced in that the Administrative Court can transfer cases to the ordinary trial process and vice versa (CPR 54.20).

▶ There is a shorter time limit than the periods of three or six years applicable to ordinary civil litigation. The law is contained in a somewhat confusing combination of section 31(6–7) of the Supreme Court (Senior Courts) Act 1981 and CPR 54.5(1)(b). Under section 31(6) the court may refuse leave to make the application or refuse to give a remedy if 'undue delay' results in 'substantial hardship to any person, substantial prejudice to the rights of any person, or would be detrimental to good administration'. However by virtue of CPR 54.5(1) the claim must be filed (i) promptly and (ii) not later than three months after the ground to make the claim first arose. In the case of a quashing order, this means the date of the decision. The time limit cannot be extended by agreement and is subject to any shorter time limit in a particular statute (CPR 54.6). The time limit can however be extended by the court (CPR 3.1(2)).

▶ The combined effect of these provisions is a two-stage filter mechanism. First a failure to apply for permission promptly, even within three months, is undue delay. The court might then extend the time limit. Secondly, if it does so, it can still refuse relief but only on the grounds specified in section 31(6). These considerations are usually examined at the full hearing stage (see *Caswell v Dairy Produce Quota Tribunal for England and Wales* [1990] 2 All ER 434).

▶ The court can refuse to grant a remedy in its discretion even when a decision is ultra vires and strictly speaking void. By contrast in ordinary litigation an ultra vires decision is treated as a nullity (*Credit Suisse v Allerdale BC* [1996]; Section 17.2). The court will not set aside a decision where, for example no injustice has been done, where the interests of third parties would be prejudiced or where intervention would cause serious public disruption (eg *R v Secretary of State for the Home Dept, ex p Swati* [1986] 1 All ER 717; *R v Secretary of State for Social Services, ex p Association of Metropolitan Authorities* [1986] 1 WLR 1). The court might also prefer a declaration to an enforceable order where enforcement might be impracticable or hinder the governmental process (see eg *R v Panel on Takeovers and Mergers, ex p Datafin plc* [1987] QB 815; *Chief Constable of North Wales Police v Evans* [1982] 3 All ER 141; *R v Boundary Commission for England, ex p Foot* [1983] at 1116). The court will also take into account whether the claimant has made full disclosure of all relevant circumstances (*R v Lancashire CC, ex p Huddleston* [1986]).

▶ A particularly important aspect of the court's discretionary power is that judicial review is intended as a remedy of last resort. The court will not normally permit judicial review if there is another remedy which is at least equally appropriate. Thus in *R (RK (Nepal)) v Secretary of State for the Home Dept* [2009] EWCA Civ 359 it was held that where a system of appeals was provided, judicial review would be permitted only in limited and exceptional cases. Here an appeal could be made only from outside the country but judicial review was not allowed.

▶ The court's approach is flexible and pragmatic. It will take account not only of the interests of the parties but of whether the matters to be decided raise issues of general importance, in which case judicial review would be more appropriate. The rule of law and the general presumption in favour of access to the courts is of particular concern. Thus in exceptional cases other remedies do not have to be exhausted. These include serious abuses of power and denial of procedural justice. (See *R (Cart) v Upper Tribunal* [2012] 1 AC 663 [33]; *R v Chief Constable of the Merseyside Police, ex p Calverley* [1986] QB 424; *R (Sivasubramaniam) v Wandsworth BC* [2003] 1 WLR 575; *R (G) v Immigration Appeal Tribunal* [2004] 3 All ER 286.)

▶ Judicial review is a limited remedy. On the one hand it can expose government wrongdoing by providing a public forum for a grievance and requiring officials to disclose information. On the other hand it cannot guarantee a just outcome for the citizen. The court cannot usually order that a particular decision be made but can only send the matter back to be decided again. Moreover, following an adverse court ruling the executive with its control of Parliament can ensure that the law is changed. For example in *Secretary of State for Justice v Jones* [2009] UKHL 22, under the Criminal Justice Act 2003 persons serving indeterminate sentences could be considered for release by the Parole Board if they could demonstrate that they were no longer a danger to the public. Due to lack of resources the Secretary of State had failed to provide the necessary training and support facilities to enable prisoners to do this. This failure was held to be unlawful. Nevertheless the claimant had no remedy. Firstly damages are not available in respect of invalid government action as such and his detention was still lawful since he had no right to be released. Moreover the detention was not arbitrary since the Parole Board hearings were not wholly an empty exercise. Thirdly the Parole Board hearings themselves were not unfair since the Board was doing the best it could in the circumstances.

19.4 Standing (*locus standi*)

The applicant must show that he has 'sufficient interest' in the matter to which the application relates (Senior Courts Act 1981, s 31(3)). Before the 1977 reforms the law was complex and diffuse, depending primarily upon which remedy was being sought. In some cases standing was limited to a person whose legal rights were affected by the decision in question.

However in *IRC v National Federation of Self-Employed and Small Businesses Ltd* [1982] AC 617, sometimes called 'Fleet Street Casuals' or the 'Mickey Mouse Case', the House of Lords, although holding that the applications had no standing on the facts, significantly liberalised the law. The applicants were members of a pressure group representing certain business interests. They challenged a decision of the Inland Revenue not to collect arrears of tax from casual print workers who were alleged to have made false claims (in some cases under the name of Mickey Mouse) on the ground that the decision was politically motivated. The following propositions were laid down:

▶ The question of standing must be decided both at the preliminary leave stage, with a view to filtering out obvious busybodies and troublemakers, and at the full hearing where the entitlement to a particular remedy is in issue.
▶ Standing is not limited to a person whose legal rights are affected by the decision in question.
▶ A majority held that 'sufficient interest' depends on the nature of the interests relevant to the statute under which the decision was made. Here the applicants failed since under the tax legislation a taxpayer's affairs are confidential and not the concern of other taxpayers, whether individuals or groups.

Lord Diplock, with some support from the others, took a broader approach based on the importance of the matter from a public interest perspective, suggesting that the more important the matter, the more generous should be the standing requirement. In some cases affecting the whole community, any citizen should have standing. Standing should not be separate from the substance of the case. It is not clear what this means since the two matters are conceptually distinct. It probably means that the stronger the merits, the more generous the standing test. Indeed Lord Diplock would have given the applicants standing had they produced evidence in support of their allegations.

Upholding the rule of law is also important, so a low threshold might be appropriate if there is no other way of calling the decision maker to account (see Rose J in *R (Bulger) v Secretary of State for the Home Dept* [2001]).

As a result of this case standing has become substantially a matter of discretion and is generous especially in environmental cases. It may be that standing will be given to anyone with a serious issue to argue and where a useful purpose would be served (eg *R (Feakins) v Secretary of State for the Environment, Food and Rural Affairs* [2004] 1 WLR 1761; *R v North Somerset DC, ex p Dixon* [1998] Envir LR 91). (The narrower approaches taken in *R v Somerset CC, ex p Garnett* [1998] JEL 161 and *R v Secretary of State for the Environment, ex p Rose Theatre Trust* [1990] 1 QB 504 are probably now unreliable.)

The courts have given standing to pressure groups certainly when they are 'associational' (see Cane, 2003), meaning that they represent people as a group who have an interest in the matter (see *R v Inspectorate of Pollution, ex p Greenpeace (No 2)* [1994] 4 All ER 329; *R (Edwards) v Environment Agency* [2004] 3 All ER 21). By contrast what Cane calls 'surrogate' groups, representing others who themselves could have standing, are less likely to succeed (see *R v Legal Aid Board, ex p Bateman* [1992] 1 WLR 711, cf. *R (Bulger) v Secretary of State for the Home Dept* (2001)), although even here an important matter might succeed (eg *R (Quintavalle) v Human Embryology and Fertilisation Authority* [2005] 2 AC 561: pressure group representing a patient, but standing not contested). A third category according to Cane comprises groups or individuals representing the general public interest. These have standing at least where there is no other way of challenging the decision (eg *R v HM Treasury, ex p Smedley* (1985): taxpayer; *R v Secretary of State for Foreign and Commonwealth Affairs, ex p World Development Movement* (1995): campaigning organisation; *R v Secretary of State for Foreign and Commonwealth Affairs, ex p Rees-Mogg* (1994): concerned citizen (former editor of *The Times*); *R (Quintavalle) v Secretary of State for Health* [2003] 2 All ER 113: anti-abortion group). Indeed the contribution of pressure groups has been welcomed as adding a valuable dimension to judicial review (*R v Secretary of State for Trade and Industry, ex p Greenpeace* [1998] Envir LR 415).

The particular remedy is also a factor. For example in *R v Felixstowe Justices, ex p Leigh* [1987] QB 582 a newspaper editor had standing for a declaration that magistrates should not hide behind anonymity, but not *mandamus* to reveal the identity of magistrates in a particular case.

Even where the claimant lacks standing the court may consider the substantive issues, albeit without granting a remedy (eg *Bulger; Rose Theatre*). Moreover, even where a person has no standing in their own right the court has a discretion in an action brought by someone with standing to hear any person, thereby broadening the scope of the process and allowing interest groups to have a say (CPR 54.17).

19.5   Choice of procedure: public and private law

The judicial review procedure applies only to 'public functions' (CPR 54.1). This implies that not all activities of government bodies are necessarily public functions and opens the possibility that some functions carried on by bodies outside government might nevertheless be public functions. Indeed contemporary political fashion favours using private bodies to deliver public services. It seems anomalous that a body carrying out functions on behalf of government should not be subject to judicial review (see the dissenting speeches of Lord Bingham and Lady Hale in *YL v Birmingham City Council* [2007] 3 All ER 957). There is no clear definition of 'public', and what is public in one context may not be so in another section. Indeed it is often suggested that judicial review should be about controlling any concentration of power rather than government as such. The debate about the legal basis of judicial review reflects this (Section 17.1.1).

The remedies provided by the Human Rights Act 1998 are also triggered by a 'public function' (Section 21.5). The meaning of public function in the two contexts is not necessarily the same. On the other hand cases in either context can be used as guidance and the same outcome has invariably been chosen (eg *Weaver v London and Quadrant Housing Trust* [2009] EWCA civ 507; *YL v Birmingham City Council (2007); Hampshire CC v Beer* [2003] EWCA Civ 1056).

The courts have refused to apply a single test but have indicated a number of factors which make a function 'public'. For judicial review purposes the focus is on the particular function that is being challenged so that a body which has a mixture of public and private functions such as a housing association is reviewable only in its public capacity. For example the eviction of a tenant housed as part of its public function can be challenged but not the eviction of a tenant it houses privately (*Weaver* (above).

It is relevant but not enough that the function in question is exercised in the public interest or that the body is important or that the decision has serious consequences for those affected by it. The main factors are as follows:

▶ Firstly where a power exercisable for public purposes is conferred directly by statute or royal prerogative it will normally be regarded as a public function (*R v Panel on*

Takeovers and Mergers, ex p Datafin plc (1987); *Scott v National Trust* [1998] 2 All ER 715: despite some statutory protection Trust's *functions* not statutory). However a body, such as an insurance company, which exercises the same commercial functions as a private body but happens to have been created by statute does not exercise public functions (*R (West) v Lloyds of London* [2004] 3 All ER 251).

▶ Secondly a function which is intermeshed with or 'underpinned' by government may be public in the sense that government bodies have control over its exercise or participate in its activities. In *R v Panel on Takeovers and Mergers, ex p Datafin plc* [1987], which is the seminal case, it was held that the Takeover Panel, a self-regulating voluntary body which acted as a City 'watchdog', was exercising public law functions. This was because it was set up in the public interest, it reported to the government and although it did not have statutory powers itself was supported by the statutory powers of the Department of Trade.

▶ How much government involvement is required is a matter of degree in the particular circumstances, making this approach highly uncertain. Relevant factors are the degree of involvement of government through finance, control or regulation and the extent to which the body in question has special powers.

See, for example *YL v Birmingham City Council* (2007): funding of a care home resident by local authority not enough without government control over the running of the home itself (Section 22.4);

Poplar Housing and Regeneration Community Association Ltd v Donoghue [2001] 4 All ER 604: housing association formed by local authority was public;

Weaver v London and Quadrant Housing Trust (2009): housing association which received government funding in return for delivering government housing policy and was intensively regulated by the government was exercising public functions in respect of decisions to evict tenants since these could not be separated from its public function of allocating social housing according to government policy. It was also relevant that the association had certain special powers and was under a statutory duty to cooperate with local authorities. However some of its functions, such as contractual arrangements with repair firms, could be private. The position of tenants who receive unsubsidised housing and pay a market rent is unclear. The dissent took a radically different approach, regarding a function as private if it used private law powers such as a landlord's power to evict a tenant. Housing associations have no special powers of eviction.

Hampshire CC v Beer (2003): farmers' market run by a farmers' cooperative is exercising public functions. Firstly it had control over a public space in the street; secondly it had previously been run by the local authority, which had now handed it over to the cooperative. This decision is questionable in the light of *Weaver*.

▶ It has been held, sometimes reluctantly, that a power which is based exclusively on contract, for example the disciplinary power exercised by sports or professional associations, is a private law power (see *R v Disciplinary Committee of the Jockey Club, ex p the Aga Khan* [1993] 2 All ER 853; *R v Football Association, ex p Football League* [1993] 2 All ER 833; *R (Heather) v Leonard Cheshire Foundation* [2002] 2 All

ER 936: retirement home owned by a charity). This seems artificial since many such bodies exercise their powers for the purpose of protecting the public in much the same way as a government agency. The reality is that the individual has no choice but to submit to the jurisdiction since the alternative is to be excluded from an area of public life. However even in the context of government proper it has been held that judicial review does not apply to a purely contractual relationship (compare *R v East Berkshire HA, ex p Walsh* [1985] QB 152: nurse employed under contract, with *R v Secretary of State for the Home Dept, ex p Benwell* [1985] QB 554: prison officer employed directly under statute). However where there is an additional element of statute or governmental policy or if the decision affects persons beyond the contractual relationship the court may treat the matter as one of public law (*McLaren v Home Office* [1990] IRLR 338; see also Hoffmann LJ in *Aga Khan favouring government control approach*).

▶ Another possible test is whether if the body in question did not exist the government would have to intervene (see *R v Chief Rabbi, ex p Wachmann* [1993] 2 All ER 249). However this is not reliable or conclusive since there is no agreement on what functions are necessary in this sense. Indeed it could apply to anything of importance. For example if all food shops closed, no doubt the government would intervene.

19.6   Exclusivity

Although originally important and controversial, this issue has now faded into the background and will be considered only briefly. Assuming that a decision concerns a public function, must the judicial review procedure always be used or can judicial review grounds be raised in another court, such as a local county court, for example in respect of the eviction of council tenants?

The Senior Courts Act does not say that challenges in other courts are forbidden and the remedies of declaration, injunction and damages are available in any court. When it was introduced in the late 1970s the courts were concerned that the new procedure should not be avoided because it is geared to the special concerns of challenging government action. The procedure was unfamiliar to lawyers, some of whom may have been reluctant or too slow to use it. The judicial review procedure is in some ways more restrictive than an ordinary action, particularly in respect of the need for permission to apply and its three-month time limit. Several cases reached the House of Lords solely on this matter, so the new procedure looked as unfriendly as the old methods.

The seminal case was *O'Reilly v Mackman* [1982] 3 All ER 1124, where prisoners sought to challenge a decision not to give them remission for good behaviour. They were outside time for judicial review and attempted to bring an ordinary civil action. Lord Diplock emphasised that a prisoner has no legal right to remission, which was an 'indulgence' from the government, but at most has a legitimate expectation that his or her case would be considered fairly. This was a matter solely of 'public law'. The House of Lords struck out their claim as an abuse of the court's process. Lord Diplock said that the judicial review procedure should normally be used in public law cases because of its safeguards which protected the government against 'groundless, unmeritorious or tardy harassment'.

Lord Diplock seemed to be staking out a position in which 'public law' was to be regarded as of special constitutional status contrary to the notion of the rule of law eulogised by Dicey (Section 6.4). Indeed *O'Reilly* ran counter to the recommendations of the Law Commission ((1976) *Law Com No 73*) and was widely criticized as over rigid (see Wade (1985) 101 LQR 182). Indeed to restrict access to the courts could be regarded as violating the rule of law. The suspicion was raised that judicial review was being limited in order to discourage challenges to government and to save money. In *Cocks v Thanet DC* [1983] 2 AC 286 decided soon after *O'Reilly* the House of Lords applied *O'Reilly* harshly to hold that a claimant who had been refused housing under homelessness legislation must use judicial review rather than a more convenient action in a local county court. This was because the claimant had no right to a home, the decision being one of discretion. (The county court now has what amounts to a judicial review function in homelessness cases (Housing Act 1996; see *Runa Begum v Tower Hamlets LBC* [2003] 1 All ER 731 at [7])).

However the cases soon drew back and there is little left of the *O'Reilly* rule today. Indeed in *O'Reilly itself* Lord Diplock suggested that there should be exceptions to the exclusivity principle but did not fully identify them. He did indicate that the judicial review procedure would not be exclusive in cases of 'collateral' challenge, where the validity of government action arises incidentally in litigation.

In *Davy v Spelthorne BC* [1984] (276). Lord Wilberforce expressed his distaste for the *O'Reilly* rule which he regarded as alien to English legal tradition (Section 5.1): 'The expressions "private law" and "public law" have recently been imported into the law of England from countries which unlike our own have separate systems concerning public law and private law. No doubt they are convenient expressions for descriptive purposes. In this country they must be used with caution for, typically, English law fastens, not upon principles but upon remedies'

The courts soon began to exploit Lord Diplock's exceptions. Thus a citizen can raise a defence in any relevant proceedings against an unlawful government claim (*Wandsworth LBC v Winder* [1985] AC 426: rent arrears; *Boddington v British Transport Police* (1998): prosecution for smoking). An ordinary civil action might also be more appropriate if the issues are mainly factual or where the public law aspects are peripheral (*Mercury Communications v Director General of Telecommunications* [1996]! All ER 575; *D v Home Office* [2006] 1 All ER 183, *Sher v Chief Constable of Greater Manchester Police* [2011] 2 All ER 364).

Roy v Kensington, Chelsea and Westminster Family Practitioner Committee [1992] 1 AC 624 further weakened *O'Reilly*. A doctor was seeking a discretionary 'practice allowance' from the NHS. He had established entitlement to some kind of allowance but not how much. The House of Lords suggested that whenever a litigant was protecting a 'private law right' he need not use the judicial review procedure. Alternatively it was held that the circumstances were so closely analogous to a private claim that as matter of discretion the action should go ahead.

Thus it is only where the citizen has no legal rights but is making a claim based entirely on the exercise of government discretion, as was the case in *O'Reilly* itself and *Cocks* (above) that the strict exclusivity principle applies. (See also *Trustees of the Dennis Rye Pension Fund v Sheffield City Council* [1997] 4 All ER 747; *British Steel v Customs and Excise Comrs* [1997] 2 All ER 366; *Cullen v Chief Constable of the RUC* [2004] 2 All ER 247, illustrating how this may turn on complex questions of statutory interpretation as to whether the citizen has a 'right' (analogous perhaps to the issue of civil rights and obligations under the ECHR (Section 21.4)).)

Thus the exclusivity rule hits vulnerable groups hardest. In *Kay v Lambeth LBC* [2006] 2 AC 465, concerning the eviction by a local authority of a former tenant, the House of Lords held that where the matter does not involve private rights, such as welfare benefit, prison and immigration cases, no other forum is available (at [30]–[31]).

However the exclusivity issue seems to have become less important. The Woolf reforms (Section 19.3) give all courts wider powers to control proceedings and require the parties to cooperate with the court in expediting proceedings. Although permission to apply is not required in an ordinary civil action, Part 24 of the CPR empowers the court to strike out a civil action at an early stage if the defendant can show that it has no reasonable chance of success. (In judicial review proceedings, however, the onus is on the *claimant* to establish a reasonable chance of success.) Moreover cases can be transferred at any time between the Administrative Court and another court. Furthermore the spread of the Administrative Court to regional centres and the judicial review jurisdiction of the Upper Tribunal suggest that public law is capable of being diffused among different courts.

The courts have emphasised that unless the procedure chosen is clearly inappropriate they will not disturb it. For example in *Clark v University of Lincolnshire and Humberside* [2000] 3 All ER 752 a student brought an action in the County Court against a decision by the University to fail her. The Court of Appeal held that she was entitled to bring a civil action. Even if judicial review was appropriate, the court would not strike out a claim in another court unless the court's processes were misused or the chosen procedure was unsuitable.

19.7　The exclusion and limitation of judicial review

19.7.1　Justiciability and 'deference'

Some matters are non-justiciable, meaning that they raise issues that the courts prefer not to engage with. It is difficult to pinpoint exactly what makes a matter non-justiciable and there is no recognised formula. It must be emphasised that the fact that an issue is politically controversial or important is itself not sufficient reason to exclude judicial review. Furthermore there may be a distinction between a matter which is wholly non-justiciable in the strict sense of being outside the court's jurisdiction and matters where the court shows 'deference' in the sense that it is unwilling to intervene except in very strong cases.

It is arguable, however, that every case is one of discretion in the particular circumstances and that there are no areas that the courts can never investigate. From this perspective the question of justiciability is an extreme example of the general principle that the level and intensity of judicial review varies with the particular context (Section 18.1) (*Huang v Secretary of State* [2007] 4 All ER 15[14]). Indeed it could be argued that the issue of justiciability is no more than the court performing its normal task of identifying the limits of a discretionary power in contexts where that power is unusually wide.

▶ Matters held to be wholly outside the court's judicial review jurisdiction are relatively few. They include the following:
▶ decisions of the High Court;
▶ the internal affairs of Parliament (Section 11.6);
▶ certain acts of state and matters of international law, including the making, and ratification of treaties (Section 9.6);

- probably political decisions at the highest level of government, such as the dissolution of Parliament and the appointment of ministers. Matters of 'high policy' are often said to be non-justiciable (see *R (Gentle) v Prime Minister* [2008]);
- the Attorney General's power to commence legal actions (*Gouriet v Union of Post Office Workers* (1978) (Section 15.6);
- perhaps the deployment of the armed forces. In *R v Jones (Margaret)* (2006) Lord Hoffmann treated it as a 'constitutional principle' that the Crown's discretion to go to war was not justiciable [65]. Lord Bingham regarded the matter as one of self-restraint. He took the view that the courts would be slow to interfere with the conduct of foreign policy or the deployment of the armed forces but did not rule it out (at [30]). In *R (Gentle) v Prime Minister [2008]* the House of Lords refused to investigate whether the decision to invade Iraq was lawful in international law (Section 9.7.1) but did not rule out intervention altogether. However in *R (Smith) v Secretary of State for Defence* [2010] 3 All ER 1067 Baroness Hale said that the deployment of the armed forces was essentially non-justiciable.

Most of the above powers are matters of royal prerogative. Before *CCSU v Minister for the Civil Service* [1985]: ban on industrial action at government surveillance centre, it was widely believed that royal prerogative powers were wholly non-justiciable. The House of Lords rejected that approach, holding that it was the content rather than the source of the power that mattered (Section 14.6.4). Because the particular matter was one of national security, the court would not interfere since the government must be the judge of what national security requires. However the court did not regard the matter as wholly non-justiciable. It was held that the government must provide supporting evidence that the matter was genuinely one of national security, which in that particular case was easy to do.

In *CCSU* Lord Roskill listed subjects he regarded as wholly non-justiciable because their nature or subject matter was not amenable to the judicial process. These included the making of treaties, defence, the prerogative of mercy, the grant of honours, the dissolution of Parliament and the appointment of ministers. Lord Roskill's list has not stood the test of time. The prerogative of mercy has been held to be reviewable (*R v Secretary of State for the Home Dept, ex p Bentley* [1993] 4 All ER 422; *A-G of Trinidad and Tobago v Lennox Phillips* [1995] 1 All ER 93). The power to make Orders in Council governing a dependent territory is reviewable (*R (Bancoult) v Secretary of State (No 2)* [2008] (Section 9.6). The power to issue a passport was held to be reviewable because it is an administrative decision affecting the right of individuals as opposed to a matter of 'high policy' (*R v Secretary of State for Foreign and Commonwealth Affairs, ex p Everett* [1989] 1 All ER 655).

The dissolution of Parliament (even though it is now statutory (Section 11.2)) and the appointment and dismissal of ministers are pre-eminently non-justiciable. They are functions of the highest level of government and are central to the democratic process. In view of their political content the legal process is clearly unsuitable for their resolution and the separation of powers requires the courts to refrain.

As *Gentle* suggests, the courts seem reluctant to treat a government power as wholly non-justiciable on a blanket basis. They prefer to look more flexibly at specific issues or particular grounds of review. In these cases the court can either refuse to go into a specific matter, intervene only in a very clear or important case or apply some grounds of review but not others. Thus the principle is that of self-restraint, or 'deference'.

The issue of deference arises especially in relation to *Wednesbury* unreasonableness (Section 18.1) and in human rights cases, where it is sometimes called 'margin of discretion' (Section 22.5.2). In *R (ProLife Alliance) v BBC* (2003) Lord Hoffmann criticised the term 'deference'. He pointed out that the matter concerns the separation of powers, namely the distinction between the role of the courts and those of the other branches of government. According to Lord Hoffmann, the courts are deferring to no one but are upholding their constitutional function (see also Lord Bingham in *A v Secretary of State for the Home Dept* (2005): 'institutional competence'). Thus it is arguable that deference, like justiciability, is not a separate doctrine but an example of the court's normal judicial review function, namely to determine the extent of the power that is under review and the weight to be attached to the justification given by the decision maker.

What general principles identify non-justiciable issues or matters calling for deference? Jowell (2009) distinguishes between two types of deference, these being firstly constitutional principles relating to the separation of powers and respect for democracy and secondly pragmatic matters based on the practical limitations of the judicial process, bearing in mind that UK judges, unlike judges in some other countries, have limited experience of political or administrative matters. Endecott (2009, 7.3) expands these into four: expertise, political responsibility, effective processes and respect for the allocated decision-making body (although the latter applies to all aspects of judicial review). In *R v Ministry of Defence, ex p Smith* [1996] Lord Bingham said that 'the greater the policy content of a decision and the more remote the subject is from ordinary judicial experience the more hesitant the court must necessarily be in holding a decision to be irrational' (at 556). Thus the court is most at home with disputes with clearly defined parties and within a framework of rules, least at home with 'polycentric' matters affecting indeterminate persons and lacking agreed guidelines.

Falling under all four of Endecott's heads, matters affecting the public at large and involving a wide and nebulous range of economic, social and political factors have traditionally been regarded as unsuited to judicial resolution since judges are most at home with defined issues and parties (see, eg *Independent Schools Council v Charity Commission for England and Wales* [2012] at [109]: 'public benefit'; Lord Hoffmann in *R (Alconbury) v Secretary of State* [2001] at [76]). Decisions which are directly made or to a lesser extent approved by a democratic assembly particularly rate deference (Section 18.1), *R v Lichniak* [2003] 1 AC 903 [14], *AXA General Insurance Ltd v HM Advocate* [2012] Section 16.2.1). For example in (*R (Farrakhan) v Secretary of State* [2002] a decision not to allow a person into the UK on public interest grounds made by the Secretary of State was deferred to on the basis that he has greater expertise and information than is available to the court and is democratically accountable for the decision. Other examples are national security (Section 24.1), the allocation of social housing: *Poplar Housing and Regeneration Community Association Ltd v Donoghue* [2001], policy towards widows: *R (Hooper) v Secretary of State for Work and Pensions* [2006] 1 All ER 487 [32] and foreign affairs, which raises issues of respect for sovereign governments beyond the reach of the courts (*R (Bancoult) v Secretary of State (No 2)* [2008] (Section 9.6.5).

The separation of powers provides a particular reason for deference. For example the courts are reluctant to interfere with the decisions of independent prosecutors but will do so exceptionally where the grounds for doing so are strong and clear (*R (Corner House Research) v Director of the Serious Fraud Office (No 2)* [2008] at [30]–[32], [58]).

Under Jowell's second head and Endecott's first are specialist decisions. These include professional judgements, aesthetic judgements such as architectural merit, moral evaluations, academic standards where judges lack training, resources and experience to choose between the competing arguments (eg high-level expert tribunals: *Page v Hull University Visitor* [1993]: no review for error of law; *R (Cart) v Upper Tribunal* [2012], *(R (Sinclair Gardens Investments) v Lands Tribunal* [2005] EWCA civ 1305: review only for difficult issues of general significance; *Cooke v Secretary of State for Social Services*[2002] 3 All ER 279 [15]–[19], *Preston v SBAT* [1975] 1 WLR 624): review only for clear error of law of general application, *(R (ProLife Alliance) v BBC* (2003): controversial matters of morality, taste and decency (Section 22.3)).

Discretionary decisions involving the allocation of scarce resources require deference under both of Jowell's heads (see *R v Cambridge HA, ex p B* [1995] and *R (Condliffe) v North Staffs Primary Health Care Trust* [2012]: medical treatment, *R (Douglas) v North Tyneside MBC* [2004] 1 All ER 709 [62]: student loan, *R (Bloggs61) v Secretary of State for the Home Dept* [2003]: protection of prisoners against attack, *R (S) v Secretary of State for the Home Dept* [2013] 1 All ER 66: taxation of prisoners' wages).

Both Jowell and Endecott take account of the limitations of the court's adversarial procedures in terms of the parties before the courts, procedural problems and the availability of information to the court (eg *R (G) v Immigration Appeal Tribunal* [2004]: delay). For example in *Copsey v WBB Devon Clays Ltd* [2005] EWCA Civ 932 [39], it was said that the court should not decide general matters such as whether an employer can keep a workforce secular since it lacks the necessary consultative procedures.

There are of course limits to deference. Hunt (2003) refers to 'due deference' meaning that the decision maker should justify the court holding back. In *Farrakhan* (above), for example it was important that the minister had carefully considered the matter see also *R (S) v Secretary of State for the Home Dept* (2013). As a minimum the courts can ensure that government processes are fair and reliable, that the decision maker is acting within its powers, that decisions have a rational basis and that fundamental rights are respected. The more serious the impact on individual rights, the less deference will be shown. At a very general level it may be the uncertainty of the absence of rules or objective standards, that most deters the courts from interfering.

19.7.2 Statutory exclusion of judicial review

Sometimes a statute attempts to exclude judicial review, thereby confronting a fundamental tenet of the rule of law that the exercise of power should be controlled by independent courts. The courts are reluctant to accept this and construe such statutes narrowly. Clear words are required to exclude judicial review, and there are even dicta, albeit unreliable, that Parliament cannot do this at all (see *R (Cart) v Upper Tribunal [2012]* at [38]). For example a provision stating that a decision shall be 'final' does not exclude review but merely prevents the decision maker from reopening the matter and excludes any right of appeal that might otherwise apply (*R v Medical Appeal Tribunal, ex p Gilmore* [1957] 1 QB 574). Even a provision stating that a 'determination of the tribunal shall not be questioned in any court of law' is ineffective to prevent review where the tribunal exceeds its 'jurisdiction' (powers). This is because the tribunal's act is a nullity and so not a 'determination'. Given that a government body exceeds its jurisdiction whenever it makes an error of law (Section 17.5) this neatly sidesteps the 'ouster clause' (*Anisminic v Foreign Compensation Commission* [1969]).

However given Parliament's ultimate supremacy, a sufficiently tightly drafted 'ouster clause' could surmount *Anisminic*. The court will take the policy of the Act into account. Here are some examples:

▶ A clause often found in statutes relating to land use planning and compulsory purchase allows challenge within six weeks and then provides that the decision 'shall not be questioned in any court of law'. The courts have interpreted this provision literally, on the ground that review is not completely excluded and that the policy of the statute is to enable development of land to be started quickly (see *R v Cornwall CC, ex p Huntingdon* [1994] 1 All ER 694).

▶ A provision stating that a particular act such as entry on a register or a certificate shall be 'conclusive evidence' of compliance with the Act and of the matters stated in the certificate may also be effective since it does not exclude review as such but makes it impossible to prove invalidity. However this may leave open the possibility of review for unfairness or unreasonableness (see *R v Registrar of Companies, ex p Central Bank of India* [1985] 2 All ER 79).

▶ In certain cases, mainly involving security, special tribunals are given judicial review powers (Sections 24.4, 24.5). Clear statutory language is required to prevent their decisions themselves being reviewable in the Administrative Court (*R (Cart) v Upper Tribunal* [2012]). For example under the Anti-Terrorism, Crime and Security Act 2001 an asylum seeker can appeal to the Immigration Appeal Tribunal against a decision of an adjudicator but only with the permission of the Tribunal (s 101). A decision to refuse permission can be challenged by a 'paper review' by a High Court judge, which is significantly more limited than normal judicial review. It was held in *R (G) v Immigration Appeal Tribunal* [2004] that in the absence of express words in a statute, judicial review could not completely be excluded. However given the intention of Parliament to deal with the serious problem of delays arising from the processing of asylum cases, the court would permit judicial review only in exceptional cases.

▶ Under the same Act there is a right of appeal to the Special Immigration Appeals Commissioners (SIAC), who include a High Court judge, against a decision of the Home Secretary to certify that a person is an 'international terrorist'. The proceedings of the commissioners are in private and evidence is sometimes not revealed to the complainant. The Act provides that any action taken by the Home Secretary may be questioned in legal proceedings only by this method (s 30). It was held in *Cart* (above) in the Court of Appeal that SIAC, not being the equivalent of the High Court, was subject to judicial review.

▶ Sometimes Parliament creates a new right and at the same time designates exclusive machinery for deciding disputes about it. This is not strictly a case of excluding judicial review since the right and the machinery are inseparable. However the court will scrutinise the machinery to establish whether it is as good as judicial review and, if this is not the case, judicial review will be available (see *A v B* [2010] 1 All ER 1167 at [21]): Investigatory Powers Tribunal for complaints against intelligence services under Human Rights Act 1998; Section 24.5).

▶ Statutes dealing with surveillance and the security services feature a clause stating that a decision cannot be challenged even on jurisdictional grounds (see Security Services Act 1989, s 5(4); Regulation of Investigatory Powers Act 2000, s 67(8)). These may exclude judicial review completely, although they do provide a right to complain to special commissioners.

Where judicial review is excluded by statute Article 6 of the ECHR may be invoked on the ground that the ouster clause prevents a fair trial in relation to a person's 'civil rights and obligations'. The fairness of the proceedings as a whole must be considered, including the judicial review stage. On the whole the courts have protected the right to a fair trial against attempts to restrict access to the courts (Section 24.4).

Summary

▶ There is a special procedure for challenging decisions of public bodies in the Administrative Court. It is highly discretionary. The procedure provides the citizen with a range of remedies to quash an invalid decision, prevent unlawful action and require a duty to be complied with. Damages may sometimes be available but under restricted circumstances. It provides machinery for protecting government against improper or trivial challenges. Leave to apply is required and judicial review will be refused where there is an equally convenient alternative remedy.

▶ Standing is flexible and increasingly liberal, although a third party may not be given standing where others are in a better position to challenge the decision.

▶ Judicial review applies only to public law functions, which usually include powers exercised by a wide range of bodies connected to the government or exercising statutory powers but does not usually exclude powers derived exclusively from contract or consent. In some cases the citizen may challenge public law powers outside the judicial review procedure on the basis of the rule of law principle that, where private rights are at stake, unlawful government action can be ignored.

▶ The remedies and procedure for judicial review are discretionary, so that even though an unlawful government decision is strictly speaking a nullity, the court may refuse to intervene. Delay, misbehaviour, the impact on third parties and the absence of injustice may be reasons for not interfering. Public inconvenience or administrative disruption are probably not enough in themselves but they might be relevant to the court's discretion when coupled with another factor such as delay.

▶ Some kinds of government power are inherently non-justiciable but more commonly the courts are deferential to certain issues for reasons relating to the separation of powers or the limitations of judicial procedures or expertise. In these cases judicial review may be limited to clear abuses of power.

▶ Sometimes statutes attempt to exclude judicial review. The courts are reluctant to see their powers taken away and interpret such provisions strictly. The Human Rights Act 1998 reinforces this.

Exercises

19.1 What are the advantages and disadvantages of the judicial review procedure from the point of view of the citizen? When may government action be challenged in the courts by means of an ordinary action?

19.2 'The expressions "private law" and "public law" have recently been imported into the law of England from countries which unlike our own have separate systems concerning public law and private law. No doubt they are convenient expressions for descriptive purposes. In this country they must be used with caution for, typically, English law fastens, not upon principles but upon remedies' (Lord Wilberforce). Discuss in the light of *O'Reilly v Mackman* [1982] and subsequent cases.

19.3 Claire, a civil servant working in the Cabinet Office, has evidence that the Prime Minister has been selling peerages to rich businesswomen in return for promises to make donations to charities specified by the Prime Minister's wife. Claire informs the head of her department, who replies that 'it's not possible, my dear'. Claire now seeks judicial review. Advise her.

19.4 James, as the father of a soldier, wants to challenge the Prime Minister's decision to reduce the number of troops fighting in Afghanistan, on the ground that the troops there are not sufficiently supported and lack resources. Advise him.

19.5 Forever Open Housing Association provides sheltered accommodation for vulnerable people. It is a charity owned by a religious sect and is part-funded and regulated by the Housing Corporation, a government agency. Mary lives in a residential home owned by Forever Open, her accommodation being paid for by the local authority under its statutory obligation to arrange for care provision for the elderly. When Mary took up residence Forever Open told her that she now had 'a home for life'. Forever Open now proposes to close the home. Advise Mary whether she can challenge this proposal in the Administrative Court.

19.6 Consider the facts of Question 17.2. Would the position be different if the Centre was operated by Quickbuck Plc, under a leasing arrangement from the council?

19.7 By statute (fictitious) the NHS is required to provide 'an effective healthcare service for all residents of England and Wales'. The statute also provides that 'the actions of any NHS hospital in relation to the provision of any service to the public shall not be questioned in any court on any ground whatsoever'. St Dave's Hospital in the English town of Holby is short of money and trained staff because of government financial cuts. The Secretary of State has issued a circular to all hospitals stating, among other things, that no further patients are to be admitted for sex-change operations and that hip replacement operations should normally be performed only on patients who play an active part in the economic life of the community.

  (i) The Holby Transsexual Rights Society, a local pressure group, objects to the circular. It discovers the contents six months after it came into effect. Advise the Society as to its chances of success in the courts.

  (ii) Frank, who is an unemployed resident in a hostel for the homeless, is refused a hip replacement operation. He wishes to bring an action in his local county court. Advise St Tony's Hospital.

  (iii) The Welsh Nationalist Party want to challenge the circular. Advise the Party.

Further reading

Allan, 'Deference, Defiance and Doctrine: Defining the Limits of Judicial Review' (2010) 60 U Toronto LR 41

Allan, 'Judicial Deference and Judicial Review: Legal Doctrine and Legal Theory' (2011) 127 LQR 91

Cane, 'Accountability and the Public/Private Distinction', in Bamforth and Leyland (eds), *Public Law in a Multi-Layered Constitution* (Hart 2003)

Endicott, *Administrative Law* (Oxford University Press 2009) chs 7.3, 10, 15.5, 15.6

Fordham, 'Judicial Review: The New Rules' [2001] PL 4

Fuller, 'The Forms and Limits of Adjudication' (1978) 92 Harvard LR 353

Halliday, *Judicial Review and Compliance with Administrative Law* (Oxford University Press 2004)

Harris, 'Judicial Review, Justiciability and the Prerogative of Mercy' (2003) 62 CLJ 631

Further reading cont'd

Hunt, 'Sovereignty's Blight: Why Contemporary Public Law Needs the Concept of "Due Deference"' in Bamforth and Leyland (eds), *Public Law in a Multi-Layered Constitution* (Hart 2003)

Jowell, 'Judicial Deference: Servility, Civility or Institutional Incapacity?' [2003] PL 592

Jowell, 'What Decisions Should Judges Not Take?' in Andenas and Fairgrieve (eds), *Tom Bingham and the Transformation of the Law* (Oxford University Press 2009)

Judicial Working Group, 'Justice outside London Report: the Administrative Court', Department of Justice 2007.

King, 'Institutional Approaches to Judicial Restraint' (2008) 28 OJLS 409

Miles, 'Standing in a Multi-Layered Constitution' in Bamforth and Leyland (eds), *Public Law in a Multi-Layered Constitution* (Hart 2003)

Rivers, 'Proportionality and the Variable Standard of Review' (2006) 65 CLJ 172

Taggart (ed), *The Province of Administrative Law* (Hart 1997) chs 1, 2, 10

Chapter 20
Administrative justice

The term administrative justice refers to a miscellaneous range of specialised bodies which make decisions affecting individuals or which resolve disputes between the individual and the government. They range from tribunals which have become essentially part of the judicial system to the regulators of many business and professional activities who combine executive, legislative and judicial power.

The constitutional issues which they raise concern the separation of powers and the rule of law the former because there are sometimes close links with the executive, the latter because they sometimes create specialised self-contained laws with their own penalties and sanctions. There are also problems of accountability since regulators are outside the central structure of ministers and Parliament. However the ordinary courts provide supervision through their powers of judicial review thus imposing the rule of law.

20.1 Tribunals

Numerous tribunals decide matters allocated to them by particular statutes. They are essentially simplified versions of courts of law and are created to provide a simpler, cheaper and more expert way of deciding relatively small or specialised disputes than the ordinary courts. These are most commonly disputes between individuals and government bodies. Tribunals deal with a range of specialised and technical matters. These include education, employment, taxation, health, land valuation, title and use, state benefits, transport, trading matters and the security services. In some cases, such as employment tribunals, they decide disputes between private persons. Immigration decisions have increasingly been entrusted to tribunals thus taking important matters of individual liberty outside the ordinary courts. They were originally called administrative tribunals, thus blurring the distinction between the judicial and executive branches and raising fears that they were not independent (see *Report of the Committee on Administrative Tribunals and Enquiries* (Cmnd 218, 1957), the Franks Report). Subsequent reforms, the most recent being the Tribunals, Courts and Enforcement Act 2007 have drawn the tribunal system more closely towards that of the ordinary courts.

Tribunals are usually claimed to have advantages of economy, speed and expertise compared with the ordinary courts – the price to be paid for this being rougher justice (Franks Report). Tribunal procedures are less formal than those of ordinary courts and do not necessarily involve lawyers. They are meant to be accessible to poorer people, with whom a substantial part of their work is concerned. However they may deal with complex legal matters, and those before them are often without legal representation, so their accessibility is questionable (see Genn, 'Tribunals and Informal Justice' (1993) 56 MLR 393). Until the recent reforms (discussed below) the tribunal system had developed haphazardly, numerous tribunals having been established over the years under separate legislation. (There is a good general outline of the development of tribunals in Lady Hale's judgement in *R (Cart) v Upper Tribunal* [2012].)

Tribunals are often presided over by a lawyer chairperson sitting with one or two lay members. They are not bound by strict rules of evidence. Most tribunals must give reasons in writing for their decisions. Although legal representation is permitted, legal aid is not available except in the case of mental health tribunals, the Employment Appeal tribunal, the Lands Tribunal and Revenue Commissioners. In accordance with the rule of law tribunals are linked into the general law by virtue of the senior courts' powers of judicial review and in many cases by rights of appeal to ordinary courts.

There is no conceptual distinction between a tribunal and a court proper. It might be important to decide whether a body is a court for the purposes of the law of contempt of court, which affects freedom of the press (Section 23.3). In this context it is irrelevant whether the body is called a court or a tribunal (see *A-G v BBC* [1981] AC 303; *General Medical Council v BBC* [1998] 1 WLR 1573). It is necessary to rely on any definition of a court in a particular statute for a particular purpose, thus illustrating the pragmatic character of the UK constitution. Confusingly some bodies have the status of a court (or 'court of record', meaning a relatively high-status court) conferred by statute but are called tribunals, for example the Employment Appeals Tribunal (Employment Tribunals Act 1996). Broadly speaking a body is likely to be regarded as a court if it exercises 'judicial' functions in the sense of being required to decide questions relating to individual rights independently.

The tribunal system has recently been overhauled. As a result of the Leggatt Report (*Tribunals for Users* (TSO 2001)), a Tribunals Service under the Ministry of Justice has been established to administer and coordinate the main tribunals and the uncoordinated plethora of tribunals has been systemised (see White Paper, *Transforming the Public Services: Complaints, Redress and Tribunals* (Cm 6243, 2004); Carnwath, 2009). The basic concerns are to rationalise the tribunal system and to strengthen the independence of tribunals from ministers and other bodies whose decisions they scrutinise and to make the tribunal system simpler and more open and user friendly.

The Tribunals Courts and Enforcement Act 2007 gives effect to the main Leggatt reforms. In *R (Cart) v Upper Tribunal* [2011] QB 120 Sedley LJ described the reforms as a landmark in the development of the UK's 'organic constitution' (at [1]). Apart from rationalising the tribunal system, the thrust of the reforms is to associate the system more closely with the judicial branch of government.

The Act creates two umbrella tribunals, which are grouped into specialist 'chambers'. These are the First Tier Tribunal and the Upper Tribunal. The Upper Tribunal is primarily an appeal body from decisions of the Lower Tribunal. The Lord Chancellor is empowered to transfer the jurisdiction of most of the existing tribunals to the new tribunals, thus rationalising and simplifying the tribunal system, The First Tier Chambers comprise, Social Entitlement, Health Education and Social Care, General Regulatory, Taxation, Immigration and Asylum, Land, Property and Housing. Employment tribunals are currently separate from the new system. The Upper Tribunal Chambers comprise the Administrative Appeals Chamber, the Tax and Chancery Chamber, the Immigration and Asylum Chamber and the Land Chamber which has first instance jurisdiction with an appeal to the Court of Appeal.

The Upper Tribunal has the status of a superior court (s 3). There is a right of appeal from First Tier decisions to the Upper Tribunal. This is only on a point of law, as opposed to fact, and permission is required from either tribunal (s 11). The right of appeal does not apply to 'excluded decisions' designated as such by the Lord Chancellor (see SI/2009/275). There is a further right of appeal, again only on a matter of law, to the Court of Appeal (Court of Session in Scotland) against a decision of the Upper Tribunal. This is also subject to a requirement for permission from either tribunal. Importantly permission has been restricted by rules made by the Lord Chancellor to an important point of principle or practice, or some other compelling reason (SI 2008/ 2834). Moreover the right of appeal does not apply to 'excluded' decisions. In this context an excluded decision includes a decision by the Upper Tribunal concerning permission to appeal to itself. In addition both levels of tribunal can review their own decisions (ss 9, 10).

The Upper Tribunal can also exercise judicial review functions in designated cases similar to those of the High Court (s 15, Section 19.1).

The members of the First Tier Tribunal are appointed by the Lord Chancellor and also include ex officio members of certain other tribunals and courts (s 4). The Upper Tribunal also comprises persons appointed by the Lord Chancellor and includes ex officio other senior office holders (s 5). In many cases the Lord Chancellor can appoint only a person selected by the Judicial Appointments Commission (see Constitutional Reform Act 2005, s 85, Sch 14). Judges of ordinary courts are ex officio members of both tiers (s 6). Lawyer members of these tribunals are known as 'Tribunal Judges'.

The Lord Chancellor's duty to uphold the rule of law under the Constitutional Reform Act 2005 applies also to tribunals under his jurisdiction. The Act (s 1) also extends to tribunals the general duty to protect the independence of the judiciary imposed on the Lord Chancellor and other ministers by virtue of Section 3 of the Constitutional Reform Act 2005, thus identifying the tribunal system with the judicial arm of government (Section 7.4).

The relationship between the tribunal system and the ordinary courts raises the constitutional issue of the tension between specialised areas of legal control and the rule of law in the sense of the aspiration that the same general law should apply to everyone (Section 6.4). Related to this is the wider question raised in *O'Reilly v Mackman* (1983) (Section 19.6) whether public law should be a distinct legal regime concentrated in a specialised judiciary or should be diffused throughout the judicial system. The decision of the Supreme Court in *R (Cart) v Upper Tribunal* [2012] concerned the right to challenge a tribunal decision by means of the general law of judicial review in a case where no right of appeal was provided.

Cart concerned whether a decision by the Upper Tribunal to refuse permission to appeal to itself was subject to judicial review. The argument against this was that the Upper Tribunal was of equivalent status to the High Court and its members included high court judges. Since the latter was not subject to judicial review neither should the Upper Tribunal be. The Supreme Court held that in principle the Upper Tribunal was subject to judicial review. It was not completely equivalent to the high court. Most importantly the constitutional principle was applied that that clear statutory language is required to exclude judicial review (see Section 19.7). However, the Supreme Court held that judicial review should be available only in limited circumstances. It favoured the approach taken by the Lord Chancellor's rules (above) which relate to appeals to the Court of Appeal from the Upper Tribunal namely that there must be an important point of principle or practice, or some other compelling reason. This test provides a filter which recognises on the one hand the limited resources available to the courts and the high status and level of expertise of the Upper Tribunal and on the other hand the need to comply with the rule of law by ensuring that there is independent scrutiny and that the tribunal system is integrated into the common law embodied in the main court system and that its decisions are consistent. Moreover, as Lord Phillips pointed out [74], [75] the claimant has had only one hearing on the substantive issues. The court did not discuss other contexts within the tribunal system where judicial review may be available. In any case judicial review is discretionary and the grounds of review are sufficiently flexible to accommodate the specialised context of particular tribunals (see Sections 19.1–19.3, 19.7).

The Council of Tribunals which previously oversaw the tribunal system and made recommendations as to procedural matters is replaced by the Administrative Justice and Tribunals Council. This remains an advisory body but its remit is extended to include the administrative justice system generally, which comprises ombudsmen and dispute resolution mechanisms within government departments and other public bodies. There is a new office, that of Senior President of Tribunals, to oversee and lead the tribunal judiciary and new Tribunals procedure Committee to make rules for tribunals.

20.2 Ombudsmen

Outside the formal tribunal system there are various mechanisms for resolving disputes between citizen and government. These include ombudsmen and internal grievance processes. The most prominent of these, and serving as a model, is the Parliamentary Commissioner for Administration (PCA).

The PCA is firmly set in the constitutional principle that the executive is primarily responsible to Parliament. It investigates, on behalf of Parliament, complaints by citizens against the central government and certain other bodies closely related to the central government (Parliamentary Commissioner Act 1967; Parliamentary and Health Services Commissioners Act 1987; Parliamentary Commissioner Act 1994). The PCA is appointed by the Crown (on the advice of the Prime Minister) and has security of tenure similar to that of a senior judge (Section 5.4.2).

Complaints must be made to an MP, who can decide whether to take the matter to the PCA. This is not subject to judicial review by virtue of parliamentary privilege and is intended to preserve the constitutional principle that the executive is responsible to Parliament. There has been considerable criticism of this rule on the ground that MPs may be reluctant to refer to the PCA in order to claim credit for themselves. Conversely MPs may be unclear about the PCA's power and refer inappropriate cases or even pass the buck by referring cases indiscriminately. The PCA also has discretion whether or not to investigate any particular case.

The PCA has no power to enforce its findings. It must report to the MP who referred the case. If it has found injustice caused by maladministration and considers that it has not been remedied, it may also lay a report before Parliament. The absence of direct enforcement powers may be advantageous in encouraging greater frankness by those being investigated. The PCA can see documents and interview civil servants and other witnesses, and the normal plea of government confidentiality cannot be used (Parliamentary Commissioner Act 1967, s 8(3)). However, Cabinet documents can be excluded (s 8(4)) and the PCA must not name individual civil servants. Investigations are private (s 7(2)).

The decisions of the PCA are subject to judicial review and are not protected by parliamentary privilege (Section 11.6; *R v Parliamentary Comr, ex p Dyer* [1994]; *R v Parliamentary Comr for Administration, ex p Balchin* [1997]).

There are considerable limitations on the powers of the PCA:

▶ Important areas of central government activity are excluded from its jurisdiction. These include foreign affairs, state security (including passports), legal proceedings, criminal investigations, government contracts, commercial activities other than compulsory purchase of land (but statutory powers exercised by contractors under privatisation arrangements are within the Ombudsman's jurisdiction), civil service employment matters and the granting by the Crown of honours, awards and privileges.

▶ The PCA can investigate only allegations of 'injustice in consequence of maladministration' (s 5(1)). Maladministration is not defined but means broadly some defect in the *process* of decision-making as opposed to its outcome: 'bias, neglect, inattention, delay, incompetence, inaptitude, perversity, turpitude, arbitrariness and so on' (the 'Crossman Catalogue', HC Deb 18 October 1966, vol 734, col 51). The PCA cannot directly question government policy or the merits of the exercise of a discretion (s 12; see *R v Local Comr for Administration, ex p Bradford City Council* [1979] QB 287).

▶ Complaints must be made in writing within 12 months of the decision being complained about.

▶ The PCA should not investigate a matter that is appropriate to a court unless in all circumstances it would be unreasonable to expect the complainant to apply to the court. The Ombudsman can take into account the complainant's personal circumstances but not the likelihood of success (*R v Local Comr for Administration, ex p Liverpool City Council* [2001] 1 All ER 462).

The House of Commons Public Administration Select Committee monitors the PCA. Reflecting the convention of ministerial responsibility, it is for the minister concerned to decide whether to give effect to the recommendations, for example by compensating the victim of the injustice or improving departmental procedures. The executive sometimes refuses to accept the PCA's findings (see Kirkham, 'Challenging the Authority of the Ombudsman: The Parliamentary Commissioner's Special Report on Wartime Detainees' (2006) 69 MLR 792). In this situation the Ombudsman can lay a special report before Parliament (s 10(3)).

Other ombudsmen include Commissioners for Local Administration, appointed by the Crown on the recommendation of the Secretary of State, who perform a similar function in respect of local government. However, where a councillor has failed to do so, individuals can complain directly to the commissioners (Local Government Act 1974). The Local Government Ombudsman also has powers to give publicity to its recommendations. Other ombudsmen operate in a similar manner in respect of particular government bodies, for example in respect of the devolved governments of Scotland, Wales (see Public Services Ombudsman (Wales) Act 2005) and Northern Ireland, the NHS, the European Parliament, the police, social housing, the legal profession and judicial appointments (Constitutional Reform Act 2005). Ombudsmen share the dominant ethos of UK government by having no power to enforce their decisions but only to report.

In addition to statutory ombudsmen there are miscellaneous non-statutory bodies exercising similar functions and making unenforceable recommendations (eg the Adjudicator's Office on tax matters, the Independent Complaints Reviewer for the Land Registry, the Charity Commission and the Banking Ombudsman). There are no formal methods of accountability relating to these bodies or controls over their appointment and dismissal. However they may count as public bodies subject to judicial review (Section 19.5).

There are also internal complaints procedures offering alternative dispute resolution (ADR) such as mediation or arbitration within government departments and agencies. These are subject to the tendency of officials in the UK to prefer the informal and secretive and the absence of a cultural awareness of what independence requires. Thus the general issue arising here is whether such internal processes are sufficiently independent to provide a fair trial in relation to a citizen's civil rights and obligations under the European Convention on Human Rights (ECHR) (Section 20.4.2).

20.3 Inquiries

Some government decisions, particularly in relation to planning and other land use matters, are taken in the name of ministers following an inquiry held by an independent inspector. In some cases, notably routine cases under town and country planning legislation, power to make the decision is delegated to the inspector. Unlike tribunal decisions that primarily concern factual or legal issues, the subject matter of such decisions may also concern controversial political issues, relating, for example to airport building or rural development. The inquiry system is therefore intended to provide an independent element as part of a wider process and is not a self-contained judicial process along the lines of a court.

Inquiries are sometimes described as 'quasi-judicial'. They follow a procedure broadly similar to that of a court but are more flexible and less formal. Formal rules of evidence do not apply. People whose interests are affected by the decision in question have a right to appear and give evidence. Others can speak at the discretion of the inspector, who can also allow cross-examination. This discretion is usually exercised liberally.

The independence and openness of inquiry procedures is partly safeguarded by the Tribunals and Inquiries Act 1992. This requires in particular that evidence must be disclosed in advance, reasons must be given for decisions and where the minister overrules the inspector the parties must be given a chance to comment and, in the case of disagreement about facts, to reopen the inquiry (see, for example Town and Country Planning (Hearings Procedure) (England) Rules 2000 (SI 2000/1624)).

Unlike tribunals, inquiries are primarily part of a larger administrative process and therefore not independent of political influence. Nevertheless provided that judicial review is available, this distinctively British process has been upheld as compliant with the right to a fair trial under the ECHR. This is because there is a substantial policy or political element involved which is appropriate for the injection of a democratic element as opposed to the impartiality expected from a court of law (see *R (Alconbury*

Developments) v Secretary of State for the Environment, Transport and the Regions [2001]). Furthermore the involvement of ministers and civil servants, with their close, secretive relationship, means that policy advice may not be subject to independent scrutiny at the inquiry (see *Bushell v Secretary of State for the Environment* [1981]).

Special inquiries can be held to investigate events of public concern, for example serious incidents or allegations of misconduct by officials. Under the Inquiries Act 2005 a minister may establish such an inquiry, decide its terms of reference and appoint the person to hold it. There is provision for such inquiries to be open and accessible but, characteristically, the chairman and the minster have wide power to limit this. The inquiry reports to the minister. A person with a direct interest in the subject of the inquiry or a close association with an interested party cannot be appointed unless the minister considers that impartiality would not reasonably be affected (s 9). The minister must make a statement to Parliament setting out the membership of the inquiry and its terms of reference (s 6).

The inquiry chairman must 'take such steps as he considers reasonable' to ensure public access to the inquiry and its evidence and the minister can restrict public access to the inquiry (ss 18, 19). In particular information must not be revealed where there is a risk of damage to the economy unless the panel is satisfied that public interest in the information outweighs the risk (s 23).

The inquiry report must be published in full subject to the minister's powers to restrict publication on grounds of 'public interest' (s 25). No time limit for publication is laid down so that a minister could delay publication for political reasons. However judicial review would be available in such circumstances. The published parts of the inquiry report must be laid before Parliament (s 26).

A constitutional difficulty with this type of inquiry arises because senior judges are often asked to hold them. The current *Leveson Inquiry* into press conduct and the relationship of the media and government is an example. Unless the inquiry is purely a fact finding one this may appear to compromise the independence of the judiciary (see Beatson, 'Should Judges Conduct Public Inquiries?' (2005) 121 LQR 221). Under section 10 of the Inquiries Act 2005 the Lord Chief Justice or the Senior Law Lord must first be consulted when it is proposed to appoint a judge to hold an inquiry.

Another form of inquiry is a Royal Commission. Again this is established by ministers, in this case under the royal prerogative. The members of a Royal Commission are usually persons with previous links with government. The report of the commission is usually laid before Parliament. Royal Commissions have no power to compel attendance or disclosure of information. They are sometimes employed to consider general constitutional issues, for example the Royal Commission on the House of Lords (Section 12.3).

A possible weakness of an inquiry or Royal Commission is that it does not provide any means of enforcement and may subvert more stringent methods of accountability. An inquiry make take many months or even years during which possible legal actions or intervention by Parliament may be suspended (eg the Saville Inquiry into the 'Bloody Sunday' killings by troops lasted 10 years). The outcome of an inquiry is not binding and while it may attract temporary publicity it may thereafter be ignored. Furthermore the terms of reference of an inquiry may be limited.

There are also Parliamentary inquiries established by Parliament under its own internal powers. These comprise a mixture of MPs and outsiders They may be more appropriate to political issues than a judicial inquiry. However, although Parliament has the power to do so evidence is not usually on oath and the politician members of the inquiry may be ill-informed, biased and unskilled at asking probing questions. This kind of inquiry was set up in July 2012 to investigate the alleged malpractices of the banking industry.

Ministers often prefer to set up non-statutory inquiries presided over by persons of their own choosing and with procedures and terms of reference set by themselves (eg the Hutton, Butler and Chilcott inquiries concerned with the invasion of Iraq and these sometimes sit in public but have no legal powers to compel witnesses to attend, to examine documents or to take evidence on oath, under which lying would be a criminal offence). For example, in January 2011 the Cabinet Secretary refused to permit the Chilcot Inquiry to make public letters sent by the then Prime Minister, Tony Blair, to George Bush, the US President.

In the interests of public confidence in good government the courts have developed the following principle in dealing with statutory government decision-making procedures: whether in the view of a 'fair-minded and informed observer' taken as knowing all the circumstances there is a 'real possibility' or 'real danger' of bias (Section 18.4). Does the appointment of inquiry chairs meet these standards, and should it? For example in 2010 a retired appeal court judge, Sir Peter Gibson, was appointed to hold an inquiry into allegations that members of the UK security services had been involved in torture. During part of the relevant time Sir Peter had been the statutory overseer of the security services and had previously investigated allegations of misconduct. He had issued reports describing the security services as 'trustworthy, conscientious and dependable'. The government has maintained that for non-statutory inquiries there is no duty to pass legally relevant tests of impartiality and independence (see *Guardian* 30 July 2010).

Illustrating that public pressures are effective, an unusually wide form of inquiry was recently established to investigate the Hillsborough Stadium Disaster of 1989 when many people were killed following the collapse of the stadium roof. Judicial Inquiries and an inquest all with limited terms of reference had failed to satisfy the relatives of the victims (Taylor, 1990; Stuart-Smith, 1998). An Independent Panel appointed by the Home Secretary and reporting to the House of Commons was given access to all documents. Its report (HC 581, 12 Sept. 2012) revealed widespread wrongdoing by the police and other agencies attempting to cover up mistakes by blaming members of the public (see *Times* 13 Sept. 2012). The success of this inquiry seemed to have been due to the independence of its membership, chaired by the Bishop of Liverpool and because, there was public access to its proceedings and unusually the government did not refuse to make information available.

20.4 Regulation

A regulator is a public official with the power to control and channel conduct in a given area. Of course all government could be described this way but regulation has the distinctive feature that specialist officials usually outside the main governmental bodies directly supervise the persons or bodies under their control and intervene not only to prevent or punish misconduct but also to impose desired policies. Regulation mainly concerns business activities but also includes charities, education bodies, health bodies and other social welfare bodies both public and private. Most regulators make binding rules, sometimes provide finance, carry out other executive functions such as investigations and consents or licences, and impose penalties thus raising questions about the separation of powers and impartiality.

There are about 670 regulatory bodies including the Bank of England, 468 local authorities and various national bodies created by statute. Most of them are quangos or non-ministerial government departments and so are to some extent independent from ministers (Sections 15.9, 15.10). There is an increasing cohort of regulators albeit with only limited powers concerned with intrusive activities by the police and other public authorities raising the age old question '*quis custodiet ipsos custodies*'. These include the Information Commissioner (Section 24.2.1), the Intelligence Services Commissioner, the Surveillance Commissioner and the Surveillance Camera Commissioner (Section 24.5) and the Commissioner for the Retention and Use of Biometric Material (Section 21.4.3).

There is no systematic method of accountability which depends on the particular statute. Analogous in this respect to tribunals, regulation creates specialised self-contained sub-systems of law which unless there is strong connection with the ordinary courts place the rule of law at risk. Regulation also illustrates the organic nature of the constitution which can be changed by the accumulation of innovations introduced over time for short-term reasons. Regulation is an example of the increasing juridification of the constitution in that the proliferation of regulatory bodies and legal mechanisms has to some extent displaced traditional modes of resolving disputes based on negotiation within personal networks.

Regulation has existed for many centuries from the days of mediaeval guilds and markets when it was a useful source of government income. During the nineteenth century factory legislation began to impose health and safety standards which protected vulnerable workers. Environmental regulation concerning pollution originated in the nineteenth century and has developed into a leading regulatory regime. The problems of complexity and overlapping of regulators was recognised in the 1970s by the Robens Report into health and safety at work (Cmnd 5034, 1972). This did not deter the subsequent proliferation of regulators.

A new form of regulation was introduced in the 1980s as part of a policy of privatization of public utilities including energy generation and supply, water, telecommunications, broadcasting and public transport. These were transferred from government ownership to private companies. It was assumed firstly that market forces produced greater efficiency than state control, and secondly that, provided that there was regulation, ownership was not important in relation to public benefit. The companies concerned were given special powers and privileges in order to lessen risks and so encourage investors. They are therefore hybrids between the public and private sector rather than genuine market participants. For some purposes they have the status of public bodies making them subject to EU directives (Section 10.3) and possibly the Human Rights Act (Section 21.4.1).

There is limited room for genuine competition in the privatised industries, so the standard justification for private enterprise is missing. Regulators are therefore a substitute for competition and their roles are complex and sometimes conflicting. Regulators provide a means of accountability to ensure that the businesses are run efficiently, they protect what competition there is, they impose public interest values, for example by protecting vulnerable groups in relation to electricity and gas supplies and they act as a tool of government policy. It has been argued in the context of media regulation that regulatory system attempts to reconcile the incommensurables of market liberalism (Section 2.3.4) and welfare liberalism (Section 2.3.5) (Vick, 'Regulatory Convergence?' (2006) 26 LS 26).

Regulation is not confined to privatised industries. Since the 1890s regulation has proliferated and some form of regulatory body affects most business and financial activity dealing, for example with consumer protection, environmental risks, social housing, data security, financial dealings and the governance of organizations such as companies. Bodies have been created to regulate standards in public life notably including members of Parliament (Section 11.7). The number of regulators fluctuates and their functions overlap.

There is a network of diverse connections made by uncoordinated legislation between regulators, local authorities, EU bodies and the central executive. There is no single model regulatory structure, the constitution of each body depending on its particular terms of reference. Patronage is a unifying feature since the members of regulatory bodies are normally appointed by ministers albeit sometimes with representative elements. Ministers can also often prescribe general policies.

The diversity and lack of coordination of regulators makes accountability unclear and incomplete as was the case originally with tribunals (Section 20.1). Sometimes the same body both funds and regulates its subjects thereby raising suspicions of conflict of interest which are not necessarily removed by internal divisions. The right to a fair trial under the ECHR may be an issue in this context (Section 17.6). Some regulators operate within the main government departments and are therefore fully accountable to Parliament through ministers (eg The Animals (Scientific Procedures) Inspectorate). The Post Office is a company wholly owned by the government but regulated by an independent Commission (Postal Services Act 2000). Many regulators are non-ministerial departments the heads of which are directly accountable to Parliament albeit without the day to day accountability provided by ministers (Section 15.8), for example The Charity Commission, the *Food Standards Agency and the various utility regulators). Some are Quangos outside the central government structure the accountability of which depends on the particular statute* (Section 15.10), for example the Environment Agency, the Pensions Regulator).

The BBC which exists under the royal prerogative and is funded by government grant financed by a licence fee charged to all television users has a curious system of semi-independent regulation in the form of the BBC Trust. This has mainly advisory powers to ensure that the BBC acts in the public interest. Its chair is appointed by the government. It is of course important that the BBC and other broadcasters are independent of political interference. Other broadcasters are financed by advertising and regulated by OFCOM, a Quango the members of which are appointed by the Secretary of State (Office of Communications Act 2002; Communications Act 2003),

> Local authorities carry out regulation in relation to social welfare, transport, public health and safety, land use and consumer protection. The Regulatory Enforcement and Sanctions Act 2008 created the *Local Better Regulation Office* appointed by the Secretary of State. The LBRTF gives guidance to local authorities which can be enforced with the consent of the Secretary of State (Section 8). Thus a non-elected body is empowered to interfere with an elected one.

There are also non-statutory regulators set up by an industry itself on a voluntary basis thus creating weak accountability and conflicts of interest, for example the Press Complaints Commission, the Advertising Standards Authority and various sports regulators. Judicial control over these bodies is problematic since they may not be regarded as 'public bodies' subject to judicial review and the Human Rights Act (Sections 19.5, 21.4).

The Regulatory Reform Act 2001 gave ministers wide powers to intervene in the organisation and powers of regulators. The Hampton Report, *Reducing Administrative Burdens: Effective Inspection and Enforcement* (2005, HM Treasury) concluded that there were too many regulators, that their powers overlapped unnecessarily and were insufficiently flexible and too burdensome. It recommended that there should be a reduced number of regulators operating on a more systematic basis with tougher penalties at their disposal. Key principles should include accountability, 'proportionate and meaningful sanctions for persistent defaulters', intervention only in clear cases based on risk, easy and cheap access to advice and avoiding duplication.

This led to the Regulatory Reform Act 2006 which gave ministers even wider powers including powers to issue codes of practice, and to alter or repeal statutes for the purposes of reorganising or abolishing individual regulators, to create criminal offences subject to limits. These abnormally wide powers are subject to the special form of parliamentary scrutiny known as the 'super affirmative procedure' (Section 13.5.3).

The McRory Report, *Regulatory Justice, Making Sanctions Effective* (2006) further widened the scope of regulation by endorsing long standing proposals for a standardised system of flexible ` administrative sanctions which regulators could apply on a sliding scale of increasing stringency. The possibility of challenge in the ordinary courts should be limited. The sanctions include persuasion, warnings, the suspension or revocation of a licence, enforcement notices requiring action to be taken, stop notices preventing actions, fixed or variable civil financial penalties such as fines and finally criminal sanctions in the ordinary courts. The criminal courts should have powers to impose penalties by way of restorative justice. The notion of administrative penalties is contrary to traditional ideas of the rule of law according to which no one should be punished except for a breach of the law established in the ordinary courts (Section 6.5).

The McRory Report, other than the proposals concerning criminal prosecutions was implemented by the Regulatory Enforcement and Sanctions Act 2008. This applies to the main national regulators but there are exceptions including the regulators of the privatised utility companies. Ministers can make Orders empowering regulators to impose civil sanctions as suggested by McRory. Safeguards include compliance with the 'regulatory principles' set out in LARA s 21. These require any person exercising a regulatory function to be 'transparent, accountable, proportionate, consistent' and to 'target cases only in which action is needed'. Regulators must publish reports of what enforcement action has been taken.

The terms of office of a regulator depends on the particular statute. A regulator is typically appointed by a minister for a fixed period which can be renewed and can be dismissed by the Secretary of State within that period on specified grounds including misconduct (see, eg Office of Communications Act 2002 Schedule). The appointment processes of many regulators are to some extent supervised by a Commissioner for Public Appointments in an attempt to ensure that powers of patronage are not abused (Section 15.9). However, characteristic of external safeguards over executive bodies, the Commission's role is only advisory. The constitutional problems raised by regulation thus exemplify the general problems of accountability namely lack of coherence which allows blame to be transferred to others, influence, patronage and secrecy (House of

Lords Constitution Committee, *The Regulatory State: Ensuring its Accountability*, HL 68 (2003–04).

> Methods of regulation vary with changing fashions in government. The traditional method, 'command and control,' consists of imposing penalties for conduct disapproved of by the regulator. This requires inspections and audits and ultimately depends on the criminal law. Unlike the case with tribunals, the discretion of the regulator means that negotiation and compromise is a regulatory tool. This led to allegations of 'regulatory capture' according to which there is a risk that regulators, anxious to be approved of, either identify with the interests of those they regulate or try to please the government in both cases compromising their independence.

From the late 1990s 'self-regulation' or 'light touch' regulation became fashionable appearing to fit the prevailing ideology of market liberalism as well as the informal networks characteristic of UK government. This involved the regulator intervening only on the basis of 'risk' and required the regulatee to monitor itself including assessment of risk. It deploys the propaganda of 'partnership' and imposes heavy administrative costs on businesses. As recent banking scandals illustrate this method of regulation increases the risk of abuse but without reducing that of regulatory capture. For example the Financial Services which until 2013 regulated banks and other financial institutions assisted the bodies that it regulated in various lobbying campaigns (*Guardian* 13 July 2012). Moreover internal methods of regulation raise the problem of bias where a regulator is a member of the governing body of the organization itself and so has a vested interest in its well-being (see *R (Kaur) v ILEX Appeal Tribunal* [2012] 1 All ER 1435 [18]–[24]: Vice President of organisation disqualified from sitting on appeal tribunal (Section 18.4)).

One response to concerns about the discretion exercised by regulators is to favour objective methods of regulation using quantitative data such as statistics devised in the light of prescribed targets or indexes. However, these may lead to unfairness and a failure to take relevant factors into account which are grounds for judicial review. An extreme version of objective regulation not used in the UK relies on what Brownsword (2005) calls a 'technical fix' whereby computer technology imbeds required patterns of behaviour in the operations of the business being regulated so that undesirable behaviour is difficult (eg speed and distance monitoring on a vehicle which cuts off power when prescribed limits are exceeded). This may be cheap and reliable as a method of control but is open to fraud, and, as Brownsword points out, puts openness and accountability at risk and arguably affronts human dignity.

Accountability has two aspects. Firstly it requires a method by which decisions can be corrected and the official punished for failure. The former is provided primarily by the courts in the same way as over other public officials. However judicial review is limited to serious failures of procedure or abuse of power and the wide discretion given to a regulator may limit the scope of judicial review (see eg *Interbrow SA v Competition Commission* [2001] EWHC Admin 367). Otherwise accountability is haphazard. There is no automatic right of appeal but a minister can provide for an appeal to a tribunal. Depending on the particular regime there are sometimes rights of appeal to the court or a special tribunal, sometimes an Ombudsman. Moreover the McRory Report (above) favoured an appeal to a tribunal rather than to the ordinary courts. There is a General Regulatory Chamber of the First Tier Tribunal (Section 5.1).

Regulators are accountable to ministers and (at least in the case of those that are non-ministerial departments) to Parliament (Section 15.10)). However, because regulators exist outside the normal chain of responsibility which applies between a minister, his or her department and Parliament there is limited opportunity for scrutiny by Parliament. Their annual reports and accounts must be presented to Parliament and their leaders often appear before Select Committees (Section 13.5). The minister's accountability may be confused because he or she is not directly responsible for the regulator's decisions except where the regulator is part of the minister's own department (Section 15.7).

Accountability also means providing the public with information and explanation. Methods of accountability such as duties to consult, to hold meetings in public and to publish information about policies and decisions depend on particular statutes (see eg Utilities Act 2000; Communications Act 2003; Postal Services Act 2000; Railways Act 2005). These devices are increasingly being used at least by the utilities regulators. As public bodies, most regulators are subject to the Freedom of Information Act 2000 which requires some information to be disclosed on request (Section 23.2.1). However exemptions in the Act, notably 'commercial confidentiality' may provide a justification for refusal.

Summary

▶ Tribunals adjudicate relatively small and specialised disputes between government and individual. They are relatively informal but subject to special safeguards to secure their independence and fairness. Recent reforms have rationalised the tribunal system and bedded tribunals more firmly into the judicial branch of government. There are other methods of administrative justice but these suffer from the absence of enforcement powers and sometimes questionable independence.

▶ A range of ombudsmen investigates complaints of maladministration against government and other bodies on behalf of the citizen. In order to preserve the constitutional principle of ministerial responsibility the Parliamentary Commissioner for Administration reports to Parliament and has jurisdiction only through an MP. Ombudsmen do not normally have enforcement powers.

▶ Internal complaints procedures raise the problem of whether they are sufficiently independent to provide a fair trial in relation to a citizen's civil rights and obligations under the ECHR.

▶ Public inquiries form part of the process for making some governmental decisions. They are presided over by independent inspectors who have an element of public participation and are subject to special safeguards. Ministers may set up special inquiries into particular events or issues. These have limited independence.

▶ The use of regulators to control a wide range of private bodies has increased in recent years. They have substantial powers combining law making, executive and judicial functions including the imposition of penalties. Regulators take several forms and their accountability is complex and uncertain.

Exercises

20.1 Are tribunals properly termed 'administrative tribunals'?

20.2 Outline the constitutional problems raised by the following:
   (i) inquiries;
   (ii) regulation.

Exercises cont'd

20.3 You are a minister with a policy of regulating the admission of students to university. What structure would you set up for dealing with complaints and how would it be accountable, if at all?

20.4 Compare the merits of the ombudsman and judicial review as methods of resolving disputes between the individual and the government.

20.5 What are the main differences in the powers of the Parliamentary and Local Ombudsmen? What are the reasons for the differences?

20.6 There have been widespread allegation in the press that politicians and civil servants have been receiving payments and other benefits such as retirement jobs and holiday homes in return for giving favours to the leaders of banks and other influential financial organizations both domestic and overseas. The government sets up an inquiry under the Inquiries Act 2005. The inquiry's terms of reference exclude any investigation into overseas organisations. The minister appoints Lord Bray a former banker, who was recently given a peerage to hold the inquiry. Lord Bray announces that members of the public may attend the inquiry in person but will have no access to any written or electronic material. He appoints two bankers with whom he has worked in the past to advise the inquiry. The eventual inquiry report largely exonerates any high level public official. However at the same time as the report is delivered to the minister another minister is photographed by the press receiving a large bundle of banknotes from an overseas diplomat in a London hotel. The minister responsible for the inquiry report postpones its publication indefinitely.

Advise the *Campaign for Cleaner Government*, a pressure group as to any legal remedies available to them in respect of these events. (Chapters on judicial review might also be consulted.)

Further reading

Ambler and Boyfield, *Reforming the Regulators* (Adam Smith Institute 2010) Black, 'De Centring Regulation: Understanding the Role of Regulation and Self- Regulation in a Post Regulatory World' (2001) 54 CLP 103

Brownsword, 'Code, Control and Choice: Why East is East and West is West' (2005) 25 LS 1

Buck, Kirkham, Thompson, 'Time for a "Leggatt-style Review of the Ombudsman System?' [2011] PL 20

Carnwath, 'Tribunal Justice: A New Start' [2009] PL 48

Laurie, 'Assessing the Upper Tribunal's Potential to Deliver Administrative Justice' [2012] PL 288

Loughlin, *Foundations of Public Law* (Oxford University Press 2010) ch 15

Le Sueur, 'Administrative Justice and the Resolution of Disputes', in Jowell and Oliver (eds), *The Changing Constitution* (7th edn, Oxford University Press 2011)

McRory, 'Environmental Regulation as an Instrument of Constitutional Change', in Jowell and Oliver (eds), *The Changing Constitution* (7th edn, Oxford University Press 2011)

Oliver, Prosser, Rawlings (eds), *The Regulatory State: Constitutional Implications* (Hart Publishing 2010)

Prosser, *The Regulatory Enterprise: Government, Regulation, and Legitimacy* (Oxford University Press 2010)

Prosser, 'Regulation and Legitimacy' in Jowell and Oliver (eds), *The Changing Constitution* (7th edn, Oxford University Press 2011)

Part VI

Fundamental rights

Chapter 21

Human rights and civil liberties

21.1 Introduction: the nature of human rights

The concept of human rights attempts to identify fundamental human interests which have a special status in the sense that they should not be violated, either at all or only in extreme circumstances. Human rights did not become a prominent legal issue in the UK until the aftermath of the Second World War, which produced a worldwide reaction against the atrocities of the Nazis.

Human rights concern basic needs such as personal freedom, privacy and freedom of religion; political interests such as freedom of expression and association; and fairness and justice, such as the right to a fair trial before an independent judge. Some of these rights conflict with others, for example freedom of the press and respect for privacy. Some may conflict with social goals such as security and the fair distribution of wealth.

Three interrelated issues underlie human rights law. Firstly what is a human right? Is it anything other than a political claim? Attitudes to this question influence the importance we attach to human rights law. The classic Enlightenment writers, notably Locke (Section 2.3.2), thought that there were certain natural rights given by God which it is the state's duty to protect. In his case these were life, health, liberty and property. For Hobbes by contrast there are no rights other than those created and enforced by law. To Hobbes 'natural rights' are essentially rational reasons for action rather than rights as such. They include primarily self-defence, 'do-as-you-would-be-done-by' and the honouring of promises. From a utilitarian perspective, Bentham regarded the notion of rights as 'nonsense on stilts' except in the sense of interests protected by particular laws.

There is no agreement as to how we identify human rights. Some claim that they are revealed by God, others that humans have a special 'dignity'. For example the UN Universal Declaration of Human Rights (Cmd 7226, 1948) is founded on the 'inherent dignity...of all members of the human family', equality, rationality and 'brotherhood' (Preamble Article 1). Others, following Kant, derive human rights from apparently self-evident rational truths such as 'equality' or 'autonomy'. For example Dworkin (*Freedom's Law* (Oxford University Press 1996) argues that certain interests, such as freedom of expression and the right to a fair trial, are non-negotiable conditions of a democratic society because they underpin equality, this being the nearest we can get to a bedrock principle. A more modest claim derives from Hume (Section 2.3.3), namely that human rights are driven by our natural sympathy for others and that we create customs underpinning particular ways of life which we desire to preserve.

Grandiose theoretical and universal claims for human rights face the difficulty that they may be too vague to be directly applied and different cultures may understand particular rights and their limits in different ways. Indeed politicians and officials drafting laws or international treaties might take refuge in vagueness as a way of producing agreement, while leaving the hard questions to be decided by others such as the courts. Indeed this was the case with the European Convention on Human Rights (ECHR) (see Marston, 'The UK's Part in the Preparation of the ECHR' (1993) 42 ICLQ 796).

This leads to the second issue. What is the legal basis for a statement of fundamental rights? The UK relies on the ECHR and the European Court of Human Rights. The Convention came into force in 1953 as an international treaty under the auspices of the Council of Europe, which was established in 1949 and has 41 members. It derives from the Universal Declaration of Human Rights, a resolution of the UN General Assembly (1948) which is not in itself legally binding. As a response to Nazi atrocities the ECHR concentrates on the protection of individual freedom against state interference rather than on what are known as 'second- and third-generation rights', these being respectively social claims such as housing and collective interests such as environmental quality. The ECHR is something of a bland compromise with many exceptions. An alternative claim relates to Dicey's version of the rule of law (Section 6.4.2), namely that human rights are inherent in the common law, which does not need the support of an international treaty.

The third issue is who should have the last word in human rights disputes? In particular should there be a bill of rights protected against being overridden by the democratic lawmaker? Even if we accept that the concept of human rights is meaningful and should be embedded in the law, nothing follows automatically from this as to what is the best mechanism for protecting it. The ultimate decision maker might, for example be a court as in the US, an elected lawmaker as in the UK or a special body as in France.

Human rights disputes differ significantly from those with which the courts traditionally deal. There is fundamental and apparently never-ending disagreement about the meaning and application of human rights concepts. Human rights cases often require the judge to assess the validity of a legal rule or government decision against a vague aspirational concept such as 'freedom of expression' and to decide the extent to which a right should be sacrificed to some important public goal, for example personal freedom against the suppression of terrorism.

Thus a human rights dispute often raises wide issues affecting society as a whole, going beyond the interests of the particular parties and which cannot be applied as rules and lack agreed criteria for decision. For this reason it is often doubted whether the legal process is an appropriate way of deciding human rights disputes. The legal process is also vulnerable to the republican attack that it gives the judge the power of arbitrary domination.

It is often claimed that the courts are most likely to produce the 'best' outcome, being independent, open and guided by intense rational analysis as a forum for public debate. However arguments about what is the best outcome merely repeat the disagreement. Unless we agree as to what counts as a best outcome, we cannot agree what mechanism is most likely to produce it. A 'best outcome' might be one produced by democratic debate. While judges are good at interpreting and applying definite rules, human rights occupy territory where judges have no special expertise, requiring them either to be political philosophers or politicians or to resort to semantic evasion. For example, serious issues about how far personal freedom should be curtailed for security reasons may turn upon the semantic question of the line between a 'deprivation of liberty' and a 'restriction on liberty' (Section 21.4). Moreover, the task of 'weighing' a human right against other aspects of the public interest may be more appropriate to a democratic body which may be able to negotiate a solution acceptable to most of those involved. Many of the cases have produced sharp disagreements between the judges.

The favourite liberal argument in favour of a court is fear of what De Toqueville called 'the tyranny of the majority'. The argument runs that 'democracy' is more than just the will of the majority and must be policed by certain basic rights of equality and freedom protected against the volatility, corruption or foolishness of the majority (see Lord Hoffmann in *R (Alconbury Developments Ltd) v Secretary of State for the Environment, Transport and the Regions* [2000] at [70]). Thus handing over power to a court is not anti-democratic but a prudent 'pre-commitment' of a majority anxious to guard against its own weaknesses, for example a panic overreaction to a supposed threat such as that of terrorism. By removing fundamental rights from its control, the majority lessens the risk that it will misuse its power. In particular a court can protect unpopular minorities. Thus in *R (Countryside Alliance) v A-G* [2008] 2 All ER 95 (114) Lady Hale remarked that 'democracy is the will of the people but the people may not will to invade those rights which are fundamental to democracy itself'.

Similarly it is often suggested that the court's power to police human rights is democratic because it was given to them by a democratic body namely Parliament (eg Lord Bingham in *A v Secretary of State for the Home Dept* [2005] [42]). However even if a democratic body gives this power to the judges, the exercise of the power does not thereby become democratic, any more than if a democratic body handed over its power to a dictator.

Waldron (1999) draws on the republican argument (Section 2.5) that we sacrifice dignity, equality and control over our lives by letting unelected judges decide whether laws are valid. The appropriate question is what mechanism can most appropriately manage disagreement? Arguably this should be a democratic assembly in which the whole community can participate on equal terms.

The Human Rights Act 1998 recognises this irreducible disagreement by trying to accommodate both sides. The Act upholds democracy by leaving the final word with Parliament while empowering the courts to put pressure on Parliament, thereby creating an accommodation in accordance with the separation of powers (Section 22.3).

There is also a characteristic Quango in the form of the Commission for Equality and Human Rights (Equality Act 2006). The Commission is required to review the protection of equality, human rights and 'mutual respect between different groups in society'. The Commission's enforcement powers concern over race, religious, sex, sexual orientation and disability discrimination where it can assist or ultimately take legal proceedings. In relation to other human rights it can only give advice to government. Its members are appointed and financed by the Secretary of State who can also remove them. As with other regulatory bodies (Section 20.4) the Commission is not therefore fully independent. Its current Chair, the distinguished philosopher Lady Onora O'Neill, advocated greater trust in officialdom and finding new methods of accountability (*Reith Lectures* 2002, Cambridge University Press).

21.2 The common law background

English lawyers have traditionally used the terminology of negative freedom (Section 2.4) and civil liberties rather than the positive language of rights. The traditional common law standpoint has been residual, namely that everyone is free to do whatever the law does not specifically prohibit. In Hobbes' language, 'freedom lies in the silence of the laws'. However, in a constitution based on unlimited parliamentary power that can readily be harnessed by political parties in thrall to vested interests, it may be difficult to ensure that the laws are indeed silent. Moreover the notion of negative freedom assumes that all freedoms are of equal value. For example, Dicey may appear complacent:

> English law no more favours and provides for the holding of public meetings than for the giving of public concerts...A man has a right to hear an orator as he has a right to hear a band or eat a bun. (1915, 353)

The common law's residual approach therefore depends on trusting the lawmaker not to enact intrusive laws and trusting the courts to interpret laws in a way sympathetic to individual liberty. This violates republican ideas by treating us as 'happy slaves' content with a kind master.

The courts have however held that some common law principles amount to fundamental rights and can be overridden only by clear statutory language (Sections 6.6, 8.4.5, 17.4). But this cannot surmount the creeping erosion of liberty by the accumulation of statutes, which, taken individually, are relatively innocuous but which add up to a formidable armoury of state powers. For example numerous provisions were enacted on behalf of the governments of 1997–2010 restricting individual liberty and increasing surveillance in order to combat antisocial behaviour and terrorism. Moreover legislation enacted to deal with a particular problem may be used for other purposes. The Terrorism Act 2000, for example was used to remove an elderly heckler from the 2005 Labour Party Conference, and the Serious Organised Crimes and Police Act 2005 to arrest a demonstrator for possession of magazine article critical of the government (see HL Deb 1 February 2006, cols 231, 239; *Guardian* 29 June 2006). Anti-terrorism powers in RIPA 2000 have been used by local government employees to spy on citizens in order to enforce minor transgressions (Section 24.5). A notorious gap in the common law was that it did not recognize a right of privacy (*Malone v MPC* [1979], Section 23.5).

It is also claimed that the common law, being open to any argument and treating all parties as equals, is especially suitable for a liberal society (Allan, *Constitutional Justice* (Oxford University Press 2001)). Indeed until the Human Rights Act 1998 the UK had resisted incorporation of the ECHR on the basis that the common law provided equivalent protection (see *Brind v Secretary of State for the Home Dept* [1991]; Lord Goff in *A-G v Guardian Newspapers (No 2)* [1998] 3 All ER 535, 660). However the two approaches are different in important respects. Firstly the ECHR requires special justification to override a right, whereas in the common law any sufficiently clearly worded statute will do. Secondly the common law, sometimes described as unprincipled, is multifactoral and utilitarian in the sense that it depends on accumulating factors pointing to or against a particular conclusion without necessarily organising these within a formal hierarchy of principles.

21.3 The European Convention on Human Rights

The ECHR has three roles under the UK constitution:

1. Individuals can petition the European Court of Human Rights in Strasbourg alleging that the state has violated their rights under the Convention. The court may award compensation and require the state to change its law. However its decisions are binding only in international law and have no direct binding force in domestic law.

Unlike the Court of Justice of the EU the court does not require domestic courts to be bound by its decisions and it does not follow a strict doctrine of precedent.

The concept of the 'margin of appreciation' was developed by the European Court as a safety valve in cases where there are significant national differences in political, religious or moral values or practices. Where the margin of appreciation applies, the European Court will not substitute its views for those of the state but asks itself only whether the national authorities were reasonably entitled to think that the interference was justifiable (eg *Handyside v UK* [1976] 1 EHRR 77: pornography, *Leander v Sweden* [1987] ECHR Ser. A 116: security, *Open Door and Dublin Well Woman v Ireland* [1992] 15 EHRR 244: abortion). Different communities may have different but justifiable blends of values and attitudes and if an international tribunal intervened it might forfeit respect. The margin of appreciation is of course limited. States cannot disregard fundamental values and standards supported by a consensus among member states and the court will review the reasonableness of the state action (eg *Marper v UK* [2008] 40 EHRR 50 [102]: retention of DNA samples).

2. As a treaty the Convention should be taken into account by domestic courts when interpreting statutes, at least where they are ambiguous. The common law should probably also be developed in the light of the Convention (*A-G v Guardian Newspapers Ltd (No 2)* [1998]).

3. The Human Rights Act 1998 incorporates the main rights listed in the Convention, *but not the Convention itself*, into UK law and provides a special mechanism for applying them. Points (1) and (2) are not affected by the Act. As Lord Bingham pointed out in *R (Al-Skeini) v Secretary of State* [2007] 3 All ER 685 [10], rights *under* the Convention differ from rights created by the 1998 Act *by reference to* the Convention.

The ECHR is primarily concerned with 'negative' rights protected against state interference as opposed to positive rights requiring state action to give effect to the right. Sometimes however a positive right exists. There are two kinds of positive right. The first is where the right requires the state to provide some positive benefit or facility such as welfare services. In a democracy courts are reluctant to impose this kind of duty on the state since it may involve choices about public spending that are regarded as more appropriate to an elected body. Moreover, some kinds of liberals may object to the impact of positive rights on the free market and the possible conflict with individual liberty and initiative ((Section 2.3.2); see Sunstein, 'Against Positive Rights' (1993) 2 EECR 35). Only in cases of extreme destitution does the ECHR enter the territory of positive rights in this sense.

There are other international treaties dealing with social and political rights, notably the UN International Covenant on Economic, Social and Cultural Rights (1976). These have not been incorporated into domestic law and contain no enforcement machinery. Some constitutions, notably those in states associated with the former Soviet Union, contain a range of economic and social rights.

The second kind of positive right does impact on the ECHR. This is where the state is required to ensure not only that it respects the right in question but also that private bodies do so. It is not enough that the state does not interfere with the right. It must also take active steps to protect the right (see Lord Steyn in *R (Ullah) v Special Adjudicator* [2004] at [34]). Such positive obligations are unlikely to be absolute and the state will be afforded a margin of discretion in carrying them out (Section 22.5.2; *R (Pretty) v DPP*

[2002] 1 All ER 1 [15]). Examples include respect for privacy and family life and freedom of expression. Thus the state must ensure not only that the media is free to inform the public but also that the privately owned press acts responsibly and respects the privacy of individuals (Section 23.3) (see Fredman, 'Human Rights Transformed: Positive Duties and Positive Rights' [2006] PL 562).

21.4 The main Convention rights

The structure of the Convention rights is as follows. Many Convention rights can be *overridden* on defined grounds relating to the public interest and the rights of others (see Arts 7–11; Art 14 (indirectly); Protocol 1, Art 1). Articles 2, 5 and 7 are *absolute*, (also called *unqualified*) but are subject to designated *exceptions which take the designated matter outside the right altogether*. Articles 3, 4(1), 6 and 12 and Protocol 1, Articles 2 and 3 are on the face of it absolute without any exceptions.

However the absolute rights are sometimes flexible. In particular their meaning may be vague. Thus the courts may use public interest arguments when they define the meaning of a right, thereby blurring the separate issues of whether there is a right at all and whether it should be overridden (eg the meaning of 'deprivation of liberty' (Section 21.4.1), 'a fair trial' (Section 21.4.2) and of freedom of religion (Section 22.5)). Even in the case of the right to life, the most fundamental of rights, although it has been stressed that an absolute right cannot be balanced against the public interest (*R (Bloggs61) v Secretary of State for the Home Dept* [2003] at [79]–[81]) the court will take into account the reasonableness of the risk assessment made by the authority in question including other demands on its resources. This relates to the larger topic of 'deference' (Sections 19.7.1, 22.5.2).

These manouvres have been justified by the repeated assertion that a principle of 'fair balance' between individual rights and the wider interests of society runs through the whole Convention (eg *MT (Algeria) v Secretary of State for the Home Office* [2010] 2 AC 110 [207], *Kay v Lambeth LBC* [2006] 2 AC 465 [32]). It has also been proclaimed that the ECHR is a 'living instrument' to be interpreted in the light of changing values and circumstances (*Austin v UK* (ECHR, 26 March 2012)). An extreme example of this approach would be to suggest that torture for a good purpose is lawful.

Under Article 15 of the Convention, states can 'derogate' (completely opt out) or 'reserve' (partly opt out) from many rights under the Convention 'in time of war or other public emergency threatening the life of the nation' but 'only to the extent strictly required by the exigencies of the situation' (Section 23.6). This does not apply to Article 2 (right to life), except in respect of a lawful act of war, Article 3 (torture and inhuman or degrading treatment or punishment), Article 4(1) (slavery or servitude) or Article 7 (retrospective punishment). The Human Rights Act 1998 reflects this (see ss 14–16). Moreover, a right may be overridden by another international obligation such as a UN resolution (see *R (Al Jedda) v Secretary of State for Defence* [2008] 1 AC 332).

The question of overriding protected rights will be discussed later in the context of the Human Rights Act 1998 (Section 22.5). In this section we shall outline the rights themselves. It must also be borne in mind that rights under particular articles may overlap. For example as well as Article 6: right to a fair trial, Article 5: personal liberty, and Article 8: privacy and family life also attract requirements of fair procedures in relevant court decisions.

21.4.1 Absolute (unqualified) rights subject to exceptions

Article 2: right to life

Except for capital punishment following criminal conviction, defence against unlawful violence, lawful arrest or prevention of unlawful escape, lawful action for quelling riot or insurrection.

Article 2 has been described as the most fundamental right requiring the highest level of scrutiny (*R (Bloggs61) v Secretary of State for the Home Dept* [2003]). It requires the state not to take life in any circumstances outside the designated exceptions. It also requires the state to provide a positive framework of laws to protect a person against a 'real and immediate risk to life' (*Osman v UK* (1998) 29 EHRR 245 [115] [116]). This duty is strongest when a person is in the custody or under the control of the state. The state must also hold an open, effective and thorough investigation into an unexplained death or serious injury to someone in its custody or care. (*See R (Reynolds) v IPPC* [2009] 3 All ER 237 [20]–[25]; *R (JL) v Secretary of State* [2009] 2 All ER 521: where there is evidence of egregious failures there should be a public hearing and legal representation.)

See *R (Middleton) v West Sussex Coroner* [2004] 2 All ER 465; *R (Hurst) v North London District Coroner* [2007] 2 All ER 1925; see also *R (D) v Secretary of State for the Home Dept* [2006] 3 All ER 946]: supervision of suicide risk; *Rabone v Pennine Care NHS Trust* [2012] 2 WLR 381: duty owed to voluntary mental patient to protect against real and immediate risk of suicide; *Van Colle v Chief Constable of Hertfordshire Police* [2006] 3 All ER 963: protection of witness; *R (AM) v Secretary of State* [2009] EWCA Civ. 219: privately run detention centre; allegations must be investigated); *Re Officer L* [2007] 4 All ER 965 police spy: no duty to protect against financial loss, *R (Gentle) v Prime Minister* [2008]: right to life of soldiers not engaged by decision to go to war in Iraq but issue of inadequate resources not addressed).

The duty depends on the fact of the particular case and is to take reasonable precautions. However the court will attach weight (deference: Section 19.7.1) to the professional judgement of the authority in question in relation to the resources available to it (*R (Bloggs61) v Secretary of State for the Home Department* [2003]: protection of prisoner against attack by other inmates: refusal to transfer to witness protection scheme: risk assessment by prison authorities upheld). Such deference does not apply where the state itself is the killer.

Article 2 has been interpreted narrowly so as not to authorise voluntary euthanasia (*R (Pretty) v DPP* [2002]): the right to life is the right not to be killed, not to have control over one's own life). In *Pretty* the court emphasised that the Convention is not meant to intervene in controversial moral issues around which there is no consensus. This is one way in which the court deals with the problem that it lacks democratic legitimacy.

Article 4(1): slavery, 4(2): forced or compulsory labour

Exceptions (to 4(2) only) are prison or parole, military service, emergency or calamity and 'normal civic obligations'.

Article 5: liberty and security of person

Except in prescribed cases in accordance with a procedure prescribed by law, this is an absolute right that cannot be overridden. The main exceptions are criminal convictions, disobedience to a court order, control of children, infection, mental health, alcoholism, drug addiction, vagrancy and in order to prevent illegal immigration or with a view to deportation or extradition. There are safeguards to ensure a speedy trial and adequate remedies against unlawful detention. A person arrested must be informed promptly of the reasons for the arrest, shall be brought promptly before a court and 'shall be entitled to take proceedings by which the lawfulness of his detention shall be decided speedily by a court and his release ordered if the detention is not lawful'.

The right to personal liberty has especially high importance and outside the exceptions Article 5 is absolute (see eg *Secretary of State for the Home Dept v JJ* [2008] 1 All ER 613 [37], [107]). However, Article 5 has been weakened by drawing a distinction between 'deprivation of liberty' and 'restrictions upon liberty'. The latter do not fall within Article 5 but fall within Protocol 4, Article 2, which the UK has not ratified, and so do not apply.

In *Austin v Metropolitan Police Comr* [2009] endorsed by the Strasbourg Court in *Austin v UK* [2012] the House of Lords held that police confinement of a crowd for two hours within a cordon on the road in uncomfortable conditions was only a 'restriction' on liberty and so was not unlawful. The Strasbourg court drawing an analogy with common temporary restrictions on movement on, for example public transport held that there was no deprivation of liberty where restrictions were unavoidable due to circumstances beyond the control of the authorities, were necessary to avert a real risk of serious injury or damage and were kept to the minimum required for that purpose (Section 23.7). Thus a public interest balancing test was applied to decide the nature of the right on the basis that the convention must reflect contemporary circumstances. In *HM v Switzerland* [2002] ECHR 39187/98 the European Court held that the placing of a child in a foster home was not a deprivation of liberty since it was done by a responsible authority in the child's own interests. These cases suggest that the underlying principle is whether the court approves of the purpose of the detention. In *Gillan v UK* [2010] ECHR App. No 158 the House of Lords held that a police 'stop and search' involving complete coercion for 30 minutes was not a deprivation of liberty (Section 24.6.4). The European Court condemned the police action under Article 8: privacy and did not decide this particular point. However it was suggested [57] that coercion of this kind did fall within Article 5. Perhaps unlike *Austin* there was no public need for the police action.

Article 7: no retrospective criminal laws

Except in respect of acts which were criminal when committed according to the general principles of law recognised by civilised nations (Section 9.6.1).

21.4.2 Rights with no exceptions

Article 3: torture or inhuman or degrading treatment or punishment

Torture consists of serious physical or psychological injury. Inhuman or degrading treatment is less (see eg *Tyrer v UK [1978] 2 EHRR 1: sensory deprivation of prisoners is inhuman treatment, Costello-Roberts v UK* [1993] 19 EHRR 112: *severe corporal* punishment is inhuman treatment. Inhumane or degrading treatment can in an extreme case include social deprivation *R (Limbuela) v Secretary of State for Social Security* [2007] 1 All ER 951: withdrawal of welfare support from asylum seekers where to do so would result in destitution). However it was emphasised in *Limbuela* that Article 3 does not confer a right to be provided with welfare services as such. There the inhuman treatment resulted from a specific exclusion of failed asylum seekers from the normal provision. Article 3 was engaged only when, taking account of all the claimant's circumstances, the claimant was reduced to a sense of despair and humiliation, for example by having no access to toilet or washing facilities (see *N v UK* [2008] 47 EHRR 865: no duty to ensure medical care).

Article 6: right to a fair trial

'In relation to civil rights and obligations and the determination of any criminal charges against them, individuals have a right to a fair trial in public before an independent and impartial tribunal established by law. The press and public may be excluded from all or any part of the proceedings in the interests of morals, public order or national security in a democratic society, where the interests of juveniles or the protection of the private lives of the parties so require, or to the extent strictly necessary in the opinion of the court in special circumstances where publicity would prejudice the interests of justice'. Judgement must be pronounced in public. However this does not apply where it would subvert the special reasons for holding the hearing in private. It is not settled whether a person may give up his right to a public hearing (see *In Re Trusts of X Charity* [2003] 1 WLR 2571).

Article 6 normally requires an adversarial procedure and 'equality of arms'((*Tariq v Home Office* [2012] 1 AC 452 [139]). There must be a hearing on all questions of fact by a body with ' full jurisdiction' (*R (Alconbury Developments) v Secretary of State* [2001]). Unlike domestic law Art 6 usually includes a right to legal representation (*R (G) v Governors of X School* [2012]).

The tribunal itself is independent. In this context the domestic law test of whether in the view of a 'fair-minded and informed observer' taken as knowing all the circumstances there is a 'real possibility' or 'real danger' of bias (Section 18.4) seems to satisfy Article 6 (see *R v Spear* [2003] 1 AC 734: courts martial: president and advocates part of military staff but independence protected).

Although Article 6 is absolute and cannot be overridden on public interest grounds the courts have introduced a public interest element into the ingredients of 'fairness'. The particular circumstances must be considered. Thus in *Secretary of State for the Home Dept v MB* [2008] 1 All ER 657 the House of Lords held that Article 6 allows a 'fair balance' to be struck between the interests of the community and those of the individual. For example in security cases a controversial 'closed material procedure' can sometimes be used where an accused person is denied the right to see all the evidence against him (Section 24.3.4).

In *Brown v Stott* [2001] the House of Lords held that a requirement to disclose the name of the driver involved in an accident was not in breach of the right against self-incrimination due to the public interest in reducing the high rate of death and injury on the roads but any unfairness must be compensated by other protection. (See also *O'Halloran and Francis v UK* [2007] 46 EHRR 397: speed cameras, duty to give information as to identity of driver; *Sheldrake v DPP* [2005] 1 AC 264: defendant must prove no risk of drink driving: not unfair since driver in best position to know. Contrast *AG's Reference (No 4 of 2002)* (ibid) (Section 24.6.2).)

In *A v Secretary of State for the Home Dept (No 2)* [2006] 2 AC 221 the House of Lords held that, in principle, evidence obtained by torture whether here or overseas was not admissible, regarding this as a 'constitutional principle'. Their Lordships disagreed as to the standard of proof. A majority held that it must be shown on balance of probabilities that the evidence was tainted, whereas the minority thought that it was enough to show that there was a 'real risk'. (See also *Secretary of State for the Home Dept v Rehman* [2003] 1 AC 153.) In Section 9.7 the Strasbourg Court held that the test is that of a real risk.

An important limit on Article 6 is that it applies only to 'civil rights and obligations'. A civil *obligation* arises where there is a legal duty towards the state, for example to pay taxes. The meaning of 'civil rights' is more difficult. The right in question must be recognized as such in domestic law. It includes but is not restricted to private law rights such as property (eg *Winterwerp v Netherlands* (1979) ECHR Ser A vol 33). However it does not apply to purely public law rights such as the right to procedural fairness or a legitimate expectation (Section 17.9), *R (Alconbury Developments) v Secretary of State* [2001].

The underlying principle seems to be that for a civil right the decision in question must involve some kind of entitlement. Therefore there is no civil right where entitlement to a benefit depends on a discretionary decision. For example in *Ali v Birmingham Corp* [2010] 2 All ER 175 a claim to be housed under homelessness legislation did not create a civil right because there was a substantial element of discretion. (See also *R (A) v Croydon LBC* [2009] 1 WLR 2577: provision of accommodation for children: no civil right.) Conversely in *Feldbrugge v The Netherlands* (1986) 8 EHRR 425 and *Salesi v Italy* (1993) 26 EHRR 187: entitlement to health insurance from the state on proof of certain facts was held to concern civil rights.)

The matter depends on the nature of the particular action. For example in *RB (Algeria) v Secretary of State* [2010] the claimant was facing deportation. The entry stay and deportation of an alien does not engage a civil right since an alien has no right to remain in the UK but depends on the discretionary powers of the Home Secretary (Section 9.3.2) (see also *R (BB) v SIAC* [2012] 1 All ER 229). Although an alien may have other rights concerning his or her treatment which might be incidentally affected, the claimant was not challenging his detention as such but only the fairness of the procedures used to deport him [90] [176][178] [228].

The removal of an existing benefit will normally engage a civil right. In *Tre Tractorer Aktebolag v Sweden* [1989] 13 EHRR 309 it was held that the revocation of a liquor licence engaged a civil right (see also *Bentham v Netherlands* [1986] 8 EHRR 1: petrol storage licence affecting operation of business). Dismissal from a particular job does not engage Article 6. However, a decision which imposes general harm on important personal or social interests including the right to work does so (See *R (G) v Governors of X School* [2012] 1 AC 167 statutory barring of a teacher from professional practice; *R (Wright) v Secretary of State* [2009] 2 All ER 129: placing of a care worker on a black list.)

The casual attitude of UK government to the qualities of independent decision making have raised issues involving Article 6. In *R (Alconbury Developments) v Secretary of State* [2001] there was a challenge to the standard procedure used by government in making planning, compulsory purchase and other land use decisions. This procedure involves an inquiry held by a semi-independent inspector who reports to the Secretary of State who may be the promoter of the decision or policy. The Court of Appeal held that the procedure violates the right to a fair trial before an independent tribunal. However the House of Lords drew back from holding that a widespread practice which fits the culture of UK government should be sacrificed. Their Lordships applied the 'curative principle' according to which the process should be looked at as a whole including any appeal or judicial review element (see also *R (G) v Governors of X School* [2012] at [84]). They held that although the procedure itself was not independent, any failure was put right because judicial review was available. A problem with this is that judicial review is not comprehensive in relation to questions of fact (Section 17.7.2) and so does not seem to satisfy the requirement of Art 6 that an independent tribunal must have full jurisdiction. However this has been dealt with by defining full jurisdiction as the virtually meaningless 'full jurisdiction to deal with the case as the nature of the decision requires' (see *Runa Begum v Tower Hamlets London BC* [2003] 1 All ER 731, 736 per Lord Bingham).In this way the limited scope of judicial review in relation to findings of fact has sometimes been held to satisfy Article 6. The courts have made a distinction between, on the one hand, a decision where a citizen has a definite entitlement on proof of certain facts (eg to a pension based on prescribed contributions) and, on the other hand, a decision where the facts are part of a larger policy or politically oriented process where the decision maker has to balance facts against competing considerations and has a discretion as to the outcome, for example a decision to build a motorway (*Alconbury*, above).

In the first 'factual' kind of case, the reach of judicial review into the facts is not far enough so that an independent procedure such as a tribunal is required which can examine all questions of fact (*Runa Begum*, above, *Tsfayo v UK* (2009) 48 EHRR 18). This type of case arises where there is 'self-regulation' within an organisation (Section 20.4). In the second 'policy' kind of case, it has been held that since respect for democratic decision making is involved, judicial review may suffice as a safety net. It can be decided which category a case falls within only by looking closely at the particular decision-making process and its goals. It is clear that the wider the view taken on the question of the meaning of 'civil right' (above), the more likely it is that the case will fall within the 'policy' category (*Runa Begum* (above) [5]).

In a criminal case Article 6 requires further safeguards. These include a right 'to be informed promptly and in a language he understands and in detail, of the nature and cause of the accusation', adequate time and facilities to prepare a defence, a right to choose a lawyer and free legal assistance 'when the interests of justice so require', a right to call witnesses and to examine opposing witnesses on equal terms and a right to an interpreter. However 'charged with a criminal offence' has been defined narrowly to exclude matters relating to sentencing and bail (*Phillips v UK* [2001] NLJ 1282; *R (DPP) v Havering Magistrates Court* [2001] 3 All ER 997).

Article 6 is primarily concerned with procedural matters. It may sometimes be difficult to distinguish procedural matters from matters of substantive law which might engage other parts of the Convention but not Article 6. For example in *Z v UK* [2002] 34 EHRR 3 a local authority was held to be in breach of Article 3 for failing to protect children but not in breach of Article 6. The domestic law of negligence had failed to protect the children, not because of any procedural immunity but because of the limited scope of negligence law itself in relation to the duties of public bodies (Section 19.2). The same applies to the non-liability of the Crown in certain cases (*Matthews v Ministry of Defence* [2003]; Section 14.5).

Article 12: right to marry and found a family according to national laws governing the exercise of the right

In *R (Baiai) v Secretary of State for the Home Dept* [2007] 4 All ER 199 it was held that the courts must be vigilant to protect the right to marry but that it carries less weight than the fundamental rights of personal liberty, freedom of expression and access to the courts. In that case a requirement of Home Office consent for non-Anglican marriages by immigrants was held invalid on the basis that the immigration authority could only interfere with the right to marry in the case of a sham marriage and it must be shown that the marriages targeted made substantial inroads into the scheme of immigration control. However 'marriage' has been narrowly interpreted as referring only to traditional marriages between biological men and women leaving it to individual states to determine policy on this sensitive issue (eg *Wilkinson v Kitzinger* [2006] *Times* 9 August: civil partnerships).

Protocol 1, Article 2: education

No person shall be denied the right to education. In the exercise of any functions which it assumes in relation to education and to teaching, the State shall respect the right of parents to ensure such education and teaching is in conformity with their own religious and philosophical convictions.

This is a limited right. It does not confer a right to be educated as such. Its primary purpose is to combat state discrimination and indoctrination. It does not require the state to provide education. It means only a right not be excluded from whatever education the state chooses to provide (*A v Head Teacher and Governors of Lord Grey School* [2004] 4 All ER 587). Nor does it include a right to state funding (*R (Douglas) v North Tyneside DC* [2004]). It treats the right as that of the parent rather than that of the child itself, an attitude that could be regarded as misplaced.

It also raises the conflict between individualistic liberalism and liberal pluralism (Section 2.3) since religious education might favour repression against individuals. It probably prevents the state from outlawing 'faith schools' but is subject to limits on the manifestation of religion (Section 21.4.3).

Moreover the UK has made a reservation:

only so far as compatible with 'the provision of efficient instruction and training and the avoidance of unreasonable public expenditure'.

Protocol 1, Article 3: free elections to the legislature at reasonable intervals by secret ballot

Although it does no directly create a right to vote this provision requires a state to justify restrictions upon voting rights (*Hirst v UK (No 2)* [2004]) (Section 12.6).

Protocol 6: abolition of the death penalty in peacetime

Although this Protocol was not itself incorporated into the Human Rights Act 1998, the Act abolished the last remaining death penalty provisions in the UK (s 21(5)).

21.4.3   Rights subject to being overridden

As we shall see (Section 22.5) the court is required according to the principle of 'proportionality' to weigh the importance of the right in question against the public interest claimed by the state and also the rights of others. In this section we shall concentrate on the rights themselves. This group of rights is vague and difficult to define. Moreover we have seen that the courts sometimes weigh competing interests even where there is no explicit requirement to do so (Section 21.4.1). For these reasons the judicial process is especially problematic in this area.

Article 8: respect for privacy, family life, home and correspondence

> Overrides. There shall be no interference by a public authority with an Article 8 right except such as is in accordance with the law and is necessary in a democratic society in the interests of national security, public safety or the economic well being of the country, for the prevention of disorder or crime, for the protection of health or morals, or for the protection of the rights and freedoms of others.

Article 8 is especially vague and wide ranging. Indeed, unlike most of the other rights which are phrased as definite entitlements, Article 8 gives only an entitlement to 'respect' meaning that decision makers must give it particular weight. It has three interlinking aspects. Firstly it protects against intrusion, surveillance and disclosure of information about oneself (Sections 22.6, 23.6). Secondly it concerns intimate family relationships. It arises, for example in immigration cases which separate partners, or close relatives or disrupt a child's education (eg *R (Aguila Quila) v Secretary of State for the Home Dept* [2012] 1 All ER 1011: forced marriages: measures excessive, see also Section 9.6.7.1). In this context, as well as giving substantive protection against disproportionate measures, Article 8 requires a fair procedure before an independent body (*IR (Sri Lanka) v Secretary of State for the Home Dept* [2011] 4 All ER 908 (Section 9.6.6). (We have seen that Art 6 is not applicable to the expulsion of aliens Section 21.4.2.)

Thirdly Article 8 embraces respect for personal autonomy and identity, including reputation (*Pfiefer v Austria* (2007) 48 EHRR 175 [33]), social relationships including employment but only in so far as it affects wider relationships, gender, sexual preferences, culture and lifestyle: 'those features which are integral to a person's identity or ability to function socially as a person' (Lord Bingham in *R (Razgar) v Secretary of State for the Home Dept* [2004] at [9]; see also *S v UK* [2008] at [19]: 'the manner in which a person presents himself to the state and to others'; *von Hanover v Germany* [2005] at [50]: 'a person's physical and psychological integrity;…the development, without outside interference, of the personality of each individual in his relations with other human beings'). There is therefore a social zone in a public context, which may fall within the scope of 'private life'.

For example *Gillan and Quinton v UK* [2010] ECHR App no 158/05: police 'stop and search' of journalists (Section 23.7.2); *Wainright v Home Office* [2003] 4 All ER 969: strip searches; *R (Purdy) v DPP* [2009]: disability and the manner of one's death; *S v UK* [2008] 25 BHRC 537: police retention of DNA samples; *Autronic AG v Switzerland* [1990] 1 EHRR 485: immigrant lifestyle; access to satellite TV from overseas; *R (AB) v Secretary of State* [2010] 2 All ER 151: refusal to transfer transsexual prisoner to woman's prison; goes to heart of identity; *R (L) v Metropolitan Police Comr* [2010] 1 All ER 113: 'enhanced criminal record certificate'; *Aguila Quila v Secretary of State for the Home Dept* [2012]: immigrant's right to settle and marry.

Article 8 applies to nuisances and environmental pollution, although the courts are likely to give considerable weight to the limited resources of public authorities and to the decisions of government agencies concerning other aspects of the public interest (*Guerra v Italy* [1998] 26 EHRR 357; *Hatton v UK* [2003] 37 EHRR 28; *Marcic v Thames Water Utilities* [2004]). It applies to the restriction of employment, where there is a stigma or social exclusion (*R (Wright) v Secretary of State for Health* [2009]: Child Abuse Register.

Article 8 is therefore very wide and susceptible to the different customs and values of individual states. It broadly reflects Mill's version of liberalism, namely that in the context of the good of society as a whole, people are happier when they choose for themselves what form of life and lifestyle to adopt (Section 2.3.3). The European Court therefore gives a 'margin of appreciation' to the individual state as to how it applies Article 8 provided that the state does not violate widely shared values (eg *Rees v UK* [1986] 9 EHRR 56: transsexual; *Olsson v Sweden* (1988) ECHR Ser. A vol. 130: child care).

The UK courts seem reluctant to treat Article 8 liberally.

▶ In *M v Secretary of State for Work and Pensions* [2006] 4 All ER 929 Lord Nicholls and Lord Mance (at [24]–[29]) took the view that 'family life' did not include same-sex couples on the ground that there was no Europe-wide consensus on this matter and that Article 8 does not confer a general right to self-determination.

▶ In *Marper v UK* [2008] the European Court condemned the UK practice of retaining indefinitely DNA samples from people arrested or charged with offences irrespective of whether they were subsequently convicted. A majority of the House of Lords had upheld the practice in *R (S) v Chief Constable of South Yorkshire Police* [2004] 4 All ER 193. Their lordships held that the practice was not a significant enough intrusion to fall within Article 8 and in any case was overridden by the public interest in detecting crime. The European Court held that the UK policy was more extreme than practices elsewhere in Europe. The difference between the two courts seems to lie mainly in the English judges placing less importance on the offence to human dignity involved (Lady Hale dissenting), and having greater confidence in the integrity and competence of the police not to misuse the power.

▶ The Crime and Security Act 2010 and the Protection of Freedoms Act 2012 Part 1 (not yet in force) respond to the European Court's decision by regulating what are still intrusive powers. Samples can lawfully be taken following an arrest or charge for a 'recordable' offence (one with a possible sentence of imprisonment) with consent. A speculative search for such material can also be carried out. Material unlawfully taken or taken in connection with a false arrest must always be destroyed. However samples can be retained indefinitely where the person was convicted of a recordable offence except for relatively minor juvenile offences. ('Conviction' includes a caution, warning or reprimand, or acquittal because of insanity or a disability.)

- In the case of a 'qualifying offence': serious crimes of violence, sexual offences and terrorist offences, samples can be retained for designated purposes such as criminal investigations or national security but in the absence of a conviction can be kept only for a limited time usually 3 years. The time limit can be extended by a District Judge or Magistrate for up to two years subject to a right of appeal to the Crown Court.
- The 2012 Act creates a 'Commissioner for the Retention and Use of Biometric Material' who is required to review the operation of the system and to give consent in certain cases. The Commissioner is appointed by and reports to the Secretary of State but appears to have no security of tenure. The Commissioner's report must be laid before Parliament but can be censored by the Secretary of State on national security and 'public interest' grounds.
- In *R (Countryside Alliance) v A-G* [2008] 2 All ER 95 it was argued that the Hunting Act 2004, which outlaws hunting wild mammals with dogs, violated Article 8 in that there was a right to participate in hunting as an aspect of countryside life and as a social activity integral to the personality. The House of Lords held that the Act does not attract Article 8 because at the heart of Article 8 is the idea of the personal and intimate whereas hunting is carried out in public. Moreover hunters were not a distinctive group so as to claim an identity analogous to an ethnic group. Some of the claimants were workers who serviced the hunt. It was held that Article 8 can apply to loss of livelihood but only where the loss of a job seriously impinges on the person's social relationships or status in society or involves loss of a home.

Article 8 protects the inviolability of the home. It does not normally confer a positive right to be provided with a home but only a right to be protected as to the use of an existing home, for example against eviction (*Kay v Lambeth LBC* [2006] at [191]–[193]; *N v Secretary of State for the Home Dept* [2005] 2 AC 296). However where a public authority evicts a tenant the court must look at all the circumstances in the light of Article 8 in order to decide whether the eviction is proportionate (*Manchester City Council v Pinnock* [2010] 3 WLR 1441: anti social behaviour of tenant's children. In that case a 9 member Supreme Court overturned three earlier House of Lords decisions. See Latham, 'Talking Without Speaking: Hearing Without listening? Evictions, the UK Top Court and the European Court of Human Rights' [2011] PL 730).

In cases involving especially vulnerable people Article 8, referring as it does to 'respect', may impose a positive duty on the state to provide a benefit (eg *R (Bernard) v Enfield LBC* [2002] EWCA 2282: disabled with children; *Anufrijeva v Southwark LBC* (2004): asylum seekers). However there must be culpability in the sense of a deliberate or negligent failure to act which has foreseeably serious consequences (*Anufrijeva*). The courts are reluctant to impose a positive obligation.

Medical treatment is a case in point. In *R (Condliffe) v North Staffs Primary Health Care Trust* [2012] the question was whether a hospital policy to refuse gastric by-pass surgery to combat obesity except in special cases to be decided solely on clinical grounds was valid in domestic law (Section 17.9.2) and also under Article 8. It was held that the court should be cautious in imposing a positive obligation where state benefits are concerned and that respect for family life was satisfied by the hospitals policy which was fair [34][40]. Cases involving the allocation of scarce resources are better decided by a democratically accountable body. (See also *McDonald v Kensington and Chelsea Royal London BC* [2011] 4 All ER 811).

There is a positive obligation on the state to enable the expression of personal lifestyles by protecting Article 8 rights against violation by private bodies (*Von Hannover v Germany* [2004] 40 EHRR 1 [57]). In *YL v Birmingham City Council* (2007]) Lady Hale (dissenting on other matters (Section 22.4.1) emphasised that the state has such a positive duty in relation to the care of the elderly. Thus the state may be required to regulate private care homes so as to ensure that they respect the Article 8 rights of their residents.

Article 9: freedom of thought, conscience and religion

> Overrides. Freedom to manifest one's religion or beliefs shall be subject only to such limitations as are prescribed by law and are necessary in a democratic society in the interests of public safety, for the protection of public order, health or morals or for the protection of the rights and freedoms of others.

This includes a right to manifest religion or belief in worship, teaching, practice and observance. In order to avoid intolerance the courts have not attempted to assess the validity of a religious belief beyond deciding whether it is genuinely held. Thus in *R (Williamson) v Secretary of State for Education and Employment* [2005] which concerned a Christian sect that practiced 'light' corporal punishment the House of Lords refused to define 'religion' in a restrictive way or pronounce on the validity of a religion but indicated that the 'manifestation' of religion, meaning the interaction with others, was subject to implicit limits based on 'seriousness, cogency and compatibility with human dignity' ([64], [76]). For this reason the practice was held to violate the ECHR.

Thus despite the importance of respect for beliefs there is a tendency towards imposing orthodoxy by assessing the claimant's practices against those of dominant groups within the community (eg *R (Begum) v Head Teacher and Governors of Denbigh High School* [2007]: extreme version of Muslim dress lawfully forbidden in school) or by giving special weight to the majority opinion represented by Parliament (eg *R (Williamson) v Secretary of State for Education and Employment* [2005], [50]–[51]: *Otto Preminger Institut v Austria* [1994] 19 EHRR 34: majority Catholic susceptibilities protected against offensive film). Moreover although Lord Bingham in *Begum* (111) emphasised the pluralistic, multicultural nature of our society, religion is often regarded – as in the Protestant tradition but certainly not universally – as essentially a private matter (*Williamson* [15]–[19]).

In the employment sphere the right to manifest religion has been held to be violated only where the employer fails to take reasonable steps to accommodate the religious requirements of the employee with its own interests. In *Copsey v WBB Devon Clays Ltd* [2005] an employee was dismissed for refusing to work on a Sunday. The employer had compelling economic reasons for Sunday working, had engaged in a long consultation process on the matter and had offered the employee an alternative position which was refused. The Court of Appeal held that in these circumstances Article 9 had not been violated. Mummery LJ appeared to go further, indicating that Article 9 was not engaged at all by requiring work which interfered with the manifestation of religion. These cases provide another illustration of the avoidance of confronting a clash between a right and other public interest concerns by defining the right narrowly.

Article 10: freedom of expression

This right shall include freedom to hold opinions and to receive and impart information and ideas without interference by public authority and regardless of frontiers. This article shall not prevent states from requiring the licensing of broadcasting, television or cinema enterprise.

Overrides. The exercise of these freedoms, since it carries with it duties and responsibilities, may be subject to such formalities, conditions, restrictions or penalties as are prescribed by law and are necessary in a democratic society in the interests of national security, territorial integrity or public safety, for the prevention of disorder or crime, for the protection of health or morals, for the protection of the reputation or rights of others, for preventing the disclosure of information received in confidence or for maintaining the authority and impartiality of the judiciary.

Freedom of expression is discussed in Chapter 23.

Article 11: freedom of peaceful assembly and association

Everyone has the right to freedom of peaceful assembly and to freedom of association with others, including the right to form and to join trade unions for the protection of his interests.

Overrides. No restrictions shall be placed on these rights other than such as are prescribed by law and are necessary in a democratic society in the interests of national security or public safety, for the prevention of disorder or crime, for the protection of health or morals or for the protection of the rights and freedoms of others. This article shall not prevent the imposition of lawful restrictions on the exercise of those rights by members of the armed forces, of the police or of the administration of the state.

Freedom of assembly is also discussed in Chapter 23.

Protocol 1, Article 1: private property

Every natural or legal person is entitled to the peaceful enjoyment of his possessions. No one shall be deprived of his possessions except in the public interest and subject to the conditions provided for by law and by the general principles of international law. The preceding provisions shall not, however, in any way impair the right of a State to enforce such laws as it deems necessary to control the use of property in accordance with the general interest or to secure the payment of taxes and or other contributions or penalties.

This protects property rights against confiscation without compensation but does not confer a positive right to acquire property (*Marckx v Belgium* (1979) 2 EHRR 330). Restrictions on the use of property imposed in the public interest, for example environmental and rent controls, are valid without compensation, although the line between use and confiscation may be difficult to draw (*Mellacher v Austria* [1989] 12 EHRR 391). Moreover the courts are not willing to use the Convention in cases where a property right is restricted by the exercise of other property rights (see *Aston Cantlow and Wilmcote with Billesley Parochial Church Council v Wallbank* [2003] 3 All ER 1213: charge to repair church roof taking effect as a common law right). Property rights probably have a lower level of protection than the other human rights and the rights of the state to override them are wider and less specific (the concept of 'fair balance' rather than proportionality is used (*Fredin v Sweden* [1991] ECHR Ser. A 192 1–69; *R (Countryside Alliance) v A-G* [2008].

21.4.4 Discrimination

Article 14: discrimination

> The enjoyment of the rights and freedoms set forth in this Convention shall be secured without discrimination on any ground such as sex, race, colour, language, religion, political or other opinion, national or social origin, association with a national minority, property, birth or other status. However by virtue of Article 16: 'Articles 10, 11 and 14 shall not prevent a state from imposing restrictions on the political activities of aliens.'

As Baroness Hale pointed out in *Re G (Adoption) (Unmarried Couple)* (2009) [122] the protection of unpopular minorities is a particular duty of the courts. Article 14 was described by Lord Nicholls in *Ghaidan v Mendosa* as fundamental to the rule of law and calling for close scrutiny ([9], [19]) and by Lady Hale as 'essential to democracy which is founded on the principle that each individual has equal value' [132].

However the ECHR does not outlaw all discrimination. Article 14 applies only where discrimination takes place in relation to one of the other Convention rights, although no such right need actually have been violated. For example although there is no right to be housed, refusing housing for discriminatory reasons is unlawful (*R (Morris) v Westminster City Council* [2005] 1 All ER 351: refusal of housing because dependent child had no immigration rights; *Ghaidan v Mendoza* [2004]: inheritance by gay partner). However a tenuous link will not suffice (*M v Secretary of State for Work and Pensions* [2006] 4 All ER 929: differential maintenance payments).

Since it refers to 'such as' Article 14 extends to forms of discrimination other than those listed (eg *A v Secretary of State* [2005]: nationality; *Ghaidan v Mendoza*: sexual orientation; *R (Douglas) v North Tyneside DC* (2004): age; *Wandsworth LBC v Michalack* [2002] 4 All ER 1136: family membership). It is not easy to identify its limits. In *R (S) v Chief Constable of South Yorkshire Police* (2004) the House of Lords took the view that the discrimination must relate to a 'personal characteristic or status' shared by the disadvantaged group as opposed to a matter of behaviour only. Article 14 was therefore not engaged by a policy of retaining DNA samples taken lawfully from suspects who were later found to be innocent since the general category of 'innocent persons' was not capable of being a protected category. In another instance 'rough sleeper' was held not to be a protected category (*M v Secretary of State for Work and Pensions [2006] 4 All ER 929*), nor was the hunting community (*R (Countryside Alliance) v A-G* [2008].

On the other hand 'overseas resident' and 'person responsible for a child under a residence order' have been held to be protected as having different legal rights and duties from UK residents and natural parents respectively (*R (Carson) v Secretary of State for Work and Pensions* [2006] 1 AC 173: claim to pension; *Francis v Secretary of State for Work and Pensions* [2006] 1 All ER 748: maternity grant). Being married is a status because it attracts special legal rights and duties and so is being unmarried (*Re G (Adoption) (Unmarried Couple)* (2009). A protected category can therefore be something voluntarily assumed.

It is difficult to see an underlying rationale in these cases such as protecting a sense of identity. However certain 'suspect categories', race and sex being pre-eminent, which are central to identity and over which the victim has no choice, enjoy a high standard of protection in that especially strong reasons are required to justify discrimination on those grounds (see Lord Walker in *Carson*; see also Lord Carson at [15]–[17], [32].

To discriminate is to treat a person worse than others who are in all relevant respects the same; in other words like cases must be treated alike. It is also discrimination to fail to treat differently persons whose situations are significantly different (*Thlmmensos v Greece* (2000) 31 EHRR 411 [44]. Since many government decisions treat different groups of people differently the problem is to decide what is a relevant respect. This relates to the purpose of the decision in question. Is it a legitimate government purpose (below)?

Both direct and indirect discrimination fall within Article 14. Indirect discrimination is where a particular group is not directly targeted but is adversely affected more than others by a restriction, for example housing conditions that are unsuited to the family lives of a particular ethnic group. Under the domestic law of discrimination (outside this book) most direct discrimination is always unlawful but the looser provisions of Article 14 apply to both kinds (see eg recognising however that they overlap).

Although Article 14 has no express overrides, discrimination is nevertheless lawful if it can be 'objectively justified'. This means that the discrimination must pursue a legitimate aim and there must be reasonable proportionality (Section 22.7), (*Belgian Linguistics Case* [1968] 1 EHRR 252. (See *R (Hooper) v Secretary of State for Work and Pensions* [2006] 1 All ER 487: widows' pensions justified as redressing past unfairness to widows; *Wandsworth LBC v Michalak* [2002] 4 All ER 1136: distant relative claiming to succeed to tenancy: restriction justified as means of rationing public resources; *A v Secretary of State* [2005]: discrimination lacked rational connection (Section 22.7.1); *In re G (Adoption) Unmarried Couples* [2009]: restriction unreasonably inflexible). One way of rationalising this is to argue that 'discrimination' in itself means making an *unjustified* distinction which violates the principle of equality. Another is to rely on the principle of balance which is said to underlie the Convention as a whole (Section 21.4).

Summary

▶ The human rights debate involves attempts to accommodate competing and incommensurable values without any coherent overarching principle to enable a choice to be made. It is therefore arguable that an elected body rather than a court should have the last word. The Human Rights Act 1998 has attempted a compromise by leaving Parliament the last word but giving the court power to influence Parliament.

▶ Freedom in the common law is residual in the sense that one can do anything unless there is a specific law to the contrary. I suggested that this is an inadequate method of safeguarding important liberties. There is a debate as to the extent to which the common law embodies the principles of the ECHR and it is suggested that there are important differences in the approaches of the two systems.

▶ The ECHR as such is not strictly binding upon English courts but can be taken into account where the law is unclear or where a judge has discretionary powers. The individual can petition the European Court of Human Rights, the decisions of which are binding in international law but, unlike those of the European Court of Justice (in relation to European Union law), are not legally binding in domestic law.

▶ The Human Rights Act 1998, while not incorporating the Convention as such, has given the main rights created by the ECHR effect in domestic law. UK legislation must be interpreted to be compatible with Convention rights but parliamentary supremacy is preserved.

Summary cont'd

▶ Most Convention rights are negative rights which restrain the state from interfering with them. Some have a positive aspect by imposing a duty on the state to ensure that the right in question is respected.

▶ Some rights, notably deprivation of liberty, are narrowly defined; others, notably privacy and family life, are broad and vague.

▶ Some of the rights are absolute and cannot be overridden by public interest considerations, although they might be defined narrowly in the light of the public interest. Other rights are subject to exceptions, and an important group of rights can be overridden on prescribed grounds of the public interest or of other rights.

▶ Some rights, notably the right to life, protection against torture and against deprivation of liberty, freedom of expression and non-discrimination have an especially high status. The right to property may have a lower level of protection than other rights.

Exercises

21.1 'Human Rights are permeated with irresolvable disagreement as to what they mean, how they apply, and as to the nature of disputes about them. The courts are therefore a hopelessly inadequate mechanism for resolving human rights problems.' Discuss.

21.2 Jones is holding a group of people in a secret location. The police arrest him. He says that his prisoners will be blown up by a bomb in one hour. Can the police use techniques of simulated drowning ('waterboarding'), which they believe to have been recommended by military intelligence services worldwide, to discover the whereabouts of the prisoners?

21.3 The common law doctrine of fairness has been said to accord with the 'spirit' of Article 6 (*Secretary of State for the Home Dept v MB* [2008] at[24]). Do you agree? What differences if any are there between the two?

20.4 Explain the scope of Article 14 of the ECHR. Does it go far enough in combating discrimination?

20.5 'Democracy is the will of the people but the people may not will to invade those rights which are fundamental to democracy itself' (Lady Hale in *R (Countryside Alliance) v A-G* [2008]). Discuss.

20.6 (i) What is meant by a deprivation of liberty under the ECHR?

(ii) Jack, who suffers from memory loss, is an outpatient at an NHS hospital. After his latest visit the hospital authorities lock Jack in a small office for three hours in order to prevent him from leaving the hospital until his wife arrives to take him home. Advise Jack, who strongly objects to this as to any rights he might have under the ECHR. What additional facts might influence your answer?

21.7 (i) Trebangor Health Authority provide fertility services only to married couples. Advise Beth a single person as to her rights under the ECHR.

(ii) Trebangor City Council refuses to provide Harry with a Council House on the ground that he is an ex offender. Mary is evicted from her council house for the same reasons. Advise Harry and Mary as to their rights under the ECHR.

(iii) Trebangor also refuses a council house to two sisters who wish to live together on the ground that they are not 'traditional families'. Advise them as to their rights under the ECHR.

Further reading

Alder, 'The Sublime and the Beautiful: Incommensurability and Human Rights' [2006] PL 697

Amos, *Human Rights Law* (Hart 2006)

Arden, 'On Liberty and the European Convention on Human Rights', in Andenas and Fairgrieve (eds), *Tom Bingham and the Transformation of the Law* (Oxford University Press 2009)

Campbell, Ewing and Tomkins (eds), *Sceptical Essays on Human Rights* (Oxford University Press 2001) chs 3, 6, 7

Elias, 'The Rise of the Strasbourgeoisie: Judicial Activism and the ECHR' *Statute Law Society* (2009)

Gearty, *Can Human Rights Survive?* (Hamlyn Lectures, Cambridge University Press 2006)

Harvey, 'Talking about Human Rights' (2004) EHRLR 500

Hill and Sandberg, 'Is Nothing Sacred? Clashing Symbols in a Secular World' [2007] PL 488

Hooker, 'Griffin on Human Rights' (2010) 30 OJLS 193

Laws, 'The Constitution: Morals and Right' [1996] PL 622

Leader, 'Freedom and Futures: Personal Priorities, Institutional Demands and Freedom of Religion' (2007) 70 MLR 713

Loughlin, *Foundations of Public Law* (Oxford University Press 2010) ch 12

McCormick, *Institutions of Law* (Oxford University Press 2007) ch 11

Poole, 'Of Headscarves and Heresies: The *Denbigh High School* Case and Public Authority Decision Making under the Human Rights Act' [2005] PL 685

Sales, 'The General and the Particular: Parliament and the Courts under the Scheme of the European Convention on Human Rights', in Andenas and Fairgrieve (eds), *Tom Bingham and the Transformation of the Law* (Oxford University Press 2009)

Waldron, *Law and Disagreement* (Oxford University Press 1999)

Williams, 'Human Rights and Law: Between Sufferance and Insufferability' (2007) 123 LQR 133

Chapter 22

The Human Rights Act 1998

The scope of the Act

As we saw in Chapter 21 the Human Rights Act 1998 (HRA) does not incorporate the European Convention on Human Rights (ECHR) as such. It gives rights (listed in Sch 1) drawn from the Convention the status of 'Convention rights', with defined consequences in UK law. All legislation must be interpreted in accordance with Convention rights and the Act provides remedies enforceable in the courts against public authorities who violate Convention rights. The Act does not override Parliamentary supremacy (Section 8.5.5). It has not incorporated Article 1 (duty to secure to everyone within the jurisdiction the rights and freedoms under the Convention) or Article 13 (effective domestic remedies for breach of the Convention). It is claimed that the Act itself achieves these aims even though Convention rights must give way to Acts of Parliament. The Act applies to all legislation whether made before or after it came into force in October 2000 (s 3(2)(a)). However it applies only to *events* that took place after it came into force. There is an exception in the case of a defence to proceedings brought by a public authority. This applies whenever the action complained of took place.

The extent to which the HRA is radical is controversial. The reasons for introducing it have never been made clear and the Act is another example of the casual nature of constitutional reform in the UK. It was not introduced as a British Bill of Rights but more as a tidying up and cost-saving operation to ensure that UK law was coordinated with the ECHR (*Rights brought Home: The Human Rights Bill* (1997) Cm 3782).

On the one hand according to Lord Hoffmann (*R v Secretary of State for the Home Dept, ex p Simms* [1999] at 412–13) the Act does little more than reinforce the existing law. Thus it provides a specific text, much of it in his view reflecting common law principles; it enacts the existing 'principle of legality' according to which fundamental rights can be overridden only by clear statutory language (Section 6.7); and it forces Parliament to face squarely what it is doing. In *R (Alconbury Developments Ltd) v Secretary of State for the Environment, Transport and the Regions [2001]* at [129] Lord Hoffmann remarked that the Act 'was no doubt intended to strengthen the rule of law but not to inaugurate the rule of lawyers'. Similarly in *R v Lambert* [2001] 3 All ER 577 03, Lord Hope emphasised the need to respect the will of the legislature and to preserve the integrity of our statute law.

On the other hand in *R v DPP, ex p Kebelene* [1999] Lord Hope emphasised that a generous approach should be taken to the scope of fundamental rights and freedoms, and in *R v Lambert* (581) Lord Slynn remarked:

> it is clear that the 1998 Act must be given its full import and that long or well entrenched ideas may have to be put aside, sacred calves culled.

More grandiosely in *A v Secretary of State* [2005] at [14] Lord Bingham said that 'the courts are charged by Parliament with delineating the boundaries of a rights based democracy'.

According to Clayton (2010) the impact of the Act has been important but limited. A restrained approach has been predominant. The Act has not changed English law in any fundamental respect although the ECHR's principle of *proportionality* has added a significant element to the law. Clayton suggests that the HRA has 'required the courts to articulate substantive values (which may be regarded as a fundamental aspect of the rule of law)'. However they were already doing this in cases such as *Anisminic* (Section 19.7), *Ridge v Baldwin* (Section 18.3) and *Conway v Rimmer* (Section 23.3). Without the power to overturn statutes it is difficult to regard the Act as a British Bill of Rights although it has been suggested that respect for the courts has a similar effect even without such a power (see Klug, 2007).

Decisions and opinions of the European Court of Human Rights must be taken into account, but they are not binding (s 2(1)). However the courts have closely followed the case law of the European Court. It has been asserted that an action cannot be unlawful under the HRA unless the UK would be liable in Strasbourg, so that the UK courts cannot develop independent human rights principles. In *R (Ullah) v Special Adjudicator* [2004], regarded as the leading case, the House of Lords held that 'the duty of national courts is to keep pace with the Strasbourg jurisprudence as it evolves over time: no more but certainly no less', and to follow a clear and consistent line of Strasbourg cases [20].

In *R (S) v Chief Constable of South Yorkshire Police* [2004] the House of Lords considered that the ECHR should be applied on a uniform basis throughout member states. This rejected the approach taken in the Court of Appeal that English law might develop its own higher standard of human rights. (See also *Ambrose (Procurator Fiscal) v Harris* [2011] 1 WLR 2435; *R (Begum) v Head Teacher and Governors of Denbigh High School* [2006] at [29]; *R (Pretty) v DPP* [2002]; *R(Gentle) v Prime Minister* [2008] at [56]; *R (Countryside Commission) v AG* [2008]; *R (Smith) v Secretary of State for Defence* [2010] 3 All ER 1067.)

This cautious approach could be defended because it supports rule of law concern with certainty, ensures that the Convention as an international agreement will be consistently applied and restrains the courts from making political judgements. On the other hand the Act itself does not suggest the *Ullah* principle and the ECHR does not require uniformity between member states (Section 22.7.2). Moreover, the Strasbourg court tends to develop broad principles rather than the facts of specific cases favoured by the common law so that UK courts might be overcautious (Clayton 2010).

The '*Ullah* principle' leaves some room for manoeuvre and to a limited extent the courts have gone outside *Strasbourg* cases. In *Manchester City Council v Pinnock* [2010] 3 WLR 1441 [48] the Supreme Court said that to be bound by Strasbourg:

> 'would destroy the constructive dialogue with the European Court which is of value to the development of Convention law. Where, however, there is a clear and consistent line of decisions whose effect is not inconsistent with some fundamental substantive or procedural aspect of our law, and whose reasoning does not appear to overlook or misunderstand some argument or point of principle, ... it would be wrong for this court not to follow that line'. (See, eg, *Barrett v Enfield* LBC [2001]: negligence liability and *R v Spear* [2003]: independence of courts martial: misunderstandings of UK law later corrected by ECtHR, *Z v UK* [2002], *Cooper v UK* [2004] 39 EHRR 8.)

Moreover the European Court allows a 'margin of appreciation' to individual states to apply the Convention to their own circumstances (Section 21.3). Where this is so the court can apply the Convention in accordance with its own values and constitutional traditions unless these violate widely shared values. Thus in *Re G (Adoption) (Unmarried Couple)* (2009) the House of Lords decided that a restriction in Northern Ireland upon unmarried couple adopting a child was contrary to Article 14 (discrimination) even though Strasbourg had not ruled on the matter [29]–[38], [116]–[121].

The UK courts approach to human rights issues does not display a clear philosophy. This is no more than one might expect from the pragmatic common law tradition coupled with the evasive nature of the Human Rights Act. Some judges, notably Lord Hope, Sir Stephen Sedley, Sir John Laws and the late Lord Steyn, appear to take a traditional liberal standpoint and welcome the notion of constitutional rights, which they claim depends on the common law as much as the Human Rights Act. Others such as Lady Hale, Lord Bingham (deceased) and Lord Hoffman (retired) also take a liberal stance but may give greater emphasis to the importance of democratic decision making. Academic commentators disagree. Ewing (2010), for example regards the Act as futile since it is permeated with discretion. Other commentators appear to support an interventionist judiciary which of course increases the influence and incomes of lawyers (see, eg Allan, 2006; Hickman, 2008; Lester, 2005; Kavanagh, 2009; Young, 2009).

The decision of the UK court can be challenged in the European court (Section 21.3). One reason why the verdicts of UK courts may be rejected by Strasbourg is that the approaches of the two courts to balancing competing interests may differ. The UK approach seems to be broad brush, pragmatic and utilitarian in the sense that the court weighs the *consequences* on either side and tries to choose the least harmful overall solution. The European Court by contrast is more likely to stress the value of the right in principle. Moreover the UK courts seem to have a tendency to trust the discretion of the police and other officials and to accept informal safeguards, whereas the European Court requires stronger safeguards (see, eg *Gillan v UK* [2010] ECHR App no 158/05 (Sections 14.1); *Marper v UK* [2008] (Section 21.4.3)).

There are also frequent dissents within the highest courts. One reason is disagreement about the proper limits of the court's intervention in particular the extent to which controversial matters should be left to the democratic process ('deference', Section 22.7.2). (See eg *Re G (Adoption) (Unmarried Couple)* (2009): Lord Walker dissenting on the ground that the matter is best left to a democratic decision maker, compare Baroness Hale [121], [122].)

22.2 Extraterritorial application

The HRA has limited effect outside UK territory. It has been emphasized that the Convention is territorial and respects international law. Indeed international relations might be destabilised if the courts interfered with matters occurring abroad. Thus the ECHR Article 1 imposes a duty on states to secure the rights in respect of everyone 'within their jurisdiction'.

In *R (Al-Skeini) v Secretary of State for Defence* [2007] the House of Lords held that the Act applied outside UK territory only where the UK is exercising governmental powers as a sovereign state in respect of territory under its control. Thus it was held (Lord Bingham dissenting) that the Act applied to the death of an Iraqi prisoner in custody on a British base in Iraq. By contrast in *R (Smith) v Secretary of State for Defence* [2010] 3 All ER 1067 a soldier serving in Iraq died of heatstroke allegedly as a result of lack of equipment. The Supreme Court held that British troops on foreign soil, outside a place over which the UK has complete control are not protected by the Act. Nor did the Act apply to the handing over of a prisoner to the Iraqi government where the UK was acting as an agent of that government and not exercising sovereign powers (see *R (Al Saadoon) v Secretary of State for Defence* (2010)). The Act does however apply to diplomatic and other activities recognised in international law as cases where there is sovereign territorial jurisdiction overseas (see *R (B) v Secretary of State for Foreign and Commonwealth Affairs* [2005] 2 WLR 618). However in a case such as *Smith* the ordinary common law would apply imposing a duty on the Crown as the soldier's employer to take reasonable care for his safety (Section 14.5; *Smith v Ministry of Defence* [2013] 1 All ER 778).

The Act may not apply to UK dependent territories. In *R v Secretary of State for Foreign and Commonwealth Affairs, ex p Quark Fishing Ltd* [2006] (Section 9.5) the House of Lords held that the Act has effect only in the UK itself. The ECHR itself can be extended to dependent territories (Art 56) but had not been so in this case. Their Lordships did not agree whether even this would suffice to attract the Act. Lord Nicholls thought that it would, Lords Bingham and Hoffmann that it would not. Lady Hale thought that the Act should in any case apply to all territories governed by the UK.

22.3 The Human Rights Act and Parliament

The HRA makes clear that the court cannot set aside an Act of Parliament or other 'primary' legislation (see ss 3(2)(b), 6(2)), thereby preserving parliamentary supremacy. For this purpose primary legislation means statutes, measures of the Church Assembly and the General Synod of the Church of England and delegated legislation that brings into force or amends primary legislation. A Prerogative Order in Council is also primary legislation for this purpose even though the courts can set it aside in judicial review proceedings on domestic grounds (s 21). (See Billings and Ponting, 'Prerogative Powers and the Human Rights Act: Elevating the Status of Orders in Council' [2001] PL 21.) Acts of the Scottish Parliament and Northern Ireland Assembly are not primary legislation (s 21; Section 14.1). The court can set aside subordinate legislation and other government decisions unless primary legislation makes it impossible to do so (s 3(2)).

If an Act of Parliament violates a Convention right, the court must therefore enforce it. However, the court can make a 'declaration of incompatibility' (s 4) which invites Parliament or the executive to change the law (Section 22.3.2). But, it has been suggested that in view of the respect shown to a court in the Human Rights Act differs little in its effect from an 'entrenched' bill of rights that empowers courts to overturn legislation (see Hiebert, 'Parliamentary Bills of Rights: An Alternative Model' (2006) 69 MLR 7).

22.3.1 The interpretative obligation

At the heart of the Act is the requirement that:

> So far as it is possible to do so, primary legislation and subordinate legislation must be read and given effect in a way which is compatible with Convention rights. (s 3(1))

Before section 3 is applied the court must decide whether the right in question has been violated. If it has, then under section 3 the governing statute must be interpreted so as to protect the right. The court must keep to the right side of the border between interpretation and law making. The government did not introduce a strong formula of the kind used in Canada, under which a statute must expressly state that it overrides the Bill of Rights (Home Office, *Rights Brought Home: The Human Rights Bill* (Cm 3782, 1997) para 2.10). Nevertheless section 3(1) was apparently intended to be a stronger provision than the traditional one of resolving ambiguities.

The judges seem to be divided as to how radical section 3 is and what the limits of interpretation are. It is clear that the ordinary principles of statutory interpretation are modified. Thus the court is not confined to cases where the provision is ambiguous (*R v A* [2001] 3 All ER 1, *Ghaidan v Mendoza* [2004]). However in *Wilson v First County Trust* [2003] the House of Lords went further in suggesting that the normal assumption that the court is seeking the intention of Parliament does not apply, and that it is for the court to make an independent judgment as to whether the language of the statute can be read in a way to make it compatible with the Convention. Similarly in *Harrow LBC v Qazi* [2004] 1 AC 938 [23] Lord Bingham said:

> The court has to arrive at a judicial choice between two possibilities, a choice which transcends the business of finding out what the legislation's words mean.

However in *R (Wilkinson) v IRC* [2006] 1 All ER 529 Lord Hoffmann [17]–[19] took a narrower stance by saying that the question was what Parliament would have intended by the words it used *in the context of* respecting the Convention thus emphasising that in a broad sense the intention of Parliament must still be respected.

The subjective nature of the different approaches was revealed in *Ghaidan v Mendoza* [2004]. A statutory provision entitled a person who had lived with a tenant 'as husband and wife' to succeed to the tenancy on the tenant's death. A majority of the House of Lords held that a homosexual relationship fell within the phrase 'living as husband and wife', which they made Convention-compatible by inserting the words 'if they were' after 'as'. The majority held that even if the ordinary meaning of the statute is clear, the court could still distort its language or read in additional wording in order to achieve a meaning that complied with the Convention. Lord Millett dissented on the grounds that the words of the statute were clear and that the majority's meaning unacceptably distorted the statute.

The boundary of the court's power depended on two factors. Firstly the interpretation must not go against the grain of the legislation in the sense of contradicting its underlying purpose. At least to this extent the intention of parliament is important. The court must look beyond the language itself and consider the policy context and legislative history of the statute in order to identify the essential features of the statutory scheme in question, which they must not violate. Secondly the courts must not make decisions for which they are not equipped in the sense of producing an interpretation that raises social or economic issues that are best left to Parliament. This relates to the issue of 'deference' (Section 19.7.1).

Although the court can stretch or add to the language of the statute it cannot repeal, delete or contradict the statutory language. Lord Millett gave the example of the word 'cat' in a statute ([72]). In some circumstances 'cat' might be read to include 'dog', for example where the care of pets was the underlying concern. However if the legislation had originally stated 'Siamese cats' and later been amended to 'cats', this route would not be possible. Thus the courts have been warned to refrain from 'judicial vandalism' (*R (Anderson) v Secretary of State for the Home Dept* (2002), 1089: Home Secretary's explicit power to interfere with sentencing process could not be circumvented; see Kavanagh, 2004).

Thus section 3 is vague and different judges might apply it differently. The following are examples (see also the table provided by Lord Steyn in *Ghaidan v Mendoza* (2004)).

- *R (Hurst) v North London Coroner* (2007). The governing statute required a coroner to investigate 'how' a deceased came by his death. In the case of deaths prior to the HRA 'how' is construed narrowly to mean 'by what means'. In the case of post-HRA deaths, 'how' means 'in what circumstances', thereby allowing a wider-ranging inquiry into deaths in custody.
- *R v Lambert* (2001). Under section 28 of the Misuse of Drugs Act 1971 it is a defence to a charge of possessing drugs for the accused to 'prove' that he neither knew of nor suspected nor had reason to suspect some fact alleged by the prosecution. This conflicts with the presumption of innocence (ECHR Art 6(2)). The House of Lords gave the phrase 'to prove' the unusual meaning of 'to give sufficient evidence'. Thus the prosecution still has the general burden of disproving the accused's claim. Lord Hope emphasised (at 604) that great care must be taken to make the revised meaning blend in with the language and structure of the statute. 'Amendment' seems to be possible as long as it does not make the statute unintelligible or unworkable (cf [80] and [81]). (See also *R (H) v London North and East Region Mental Health Review Tribunal* [2001] EWCA Civ 405.)
- *R v A* (2001) (perhaps the most radical example). The Youth Justice and Criminal Evidence Act 1999 prohibited evidence in rape cases of the alleged victim's previous sexual experience without the court's consent, which could be given only in specified circumstances (s 41(1)). It was held that the court could construe the Act so as to permit evidence necessary to make the trial fair since that was the general object of the Act. Thus additional provisions, 'subject to the right to a fair trial', could be implied into unambiguous language beyond the normal limits of statutory interpretation even if this strained the normal meaning (see Lord Steyn's speech). However the court cannot override provisions that specifically contradict Convention rights.
- *S (Children) (Care Plan)* [2002] 2 All ER 192. The power of the court to intervene in local authority care proceedings could not be added to the Children Act 1989; the court cannot depart substantially from a fundamental feature of a statutory scheme, particularly if it has practical consequences which the court cannot evaluate (s 38). Similarly in *Poplar Housing and Regeneration Community Association v Donoghue* [2001] the term 'reasonable' could not be inserted into a statute which gave a landlord an absolute right to evict a tenant.
- *Bellinger v Bellinger* [2003] 2 All ER 593. A statute could not be interpreted so as to treat a transsexual as female for marriage purposes since this would raise wide social issues that a court is not equipped to confront (cf Gender Recognition Act 2004).
- *Cachia v Faluyi* [2002] 1 All ER 192. A provision in the Fatal Accidents Act 1976 that not more than one 'action' shall lie in respect of the same subject matter arose when a firm of solicitors issued a writ in respect of the death of the claimant's wife in a road accident but then disappeared before it could be served. A second firm issued a new writ several years later. Under domestic law the second writ would probably be invalid. However under the HRA the Court of Appeal read 'action' in an unorthodox way to mean 'served process'. Brooke LJ remarked [20]. that this was a very good example 'of the way in which the 1998 Act now enables English judges to do justice in a way that was previously not open to us.'
- In *R (Wilkinson) v IRC* (2006) the House of Lords held that section 262 of the Income and Corporation Taxes Act 1988 (widow's tax allowance) could not be interpreted to include a widower.

Section 3 seems to assume that the meaning of the Convention is a given against which UK law can be measured. However, even though the decisions of the European Court give some assistance, the meaning and scope of a Convention right is often vague. Indeed as a 'living instrument' the meaning of the Convention is always evolving. Thus interpretation is against a moving target. The enterprise may be self-defeating since a Convention provision could be 'read down' to conform to existing UK law as well as a UK law being 'read up' to conform to the Convention.

22.3.2 Declaration of incompatibility

Where it is not 'possible' to interpret primary legislation in line with a Convention right, the Supreme Court, the Court of Appeal, the High Court and certain other courts of equivalent status may – but are not required to – make a 'declaration of incompatibility' (s 4). This is at the heart of the accommodation between law and democracy made by the Act. A declaration of incompatibility invites Parliament to consider whether to change the law. It has no effect on the validity of the law in question and is not binding on the parties (s 4(6)).

For this reason the Act is sometimes described as a 'partnership' or a 'constitutional dialogue' between the three branches of government. It respects the separation of powers by making specific provisions concerning the relationship between the three branches (see Lord Hobhouse in *Wilson v First County Trust* (2003)).

A declaration of incompatibility triggers a 'fast-track' procedure that enables a minister, by statutory instrument subject to the approval of Parliament, to make such amendments as he or she considers necessary to remove the incompatibility. Ministers are not bound to obey a declaration of incompatibility. Judicial review may lie in respect of an irrational refusal to do so although the court would be unlikely to interfere with the province of Parliament (Section 19.7.1). Subordinate legislation that conflicts with a Convention right can be quashed by the court and reinstated in amended form under this procedure. The fast-track procedure can also be used where an incompatibility arises because of a ruling by the European Court of Human Rights and a minister considers that there are 'compelling reasons' for proceeding (s 10). It does not apply to measures of the Church of England.

A declaration of incompatibility is a last resort (*R v A* (2001) [108]) and should not be used in order to avoid the task of interpreting the statute to comply with the Convention (Lord Steyn in *Ghaidan v Mendoza* (2004 [39])).

The declaration of incompatibility therefore gives the court a constitutional role detached from the outcome of the particular case. This is sometimes described as a 'constitutional dialogue' between the three branches but if so it is a limited and formalised one in which the executive is required to take it or leave it. Moreover in two cases a declaration of incompatibility was refused on the narrow ground that the outcome of the cases did not damage the interests of the claimant (*R (H) v Secretary of State for Health* [2006] 1 AC 441; *Secretary of State for the Home Dept v Nasseri* [2009] 2 WLR 1190). This seems questionable.

22.3.3 Statement of compatibility

Under section 19 a minister in charge of a bill in either House of Parliament must, before the second reading of the bill, (i) make a statement to the effect that in his or her view the provisions of the bill are compatible with Convention rights (a 'statement of compatibility') or (ii) make a statement to the effect that although he or she is unable to make a statement of compatibility the government nevertheless wishes the House to proceed with the bill. The statement must be in writing and published in such manner as the minister considers appropriate.

Apart from putting political pressure on the government, the effect of a statement of compatibility is not clear. As a statement of the opinion of the executive, the courts should not defer to it when interpreting the legislation in question (*Wilson v First County Trust (2003)*). Indeed a statement of compatibility means little where the statute in question confers a wide discretion on the executive or the police. Moreover because the statement applies only to the second reading it does not cover amendments that might be included at later stages.

22.4 The executive and judiciary: remedies

A 'public authority', including the executive and the courts, is liable for failing to comply with a Convention right. By virtue of section 6(1) 'it is unlawful for a public authority to act in a way which is incompatible with a Convention right'. For this purpose an 'act' includes a failure to act but does not include a failure to introduce or lay before Parliament a proposal for legislation or make any primary legislation or remedial order (s 6(6)).

However liability is excluded by s 6(2) if (a) 'as a result of one or more provisions of primary legislation, the authority could not have acted differently' or (b) 'in the case of one or more provisions of, or made under, primary legislation which cannot be read or given effect in a way which is compatible with the Convention rights, the authority was acting so as to give effect to or enforce those provisions'. The difference between (a) and (b) is that under (b) an authority might be able to act differently but nevertheless has a defence if it is enforcing a statute, for example evicting a tenant or collecting taxes.

There is a wide and a narrow way of reading s 6(2)b. In earlier cases (see, eg *Doherty v Birmingham City Council* [2009] 1 AC 367: eviction from gypsy site: *Wilkinson v IRC* (2006) (above), the House of Lords held that if a statutory provision of this kind was being enforced the court should look no further other than to apply the domestic law of *Wednesbury* unreasonableness. However in *Manchester City Council v Pinnock* (2010): eviction from council house, the Supreme Court, following Strasbourg and unusually overruling previous House of Lords cases, held that the particular circumstances must be scrutinised in all cases to see whether a Convention right has been violated.

Section 6 effectively adds another ground to judicial review. However because Prerogative Orders in Council are primary legislation for the purposes of the Act only domestic grounds of review are available for these (Section 22.3.1). In addition to remedies under section 6, acts of the devolved regimes in Scotland, Wales and Northern Ireland are automatically invalid if they violate Convention Rights since they are outside the devolved powers (Section 16.2.1).

The HRA must be applied by all courts. Section 7 entitles a 'victim' to bring proceedings in respect of an act which is unlawful under section 6 and also to rely on Convention rights in any legal proceedings. However, a minister can make rules designating an 'appropriate court or tribunal' for the purposes of an action under the

Act (ss 7 (2),(9),(10),(11)). This power has been exercised principally in relation to special tribunals concerning immigration, asylum and other cases involving national security matters. However by means of judicial review the ordinary courts can ensure that the designated tribunal provides an adequate process for protecting the right in issue (see *A v B* [2010] 1 All ER 1167 (Sections 19.7.2, 23.3). Reflecting judicial independence, decisions made by courts and tribunals can be challenged only by appeal or judicial review (s 9).

The onus is on the claimant to show that a law or decision does not comply with the Convention (*Lambeth BC v Kay* (2006)) and that he or she is a 'victim'. 'Victim' has the same meaning as in cases brought before the ECHR (s 7(7)). The claimant or a close relative must be directly affected, or at least very likely to be affected, by the action complained of (see *Klass v Federal Republic of Germany* (1979) 2 EHRR 214; *Open Door and Dublin Well Woman v Ireland* (1992) 15 EHRR 244). There is no standing for non-governmental organisations (NGOs) representing collective or public interests. Thus in a judicial review case an NGO unless perhaps it comprises victims can challenge a decision only on domestic grounds (s 7(3)). It appears that a public authority cannot be a victim against another public authority since in ECHR terms both are part of the 'state' (see *Aston Cantlow and Wilmcote with Billesley Parochial Church Council v Wallbank* [2003] 3 All ER 1213). In ordinary judicial review law the courts can review decisions of one public body against another. In principle this restriction seems unjustifiable.

Under section 8 the court can award any of the remedies normally available to it 'as it considers just and appropriate'. Damages can be awarded only by a court which has power to award damages or order compensation in civil proceedings (eg not criminal courts and other specialist courts) and then only if the court is satisfied that 'the award is necessary to afford just satisfaction to the person in whose favour it is made' (s 8(4)). The phrase 'just satisfaction' is part of the jurisprudence of the ECHR and the court must take into account the principles applied by the ECHR in awarding compensation (s 8(4)). However, apart from insisting that there must be substantial loss or injury these do not give clear guidance and the court has considerable discretion (*Z v UK* (2002) 34 EHRR 3; *Damages under the Human Rights Act 1998* (Law Com No 266, 2006); *Cullen v Chief Constable of the RUC* (2004)). In order to safeguard judicial independence, where an action for damages is brought in respect of a judicial act, meaning in this context an act of a court, there is no liability in respect of an act in good faith except for an unlawful arrest or detention. The action must be brought against the Crown with the judge concerned being made a party (HRA, ss 9(3)–(4)).

22.5   Public authorities

The ECHR applies to states, and some of its articles, notably Articles 8 and 10, are directed explicitly to public authorities. TheHRA can be directly enforced only against a public authority (s 6(1)). The law as to what is a public authority is unclear and controversial reflecting the absence of a coherent concept of the state in UK law.

The Act singles out some particular cases but does not provide a general definition. Thus 'public authority' includes a court or tribunal (s 6(3)). However, Parliament or a person exercising functions in connection with proceedings in Parliament is not a public authority (s 6(3)). Public authority' also includes anybody 'certain of whose functions are functions of a public nature' (s 6(3)b). An individual can be a public authority (*A v Head Teacher and Governors of Lord Grey School* [2004] 4 All ER 587).

It has emerged that there are two kinds of public authority. Firstly there are bodies, such as central and local government and the police, which are inherently public. These are known as 'core' public authorities. All the activities of these bodies fall within the HRA. Secondly there are 'functional' or 'hybrid' public authorities. These include private or voluntary bodies whose activities interrelate with those of the government. Functional public authorities may perform some functions on behalf of the government but also perform private functions. The 'private acts' of hybrid public bodies do not fall within the HRA (s 6(5)).

Thus in the case of hybrid public authorities the court must look not only at the particular *function* but also at the particular *act* within that function which is claimed to invade a Convention right. For example the provision of social housing under government control was held to be a public function, as was the act of evicting a tenant in furtherance of government policy. It was suggested however that other acts within the same overall function, such as managing repair contractors, might not be public acts (*Weaver v London and Quadrant Housing Trust* [2009] EWCA Civ. 507).

This can be compared with the approach taken in domestic judicial review cases (Section 19.5). In judicial review contexts the function must apparently be looked at in the case both of core and of hybrid bodies. In human rights cases this applies only to hybrid bodies. In relation to hybrid bodies although the courts have emphasised that the purpose of the two regimes is not the same (the Human Rights Act having the more limited purpose of following the ECHR) they have usually applied the same authorities in both contexts.

It has been argued that a broad view should be taken of what is a public function so as to subject a wide range of powerful bodies to the Act. This has been endorsed by the Joint Committee on Human Rights (Seventh Report, 2003–04, HL 39, HC 382). On the other hand it has been suggested that private bodies should be subject to less onerous obligations than public bodies narrowly defined (see Oliver, 'Functions of a Public Nature and the Human Rights Act' [2004] PL 329; cf Sunkin, 'Pushing Forward the Frontiers of Human Rights Protection' [2004] PL 643).

The approach of the ECHR seems to be based on whether the particular act is carried out under the control of the government or on behalf of the government (*Sigurjónnson v Iceland* (1993) 16 EHRR 462). The UK courts have broadly followed this approach. They have also been influenced by the belief that a body which is itself a public authority cannot claim human rights against another public authority. This is particularly significant in relation, for example to religious bodies and charities that protect vulnerable minorities. There is no single criterion. The matter depends on a combination of factors relating the body in question to the government. These include in particular the extent of government control over the body and, whether it has any special powers (see also Section 19.5). The matter remains controversial.

In *Aston Cantlow and Wilmcote with Billesley Parochial Church Council v Wallbank* (2003) the House of Lords held, overruling the Court of Appeal, that a parochial church council of the Church of England is not a core public authority even though the Church of England has a close connection with the state and has many special legal powers and privileges. A core public authority must be 'governmental' in the sense that its activities are carried out on behalf of the general public interest, whereas the Church of England primarily benefits its own members.

However, some aspects of the Church of England might fall into the category of *functional* public authority, for example functions in connection with marriages and funerals since these involve public rights. The case itself concerned the statutory right of a parochial church council to force a house owner to pay for the repair of a church roof under an obligation acquired with the property. A majority held that this was a private function, being the enforcement of a property right for the primary benefit of churchgoers. Lord Scott, dissenting, thought that this was a 'public' function in that it involved historic conservation for the benefit of the community enforced by special powers.

YL v Birmingham City Council [2007] 3 All ER 957 is the other main authority. The House of Lords held that a privately owned care home was not exercising a public function for human rights purposes in relation to a resident who was placed there and financed by a local authority acting under its statutory duty to care for the vulnerable. The majority took the view that there was not a sufficiently close operational connection between the home and the government to attract the HRA. The home had no special powers, was not acting as the agent of the government and the relationship between the home and its resident was the same whether or not the resident was supported by the local authority. The local authority funded the individual resident and not the home as such.

Lord Bingham and Lady Hale dissented, taking a fundamentally different approach. This was based on the principle that the state had taken on itself the function of caring for the elderly and that it should make no difference so far as human rights were concerned whether this was done through a private agency or directly by the state itself. Lady Hale emphasised the positive duty of the state to ensure that Article 8 rights were protected, arguing that this can best be achieved by imposing liability directly on the private agency. This leads to the question of 'horizontality' (Section 21.4.2).

In *Poplar HARCA v Donoughue* (2001) the Court of Appeal held that a housing association set up by a local council to take over its rented property was a public authority at least in relation to the eviction of former council tenants. The court stressed that there was no single test but that the matter depended on accumulating factors showing 'publicness'. The court gave weight to the historical connection between the authority and the association. Moreover, the local authority remained involved with the running of the association and it is questionable in the light of *YL* whether the contracting out of a government function to an existing profit making body would remain public.

In *Weaver v London and Quadrant Housing Trust* (2009) the Court of Appeal rejected the historic connection approach. It held that a housing association that received government funding in return for delivering government housing policy was exercising public functions both for judicial review and HRA purposes in respect of decisions to evict tenants. It was intensively regulated by the government and under a statutory duty to cooperate with local authorities. Eviction decisions although governed by ordinary private law could not be separated from its public function of allocating social housing according to government policy. It was also relevant that the association had certain special powers and was under a statutory duty to cooperate with local authorities. However some 'acts', such as contractual arrangements with repair firms, could be private and the position of tenants who receive unsubsidised housing and pay a market rent is unclear. The dissent took a radically different approach, regarding a function as private if it used private law powers such as a landlord's power to evict a tenant.

Thus confusion remains and it is unclear to what extent a body which contracts with government to provides services under privatization policies is subject to the Human Rights Act.

22.6 Horizontal effect

On the face of it the HRA gives a remedy only against a public authority. However it is arguable that the Act sometimes has 'horizontal effect' in the sense that private persons as well as public bodies may be required to respect human rights. Even private legal relationships are created and defined by the state, which could therefore be regarded as responsible for ensuring that the law meets the minimum standards appropriate to a democratic society. For example it would be anomalous if there were a right of privacy against an NHS hospital and not a private hospital. Unfortunately the UK courts have not yet directly ruled on the question of horizontal effect and have sometimes ignored the issue (see eg *Aston Cantlow* and *YL v Birmingham City Council* [2007]; Section 22.5). In *Manchester City Council v Pinnock* (2010) [50] the Supreme Court refused to enter into the question of whether a private landlord would be bound to respect the right to family life when making eviction decisions. (Section 21.4.3).

These are arguments both for and against horizontality.

▶ According to section 7 a claim under the Act can be made only by a person who would be a 'victim' for the purposes of Article 34 of the Convention if proceedings were brought in Strasbourg (s 7(1)(b), (7)). Under Article 34 a claim in Strasbourg can be made only against a party to the Convention, usually a state. It has therefore been argued that since the purpose of the HRA is to give effect to the ECHR, by their nature Convention rights are directed only against the state (Buxton, 2000).

▶ The Act does not include Article 1 of the ECHR, which requires states to 'secure to everyone within their jurisdiction' the rights and freedoms conferred by the Convention.

▶ On the other hand it can be recalled that the HRA does not incorporate the Convention as such but makes certain rights taken from the Convention enforceable in the courts (s 1).

▶ All legislation must be interpreted according to the Convention, even that applying to private relationships. In *Ghaidan v Mendoza* (2004) the House of Lords applied Article 14 (discrimination) to legislation which discriminated against homosexual couples occupying property owned by private landlords (see also *Wilson v First County Trust* (2003).

▶ By virtue of section 6 the courts are public authorities. It is arguable that a court would act 'unlawfully' if it did not apply Convention rights in every case before it, even between private persons (see Sedley LJ in *Douglas v Hello!* [2001] 2 All ER 289; Section 23.6). However, the victim's right would be against the court itself, not directly against the other private party. It is therefore difficult to see how the court could award damages. Moreover section 6 could also be interpreted as applying only to the court's own practice and procedure.

▶ A less extreme version of the above is that while section 6 cannot create a new cause of action against a private body, it can require the court to apply Convention rights in the context of *existing* causes of action or in respect of the court's own powers to make orders and grant remedies (see *Wilson v First County Trust* (2003) at [174]; Baroness Hale in *Campbell v MGN Ltd* [2004] 2 All ER 995 [133]). The matter would therefore have to arise in the course of other legal proceedings into which a human rights dimension could be implied. For example a court might be entitled to refuse to give a possession order to a private landlord who attempted to evict a tenant from her home (*R (McLellan) v Bracknell Forest BC* [2002] [42]). The weakness of this approach seems to be that it is random in that it depends on the matter falling into an existing category of UK law.

▶ Particular Convention rights may include a positive obligation on the state to protect the right and to require private persons to respect it (*Kroon v The Netherlands* (1995) 19 EHRR 263). This has been recognised in the case of Article 2 (right to life); Article 3 (torture and inhuman or degrading treatment: *Z v UK* (2002), *X and Y v Netherlands* (1985) 8 EHRR 235, *A v UK* [1998] 27 EHRR 611; Article 8 (privacy: *Douglas v Hello!* (2001) [91]; *Thompson v News Group Newspapers* [2001] 1 All ER 908; Article 9 (freedom of religion: *R (Williamson) v Secretary of State for Education and Employment* (2005) [4], [86]. However this positive obligation is not absolute and the court will give the government a substantial margin of discretion in relation to the measures it takes (Section 22.7.2).

▶ Particular provisions of the Act itself may have horizontal effect in their own right, notably section 12, which requires the court to have regard to the interests of press freedom (Section 23.3).

▶ The courts might develop the common law on the basis that the ECHR encapsulates values of general import. In *Campbell v MGN Ltd* [2004] the House of Lords used Articles 8 and 10 of the ECHR to reconfigure the common law in respect of privacy in relation to press freedom (see Section 22.6). The majority did not seem to think that the matter strictly fell within the HRA ([17]–[19], [26], [49]).

22.7 Overriding protected rights: proportionality

Any workable code of fundamental rights must be expressed in general language and with sufficient filters or exceptions to permit governments to act in the public interest or to resolve conflicts between rights. It is tempting to seek an overarching principle that would balance or combine the human right with a competing interest under some overall concept of common good. However it is doubtful whether any such overriding principle is possible. Indeed in *R (S) v Chief Constable of South Yorkshire Police* (2004) Sedley LJ in the Court of Appeal pointed out that strictly speaking the notion of 'balancing' individual rights against the public interest means that the latter will always prevail.

Moreover there are competing approaches as to what human rights are about. In one view, that of liberal individualists, human rights concern a zone of individual freedom which might exceptionally be overridden in the public interest, but recognising the sacrifice involved. On the other hand communitarians and republicans, favouring 'positive freedom', might argue that human rights in themselves are valuable only as part of some greater good. For example in *Gough v Chief Constable of Derbyshire* [2001] 4 All ER 289 Laws LJ said:

> rights are divisive, harmful, ultimately worthless, unless their possession is conditional upon the public good (at 321) it is inherent in the nature of the right itself that the individual who

claims its benefit may have to give way to the supervening weight of other claims...the right's practical utility rests upon the fact that there can be no tranquility within the state without a plethora of unruly individual freedoms. (at 320)

There are two ways of accommodating competing public interest considerations. Firstly the right itself could be narrowly defined Secondly, many of the rights are made subject to specific justifications for overriding them (overrides).

In *R (Begum) v Head Teacher and Governors of Denbigh High School* [2007] AC 100 the House of Lords took both approaches. It was held that a ban on the wearing of a strict form of Muslim dress at school was not an unlawful interference with freedom of religion (Art 9). A majority held that the right to religious freedom was not infringed at all since mainstream Muslim opinion did not require this form of dress the child had chosen to attend the school in question and could have attended another, more flexible school [34]. Perhaps uncomfortable with the reality of this, Lord Nicholls and Baroness Hale held that the right had been infringed but that the decision was 'objectively justified' under one of the prescribed overrides, namely 'the rights of others', these being the social purpose of fostering a sense of community by means of a dress code. This case provides an illustration of the subjective and impressionistic nature of the balancing exercise and also the importance of mainstream opinion. (See Mc Goldrick, 'Extreme Religious Dress: Perspectives on Veiling Controversies' in Hare and Weinstein (eds), *Extreme Speech and Democracy* (Oxford University Press 2009).)

A right may be defined narrowly by bringing public interest concerns to bear. Right can be narrowly seen in respect of the meaning of 'deprivation' of liberty as opposed to 'restriction' of liberty (*Austin v UK* (2012) Section 21.4.1). Usually this works against the claimant since he has to bring him or herself within the scope of the right in question, whereas in the case of the separate public interest overrides it is for the state to justify interfering with the right on the basis of proportionality. On the other hand sometimes this might work in the claimant's favour since, as Lord Hoffmann pointed out (at in *Secretary of State for the Home Dept v JJ* (2008) [44]) a narrow definition of deprivation of liberty may make it more difficult for the state to justify overriding it.

The law might react to political pressures. For example the meaning of 'torture or inhuman and degrading treatment' might be redefined according to changing sensibilities (*Chalal v UK* (1996); *Z v UK* (2002)). Discrimination (Section 21.4.3) embodies the notion of a reasonable balance between competing concerns and are receptive to changing attitudes. The 'living instrument', nature of the ECHR means that the rights themselves change with the times (eg *Ghaidan v Mendoza* (2004): homosexual partners).

Under Articles 8–11 and Protocol 1, Article 1 the court is required to balance the right against a specified override. The overrides vary with the particular article but in all cases include public safety, public order, the prevention and detection of serious crime, the protection of health and morals and the protection of the rights of others. This is broadly understood to include the rights of the public generally to have fair, reasonable and effective laws (*Kokkinakis v Greece* [1993] 17 EHRR 397). Sometimes one human right may conflict with another, for example freedom of expression and privacy (Section 23.6), but the Convention contains no guidance as to any ranking order.

Firstly the restrictions must be 'prescribed by law' or 'in accordance with the law', terms which apparently mean the same. This imports traditional rule of law ideas. Thus the restrictions must be authorised by domestic law but, more than that, they must not involve wide discretion and must be made in accordance with a regular, democratic and accessible lawmaking process and preferably not by judicial extension of the law (see *R (Purdy) v DPP* (2009): guidance as to prosecution policy for assisted suicide; *R (Laporte) v Chief Constable of Gloucestershire* [2007] 2 AC 105 [52]: policing demonstrations (Section 22.8.1); *Gillan v UK* (2010): stop and search powers). The applicant must be able reasonably to foresee that the conduct in question would be unlawful and there must be adequate safeguards, including independent and accessible courts. The common law is particularly vulnerable to claims of uncertainty (see *R v Goldstein* (2006): public nuisance).

Secondly the restrictions must be 'necessary in a democratic society'. This is the foundation of the central doctrine of 'proportionality'. Proportionality also applies in other contexts in particular where the state has a positive duty to protect a right against interference by others, in order to avoid placing undue burdens on the government. This applies even to the 'absolute' rights (*R (Pretty) v DPP* (2002) [90]) (see also Section 18.1).

22.7.1   Proportionality

Proportionality has four aspects (see R v Secretary of State for the Home Department ex parte Daly (2001), Huang v Secretary of State for the Home Department (2007), 2 All ER 1089).

1. The objective justifying the interference is sufficiently important to justify limiting the right. This means an interest, sometimes called a 'pressing social need' which is more than merely 'useful', 'reasonable' or 'desirable' (*Handyside v UK* (1976); *R (Laporte) v Chief Constable of Gloucestershire* (2007) [52]; *Brown v Stott* (2001) combating drink driving; R (*Williamson*) *v Secretary of State* (2005) [79]: child welfare; *R (Begum) v Head Teacher and Governor of Denbigh High School* (2007): social cohesion).

2. The interference with the right must be rationally connected to the objective. This is stricter than ordinary *Wednesbury* unreasonableness (Section 18.1). It requires the government action to be accurately targeted. In *A v Secretary of State* (2005) a statute failed this test. The Anti-Terrorism, Crime and Security Act 2001 authorised the indefinite detention of a foreign national whose presence in the UK the Home Secretary reasonably believes is a risk to national security and whom he reasonably suspects is a terrorist, unless the person voluntarily leaves the country. The government claimed that these powers were necessary because it would otherwise be impossible to deal with suspects who were too dangerous to be at large but against whom no criminal charges could be brought since a non-national could not be deported to a place where he or she would be at risk of torture or inhuman or degrading treatment (*s 9*). The House of Lords held by an 8 to 1 majority that the measure, although satisfying the *Wednesbury* test went too far in some respects and not far enough in others. The statute was discriminatory and disproportionate in

singling out foreign nationals since the threat was no less from British terrorists and foreign nationals who were also a danger when abroad.

3. The restriction must go no further than is necessary to achieve the purpose. For example in *A* (above) the terrorist threat could have been dealt with by less intrusive means such as intensive surveillance. In *McVeigh v UK* [1983] 5 EHRR 71 the European Court held that an emergency restriction on travel did not justify a refusal to let the claimants contact their wives. *In re G (Adoption) (Unmarried Couples)* (2009) the House of Lords held that, although the question of whether an unmarried couple were suitable as adoptive parents was relevant, it was disproportionate to adopt a blanket policy rejecting all such couples as opposed to considering each case on its merits (see also *R (Aguila Quila) v Secretary of State for the Home Dept* (2012): blanket policy of refusing entry into UK to underage partners to deal with forced marriages).

4. Whether the interference strikes a 'fair balance' between the rights of the individual and the interests of the community.

Thus in the end, proportionality requires the court to make a subjective judgement as to whether an interference is justified on the basis of a scrutiny of all the circumstances. For example in *R (BBC) v Secretary of State for Justice* (2012) the BBC was not permitted to film an interview with a terrorist suspect who had been detained without charge for 7 years awaiting deportation. The Divisional Court held that this was not proportionate. Tests 1 and 2 (purpose and rational connection were satisfied but the crucial fourth test of fair balance was not since a face to face interview was important in the circumstances to freedom of expression (Section 23.1) and the government could not provide evidence of concrete harm).

A right can be overridden on the ground of the public cost in giving effect to it only in clear and weighty cases. For example in *R (AB) v Secretary of State for Justice* [2010] 2 All ER 151 it was held that a refusal to move a transsexual prisoner to a woman's prison could not be justified on the basis of cost and in *Aguila Quila* (above) the Supreme Court rejected the government's argument that it would be too expensive to screen individual applicants. It is also important under this head to provide safeguards to protect the right in question such as an appeal (see *R v Shaylor* [2002] 2 All ER 477: freedom of expression; *Gaskin v UK* (1990) 12 EHRR 36 access to personal information). It has been suggested that the UK courts are more willing to take a broad brush balancing approach than is the case in other European countries (Gould *et al*, 2007; see Section 22.1).

Sometimes the competition is between two individual protected rights. A problem here is to decide how much weight each should have in the 'balancing exercise'. For example is freedom of expression (Art. 10 more important than privacy (Art 8) or freedom of religion (Art 9)) (Section 23.5). The court's approach seems to be utilitarian (Section 2.3.3). Thus the starting point is to treat each right as equal then to look at each in turn in the particular circumstances, comparing the consequences to the individual and those to other people and the public interest and choosing what is overall the lesser evil (eg *HM Advocate v Murdoch* [2010] 3 WLR 814: police records concerning a witness: right to a fair trial outweighed privacy, *R (L) v Metropolitan Police Comr* (2010): 'enhanced criminal records certificate affecting job as school assistant: risk to children outweighed privacy'. *Campbell v MGN* [2004]; privacy outweighed press freedom where matter was not of serious concern to public.

Important illustrations of proportionality can be found in particular contexts (see, for example Sections 9.6.7.2, 23.6, 23.7).

22.7.2 Margin of discretion/deference

Normally the court itself decides whether the interference is proportionate. The European doctrine of margin of appreciation which restrains the court from interfering in certain cases (Section 21.3) has no application in domestic law (*R v DPP, ex p Kebilene* (2000) at 380–81). However the courts sometimes leave a discretionary area of judgement to ministers and Parliament in a similar way. This is the 'margin of discretion' or 'deference'. The courts do not wish to exceed their proper constitutional role or to interfere in matters where they have no experience or expertise or to which legal processes are unsuited. A similar principle applies in domestic judicial review cases (Section 19.7.1) and in EU law.

Thus in *R (Mahmood) v Secretary of State for the Home Dept* [2001], Lord Phillips MR said that:

> the court will bear in mind that, just as individual states enjoy a margin of appreciation which permits them to respond, within the law, in a manner that is not uniform, so there will often be an area of discretion permitted to the executive of a country before a response can be demonstrated to infringe the Convention…The court will ask the question, applying an objective test, whether the decision maker could reasonably have concluded that the interference was necessary to achieve one or more of the legitimate aims recognised by the Convention [38].

The margin of discretion/deference applies mainly to the question whether the government is entitled to override the right on a public interest ground (*R (S) v Chief Constable of South Yorkshire Police* [2004] at [27], [64]). In cases where a right is vaguely defined it could also influence the court's decision as to extent of the right (see *R (Gentle) v Prime Minister* [2008]: decision to invade Iraq; did not engage right to life).

Where deference applies the court will interfere only if the decision is clearly flawed. However there is uncertainty both as to when deference should apply and to its limits. In *Huang v Secretary of State* (2007) Lord Bingham thought that the principle of deference was relatively easy to apply but difficult to identify in theory and that it depends heavily on the context. Some writers refer to 'due deference' meaning that the government must justify the trust placed in it in the particular context, for example by showing that it has carefully considered the human rights implications. This makes human rights law closely resemble domestic judicial review.

Because all public authorities are obliged to respect Convention rights unless overridden by primary legislation (Section 21.2) there seems to be no place in human rights cases for any matter to be absolutely non-justiciable. Indeed in *R (BBC) v Secretary of State* (2012) [53] the Divisional Court thought that the matter was essentially that of giving 'appropriate weight' to the views of the government but the final decision is for the court.

The kinds of cases where deference is required are similar to those applying in domestic judicial review (Section 19.7.2). In human rights cases the most important concern is to avoid trespassing on the democratic territory of Parliament. The width of the margin of discretion depends on the importance of the right, the importance of the public interest in question and the democratic content of the decision. The margin is greatest in relation to Parliament itself. Thus in *R (S) v Chief Constable of South Yorkshire Police* [2004] Lord Woolf said [16]:

> I regard it as being fundamental that the court keeps at the forefront of its consideration its lack of any democratic credentials.

The margin is not applied automatically. The government must provide some rational support for its actions (*R v Shaylor* 2002) [61]; *Matthews v Ministry of Defence* [2003]). In the context of the 'margin of appreciation' the Strasbourg Court has emphasised that it may depend upon whether the matter has been subject to considered democratic deliberation as opposed to 'unquestioning and passive adherence to a historic tradition' (*Hirst v UK (No 2)* (2004). The court might be influenced by the extent to which a controversial government decision has been debated in Parliament or is supported by international Conventions, expert opinion and so on. Thus in *R (Animal Defenders International) v Secretary of State for Culture, Media and Sport [2008] 1 AC 1312 which concerned censorship of political advertising it was important that issue had been fully debated in Parliament.* Some writers refer to 'due deference' meaning that the government must justify the trust placed in it, for example by showing that it has carefully considered the human rights implications. This makes human rights law closely resemble domestic judicial review.

The guide to deference provided by Laws LJ (dissenting) in *International Transport Roth GmbH v Secretary of State for the Home Dept* [2003] 3 WLR 444 [83]–[87] is often cited. The case concerned a scheme to fine truckers for every illegal immigrant discovered in their vehicles. A majority of the Court of Appeal held that this violated the right to a fair trial under the HRA. Laws LJ took account of the following factors to justify refusal to intervene in decisions made by what he called 'the democratic powers':

▶ great deference paid to an Act of Parliament as the highest level of authority;
▶ more scope for deference where the Convention itself requires a balance to be struck than in the case of the unqualified rights, but even here there may be some scope for deference in defining the right, for example deprivation of liberty (see Section 20.3);
▶ greater deference in relation to matters peculiarly within the responsibility of the executive such as security, defence and immigration. Less deference in relation to matters directly concerning the courts;
▶ deference to matters especially within the expertise of the democratic powers such as macro-economic policy.

The margin of discretion is particularly strong in areas involving controversial political or ethical issues which depend on moral or political value judgements (eg *R (Countryside Alliance) v A-G* [2008]: hunting; *R (ProLife Alliance) v BBC* [2003]: taste and decency). It is also strong in relation to legislation intended to meet general welfare goals such as health or housing, these being matters of priority appropriate to democratic decision.

In *Poplar Housing and Regeneration Community Association v Donoghue* [2001], a housing case, Lord Woolf LCJ remarked that:

> the economic and other implications of any policy in this area are extremely complex and far reaching. This is an area where in our judgement the courts must treat the decisions of Parliament as to what is in the public interest with particular deference. (at [69])

> (See also *R (Sinclair Collis Ltd) v Secretary of State for Health* [2012] 2 WLR 304: an EU case concerning a ban on tobacco sales: intensity of review depends on democratic content of decision).

On the other hand some matters are so important as to fall outside any margin of discretion. Here the court will do the interest balancing itself. These include the right to life at least where the state directly takes life (Section 21.4.1); deprivation of liberty (*Hillingdon BC v Neary* [2011] 4 All ER 585: a fundamental constitutional right [23] 24]); discrimination (Baroness Hale in *Ghaidan v Mendoza* [2004]); the right to a fair trial (*R v A* [2001]), In *A v Secretary of State for the Home Dept* [2005], a majority of the House of Lords deferred to the government as to whether the terrorist threat provoked by 9/11 amounted to an emergency so as to justify derogating from the detention without trial provisions of the ECHR since this was a matter of political judgement. However, it was held that the court could decide whether the detention powers themselves were proportionate since personal liberty was directly at issue (see Lord Bingham [39]–[42]).

The judges have sometimes disagreed as to whether deference should be given. This suggests that their own political views as to the importance of the right are relevant. For example in *A* (above) Lord Walker dissented on the ground that the government is the best judge of a security risk and Lord Hoffmann held that the court could decide whether there was an emergency since to allow the executive to do so threatened the rule of law. In *R (ProLife Alliance) v BBC* [2003] which concerned a ban on an upsetting party political broadcast, while the majority deferred to the judgement of the BBC, Lord Scott dissented because of the importance of free speech for democracy. In *Re G (Adoption) (Unmarried Couple)* (2009): the majority did not apply a margin of discretion to Northern Ireland legislation preventing unmarried couples from adopting because of the duty of court to combat discrimination. Lord Walker dissented on grounds of respect for cultural differences which should be resolved democratically.

The law relating to proportionality and in particular to deference therefore brings the courts directly into the political arena.

Summary

▶ The HRA, while not incorporating the ECHR as such, has given the main rights created by the ECHR effect in domestic law. UK legislation must be interpreted to be compatible with Convention rights, and public bodies other than Parliament must comply with Convention rights. The courts must take the decisions of the ECHR into account but are not bound by them. However the UK courts take a cautious approach and follow Strasbourg closely.

▶ The Act is territorial and applies outside the UK only exceptionally.

Summary cont'd

▶ Parliamentary supremacy is preserved in that Convention rights must give way where they are incompatible with a statute. The courts have taken a moderate approach in relation to the obligation to interpret statutes, 'so far as it is possible to do so', to be compatible with Convention rights. However there are differences of emphasis between judges as to the assumptions on which interpretation should be approached, in particular the extent to which established English law should be respected.

▶ Where primary legislation is incompatible the court can draw attention to violations by making a declaration of incompatibility. There is a 'fast-track' procedure available in special circumstances to enable amendments to legislation to be made. The government must be explicit as to any intention to override Convention rights.

▶ The HRA can be directly enforced only against public authorities and by a 'victim' defined in accordance with the case law of the European Court.

▶ 'Public authority' includes all the activities of government bodies proper and courts and tribunals, but in relation to bodies that have a mixture of public and private functions (eg social landlords) only to their public 'acts'. The courts seem to be taking a similar approach to the question of what constitutes a public function as in judicial review cases.

▶ 'Horizontal effect' may be direct, where the court is required to enforce a right against a private person, or indirect, where the state is required to protect against violations by private persons. It is not clear how far the Act has horizontal effect, although there are several devices that might enable it to do so.

▶ Some Convention rights can be overridden by prescribed public interest concerns or other rights and a principle of fair balance runs through the Convention as a whole. The courts are guided by the concept of proportionality. While these devices help to structure and rationalise decision making they do not remove the need for the court to make a subjective political judgement.

▶ The courts have applied the notion of 'margin of appreciation' or 'margin of discretion', particularly in the context of decisions made by elected bodies (see also Section 19.7.1). The width of the margin depends on various factors, chief among which are the importance and extent of the particular right that is violated in relation to the seriousness of the public harm if the right were not overridden, and the extent to which the matter involves controversial political, social or economic choices. It remains controversial whether the courts provide the best method of protecting fundamental rights.

Exercises

(You should also refer to material in Chapters 21 and cases in Chapter 9.)

22.1 What is meant by describing the HRA as creating a 'constitutional dialogue'? Do you agree with this description?

22.2 Has the Human Rights Act created a British bill of rights?

22.3 According to Lord Bingham the court's role under the Human Rights Act is democratic because Parliament has given the courts 'a very specific wholly democratic mandate' (*A v Secretary of State for the Home Dept* [2005] at [42]. Do you agree?

22.4 Explain and compare the constitutional significance of the declaration of incompatibility and the statement of compatibility.

22.5 'My impression is that two factors are contributing to a misunderstanding of the remedial scheme of the 1998 Act. First there is the constant refrain that a judicial reading down or reading in would flout the will of Parliament. The second factor may be an excessive concentration on linguistic factors of the particular statute' (Lord Steyn in *Ghaidan v Mendoza* [2004]). Explain and critically evaluate this statement.

22.6 That the Act 'was no doubt intended to strengthen the rule of law but not to inaugurate the rule of lawyers'. *R (Alconbury Developments Ltd) v Secretary of State for the Environment, Transport and the Regions [2001] at* [129] Lord Hoffmann. Explain and consider whether Lord Hoffmann has been proved right.

22.7 Advise on the chances of success of challenges to each of the following under the HRA:
  (i) the failure of the Ministry of Defence to provide adequate water purification facilities in UK army bases in Afghanistan creating a risk of lethal illness;
  (ii) the refusal of the army authorities to give home leave to a British soldier to enable him to attend his grandmother's funeral;
  (iii) the failure of the British army to provide protective combat equipment comparable to that provided to the soldiers of other countries;
  (iv) the expulsion of Mary from Utopia, a British dependent territory on the ground that she committed serious offences as a child. Mary claims that she will face a forced marriage in the only other country where she has a right to live;
  (v) The expulsion of George from the UK for violating immigration law. George is married to Martha a British citizen who is unwell and cannot support their two young children alone. Would your answer differ if George was being extradited to the USA on a charge of conspiracy to disrupt the US government?

22.8 Advise on the chances of a successful challenge to the following:
  (i) a decision by the NHS to refuse a life-extending drug to elderly people suffering from certain terminal illnesses on the grounds that the cost is not worth the benefit and the funding is desperately needed for medical supplies in support of military interventions against non-democratic states;
  (ii) a government order to slaughter a flock of birds which are owned by a religious community to which the birds are sacred. The government's reason is that the presence of the birds creates a risk to human health. The community leaders believe that any risk can be minimised by suitable protective measures.

22.9 Matthew who is serving a long prison sentence for a banking fraud requests to be moved to a prison nearer his home so that his young children will not lose touch with him. He also claims that he is at risk of death in his present prison because some of his fellow prisoners were victims of his crime. The prison authorities refuse this request on the ground that moving him is too expensive and the risk to him can be minimised by keeping him in solitary confinement. Matthew requests a hearing before an independent body. This request is also refused.

22.10 A statute (fictitious) provides that 'a landlord may evict a tenant where the occupation of the premises by the tenant is not sustainable'. Trebangor Council evicts Mary who has occupied a home owned by the Council for many years together with her elderly mother and two children. The reason the council gives for the eviction is that there is a housing shortage in the area and that Mary is a troublemaker with a record of anti-social behaviour. Mary's mother can be accommodated in a care home. Mary wishes to challenge her eviction under the HRA. Advise her.

What would be the position if Mary's landlord was a private landlord but the facts were the otherwise the same?

Further reading

Allan, 'Human Rights and Judicial Review: A Critique of "Due Deference"' (2006) 65 CLJ 695

Beatson, Grosz, Hickman and Singh, *Human Rights: Judicial Protection in the UK* (Sweet & Maxwell 2008)

Buxton, 'The Human Rights Act and Private Law' (2000) 116 LQR 116

Buxton, 'The Future of Declarations of Incompatibility' [2010] PL 261

Clapham, *Human Rights Obligations of Non State Actors* (Oxford University Press 2006)

Clayton, 'The Human Rights Act: the Good the Bad and the Ugly' *Administrative Law Bar Association*, Summer Conference 2010

Ewing, *Bonfire of the Liberties: New Labour, Human Rights and the Rule of Law* (Oxford University Press 2010)

Ewing and Than, 'The Continuing Futility of the Human Rights Act' [2008] PL 668

Fenwick, Phillipson and Masterman (eds), *Judicial Reasoning under the Human Rights Act* (Cambridge University Press 2007)

Gardbaum, 'How Successful and Distinctive is the Human Rights Act? An Expatriate Comparativist's Assessment' (2011) 74 MLR 195

Gould, Lazarus, Swiney, *Public Protection, Proportionality and the Search for Balance,* Ministry of Justice (2007).

Hickman, 'Constitutional Dialogue, Constitutional Theories and the Human Rights Act 1998' [2005] PL 306

Hickman, 'Public Law after the Human Rights Act' (Hart Publishing 2010)

Hickman, 'The Courts and Politics after the Human Rights Act' [2008] PL 84

Hickman, 'The Substance and Structure of Proportionality' [2008] PL 694

Hiebert, 'Governing under the Human Rights Act: the Limitations of Wishful Thinking' [2012] PL 27

Irvine, 'A British Interpretation of Convention Rights' [2012] PL 236

Jowell, 'Judicial Deference and Human Rights: A Question of Competence', in Craig and Rawlings (eds), *Law and Administration in Europe* (Oxford University Press 2003)

Kavanagh, 'The Elusive Divide between Interpretation and Legislation under the Human Rights Act 1998' (2004) 24 OJLS 259

Kavanagh, 'The Role of Parliamentary Intention in Adjudication under the Human Rights Act 1998' (2006) 26 OJLS 179

Kavanagh, *Constitutional Review under the Human Rights Act* (Cambridge University Press 2009)

Kavanagh, 'Judging the Judges under the Human Rights Act' [2009] PL 287

Klug, 'A Bill of Rights: Do We Need One or Do We Already Have One?' [2007] PL 701

Lakin, 'How to Make Sense of the Human Rights Act 1998: The Ises and Oughts of the British Constitution' (2010) 30 OJLS 399

Lester, 'The Utility of the Human Rights Act: A Reply to Keith Ewing' [2005] PL 249

Lester and Beattie, 'Human Rights and the British Constitution' in Jowell and Oliver (eds), *The Changing Constitution* (Oxford University Press 2007)

Lewis, 'The European Ceiling on Human Rights' [2007] PL 720

Mead, 'Outcomes Aren't All : Defending Process Based Review under the Human Rights Act' [2011] PL 61

Nicol, 'Law and Politics after the Human Rights Act' [2006] PL 722

Phillipson, 'Deference, Discretion and Democracy in the Human Rights Era' (2007) 40 CLP 57

Phillipson and Williams, 'Horizontal Effect and the Constitutional Constraint' [2011] 74 MLR 878

Further reading cont'd

Sales, 'The General and the Particular: Parliament and the Courts under the Scheme of the European Convention on Human Rights', in Andenas and Fairgrieve (eds), *Tom Bingham and the Transformation of the Law* (Oxford University Press 2009)

Sales, 'Strasbourg Jurisprudence and the Human Rights Act: A Response to Lord Irvine' [2012] PL 253

Sales and Ekins, 'Rights-Consistent Interpretation and the Human Rights Act' 1998 (2011) 127 LQR 217

Shah and Poole, 'The Impact of the Human Rights Act on the House of Lords' [2009] PL 347

Steyn, 'Deference: A Tangled Story' [2005] PL 346

Symposium, 'Can Human Rights Survive?' [2007] PL 209

Wilde, 'The Extraterritorial Application of the Human Rights Act' (2005) 65 CLJ 47

Williams, 'A Fresh Perspective on Hybrid Public Authorities under the Human rights Act: Private Contractors, Rights-Stripping and Chameleonic Horizontal Effect' [2011] PL 139

Wright, 'Interpreting Section 2 of the Human Rights Act: Towards an Indigenous Jurisprudence of Human Rights' [2009] PL 595

Young, 'Is Dialogue working under the Human Rights Act?' [2011] PL 773

Young, 'In Defence of Due Deference' (2009) 72 MLR 554

Chapter 23
Freedoms of expression and assembly

Introduction: justifications for freedom of expression

The arguments for freedom of expression were outlined by Lord Steyn in *R v Secretary of State for the Home Dept ex parte Simms* [2000] at [34]–[41], see also *R (BBC) v Secretary of State for the Home Dept* [2012] at [35]–[43]. They are of two kinds. The first kind, from a liberal position, regards freedom of expression as an end in itself: a defining characteristic of a human being. Individuals are regarded as capable of 'making up their own minds about what is good or bad, true and false and are properly entitled to participate equally in politics'.

The second kind of justification associated with republicanism (Section 2.5) regards freedom of expression as *instrumentally* valuable, that is valuable as a means by which to pursue some other valuable end. The ends in question were identified by Mill (Section 2.3.3) as democracy, self-fulfillment and the testing of truth.

As regards democracy Lord Steyn (above) emphasised freedom of expression in informing debate, as a safety valve to encourage consent and as a brake on the abuse of power. Democracy can flourish only in circumstances where there is a free press with access to government Thus in *Hector v A-G of Antigua and Bermuda* [1990] 2 All ER 103 Lord Bridge said that 'in a free democratic society ... those who hold office in government must always be open to criticism. Any attempt to stifle or fetter such criticism amounts to political censorship of the most insidious and objectionable kind.' However in *R v Shaylor* [2002] Lord Hutton suggested, redolent of the 'dignified constitution' (Section 1.6), that freedom of expression might undesirably weaken confidence in those who govern us (although the opposite might be said). Free expression requires not only the right to criticise government and challenge orthodoxy but also fair opportunities at elections and other public debates (*Handyside v UK* [1976]; *Bowman v UK* [1998]; *Castells v Spain* [1992] 14 EHRR 445.

An issue here is whether freedom of expression should apply to those who reject democracy itself. In *Kuznetov v Russia* [2008] ECHR 10877/04 [45] the Strasbourg court appeared to suggest that freedom of assembly could be restricted if rejection of democratic principles are involved. However it is arguably wrong to exclude discussion of other possible forms of government.

The liberal argument that freedom of expression provides a means to the end of self-development starts with the proposition that the proper end of humanity is the realisation of individual potential which cannot flourish without freedom of expression. However self-development also requires protection for privacy, so there is a conflict between these fundamental human needs (*Von Hannover v Germany* [1995]).

The argument that freedom of expression facilitates the pursuit of truth and the acquisition of knowledge suppressed by official orthodoxy was expressed in the seventeenth century by John Milton in his *Areopagitica*. Mill argued that 'truth', which he equated with the general good, can best be discovered and preserved by constant questioning. However this provides relatively weak support since truth is not always necessarily conducive to the general welfare. Karl Popper states, free critical discussion at least provides a means by which to eliminate errors in our thinking and thus to move towards ever more plausible working hypotheses but never incontrovertible truths (*The Open Society and Its Enemies* (Routledge, 1996)). However, it could be argued most obviously in relation to elections that freedom of expression allows the loudest (best funded) voice to prevail. According to the philosopher of science from a liberal perspective, one point of freedom of expression is arguably to keep diversity and disagreement alive. Thus Bollinger suggests that freedom of expression facilitates 'the development of [a] capacity for tolerance' ('The Tolerance Society' [1990] CLR 979). A capacity for tolerance weakens 'a general bias against receiving or acknowledging new ideas' (ibid). As Locke recognised (*On Tolerance* (1698)) it is particularly valuable as a means of keeping the peace in large and complex societies containing people with varied beliefs and interests.

Freedom of expression is not absolute Not all aspects of it are equally important and it may be overridden by other factors (Section 23.2). This leads to the danger, identified by Berlin (Section 2.4), of freedom of expression being regarded as a 'positive freedom' conditional upon those in power assessing its worthiness. Thus in *City of London Corp v Samede* [2012] 2 All ER 1039 [41] Lord Neuberger MR warned against giving particular weight to matters which the judge considers to be especially important or with which he agrees.

Mill distinguished between causing *harm* which should be prohibited and causing *offence* which should not. Indeed being offended or shocked might be considered good, as stimulating thought (see Lord Scott (dissenting) in *R (Prolife Alliance) v BBC* [2003] (Section 23.3)). However, it is not clear what counts as harm. Mill took harm to mean interfering with someone's rights or interests but this begs the questions of what counts as an 'interest'. Am I harmed if I am seriously upset or offended by someone attacking my religion? This raises the difficult issue of 'hate speech' (Section 23.6).

Freedom of expression includes both the *content* of what is said and the form and place where it is expressed. In R (*ProLife Alliance*) v BBC [2003] which concerned a ban on a televised party political broadcast regarded as offensive, Lord Hoffmann drew a distinction between a complete ban and refusing to give someone a platform to disseminate offensive material. Just as no one has a right to have his or her work published by a particular publisher, no one has a right to appear on television. He emphasised the pervasive influence of television, with the implication that protective measures are especially justified. Lord Scott dissenting thought that this analogy may be unreal given the importance of television as a medium of political communication and the state's positive duty to ensure the dissemination of opinion.

In *R (BBC) v Secretary of State* [2012] the government had refused to allow a live interview by the BBC with a person who had been detained for 7 years without charge pending extradition. In overruling the government's refusal as disproportionate the Divisional Court emphasised the watchdog role of the press and the importance of the immediacy and personal nature of television. No countervailing security consideration was raised by the government relating to the particular circumstances. General objections to giving publicity to suspected terrorists were not enough.

23.2 The legal status of freedom of expression

Article 10 of the European Convention on Human Rights (ECHR) defines freedom of expression as:

> freedom to hold opinions and to receive and impart information and ideas without interference by public authority and regardless of frontiers. This article shall not prevent states from requiring the licensing of broadcasting, television or cinema enterprise.

The extent of freedom of expression is influenced by the sort of expression approved of by the state. Thus some kinds of expression are given greater weight than others. Great weight is given to political expression through the media since this is regarded as essential to democracy (Lord Bingham in *McCartan Turkington Breen v Times Newspapers* [2001] at 290–91). The European Court has stressed that freedom of political debate is at the very core of the concept of a democratic society which prevails throughout the Convention (see *Castells v Spain* (1992); *Jersild v Denmark* [1994] 19 EHRR 1). Great weight is also given to open justice in the form of the publication of fully reasoned court judgments since this is a means of holding the judiciary to account *(R (Mohammed) v Secretary of State for Foreign Affairs* [2010]; Section 23.3).

Less weight is given to commercial expression such as advertising and possibly the least weight is given to lifestyle matters such as pornography (*City of London Corp v Samede* [2012] at [41]: 'political and economic views are at the top end of the scale, pornography and vapid tittle-tattle towards the bottom'). In *R v Secretary of State for the Home Dept, ex p Simms* [1999] a prisoner was entitled to have access to a journalist in order to publicise his claim that he was wrongly convicted but Lord Steyn thought that he would not have had such access to indulge in pornography or even in a general political or economic debate (see also *R (British American Tobacco UK Ltd) v Secretary of State for Health* [2004] EWHC 2493: advertising; *'Miss Behavin' v Belfast City Council* [2007] 3 All ER 1007: sexual services). It is not clear how much weight is given to cultural matters such as theatre and works of art. However where these conflict with religious susceptibilities, at least those of influential sections of the community, it seems that the latter carry greater weight (*Otto Preminger Institut v Austria* [1994]).

Some statutes give specific protection to political freedom of expression. The main examples are the Bill of Rights 1688, the Parliamentary Papers Act 1841 (Section 11.6.3) and the Defamation Acts 1952 and 1996 (Section 23.4). The Education (No 2) Act 1986, imposes a duty on universities to protect freedom of speech on their premises. Sometimes statutes protect freedom of expression against some general restriction (eg Environmental Protection Act 1990, s 79(6A): noise controls: political demonstrations exempted).

Article 10 confers the right of freedom of expression subject to 'duties and responsibilities'. These entitle the state to limit freedom of expression for the following purposes. The court must balance these against freedom of expression in the particular circumstances of each case according to the principle of *proportionality* (Section 22.7.1):

- national security;
- territorial integrity or public safety;
- prevention of disorder or crime;
- protection of health or morals;

▶ protection of the reputation or rights of others. Thus freedom of expression may be compromised by the right to a fair trial (Art 6), privacy (Art 8) and freedom of religion (Art 9).
▶ preventing the disclosure of information received in confidence;
▶ maintaining the authority and impartiality of the judiciary.

▶ Numerous statutes and common law principles have restricted freedom of expression for the following main purposes. These conform to Article 10 in principle. However any restriction must be proportionate in the specific circumstances.
▶ security public order and safety;
▶ reputation;
▶ protection of personal data, for example medical records and student records held by universities (Data Protection Act 1998);
▶ sexual morality (Obscene Publications Act 1959: 'deprave and corrupt' subject to defence of artistic merit), Cinemas Act 1985 local authorities licensing of cinema performances, Video Recordings Act 2010);
▶ child protection, particularly in relation to reporting court proceedings (Children Act 1989, s 97(2); Magistrates Courts Act 1980, s 69(2)(c); see *Pelling v Bruce-Williams* [2004] 3 All ER 875; *Re Webster (A Child) (No 1)* [2006] EWHC 2733);
▶ combating racial, religious and sexual hatred;
▶ the independence of judicial proceedings (below);
▶ protection against misleading advertising and professional claims;
▶ intellectual property such as copyright.

23.3 Press freedom and censorship

In the eighteenth century Blackstone introduced the distinction between 'prior restraint – censorship', requiring government approval in advance, and punishing the speaker after the event (*Commentaries* (1765) III, 17). Prior restraint is regarded as an especially serious violation of freedom of expression because it removes from the public sphere the possibility of assessing the matter, whereas punishment may be regarded as a legitimate compromise between competing goods. Prior restraint should therefore be only a last resort particularly in the case of news, 'which is a perishable commodity' (see *Observer and Guardian Newspapers v UK* [1992] 14 EHRR 153). Indeed in *Open Door and Dublin Well Woman v Ireland* [1992] 15 EHRR 244 five judges thought that prior restraint should never be tolerated. On the other hand if there are serious penalties such as fines for publication after the event, these are likely to have a 'chilling' effect by discouraging publication so that Blackstone's distinction may be somewhat illusory.

As we have seen political expression is especially important both as a means of holding government to account and participating in democracy. By virtue of its 'duties and responsibilities' under Article 10 the press is the public's watchdog for this purpose. Thus Lord Bingham in *McCartan Turkington Breen v Times Newspapers Ltd* [2001] 2 AC 277 stressed the importance of a free, active, professional and inquiring media to a modern participatory democracy, pointing out that ordinary citizens cannot usually participate directly but can do so indirectly through the media (290–91). The European Court has held that the state has a duty to safeguard the free flow of information and opinion through the media even in respect of objectionable opinions. *(See Jersild v Denmark* [1994]: television interview was entitled to include racist views provided that interviewer did not associate himself with them. See also *Lingens v Austria* [1986] 8 EHRR 407, *Castells v Spain* (1992) [43]).

The European Court has emphasised that press freedom, includes the need to give some journalistic latitude in order to prevent the chilling effect of vague restrictions which may discourage the media from bold investigations of wrongdoing among the powerful. (See *Thomas v Luxemburg* [2003] 36 EHRR 359, 373; *Fressoz v France* [1999] 5 BHRC 654, 656; *Selisto v Finland* [2006] 44 EHRR 144, 161.)

An important aspect of press freedom concerns open justice in court proceedings as a means of holding the judiciary to account. The press has a duty to report on matters before a court subject to particular exclusions which must be justified under the proportionality principle either on public interest grounds or to protect other rights such as privacy (Section 23.5). Thus in *R (Mohammed) v Secretary of State for Foreign Affairs* [2010] the government unsuccessfully challenged the disclosure in a court judgment of evidence concerning the government's alleged complicity in torture. The Court of Appeal emphasised that the court has a public duty to be open and that, without the commitment of an independent media, the operation of the principle of open justice would be irremediably diminished and democracy and the rule of law threatened [38] [41] [57] [134] [180] [184].

(See also *Sunday Times v UK* [1979] at [65], *AH v West London Mental Health Tribunal* [2011] UKUT 74, *Independent News and Media Ltd v A* [2010] EWCA Civ 343), *Re S (A Child)* [2004] 4 All ER 683 [602]–[604]; *Re Webster (A Child) (No 1)* [2006] EWHC 2733: press but not the public were permitted to attend a high-profile case involving childcare proceedings; Ministry of Justice, *Confidence and Confidentiality: Openness in Family Courts – A New Approach* (CP 10/07, 2007), Davies,' The Rights Approach to the Right to a Public Hearing' [2012] PL 11.)

Press comment is restricted on pending trials that create a 'substantial risk' that the course of justice will be seriously impeded or prejudiced (Contempt of Court Act 1981, s 2; There is an important defence that the publication contains a discussion in good faith of public affairs where the risk of prejudice is merely incidental to the discussion. (See *Sunday Times v UK* [1979] 2 EHRR 245, *A-G v English* [1983] 1 AC 116.)

There is an archaic common law offence of 'scandalising the judiciary' by making personal criticisms of a judge. For example the Attorney General for Northern Ireland threatened to prosecute the former minister Peter Hain for referring in his memoirs to. the 'high handed and idiosyncratic behaviour' of a certain judge (*Times* 10 May 2012).

Press freedom is protected by sections 3 and 32 of the Data Protection Act 1998 which exempts journalistic, literary or artistic material processed 'with a view to publication' from the protection given to personal data by the 'data protection' principles of the Act. These principles concern fairness in obtaining and processing data, use, accuracy and the access of subjects to the data. The exemption currently applies where the data controller having regard in particular to the special importance of the public interest in freedom of expression, reasonably believes that publication would be in the public interest. However the Leveson Report (below) downgrades the exemption. Leveson proposes that the exemption be limited to cases where the material is *necessary* for publication and that it should apply only where the public interest outweighs the interest of privacy the two being assumed to start with equal weight. This could seriously chill freedom of expression.

The media is not uniformly regulated. There is significant state censorship over broadcasting including a general power to require announcements or to ban broadcasts exercisable by the Secretary of State (Broadcasting Act 1990, s 10; BBC Licence Agreement). There are also specific requirements, including impartiality and taste, policed by the Office of Communications (OFCOM), which replaced a variety of other bodies (Communications Act 2003). The BBC is not regulated by OFCOM but has an internal regulator in the form of the BBC Trust which is nominally independent of both management and government but has a confused overlap with both. Its Chair is appointed by the government and the Trust appoints the Director General of the BBC. Broadcasting regulation can be justified in that, unlike the print media, access to the airwaves is limited being effectively a government controlled monopoly offering the public limited choice. However technical developments including the internet have opened up so many different outlets that regulation may be less appropriate. Where there is a regulatory mechanism the courts are reluctant to impose their own judgements, short of reviewing unreasonable decisions. In *R (ProLife Alliance) v BBC* [2003] a majority of the House of Lords using the notion of deference (Section 19.7) left it to the BBC to decide whether a requirement to ensure that programmes do not offend 'good taste and decency' overrode the right to freedom of expression of the Alliance, who wished to include in an election broadcast images of the process of abortion. By taking this line their Lordships accepted that even political expression could be restricted on the ground of taste alone (see also *R v Broadcasting Standards Commission, ex p BBC* [2001] QB 885, *R (Animal Defenders International) v Secretary of State* [2008], *Appelby v UK* [2003] 37 EHRR 783).

Lord Scott dissented on classical liberal grounds. Far from wishing to protect the public against offence he claimed that 'the public in a mature democracy are not entitled to be offended by the broadcasting of such a programme'.... a ban would be 'positively inimical to the values of a democratic society to which values it must be assumed that the public adheres' [98]. ... a broadcaster's mindset that rejects a party election television programme on the ground that large numbers of the voting public would find the programme 'offensive' denigrates the voting public, treats them like children who need to be protected from the unpleasant realities of life, seriously undervalues their political maturity and can only promote (voter apathy)' [99].

By contrast with the broadcast media, since the abolition in 1695 of state licensing of printing presses, the government has no censorship powers over the printed word. This is regarded as an essential safeguard for the press against state interference. The Press Complaints Commission, a voluntary body controlled by the industry itself, has no investigatory or enforcement powers and is widely regarded as lacking independence.

However the *Leveson Report* (HMSO 29 November 2012) has recommended a form of state regulation. The report was a response to substantial abuses by journalists of the privacy of individuals primarily by hacking e mails and mobile phones. Leveson stressed that there should be no power to prevent publication and no direct government regulation of the press. He recommended that a new 'independent self-regulatory' body should be created by the industry. Its process and membership should be independent of press and government interests (*Guardian* 30 December 2012). It should be appointed by a panel which has a substantial majority 'demonstrably independent' of press and government interests. The regulator should have powers to arbitrate disputes, investigate complaints and to investigate on its own initiative. It could also receive 'third party complaints' from the public (something that might open the floodgates!). It should draw up a press code of conduct dealing with privacy and accuracy. It would be empowered to impose penalties including fines of up to £1,000,000 and requirements to correct and apologise. The scheme would be voluntary but those who join it would have the incentive of reduced liability to damages and costs in the courts. (This would require statutory enactment. Moreover it has been suggested that penaiisng those who do not join the regulator would violate Art. 10 of the ECHR).

The Leveson Report raises two main problems. Firstly in order to reassure the public as to the independence, effectiveness and integrity of the regulator Leveson thought that safeguards are required in the form of a statutory body. This body would not directly regulate the press but would 'validate' or ' recognise' the regulator as regards its composition, standards and the extent to which the press signed up to it. It would also act as a 'backstop' if voluntary regulation failed although precisely how and in what circumstances is unclear. It is arguable that such a body indirectly threatens freedom of expression by amounting to a form of state licencing which gives the executive influence over the press. The government responded to this in March 2013 by proposing that the regulator be validated by royal charter rather than statute. In a manner common to constitutional reform this was devised in private negotiations between the political parties. Since, as an exercise of the prerogative a royal charter is a form of law uniquely under the control of ministers this does nothing to protect the press. However it is proposed in the Enterprise and Regulatory Reform Bill that a royal charter cannot be amended except under its own terms in this case a requirement of a two-thirds vote in Parliament (of course this lock could be removed by an ordinary statute). Under the proposed charter a separate body to appoint the regulator is included and neither this body nor the regulator itself must be subject to press or government control. The newspaper industry would appoint one member of the panel that appoints the regulator but has no veto over any appointments. The Code of Conduct would be written by a committee comprising one third editors, journalists, and lay persons. The Charter is vague or as to who appoints the appointment panel. As usual there seems nothing to prevent this being recruited from the personal networks of the powerful.

The second problem is that Leveson made no proposals for regulation of internet media such as blogs and social networks. Like the press the internet is subject to the general law but its regulation raises formidable practical problems primarily because of the vast number of sources difficult to identify many of which are overseas and outside the reach of the law.

The courts have general prior restraint powers in the form of an injunction, carrying imprisonment for contempt of court. The Attorney General can seek an injunction in the name of the public interest, most notably in the case of publications that risk prejudicing legal proceedings such as newspaper comments on matters related to pending litigation (contempt of court) and in the interests of government confidentiality or national security (Section 24.3). A temporary injunction pending a full trial can be granted on the basis that there is an arguable case, since once material is published there is no turning back. A temporary injunction prevents anyone, whether a party or not, publishing the material with the intention to impede the court's purpose in granting the injunction (*A-G v Observer Ltd* [1988] 1 All ER 385; *A-G v Times Newspapers Ltd* [1991] 2 All ER 398). This can include a 'super-injunction' which prevents reports even of the fact that the injunction has been granted (Section 11.6.3). However an injunction will be granted only if it serves a useful purpose. Once material becomes public, even if unlawfully, the press has a duty to disseminate it and further restraint cannot be justified (see *Observer and Guardian Newspapers v UK [1992] 14 EHRR 153*).

The importance of press freedom was reinforced by section 12 of the Human Rights Act 1998. This provides firstly that a court order limiting the 'Convention right of freedom of expression' cannot normally be granted in the absence of the respondent. This affects interim injunctions which might be sought as an emergency measure. Secondly section 12 prevents an interim order being made unless the applicant is likely to establish that publication should not be allowed. Thirdly section 12 requires the court to have particular regard to freedom of expression and,

> where the proceedings relate to material which the respondent claims or which appears to the court to be journalistic, literary or artistic material (or to conduct connected with such material), to [have regard to] (a) the extent to which (i) the material has, or is about to, become available to the public; or (ii) it is, or would be, in the public interest for the material to be published; and (b) any relevant privacy code.

However even after the Human Rights Act 1998 the UK courts have taken a generous approach to injunctions. In *A-G v Punch* [2003] 1 All ER 396, a magazine published a series of articles by David Shaylor, a former member of the security services against whom a prosecution under the Official Secrets Act was pending for disclosing information about intelligence operations. The House of Lords upheld an injunction which prevented publication of any material obtained by Mr Shaylor in the course of or as a result of his employment in the security services even though their lordships were critical of the chilling effect of restrictions that are not precisely targeted [61]–[63].

In *Douglas and Zeta-Jones v Hello! Ltd* [2001] 2 All ER 289 the Court of Appeal held that section 12 merely ensures that the competing rights in question are taken into account at the interim stage. In *Cream Holdings v Banerjee* [2004] 4 All ER 618 the House of Lords held that the normal threshold is that the applicant would 'more likely than not' succeed at the trial. However the approach must be flexible; for example if publication would cause serious harm, a lower threshold would be justified (eg *Thompson and Venables v News Group Newspapers Ltd* [2001]: disclosure of new identities of released prisoners at risk of threats to life).

It is important that the confidentiality of those who supply information to the press is protected. In *R v Central Criminal Court, ex p Bright, Alton and Rusbridger* [2001] 2 All ER 244 the Court of Appeal quashed a production order sought by the Crown against the editors of the *Guardian* and the *Observer* to disclose information received from David Shaylor, a former MI5 agent. It was held that disclosure would inhibit press freedom without there being a compelling reason for the disclosure.

The press also has statutory protection. Section 10 of the Contempt of Court Act 1981 protects the anonymity of a publisher's sources of information except where the court thinks that disclosure is necessary on the grounds of the interests of justice, national security or the prevention of crime and disorder. Section 10 enables the court to exercise a discretion between the competing concerns. Before the Human Rights Act 1998 the courts interpreted the exceptions broadly against the press, influenced by the common law idea that the press should have no special privileges (eg *X Ltd v Morgan Grampian Publishers Ltd* [1991] 1 AC 1: commercial interest outweighed press freedom). This was strongly criticised by the European Court in *Goodwin v UK* [1996] 22 EHRR 123 on the ground that the protection of journalistic confidentiality is crucial to press freedom. It has also been held that where national security or wrongdoing is involved the court will usually order disclosure (*X v Morgan Grampian* [1991]; *Ashworth Hospital v MGN*

Ltd [2001] 1 All ER 991). However in *John v Express Newspapers Ltd* [2000] 3 All ER 257, which concerned the leaking of legal advice, it was held following *Goodwin* that a confidential source should be publicly disclosed only as a last resort (see also *Financial Times v UK* [2009] *Times* 16 December: sources should be protected unless clear evidence of damage or harmful intent).

It has often been suggested that freedom of the media encourages indirect censorship by private commercial forces controlling the press or broadcast media which are intolerant of minority opinions. A free press is necessarily influenced by commercial concerns favouring a conformist majority by the need to sell newspapers or advertising space. There is also the possibility that control of an uncomfortably large share of the media might be concentrated in a single owner. To some extent this is regulated by the Communications Act 2003, which empowers the Secretary of State to refer a takeover or a merger to the Office of Fair Trading, which in turn can refer the matter to the Competition Commission.

23.4 Press freedom and reputation: defamation

Defamation concerns personal reputation, which is protected by the ECHR (Art 8). In *Reynolds v Times Newspapers Ltd* [2001] 2 AC 127 Lord Nicholls described reputation [as] 'an integral and important part of the dignity of the individual' (201). Apart from its role in ensuring that those who rule us are accountable, freedom of expression is also part of individual dignity. Moreover both interests secure autonomy by providing protection against arbitrary interference. Hence agonising and politically controversial choices must be made between conflicting rights with no agreed method of choosing between them.

Material is defamatory if it reflects on the claimant's reputation so as to lower him or her in the estimation of right-thinking members of society generally (*Sim v Stretch* [1936] 2 All ER 1237) or tends to cause the claimant to be shunned or avoided (*Youssoupoff v Metro-Goldwyn-Mayer Pictures Ltd* [1934] 50 TLR 581) or would bring the claimant into ridicule or contempt (*Dunlop Rubber Co Ltd v Dunlop* [1921] 1 AC 637).

A claimant must prove that the relevant material (i) is defamatory, (ii) has been published and (iii) refers to him or her. The Defamation Bill 2012, an object of which is to safeguard freedom of expression, adds that the statement must have caused serious harm. Publication means merely communication to another person, so each time an item is passed on (eg from journalist to newsroom to a newsagent) there is a separate publication. This might be regarded as highly unfair to news vendors, etc. who innocently pass on the material. The Defamation Bill partly protects such secondary publishers by allowing actions against them only where it would not be reasonably practicable to sue the author, editor or a commercial publisher.

Defamatory publications take one of two forms: namely, libel and slander. Material is libellous if it is published in a permanent form, for example writing or another recorded medium. It is slanderous if it takes a less than permanent form, for example word of mouth.

In general the press is subject to the law of defamation in the same way as anyone else. English law is widely regarded as relatively unsympathetic to the press and English courts are often chosen as a forum for defamation actions as opposed, for example to the US, where freedom of expression is enshrined in the Constitution. The main relevant difference is that in English law the defendant media have to prove the truth of any allegations they make, whereas more usually the onus is on the claimant to prove that the allegation is false.

However defamation law recognises the importance of freedom of expression. To this end there are various defences. These include:

1. *truth (or justification).* Subject to an exception under section 8 of the Rehabilitation of Offenders Act 1974 this can be pleaded even where a defendant has been actuated by malice (ie spite or ill will). The publication as a whole must be considered, so the truth of part is no defence;
2. *absolute privilege.* Liability cannot be imposed in the course of:
   (i) parliamentary proceedings (Section 11.6.3);
   (ii) contemporaneous reports of judicial proceedings (Defamation Act 1996, s 14. (c) high level official communications (*Chatterton v Secretary of State for India* (1895) 2 QB 189)).
3. *qualified privilege.* This applies only where the defendant honestly believes what he or she says to be true. Traditionally qualified privilege has applied where the defendant meets the following two requirements (see Lord Nicholls in *Reynolds* (2001) 194–95, 200):
   (i) the defendant has an interest or a duty (legal, social or moral) to communicate the relevant material to another or others;
   (ii) the recipient of the material must have a corresponding interest or duty to receive it (eg *Clift v Slough BC* [2009] 4 All ER 756: circular about anti-social staff member circulated more widely than necessary). This important matter is discussed further below (Section 23.4.2);

   Qualified privilege also applies to a range of 'fair and accurate' reports of official proceedings worldwide including legislatures, courts, inquiries and international organisations. Some including copies of government information notices, reports of public meetings and company meetings are subject to explanation or correction (Defamation Act 1996, s 15). The Defamation Bill proposes minor changes to this.
4. *fair comment* (recently renamed *'honest comment'* or *'honest opinion'*). This protects honest expressions of opinion on matters of public interest. The defence can be defeated by a showing that the defendant was actuated by malice. Important support to freedom of expression was provided in *British Chiropractic Association v Singh* [2010] EWCA Civ 350. The Court of Appeal held that a statement in a scientific journal concerning contested scientific conclusions was to be treated as an expression of opinion not a statement of fact. Thus the defendant would not be faced with the virtually impossible task of proving that the statement was true. The Court remarked that to treat matters of scientific controversy as matters of fact would be a disproportionate interference with freedom of expression: an Orwellian Ministry of Truth (see [18]–[23]). Similarly in *Joseph v Spiller* [2011] 1 All ER 947 the Supreme Court held that the comment need not identify the facts on which it was based in detail but must identify in general terms what led the commentator to make the comment so that the reader could understand what it was about and call for further explanation. The Defamation Bill reinforces this by giving qualified privilege to material in peer reviewed scientific and academic journals.

Two further features of the law protect freedom of expression. First the institution of the jury and second the limited availability of an injunction. Defamation actions (which are heard in the High Court) are usually tried with a jury, which is regarded as providing a safeguard against official repression (see Fox's Libel Act 1792). On the other hand the jury's power to decide the amount of damages has sometimes resulted in large awards that have a chilling effect on freedom of expression suggesting that the jury is not an effective guarantor of freedom of speech. However under section 8 of the Courts and Legal Services Act 1990 the Court of Appeal has the power, where a jury has awarded 'excessive' compensation, to substitute a lower sum. In *Rantzen v Mirror Group Newspapers Ltd* [1994] QB 670, the award was reduced from £250,000 to £110,000. While the Court based its decision on the Act, it also justified it by reference to Article 10 of the ECHR (see *Tolstoy Miloslavsky v UK* [1995] 20 EHRR 442). In *John v Mirror Group Newspapers Ltd* [1996] 3 WLR 593 the Court of Appeal held that awards of exemplary or punitive damages going beyond compensation could be recovered only where the defendant knowingly or recklessly published untruths having cynically calculated that the profit accruing from the publication would be likely to exceed any damages. Lord Bingham, stated that 'freedom of expression should not be restricted by awards of exemplary damages save to the extent shown to be strictly necessary for the protection of reputations' [58].

The Defamation Bill gives the judge a wide power to dispense with a jury in order to reduce the costs of litigation and to discourage 'libel tourism'.

In support of freedom of speech the judiciary has long been reluctant to grant injunctions in defamation cases. Hence this remedy will not be granted unless the plaintiff can satisfy a number of exacting conditions, in particular that there is no ground for supposing that the defendant may avoid liability by pleading truth, privilege or fair comment (*Bonnard v Perryman* [1891] 2 Ch 269). Furthermore judges are grudging in their readiness to grant interim (or interlocutory) injunctions which restrain the offending expression pending a full trial (ibid). Such injunctions are only granted where (i) a court is satisfied that publication will result in immediate and irreparable injury and (ii) damages would not provide an adequate remedy (*Monson v Tussauds Ltd* [1894] 1 QB 671; see also HRA 1998, s 12 (Section 22.3)).

23.4.1 Public bodies

In recent years two more features of defamation law have been modified by the judiciary with a view to establishing an appropriate balance between press freedom and reputational interests compatible with the ECHR. These concern public bodies and qualified privilege.

In *Derbyshire CC v Times Newspapers Ltd* [1993] [1993] 1 All ER 1011 the House of Lords held that a local authority and other public bodies cannot sue in defamation. The *Sunday Times* published an allegation of mismanagement of pension funds by the Council. Lord Keith explained that: 'it is of the highest public importance that a democratically elected body…should be open to uninhibited public criticism' (1017). The House of Lords did not base its decision on the ECHR but found support in 'the common law of England'. The same principle applies to political parties (see *Goldsmith v Bhoyrul* [1997] The Times, 20 June, 493).

However, one feature of the case suggests that Lord Keith's commitment to democracy may be half-hearted. Lord Keith indicated that individual public officials can sue in defamation on the same basis as private individuals. The House of Lords has thus been criticized for failing to follow the US Supreme Court's lead in *New York Times Co v Sullivan* [1964] 376 US 254 by introducing the 'actual malice' rule into UK law in relation to individuals. This rule protects statements against both public institutions and individual public officials made in the absence of malice and with knowledge that they are false. This would have helped to protect political expression and would have brought the law of defamation into closer alignment with the European Court of Human Rights. This treats Article 10 as requiring three distinctions; namely political figures should receive less protection from defamation law than private individuals and governmental bodies (and political parties) should receive even less protection from the law than political figures (see *Lingens v Austria* [986]; *Castells v Spain* (1992); *Oberschlick v Austria* [1995] 19 EHRR 389).

23.4.2 Responsible journalism

As we saw above (Section 23.4) the defence of qualified privilege has traditionally required a reciprocal relationship between the publisher of the statement and the recipient, namely that there must be an interest or duty (legal, social or moral) to communicate the material and a corresponding interest or duty to receive it. This has caused difficulty vis-à-vis material communicated to the public at large and. judges have been reluctant to create an open-ended 'public interest' defence. However in *Reynolds v Times Newspapers Ltd* [2001] the House of Lords held that qualified privilege can in some circumstances be pleaded where political material is disseminated to the general public. Their Lordships emphasised that such material would still have to fall within the criteria for reciprocity in the sense that there must be a public interest in the material in question. Lord Nicholls stated:

> through the cases runs the strain that, when determining whether the public at large had a right to know the particular information, the court has regard to all the circumstances. The Court is concerned to assess whether the information was of sufficient value to the public that, in the public interest, it should be protected by the privilege in the absence of malice. (at 195)

To this his Lordship added a (non-exhaustive) list of considerations namely (i) the seriousness of the allegation(s); (ii) the nature of the information and the extent to which the matter is a matter of public concern; (iii) the source of the information; (iv) the steps taken to verify the information; (v) the status of the information; (vi) the urgency of the matter; (vii) whether comment was sought from the claimant; (viii) whether the relevant publication contained the gist of the claimant's side of the story; (ix) the tone of the article; and (x) the circumstances of the publication (at 205).

Reynolds applies to anyone but is of course of special concern to the media. It is open to at least two criticisms. Firstly it means that judges define standards of good journalistic practice and decide what the public should know. It is far from obvious that this is a task that they are well equipped to undertake. Secondly it produces uncertainty and so the chilling effect. In particular there is no agreement as to what 'public interest' means. Is it, for example limited to matters which directly affect the public? If not what else is included?

Following criticism in New Zealand of the chilling effect of *Reynolds* (*Lange v Atkinson* [1998] 3 NZLR 424) later cases have treated the *Reynolds* defence as one of 'responsible journalism' sometimes called '*Reynolds* privilege and' as liberalising in favour of press freedom. It has been emphasised that the requirements of good journalistic practice should not be applied strictly but are general guidelines, allowing latitude for editorial judgement each case depending on its particular circumstances (*Jameel v Wall Street Journal Europe* [2006] 4 All ER 1279 [46], [50], [57]). In *Flood* the Supreme Court held that the journalist had a duty of verification to the extent that there must be a reasonable basis for the facts published but need not exhaustively investigate whether the facts were true. Thus the *Reynolds* defence gives the court considerable discretion thereby focusing on the judge's attitude to the press.

In *Jameel v Wall Street Journal Europe* [2006], the publication of a blacklist of businesses suspected of terrorist involvement revealing Saudi cooperation with USA and based on information from within the US and Saudi governments was held to be protected. Lord Hoffmann summarised the requirements of *Reynolds* as that the article as a whole should be on a matter of public interest [48], that the defamatory statement should be part of the story and make a real contribution to it [51] and that the steps taken to gather and publish the information should be reasonable and fair [53] [147].

By contrast in *Grobbelar v Mirror group Newspapers* [2001] 2 All ER 437 a newspaper campaign accused a footballer of taking bribes based on information from a business associate. The newspaper had made an unqualified assertion of guilt, stood to make a large profit from its campaign and relied on a dubious source. The Court of Appeal held that the newspaper should not be protected since far from there being a chilling effect on freedom of expression the protection of publication would encourage the press to be less thorough and their exposes more sensational [39]–[47].

In *Flood v Times Newspapers* [2012] SC 11 the Supreme Court upheld a publication concerning allegations of police corruption in the form of selling sensitive information about extradition to Russian oligarchs. The information had been obtained from leaks within the police service. The public importance of the issues justified publishing the alleged facts behind the allegations and naming the person concerned since otherwise suspicion might fall on other police officers. The claimant was later exonerated but the original report remained on the newspaper's website. The Court of Appeal had held that the privilege no longer applied but the Supreme Court has not yet decided the issue.

Reportage is an aspect of the Reynolds defence. This applies to a person including a journalist who merely repeats an allegation made by another, for example a statement that accusations have been made against X. There is a defence if it can be shown clearly that when read as a whole the author did not in any way support the statement in question. Thus very careful journalistic expression is required (*Chapman v Orion Publishing Group* [2008] 1 All ER 750; *Galloway v Telegraph Group* [2006] EWCA Civ 17).

Thus there are three levels of journalistic standard: first 'reportage' where it suffices to show that the allegations have been made and there is a public interest in knowing that fact. Secondly the publication of evidence behind allegations. This must be justified on stronger public interest grounds and the information must be checked as reasonably reliable. Third the publication of the identity of the person concerned must be specifically justified (as in *Flood*). *The Defamation Bill proposes a separate defence of 'responsible publication' on matters of public interest.*

23.5 Press freedom and privacy

The issue of public interest strongly arises in connection with the right to privacy. Article 8 of the ECHR states that 'everyone has a right to respect for his family and private life'. Privacy relates among other things to dignity, independence and self-respect and the desire to control personal information (Section 21.4.3). There is therefore a clash with Article 10.

Article 8 forbids a 'public authority' from interfering with privacy. Newspapers are privately owned, so the protection of privacy against the press is an example of the possible horizontal impact of the Human Rights Act (Section 22.6). Before the Human Rights Act 1998 English law had no separate right to privacy and was accordingly in violation of the ECHR (*Malone v UK* [1984] 7 EHRR 14). At best privacy was regarded as a value that influences specific causes of action, most importantly breach of confidence which originally concerned wrongful disclosure of information arising out of a confidential relationship (eg *Wainright v Home Office* [2003] 4 All ER 969; *Kaye v Robertson* [1991] FSR 62).

Under the influence of Human Rights Act the law of confidence has become assimilated into the more general right of privacy by becoming detached from the need to show a specific confidential relationship. An injunction can be obtained where the following three conditions are satisfied (*A-G v Guardian Newspapers (No 2)* [1998] 3 All ER 535):

1. The information is confidential in character. In *Campbell v MGN Ltd* [2004] the House of Lords held that privacy lay at the root of breach of confidence. It was suggested that information is confidential whose disclosure violates 'a reasonable expectation of privacy'. This test was preferred to the stronger one used in some jurisdictions that the disclosure be highly offensive to a person of ordinary susceptibilities (see [21]–[22], [83], [134]–[135]). This includes not only the content of the information but also the situation or relationship in which it is revealed, for example in the home or in a diary. A matter might still be protected even in a public place.
2. The information must have been imparted in circumstances imposing an obligation of confidence; for example it was imparted for a limited purpose. Earlier cases requiring a specific confidential relationship such as family or employment no longer apply (although such a relationship, for example between ministers and civil servants, will still be sufficient). The claimant must however establish that the relevant information was acquired in circumstances where a reasonable person would have realised that it was confidential.
3. There must be an unauthorised use of the relevant information by the confidant or a third party with knowledge of the confidence and for a purpose other than that for which it was imparted (eg HRH *Prince of Wales v Associated Newspapers* [2007] 2 All ER 139: diaries written by the Prince making disparaging remarks about overseas dignitaries).

There is a defence (i) that disclosure of the relevant material was in the public interest and (ii) that this outweighs the interest in preserving confidentiality.

Privacy must therefore be balanced against the right to freedom of expression. In cases involving press intrusion privacy is currently given a high level of protection (see *Von Hannover v Germany* [2004] 40 EHRR 1). The main technique used by the courts when a conflict arises, is to start by treating the competing rights as having equal weight then, to look at the impact on each right in turn, asking whether the harm done to the privacy interest is *in its own terms* more serious than the harm done to freedom of expression. However it must be remembered that press freedom is important *in itself* irrespective of the content of the particular press report.

This rough utilitarianism founders upon the problem that there is no common denominator against which to compare the harms and no agreement as to the proper relationship between a person's private and public lives. It is sometimes believed that privacy has been strengthened at the cost of restricting press freedom. On the other hand the public interest in open justice has been strongly asserted. As usual the judges must make a subjective choice. The uncertainty generated by this risks inhibiting freedom of expression.

The following examples of the 'balancing exercise' illustrate its subjective nature.

In *Campbell v MGN Ltd* [2004] the *Daily Mirror* had published information and photographs about the treatment for drug addiction undergone by a famous fashion model. The House of Lords regarded freedom of expression and privacy as of equal importance and looked closely at all the circumstances with the aim of producing the least harmful outcome. Lord Hoffman remarked (at [51]) that the law had shifted in emphasis from the notion of good faith to that of protecting autonomy and dignity and the control of information about one's private life (see also *Von Hannover v Germany* [2004]). It was held first that the fact the claimant had been a drug addict was not protected since she had repeatedly told the media that she was not on drugs, and to that extent had given up her privacy. However it was also held that the details of her treatment should not have been published since these were inherently private and personal in nature. Importantly there were no political or democratic values in issue of a kind which supported press freedom. Lords Nicholls and Hoffmann dissented, taking a wider view of press freedom, that a newspaper should be able to add colour and detail to its reporting and that journalists should be entitled to some latitude in the wider interests of a healthy press. A restrictive approach might inhibit the press and so hamper democracy.

In *JIH v News Group Newspapers Ltd* [2011] the Court of Appeal said that no special treatment should be given to public figures or celebrities. However where publication of the information was permitted an anonymity order could be made, but only where there was a clear case for doing so.

In *Moseley v Mirror Group Newspapers* [2008] EWHC 1777, what would otherwise have been protected as a private sex party was lawfully made public on the basis that the court considered it to have Nazi overtones.

In *HRH Prince of Wales v Associated Newspapers* [2007] the Court of Appeal prohibited the press from publishing extracts from the personal journals of the Prince of Wales. These contained his impressions of the appearance and character of the Chinese leaders during an official visit to China. Factors to be taken into account include the fact that the information was leaked by an employee in breach of contract. It is a matter of public interest in itself that confidential employment relationships be protected. It was also relevant that the information made only a 'minimal' contribution to the public interest.

In *Re S (A Child)* (2004) the competition was between press freedom in reporting the identity of the parties in court proceedings and the privacy of a child in care whose mother had been convicted of murdering his brother. The Court of Appeal preferred the press interest. It held that the importance of open justice and drawing public attention to child abuse outweighed the child's interest since the additional publicity would cause relatively limited upset over and above that which had already occurred.

In *W(B) v M (Official Solicitor)* [2011] 4 All ER 1295 the clash was between open justice and concern for a child in a minimally conscious state where the child's mother applied to the court to withhold life support. The Court of Protection balanced the public interest against the privacy of the family by permitting the press to report the evidence and arguments but not the identities of the parties. The public interest in medical cases was in the general issues not in the individuals concerned and there was no analogy with 'celebrity' cases.

The reputation of accused persons seems to carry limited weight. In *Re Guardian News and Media Ltd* [2010] 2 All ER 799 the Supreme Court overturned an anonymity order which had prevented publication of the names of terrorist suspects whose assets had been frozen by the court pending further proceedings. In view of public concerns about terrorism the information was of public interest and any damage to reputation was not specific. It was assumed that the public are capable of understanding the difference between accusation and guilt.

Similarly in *A-G's Reference (No 3 of 1999)* [2010] UKHL 34 the House of Lords permitted the BBC to publish the name of a person who was subject to a retrial for rape as a result of a previous trial in which DNA evidence had been wrongly excluded. The public interest in open justice outweighed the harm to the claimant's reputation. The issue of DNA evidence was one of public concern and there were procedures available to safeguard the right to a fair trial.

23.6 'Hate speech'

Hate speech involves attacks on racial, ethnic, religious or cultural groups, including lifestyle matters such as sexuality. Hate speech may also be directed at other vulnerable groups such as the elderly and the disabled. Hate speech involves matter that shocks or offends, thereby raising the overrides of public morality and the rights of others and providing a hard test of the rationales for freedom of expression. It could be argued along with Mill that being offended or shocked is not harmful since it challenges orthodoxy and does not limit freedom. On the other hand there is an argument for suppressing the expression of opinions that offend others where there is a risk to public safety or the welfare of vulnerable groups. However this leads to oppressive or lazy enforcement since it is often cheaper and easier to suppress a speaker than to police those who cause a disturbance because they are offended.

The notion of ideas and information as underlying freedom of expression has enabled it to be claimed that some forms of hate speech should not be protected since they contain no worthy ideas. For example in *Otto Preminger Institut v Austria* [1994] the state seized a film depicting Christ and his mother as in league with the Devil. The Court said that:

> in the context of religious opinion and beliefs...may legitimately be included an obligation to avoid as far as possible expressions that are gratuitously offensive to others and thus an infringement of their rights, and which therefore do not contribute to any form of public debate capable of furthering progress in human affairs.

Pornography is also susceptible to this argument. For example the publication of material that is likely to deprave and corrupt a significant proportion of those exposed to it is prohibited (the 'harm' principle) but subject to a defence of literary or artistic merit (Obscene Publications Act 1959). However, this elevates the truth rationale for freedom of expression at the expense of that of self-fulfilment and comes close to Berlin's fear of 'positive freedom' (Section 2.4).

As usual the law must find an accommodation. One way of doing so is by attempting to distinguish between expressing opinions, however distasteful, and inciting unlawful or harmful behaviour (see Section 23.7.3). However, in the case of particularly vulnerable groups this line is breached and some forms of expression that are offensive to such groups are also prohibited. The law is sensitive to particular historical circumstances. For example there is protection in respect of racial and religious hate expression but not age, gender, disability or class hate expression as such. These fall within more general offences (Section 23.7.3).

In respect of some forms of communication which are especially open to abuse, offense is prohibited generally. Thus the Communications Act 2003 while having social inclusion as one of its aims makes it an offence to send online or by telephone any 'grossly offensive message' (s 127(1)). The same Act imposes restrictions on the broadcast media as does the Charter of the BBC (Section 23.3).

23.6.1 Racism

Racism has been so widely condemned throughout Europe as to amount to a special case. The International Convention on the Elimination of All Forms of Racial Discrimination (1965) (CERD) has been ratified by most members of the Council of Europe (not Ireland, Lithuania or Turkey). Article 4 of this Convention requires signatories to create offences in relation to:

> all dissemination of ideas based on racial supremacy or hatred, incitement to racial discrimination, as well as acts of violence or incitement to such acts against any race or group of persons of another colour or ethnic origin.

Article 4 also requires states to have 'due regard' to (among other things) the right to freedom of opinion and expression.

The main offences are contained in sections 17–23 of the Public Order Act 1986. A person is guilty if he or she uses:

> threatening, abusive or insulting words or behaviour or displays written material which is threatening, abusive or insulting if (a) he intends to stir up racial hatred or, (b) having regard to all the circumstances, such hatred is likely to be stirred up thereby. (s 18)

Race includes colour, race, nationality and ethnic or national origins (s 17). An ethnic group can be defined by cultural as well as physical characteristics (see *Mandla v Dowell-Lee* [1983] 1 All ER 1062: Sikhs; *Commission for Racial Equality v Dutton* [1989] QB 783: gypsies but not other travellers).

The offences can be committed in public or private places except exclusively within a dwelling (s 18(2)(4)). Public disorder is not required nor is the presence at the time of any member of the targeted racial group. For example the offence could apply to an academic paper read to an audience in a university or club. However there is a defence if the accused did not intend to stir up racial hatred and did not intend his or her words or behaviour to be, and was not aware that it might be, threatening, abusive or insulting (s 18(2)(5)).

It is also an offence to publish or distribute written material in the same circumstances (s 17) and to possess racially inflammatory material (s 23). Similar provisions apply to a public performance of a play (s 20), to distributing, showing or playing recordings and to broadcasting or cable services except from the BBC and ITC (ss 22(7), 23(4)). Broadcasting bodies are governed by special systems of regulation. Contemporaneous reports of parliamentary, court or tribunal proceedings are exempted (s 26).

The offences are arrestable and the police have wide powers of entry and search (s 24). The consent of the Attorney General is required for a prosecution, which might be regarded as a safeguard for freedom of expression (s 27).

There are increased sentences for offences of assault, criminal damage, public order and harassment committed wholly or partly with religious or racial motivations (Crime and Disorder Act 1998, ss 28, 32). At the time of committing the offence or immediately before or after, the offender must demonstrate hostility towards the victim based on the victim's membership (or presumed membership) of a racial or religious group.

23.6.2 Religion

In the context of religion, causing offence seems to justify restricting freedom of expression. Religion is defined to include any spiritual belief but it is not confined to belief in a supernatural entity and can include atheists (*Campbell and Cozens v UK* [1982] 4 EHRR 293). However it must be consistent with basic standards of human dignity and its 'manifestation' must be cogent, serious, cohesive and important (*R (Williamson) v Secretary of State for Education and Employment* [2005] at [23–4]. This invites the decision maker to impose his or her own view as to what is important (see also Charities Act 2006, s 2(3): need not involve belief in a god). Article 9 of the ECHR concerns freedom of religion (Section 21.4.3). This overlaps with Article 10 but the two may conflict where freedom of expression is used to pressurise a religion or its supporters. The Human Rights Act 1998 requires courts to have particular regard in matters involving religious organisations to the importance of freedom of thought, conscience and religion (s 13). This could be read as authorising religious organisations to violate other rights such as privacy or to discriminate on religious grounds.

The European Court appears to give states a wide margin of discretion in respect of religious matters. In *Otto Preminger Institut v Austria* [1994] the state seized a film depicting Christ and his mother as in league with the Devil which offended the Roman Catholic majority in the Tyrol. The Court held that the seizure was lawful for the purpose of protecting the rights of others. This seems to come close to censorship based on majority sentiment. (See also *Wingrove v UK* [1997] 24 EHRR 1: homoerotic imagery discomforting to some Christians; ban upheld with strong dissent.) Christianity at least seems to be given a privileged status (eg *Choudhury v UK* [1991] App No 174/39/90: state not required to protect other religions). Although the Church of England is closely associated with the state, Christianity as such is not part of English law (*Bowman v Secular Society* [1917] AC 406). The main restriction on freedom of speech concerning religion namely the common law offences of blasphemy and blasphemous libel which favoured Christianity were abolished by the Criminal Justice and Immigration Act 2008 (s 79).

The Racial and Religious Hatred Act 2006, adding Part 3A to the Public Order Act 1986, creates various offences of intention to stir up religious hatred broadly similar to but narrower than those applying to racial hatred (Section 23.7.1). Religious hatred means hatred towards a group of persons defined by reference to religious belief or lack of religious belief. Thus atheists are protected by the Act. Religion is not defined. Threatening words or behaviour are required and there must be a direct intention to stir up hatred not merely that hatred is likely. As with other public order offences, conduct taking effect entirely within a private dwelling is excluded.

The Act attempts to protect freedom of expression by stating that:

> nothing in this Part shall be read or given effect in a way which prohibits discussion, criticism or expressions of antipathy, dislike, ridicule, insult, or abuse of particular religions or the beliefs or practices of their adherents, or of any other belief system or the beliefs of its adherents, or proselytising or urging the adherents of a different religion or belief system to cease practising their religion or belief system.

Since the offence requires threatening words or behaviour it may be that this provision limits the offence to personal abuse. Can threats of hellfire be used as part of an evangelising recruitment drive? Under the Anti-Terrorism, Crime and Security Act 2001 the penalties for certain offences involving assault, property damage, public order and harassment are increased where there is a religious motivation along the same lines as those applying to racially aggravated offences (s 39).

Under section 74 of the Criminal Justice and Immigration Act 2008 this group of offences has been extended to stirring up hatred on the ground of sexual orientation. Again there is some protection for freedom of expression. By virtue of Schedule 16 the discussion or criticism of sexual conduct or practices or the urging of persons to refrain or modify such conduct or practices shall not be taken of itself to be threatening or intended to stir up hatred.

23.6.3 Political protest

Under the ECHR the limits of permissible criticism are wider with regard to the government than in relation to a private citizen or an individual politician (*Castells v Spain* (1992) [46]).

The old common law harshly penalized dissent. The offence of seditious libel consisted of publishing material with the intention to incite hostility towards the government or its institutions or possibly to promote hostility between different classes of 'Her Majesty's subjects' (*R v Burns* [1886] 16 Cox CC 395). Seditious libel has now been abolished but echoes remain in the broad discretionary powers that modern law gives to the police under which disagreement with government policy might be regarded by a police officer as evidence of unlawful intent.

There are other offences related to sedition that are little used but because of their vague language remain potential threats against political dissenters. The Incitement to Disaffection Act 1934 makes it an offence maliciously and advisedly to endeavour to seduce any member of the armed forces from his or her duty or to aid, counsel or procure him or her to do so. The Police Act 1996 creates a similar offence in relation to the police (s 91) and the Aliens Restrictions (Amendment) Act 1917 prohibits an alien from attempting to cause sedition or disaffection and also from promoting or interfering in an industrial dispute in an industry in which he or she has not been employed for at least two years immediately before the offence. It is questionable whether these provisions, particularly the latter, are compliant with the Human Rights Act 1998. Anti-terrorism legislation also imposes wide restrictions on political expression by virtue of its broad definition of terrorism (Terrorism Act (TA) 2000; Section 24.7.1).

23.7 Freedom of assembly: demonstrations and meetings

Article 11 of the ECHR confers a right to freedom of assembly and association. This is subject to the following overrides: national security or public safety, the prevention of disorder or crime, the protection of health or morals, or the protection of the rights and freedoms of others. Also, 'this article shall not prevent the imposition of lawful restrictions on the exercise of those rights by members of the armed forces, of the police or of the administration of the state'.

The right of freedom of assembly applies mainly to assembly for political purposes but not to assemblies for sports or other recreational purposes (*R (Countryside Alliance) v A-G* [2008] at [58], [119]; see also *Anderson v UK* [1997] 25 EHRR 172). Freedom of assembly is closely related to freedom of expression. Indeed the right to meet in public is particularly important because, unlike many other forms of expression which depend on access to the media and therefore on money or influence, this right is open to all.

The main limits on freedom of assembly concern the protection of property rights and the protection of the public against violence. However, in *Kuznetov v Russia* [2008] at [45] the Strasbourg court appeared to suggest that freedom of assembly could be restricted if rejection of democratic principles are involved.

The law has developed as a series of pragmatic responses to particular problems and political agendas and has become relentlessly more restrictive in recent years. For example the Public Order Act 1936 was a response to fears of fascism and communism. It was superseded by the Public Order Act 1986, which was provoked by race riots. Further legislation has been aimed at miscellaneous targets of the government of the day. These included anti-nuclear demonstrations, hunt saboteurs, travellers, 'stalkers', football hooligans, anti-war demonstrators, terrorists and animal rights groups (see Criminal Justice and Public Order Act 1994, ss 60, 60AA; Protection from Harassment Act 1997; Crime and Disorder Act 1998; Football (Offences and Disorder) Act 1999; Football (Disorder) Act 2000; Serious Organised Crime and Police Act 2005; Terrorism Acts 2000, 2006). Whether or not all of these are legitimate causes for concern the legislation may be drafted loosely enough to include wider political activities, thereby attracting human rights arguments based on uncertainty, proportionality and discrimination.

This illustrates the weakness of the traditional residual approach to liberty under which according to Dicey the right to hold a public procession is in principle no different from the right to eat a bun. The notion that everything is permitted unless forbidden is particularly ironic in the case of public meetings. All meetings and processions take place on land. All land, even a public highway, is owned by someone, whether a private body, a local authority, the Crown or a government department. Holding a meeting without the consent of a private owner is a trespass so that the owner can bring a civil action to evict the trespasser (see *Harrison v Duke of Rutland* [1893] 1 QB 142).

In the case of the public highway the traditional view was that the public has a right only to 'pass or repass' on a highway (ie to travel) and also to stop on the highway for purposes that are reasonably incidental such as 'reasonable rest and refreshment' (*Hickman v Maisey* [1900] 1 QB 752). In *Hubbard v Pitt* [1976] QB 142, for example the Court of Appeal held that peaceful picketing by a protest group who distributed leaflets and questionnaires was not a lawful use of the highway. Dicey thought that a procession, but not a static meeting, would usually be lawful because processions comprise a large number of individuals exercising their right to travel at the same time.

In *DPP v Jones* [1999] 2 All ER 257 the House of Lords upheld a right of peaceful demonstration by environmentalists on the highway at Stonehenge. Lord Irvine LC asserted that the law should now recognise that the public should have a right to enjoy the highway for any reasonable purpose provided that the activities did not constitute a nuisance and did not obstruct other people's freedom of movement. Lord Hutton considered that the common law should now recognise that the right of assembly, which is one of the fundamental rights of citizens in this country, is unduly restricted unless it can be exercised 'in some circumstances' on the public highway. Lords Hope and Slynn dissented, Lord Hope because of the effect of such a right on property owners who were not before the Court to defend their interests, Lord Slynn because of a reluctance to unsettle established law. (See also *Tabernacle v Secretary of State for Defence* [2009] EWCA Civ 23: protest camp held regularly over 20 years without disruption: eviction unlawful.)

Jones was decided before the Human Rights Act 1998 came into effect. As regards public land the matter now depends on proportionality, balancing the right of assembly against the interests of the property owner and other aspects of the public interest. The outcome of the cases suggests that the right to assembly is outweighed if substantial interference with others is involved. In *City of London Corp v Samede* [2012] the *Occupy Movement* demonstrating against corporate greed set up a camp for several weeks in an open space outside St Paul's Cathedral in London. The land was owned by the claimant to a public body who sought to remove the tents. It was held that it was proportionate to remove the tents. The occupation raised health risks and caused disruption including to local businesses which was continuing for an indefinite time and there would be no defence to an action for trespass in domestic law. Moreover the particular location was not vital to the political causes being espoused and there had been no attempt to prevent a demonstration as such. (See also *Mayor of London v Hall* [2011] 1 WLR 504: protest camp lawfully evicted from Parliament square other than long-term protestor whose occupation did not cause disruption.)

In the case of privately owned land such as many retail parks and shopping centres the Human Rights Act may not apply (Section 22.5) so that property rights dominate the issue and the law of trespass might be used to restrict political activity. A private owner can require anyone to obey whatever restrictions the owner wishes to impose and can exclude anyone from the premises. Whether the Human Rights Act could impose a positive duty on the state to protect freedom of assembly in such places on the basis that they are in effect public spaces is questionable. In *Appelby v UK* [2003] the European Court held that the owner of a shopping mall could prevent environmental campaigners from setting up a stall and distributing leaflets. However the Court stressed that they had other means of communicating their concerns. And that any restrictions must have a rational justification (See Mead [2013] PL 100).

Under the Serious Organised Crimes and Police Act 2005 it is an offence to trespass on a site in England and Wales or Northern Ireland designated by the Secretary of State (s 128). Except in the case of land owned by the Crown, which covers most central government land, and by the Queen or the immediate heir to the throne in their private capacity, this power can be used only in the interests of national security. However the courts are reluctant to interfere with the government's view as to what national security requires.

23.7.1 Statutory police powers

The police have wide powers to regulate public meetings and processions. These are supplemented by powers relating to particular places (Seditious Meetings Act 1817, s 3: meetings of 50 or more people in the vicinity of Westminster when Parliament is sitting; Serious Organised Crime and Police Act 2005). The main general police powers are as follows:

▶ The organiser of a public procession intended (i) to demonstrate support for or opposition to the views or actions of any person or body of persons, (ii) to publicise a campaign or cause or (iii) to mark or commemorate an event must give advance notice to the police (Public Order Act 1986, s 11). There are certain exceptions. These include:

    (i) processions commonly or customarily held in the area. This only applies if the route remains the same. It is not enough that the time and place of commencement are the same (*Kay v Metropolitan Police Comr* [2007] 4 All ER 31: mass cycle ride through London);

    (ii) funeral processions organised by a funeral director in the normal course of business;

    (iii) cases where it is not reasonably practicable to give advance notice (eg a spontaneous march).

▶ There is no power to ban a procession for failing to give notice. However, if a 'senior police officer' reasonably believes (i) that any public procession may result in serious public disorder, serious damage to property, or serious disruption to the life of the community or (ii) that the purpose of the organisers is to intimidate people into doing something they have a right not to do, or not doing something they have a right to do, the senior officer can impose such conditions as appear to him or her to be necessary to prevent such disorder, damage, disruption or intimidation, including conditions as to the route of the procession or to prohibit it from entering any public place specified in the directions (Public Order Act 1986, s 12). A 'senior police officer' is either the Chief Constable, Metropolitan Police Commissioner or the senior officer present on the scene (s 12(2)). Intimidation requires more than merely causing discomfort and must contain an element of compulsion.

▶ All public processions or any class of public procession can be banned if the Chief Constable or Metropolitan Police Commissioner reasonably believes that the power to impose conditions is not adequate in the circumstances (Public Order Act 1986, s 13). The decision is for the local authority with the consent of a Secretary of State (in practice the Home Secretary), thus injecting a nominal element of democracy.

▶ There are police powers to impose conditions upon public meetings for the same purposes as in the case of processions (Public Order Act 1986, s 14). For this purpose a public assembly is an assembly of 20 or more people in a public place which is wholly or partly open to the air (s 16). Unlike processions the police have no general power to ban a lawful assembly but can control its location and timing and the numbers attending.

▶ Section 70 of the Criminal Justice and Public Order Act 1994 (inserting ss 14A–C into the Public Order Act 1986) confers power on a local authority with the consent of the Secretary of State to ban certain kinds of assembly. This includes private land and buildings where the public is invited, for example ancient monuments such as Stonehenge, meeting rooms, shops, sports and entertainment centres and libraries. The Chief Constable must reasonably believe that an assembly (i) is a 'trespassory' assembly likely to be held without the permission of the occupier or outside the public's rights of access and (ii) may result in serious disruption to the life of the community or may result in significant damage to land, buildings or monuments of historical, architectural or scientific importance. A ban can last for up to four days within an area of up to five miles. The ban covers all trespassory assemblies and cannot be confined to particular assemblies.

▶ Under the Serious Organised Crime and Police Act 2005 it is an offence to organise or take part in a demonstration within a designated area without police permission, for which written notice must be given if reasonably practicable at least six clear days in advance and in any case not less than 24 hours in advance. In relation to 'taking part' a demonstration can be by one person. If proper notice is given the police must give authorisation but this can be subject to conditions, including limits on the number of people who may take part, noise levels and the number and size of banners and placards. These provisions do not apply to public processions which fall within the Public Order Act 1896 or to lawful trade union activity.

▶ Anti-terrorism powers have been used in connection with political demonstrations (*Gillam and Quinton v UK* [2010] Section 24.6.4).

23.7.2 Common law police powers

Where a breach of the peace is taking place or imminent the police have a wide common law power to arrest anyone who refuses to obey their reasonable requirements (*Albert v Lavin* [1982] AC 546). The power to prevent a breach of the peace includes a power to remove a speaker (*Duncan v Jones* [1936] 1 KB 218) and a right of entry to private premises (*Thomas v Sawkins* [1935] 2 KB 249). A charge of obstructing the police is also possible (Police Act 1996, ss 8, 9(1)) and magistrates can 'bind over' a person to keep the peace.

Before the Human Rights Act 1998 the courts were reluctant to interfere with police discretion. The main consideration was efficiency in giving the police the power to control the disturbance as they saw fit within the resources available to them. Therefore even where a peaceful and lawful meeting is disrupted by hooligans or political opponents the police could prevent a likely breach of the peace by ordering the speaker to stop in preference to controlling the troublemakers (*Duncan v Jones* [1936]).

Although the police must act even-handedly (*Harris v Sheffield United Football Club* [1988] QB 77 at 95) there is a risk that they will exercise their discretion in favour of interests supported by the government. A *Guardian* investigation revealed that the police had been targeting thousands of political campaigners over many years (27 October 2009). For example during the miners' strike of 1983 the police restricted the activities of demonstrators in order to protect the 'right to work' of non-strikers, going as far as to escort non-strikers to work. A result of these events is that police reputation for impartiality has been damaged. (See also *R v Coventry City Council, ex p Phoenix Aviation* [1995]: duty to protect business interests.) On the other hand in *R v Chief Constable of Sussex, ex p International Traders Ferry Ltd* [1999] 1 All ER 129 and *R v Chief Constable of Devon and Cornwall Constabulary, ex p Central Electricity Generating Board (CEGB)* [1981] 3 All ER 826 police restrictions on lawful business activities favoured animal rights and anti-nuclear protestors respectively. In both cases it was held that the matter was one of discretion.

A breach of the peace means violence or threatened violence (see *R v Howell* [1982] QB 415; *R (Laporte) v Chief Constable of Gloucestershire* [2007] 2 AC 105 [27]). In *McLeod v UK* [1998] 27 EHRR 493 the European Court held that breach of the peace powers can satisfy the test of legality (Section 21.4.3) only where the individual causes or is likely to cause harm or acts in a manner the natural consequences of which would be to provoke violence in others.

Under the ECHR, the police are required to give priority to freedom of expression as long as the person concerned does not himself commit a wrongful act, unless there is a serious risk of disruption. In *Plattform 'Arzte fur das Leben' v Austria* [1988] 13 EHRR 204 the ECtHR held, in the context of an anti-abortion demonstration, that there was a positive duty to protect a peaceful demonstration even though it might annoy or give offence to persons opposed to the ideas and claims which it is seeking to promote (see also *Ezelin v France* [1991] 14 EHRR 362; *McLeod v UK* [1998]).

The English courts have recently given mixed protection to the right to demonstrate.

▶ In *R (Laporte) v Chief Constable of Gloucestershire* (2006) the police had stopped, searched and then turned back with a police escort a coachload of anti-Iraq war protesters who were travelling to a demonstration at a military site. Although this took place several miles from the site, the police claimed that their powers extended to taking action whenever they reasonably anticipated that a breach of the peace was likely, whether committed by the persons in question or by others. The House of Lords, invoking the importance of freedom of expression, held that the common law power to prevent a breach of the peace was confined to a situation where the breach of peace was actually taking place or was imminent. It was also held that that freedom of expression should be limited only as a last resort and the police should attempt initially to target the actual troublemakers. Lord Bingham regarded *Moss v McLachlan* [1985] 1 RLR 76, where demonstrators were also turned back, as a borderline example of imminence, recognising that the police must have some discretion.

▶ In *Wood v Metropolitan Police Comr* [2009] it was held that the retention by the police of photographs of demonstrators not suspected of any offence was an unlawful infringement of privacy. Lord Collins stressed the chilling effect of the practice on the exercise of lawful rights such as the right to protest.

▶ But in *Austin v Metropolitan Police Comr* [2009] 3 All ER 455 during a political demonstration the police detained a crowd, including bystanders, behind a cordon on the highway for two hours in conditions of discomfort in order to prevent a violent demonstration ('kettling'). Previous attempt to disperse the crowd had been met with violence. It was held that the actions of the police did not constitute a 'deprivation of liberty' under the ECHR but only a 'restriction' of liberty which is not protected as such. (Section 21.4.1). The police action was also lawful at common law as necessary to keep order at the time.

▶ *Austin* was upheld by the Strasbourg court in *Austin v UK* [2012]. The court considered held that there was no deprivation of liberty within Article 5 since the' kettling' was justified as a last resort to prevent serious disorder. However, the court stressed the importance of freedom of assembly and that crowd control should be used only where necessary to prevent serious injury or damage. It is unclear how far the police have a margin of discretion, in particular the extent to which police resources can be taken into account in assessing the necessity of the police action.

23.7.3 Public order offences

Specific public order offences strike primarily at people who intentionally cause violence, but sometimes go beyond that. They overlap, allowing police discretion in relation to the penalties. Moreover the police and in some circumstances police support officers can arrest on the basis of reasonable suspicion for any offence (Police and Criminal Evidence Act 1984 (PACE), s 24, as modified by Serious Organised Crimes and Police Act 2005). Even minor punishments or disciplinary measures might be condemned under the ECHR as disproportionate or uncertain and so chilling the right of assembly (*Ezelin v France* (1991)).

The main offences are as follows:

1. Under the Highways Act 1980 it is an offence to obstruct the highway and the police can remove the offender (s 137). It is not necessary that the highway be completely blocked or even that people are inconvenienced. Here the accused's intentions are irrelevant (*Arrowsmith v Jenkins* [1963] 2 QB 561 *Homer v Cadman* [1886] 16 Cox CC 51; *Hirst and Agu v West Yorkshire Chief Constable* [1986] 85 Crim App Rep 143). However in the light of the Human Rights Act a non-obstructive peaceful demonstration would probably not be unlawful (Section 23.7). There are also numerous local statutes and bylaws regulating public meetings in particular places.

2. The Public Order Act 1986 creates several offences, replacing a clutch of ancient and ill-defined common law offences (rout, riot, affray and unlawful assembly). However the old case of *Beatty v Gillbanks* [1882] 9 QBD 308, often cited as an endorsement of freedom of assembly, may still apply to them. A temperance march by the Salvation Army was disrupted by a gang, known as the Skeleton Army, sponsored by brewery interests. The organisers of the march were held not to be guilty of the offence of unlawful assembly (replaced by the Public Order Act 1986) on the ground that their behaviour was in itself lawful and the disruption was caused by their opponents. Thus even though in one sense the Salvationists were provoking their opponents the court was in effect ascribing moral blame.

   The offences under the Public Order Act 1986 are as follows (in descending order of seriousness):

   ▶ *riot* (s 1). Where 12 or more people act in concert and use or threaten unlawful violence for a common purpose, each person using violence is guilty of the offence;

   ▶ *violent disorder* (s 2). At least three people acting in concert and using or threatening unlawful violence;

   ▶ *affray* (s 3). One person suffices. Using or threatening unlawful violence is sufficient, but threats by words alone do not count;

▶ The above offences may be committed in public or in private and the conduct must be such 'as would cause a person of reasonable firmness present at the scene to fear for his personal safety'. No such person need actually be on the scene. The defendant must either intend to threaten or use violence or be aware that his or her conduct may be violent or threaten violence (s 6). 'Violence' is broadly defined to include violent conduct to property and persons and is not restricted to conduct intended to cause injury or damage (s 8);

▶ *fear or provocation of violence* (s 4). A person is guilty who uses 'threatening, abusive or insulting words or behaviour or distributes or displays any writing, sign or visible representation that is threatening, abusive or insulting'. The offence can be committed in a public or a private place except exclusively within a dwelling or between dwellings (s 8). The meaning of 'threatening, abusive or insulting' is left to the jury (see *Brutus v Cozens* [1973] AC 584) but the accused must be aware that his words are threatening, abusive or insulting (s 6(3)). The act must be aimed at another person with the intention either to cause that person to believe that immediate unlawful violence will be used or to provoke that person into immediate unlawful violence. Alternatively the accused's conduct must be likely to have that effect even though he or she does not so intend.

The violence must be likely within a short time of the behaviour in question. Before the Human Rights Act it was held that whether the other person's reaction is reasonable is irrelevant, so the principle that a speaker 'takes his audience as he finds it' seems to apply. Thus provoking a hostile or extremist audience would be an offence, provided that the words used or act performed is to the knowledge of the accused threatening, abusive or insulting to that particular audience (*Jordan v Burgoyne* [1963] 2 QB 744, *R v Horseferry Road Metropolitan Stipendiary Magistrate Court, ex p Siadatan* (1991)). Today the proportionality concept might make a difference.

▶ *threatening, abusive or insulting behaviour or disorderly behaviour with intent to cause harassment, alarm and distress where harassment, alarm or distress is actually caused* (s 4A) (inserted by the Criminal Justice and Public Order Act 1994). This offence and section 5 threaten freedom of expression in that they move away from the important safeguards that the conduct in question must be threatening, abusive or insulting and involve violence. Thus these provisions are arguably disproportionate, applying also to 'disorderly behaviour', an expression which is not defined;

▶ *harassment, alarm, or distress* (s 5). Section 5 also applies to threatening, abusive or insulting behaviour or disorderly behaviour. It requires only that a person who actually sees or hears the conduct must be likely to be caused harassment, alarm or distress and does not require an intent to cause harassment or alarm or actual harassment, alarm or distress. Violence is not involved. However, there are the defences that (i) the accused had no reason to believe that any such person was present; (ii) he did not intend or know that his words or actions were threatening, abusive or insulting, or disorderly (see *DPP v Clarke* [1992] Crim LR 60) and (iii) his conduct was 'reasonable'.

The police have a summary power of arrest in relation to all the above offences but under section 5 must first warn the accused to stop. The conduct before and after the warning need not be the same.

It is unlikely that the offences under sections 1–4 are contrary to the ECHR in that they aim at preventing violence. Sections 4A and 5 are more vulnerable. In addition to 'threatening' behaviour they target abusive, insulting and disorderly behaviour which leads to no more than distress. This arguably runs counter to the view of the European Court that conduct which shocks and offends is a price to be paid for democracy (Section 23.1).

3. Section 1 of the Public Order Act 1936 prohibits the wearing of political uniforms in any public place or public meeting without police consent, which can be obtained for special occasions. 'Uniform' includes any garment that has political significance, for example a black beret (*O'Moran v DPP* [1975] 1 All ER 473). Political significance can be identified from any of the circumstances or from historical evidence.

4. Aggravated trespass gives the police a weapon against political demonstrators. Aimed originally at anti-hunting protestors, it occurs where a person who trespasses on land in the open air does anything which in relation to any lawful activity that persons are engaging or about to engage in on that land or on adjoining land is intended to have the effect (i) of intimidating those persons or any one of them so as to deter them or any one of them from engaging in that lawful activity; (ii) of obstructing that activity or (iii) of disrupting that activity (Criminal Justice and Public Order Act 1994, s 68). For this purpose a lawful activity is any activity that is not a criminal offence or a trespass (s 68(2)). There is no defence of reasonableness and violence is not required. The police can order a person who is committing or has committed or intends to commit an offence to leave the land (s 69). it is an offence to return within three months. It is not clear whether passive conduct such as lying down would be an offence.

5. Under the Protection from Harassment Act 1997 as amended by the Serious Organised Crime and Police Act 2005 a course of conduct (meaning conduct on at least two occasions relating to one person or on one occasion in the case of two or more persons) which the perpetrator knows or ought to know amounts to or involves the harassment of another is an offence. The test is whether a reasonable person in possession of the same information as the accused would think the conduct likely to cause harassment (s 1(2)). Aimed originally at animal rights activists, this provision can be used against political demonstrations in general. Harassment is a wide term. It includes a course of conduct intended to persuade any person not to do something lawful or to do something unlawful and can include 'collective' harassment by a group (Criminal Justice and Police Act 2001, s 44). Thus the anti-abortion protesters in *DPP v Fidler* [1992] 1 WLR 91, who were acquitted because they intended to persuade rather than to prevent women entering an abortion clinic, would now probably be convicted. There are defences of preventing or detecting crime and acting under lawful authority and a broad defence of 'reasonableness' (s 1(3)(c)). This may allow the press to claim that its duty to inform the public overrides the victim's right of privacy. It may also allow religious enthusiasts to evangelise (cf Section 23.6.2).

6. The Terrorism Act 2006 outlaws the publication or dissemination of a statement which directly or indirectly encourages terrorism (ss 1, 2). Encouragement includes 'glorifying' (which includes praising or celebrating) the commission or preparation (whether in the past, or in the future or generally) of acts of terrorism in such a way that members of the public could be expected to infer that they should emulate the

conduct in question in existing circumstances. However the accused must intend or be reckless as to the consequences of publication and there is a defence that the statement did not express his or her views and did not have his or her endorsement. The definition of terrorism is wide. Terrorism includes any act or the threat of an act that involves serious violence against a person or property or which endangers life or creates a serious risk to the health or safety of the public or a section of the public or seriously disrupts or interferes with an electronic system. The action must be intended to advance a political, religious or ideological cause (Terrorism Act 2000 Section 23.7.1, Counter Terrorism Act 2008 adds 'racial' to this list). The action must be designed to influence the government or coerce the public or a section of it or an international governmental organisation (added by TA 2006, s 34).

Summary

- The justifications for freedom of expression concern the advancement of truth, the protection of democracy and the rule of law, and self-fulfilment. Press freedom is particularly important in a democracy. Freedom of expression involves the state not only abstaining from interference but in some cases, particularly in relation to the press, taking positive steps to protect freedom of expression.

- Freedom of expression may conflict with other rights, notably religion and privacy. It may also be overridden by public interest concerns such as the integrity of the judicial process.

- We distinguished between prior restraint (censorship) and punishments after the event. UK law has some direct censorship by the executive in relation to the broadcast and film media. More general powers of censorship are available by applying to the courts for injunctions. These may be too broad in the light of the Human Rights Act 1998.

- Defamation protects a person's interest in reputation. Public bodies are not protected by the law of defamation, although, perhaps unjustifiably, individual public officials are. The protection of qualified privilege is available to the press, although its scope is uncertain.

- English domestic law has no distinct right of privacy which protects interests in self-esteem, dignity and autonomy. Breach of confidence covers some but not all of the ground. However under the Human Rights Act 1998 freedom of expression must be balanced against privacy as an independent right. Both have equal weight in the abstract and the court will compare the seriousness of the consequences in the individual circumstances. Protection for press freedom is based on establishing a public interest in disclosure.

- The relationship between freedom of expression and offence is particularly difficult. Although offence is generally not protected against freedom of speech, this may not apply to religious feelings.

- There are specific protections against hate speech in relation to race, religion and sexual orientation. These have savings to protect freedom of expression but the line is difficult to draw.

- The law relating to public meetings and processions sets freedom of expression and assembly against public order. This is characterised by broad police discretion. A range of statutes responding to perceived threats have created various offences that restrict freedom of expression and give the police extensive powers to regulate public meetings and processions and demonstrations by individuals and groups. The police also have wide common law powers to prevent imminent breaches of the peace. Under the Human Rights Act 1998 these powers must be exercised in accordance with the principle of proportionality in order to safeguard freedom of expression and association.

Exercises

23.1 Section 127 (1) of the Communications Act 2003 makes it an offence to send online or by telephone a message or other matter that is 'grossly offensive or of an indecent obscene or threatening character. This does not apply to programmes provided by broadcasters' (s 127 (4) (eg BBC, ITV, Sky)). Discuss in relation to freedom of expression.

23.2 'The independence of lawyers and other professionals is not compromised by government regulation: why should this not apply also in relation to the press?' Discuss in the context of the Leveson Report.

23.3 The BBC proposes to hold a radio interview on 'Today', a widely respected public affairs programme, with Lord Downton a leader of an extremist organization that rejects democracy in favour of military rule. Lord Downton is also a leading member of a religion that worships Homer Simpson a cartoon character in a popular TV show. The government acting under royal prerogative powers contained in the BBC Charter orders the BBC not to broadcast the interview. Advise the BBC.

23.4 'The common law recognises that there is a right for members of the public to assemble together to express views on matters of public concern and I consider that the common law should now recognise this right, which is one of the fundamental rights of citizens in this country, is unduly restricted unless it can be exercised in some circumstances on the public highway' (Lord Hutton in *DPP v Jones* [1999]). Discuss whether there is such a right and what its limits are.

23.5 The *Daily Rant* a popular newspaper was given from an anonymous source documents containing the names and copies of confidential tax returns of a number of leading business executives. The documents indicated that all had paid unusually low amounts of tax. Some of the persons concerned had recently given large donations to the ruling political party. The source also mentioned that one of the executives was rumoured to indulge in bizarre sexual practices in company with a leading politician. Advise the Editor whether he should publish all or some of the material and if so what steps he should take against possible legal liability.

23.6 'A function of free expression is to invite dispute. It may indeed best serve its purpose when it induces a condition of unrest, creates dissatisfaction with conditions as they are and even stirs people to anger' (Mr Justice Douglas in *Terminiello v Chicago* [1949]). To what extent does English law recognise this?

23.7 A prominent Anglican bishop has been invited to address a rally which the local diocese holds each year following a procession. This year the rally is held in Camp Park. Police permission has not been sought. A press release announces that the Bishop will argue that homosexuals should not be allowed to marry. He will also claim that Christianity is a distinctively European religion and that unbelievers deserve to be 'run out of the country'. A rival group, Christians for Tolerance (CT), proposes to attend the rally travelling by coach. Fearing that there may be violence at the rally, and having insufficient resources to provide adequate policing at the rally itself, the police stop the CT coach at a motorway service area some five miles from the park. They refuse to allow any passengers to disembark and detain the coach for about three hours, by which time the rally has finished. Discuss the legality of the police action. Has the bishop committed any offense by making his address?

23.8 Members of the Freedom for Peace Party hold a demonstration and distribute leaflets outside an army recruitment office in a shopping centre in Westchester every Saturday morning. The centre is owned by an insurance company. The leaflets include appeals not to join the army and praise the seventeenth-century Leveller movement, which was prepared to fight for equality and democracy. Last week security guards, ordered the leaflet distributors to leave and when they refused to do so detained them until the police arrived. Discuss the legality of these events. What, if any, offences have been committed?

Further reading

Ahdar and Leigh, *Religious Freedom in the Liberal State* (Oxford University Press 2005)

Barendt, *Freedom of Speech* (2nd edn, Oxford University Press 2005)

Blom-Cooper, 'Press Freedom: Constitutional Right or Cultural Assumption?' [2008] PL 260

Cram,' The Danish Cartoons, Offensive Expression and Democratic Legitimacy', in Hare and Weinstein (eds), *Extreme Speech and Democracy* (Oxford University Press 2009)

Errera, 'The Twisted Road from *Prince Albert* to *Campbell*, and Beyond: Towards a Right of Privacy?', in Andenas and Fairgrieve (eds), *Tom Bingham and the Transformation of the Law* (Oxford University Press 2009)

Fenwick, 'Marginalising Human Rights: Breach of the Peace, "Kettling", the Human Rights Act and Public Protest' [2009] PL 737

Finnis, ' Endorsing Discrimination between Faiths: A Case of Extreme Speech?' in Hare and Weinstein (eds), above

Greenawalt, 'Free Expression Justifications' (1989) 89 CLR 119

Hare, 'Blasphemy and Incitement to Religious Hatred', in Hare and Weinstein (eds), above see also Hare [2006] PL 52

Leigh, 'Homophobic Speech, Equality Denial and Religious Expression', in Hare and Weinstein (eds), above

Malik, 'Extreme Speech and Liberalism', in Hare and Weinstein (eds), above

Moreham, 'Privacy in the Common Law: A Doctrinal and Theoretical Analysis' (2005) 121 LQR 628

Morgan, 'Privacy in the House of Lords Again' (2004) 120 LQR 563

Williams, 'Hate Speech in the United Kingdom: An Historical Overview', in Hare and Weinstein (eds), above

Chapter 24

Exceptional powers: security, state secrecy and emergencies

Introduction: security and the courts

The rule of law requires that government powers be defined by clear laws and that there should be safeguards for individual freedom. Liberal democracy requires that citizens should be fully informed as to what government is doing. As against this the Hobbesian minimum duty of the state is to safeguard human life by keeping order (Section 2.3.1). This may involve facing unpredictable events and acting secretly. Hobbes believed that the people must entrust open-ended and absolute powers to government. He thought that the risk of government abusing its power was a price worth paying for security.

Wide emergency powers are particularly prone to abuse. For example, political pressures may encourage a government to introduce legislation that removes normal safeguards on the ground that the seriousness of the threat requires speedy and decisive action. This could be a cloak for appeasing the mob, particularly where the emergency involves threats from outsiders or minorities. Moreover it is easier and cheaper to bypass the rule of law than to raise policing standards. History tells us that governments may use the excuse of an emergency as a means of reinforcing their own positions. Marshal J (in *Skinner v Railway Labor Executives' Association* [1989]) remarked:

> When we allow fundamental freedoms to be sacrificed in the name of real or perceived exigency, we invariably come to regret it. (at [635]–[636])

Emergency laws may violate the rule of law and democracy in several respects:

- There may be a temptation to use oppressive methods such as torture or detention without trial in order, for example to prevent terrorist attacks. Torture is absolutely prohibited by the European Convention on Human Rights (ECHR) (see Section 20.4.2).
- Parliamentary scrutiny of legislation may be rushed or truncated so that the laws are effectively made by a small group within the executive without the wide process of consultation and checks and balances which both the rule of law and democracy require.
- Vaguely defined powers such as random stop and search powers may target ill-defined groups because the needs of an emergency favour flexibility. The judicial review doctrine that powers must be used reasonably and for proper purposes may be frustrated by the wide terms in which the powers are conferred.
- Safeguards such as judicial review might be restricted.
- Requirements of secrecy in court proceedings may lead to exclusion of the press.
- Evidence in legal proceedings may be restricted.
- Jury trial has been removed in some cases (Northern Ireland (Emergency Provisions) Act 1978).
- Intrusive surveillance is authorised. For example, on the pretext of community protection against local anti-social behaviour, in 2009 the West Midlands police

established large-scale CCTV surveillance in a predominantly Muslim area of Birmingham without local oversight and concealing its true purpose, which was national counter-terrorism (*Guardian* 1 October 2010).

▶ Powers of detention without going before a court might be extended.

▶ Minorities might be targeted on the basis that those who do not support majority values are a security risk. For example Lord Rooker, a Home Office minister, stated that:

> in a tolerant liberal society, if we are not guarded we will find that those who do not seek to be part of our society will use our tolerance and liberalism to destroy that society. (HL Deb 27 November 2001, col 143)

▶ Measures originally introduced to meet an emergency become permanent. Typically emergency measures should contain a 'sunset clause' under which the measure expires on a given date unless renewed by Parliament.

▶ The executive is given power to alter existing laws without adequate democratic scrutiny.

▶ Measures intended to deal with serious threats are used against trivial offences or for political purposes. Laws cast in wide terms are not necessarily ambiguous, so ministerial reassurances about the scope of the legislation cannot be used as an aid to interpretation under the *Pepper v Hart* doctrine (Section 7.7.2).

A state can derogate from some Articles of the ECHR in times of war or other public emergency threatening 'the life of the nation' (Art 15; Human Rights Act 1998, ss 1(2), 14, 15). The state must show that the threat is current or imminent, that the measures do not go beyond a necessary response to the emergency and that other international obligations are not violated. There must also be the safeguard of judicial review by an independent court (*Chahal v UK* (1996). The European Court has given states a wide margin of discretion (Section 22.7.2) and is reluctant to attribute improper motives to a government. (See *Lawless v Ireland (No 3)* [1961] 1 EHRR 15; *Brannigan and McBride v UK* [1993] 17 EHRR 539; *Klass v Federal Republic of Germany* [1979] 2 EHRR 714; *Brogan v UK* (1989).

Article 2 (the right to life) cannot be derogated from except in respect of deaths resulting from lawful acts of war, nor can Article 3 (torture and inhuman and degrading treatment). Article 4(1) (slavery), Article 7 (retrospective punishment) and Protocol 6 (capital punishment).

The definition of 'emergency' is not clear. The criteria are that the threat be actual or imminent, that its effects involve the whole nation, that the organised life of the community is at risk and that the crisis be exceptional so that normal measures are plainly inadequate (see *Lawless v Ireland (No 3)* [1969], *A v Secretary of State for the Home Dept* [2005].

In *A v Secretary of State for the Home Dept [2005]*, a majority of the House of Lords deferred to the government's view that an emergency existed in the shape of the terrorist threat following 9/11 (see Section 22.7.1). Lord Hoffmann took a different view. He suggested that an emergency existed only when the basic principles of democracy and the rule of law were threatened and that a high risk of terrorist attack was not in itself evidence of this. Indeed he suggested that government measures of the type in issue were a greater threat to democracy.

In deciding whether an exceptional interference with a Convention right is justified, the courts are particularly concerned with safeguards to prevent an abuse of power.

These try to strike a balance by requiring certain non-negotiable standards based on the rule of law. They include:

- powers being defined in detail by clear publicly announced laws (see *R (Gillan) v Metropolitan Police Comr* [2006] at [31]);
- the safeguards of access to a lawyer and judicial supervision;
- the right to a fair trial, including the right to challenge evidence (*Secretary of State for the Home Dept v MB* [2008];

Traditionally the UK courts have regarded matters of national security as non-justiciable, relying on ministerial accountability to Parliament as a safeguard (eg *Liversidge v Anderson* [1942] AC 206 but note Lord Atkin's classic dissent). According to Lord Diplock in *Council of Civil Service Unions (CCSU) v Minister for the Civil Service* [1985], 'national security is par excellence a non-justiciable question. The judicial process is totally inept to deal with the type of problems which it involves.' For example the courts have limited access to the specialised knowledge that security matters require, some of which must be secret. However even in the *CCSU* case the government had to show that it was acting in good faith and that the matter (the effectiveness of GCHQ, the government's centre for the interception of electronic communications) was genuinely one of national security.

In recent years the UK courts have been more willing to interfere with national security powers, at least on the level of broad principle. The jurisprudence of the ECHR has invited the courts to apply the proportionality principle, thus increasing the intensity of review. On the other hand at the level of detail the 'margin of discretion' enables the courts to defer particularly to the government's use of information, its assessment of risk and its use of secrecy since these are matters with which judicial experience is not comfortable (see Poole, 2008).

24.2 State secrecy: access to information

There are two aspects to state secrecy. The first concerns a right of access to information held by government. Under the ECHR freedom of expression does not in general *require* a person to give information (*Leander v Sweden* [1987] 9 EHRR 433). Access to government information as such is therefore not protected by the ECHR. There is however a right to information under Article 2 (right to life (Section 21.4.1), Article 6 (right to a fair trial) and Article 8: respect for family life (Section 21.4.3), for example *Guerra v Italy* (1998): environmental risks; *Gaskin v UK* (1990): adoption records, applied restrictively in *Gunn-Russo v Nugent Care Housing Society* [2001] EWHC Admin 566).

Apart from cases where the principles of natural justice apply (Section 18.3) the common law gives no right to information. Indeed in *Burmah Oil Co Ltd v Bank of England* [1980] AC 1090 at 1112, Lord Wilberforce did not believe that the courts should support open government.

There are however certain statutory rights to information, of which the Freedom of Information Act 2000 is the most general. On the other hand there are also particular doctrines, such as public interest immunity (Section 24.3.3) and the absence of a general duty to give reasons for government action (Section 18.5), that reinforce state secrecy.

The second aspect of secrecy concerns claims by the state to suppress information held by others, such as the media. Here the state is interfering with common law rights and also the right of freedom of expression under Article 10 of the ECHR. The onus is therefore on the state to justify its intervention. In relation to government information secrecy is reinforced by statutes, notably the Official Secrets Act 1989 forbidding disclosure of certain information, by the civil law of breach of confidence and by employment contracts.

Arguments in favour of 'open government' include the following:

▶ *democratic accountability*: officials should be accountable to well-informed public opinion;
▶ *autonomy*: people should be able to exercise informed choice in relation to their own affairs;
▶ *justice*: in being able to correct false information;
▶ *direct public participation*: in decision making, as a republican idea based on equality and dignity;
▶ *public confidence*: in government.

Arguments in favour of government secrecy include the following:

▶ release of certain kinds of information might cause serious harm, for example to national security, crime prevention, and some economic information;
▶ the protection of vulnerable persons such as the mentally ill and children;
▶ expense and delay, bearing in mind that seekers of information may be cranks, enemies or maniacs;
▶ freedom of information perhaps weakening ministerial responsibility to Parliament;
▶ frankness within government, for example the danger of policy making being inhibited by premature criticism or the quality of debate being diluted by the temptation to play to the gallery;
▶ public panic if disclosures are misunderstood;
▶ self-importance and self-protection by public officials: without secrecy it might be more difficult to make public appointments;
▶ the mystique of government (the 'dignified constitution'), emphasised by Bagehot as a source of stability (see Section 5.1);
▶ contemporary policies of privatisation and encouraging public bodies to follow commercial practices, including 'commercial confidentiality', also militate against openness in favour of a protective, defensive culture.

24.2.1 The Freedom of Information Act 2000

The scope of the Freedom of Information Act 2000 is potentially wide. Subject to many exemptions, the Act requires public authorities in England, Wales and Northern Ireland (see also Freedom of Information (Scotland) Act 2002) to disclose information on request and also to confirm or deny whether the information exists (s 1). This is supervised and enforced by an Information Commissioner, who also has advisory and promotional functions. As so often in the UK constitution the Act depends heavily on the ability of the Information Commissioner, a government appointee, to stand up to the government and to be adequately resourced by government.

Under Schedule 1 central government departments (but not the Cabinet, the royal household or the security services), Parliament, the Welsh Assembly (but not the Scottish government (s 80)), local authorities, the police, the armed forces, state educational bodies and NHS bodies are automatically public authorities, as are a long list of other specified bodies, including companies which are wholly owned by these bodies (s 6).

The Secretary of State may also designate other bodies, office holders or persons as public authorities which appear to him to be exercising 'functions of a public nature' or who provide services under a contract with a public authority whose functions include the provision of those services (s 3(1)). This might include a voluntary body acting on behalf of a government agency. The designation is controversial in relation to bodies, such as Network Rail (not currently listed), constituted as private companies and run on business lines but with the government holding an interest The Secretary of State can however limit the kind of information that the listed bodies can disclose (s 7). For example journalistic material held by the BBC is exempt. Where a body holds information for mixed purposes only some of which are exempt there need be no disclosure (*BBC v Sugar (No 2)* [2012] *Times* Feb 28).

The Act gives a right to any person to request in writing (s 8) information held by the authority on its own behalf or held by another on behalf of the authority (s 3(2)). The person making the request is entitled to be told whether or not the authority possesses the information (duty to confirm or deny) and to have the information communicated to him or her (s 1(1)). Reasons do not normally have to be given for the request. However disclosure can be refused if the applicant has not provided such further information as the authority reasonably requires to enable the requested information to be found (s 1), although the authority must provide reasonable advice and assistance (s 16). A request can also be refused if the cost of compliance exceeds a limit set by the Secretary of State or where the request is vexatious or repetitive (s 14). A fee regulated by the Secretary of State can be charged (s 9). The authority must respond promptly and within 20 working days, although there is no penalty for failure to do so (s 10). However if the matter might involve an exemption there is no time limit other than a 'reasonable' time to make a decision. Thus the right to information is far from absolute and there is considerable scope for bureaucratic obfuscation and delay and for lying as to the existence of a document.

The Information Commissioner can require the authority to disclose information either on her or his own initiative (enforcement notice, s 52) or on the application of a complainant whose request has been refused (decision notice, s 50). Reasons must be given for a refusal and the Commissioner can where appropriate inspect the information in question and also require further information. An authority can refuse to disclose to the Commissioner any information which might expose it to criminal proceedings other than proceedings under the Act itself. Both sides may appeal to the Information Tribunal on the merits, with a further appeal to the High Court on a point of law (s 57). The right to information can be enforced by the courts through the law of contempt but no civil action is possible (s 56).

The right to information under the Act is subject to many exemptions (Part II). These apply both to the information itself and usually to the duty to confirm or deny (but in looking at each exemption the distinction should be borne in mind). Some exemptions are absolute exemptions for whole classes of information. Others require a 'prejudice' test relating to the particular document. However this is less onerous for the government than the 'substantial prejudice' that was originally envisaged in the White Paper (*Your*

Right to Know: Freedom of Information (Cm 3818, 1997)). Some exemptions are vague, encouraging delaying tactics by officials.

The absolute exemptions are as follows:

▶ information which is already reasonably accessible to the public even if payment is required (s 21);
▶ information supplied by or relating to the intelligence and security services (s 23). A minister's certificate is conclusive, subject to an appeal to the Tribunal by the Commissioner or the applicant, which in respect of the reasonableness of the decision is limited to the judicial review grounds (s 60);
▶ information contained in court records widely defined (s 32);
▶ information protected by parliamentary privilege (s 34). In *Corporate Officer of the House of Commons v Information Comr* [2009] an attempt to prevent disclosure of MPs' expenses claims on the grounds of parliamentary privilege was unsuccessful (Section 11.6.2). However information held by Parliament is exempt if the Speaker or in the case of the House of Lords the Clerk of the Parliaments so certifies (s 34(1));
▶ information that would prejudice the conduct of public affairs in the House of Commons or the House of Lords (s 36);
▶ certain personal information, although some of this is available under the Data Protection Act 1998 (s 40(1)(2));
▶ information the disclosure of which would be an actionable breach of confidence (s 41);
▶ information protected by legal obligations such as legal professional privilege or European law (s 44);
▶ communications with the sovereign, the heir to the throne and the second in line to the throne (see below).

In other cases the exemption applies only where it 'appears to the authority' that 'the public interest in maintaining the secrecy of the information outweighs the public interest in disclosure' (s 2(1)(b)). The balance is therefore tipped in favour of disclosure. However because this test is subjective the Commissioner's powers may be limited to the grounds of judicial review.

The main exemptions of this kind are as follows:

▶ information which is held at the time of request with a view to being published in the future (s 22). No particular time for publication need be set although it must be reasonable that the information be withheld;
▶ information required for the purpose of safeguarding national security. There is provision for a minister's certificate as under section 23 (above);
▶ information held at any time for the purposes of criminal proceedings or investigations which may lead to criminal proceedings or relate to information provided by confidential sources (s 30). This would include many inquiries into matters of public concern;
▶ information the disclosure of which would or would be likely to prejudice defence, foreign relations, relations between the UK devolved governments, the House of Commons or the House of Lords, law enforcement widely defined to include many official inquiries, the commercial interests of any person including the public authority holding the information, or the economic interests of the UK (ss 26–29, 31);
▶ audit functions;

- communications with the royal family. However the Constitutional Reform and Governance Act 2010 has removed the public interest test as regards communications with the sovereign, the heir to the throne and the second in line to the throne, thus giving these communications absolute exemption. This protects correspondence from the Prince of Wales, who as heir the throne is required to be politically neutral, but has allegedly lobbied ministers in order to influence government policy *Guardian* 26 June 2010), health and safety matters;
- environmental information (this is subject to special provisions; see Section 24.2.2);
- information concerning the 'formulation or development' of government policy (s 35). This includes all communications between ministers, Cabinet proceedings, advice from the law officers and the operation of any ministerial private office. It also seems to include advice from civil servants. However once a decision has been taken statistical background information can be released;
- other information which 'in the reasonable opinion of a qualified person' would or would be likely to prejudice collective ministerial responsibility or which would or would be likely to inhibit 'free and frank' provision of advice or exchange of views or 'would otherwise prejudice or be likely to prejudice the effective conduct of public affairs' (s 36). This would again ensure that civil service advice remains secret. A 'qualified person' is the minister or other official in charge of the department. Because the test is subjective it appears that the Commissioner would have no power to intervene except where the qualified person's decision was 'unreasonable'. A question here would be whether the minimal *Wednesbury* version of unreasonableness (see Section 18.1) would apply.

Moreover ministers have a general power to override the Commission's enforcement powers. In the case of information held by the central government, the Welsh Assembly and other bodies designated by the Secretary of State, an 'accountable person' (a Cabinet minister or the Attorney General, or their equivalents in Scotland and Northern Ireland) can serve a certificate on the Commissioner 'stating that he has on reasonable grounds formed the opinion' that there was no failure to comply with the duty to disclose the information (s 53). Reasons must be given and the certificate must be laid before Parliament. The certificate would also be subject to judicial review.

For example in 2012 the Health Secretary Andrew Lansley vetoed publication of the government's assessment of the risks of health service reforms. The Attorney General blocked an attempt to require the government to publish letters sent to it by Prince Charles (before absolute immunity for such letters (above) came into effect) on the ground that publication would weaken public confidence in the monarchy (*Guardian* 7 October 2012). Ministers have also vetoed publication of the minutes of cabinet meetings prior to the invasion of Iraq (*Guardian* 31 2012).

24.2.2 Other statutory rights to information

Other statutory rights to information are characterised by broad exceptions and weak or non-existent enforcement mechanisms. None of them gives access to the contemporary inner workings of the central government. The most important of them are as follows:

- historical records. Part VI of the Freedom of Information Act 2000 has replaced a series of Public Records Acts. A government document becomes a historical record after 20 years (reduced from 30 years by the Constitutional Reform and Governance

Act 2010, Sch 7). At which point, subject to certain exemptions (mainly relating to matters such as legal proceedings and other investigations which directly affect individuals), the document is placed in the National Archives available to the public;

▶ personal information relating to the applicant held on computer or in structured manual records (Data Protection Act 1998). This is enforced by the Information Commissioner. However the Act exempts much government data, including national security matters, law and tax enforcement matters and data 'relating to the exercise of statutory functions';

▶ local government information. The Local Government (Access to Information) Act 1985 gives a public right to attend local authority meetings, including those of committees and subcommittees, and to see background papers, agendas, reports and minutes. There are large exemptions, which include decisions taken by officers, confidential information, information from central government, personal matters excluded by the relevant committee and 'the financial or business affairs of any person'. The Act appears to be easy to evade by using officers or informal groups to make decisions. It is not clear what counts as a background paper;

▶ the Public Bodies (Admission to Meetings) Act 1960 gives a right to attend meetings of parish councils and certain other public bodies. The public can be excluded on the grounds of public interest (see *R v Brent HA, ex p Francis* [1985]);

▶ the Access to Personal Files Act 1987 authorises access to local authority housing and social work records by the subject of the records and in accordance with regulations made by the Secretary of State (see also Housing Act 1985, s 106(5));

▶ the Environmental Information Regulations 2004 (SI 2004/3391) implementing EC Directive 2003/4/EC require public authorities to disclose certain information about environmental standards and measures. This is enforced by the Information Commissioner under the Freedom of Information Act 2000. The information must be made available within 20 days on request but there are no specific requirements as to how this is to be done. A charge can be made. Requests can be refused on grounds including manifest unreasonableness or a too general request, confidentiality, increasing the likelihood of environmental damage, information voluntarily supplied unless the supplier consents, international relations and national security. Under the Aarhus Convention (*Access to Information, Public Participation in Decision Making and Access to Justice in Environmental Matters* (Cm 4736, 1998)) the government is required to make regulations giving a general right to environmental information subject to exceptions on public interest grounds.

24.3 Disclosure of government information

24.3.1 The Official Secrets Act 1989: criminal law

The Official Secrets Act 1989 protects certain kinds of government information from unauthorised disclosure. It was enacted in response to long-standing and widespread criticism of section 2 of the Official Secrets Act 1911, which covered all information, however innocuous, concerning the central government and allowed no defence on public interest grounds (see *Departmental Committee on Section 2 of the Official Secrets Act 1911* (Cmnd 5104, 1972), the Franks Report). A series of controversial prosecutions culminated in the trial of Clive Ponting in 1995, where a civil servant who gave information to an MP concerning alleged governmental malpractice during the Falklands War was acquitted by a jury against the judge's summing up. Ponting's acquittal meant that the government could no longer resist reform.

Section 1 of the 1911 Act, which concerns spying activities, remains in force but section 2 has been repealed. The Official Secrets Act 1989 is narrower but more sharply focused.

It identifies four protected areas of government activity and provides defences which vary with each area. The aim is to make enforcement more effective in respect of the more sensitive areas of government. In each case it is an offence to disclose information without 'lawful authority'. In the case of a Crown servant or 'notified person' (below) this means 'in accordance with his official duty' (s 7). In the case of a government contractor, lawful authority means either with official authorisation or disclosure for the purpose of his or her functions as such, for example giving information to a subcontractor.

In the case of other persons who may fall foul of the Act, such as a former civil servant, lawful authority means disclosure to a Crown servant for the purpose of his or her functions as such (ss 7(3)(a), 12(1)), for example to a minister or the Director of Public Prosecutions but not a member of Parliament or the police since these are not Crown servants. Alternatively lawful authority means in accordance with an official authorisation, presumably by the head of the relevant department (s 7(3)(b), 7(5)).

The protected areas are as follows:

▶ *Security and intelligence (s 1).* This applies (i) to a member or former member of the security and intelligence services; (ii) to anyone else who is 'notified' by a minister that he or she is within this provision; (iii) to any other existing or former Crown servant or government contractor. In the cases of (i) and (ii) any disclosure is an offence unless the accused did not know and had no reasonable cause to believe that the information related to security or intelligence. The nature of the information is irrelevant. In the case of (iii) the disclosure must be 'damaging' or where the information or document is of a kind where disclosure is likely to be damaging (s 1(4)). 'Damaging' does not concern the public interest generally but means only damaging to 'the work of the security and intelligence services'. This might include, for example informing MPs that security agents are breaking the law. It is a defence that the accused did not know and had no reasonable cause to believe that the disclosure would be damaging;

In *R v Shaylor* [2002] the House of Lords held that section 1 did not violate the right to freedom of expression. The accused, a former member of the security services, had handed over documents to journalists which according to him revealed criminal behaviour by members of the service. His motive was to have MI5 reformed in order to remove a public danger. The House of Lords held that the interference with the right to freedom of expression was proportionate. The main reason for this was that the restriction was not absolute. It allowed information to be released with 'lawful authority', thereby inviting the claimant to approach a range of 'senior and responsible crown servants' such as the Metropolitan Police Commissioner and the Security and Intelligence Commission ([103]). The consent of the Attorney General is required for a prosecution, although it is questionable whether this provides independence.

Lord Hutton ([99]–[101]) went further than the others in stressing that the need to protect the secrecy of intelligence and military operations was justified as a 'pressing social need' even where the disclosure was not itself harmful to the public interest (cf Lord Scott [120]). This was to protect confidence in the security services. Moreover an individual whistleblower may not be sufficiently informed of the consequences of his actions. Lord Hutton [105]–[106] also rejected the argument that senior officials or politicians might be reluctant to investigate complaints of wrongdoing, holding that the court must assume that the relevant legislation is being applied properly. By contrast Lord Hope asserted that 'institutions tend to protect their own and to resist criticism from wherever it may come' [70]).

The Court of Appeal had left open the possibility that a defence of necessity might apply to the Official Secrets Act 1989. This would apply only in extreme circumstances where disclosure was needed to avert an immediate threat to life or perhaps property. The House of Lords did not comment on this issue.

- *Defence (s 2).* This applies to any present or former Crown servant or government contractor. In all cases the disclosure must be damaging. Here damaging means hampering the armed forces, leading to death or injury of military personnel or leading to serious damage to military equipment or installations. A similar defence of ignorance applies as under section 1;
- *International relations (s 3).* Again this applies to any present or former Crown servant or government contractor. Two kinds of information are covered: (i) any information concerning international relations; (ii) any confidential information obtained from a foreign state or an international organisation. The disclosure must again be damaging. 'Damaging' here refers to endangering the interests of the UK abroad or endangering the safety of British citizens abroad. The fact that information in this class is confidential in its 'nature or contents' may be sufficient in itself to establish that the disclosure is damaging (s 3(3)). There is a defence of ignorance on the same basis as under section 1 (s 3(4));
- *Crime and special investigation powers (s 4).* This applies to present or former Crown servants or contractors and covers information relating to the commission of offences, escapes from custody, crime prevention, detection or prosecution work. 'Special investigations' include telephone tapping under a warrant from the Home Secretary and entering on private property in accordance with a warrant under the Security Services Act 1989 (see Section 23.4). Section 4 does not require that the information be damaging as such because damage is implicit in its nature. There is however a defence of 'ignorance of the nature' of the information (s 4(4)–(5)).

Section 5 makes it an offence to pass on protected information, for example by the press. Protected information is information falling within the above provisions which has come into a person's possession as a result of (i) having been 'disclosed' (whether to him or another) by a Crown servant or government contractor without lawful authority; or (ii) entrusted to him in confidence; or (iii) disclosed to him by a person to whom it was entrusted in confidence. This does not seem to cover someone who receives information from a former Crown servant or government contractor. If this is so the publisher of the memoirs of a retired civil servant may be safe, although the retired civil servant herself will not (but see *Lord Advocate v The Scotsman Publications Ltd* [1990], where section 5 was applied). Nor does the section seem to apply to a person who accidentally finds protected information (eg a civil servant leaves her briefcase in a restaurant). Could this be regarded as a 'disclosure'? It is an offence for a Crown servant or government contractor not to look after the protected information and for anyone to fail to hand it back if officially required to do so (s 8).

The Crown must prove that the accused knew or had reasonable cause to believe that the information was protected under the Act and that it came into his or her possession contrary to the Act. In the case of information in categories (1), (2) and (3) above the Crown must also show that disclosure is 'damaging' and that he or she knew or had reasonable cause to believe that this was so.

24.3.2 Civil liability: breach of confidence

As we saw in Chapter 23 the publication of information given in confidence can be prevented by means of an injunction. The Crown can take advantage of this. However a public authority must show positively that secrecy is in the public interest, which the court will balance against any countervailing public interest in disclosure. A public authority can rely on a public interest in disclosure in order to override private confidentiality even where the information has been given only for a specific purpose (see *Hellewell v Chief Constable of Derbyshire* [1995] 4 All ER 473; *Woolgar v Chief Constable of the Sussex Police* [1999] 3 All ER 604).

A civil action for breach of confidence may be attractive to governments since it avoids a jury trial, can be speedy and requires a lower standard of proof than in a criminal case. Indeed under the common law a temporary injunction, which against the press may destroy a topical story, could be obtained from a judge at any time on the basis merely of an arguable case (*A-G v Guardian Newspapers* [1987]).

In *A-G v Guardian Newspapers Ltd (No 2)* [1990] (*Spycatcher*) the House of Lords in principle supported the interests of government secrecy. Peter Wright, a retired member of the security service, had published his memoirs widely abroad revealing possible criminality within the service including a plot to destabilise the Labour government. Their Lordships refused to grant a permanent injunction but only because the memoirs were no longer secret. It was held that the relationship between the member of the security service and the Crown was one of confidence for life and that the Crown could probably obtain compensation from Wright and from newspapers (see also *A-G v Blake* [1998] 1 All ER 833).

The position is probably the same under the Human Rights Act 1998, subject to the limited protection provided by section 12 of the Act (Section 23.3). In *Observer and Guardian Newspapers v UK* [1992] the ECHR, with a strong dissent from Morenilla J, held that in the area of national security an injunction is justifiable to protect confidential information even where the content of the particular information is not in itself harmful (see also *Sunday Times (No 2) v UK* [1992]; *A-G v Jonathan Cape Ltd* [1975].

The exposure of 'iniquity' (serious wrongdoing or crime) by government officers can justify disclosure (eg *Lion Laboratories v Evans* [1985] 1 QB 526). In *Spycatcher* serious iniquity was not established and it remains to be seen whether 'iniquity' overrides national security. The method of disclosure must be reasonable and the discloser must probably complain internally before going public (*Francombe v Mirror Group Newspapers* [1984] 2 All ER 408).

A common response by UK officials to those who disclose official wrongdoing is to condemn the whistleblower (see Committee on Standards in Public Life, consultation paper, *Getting the Balance Right*, 2003). For example Steve Moxon, a civil servant who had revealed irregularities in the processing of immigration visas to the press leading to the resignation of the responsible minister, was dismissed for 'an irretrievable breakdown in trust' (*Independent*, 2 August 2004).

24.3.3 Public interest immunity

An important aspect of government secrecy concerns the doctrine once called 'Crown privilege' and now 'public interest immunity' (PII). A party to a legal action is normally required to disclose relevant documents and other evidence in his or her possession. Where PII applies, such information must not be disclosed. In deciding whether to accept a claim of PII, the court is required to 'balance' the public interest in the administration of justice against the public interest in confidentiality. At one time the courts would always accept the government's word that disclosure should be prohibited. However as a result of *Conway v Rimmer* [1968] AC 910 the court itself does the balancing exercise.

Public interest immunity applies both to civil and to criminal proceedings (see Criminal Procedure and Investigations Act 1996, ss 3(6), 7(5)). Any person can raise a claim of PII. Claims are often made by ministers following advice from the Attorney General, ostensibly acting independently of the government. It appears that a minister is not under a duty to make a claim even if he or she believes that there is a public interest at stake but must personally do an initial balancing exercise. In *R v Brown* [1993] the court emphasised that it was objectionable for a minister automatically to accept the Attorney General's advice.

Where a PII certificate is issued the person seeking disclosure must first satisfy the court that the document is likely to be necessary for fairly disposing of the case, or in a criminal case of assisting the defence – a less difficult burden (see *Air Canada v Secretary of State for Trade (No 2)* [1983] 2 AC 394; *Goodridge v Chief Constable of Hampshire Constabulary* [1999] 1 All ER 896; Criminal Procedure and Investigations Act 1996, s 3). The court can inspect the documents at this stage but is reluctant to do so in order to discourage 'fishing expeditions' (*Burmah Oil Co Ltd v Bank of England* [1980]. The court will then 'balance' the competing public interests involved, at this stage inspecting the documents. The court will give great weight to statements by ministers, particularly in relation to security issues, where the separation of powers and the court's relative lack of expertise require deference to the executive (see Section 23.1). The decision is however for the court, taking into account all the circumstances.

Grounds for refusing disclosure include, for example national security, the protection of anonymous informers or covert surveillance operations (*Rogers v Secretary of State for the Home Dept* [1973] AC 388; *D v NSPCC* [1978] AC 171), financially or commercially sensitive material such as communications between the government and the Bank of England and between the Bank and private businesses (*Burmah Oil v Bank of England* [1980]), and relationships with foreign governments.

It has also been said that preventing 'ill-informed or premature criticism of the government' is in the public interest (*Conway v Rimmer [1968]*). There is no automatic immunity for high-level documents such as Cabinet minutes but a strong case must be made for their disclosure (see *Burmah Oil Co Ltd v Bank of England* [1980], *Air Canada v Secretary of State for Trade(No 2)* [1983]).

The desire to protect candour and frankness within the public service is arguably not a sufficient justification (*Conway v Rimmer* [1968], 957, 976, 993–95; *R v West Midlands Chief Constable, ex p Wiley* [1994] 1 All ER 702; *Williams v Home Office (No 2)* [1981] 1155; *Science Research Council v Nasse* [1980] AC 1028 at 1970: candour a 'private' interest; but *Burmah Oil Co Ltd v Bank of England* [1980] (1132) disagrees).

A distinction has been made between 'class claims' and 'contents claims'. In a class claim, even if the contents of a document are innocuous, the document should still be protected because it is a member of a class of documents whose disclosure would prevent the efficient working of government, such as policy advice given by civil servants or diplomatic communications. *In R v West Midlands Chief Constable, ex p Wiley* [1994] it was claimed that evidence given to the Police Complaints Authority was protected by class immunity. The House of Lords rejected this blanket claim, holding that immunity depended on whether the *contents* of the particular document raised a public interest, which on the facts they did not. It is not clear whether the notion of a class claim as such survives this decision since their Lordships rejected the claim only in relation to that particular class of document. However Lord Templeman remarked (at 424) that the distinction between a class and a contents claim loses 'much of its significance'.

In *R v H and C* [2004]) *Times* 6 Feb. the House of Lords specified principles that must be applied, at least in a criminal case, to minimise unfairness. The government must show a pressing social need that cannot be met by less intrusive means. The parties must be given an opportunity to argue the reasons for the claim in open court and also for the procedure to be adopted. As much as possible of the material must be disclosed. Where a conviction is likely to be unsafe as a result of PII the trial must probably be discontinued. Lord Bingham remarked that it is axiomatic that if a person charged with a criminal offence cannot receive a fair trial, he should not be tried at all. The court should consider possible safeguards which would allow the material to be disclosed such as anonymity or inspection in a special place, or producing s summary (*R v West Midlands Chief Constable, ex p Wiley* [1994]).

If a PII claim is successful the evidence cannot be used at all (*Al Rawi v Security Service* [2012]). If the PII claim fails the material must be disclosed unless the person holding it concedes the issue to which it relates. A 'closed material procedure' (below) cannot be used instead. Thus whatever the outcome there may be unfairness. A claimant may not get the evidence he needs, but in order to protect its secrecy the state may be unable to defend itself. PII as such has been held not to violate the ECHR provided that the trial overall is 'fair' (*Edwards and Lewis v UK* [2003] 15 BHRC 189; *Rowe and Davies v UK* [2001] 30 EHRR 1; *Jasper v UK* [2000] 30 EHRR 401; *Fitt v UK* [2000] 30 EHRR 480).

R (Mohamed) v Secretary of State for Foreign and Commonwealth Affairs [2010] a British prisoner in Guantanamo Bay, sought judicial review of a refusal by the Foreign Office to reveal the contents of information which it had obtained from the US relevant to the claimant's defence against a prosecution in the US for terrorism. In particular the information might have suggested that UK officials turned a blind eye to torture carried out by US officials. The Foreign Office sought a PII in respect of certain passages in the court's judgement in previous cases which included the information in question.

The Court of Appeal emphasised that only in exceptional circumstances would it override a ministerial statement in a security matter but these were such circumstances. The rule of law and freedom of the press in relation to open justice strongly required disclosure. Moreover the government's reasons for its claim were inaccurate and misleading. According to Lord Judge LCJ there was nothing secret in the material, which carried no threat to national security since it contained nothing that would help a terrorist. Moreover the government's claim that, if it revealed the information, the US would not cooperate in intelligence matters in future had no basis, particularly as the information had already been published in legal proceedings in the US.

24.3.4   Closed material procedure and special advocates

In cases involving secret evidence, for example from undercover agents or informers, such as security cases decided by the Special Immigration Appeal Commission (SIAC), terrorism cases and hearings by the Parole Board, the court can use material not disclosed to the accused. This denial of open justice confronts the rule of law in the form of the right to a fair trial and 'equality of arms' under Article 6 of the ECHR, the right to personal freedom under Article 5(4) and the right of freedom of expression under Article 10 of the ECHR in the sense of the public right through the press to be informed of what is being done in its name. (See Lord Dyson in *W(Algeria) v Secretary of State* [2012] at [35] and in *Tariq) v Home Office* [2012] 1 AC 452 [139]). Article 8, respect for family life may also be in issue. Articles 8 and 10 can be overridden on national security grounds subject to the test of proportionality. Although Articles 5 and 6 have no express overrides, the notion of a fair trial is itself affected by public interest considerations (Section 21.4.2 and see *R (BB) v SIAC* [2011] 4 All ER 210 [19]). Unlike decisions of the Investigatory Powers Tribunal (Section 24.4). decisions of SIAC are subject to judicial review (*R (Cart) v Upper Tribunal* [2010] 1 All ER 908).

A method of accommodating the conflicting concerns of fairness and security is the device of a 'special advocate'. This is a lawyer appointed by the court subject to security vetting who acts on the accused's behalf and might see the material but without disclosing it to the parties. A special advocate has no duty to give information to the claimant or to take instructions from the claimant. Thus the claimant may not be able to give adequate instructions to his lawyer. This device therefore creates serious problems of fairness and raises ethical issues relating to the confidence inherent in the lawyer–client relationship. In *R (Roberts) v Parole Board* [2006] 1 All ER 39, Lord Bingham described the closed material procedure as 'taking blind shots at a hidden target' ([18]) and thought that it could be used only where no serious unfairness was involved, for example where the relevant information could be edited or was not relied upon ([19]). Closed material procedure has been accepted in cases designated by statute before special security tribunals (Section 23.4) provided that the person affected is given an

opportunity to answer the case against him (*A v UK* (2009) 49 EHRR 625 [216–220].
Thus in *Tariq v Home Office* [2012] the Supreme Court upheld closed procedure in
a case where the claimant who had been suspended from work as an immigration
officer on alleged security grounds was alleging racial and religious discrimination
before an Employment Tribunal. This was because the nature of his employment
involved security vetting and the tribunal's procedure was sufficiently flexible to
provide safeguards to ensure fairness (see also *Leander v Sweden* [1987] 9 EHRR 433
(Art 8)).

However in *Al Rawi v Security Service* [2012] the Supreme Court refused to allow
the use of closed material procedure in an ordinary civil action, in that case an action
against the government for alleged complicity in torture. The court relied on the
common law principle of the rule of law as well as on the ECHR. It was held the court
has no inherent power to order the use of closed material. Any such power must come
from Parliament.

There are limits to the use of closed material. The trial not be seriously unfair. In
particular a defendant must always have access to enough material to be able to answer
the allegations against him. The overall test is whether the person concerned is given
sufficient information about the allegations against him to enable him to give effective
instructions (*A v UK* (2009) 26 BHRC 1), *Secretary of State for the Home Dept v AF* [2010]
2 AC 269 [59]). Relevant factors include the nature of the case, what steps had been
taken to explain the detail of the allegations and a summary of the closed material, how
effectively the special advocate was able to act on behalf of the controlled person and
what difference disclosure would make.

It seems that interference with a basic right cannot be made on the ground of closed
evidence alone. In *BM v Secretary of State for the Home Dept* [2010] 1 All ER 847 the
minister ordered the claimant to move to another city under a Control Order, alleging
that there was a risk that he might abscond. The court set aside the minister's decision
on the ground that the 'open material' showed no support for the allegation.

In *W (Algeria) v Secretary of State* [2012] it was the government who objected to the
closed material procedure where witnesses in a deportation case before SIAC would
give evidence only in secret because they feared for the safety of their families. The
Supreme Court held that, as the lesser evil, closed procedure could be used. Lord Dyson
[38] held that this applied only where Articles 2 (life) and 3 (torture) of the ECHR were
at issue and not to protect art 8 (privacy and family life).

The Justice and Security Bill proposes to give a minister power to request closed
procedure in any action against the government. The application can be in secret and
the court must accept the request if it considers that the matter would be damaging
to national security. Other powers to exclude material must be ignored. The rationale
behind this is that under PPPI law (Section 24.3.3) the alternative may be no trial at all.
(See also Joint committee on Human Rights, *Counter Terrorism Policy and Human Rights,
(Sixteenth Report)* HL 64, HC 395 (2010), Commons Constitutional Affairs Committee,
The Operation of SIAC and the Use of Special Advocates (Seventh Report, HC 2004–05,
323–I).)

24.4   The security and intelligence services

The 'secret services' comprise the security services, the intelligence services and
the government communications centre, GCHQ. Traditionally they have operated

under the general law without special powers other than the possibility of royal prerogative power. They were in principle accountable to ministers, ultimately the Prime Minister, but there was no formal mechanism for parliamentary accountability. Their role has been primarily that of information gathering. Where powers of arrest or interference with property were required, the assistance of the police was requested. However, the *Spycatcher* litigation (see Section 24.3.2) brought to a head recurrent concerns that security agents were out of control and unaccountable and they have now been placed within a statutory framework. This relies heavily on the discretionary powers of ministers but contains certain safeguards, albeit judicial review is restricted.

The security services (formerly MI5) deal with internal security (Security Services Act 1989 as amended by Intelligence Services Act 1994). They report to the Prime Minister. Their responsibilities include

> the protection of national security and, in particular, its protection against threats from espionage, terrorism and sabotage, from the activities of agents of foreign powers, and from actions intended to overthrow or undermine parliamentary democracy by political or violent means. (s 1)

Section 1(3) includes the safeguarding of 'the economic well-being of the UK against threats posed by the actions or intentions of persons outside the British Islands'. This is extremely wide and could extend, for example to the lawful activities of environmental non-governmental organisations (NGOs). The Security Services Act 1996 extends the functions of the security services to include assisting the police in the prevention and detection of serious crime. This includes the use of violence, crimes resulting in substantial financial gain, conduct by a large number of persons in pursuit of a common purpose or crimes carrying a sentence of three years or more. This is wide enough to include political public order offences and industrial disputes and may violate ECHR notions of clarity and proportionality.

The intelligence services (formerly MI6 now SIS and GCHQ) deal with threats from outside the UK. They are governed by the Intelligence Services Act 1994. They are under the control of the Foreign Office but also report to the Prime Minister. Their functions are 'to obtain and provide information relating to the actions and intentions of persons outside the British Islands' and 'to perform other tasks relating to the actions and intentions of such persons'. GCHQ monitors electronic communications and 'other emissions' and can provide advice and information to the armed forces and other organisations specified by the Prime Minister. Reflecting the ECHR their powers are limited to national security, with particular reference to defence and foreign policies, the economic well-being of the UK in relation to the actions and intentions of persons outside the British Islands and the prevention and detection of serious crime (ss 1(2), 3(2)).

Neither service must take action to further the interests of any political party (Security Services Act 1989, s 52(2); Intelligence Services Act 1994, s 2(3)).

Under sections 5 and 6 of the Intelligence Services Act 1994 all the intelligence agencies can enter property or interfere with wireless telegraphy under a warrant issued by the Secretary of State or Scottish ministers. Contravention is 'unlawful' but not a criminal offence. In the case of SIS and GCHQ a warrant cannot relate to property in the UK but the Secretary of State can authorise SIS and GCHQ to carry out actions overseas that would be a crime or civil wrong in the UK (s 7). (This does not of course affect any liability in the overseas country concerned.) In relation to the police support role of the security service a warrant can be issued only in the case of more serious crimes (see Security Services Act 1994, s 5 as amended by Security Services Act 1996). The security services also have powers to intercept communications (Section 23.5).

24.5 Surveillance

The problem of the state amassing information about individuals is of increasing concern because of increasingly sophisticated surveillance and data storage and transfer technology. Proposals innocuous in themselves, are viewed with suspicion not only because of the risk of abuse of power but also because of the accidently misuse of information in the hands of low level officials such as local government employees. After the Human Rights Act 1998 safeguards have been introduced but the powers of the ordinary courts are limited and officials have wide discretionary powers. Heavy reliance is placed upon government appointed part-time Commissioners with limited resources to regulate the use of these powers.

The European Court of Human Rights has held that under Article 8 of the ECHR (privacy) there must be safeguards in respect of surveillance. These must include clearly defined limits on the power and supervision by an independent court (*Malone v UK* (1984); *Khan v UK* [2001] 31 EHRR 1016). Moreover retaining data falling within Article 8 after it has been used for the authorised purposes is a violation unless there is a particular reason for suspicion against that person (*Amman v Switzerland* [2000] ECHR App no 27798/95). In *Halford v UK* [1997] IRLR 471 it was held that the UK was in breach of Article 8 by failing to regulate the use of interception devices by employers. In *JH Ltd v UK* [2001] *Times* 19 Oct. the European Court held that bugging in a police station was a violation of the right to privacy.

The Regulation of Investigatory Powers Act 2000 (RIPA), which largely supersedes the Interception of Communications Act 1985, responds to the ECHR. It includes not only the police and intelligence services but also the revenue and military services and can be extended by the Secretary of State to other public bodies such as local councils. RIPA authorises telephone tapping and intercepting electronic data such as emails and websites both on public and private systems. It also creates new powers of surveillance by making clear that certain forms of interception and uses of information are lawful, including bugging devices. However, notwithstanding the Act, eavesdropping upon lawyer–client communications may still be unlawful as an affront to the rule of law (*R v Grant* [2005] 3 WLR 437 [52]).

RIPA distinguishes between 'directed surveillance' which is covert surveillance undertaken as part of a specific operation to obtain private information about a person (s 26) and 'intrusive surveillance'. Intrusive surveillance is covert surveillance carried out in relation to anything taking place on residential premises or in a private vehicle where there is an individual planted or a covert surveillance device is used. Intrusive surveillance can be carried out only in the interests of national security or for preventing or detecting serious crime or in the interests of the economic well-being of the country. RIPA also regulates the use of covert human intelligence (ss 26, 29). This includes undercover officers, spies and informers.

Intrusive surveillance must be authorised by the heads of the government agency in question. In the case of the police and customs agencies there must also be the approval of a Surveillance Commissioner (s 36). Authorisation by the armed services, the intelligence services and the Ministry of Defence requires the approval of the Secretary of State. The authorising officer can appeal to the Chief Surveillance Commissioner against a refusal by a Commissioner, but not by the Secretary of State, to approve an authorisation. A person 'aggrieved' by an authorisation can complain to the Investigatory Powers Tribunal (s 65).

Directed surveillance and use of covert human intelligence can be authorised by a range of public bodies designated by the Secretary of State, including government agencies, the police and local authorities (see SI 2003/3171). It can be used if 'necessary' and 'proportionate' for a wide range of purposes within the overrides to Article 8 of the ECHR (s 28). These purposes include national security, the prevention and detection of serious crime, the safeguarding of the economic well-being of the country and – but only in the case of conduct other than interception – the safeguarding of public health, public safety, tax collection, protecting life and health in emergencies and 'other purposes specified by the Secretary of State' (s 22).

Low-level public bodies such as local councils have been using these powers casually. Local authorities allegedly authorised directed surveillance powers more than 8,500 times during 2008 and 2009 to combat relatively trivial matters such as dropping litter, car parking and sickness claims. Less than 5 per cent resulted in prosecutions (see *Guardian* 24 May 2010). However The Protection of Freedoms Act 2012 ss 37, 38 (not yet in force) introduces a requirement for approval by a magistrate of local authority authorisations for the disclosure of communications data, surveillance and covert human intelligence.

By virtue of section 1(1) of RIPA it is an offence intentionally and without lawful authority to intercept a communication while it is being transmitted by means of a public postal service or a public telecommunications system, including e mail. It is also an offence intentionally and without lawful authority to intercept a communication transmitted through a private telecommunications system (eg a company network, cordless phone or pager) except by the controller of the system or with his or her consent (*R v Sargent* [2003] 1 AC 347).

The obtaining and use of electronic 'communications data' (emails) can be authorised by a wide range of officials without prior judicial control (RIPA, Part 1, ch 2). Communications data does not include the content of a message but includes 'traffic information' such as billing data and the source and destination. The Secretary of State can require persons operating public postal or telecommunications systems (which includes Internet service providers) to keep a reasonable 'interception capability' (s 12(1)) and to provide traffic data to designated public officials on demand (s 22(4)). However blanket storage of personal information unrelated to a specific investigation may violate the ECHR.

RIPA empowers anyone in lawful possession of intercepted information to require the disclosure of the key to protected (encrypted) data on the grounds of national security, serious crime and, more dubiously, that it is necessary for the performance of a public function (s 49). The UK is the only leading democracy to allow this. A disclosure notice must be authorised by a circuit judge, who must be satisfied that there is no other means of obtaining the required information and that the direction is proportionate to what is sought to be achieved. A disclosure notice requested by the police, the security services or the customs and excise commissioners can also contain 'tipping off' provisions imposing a lifelong secrecy requirement as to the existence of the notice (s 54).

The ordinary courts are largely excluded. Evidence cannot normally be given suggesting that there has been telephone tapping, lawful or otherwise (RIPA, ss 17, 18). Information obtained by telephone tapping is not therefore admissible. However, information obtained from telephone tapping can be used in police interviews and presumably by the executive for other purposes (*R v Sargent* [2003] 1 AC 347). Information obtained by other bugging devices, and undercover agents is admissible in court (*R v Khan (Sultan)* [1996] 3 All ER 289).

There are limited independent safeguards. The Secretary of State is responsible for ensuring that interception warrants are issued for proper purposes (s 15). The Directors General of each of the security and intelligence services are responsible as both poacher and gamekeeper for the efficiency of their service and for making 'arrangements' for securing that information is neither obtained nor disclosed 'except in so far as is necessary for the proper discharge of its functions' or, in the case of disclosure, for the prevention or detection of serious crime.

RIPA creates an Investigatory Powers Tribunal to hear allegations of misuse of power by the security and intelligence services and by the police and other bodies (s 65). In human rights cases it has been designated as the only forum for human rights challenges against any of the intelligence services (Human Rights Act 1998, s 7). The Tribunal may award compensation and quash warrants or authorisations and order records to be destroyed (ibid). The Tribunal is required to apply judicial review principles (s 67). In view of the wide powers involved this affords only a low level of review.

There is also an Intelligence Services Commissioner who reviews the exercise of the various powers of investigation and use of material by the Security Services (s 59). The Justice and Security Bill extends this to the armed forces and Mod. The Commissioner, who must be a senior judge, has no enforcement powers and reports to the Prime Minister, who must lay the Commissioner's annual reports before Parliament. Interception of Communications Commissioners (s 57) have similar status and functions.

Decisions of the Tribunal and the Commissioners cannot be questioned in the courts even on jurisdictional grounds (Intelligence Services Act 1994, s 5(4); RIPA, s 67(8)). However in *A v B* [2010] the Supreme Court held that the tribunal's processes provide adequate safeguards.

Where it does not decide in favour of the complainant, the Tribunal may refer a matter to the Commissioner to investigate 'whether the service has in any other respect acted unreasonably in relation to the complainant or his property'. The Commissioner may then report to the Secretary of State, who can make an award of compensation (Schedule 1(7)).

There is an Intelligence and Security Committee composed of backbench members of both Houses, which examines the spending, administration and policy of the intelligence services (Intelligence Services Act 1994, s 11). However, this is nominated by the Prime Minister and is not strictly speaking a committee of Parliament with a duty to Parliament itself. Its annual report is laid before Parliament but can be censored by the Prime Minister after consultation with the Committee. The Justice and Security Bill puts the Committee on a statutory basis and provides for a 'memorandum of understanding' between the committee and the government in relation to the scrutiny of operational matters.

The use of covert surveillance devices by the police is also regulated by the Police Act 1997 and the two regimes overlap. Part III of the 1997 Act authorises the police to interfere with property for the purpose of preventing or detecting 'serious crime'. For this purpose serious crime means crimes involving violence, substantial financial gain or conduct by a large number of persons in pursuit of a common purpose (s 93(4)). Thus political groups may be vulnerable. The action must be 'necessary' and 'proportionate'. The exercise of the power must be authorised by a designated senior police officer, military officer, customs and revenue officer or officer of certain other law enforcement agencies.

In certain cases the authorisation must be by a *Surveillance Commissioner* (s 91). This includes dwellings, hotel bedrooms and offices and matters likely to involve legal professional privilege, confidential personal information or confidential journalistic material. Where residential premises are involved these would also constitute 'intrusive surveillance' under RIPA. The 1997 Act also imposes duties on private communication providers such as internet service providers to cooperate with the authorities.

Apart from the general law of privacy (Section 23.5) there are no restrictions on CCTV cameras in public places. The Protection of Freedoms Act 2012 Part 2 introduces a familiar weak version of regulation. The Act requires the Secretary of State to prepare and publish a Code of Practice containing guidance about the use of surveillance cameras and information obtained from them. Various local government bodies must 'have regard to' the code when exercising their functions. The Code is admissible as evidence but is not directly enforceable (s 33). A Commissioner is to have advisory powers and to publish an annual report to be laid before Parliament.

24.6 Emergency powers

As we saw in Chapter 23 the police have a general power to prevent a breach of the peace. There is no legal obstacle to the armed forces or indeed anyone else being used in support of this. Indeed perhaps everyone has a duty to aid the civil power in quelling a disturbance (*Charge to the Bristol Grand Jury* [1832] 5 C & P 535). An individual, whether policeman, soldier or private person, acting in self-defence is however liable for the excessive use of force, thus illustrating Dicey's version of the rule of law (see Section 6.4.2). The force used must be no more than is reasonable in the circumstances for self-defence or the defence of others (see Criminal Law Act 1967, s 3). In deciding what is reasonable the court will take into account the pressure of the circumstances (see *A G for Northern Ireland's Reference (No 1)* [1975]; *McCann v UK* [1995]). However obedience to orders as such is probably not a defence (*Keighley v Bell* [1866]) but should be taken into account as an aspect of reasonableness.

Under the royal prerogative the armed forces can be deployed at the discretion of the Crown and the Crown can also arm the police (Section 14.6.1). The Crown may also enter private property in an emergency but must pay compensation for any damage caused other than in wartime (War Damage Act 1965; *Saltpetre Case* [1607]; *A-G v De Keyser's Royal Hotel* [1920].

Beyond this is the possibility that where there is such a serious disruption to public order that the courts cannot function, the military may assume control under a state of martial law. Dicey denied that martial law is part of English law (1915, ch 8). However the concept has been used and indeed applied where the courts were still sitting in relation to colonial territories (*Marais v General Officer Commanding* [1902] AC 109). Martial law was declared in Ireland in 1920 and the House of Lords accepted the possibility that the courts could in principle control the activities of the military under martial law (*Re Clifford and O'Sullivan* [1921] 2 AC 570).

Exceptional executive powers can be conferred by emergency regulations (Civil Contingencies Act 2004). This might override any overlapping prerogative powers (see Section 14.6.5). Regulations can be made by Order in Council, or if this would cause serious delay by a senior minister, if the relevant authority is satisfied that an emergency exists or is imminent, that there is an urgent need to deal with it and that existing legislation is inadequate for the purpose. Thus there need be no declaration of a formal state of emergency or approval by Parliament to trigger the powers. However, the powers lapse unless approved by Parliament within 7 days (s 27) and must be renewed at 30-day intervals (s 27(4)).

An emergency is more widely defined than for the purpose of derogating from the ECHR (Section 24.1). An emergency means:

> an event or situation which threatens serious damage to human welfare or the environment in the United Kingdom or in a part or region, or war or terrorism which threatens serious damage to the security of the United Kingdom. (s 19(1))

These threats are widely drawn. Human welfare includes loss of life, illness or injury, homelessness, property damage, disruption of supplies of money, food, water, energy and fuel, or disruption of a communication system, facilities for transport or health services. Environmental damage is limited to biological, chemical or radioactive contamination or disruption to or destruction of plant or animal life (ss 19(2)–(3)). An emergency might include, for example a general strike, a natural disaster or epidemic or terrorist threat.

Parliament must meet within 5 days and the regulations lapse unless approved by Parliament within 7 days and in any event after 30 days. In both cases they can be renewed (ss 26, 27).

The Act allows ministers to alter statutes. It confers powers to deploy the armed forces, to require people to perform unpaid functions and to provide information, to restrict freedom of movement and assembly, to take or destroy property without compensation (s 22) and to extend the power to detain without trial. There are safeguards based on the ECHR. These include proportionality and compliance with Convention rights. The powers can be used only for the specific purpose of dealing with the threats created by the emergency. There can be no military conscription or outlawing of industrial action. No offence can be created except one triable summarily by magistrates or the Sheriff's Court in Scotland and not punishable with more than three months' imprisonment. Criminal procedure cannot be altered, nor the Human Rights Act 1998 (s 23). Judicial review is not specifically preserved but 'regard' must be had to its importance (s 22(5)).

24.7 Anti-terrorism measures

The UK's anti-terrorism laws illustrate the phenomenon of 'creep' as increasingly wide powers introduced in response to specific events becoming absorbed into the general law. They also illustrate the importance of safeguards comprising access to independent courts, monitoring bodies and parliamentary mechanisms. However these reassuring forms may help to legitimise harsh laws.

Terrorist actions have features going beyond ordinary crimes and so require special legislation. These include dispersed, secretive and fragmented elements sometimes involving many participants and with a political and international dimension, the need for precautionary action at an early stage due to the risks to the public involved, a close relationship with human rights, the need for secrecy and specialist expertise with resulting limitations on judicial review (see Walker 2011).

In order to legitimize special measures the rhetoric of 'war on terrorism' is substituted for that of law enforcement. This rhetoric may encourage the very terrorism that it seeks to combat. Moreover, the width of the powers means that they may be used against non-violent people whose activities the government dislikes or whom the police or local officials find it convenient to target. For example anti-terrorist legislation was used to remove a member who objected to the invasion of Iraq from a Labour Party conference (*Guardian* 8 October 2005).

Special anti-terrorism laws were originally enacted as emergency provisions in response to the conflict in Northern Ireland (see Northern Ireland (Emergency Provisions) Act 1978 (EPA), Prevention of Terrorism (Temporary Provisions) Act 1974 (PTA). These Acts created two distinct anti-terrorism regimes in the UK since there were now additional measures in Northern Ireland (eg trial without a jury and detention without trial). The EPA and PTA were intended to be temporary and only apply to terrorism cases but were repeatedly re-enacted, extended and modified. Some of the powers in the PTAs and EPAs were mirrored in new laws to deal with ordinary crime in the UK as a whole. Thus the extraordinary powers had become ordinary.

In response to the peace process in Northern Ireland a review of the anti-terrorism laws was undertaken to ensure they were suitable for countering future terrorism threats. In 1996 the Lloyd Report (*Inquiry into Legislation against Terrorism* (Cm 3420, 1996)) recommended wide-ranging changes, including the harmonisation of anti-terrorism laws across the UK, the expansion of these powers to all domestic and international terrorism and a new definition of terrorism. Many of these recommendations were enacted in the Terrorism Act 2000 (TA) which applied to the whole of the UK.

After the attacks in the US in September 2001 the TA was considered to be inadequate. In 2001 the Anti-Terrorism, Crime and Security Act 2001 (ATCSA) was enacted in unseemly haste. It was controversial, in particular introducing indefinite detention of non-UK nationals who could not be deported because they faced ill-treatment overseas (Section 9.6.7.3) (s 23). In *A v Secretary of State for the Home Dept* [2005] in a landmark judgement regarded by some as vindicating the rule of law but by others as a dangerous usurpation of the responsibility of the government (Campbell, 2009), an eight-to-one majority of the House of Lords held that the indefinite detention of aliens was disproportionate and discriminatory. The government's inability to secure the re-enactment of indefinite detention led to the Prevention of Terrorism Act 2005, which introduced an alternative namely Control Orders which amounted to restrictions on movement sometimes tantamount to house arrest. These applied to citizens and non-citizens alike. However, Control Orders have proven almost as controversial (see *Secretary of State for the Home Dept v JJ* [2008] and are currently being replaced (Section 24.6.5).

The panic-fuelled retreat from human rights norms that typifies anti-terrorism legislation has generated considerable litigation and was continued in the legislation introduced after the London bombings in July 2005. The Terrorism Act 2006 extended pre-charge detention (s 23) and introduced new offences that are widely feared to restrict free speech (ss 1–3) (Section 23.7.3). It also introduced the offences of preparation of terrorist acts (s 5) and training for terrorism (s 6). The Treasury has power to freeze the assets of suspected terrorists (ATCSA 2001; see Section 24.6.6). The Counter Terrorism Act 2008 introduced measures which largely tightened up existing powers.

There has since been a slight liberalising of the law. The Terrorism Prevention and Investigatory Measures Act 2011 replaces the controversial Control Orders with ostensibly less restrictive measures (Section 24.6.5). The Protection of Freedoms Act 2012 responds to the rejection by the Strasbourg court of wide powers of stop and search which police were using against political demonstrators (Section 24.6.2).

24.7.1 Definition of terrorism

The definition of terrorism (TA 2000, s 1) is complex, 'sweepingly broad and extraordinarily vague' (Richards J in *R (Kurdistan Workers' Party) v Secretary of State for the Home Dept* [2002] EWHC 644). It has three elements.

Firstly there must be an act or the threat of an act that falls into one of five categories:

▶ serious violence against a person;
▶ serious violence against property;
▶ endangers life;
▶ serious risk to the health or safety of the public or a section of the public;
▶ seriously disrupts or interferes with an electronic system.

Secondly the action must be intended to advance a political, religious or ideological cause. (The Counter Terrorism Act 2008 adds 'racial' to this list.)

Thirdly the action must be designed to influence the government or coerce the public or a section of it or an international governmental organisation (added by TA 2006, s 34). It is not necessary for the action to be carried out on UK soil, against a UK citizen or property owned by a UK citizen.

The breadth of the definition means that attacks or threats against any government anywhere can be investigated by British police. This would include people resident in the UK who are active political agitators against other states. Thus it is possible that the TA could be used to police international politics, raising grave questions of traditional liberties. The vagueness of the definition means that it could include a wide variety of actions and persons, some of which might not necessarily be a significant threat to national security. For example the definition could apply to environmental protestors who chain themselves to trees in order to obstruct the building of a motorway through a wildlife habitat.

This breadth of definition would therefore permit the use of the legislation in situations where the low threat of violence does not justify specialised powers and offences. During the Terrorism Bill's passage through Parliament, Jack Straw, the Home Secretary, conceded that the definition granted considerable discretion to the enforcement agencies (SC Deb (D) 18 January 2000, col 22). Given the breadth of the definition, the ministers and the police have the key roles in deciding who is or is not a terrorist.

24.7.2 Proscription

One of the key elements of the anti-terrorism regime is the banning of terrorist organisations. It is an offence to belong to or to support a proscribed organisation (TA 2000, ss 11, 12). The proscribed organisations are listed in Schedule 2 of the TA 2000 or have the same name as one listed or are proscribed by statutory instrument. The organisation remains proscribed irrespective of any change in name (TA 2006, s 21).

The Home Secretary can add other organisations to the list if she believes the organisation is 'concerned in terrorism' (TA 2000, s 3; TA 2006, s 21). This means committing or participating in acts of terrorism, preparing for terrorism, promoting, encouraging or unlawfully 'glorifying' terrorism or otherwise being concerned with terrorism. Glorifying terrorism, which includes praise or celebration, is unlawful if it can reasonably be inferred to refer to conduct that should be emulated in present circumstances. The Home Secretary does not apparently have to show reasonable grounds for her belief.

It is an offence to be or to profess to be a member of a proscribed organisation (s 11) or to invite support for a proscribed organisation (s 12). In *A G's Reference (No 4 of 2002)* [2005] 1 AC 264 the House of Lords did not decide whether this very wide provision violated the right of freedom of expression although Lord Bingham thought that it would be justified as proportionate [54]. However, s 11 (2) imposes a burden of proof on the accused to show that he has not taken part in the activities of the organisation at a time when it was proscribed. This was held to be unfair as a violation of Article 6 of the ECHR (right to a fair trial).

The organisation or someone affected by the proscription can apply to the Secretary of State to de-proscribe the organisation. There is a further right of appeal to the Proscribed Organisations Appeal Commission (POAC) established under the TA 2000 but this appeal can only apply the rules of judicial review (s 5). The POAC is appointed by the Lord Chancellor and includes an appellate court judge. The Lord Chancellor can make rules permitting its proceedings to be held in secret and for evidence to be withheld from the parties and their representatives (TA 2000, Sch 3). There is a further right of appeal to the Court of Appeal but this requires the permission of the Court (s 6). Judicial review is otherwise excluded.

It is an offence to express support or invite support for a proscribed organisation, to address a meeting (of three or more persons) with the purpose of encouraging support for a proscribed organisation or furthering its activities, or to arrange or help to arrange a meeting which the person knows supports or furthers the activities of a proscribed organisation or which is addressed by a person who belongs to or professes to belong to a proscribed organisation, irrespective of the subject of the meeting (s 12). In the case of a private meeting there is a defence that the person has no reasonable cause to believe that the address would support a proscribed organisation or further its activities.

A remnant of the legislation's roots in the Northern Ireland conflict (where mass parades were held with men and women in paramilitary uniforms of flak jackets and berets) is the crime of wearing clothing or an item in public that would arouse reasonable suspicion the person is a member of a proscribed organisation (s 13). These laws on proscription are serious restrictions on freedom of expression and were controversial when they were first enacted but have come to be viewed as necessary and are among the least problematic of the anti-terrorism laws.

24.7.3 Arrest and pre-charge detention

A constable may arrest without warrant and search a person whom he reasonably suspects to be a terrorist, that is someone who has committed a terrorist offence or is concerned in the commission, preparation or instigation of acts of terrorism (ss 41, 43(2)). It is not clear whether 'reasonably suspects' has the same meaning as 'suspects on reasonable grounds', which is the text for an ordinary arrest. Arguably 'reasonably' in this context means in accordance with proportionality. Unlike ordinary powers of arrest this power does not tie the arrest to a specific offence (*R v Officer in Charge of Police Office Castlereagh Belfast, ex p Lynch* [1980] NI 126). Significant in the context of liberal values of human dignity, the officer does not need to disclose to the arrestee the grounds for his suspicions (*Oscar v Chief Constable RUC* [1992] NI 290).

Once the person has been arrested he or she can be detained for questioning without charge for up to 28 days (Sch 8 as extended by TA 2006, s 23). In *Brogan v UK* [1989] the European Court of Human Rights held a similar power to be in breach of the Convention requirement that a suspect must be brought promptly before a court (Art 5) and that a suspect should be brought before a judge within a maximum of four days after their arrest. Section 23 of the Terrorism Act 2006 was intended to end this difficulty and is in accordance with a narrow interpretation of *Brogan*. The Act creates a series of increasing powers. A suspect can be detained for up to 48 hours by the police alone. To detain a person from 48 hours up to 14 days, the police must apply to a lower level court. For detention up to 28 days they must apply to a senior judge (Sch 8). Permission can be granted if the detention is necessary to obtain or preserve evidence or to carry out an examination or analysis and the investigation is being conducted diligently and expeditiously (ibid) but again the police investigation does not need to be tied to a specific crime. The detention must be reviewed regularly. The accused is entitled to legal representation but can be excluded from any part of the hearing and sensitive material can be withheld from the accused and his or her advisors (ibid). The Act also includes provision for questioning a terrorist suspect after being charged, which does not apply to ordinary charges (ss 22–24).

24.7.4 Stop and search

Under section 43 of the Terrorism Act 2000 a constable may stop and search anyone whom he reasonably suspects to be a terrorist. He may also search any vehicle stopped either under this power or if he reasonably suspects that it is being used for terrorism and anything on or on the vehicle or carried by the driver or passengers (Protection of Freedoms Act 2012, s 60 (2) (3)).

More controversially under sections 44–45, within an area authorised by a senior officer if he thinks it 'expedient' for the prevention of acts of terrorism, a policeman in uniform can stop and search any person for articles of a kind that could be used in connection with terrorism. Reasonable grounds are not required either for the authorisation or the search. (By contrast under the general law, except after an arrest, search powers normally require a warrant specifying the nature of the material to be searched for (see Police and Criminal Evidence Act 1984, Part II)). Safeguards include a requirement for confirmation by the Home Secretary and a provision that the authorisation has a limited life of 28 days.

In *R (Gillan) v Metropolitan Police Comr* [2006] a policeman used section 44 against a student demonstrator and a journalist at an arms sale fair supported by the government. The House of Lords held that this limited and temporary restraint was not a deprivation of liberty within Article 5 of the ECHR (Section 21.4.1) and as an interference with privacy was justified because the proportionality test should be applied lightly in terrorist cases. *Gillan* was subsequently condemned by the ECHR (*Gillan and Quinton v UK* [2010]). It was held that section 44 engaged at least Article 8 of the ECHR as a clear interference with privacy. It was held that the power was too vague and lacked essential safeguards, including judicial supervision. It was not therefore 'in accordance with the law'.

Section 61 (not yet in force) of the Protection of Freedoms Act 2012 replaces section. 44 with more restricted powers. It is questionable whether these are sufficient to satisfy the *Gillan* judgement within areas designated by a senior officer, where he or she *reasonably* suspects that terrorism may take place a constable in uniform can search vehicles, their contents, drivers, passengers and pedestrians. The power can be exercised only to discover evidence of terrorism but the constable need not have reasonable grounds (s 61 (5)). Thus the main difference between this provision and section. 44 is that the authorization must be based on reasonable grounds and not merely 'expedient'. The Secretary of State must prepare and publish a code of practice to which a police officer must have regard when exercising these powers (s. 62).

Under section 42 of the Terrorism Act 2000 a magistrate may issue a search warrant for the search of any premises if a constable has reasonable grounds to suspect that a person concerned with the commission, preparation or instigation of acts of terrorism is to be found there. The Counter Terrorism Act 2008 adds a power to remove documents, including electronic data, for examination and retain them for up to 96 hours (s 1).

Under section 89 a member of the armed forces on duty or a constable may stop any person so long as it is necessary in order to question him for the purpose of ascertaining that person's identity or movements and what he or she knows about a recent explosion or incident.

24.7.5 Terrorism prevention and investigation measures

The controversial power to impose Control Orders (Section 24.6) has been replaced by powers to impose more limited restrictions on the movements of terrorist suspects by avoiding outright deprivation of liberty with its unclear meaning (Section 21.4). Under the Terrorism Prevention and Investigatory Measures Act 2011 the Secretary of State can impose a TPIM notice subject to a two year time limit which can be extended for a further year. The Secretary of State must have a reasonable belief that the person concerned is or has been involved in terrorism and must reasonably consider that the measures are necessary to protect the public from a risk of terrorism and are necessary for purposes connected with preventing or restricting the individual's involvement in terrorism. The prior permission of the court is required except in urgent cases when the matter must be referred to the court immediately after imposing the restriction. However, the court can refuse permission only if the measure is 'obviously flawed' on the basis of judicial review principles.

A TPIM notice can impose residence conditions including an overnight curfew, travel restrictions which prevent the subject leaving or entering a specified area and requiring compliance with police directions, restrictions on access to bank accounts and the transfer of assets abroad, restrictions on the use of electronic communication devices, restrictions on communication or association with others, restrictions on work or study.

A subject can also be required to report to a police station and to allow photographs to be taken, to wear a tracking device and to allow official access to his home.

The Secretary of State must report to Parliament every three months as to the use made of these powers and must appoint an 'independent' reviewer yearly (s 20). The powers expire after 5 years but can be extended for another 5 years subject to an affirmative vote of both Houses of Parliament (s 21).

24.7.6 Terrorist assets

Under section 1 of the Anti-Terrorism, Crime and Security Act 2001 a magistrate in civil proceedings brought for the purpose can order the forfeiture of cash which is intended to be used for terrorist purposes or which belongs to a proscribed organisation or which is or represents property obtained through terrorism. Under sections 4 and 5 of the ATCSA the Treasury can freeze the assets of any person resident in the UK or any UK citizen or company if it reasonably believes (i) that action to the detriment of the UK economy (or part of it) has been or is likely to be taken or (ii) that action constituting a threat to the life or property of one or more UK nationals has been or is likely to be taken, in both cases either by an overseas government or by an overseas resident. The freezing order can prevent benefits being paid to the government or resident in question or to any person the Treasury reasonably believes has assisted or is likely to assist them. These powers are therefore not limited to terrorists but could, for example be used to protect trade interests against overseas competition. They include power to require public bodies to disclose confidential information, again not limited to terrorist offences (s 17).

By virtue of Orders in Council made under the United Nations Act 1947 the Treasury has power to give directions for the freezing of terrorist assets in order to give effect to various United Nations Conventions (see Resolution 1373, 2001). This drastic power can involve placing serious restrictions as to every expenditure upon the persons concerned other than for essential needs. The Order can be made without judicial permission.

The Counter Terrorism Act 2008 introduces special High Court proceedings for setting aside the use of these powers. These provisions include what have now become commonplace powers to exclude parties and sensitive evidence and for using the device of a special advocate. However the Treasury is obliged to disclose to the Court all relevant material both for and against its case. The Court is limited to applying judicial review principles.

In *HM Treasury v Ahmed* [2010] the Supreme Court held that an order made under the 1947 Act which triggered asset freezing on 'reasonable suspicion' was invalid as violating the principle of legality, under which only clear statutory language can deprive a person of property (Section 6.6). The Terrorist Asset Freezing (Temporary Provisions) Act 2010 retrospectively validated the use of these powers. The Terrorist Asset-Freezing Etc Act 2011 puts the reasonable suspicion test into full statutory form.

Where a person has been convicted of certain funding and money laundering offences the court concerned may order assets connected with the offence to be seized (Terrorism Act 2000, s 23). The Counter Terrorism Act 2008 has extended this power and introduces provisions for compensating the injured out of the convicted person's assets.

24.7.7 Other terrorist offences and powers

1. the encouragement of terrorism and dissemination of terrorist publications (TA 2006, ss 1, 2);
2. preparation of terrorist acts (TA 2006, s 5). This is not confined to a specific act of terrorism but could include, for example buying materials capable of being made into bombs;
3. giving or receiving instruction or training for terrorism (TA 2006, s 6). This is also wide, including the use of any method or technique for doing anything that is capable of being done for the purpose of terrorism (s 6(3)(b)). For example it could include IT skills. However the instructor must know that the pupil intends to use the skills for terrorist purposes;
4. attendance at a place used for terrorist training;
5. offences relating to radioactive devices or materials for terrorist purposes (ss 9–11);
6. the Secretary of State can authorise the taking of land or a road closure or restriction if he or she considers it necessary for the preservation of peace or the maintenance of order (ss 91, 94). A member of the armed forces on duty or a constable may order a road closure or restriction if he considers it immediately necessary for the preservation of peace or the maintenance of order (s 92);
7. the Counter Terrorism Act 2008 introduces increased penalties for any offence with a terrorist connection;
8. the Counter Terrorism Act 2008 confers wide powers on any person to disclose information to any of the intelligence services for the purpose of its functions (s 19), with a corresponding power given to the intelligence services also to disclose information. This does not appear to be limited to terrorist offences.

Summary

▶ The courts give the executive a wide margin of discretion in relation to security matters. Under the ECHR there is also a wide margin and states can derogate from some of its provisions in the event of an emergency. However the courts protect fundamental rights by requiring safeguards, in particular independent judicial supervision.

▶ There is no general right to the disclosure of governmental information. The Freedom of Information Act 2000 confers a right to 'request' the disclosure of documents held by public authorities. However this can often be overridden by the government and is subject to many exceptions, particularly in relation to central government policy.

▶ There are certain statutory rights to the disclosure of specified information but these are outnumbered by many statutes prohibiting the disclosure of particular information.

▶ Under the Official Secrets Act 1989 defined categories of information are protected by criminal penalties. Except in the case of national security, the information must be damaging. There is also a defence of ignorance.

▶ The law of confidence requires the court to balance the public interest in openness against the public interest in effective government. The balance is struck differently according to context.

▶ The courts have endorsed the importance of freedom of expression and a public body is required to show a public interest in secrecy. The main remedy is an injunction. Third parties such as the press are not directly bound by an injunction but might be liable for contempt of court if they knowingly frustrate its purpose.

Summary cont'd

▶ Public interest immunity allows the government to withhold evidence. The court makes the decision on the basis of 'balancing' the public interest in the administration of justice against the public interest in effective government. The courts' approach to public interest immunity is affected by the Human Rights Act 1998, which requires that any claim preserve the essentials of the right to a fair trial.

▶ Proceedings might be 'closed' proceedings, where the defendant is denied direct access to the evidence against him and the public and press are excluded. Again the essentials of the right to a fair trial must be preserved. There is also a conflict with the rule of law and Article 10 of the ECHR (freedom of the press). The device of a special advocate might be used.

▶ The security and intelligence services are subject to a certain degree of control, largely outside the ordinary courts.

▶ There is regulation of electronic and other forms of surveillance by the police and other law enforcement agencies, also outside the ordinary courts. The overlapping regimes of the Police Act 1997 and the Regulation of Investigatory Powers Act 2000 give the government wide powers of interception and surveillance subject to procedural safeguards and to limits derived from the ECHR as to permissible purposes and proportionality.

▶ In an emergency the police, supported by the armed forces, may take action to keep the peace and can use reasonable force in self-defence and the defence of others. It is questionable whether martial law as such is part of English law. The Civil Contingencies Act 2004 gives the executive wide powers to deal with an emergency. These are subject to control by Parliament and safeguards based on the ECHR.

▶ Increasingly restrictive anti-terrorist measures have been introduced in response to a series of threats and incidents. These have sometimes required derogation from the ECHR protection for personal liberty. They also involve restrictions on the right to a fair trial. The courts have condemned a significant number of these powers and criticised others. However there is no consensus on how to accommodate security and respect for freedom.

Exercises

24.1 Tony, a US citizen, and Gordon, a UK citizen, are arrested by the police on suspicion of being associated with an international terrorist group. The police suspect that certain incriminating information which they received from the US may have been extracted from Tony by torture. Gordon is released but Tony is detained under a certificate issued by the Home Secretary stating that he is suspected of being a terrorist. Tony demands to see the evidence against him. He also asks for a lawyer but the request is refused. He is offered a special advocate as a representative. Discuss.

24.2 Simon is the leader of an animal rights campaigning organisation. The police receive an anonymous message that the organisation proposes to enter the headquarters of a drugs company (known to donate large sums to the ruling political party) in order to distribute animal rights leaflets. A policeman stops Simon in the street and searches him but finds nothing relevant to the allegation. The policeman then arrests Simon on the ground that he is a terrorist. Simon is detained for 14 days without charge and without going before a court. The Home Secretary, who knows Simon as a prominent critic of the government, issues a TPIM against Simon 'as a matter of urgency'. This requires that neither Simon nor any member of his group carry out any political activity anywhere, that Simon be confined to his home for 14 hours every day and that he does not use a mobile phone or a computer.

Advise Simon as to the legality of these actions.

Exercises cont'd

24.3 While on holiday in Devon the Prime Minister accidentally leaves his personal diary on a train. Another passenger finds it and is delighted to see that it contains disparaging remarks about the Prime Minister's Cabinet colleagues. He hands it in at the office of the *Sunday Stir*. The Editor informs the Prime Minister's Office that extracts from the diary will be published in next Sunday's edition. Advise the Prime Minister as to any legal remedy he might have.

24.4 Derek, a civil servant in the Department of Health, believes that the Cabinet minister in charge of his department has been ordering government statisticians to alter the latest NHS performance figures in order to show that government policies are bearing fruit. Derek gives this information to the editor of the *Daily Whinge*, who contacts the relevant minister for his comments. The Attorney General immediately applies for a temporary injunction and commences an action for breach of confidence against Derek. Derek requests the production of letters between civil servants and the minister (the existence of which he learned from an anonymous email) which he claims would support his version of events. The government issues a PII certificate on the ground that the information is in a category the disclosure of which would inhibit free and frank discussion within the Cabinet. The minister who signed the certificate did not examine the information personally but relied on advice from the Attorney General that the 'certificate will cover us for all Cabinet-level documents'.
 (i) Advise Derek.
 (ii) Advise the Attorney General whether he can prosecute Derek under the Official Secrets Act 1989.

24.5 Tom has recently retired from a senior post in the intelligence services. He possesses recordings of conversations by service officials which suggest that senior ministers have requested them to fabricate evidence supporting a proposed invasion of an African country. He wishes to pass the recordings to Jerry, a journalist. Advise Tom whether he and Jerry are at risk of conviction under the Official Secrets Act 1989.

24.6 'Terrorist threats and actions test the Executive's commitment to the rule of law and good governance. Because of the extreme powers given by such extraordinary legislation, there is an incumbent requirement to provide limits to its terms, scope and life span' (Thomas, 'Emergency and Anti-Terrorist Powers 9/11: USA and UK' (2003) 26 Fordham Int'l LJ 1993). Does the current law meet these requirements?

24.7 Vera a police officer observes Lewis leaving a cafe which is known as a place where various anti-government groups meet and which also provides a meeting place for asylum seekers. Lewis is carrying a large parcel under his arm and is wearing a badge proclaiming the slogan 'We stop at Nothing to Win'. Vera believes that the slogan is that of KILL, an anarchist organisation recently proscribed under anti-terrorist legislation. She stops Lewis and searches both him and his parcel. The parcel turns out to contain football kit and the slogan is that of a local football club although it is the same as that of KILL. Advise as to the legality of Veras's actions on the alternative assumptions that the Protection of Freedoms Act has and has not come into force. Has Lewis committed any offence?

Further reading

Akdeniz, Taylor and Walker, 'Regulation RIPA 2000 (1): Bigbrother.gov.uk: State Surveillance in the Age of Information and Rights' [2001] CLR 73
Arden, 'Human Rights in the Age of Terrorism' (2005) 121 LQR 609
Barak, 'Human Rights in Times of Terror: A Judicial Point of View' (2008) 28 LS 492

Further reading cont'd

Barendt, 'Incitement to and Glorification of Terrorism', in Hare and Weinstein (eds), *Extreme Speech and Democracy* (Oxford University Press 2009)

Bates, 'Anti-Terrorism Control Orders: Liberty and Security Still in the Balance' (2009) 29 LS 9

Birkinshaw, 'Regulating Information', in Jowell and Oliver (eds), *The Changing Constitution* (7th edn, Oxford University Press 2011)

Bonner, *Executive Measures, Terrorism and National Security: Have the Rules of the Game Changed?* (Ashgate 2008)

Cabinet Office, *The National Security Strategy of the UK* (Cm 7291, 2008)

Choudhury, The Terrorism Act 2006: Discouraging Terrorism', in Hare and Weinstein (eds) (above)

Clayton and Tomlinson, 'Lord Bingham and the Human Rights Act: The Search for Democratic Legitimacy During the "War on Terror"', in Andenas and Fairgrieve (eds), *Tom Bingham and the Transformation of the Law* (Oxford University Press 2009)

Dickson, 'Law versus Terrorism: Can Law Win?' [2005] EHRLR 12

Dyzenhaus, *The Constitution of Law: Legality in a Time of Emergency* (Cambridge University Press 2008)

Feldman, 'Human Rights, Terrorism and Risk: The Roles of Politicians and Judges' [2006] PL 364

Gearty, 'Human Rights in an Age of Counter Terrorism: Injurious, Irrelevant or Indispensible?' (2005) 58 CLI 25

Hazell and Busfield-Birch, 'Opening the Cabinet Door: Freedom of Information and Government Policy Making' [2011] PL 260

Ip, 'The Rise and Spread of the Special Advocate' [2008] PL 717

Kostakopoulou, 'How to Do Things with Security Post 9/11' (2008) 88 OJLS 317

Poole, 'Courts and Conditions of Uncertainty in Times of Crisis' [2008] PL 234

Tomkins, 'National Security and Due Process of Law' (2011) 64 CLP 215

Walker, *Terrorism and the Law* (Oxford University Press, 2011)

Walker, 'The Judicialisation of Intelligence in Legal Process' [2011] PL 235

Walker, 'The Legal Definition of Terrorism in the United Kingdom and Beyond' [2007] PL 331

Walker and Broderick, *The Civil Contingencies Act 2004* (Oxford University Press 2006)

White Paper, *The United Kingdom's Strategy for Combating International Terrorism* (Cm 7547, 2009)

Index

Printed and bound in Great Britain by
TJ International Ltd, Padstow, Cornwall